NORTHERN ETHNOGRAPHIC LANDSCAPES

Perspectives from Circumpolar Nations

Mist hangs over the abandoned Sámi summer camp at Kvænangsfjellet mountain, Norway.

Northern Ethnographic Landscapes

Perspectives from Circumpolar Nations

IGOR KRUPNIK, RACHEL MASON,
AND TONIA W. HORTON, EDITORS

Published by the

**Arctic Studies Center,
National Museum of Natural History,
Smithsonian Institution**
Washington, D.C.

In collaboration with
The National Park Service

ISBN 0-9673429-7-X
Library of Congress Cataloging-in-Publication Data

Northern ethnographic landscapes : perspectives from circumpolar nations / Igor Krupnik, Rachel Mason, and Tonia W. Horton, editors.
    p. cm. — (Contributions to circumpolar anthropology ; v. 6)
Includes bibliographical references and index.
ISBN 0-9673429-7-X (alk. paper)
1. Ethnology—Arctic regions. 2. Human geography—Arctic regions. 3. Landscape assessment—Arctic regions.
4. Landscape protection—Arctic regions. 5. Environmentally sensitive areas—Arctic regions. 6. Arctic
regions—Environmental conditions. I. Krupnik, Igor. II. Mason, Rachel, 1954- III. Horton, Tonia W. (Tonia Woods)
IV. Series: Contributions to circumpolar anthropology ; 6.

GN673.N67 2004
306'.0911'3—dc22
                  2004024361

∞ The paper used in this publication meets the minimum requirements of the American National Standard For Information Sciences—Permanence of Paper for Printed Library Materials, ANSI Z39.48-1992.

This publication was supported by a grant from the National Park Service, Alaska Regional Office.

Technical Editor: Thetus H. Smith
Cover design: Raissa Macasieb-Ludwig
Series design: Anya Vinokour
Production editor: Elisabeth Ward
Printed in Canada.

This publication is Volume 6 in the Arctic Studies Center series, *Contributions to Circumpolar Anthropology*, produced by the Arctic Studies Center, National Museum of Natural History, Smithsonian Institution.

THIS SERIES IS MADE POSSIBLE IN PART BY THE JAMES W. VANSTONE (1921–2001) ENDOWMENT.

Cover: *Cape Espenberg, Alaska. During the last 6,000 years, storm surges and winter winds sculptured sands deposited from offshore currents into the beach ridges of Cape Espenberg on the southern shore of Kotzebue Sound, Alaska. The cape was inhabited by the Pittagmiut, a group of North Alaskan Iñupiat people in the 19th century. In late May or early June the entire population of 400 people would be located along the cape hunting for bearded seals in the offshore ice. The long expanse of coastline from the cape to the current community of Deering is known as Saniniq, meaning "shallow ocean." National Park Service Photo.*

PUBLISHED BY: Arctic Studies Center, National Museum of Natural History Smithsonian Institution
10ᵗʰ and Constitution Avenue, N.W., Washington, D.C. 20013-7012 ▪ (202) 633-1887phone ▪ (202) 357-2684 fax ▪ www.mnh.si.edu/arctic

DISTRIBUTED BY: University of Alaska Press, P.O. Box 756240, Fairbanks, Alaska 99775-6240
Toll-free in the U.S.: 1 (888) 252-6657 ▪ (907) 474-5831 phone ▪ (907) 474-5502 fax ▪ E-mail fypress@uaf.edu ▪ www.uaf.edu/uapress

contents

Part One

State Policies: Perspectives from Four Arctic Nations

Part Two

Protecting the "Invisible": Stories from the Arctic Zone

Part Three

Regional Approaches to Documentation and Protection

Part Four

Comparative Perspectives

contributors

Thomas Andrews has conducted research in the northern Yukon and in the Canadian Northwest Territories since the late 1970s. His many publications include articles on Aboriginal land management systems, community-based resource management in the Northwest Territories, local cultural landscapes, ethnoarchaeology, and sacred sites. Since 1990, he has worked at the Prince of Wales Northern Heritage Centre, in Yellowknife, Northwest Territories, where he currently holds the position of Territorial Archaeologist.

Herbert O. Anungazuk is an Iñupiaq from Wales, Alaska. Since 2003, he has worked as a Cultural Anthropologist for the Cultural Resources Team of the National Park Service in Anchorage, Alaska. Before that, beginning in 1993, he was a Native Liaison and Heritage Specialist with the NPS Alaska Office. His knowledge of Iñupiaq language and culture, along with traditional skills acquired from elders over decades, facilitate his work as a researcher, liaison and interpreter.

Olga Balalaeva is a researcher in folklore and ethnology of the Peoples of the North and in Finno-Ugric Studies. She has served as Senior Scientific Researcher, Folklore Department, A.M. Gorky Institute of World Literature, and as scientific consultant to State Committee of the North and the Arctic Science Committee of the Russian Federation. She has been engaged in fieldwork among the Khanty since 1988.

Arthur Bjorgvin Bollason was Director of the Saga Centre, Hvollsvollur, Iceland in 1999–2003. After completing Master's degree research in Germany, he be-

came the Icelandic radio's national correspondent for German affairs, was a researcher at the Arni Magnusson Institute, and will be the co-chief editor for a new German translation of the Complete Saga of the Icelanders. A sometimes television host, poet, and tourist guide, he now works for Icelandair in Germany.

Susan Buggey has been active in research, evaluation, and writing on cultural landscapes for 25 years. Former Director of Historical Services for Parks Canada, she is now an Adjunct Professor in the School of Landscape Architecture at the Université de Montréal in Monreal, Canada. She writes extensively on landscapes associated with the history of Aboriginal peoples and the associative values of cultural landscapes.

Heather Burke has over thirteen years experience as a consultant archaeologist, working in New South Wales, Queensland, South Australia and the Northern Territory. Her particular skills are in the fields of site recording and significance assessment, for both historical and Aboriginal archaeological sites, the assessment and recording of standing structures and mining heritage, and the interpretation and presentation of heritage sites. She has authored several publications on Aboriginal archaeology in Australia.

Donald G. Callaway is the Senior Cultural Anthropologist in the Alaska Regional Office of the National Park Service. He has conducted fieldwork and research in rural Alaska for the last 19 years and, over the last decade, in the Russian Far East. A cultural anthropologist by his training, he also held post-doctoral fellowships in statistics at UC Berkeley and in health issues at the Institute on Aging and Oregon Health Sciences in Portland, Oregon. His primary fields of interest include applied anthropology, formal methods, network analysis, and oral histories.

Susan W. Fair was a folklorist and Native art historian; she conducted independent research and wrote extensively on Alaska Native art and culture. Her relationship with the Iñupiat village of Shishmaref, in Northwest Alaska, was particularly close. In the 1970s and early 1980s, she was a certified appraiser of Native American and Alaska Native art. In Alaska, she curated several prominent installations of Native art and ethnographic collections. At the time of her death in 2003, she held a joint teaching/research appointment at the University of Arizona Tucson.

Torvald Falch is Deputy Director General, Department of Environment and Cultural Heritage, Sámi Parliament of Norway in Vuonnabáhta (Varangerboten), Norway. He has a Masters' degree in political sciences from the University of Oslo and he has worked for the Sámi Parliament's Department of Cultural Heritage since 1994. He is responsible for the management and documentation of Sámi cultural sites and landscapes in Norway, as well as for the general political liaison in actions concerning cultural heritage, biological diversity, sustainable development, and environmental issues.

Natalia Fedorova is Senior Research Fellow at the Institute of History and Archaeology of the Urals Division of the Russian Academy of Sciences in Ekaterinburg, Russia. Since 2003, she is also Deputy Director of the Museum and Exhibit Center in Salekhard, Yamal. Her recent studies are focused upon the prehistoric cultures of the West Siberia boreal forest and Arctic zone, medieval and antique metal artwork, and culture contacts in Central (Inner) Eurasia. She authored six books and more then fifty papers on West Siberian archaeology and art history.

William W. Fitzhugh is Director of the Arctic Studies Center and Curator at the Department of Anthropology, National Museum of Natural History, Smithsonian Institution, in Washington, DC. His interests include pre-

history and environmental archaeology, maritime adaptations, and culture contacts. He has organized several special exhibit projects, such as *Inua* (1982); *Crossroads of Continents* (1988); *Ainu* (1999); and *Vikings* (2000).

Ingegerd Holand works as Adviser on Sámi (Saami) cultural heritage and resource management at The Norwegian Directorate for Cultural Heritage (Riksantikvaren) in Oslo, Norway. She was born in Kvænangen, Northern Norway, in a Coastal Sámi comunity, and is an archaeologist by profession, educated in Tromsø as well as in London. Her research and work has previously included both mainstream Scandinavian archaeology and Sámi archaeology, while her present job involves responsibility for all Sámi monuments, including landscape preservation.

Tonia Woods Horton is a landscape architect and ethnohistorian. She was the first manager for the Cultural Landscapes program in the Alaska Region, National Park Service, from 1998 to 2004. She directed projects through Alaska's fifteen national parks with a special focus on ethnographic landscapes. She holds degrees in landscape architecture, and in American Indian and environmental history. Currently she is an assistant professor of landscape architecture at Pennsylvania State University.

Galina P. Kharyuchi is senior researcher at the Center for Humanitarian Research on Indigenous Minority Peoples of the North in Salekhard, northern Russia. She was born to a Nenets reindeer-herding family in the Gydan tundra along the Arctic coast of West Siberia. She graduated from teacher's college and worked for several years as an educator in her native area, prior to becoming professional ethnographer. She has a degree in history and anthropology, and she writes extensively on indigenous nations of West Siberia and her native tundra Nenets people, in particular.

Igor Krupnik, Arctic ethnologist at the Arctic Studies Center, Smithsonian Institution in Washington, DC, is currently coordinator of various international projects studying the impacts of global climate change and the preservation of cultural heritage, and ecological knowledge of northern Native people. He writes extensively on Arctic peoples and he is the general editor of the Smithsonian *Contributions to Circumpolar Anthropology* series.

Ellen Lee is Director of the Archaeological Services Branch of Parks Canada, an organization responsible for the national parks and national historic sites programs of Canada. She has written on a range of topics related to cultural landscapes and the commemoration of Aboriginal history in Canada, and maintains an interest in the overlapping of cultural and natural values for protected area management. Her most recent publication is "Managing the Intangible" (co-authored with A. English), in *The Full Value of Parks and Protected Areas: From Economics to the Intangible* (2003).

Rachel Mason is a cultural anthropologist with the National Park Service, Alaska Regional Office. She has worked in Alaska since 1986, most extensively in the Kodiak Archipelago and the Aleutian Islands. Prior to her current employment at the NPS, she worked as a technical advisor to the Federal Subsistence Management Program for the U.S. Fish and Wildlife Service. Her research interests include Alaska Native cultures, subsistence, and commercial fisheries.

Anita Maurstad has performed research on small-scale fishing in northern Norway since the late 1980's. She has a doctorate in resource management, and her publications focus on culture and knowledge management in small-scale fisheries, paying special attention to its interaction with science and fisheries management. Formerly a research associate by the Norwegian College of Fisheries Science since 1997, she is now associate professor at Tromsø Museum, Department for Contemporary Cultural History.

Pavel M. Shul'gin is Deputy Director of the Russian Research Institute for Cultural and Natural Heritage in Moscow, since 1992. His research interests include various issues in economic, legislative, and regional development that relate to the conservation and use of heritage resources in Russia. His numerous publications have advanced the concept of the so-called "unique historical territories," that is, regions, for which heritage preservation should be regarded as a top economic and social priority.

Marianne Skandfer has a Ph.D. in archaeology from the University of Tromsø. She is currently a post-doctoral fellow at the University of Tromsø in Tromsø, Norway. Her research interest is in north Fenno-Scandian archaeology, including Stone Age, early ceramics, and the emergence of Sámi ethnicity. Between 1997 and 1999 she worked as an executive officer in the Department of Sámi Cultural Heritage in the Sámi Parliament in Norway.

Claire Smith is a Senior Lecturer in Archaeology at Flinders University, Adelaide, Australia. Her main research focus is on archaeological field methods and on Indigenous archaeology. She has conducted fieldwork in the Barunga region of southern Arnhem Land since 1990, and has on-going excavation projects in the Barunga region, Northern Territory and in Burra, South Australia. Her major publications include the co-edited volume *Indigenous Cultures in an Interconnected World* (2000) and the authored book, *Country, Kin and Culture. Survival of an Aboriginal Community* (in press).

Elisabeth I. Ward is a graduate student at the University of California, Berkeley, Scandinavian Studies Department. Drawing on her maternal Icelandic heritage, Elisabeth has actively pursued her interest in the Icelandic language and culture. After completing a Master's degree in Anthropology at George Washington University, she became Assistant Curator and Co-editor for the Smithsonian Institution millennial exhibition, *Vikings: The North Atlantic Saga*, a position she held from 1998 until 2003.

Andrew Wiget is professor and Director of the New Mexico Heritage Center at New Mexico State University. He has been involved in cultural conservation work and land claims cases with Native American tribes for twenty years. Since 1992, he has partnered with Olga Balalaeva in conducting ethnographic field research and engaging in applied work among the Khanty of western Siberia.

list of figures

abbreviations

ADFG	Alaska Department of Fish and Game, USA
AMNH	American Museum of Natural History, New York, USA
ANCSA	Alaska Native Land Claims Settlement Act, 1971, USA
ANILCA	Alaska National Interest Lands Conservation Act, 1980, USA
ASC	Arctic Studies Center, Department of Anthropology, Smithsonian Institution, Washington, D.C.
ATV	All terrain vehicle
BIA	Bureau of Indian Affairs, U.S. Department of the Interior, Washington, D.C., USA
CEAA	Canadian Environmental Assessment Act, 1996, Canada
CIS	Commemorative Integrity Statement, Canada
CLI	Cultural Landscape Inventory, National Park Service, USA
CPAWS	Canadian Parks and Wilderness Society, Canada
CRM	Cultural Resource Management
ERI	Ethnographic Research Inventory, US National Park Service
EVOS	Exxon Valdez oil spill, USA
GIS	Geographic Information System
GPS	Geographic Positioning System
HSMBC	Historic Sites and Monuments Board of Canada
ILO	International Labour Organization
ILUA	Indigenous Land Use Agreement, Australia
IPS	Indigenous Peoples' Secretariat
KMAO	Khanty-Mansi Autonomous Area, Russia
NAGRPA	Native American Graves Protection and Repatriation Act, 1990, USA
NHP	National Historic Park, USA
NHPA	National Historic Preservation Act, 1966, USA
NHS	Natioanl Historic Site, Canada
NAA-SI	National Anthropological Archives, Smithsonian Institution, USA
NPP	National Park and Preserve, USA
NPS	National Park Service, U.S. Department of the Interior
NWT	Northwest Territories, Canada
RAIPON	Russian Association of the Indigenous Peoples of the North, Russia
RRICNH	Russian Research Institute for Cultural and Natural Heritage, Moscow, Russia
TCP	Traditional Cultural Properties
TEK	Traditional Ecological (Environmental) Knowledge
USFWS	United States Fish and Wildlife Service
USGS	United States Geological Survey
WACH	Western Arctic Caribou Herd, Alaska

1 / *Mt. Drum in Wrangell-St. Elias National Park, Alaska. The Ahtna Athapaskans living in this area called this 12,010-foot peak "Upriver K'elt'aeni." Nearby Mount Sanford is Downriver K'elt'aeni, while Mt. Wrangell is simply K'elt'aeni. Many Athapskans tend to render all directions as "upriver" or "downriver." The name K'elt'aeni seems to mean "The One That Controls," apparently referring to the weather.*

foreword

Today, few scholars would question the importance of "landscape" as an integrating concept in understanding cultural traditions. Landscape approaches have been applied for several decades in European and North American scholarship. In American anthropology, landscape theory has been influenced strongly by Julian Steward's concept of cultural ecology and more recently by increasingly integrative approaches combining environmental studies, ecology, history, and anthropology. More recent movements toward understanding ethnographic landscapes are being fostered by growing collaboration between scientists and native partners in studies of climate and environmental change, natural resource distribution, subsistence practices, and many other topics having a geographic component. The extension of such studies into historical periods and the deep past and growth in scientific knowledge of paleoenvironments and effects of climate change expand these frontiers still further.

Native American groups, especially in North America, are playing an important role in advocating that these concepts of cultural and ethnographic landscape be included into government programs and management policies. Nevertheless, it is encouraging to discover a government agency building such an idea into its management policy. Unlike other nations that have recognized the importance of culture (admittedly, often a "national" culture, not always "cultures"), the United States has not had a distinguished record of heritage preservation in general or of cultural preservation in particular. Such themes have generally been relegated to museums, scholars, and private interest groups rather than governments. Therefore, I was

delighted when Ted Birkedal of the Alaska Office of the National Park Service (NPS) expressed interest in having the Arctic Studies Center collaborate with the NPS to conduct a study of how the concept "ethnographic landscapes" was being utilized in scientific literature and government policy in the circumpolar region. The Arctic Studies Center was familiar with how park systems operate among many arctic nations and was actively conducting research and educational program throughout this region. As the editors explain in their introduction, the initial idea was to provide a state-of-the-art overview that could be used by the NPS in their policy formation process. While it took us several years to design the study and identify partners, this publication represents the perspectives of specialists involved in key organizations and projects. The result is, of course, only a sampling of thought and practice as applied to the arctic and subarctic region.

The Arctic Studies Center has been pleased to collaborate with the National Park Service's Alaska Office in this effort by bringing together a body of new knowledge and practice in the field of heritage preservation. The inclusion of ethnographic and cultural landscapes as valuable elements of national heritage conservation provides an important new opportunity for recognizing the contributions of culture, ethnography, and the traditions of indigenous arctic residents; it also provides an important perspective for understanding cultural similarities and differences around the globe.

William W. Fitzhugh, Director
Arctic Studies Center

2/ Masik site at the entrance to Mechigmen Bay, Chukchi Peninsula, Siberia. This ancient whaling settlement was abandoned around 1950; but family visits, memories, and stories associated with the site keep the old landscape alive.

introduction
Landscapes, Perspectives, and Nations

IGOR KRUPNIK, RACHEL MASON,
AND SUSAN BUGGEY

The creation of this book is a remarkable story worth sharing with its readers. In the late 1990s, the Cultural Resources office of the U.S. Department of Interior's National Park Service (NPS) in Anchorage, Alaska, considered contracting a junior archaeologist or a graduate student for a fairly standard service: producing an overview of the current literature and policy documents about cultural and ethnographic landscape preservation in some northern countries. Money was available and the terms of reference were clear; nobody believed that it would take more than a few months to produce a 50-60 page report for the agency's internal use only.

The NPS' Alaska Regional Office was eager to look at other nations' policies on ethnographic landscapes for several reasons. By that time, several federal and state legislative actions, NPS-led initiatives pertaining to Native Americans' heritage and ancestral lands, had been adopted. Many collaborative projects with Native communities were under way, both in Alaska and elsewhere in the United States. After several decades of protecting '"historic sites"—historic monuments and buildings, battlefields, archaeological ruins, and remains along pioneer trails—the NPS finally acknowledged the need to extend protective status to heritage places that may have, but equally *may not* have any visible traces of human activities.

This recognition opened the way for a new vision of heritage preservation that was far more suitable to the Native American perspective. It included physical landscapes with great value to indigenous people, reflected in their associated myths, stories, rituals, and spiritual practices. As a result, new terms, such as "historic properties," "tribal preservation," and "indigenous cultural (or ethnographic) landscapes" appeared on the Native American public agendas and in NPS documentation alike (cf. Parker 1990; Stoffle et al. 1997). In 1990, the NPS institutionalized a distinct Cultural Landscapes Program that addressed serious inadequacies in national preservation policies, particularly affecting the lands that were of special value to Native Americans (see Horton, this volume). It was clear that this area would require innovative approaches in management and protection. In fact, the new notion of 'ethnographic landscapes' would become one of the most contentious policy issues for years to come.

At the federal level, the Native American Graves Protection and Repatriation Act (NAGPRA) of 1990 symbolized a huge step in recognizing the cultural presence of Native Americans on their ancestral lands and in requiring by law that all human remains and funerary items discovered on federal grounds be repatriated to associated tribes. Two years later, the 1992 amendment to the National Historic Preservation Act (NHPA) of 1967 required that places significant to Native Americans be conserved with other culturally significant sites that are part of a diverse national heritage. In 1996, Executive Order 13007 explicitly protected Native Americans' access to their sacred sites provided under the American Indian Religious Freedom Act (AIRFA) of 1978 (Mason, this volume). In Alaska, negotiations between the NPS and Russian park managers had been under way since the late 1980s to establish a new joint "Beringia International Park" on both sides of the Bering Strait. Key among its many declared functions was the protection of landscapes, monuments, and the subsistence activities of indigenous people as well as their ties to the ancestral lands and their historical connections to each other. The "Shared Beringia Heritage Program," established in 1991 under the NPS Alaska office, offered strong support to such ties and connections through research, conferences, and cultural exchanges across the Bering Strait (Beringian Heritage 1989; Callaway 2003; Vdovin 1990).

Those transitions in U.S. attitudes toward indigenous lands and landscapes went hand-in-hand or were often preceded by similar developments in Canada (Buggey 1999, this volume), Norway (Holand, this volume), and several other countries, particularly Australia and New Zealand. The crucial role of UNESCO cannot be overestimated, notably since 1992, when it introduced the term "cultural landscapes" to its operational guidelines pertaining to the World Heritage Convention of 1972. It recognized them as "the combined works of nature and of man" and "the interaction between humankind and nature," and it officially acknowledged that "the protection of traditional cultural landscapes is . . . helpful in maintaining biological diversity" (UNECSO 1996:cl. 36–38). By 2002, about thirty cultural landscapes were inscribed on UNESCO's 'World Heritage List (Fowler 2003:ch.3).[1] Scientific literature was bubbling up with new monographs, conference proceedings, and project reports, including three seminal international volumes on cultural landscapes published under the *One World Archaeology* series (Carmichael et al. 1994; Smith and Wobst, in press; Ucko and Layton 1999; see also Alanen and Melnick 2000; Bender 1992; Feld and Basso 1996; Hirsch and O'Hanlon 1995; Mitchell 1994; Thompson 1995; Tilley 1994). At the same time, the NPS Alaska office supported several field programs aimed at docu-

menting Native Alaskan oral traditions associated with protected landscapes around the prospective 'Beringia' Park and elsewhere across the state (Simon and Gerlach 1991; Fair and Ningeulook 1994; Schaaff 1996; Fair, this volume; Callaway, this volume). New data and expertise argued strongly in favor of shifting the NPS' focus toward ethnographic landscapes as the next cutting edge in its activities, particularly in the areas critical to Native Americans' lives, history, and heritage.[2]

Despite all these factors and the establishment of a special "Cultural Landscapes Program" at the NPS Alaska office (which recognized ethnographic landscapes as a particular focus of its activities in 1998), several gray areas remained. No clear instructions existed on how to deal with ethnographic landscapes and the associated traditions of indigenous people, from the park management perspective. A tentative definition of what constitutes an "ethnographic landscape,"[3] developed under the NPS guidelines, proved to be of limited management value. National Register Bulletin 38 (Parker and King 1990), part of a series that was so instrumental in developing the NPS cultural landscapes framework, offered little help, since its primary focus remained physical landscapes. Anthropologists working with northern Native communities were quick to point to the whole spectrum of invisible indigenous legacies associated with ethnographic landscapes—myths, dreams, personal stories and names, place-names, teaching and initiation practices. Without Native people's participation, those legacies remained hidden to park managers and were not listed on their preservation mandates. Therefore, new expertise was needed and more information had to be collected to tackle the ethnographic landscape challenge, for both theoretical and practical purposes.

A Book Project Emerges

The initial idea of contracting with a student to do a brief in-house review was quickly abandoned, and the NPS opted to collaborate with the Arctic Studies Center (ASC) of the Smithsonian Institution in Washington, D.C. By that time, the ASC was conducting its own heritage landscape studies and site surveys in Canada (Labrador), Alaska, and Russia (Yamal Peninsula in West Siberia). The ASC also had a long history of cooperation with the NPS, particularly with its Alaska office. Smithsonian anthropologists promptly suggested that the project be turned into an international venture and that it present authentic visions and voices from many northern nations besides the U.S., including Canada, Russia, and the Scandinavian countries. The appearance of a Parks Canada special report, *An Approach to Aboriginal Cultural Landscapes* (Buggey 1999), with its trove of information on the Canadian approach to heritage landscape preservation, made such an idea even more appealing.

For about a year the main vision for the study centered on an international workshop, with speakers from several countries presenting their national policy papers. In 2000, Igor Krupnik, the ASC ethnologist, introduced a new scenario for the project. Instead of a conference to be held in Washington, D.C. or Anchorage, Krupnik suggested producing an edited volume of invited papers written by scholars and managers from several northern nations. Such an international collection of articles would be published jointly by the ASC (Smithsonian Institution) and the NPS. The main incentive to prospective contributors would be the potential to demonstrate a circumpolar diversity of perspectives and approaches to ethnographic landscapes in a single book. This approach positioned the U.S.-Alaskan heritage preservation policy as an important component (if not the key magnet) of the book, something not envisioned under the original plan. The NPS gladly accepted this new vision. Two of its Alaskan ethnographers, Rachel Mason and Donald Callaway, and the manager of the Alaskan NPS cultural landscapes program, Tonia Horton, agreed to write papers for the book, and Mason and Horton became its co-editors. Krupnik, was named the lead editor for the volume, and he went on trips to Russia (Fall of 2000), and to Norway and Canada (Spring of 2001) to look for possible authors.

The response to a joint international volume on ethnographic landscape preservation was overwhelmingly enthusiastic, even though most of the invited authors had never met and often had never heard of each other's work in the same field. By late 2002 the book's core had been assembled with contributions from the U.S., Canada, Russia, Norway, Iceland, and Australia (see below). Authors include park management specialists, heritage administrators and scholars, cultural anthropologists, and indigenous researchers (see Contributors list). It took two more years to complete the project and to produce this volume as a part of the new Smithsonian series, *Contribution to Circumpolar Anthropology*, published by the ASC.

Indigenous/Aboriginal Approach to Landscape

As has been asserted repeatedly, indigenous peoples in many parts of the world view landscapes in ways common to their experience but different from Western views on land, landscape, and historic heritage (Buggey 1999:1).[4] Indigenous people view the relationship between people and places in holistic and often openly spiritual terms, rather than seeing it primarily in terms of material interests and ownership/property rights. This does not mean that they have no material interests in land and landscapes, or that their subsistence use of land and landscape lacks any notion of land ownership, based on tribal, clan, or family ties. The difference is, first and foremost, in the priorities that indigenous people put into their perspective on landscape—or, for that matter, the seascape, i.e., the waters they use or travel through. Most indigenous communities, particularly hunter-gatherers and herders, regard themselves as an integral part of the holistic and living landscape. Within this worldview, people are at one with the landscape, which also includes animals, plants, known and mythological ancestors, and various supernatural beings, like animal keepers, malignant spirits, and non-empirical creatures. The spirits of all these entities inhabit the landscape, which—according to indigenous views—is a multi-faceted and densely populated place, well beyond humans' daily presence.

Traditional aboriginal cosmologies similarly saw a relationship of the earth and sky, the elements, the directions, the seasons, the life species, and mythic transformers to the lands that people have occupied since ancient times. All those elements were also connected via journeys or paths through space and time that once were accessible to humans' mythological ancestors and that still are/were accessible to shamans and even to some ordinary people through dreams, initiations, or visionary revelations. In this perspective, land and landscapes are revered in total as well as in specific physical incarnations, such as mountains, lakes, rocks, stones, capes, trees, etc. Those physical incarnations are primarily, though not exclusively, regarded as places of connectivity, nodes of spiritual power, or markers of paths and journeys related to ancestors, shamans, animal spirits, or supernatural beings.

This is, of course, a condensed and a bit idealized compilation of what may be called "aboriginal world views" (Buggey 1999:1–3). In reality, views on landscape differ substantially from one group to another and also change through time. Even classical tribal ethnographies of the nineteenth and early twentieth centuries often documented only fragments or traces of the elements of this generic complex. Introduced religions, particularly Christianity, and later, modern education, also made huge inroads in indigenous perspectives in many northern areas; both contributed substantially to the erosion of the old holistic visions (Krupnik and Vakhtin 1997). Nevertheless, traditional knowledge in the form of myths, narratives, place-names, and ecological lore, bequeathed through oral tradition from generation to generation, has embodied and preserved indigenous people's relationship to the land, from the ancestral times to the present. Such a holistic view is often cited as a key in understanding indigenous conceptualization of the land, the landscape, and its cultural resources (Stoffle and Evans 1990; Stoffle et al. 1997:232). Today's northern people differ greatly in terms of their individual knowledge and ability to articulate their specific ties to the land; but they voice their unity with the land immediately when confronted with another view of the same landscape espoused by resource and heritage managers, government people, and scientists.

Besides their specific vision of the land and landscapes, indigenous northern people have a particular view of history (cf. Buggey 1999:3). Their approach to history is primarily through cosmology, narratives, genealogies, and places—rather than through written records, fixed dates, and established time sequences. Elements of the land often become markers of time and of past events, particularly through place- names and associated stories that are remembered and transmitted to younger generations. Under this vision, the land is "like a book" to indigenous people (see Andrews, this volume); it is their most solid chronicle and a tribal register that unites group members through shared memories, residence, and affiliation. The land also acts as an ever-present teaching ground, a classroom to which the elderly and the learned bring the young and the uneducated.

With this in mind, we would like to endorse the following definition of indigenous "ethnographic landscape" that was formulated earlier by one of the co-authors of this Introduction (Buggey 1999:27):

> An 'ethnographic landscape [or 'aboriginal cultural landscape'] is a place valued by an Aboriginal group (or groups) because of their long and complex relationship with that land. It expresses their unity with the natural and spiritual environment. It embodies their traditional knowledge of spirits, places, land uses, and ecology. Material remains of the association may be prominent, but will often be minimal or absent.

The key components to this definition—long and complex relationship between people and land; the idea of people's *unity* with both natural and spiritual environment; the expression of people's ties to the landscape primarily through their cultural knowledge; and the unimportance of material remains in supporting such ties—are all critical indicators. They fuse into that which anthropologists call the "living group identity," that is, a cognized feeling of *today's* cultural specificity and belonging, actively transmitted within the community and among the generations. We believe, this is the pillar in approaching indigenous cultural (ethnographic) landscapes, rather than the constructs commonly used by heritage managers, such as "historic memory," "testimonies to past glory," "monuments of human creativity," "aesthetic values," and others. In many well documented cases, such a vision collided with the indigenous approach to land, landscape, and history—almost universally with great loss and harm to indigenous people (cf. Keller and Turek 1998). Recently, however, the trend is gradually being reversed—whether the issue at stake is a claim to land-use or to specific resources, access to land for particular spiritual purpose, or a government-initiated designation of lands as wildlife sanctuaries, parks, or heritage areas.

The concept of "northern wilderness" that had served for decades as the cornerstone for all approaches to landscape protection was the first to change its status, as illustrated by several chapters in this volume. Whether focused on the pristine nature of vast northern expanses or on "untouched" arctic ecosystems, it argued for northern lands to be protected for the purpose of nature preservation, or as the nation's treasure, or for the sake of future generations—that is, independent and irrespective of its residents, northern peoples, as well as of their values, memories, traditions, and their current use of the land. While still popular with the broad public, some conservationist groups, and tourist agencies alike, the "northern wilderness" paradigm is quickly losing its appeal among parks- and heritage managers in many northern countries (see several papers in Catton 1997 and Burks 1994, specifically Turner 1994; Muk and Byaliss-Smith 1999; also chapters by Buggey, Callaway, Horton, Mason, Shul'gin, Ward and Bollason, Wiget and Balalaeva, this volume).

The recognition of indigenous landscapes—via the score of new policies and projects described in this book—constitutes a milestone in this transition. The designation and protection of certain landscapes, because of their specific cultural meaning to *indigenous people*, paves the way to a far more respectful and informed approach to aboriginal cultures and to the general heritage of all local peoples. It applies to every northern nation whose preservation practices are described in this book. It also elevates the status of aboriginal views on landscape and land-human relationships to the sphere of legislative actions, management instructions, budget allocations, and daily work of the respective governmental agencies. As heritage managers, scholars, cultural anthropologists, and citizens, we applaud such a transition.

The Structure of the Volume

As chapters of this volume were gradually taking shape, it became clear that the book would address three different perspectives, or levels, in northern ethnographic landscape preservation. The first level analyzes what may be called "national doctrines": the established official approaches and management systems of individual polar countries, like Canada, the U.S., Russia, and others. This represents a view from the top, a reflection of the general ideology that is usually developed and espoused by the main national preservation agency or associated research institutions. At the opposite end of the spectrum is a specific bottom view that comes from the "foot soldiers" in the trenches, such as park managers and researchers, engaged in particular local programs or projects. Those local experiences illustrate the true diversity and on-the-ground realities that are often hard to grasp from major national policy documents. Finally, the middle stands for a regional perspective in management that comes from local hubs and regional agencies, and is shaped by decades of accumulated practical studies and management decisions. It also represents unique blends of local histories, administrative politics, and population mixtures typical of each major northern region.

Most of our authors have worn several hats during their professional careers, and each person has his or her heartfelt story about ethnographic landscape research or management to share. No individual chapter in this volume, therefore, speaks for only one particular "beast". Still, we found it useful to group the papers along *national*, *local*, and *regional* lines, and to organize the book in three main sections, according to those major visions.

Part 1: State Policies from Four Arctic Nations

Part One is made up of five papers. Arranged geographically, each paper represents a nation: Canada (Susan Buggey), the U.S. (Rachel Mason and Tonia Horton), Norway (Ingegerd Holand), and Russia (Pavel Shul'gin). Altogether those four countries cover almost eighty-five percent of the circumpolar land area. We regret our lack of information on ethnographic landscape policies in Greenland, Sweden, and Finland; a paper by Elisabeth Ward and Arthur Bollason (see below) at least partially represent the situation in Iceland. The two papers covering heritage landscape preservation in Alaska comes from the realities of the U.S. National Park Service system that recognizes "cultural landscapes" and "ethnographic landscapes" as two *separate* programs. Similarly, the two institutionalized visions on heritage landscapes in Norway are represented by the main governmental heritage agency, *Riksantikvaren* (Holand, this section), and by the Sámi Parliament (Falch and Skandfer, below).

Part 2: Protecting "The Invisible": Ethnographic Landscape Stories Across the Arctic Zone

Part Two is made up of seven chapters, which follow a thematic, rather than a geographic, progression. They illustrate the richness and variety of local ethnographic landscapes; each paper describes a specific research, documentation, or a local management effort.

The section starts with ethnographic landscapes having the greatest physical visibility of human traces on the ground, such as material constructions built for subsistence activities in the boreal marshland areas of West Siberia (Andrew Wiget and Olga Balalaeva) or at

indigenous ritual sites across the Siberian tundra used by nomadic reindeer herders (Galina Kharyuchi). It moves to a more complex overlap of indigenous and managerial perspectives on protected landscapes in Alaska (Donald Callaway), with their conflicting intertwinement of uses, boundaries, markers, and regimes. A different mixture is presented by the story of a complex multi-layer heritage landscape of a contemporary Native community, the village of Sivuqaq/Gambell on St. Lawrence Island, Alaska (Igor Krupnik). Here, the overlapping traces of earlier ethnographic landscapes are engrained both in remains and in human memories stretching back to the past The section progresses to even more intangible markers of human presence on the land, such as Native place-names from the Seward Peninsula in Northwest Alaska (Susan Fair), and to virtual heritage landscapes re-created by projecting medieval Icelandic saga stories onto the twenty-first century terrain (Elisabeth Ward and Arthur Bollason). In the two latter cases, the ethnographic landscape barely exists beyond the human mind; it is being created and transmitted by the sheer power of community memory and its adherence to the ancestors' traditions. The last paper presents the most extreme case of "invisible" heritage landscape, almost beyond today's park managers' imagination. It deals with the purely mental constructs of ocean fishing grounds and "seascapes" of the ocean bottom off the coast of northern Norway (Anita Maurstad). These products of generations of accumulated fishermen's knowledge are both the most elusive and the hardest types of "scapes" to manage, as they literally cease to exist at the moment the fishermen leave the place.

Part 3: Regional Approaches to Ethnographic Landscape Documentation and Protection

Part Three has four chapters, which are, again, organized geographically to cover Canada, U.S., Russia, and Norway. In this section the authors present more targeted regional reviews peppered with individualized experience from the ongoing heritage landscape programs in the Canadian Northwest Territories (Tom Andrews), in two Alaskan National Parks (Tonia Horton), in the Russian Yamal Autonomous Area, in northern West Siberia (Natalia Fedorova), as well as from the work of the Sámi Parliament and of its former Sámi Cultural Heritage Council on the protection of the Sámi heritage landscapes in Norway (Torvald Falch and Marianne Skandfer). We believe that those four chapters, framed by years—often, decades—of their authors' involvement in local research and documentation/preservation efforts, will be both illustrative and indicative of current trends across the circumpolar North. We hope that further writers and publishers explore this vast body of northern landscape management expertise that we cannot explore here beyond a few selected stories.[5]

Part Four and Epilogue

The final section offers our readers a look at heritage landscapes preservation outside the northern polar zone. In a book about northern landscapes, we had space for just one compelling perspective from outside the Arctic—a paper about the management of aboriginal heritage landscapes and seascapes in Australia (Claire Smith and Heather Burke). We believe that the Australian experience is particularly relevant to heritage management in the North, not only because the Australians pioneered the idea of indigenous heritage landscapes, but also because so much in Australian indigenous landscapes is about 'invisible' elements such as myths, dreams and 'dreamlands,' place-names, ancestral journeys, story-scapes, and knowledge initiation rites.

The volume concludes with an Epilogue by Ellen Lee, Director of the Archaeological Service Branch of Parks Canada. Her remarks review some of the many institutional hurdles and bottlenecks in heritage landscape preservation and in carrying the message out to the general public and to policy-makers. It reiterates the key line of every chapter in this volume that points to partnership with northern aboriginal communities as the best strategy to better document and to protect the invisible heritage of their lands.

Lessons and Messages

As always, the edited chapters and the final printed volume represent only a fraction of what has been assembled and reviewed during our project. As we perused the many paper drafts, agency reports, and secondary literature, several themes emerged as common experiences from across the northern regions. In the final section of this Introduction, we want to share a few critical lessons we learned through this process. We also consider these points as our key messages to park managers, researchers, and to general readers interested in the issues of northern ethnographic landscapes policies, preservation, and documentation.

Definition

Our first message is that there is a common understanding among researchers and managers in many northern countries about what constitutes an *ethnographic* landscape. But neither a good working definition nor a practical management approach transcends the boundaries of the respective nations. Landscape scholars and managers quote each other's policy documents and papers actively, but their daily operations take place in the legal and administrative spaces of their respective national systems. Of the four national approaches reviewed in our volume—those of Canada, the U.S., Norway, and Russia—two national systems (the U.S. and Russia) use the term "ethnographic landscape," whereas two other systems (Canada and Norway) stick to the term "cultural landscape" instead, with the added terms "aboriginal" and "Sámi," respectively. This demonstrates that true convergence of policies and approaches is still far ahead of us, if ever attainable, given the diversity of peoples, traditions, politics, and histories across the circumpolar zone.

In every northern country landscape managers and scholars now agree that the preservation of "ethnographic landscapes" is of critical importance to its Native residents. In the long run, it may be as crucial to the continuity of their cultures and identities as physical access to ancestral lands, in terms of subsistence activities, mobility, and use of traditional resource and community sites (Parker 1990). However, little public understanding and a great deal of managerial discord exist about what actually constitutes an indigenous "ethnographic landscape" and how such a landscape can be protected.

One may argue that there is only a minor semantic difference between the American vision of "ethnographic landscape" and the Canadian "aboriginal cultural landscape," and that the more distinctive Norwegian and Russian definitions fall more or less within the same realm. But the seemingly minor semantic distinctions may conceal more important practical differences. For example, under the U.S. National Park Service, ethnographic landscapes are just one of *four* recognized types of cultural landscapes (in addition to historic sites, historic designed landscapes, and historic vernacular landscapes—see papers by Mason and Horton, this volume). Ethnographic landscapes, defined herein by the NPS as "containing a variety of natural and cultural resources that associated people define as heritage resources," are clearly perceived as a combination of certain valuable *resources* that have to be identified, listed, and protected. The NPS' Ethnography Program, however, uses a different definition that presents an ethnographic landscape as "a relatively contiguous area of interrelated places that the members of contemporary social groups define as meaningful because it is inextricably and traditionally linked to their own local or regional histories, cultural identities, beliefs, and behaviors." Under that vision, the focus is upon certain "contiguous areas" and places that must be, similarly, identified and protected.

Canada's definition sees a cultural landscape as "any geographical area that has been modified, influenced, or given special cultural meaning by people" (Parks Canada 1994:119). In contrast to the U.S. definition, it stresses the role of human impact upon the land-

scape. Within this wide scope, it generally follows the anthropologically-inspired typology of the UNESCO World Heritage Convention (UNESCO 1996, cl.39). Common grounds are quite obvious; but one has to have extensive insider knowledge to grasp the practical differences.

Though accepted in their respective management systems, those definitions are but a starting point. They co-exist with several other related terms that sometimes offer a more instrumental perspective, such as "sacred landscape" (Carmichael 1994), "sacred sites" (Balalaeva 1999), "sacred places" (Kelley and Francis 1994), "spiritual (or ceremonial) lands," "spiritual geography" (Griffith 1992), "symbolic landscape" (Burley 1991; Schanche 1995), "ancestral lands," "holy lands" (Spicer 1957), "holy grounds" (Schlee 1990), "storyscapes" (Stoffle et al 1997), and others.[6] They also lack a *functional* aspect indicative of the specific origin or uses of an ethnographic landscape. Every typology has certain gray areas of ambiguity; some authors argue that *all* socially relevant landscapes are symbolic and historical (Cosgrove 1989; Ingold 1991).

Definitions inevitably have limited operational value and have to be elaborated by specific identification guidelines that address the distinctive qualities of different types of landscapes. In terms of implicit guidelines for identifying and especially for managing areas that could be labeled *ethnographic* versus other recognized types of cultural landscapes, much work is urgently needed. We cannot offer a plausible response to this challenge, besides pointing out that various symbolic landscapes have an interwoven and even conflicting history, and that flexibility, openness, and consultations are the best tools in dealing with "virtual realities," such as ethnographic landscapes.

Knowledge

Although both the title of this book and the various policy and management systems it represents feature the terms "lands" and "landscapes," the real subject is, in fact, knowledge. It is the human knowledge about the landscape, preserved and transmitted by its residents (or, often, former residents), that gives its magic touch to northern lands and waters. Verbalized human tradition transforms the vast and mostly unpopulated arctic areas with no signs and street markers, or a terrain dotted with anonymous archaeological remains, into meaningful cultural space.

We believe that such an explicit focus on human knowledge and tradition is critical in developing policies regarding ethnographic landscape preservation. Unlike a physical landscape, an ethnographic landscape is alive and meaningful as long as it is supported by viable and accessible cultural knowledge. In a reverse statement, the extinction of cultural knowledge associated with a certain landscape returns it to the status of wilderness or makes it an empty land with barely seen remnants of former occupation.

We would argue that in practical managerial terms it is, therefore, as important to preserve and support the knowledge about the land (through documentation, education, and other heritage efforts) as it is to establish a vigorous protective regime for the land itself. A compelling example comes from the fishermen's knowledge of seascape (Maurstad, this volume). When the fishermen are gone, and their knowledge of bays, currents, ocean floor, and specific fishing sites is lost, the age-built cultural seascape reverts back to the "wild" ocean or is reduced to a nautical chart. There would be, in fact, nothing more to protect than lighthouses and fish stocks.

The focus on human knowledge, rather than on the land or landscape itself, offers new prospects for long-term preservation and even for a restoration of certain ethnographic landscapes. Indeed, knowledge preserved in writing or orally within the present or former residential community may bring new life to the old cultural landscape. Old knowledge is the only path to restore cultural value to the landscape that has lost its original meaning for its current residents and land managers. The unique preservation of early medieval oral histories (sagas) in Iceland helped revitalize "virtual

ethnographic landscapes" of the past and turn them to today's use for tourism and heritage education (Ward and Bollason, this volume). Therefore, today's investment in documenting the knowledge related to northern ethnographic landscapes may be the best and the most sound policy to assure their continuity in the future.

Cooperation

As many papers in this volume illustrate, documenting ethnographic landscapes is a collaborative process. There is a huge mental gap to bridge and a great distance to cover between the offices of heritage preservation agencies (even those located in the northern regions) and the indigenous communities who created and maintained local ethnographic landscapes over generations. Here nothing can be done without true collaboration, mutual trust, and respect. Cultural sensitivity is crucial in approaching the most invisible aspects of Native legacy related to ethnographic landscapes and to people's bonds to their ancestral lands.

Whereas heritage managers may address local communities directly and often do a thorough job in collecting knowledge about landscapes, we believe that three other groups of players are critical to this process. The first are respected indigenous experts, usually elders. They embody local heritage and tradition, and they act as the most legitimate and authoritative spokespersons for their communities. Cultural anthropologists, with established ties to local groups and extensive first-hand knowledge of their tradition, make up the second group. Local educators, particularly those from within the Native communities, are the third type of players. Their role in landscape documentation and preservation is absolutely critical, though greatly underestimated. Their main input is in formatting the knowledge of elders (and of anthropologists) into stories and texts appealing to the younger generations of Native people, who will be the bearers and protectors of local ethnographic landscapes for decades to come.

Through our personal experience—and more than

ever, after this volume—we believe that no documentation and no protection of ethnographic landscapes can be successful without the full involvement of local communities. We regard this as the key message of our collective effort and we want it to be heard clearly by policy-makers, heritage professionals, and public alike.

Acknowledgements

This *Northern Ethnographic Landscapes* volume is an outcome of collaboration between the NPS Alaska Regional Office in Anchorage and the Smithsonian Arctic Studies Center. This book would never have materialized if not for friendly guidance as well as the logistical and financial backing of the NPS in Alaska. Within the NPS Alaska Regional Office we are especially grateful to Ted Birkedal, Cultural Resources Team Manager, and to Steve Peterson, Senior Historical Architect. They developed the initial concept of a report on international practices in northern ethnographic landscapes documentation and they have supported the project through every stage of its implementation. Donald Callaway, Senior Cultural Anthropologist, was our NPS project liaison. At the Smithsonian, William W. Fitzhugh, the ASC Director, was always a source of friendly encouragement and insight; Stephen Loring and Aron Crowell shared their knowledge and offered good advice. We thank you all.

Several more people were instrumental in introducing prospective contributors, sharing their expertise, and providing other forms of support. In Alaska, we are grateful to Judy Gottlieb, the NPS Associate Regional Director for Subsistence and Partnerships, in Anchorage; and to Leigh Selig, then Assistant Superintendent, Western Arctic National Parklands, in Nome. In Canada, we thank Ellen Lee and Hélène Chabot at Parks Canada in Ottawa; Norman Hallendy in Carp, Ontario; and Rick Armstrong at the Nunavut Research Institute in Iqaluit, Nunavut. In Norway, we received great support from Ole Grøn at the Norwegian Institute for Cultural Heritage Research (NIKU) in Oslo; Audhild Schanche at the Nordic Sámi Institute and Alf Isak Keskitalo at the Guovdageaidnu Municipal Museum in Kautokeino; Bjørnar Olsen and Henry Minde at the University of Tromsø in Tromsø; Terje Brantenberg and Ivar Bjørklund at the Tromsø Museum, Tromsø. In Russia, Krupnik's trip to Salekhard in fall of 2000 was supported by the Science Department of the Yamal Area administration, and was facilitated by Natalia Fedorova, Sviatoslav Alekseev, and Aleksei Zen'ko.

While working on this volume, we lost one of its most devoted contributors, the Alaskan folklorist and art historian Susan Fair, who passed away in 2003. We are fortunate that Susan's colleague, Herbert Anungazuk from the NPS Alaska Office, graciously prepared a tribute to Susan's legacy for this collection.

We are grateful to many colleagues who kindly offered their photos for section and text illustrations. These visual contributions by Thomas Andrews (Yellowknife, Canada), Sergei Bogoslovskii (Moscow, Russia), Donald Callaway and Thetus Smith (Anchorage, Alaska), David Dector (Jerusalem, Israel), William Fitzhugh (Washington, D.C.), Ingegerd Holand (Oslo, Norway), and John Hood (Harrow, UK) are very much appreciated.

Our special thanks go to the volume's editorial and production team. Thetus H. Smith, our style- and technical editor from the NPS Alaska Office, was instrumental in bringing individual papers into one consistent format for the volume. Georgene Sink in Anchorage assisted with translation of the Russian papers, and Cara Seitcheck and Katherine Rusk in Washington offered their editorial skills. Elisabeth Ward and Iris Hahn-Santoro at the ASC and Bryan Hood in Tromsø assisted in translation and editing of Torvald Falch and Marianne Skandfer's paper, delivered in Norwegian. We thank Elisabeth Ward, our volume production editor (now at Berkeley); Kathleen Paparchontis, who prepared the Index for the volume; and Raissa Macasieb-Ludwig, who prepared the illustrations for the book.

Finally, we salute all our volume contributors. Our common journey, from the outset of the project to the printing of the book, took several years to accomplish. We would never have made it if not for their enthusiasm, patience, and comradeship that helped coalesce many individual studies in several languages and countries into a collective vision on ethnographic landscapes preservation across the circumpolar North.

Notes

1. As of 2002, 29 cultural landscapes have been nominated from 23 countries (World Heritage Convention 2002). As of this writing, there were 15 sites officially registered as "cultural landscapes" and two sites listed as "archaeological landscapes," in addition to 23 "mixed" properties (of which most feature "outstanding cultural values") on the overall list of 788 "world heritage properties" (http://whc.unesco.org/pg.cfm?cid-31).

2. This turned out to be the right prediction, as the issue of indigenous ethnographic landscapes became the key theme for the 29th Annual Meeting of the Alaska Anthropological Association in Anchorage in 2002 (titled "Lands, Landscapes and Landmarks") as well as for "WAC-5," the 5th World Archaeological Congress in Washington, D.C. in 2003.

3. According to the NPS definition, an ethnographic landscape is a landscape that contains "a variety of natural and cultural resources that associated people define as heritage resources. Examples are contemporary settlements, religious sacred sites and massive geological structures. Small plant communities, animals, subsistence and ceremonial grounds are often components" (Birnbaum 1994:2; Hardesty 2000:182; see also chapters by Mason and Horton, this volume).

4. The literature on the issues of indigenous worldviews and landscapes is indeed enormous. The most commonly quoted sources include Basso 1996; Berkes 1999; Brody 1981; Frey 2001; Kelley and Francis 1994. For the Northern indigenous people see Fienup-Riordan 1994; Hallendy 2000; Kari and Fall 1987/2003; Kawagley 1995; Nelson 1986; Nelson et al. 1982; Tanner 1979. International collections, with extensive bibliographies include Feld and Basso 1996; Grim 2001; Hirsch and O'Honlon 1995; Irimoto and Yamada 1994; Mills and Slobodin 1994.

5. Again, we regret that the limits of our volume prevent us from presenting regional data from other northern countries as well as from other areas within the four nations covered in the book, like Nunavut in Canada (Hallendy 2000; Heyes 2002), or Chukotka in Russia, for which a lot of information is available

6. See also specific northern/Arctic terms, such as 'memoryscapes' (Nuttal 1991), 'culturescapes' (King 2002), 'visioscapes' (Sejersen 2004). One could argue that some of these terms refer to different *levels* of aboriginal ethnographic landscapes and, thus, may be organized typologically, if not hierarchically. For an attempt to produce such an hierarchy of cultural (ethnographic) landscapes of Southern Paiute people of the Grand Canyon area see Stoffle et al. 1997.

References

Alanen, Arnold R., and Robert Z. Melnick, eds.
2000   *Preserving Cultural Landscapes in America.* Baltimore and London: John Hopkins University Press.

Balalaeva, Olga
1999   Sviashchennye mesta khantov Srednei i Nizhnei Obi (Sacred sites of the Khanty People along the Middle and Lower Ob River). In *Ocherki istorii traditsionnogo zemlepol'zovaniia khantov (materially k atlasy)* (Studies in the history of traditional land-use of the Khanty People), pp. 139–56. Ekaterinburg: Tezis.

Basso, Keith
1996   *Wisdom Sits in Places: Landscape and Language Among the Western Apache.* Albuquerque: University of New Mexico Press.

Bender, Barbara, ed.
1993   *Landscape: Politics and Perspectives.* Oxford: Berg.

Beringian Heritage
1989   *Beringian Heritage. A Reconnaissance Study of Sites and Recommendations.* International Park Program. Denver: National Park Service.

Berkes, Fikret
1999   *Sacred Ecology. Traditional Ecological Knowledge and Resource Management.* London: Taylor and Francis.

Birnbaum, Charles A.
1994   *Protecting Cultural Landscapes: Planning, Treatment and Management of Historic Landscapes.* Preservation Brief 36. Washington, D.C.: National Park Service.

Brody, Hugh
1981   *Maps and Dreams. Indians and the British Columbia Frontier.* New York: Pantheon Books.

Buggey, Susan
1999   *An Approach to Aboriginal Cultural Landscapes.* Ottawa: Historic Sites and Monuments Board of Canada, Parks Canada.

Burks, David Clarke, ed.
1994   *Place of the Wild.* Washington, DC and Covelo,

CA: Island Press and Shearwater Books.

Burley, David V.

1991   Chiefly Prerogatives Over Critical Resources: Archaeology, Oral Traditions and Symbolic Landscapes in the Ha'apai Islands, Kingdom of Tonga. In *Culture and Environment: A Fragile Coexistence*, R.W. Jamieson, A. Abonyi, and N. Miran, eds., pp. 437–43. Calgary: University of Calgary.

Callaway, Donald

2003   Beringia: Visions of an International Park in Difficult Times. *Alaska Park Science* (Winter):3–11. Anchorage

Carmichael, David

1994   Places of Power: Mescalero Apache Sacred Sites and Sensitive Areas. In *Sacred Sites, Sacred Places*. D.L. Carmichael, J. Hubert, B. Reeves, and A. Schanche, eds., pp.89–97. *One World Arcaheology* 23. London and New York: Routledge.

Carmichael, David L., Jane Hubert, Brian Reeves, and Audhild Schanche, eds.

1994   Sacred Sites, Sacred Places. *One World Archaeology* 23. London and New York: Routledge.

Catton, Theodore

1997   *Inhabited Wilderness. Indians, Eskimos, and National Parks in Alaska*. Albuquerque: University of New Mexico Press

Cosgrove, D.

1989   Geography is Everywhere: Culture and Symbolism in Human Landscapes. In *Horizons in Human Geography*, D. Gregory and R. Walford, eds., pp. 118–35. London: Macmillan.

Fair, Susan W., and Edgar N. Ningeulook

1994   *Qamani: Up the Coast, In My Mind, In My Heart*. Manuscript, Alaska Support Office, National Park Service, Anchorage, Alaska.

Feld, Steven and Keith H. Basso, ed.

1996   *Senses of Place*. Santa Fe, NM: School of American Research Press.

Fienup-Riordan, Ann

1994   *Boundaries and Passages. Rule and Ritual in Yup'ik Eskimo Oral Tradition*. New Brunswick and London: Rutgers University Press

Fowler, P.J.

2003   World Heritage Cultural Landscapes 1992–2002. *World Heritage Paper* 6. Paris: UNESCO, World Heritage Centre.

Frey, Rodney, in collaboration with the Schitsu'umsh

2001   *Landscape Traveled by Coyote and Crane. The World of the Schitsu'umsh (Coeur d'Alene Indians)*. Seattle: University of Washington Press.

Gosden, Chris

1989   Prehistoric Social Landscapes of the Arawe Islands, West New Britain Province, Papua New Guinea. *Archaeology in Oceania* 24(2):45–58.

Griffith, James

1992   *Beliefs and Holy Places: The Spiritual Geography of the Primeria Alta*. Tucson: University of Arizona, Bureau of Applied Research in Anthropology.

Grim, John, ed.

2001   *Indigenous Traditions and Ecology: The Interbeing of Cosmology and Community*. Cambridge, MA: Harvard University Press.

Hallendy, Norman

2000   *Inuksuit. Silent Messengers of the Arctic*. Vancouver and Toronto: Douglas & McIntyre and University of Toronto Press.

Hardesty, Donald L.

2000   Ethnographic Landscapes: Transforming Nature into Culture. In *Preserving Cultural Landscapes in America*. A.L. Alanen and R.Z. Melnick, eds., pp. 169–85. Baltimore: Johns Hopkins University Press.

Heyes, Scott

2002   Protecting the Authenticity and Integrity of Inuksuit within the Arctic Milieu. *Études/Inuit/Studies* 26(1–2):133–56.

Hirsch, Eric, and Michael O'Hanlon, eds.

1995   *The Anthropology of Landscape: Perspectives on Place and Space*. Oxford: Clarendon Press.

Ingold, Tim

1993   The Temporality of the Landscape. *World Archaeology* 25(2):152–74.

Irimoto, Takashi, and Takako Yamada, eds.

1994   *Circumpolar Religion and Ecology. An Anthropology of the North*. Tokyo: University of Tokyo Press.

Kari, James, and James A. Fall, comps.

1987 *Shem Pete's Alaska. The Territory of the Upper Cook Inlet Dena'ina*. Fairbanks: Alaska Native Language Center, University of Alaska. 2nd edition 2003, Fairbanks: University of Alaska Press.

Kawagley, Oscar A.

1995   *Yupiaq Worldview: A Pathway to Ecology and Spirit*. Prospect Heights, Ill:Waveland Press.

Keller, Robert H., and Michael F. Turek

1998   *American Indians and National Parks*. Tucson: University of Arizona Press

Kelley, Klara Bonsack, and Harris Francis

1994   *Navajo Sacred Places*. Bloomington and Indianapolis: Indiana University Press.

King, Alexander D.

2002   Reindeer Herders' Culturescapes in the Koryak Autonomous Okrug. In *People and the Land: Pathways to Reform in Post-Soviet Siberia*. E. Kasten, ed., pp. 63–80. Berlin: Dietrich Reimer Verlag.

Krupnik, Igor, and Nikolai Vakhtin

1997   Indigenous Knowledge in Modern Culture. Siberian Yupik Ecological Legacy in Transition. *Arctic Anthropology* 34(1):236–52.

Mills, Antonia, and Richard Slobodin, eds.

1994   *Amerindian Rebirth. Reincarnation Belief Among*

North American Indians and Inuit. Toronto: University of Toronto Press.

Mitchell, W.J.T., ed.
1994   *Landscape and Power.* Chicago: University of Chicago Press.

Mulk, Inga-Maria, and Tim Bayliss-Smith
1999   The Representation of Sámi Cultural Identity in the Cultural Landscapes of Northern Sweden: The Use and Misuse of Archaeological Knowledge. In *The Archaeology and Anthropology of Landscape. Shaping Your Landscape.* P.J. Ucko and R. Layton, eds., pp.358-96. *One World Archaeology* 30. London and New York: Routledge.

Nelson, Richard K.
1986   *Make Prayers to the Raven: Koyukon View of the Northern Forest.* Chicago: University of Chicago Press.

Nelson, Richard K., Kathleen H. Mautner, and G. Ray Bane
1982   *Tracks in the Wildland. A Portrayal of Koyukon and Nunamiut Subsistence.* Fairbanks: University of Alaska Fairbanks, Cooperative Park Studies Unit.

Nuttal, Mark
1991   Memoryscape: A Sense of Locality in Northwest Greenland. *North Atlantic Studies* 1(2):39-50.

Parker, Patricia L.
1990   *Keepers of the Treasures. Protecting Historic Properties and Cultural Traditions on Indian Lands.* Washington, D.C.: National Park Service, Interagency Resource Division.

Parker, Patricia L., and Thomas F. King
1990   Guidelines for Evaluating and Documenting Traditional Cultural Properties. *National Register Bulletin* 38. Washington, D.C.: National Park Service

Parks Canada
1994   *Guiding Principles and Operational Policies.* Ottawa: Department of Canadian Heritage

Schaaf, Jeanne, ed.
1996   *Ublasaun. First Light. Inupiaq Hunters and Herders in the Early Twentieth Century, Northern Seward Peninsula, Alaska.* Anchorage: National Park Service.

Schanche, Audhild
1995   Det symbolske landskapet - landskap og identitet I sámisk kultur. *Ottar* 4:38-47.

Schlee, Günther
1992   Ritual Topography and Ecological Use. The Gabbra of the Kenyan/Ethyopian Borderlands. In *Bush Base: Forest Farm—Culture, Environment and Development*, E. Croll and D. Parker, eds., pp. 110-28.London and New York: Routledge.

Sejersen, Frank
2004   Horizons of Sustainability in Greenland: Inuit Landscapes of Memory and Vision. *Arctic Anthropology* 41(1):71-89.

Simon, James J.K., and Craig Gerlach

1991   *Reindeer Herding Subsistence and Alaska Land Use in the Bering Land Bridge National Preserve, Northern Seward Peninsula, Alaska.* Anchorage: National Park Service.

Smith, Claire and H.M. Wobst
n.d.   Indigenous Archaeologies: Decolonising Theory and Practice. *One World Archaeology* 47. London and New York: Routledge (in press).

Spicer, Edward H.
1957   Worlds Apart: Cultural Differences in the Modern Southwest. *Arizona Quarterly* 13(3):197-203.

Stoffle, Richard W., and Michael J. Evans
1990   Holistic Conservation and Cultural Triage: American Indian Perspectives on Cultural Resources. *Human Organization* 49(2):91-9.

Stoffle, Richard W., David B. Halmo, and Diane E. Austin
1997   Cultural Landscapes and Traditional Cultural Properties: Southern Paiute View of the Grand Canyon and Colorado River. *American Indian Quarterly* 21(2):229-49.

Tanner, Adrian
1979   *Bringing Home Animals: Religious Ideology and Mode of Production of the Mistassini Cree Hunter.* London: Hurst.

Thompson, George F.
1995   *Landscape in America.* Austin: University of Texas Press

Tilley, Christopher
1994   *A Phenomenology of Landscape. Places, Paths and Monuments.* Oxford and Providence: Berg.

Turner, Jack
1994   The Quality of Wilderness: Preservation, Control, and Freedom. In *Place of the Wild*. D.C. Burks, ed., pp. 175-89. Washington, D.C. and Covelo, CA: Island Press and Shearwater Books.

Ucko, Peter J., and Robert Layton, eds.
1999   The Archaeology and Anthropology of Landscape. Shaping Your Landscape. *One World Archaeology* 30. London and New York: Routledge.

UNESCO
1996   *Operational Guidelines for the Implementation of the World Heritage Convention.* Paris: UNESCO.
1998   *Natural Sacred Sites: Cultural Diversity and Biological Diversity.* Proceedings of the First International UNESCO Seminar. Paris: UNESCO
2002   *Sites Inscribed on the World Heritage List. World Heritage Convention.* Paris: UNESCO.

Vdovin, Boris I., comp.
1990   *Tekhniko-ekonomicheskoe obosnovanie sozdaniia kompleksa osobookhraniaemykh territorii i akvatorii v raione Beringova proliva* (Building a network of protected landscapes and seascapes in the Bering Strait area: technical and economic assessment study). Report. St. Petersburg: Lengiprogor.

3/ Ezogokwoo ('bones of Ezo's people'), a sacred place and the site of a major battle between the Dogrib and a neighbouring group, Northwest Territories, Canada.

part 1

STATE POLICIES—PERSPECTIVES FROM FOUR ARCTIC NATIONS

An Approach to Aboriginal Cultural Landscapes in Canada

SUSAN BUGGEY

Indigenous peoples in many parts of the world view landscape in ways common to their experience and different from the Western perspective of land and landscape. The relationship between people and place is conceived fundamentally in spiritual terms rather than primarily material terms. Many indigenous people consider all the earth to be sacred and regard themselves as an integral part of this holistic and living landscape. They belong to the land and are at one in it with animals, plants, and ancestors whose spirits inhabit it. For many, places in the landscape are also sacred, as places of power, of journeys related to spirit beings, of entities that must be appeased. Laws and gifts from these spirit beings shaped the cultures and day-to-day activities of Aboriginal peoples in Canada's North. Intimate knowledge of natural resources and ecosystems of their areas, developed through long and sustained contact, and respect for the spirits that inhabit these places, molded life on the land. Traditional knowledge, in the form of narratives, place names, and ecological lore, bequeathed through oral tradition from generation to generation, embodies and preserves the relationship to the land. Landscapes "house" these stories, and protection of these places is key to their long-term survival in Aboriginal culture.

In Canada's North, Aboriginal peoples have occupied the harsh, varied environment for millennia. A diversity of historical experience across time and place, as well as differing current situations, marks the relationships of people with the region. Today Indians, Inuit, and Métis comprise approximately fifty First Nations, speaking predominantly Athapaskan and Inuktitut in about sixteen different languages. The area is divided politically into three territories: Yukon in the west, Northwest Territories in the center, and Nunavut in the east. Aboriginal rights and settlement areas are defined by comprehensive land claims agreements negotiated between Aboriginal peoples and the federal government and based on traditional use and occupancy of lands. Provisions in each claim differ. Agreements concluded in the past decade include chapters relating to environment, heritage, and cultural resources that provide part of the planning context for national historic sites (Lee 1997). The Royal Commission on Aboriginal Peoples, established in 1991, examined the relationship between Aboriginal peoples and Canadian society in general, including government, over time and throughout the country. Its massive report (Canada 1996) articulated Aboriginal worldviews, traditions of knowledge, issues, and recommendations that have situated, or placed in context, subsequent considerations of Aboriginal heritage. The Supreme Court of Canada decision in the Delgamuukw case (1997) marked legal acceptance of Aboriginal oral history related to a group's traditional area along with wider implications for Aboriginal rights related to land ownership.

To recognize the values of Aboriginal cultural landscapes (Fig. 4) and to commemorate these places, identification and evaluation have to focus on Aboriginal worldviews, rather than on those of non-indigenous cultures of Western civilization and Western scientific tradition. In Canada, national heritage falls under the purview of the Minister of the Environment. The minister is advised on the identification of national historic significance by the Historic Sites and Monuments Board of Canada (HSMBC), a statutory body composed of representatives of the ten provinces, three territories, and three national heritage agencies. Parks Canada, a federal government agency reporting to the Minister of the Environment, administers the program of national historic commemoration. Historically, the history of Aboriginal peoples has been underrepresented in its National Historic Sites system, but it is now one of the priority themes. For a decade, an ongoing dialogue involving many parties has been exploring ways to address this neglected aspect of Canada's history. By 1997-98 the HSMBC had specifically identified the need for an appropriate framework based on "nature, tradition, continuity, and attachment to the land [. . .] as the defining elements in determining historic significance" and on "considering groups for commemoration [and] focusing on the importance of place to the Aboriginal group" (HSMBC Minutes July 1998). This paper focuses on Canada's North, but it derives from a national context (Buggey 1999). It situates Aboriginal worldviews and place in relation to the field of cultural landscapes and to national historic site designations related to the history of Aboriginal people. Various aspects were explored with about fifty people, who include Parks Canada; provincial and territorial staff in all parts of the country; consultants with extensive experience in working with Aboriginal communities; and Aboriginal people in umbrella organizations and various other positions. The paper presents guidelines that Canada has developed for the identification of Aboriginal cultural landscapes of national historic significance.

4/ *Some landscapes important to the history of Aboriginal people in Canada.*

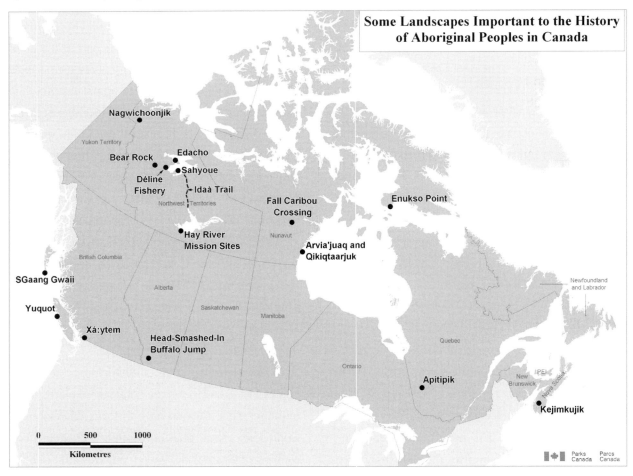

Aboriginal Worldviews

To understand the northern landscape requires an understanding of the related cosmologies. Aboriginal cosmologies relate earth and sky, the elements, the directions, the seasons, and mythic transformers to lands Aboriginals have occupied since ancient times. Guided by these cosmological relationships, many have creation stories related to their homelands, and they date their presence in those places to times when spirit beings traversed the world, transformed themselves at will between human and animal form, created their ancestors, and contoured the landscape. For the Beaver people of the subarctic, for example, the creation story focused on Muskrat, the diver who brought a speck of dirt from the sea bottom to the earth's surface, at a point that represented the coming together of trails from the four directions. It focused equally on Swan, who flew into the sky and brought back the world and the songs of the seasons. Transformed in vision quest from the boy Swan to culture hero Saya, who travels across the sky as sun and moon, he was the first man to follow the trail of animals and thus established the relationship between hunters and their game. Hunters slept with their heads to the east, the direction of the rising sun, so that they might dream their hunt along the trail of the sun before they experienced it on the physical trail across the land (Ridington 1990:69–73, 91–3).

Certain places embody these cosmological contexts. The stages of the journeys and exploits of culture heroes, such as Yamoria and his namesakes of several groups through the Mackenzie Basin of the Northwest Territories, can be related to specific features in the landscape (Andrews 1990). These narratives vary from group to group, but their climax occurs at the same geographical point, Bear Rock on the Mackenzie River (Fig. 5), where the several features of the mountain and the archaeological evidence concur in long association. Many Dene regard Bear Rock as a sacred site, and its symbolic importance is reflected in its selection as the logo of the Dene Nation, which represents the relation between the Dene and Deneneh (Hanks 1993). The Gwich'in cycle of stories of the trickster Raven records how the hollows in the landscape known today at Tsiigehtchic in the Northwest Territories are his camp and bed (Gwich'in Social and Cultural Institute 1997:800–7). In northern Quebec, sites associated with the travels of the giant beaver still in transformation mode populate the demographically vacant map (Craik and Namagoose 1992:17–21).

Cosmological relationships and associations with spirit beings identify places of power, where the combination of spirits and place creates environments favorable for spiritual communication. Identification of sites along two trails in the Dogrib landscape in the Northwest Territories, for example, differentiated five categories of sacred sites to which Dogrib elders accorded recognition:

—Places where the activities of culture heroes are associated with landscape features;

—Sites inhabited by giant, usually malevolent and dangerous, "spirit animals;"

—Locations where the dreaming activities of culture heroes intersected the landscape;

—Places where important resources, such as stone and ochre, are found;

—Graves.

Twenty sacred sites associated with culture hero Yamòzhah and his exploits in making the land safe were identified along the Idaà Trail (Andrews et al. 1998:307–14; Andrews, this volume).

The cosmological and mythological associations of sacred places and the continuing cultural relationship to the spirits and power of these places characterize many landscapes important to Aboriginal people in Canada. Traditional knowledge relates contemporary cultures directly to traditional places. Social structure, economic activity, language, rituals, and spiritual beliefs preserve cultural memory through intangible traditions related to place. Seeing places as markers of identity requires looking at them through the worldview and experience of the peoples associated with them. As the report *Rakekée Gok'é Godi: Places We Take Care Of* states,

> [o]ne of the most important themes in understanding Sahtu Dene and Métis history is the relationship between culture and landscape. Virtually all of Sahtu Dene and Métis history is written on the land. As such, the places and sites, which commemorate this relationship, are an integral part of Sahtu Dene and Métis identity (Sahtu 2000:14).

Narratives and place names bequeathed from generation to generation relate these spiritual associations directly to the land.

> The Sahtu Dene narratives create a mosaic of stories that envelop the cultural landscapes of Grizzly Bear Mountain and Scented Grass Hills. The web of "myth and memory" spread beyond the mountains to cover the whole western end of Great Bear Lake, illustrating the complexity of the Sahtu Dene's landscape tradition (HSMBC Minutes November 1996).

The complexity and intensity of Aboriginal belief and tradition mark the continuous living relationship people have with the land, and the concept of "land" includes water and sky as well as earth. The interrelationships of people, animals, and spirits—as well as kinship and language attachments to place—are spiritual, mental, and emotional aspects of living with a particular environment. Traditional life, rooted in intimate knowledge of the natural environment, focused on seasonal movement, which was patterned by movements of animals, marine resources, and the hunt. Uses and activities, from harvesting and social gatherings to rituals and ceremonies, are core expressions of relation to the land. Kinship, social relationships, and reciprocal obligations linked people in this complex round sustained for centuries. These defining attributes of Aboriginal peoples' attachments to land are more important to them than place as physical resource.

The inter-connectedness of all aspects of human life with the living landscape—in social and spiritual relationships as much as in harvesting—continuously through time roots Aboriginal cultures in the land. A working definition declares that

> An Aboriginal cultural landscape is a place valued by an Aboriginal group (or groups) because of their long and complex relationship with that land. It expresses their unity with the natural and spiritual environment. It embodies their traditional knowledge of spirits, places, land uses, and ecology. Material remains of the association may be prominent, but will often be minimal or absent (Buggey 1999:27).

The associated people will not necessarily be only current occupiers or users of the land, but may also include those who have a historic relationship still significant to their culture, such as the Huron-Wendat of Quebec to the territory in southern Ontario that they left in the mid-seventeenth century. As well, other people than the associated group (or groups) may have used these landscapes and may attach values to them.

Cultural Landscapes

In identifying cultural landscapes of national historic significance, Canada follows UNESCO's approach. After nearly a decade of debate about the nature of cultural landscapes and their potential outstanding universal value, in 1992 UNESCO's World Heritage Committee, the administrative body for the World Heritage Convention, agreed that "the term 'cultural landscape' embraces a diversity of manifestations of the interaction between humankind and the natural environment" (UNESCO 1996a:37). UNESCO's guidelines focus on this interaction between societies and the natural world that shapes the cultural landscape. In addition to this defining characteristic, it lists a tripartite categorization of landscapes:

> —The clearly defined landscape designed and created intentionally by man;
>
> —The organically evolved landscape: relict or continuing;
>
> —The associative cultural landscape.

These provide an elementary identification of types as

5/ *Bear Rock, on the Mackenzie River, Northwest Territories, is the subject of important traditional teachings and a sacred site to the Dene people.*

aids in the identification of where values lie. The third type, the associative cultural landscape, is justified for inclusion on the World Heritage List "by virtue of the powerful religious, artistic or cultural associations of the natural element rather than material cultural evidence, which may be insignificant or even absent" (UNESCO 1996a:39iii). Cultural landscapes associated with indigenous peoples are most likely to fit in this category.

Associative cultural landscapes mark a significant move away from conventional heritage concepts rooted in physical resources, whether the monuments of cultural heritage or wilderness in natural heritage. They also accentuate the indivisibility of cultural and natural values in cultural landscapes. The 1995 Asia-Pacific workshop on associative cultural landscapes, held for UNESCO, elaborated on their essential characteristics:

Associative cultural landscapes may be defined as large or small contiguous or non-contiguous areas and itineraries, routes or other linear landscapes—these may be physical entities or mental images embedded in a people's spirituality, cultural tradition and practice. The attributes of associative cultural landscapes include the intangible, such as the acoustic, the kinetic and the olfactory, as well as the visual (Australia ICOMOS 1995:4).

Associative cultural landscapes are, then, defined by cultural values related to natural resources. The range of natural features associated with cosmological, symbolic, sacred, and culturally significant landscapes may be very broad: mountains, caves, outcrops, coastal waters, rivers, lakes, pools, hillsides, uplands, plains, woods, groves, trees. While the physical resources are largely natural, cultural values transform these places from natural to cultural landscapes. In language, narratives, sounds, ceremonies, kinship relationships, and social customs are found cohesive evidences of cultural meanings.

The emergence of cultural landscapes as an integral part of cultural heritage coincided with international recognition in the natural heritage community that areas long identified as pristine wilderness and celebrated for their ecological values untouched by human activity are the homelands of indigenous peoples and are shaped by long-term, sustainable human occupation. Their management of those landscapes has often altered the original ecological system, but it has equally contributed to the biological diversity that has long been regarded as a prime value of wilderness (McNeely 1995). Anthropologists and Aboriginal people working on traditional use studies and undertaking to reestablish cultural landscapes on the West Coast have applied this dilemma to ways of seeing west coast landscapes: in contrast to the visitor and the scientist, who perceive wilderness in Gwaii Haanas (Fig. 6), the Haida people see their homeland, Haida Gwaii, rich with the historical and spiritual evidences of their centuries-long occupation.

Defining cultural landscapes as "[a]ny geographical area that has been modified, influenced, or given special cultural meaning by people" (Parks Canada 1994a:119), Parks Canada overtly recognizes cultural landscapes characterized by the intangible values that indigenous peoples attach to landscape. According heritage status to places with spiritual associations in the absence of material remains acknowledges human values crucial to the identities of these peoples. It is also explicitly accepted that the associated peoples identify such places and values. Most provinces have developed an approach to cultural landscapes (e.g., Ontario: http://www.culture.gov.on.ca/english/culdiv/ heritage/landscap.htm and Nova Scotia: http:// museum.gov.ns.ca/mnh/nature/nhns/t12/t12-2.htm). Both the provinces and the territories, however, have generally used an archaeological rather than a cultural landscape approach to the commemoration of Aboriginal heritage and have not designated places as Aboriginal cultural landscapes. They recognize, though,

that some designated sites, such as Writing-on-Stone Provincial Park in Alberta and White Mountain on Lake Mistassini in Quebec, have cultural landscape values. British Columbia's traditional use studies program (British Columbia 1996) and Yukon's address to Aboriginal values of place in its planning processes are examples of other approaches to recognizing cultural landscapes. Aboriginal decision-makers, as well, have their own approach, including toponymy for the management of symbolic values.

National Historic Site Designations of Aboriginal Cultural Landscapes

During the past thirty years, the Historic Sites and Monuments Board of Canada has recommended a number of places associated with the cultures of Aboriginal peoples for designation as national historic sites. The movement from viewing objects through perspectives of art history and archaeology, characteristic of the HSMBC's experience in commemorating Aboriginal history from the late 1960s through the 1980s, to seeing cultural landscapes associated with living peoples, mirrors the historiography of the various decision periods. As early as 1969, the board recognized the Inuksuit at Enusko Point, Baffin Island, Nunavut, as being of national significance. In keeping with the perspective of the time, it saw them primarily as archaeological artifacts, rather than holistically as part of a multi-dimensional cultural landscape (Stoddard 1969). A range of other designated sites in several parts of the country reflects this scientific approach to the identification of values, which situated them within the traditional scholarly disciplines of archaeology, history, or art history. Their scope, boundaries, and significance were normally described by the archaeological investigations that had been carried out, sometimes accompanied by professional historical or ethnological studies; and their values were defined by such established criteria as the exceptional or outstanding example of a culture (Federal Archaeology Office 1998a, App. B). Limited scale often characterized them, as at the fish weir at Atherley Narrows (Mnjikaning) in

Ontario or the mysterious Cluny Earthlodge Village in Alberta. Some sites were designated for their historical significance as defined by Canadian national history, such as Batoche for its role in the North West Rebellion/Resistance of 1885. Other places became national historic sites because of their cultural expression as art, for example the Peterborough petroglyphs in Ontario or Nan Sdins, the Haida village in British Columbia. A few large sites, such as Port au Choix in Newfoundland and Debert/Belmont in Nova Scotia, were identified for their culture history, which was analyzed through archaeological evidence, not through cultural associations. The practice of designating sites related to the history of Aboriginal peoples primarily based on archaeological evidence reflected standard approaches in the heritage community nationally and internationally. Since then, while there has been no move to diminish archaeological values, institutional standards have moved to ensure the participation of associated living communities in the identification of perspectives and values, as well as in the management of cultural landscapes.

6/ Mortuary or memorial poles in the village of Nan Sdins on SGaang Gwaii Island, in Haida Gwaii, British Columbia, homeland of the Haida people.

The Perspective of the 1990s

Recognizing that the history of Aboriginal peoples was under-represented in the National Historic Sites system, in 1990–91 the board explored issues and a preliminary classification of sites related to the commemoration of the history of Native people. That year the board recommended that

> sites of spiritual and/or cultural importance to Native peoples, generally should be considered to be eligible for designation as national historic sites even when no tangible cultural resources exist, providing that there is evidence, garnered through oral history, or otherwise, that such sites are indeed seen to have special meaning to the culture in question and that the sites themselves are fixed in space (HSMBC Minutes February 1990).

Background papers identified that "from a

Native perspective commemorative potential seemed to derive from one or a combination of the following: the traditional and enduring use of the land; the relationship between the people and the land; and recent events in a first nation's history, such as its relationships with newcomers" (Goldring and Hanks 1991). Inspired by a presentation on the Red Dog Mountain and the Drum Lake Trail in the western Northwest Territories, the HSMBC took particular interest in exploring the significance of mythical or sacred sites and in the potential of "linear sites or trails encompassing a number of tangible resources . . . and emphasizing linkages between a people and the land" (HSMBC Minutes March 1991). As a result of formal and informal consultations during 1990–91, it was apparent that any framework for addressing Aboriginal history

—Must conform with emerging prescriptions in successive northern land claims regarding heritage and cultural sites (Lee 1997);

—Must respect Aboriginal worldviews encapsulated in the enduring relationship between people and the land.

—To achieve the latter objective, must recognize [w]hat distinguishes Native Peoples' understanding . . . is the extent to which the human relationship with places has ethical, cultural, medicinal, and spiritual elements, which are interwoven with patterns of economic use. Stories are told about particular parts of the land, spiritual powers exist in certain places that are absent elsewhere, and teachings are annexed to specific places in ways that have little counterpart in non-Native society. In Native cultures, these attributes are often more important than the physical, tangible remains of past human use of land (Goldring and Hanks 1991:14).

By 1991, therefore, the board had already before them a basic outline of perceptions, issues, and structures for approaching northern Aboriginal sites that would gradually and increasingly direct their considerations and recommendations on the commemoration of the history of Aboriginal peoples for the rest of the decade. The decision not to proceed with a study of petroglyphs and pictographs and to shift resources to community-based studies marked a key stage. In moving from a focus in scientific knowledge to a focus in Aboriginal traditional knowledge, from types of sites (e.g., trails, sacred sites) to places that embody traditional narratives and spiritual meaning along with economic use, and from criteria to guidelines for directing their assessments, the board began to evolve an approach to commemorating the history of Aboriginal peoples that is based both in Aboriginal values and in the significance of Aboriginal places to all Canadians. The concept of cultural landscapes, rooted in the interaction of culture and the natural environment in all its dimensions, epitomizes this approach.

Consultation and Participation

One of the key implications of the redefinition in approaching landscapes in the 1990s is the involve-

ment of associated peoples directly in the selection, research design, designation, and management of places of heritage significance. The 1980s saw transition in research strategies from culture history to ethno-archaeology in studies, for example, of the Mackenzie Basin in the Northwest Territories and of Stó:lō sites in British Columbia (Hanks and Pokotylo 1989; Lee and Henderson 1992). The more active involvement of Dene and Métis in the former area reflects in part a response to the fact that "the Dene are tired of being simply the object of inquiry and are becoming inquirers in their own right" (Hanks and Pokotylo 1989:139). The Traditional Environmental Knowledge Pilot Project of the Dene Cultural Institute, started in 1989, exemplifies participatory action research, in which indigenous peoples have primary involvement in the direction of studies that serve their needs, including research design and implementation, "the accepted approach to the study of TEK" (Johnson 1995:116). The active involvement of Aboriginal people, particularly elders, has refocused the investigative effort from the analysis of physical resources to recognition of the holistic and essentially spiritual relationship of people and land.

Experience in the 1990s endorses the crucial nature of this role. When the petroglyphs at Kejimkujik National Park, Nova Scotia, were initially identified for commemoration, they were seen as the primary cultural resources of the park. Consultation with the Mi'kmaq people reoriented the commemorative focus from the single resource type to the whole park area. Arguing the "strong sense of connection between people and place," the background paper, prepared jointly by representatives of the Mi'kmaq people and Parks Canada's Atlantic regional office, proposed three bases for commemoration of the "cultural landscape" of the region:

—The 4000 year history of traditional land use in which the archaeological resources were largely undisturbed;

—The natural environment of the park that enhanced an understanding of Mi'kmaq spirituality with the land;

—The petroglyph sites, which are a significant part of Mi'kmaq cultural and spiritual expression (Mi'kmaq 1994).

Equally, when Parks Canada initiated a commemorative integrity exercise at Nan Sdins (Ninstints) National Historic Site, British Columbia, consultation with the hereditary chiefs argued for recognition of heritage values that identified not only the achievements of Haida art and architecture represented by the village—the focus of the National Historic Site and World Heritage Site designations—but also "the history of a people in a place:"

—The continuing Haida culture and history;

—The connectedness of the Haida to the land and the sea;

—The sacredness of the site;

—Its role as the visual key to the oral traditions of the Haida over thousands of years (Dick and Wilson 1998).

Both examples demonstrate Parks Canada's move to implement three principles resulting from the National Workshops on the History of Aboriginal Peoples in Canada in 1992–94:

—Fundamental importance of Aboriginal traditional knowledge to the understanding of the culture and history of all indigenous peoples;

—Meaningful participatory consultations with Aboriginal groups;

—Aboriginal peoples' taking a leading role in presenting their history and culture (Parks Canada 1994b).

Involvement of Dogrib elders in extensive studies along the Idaà Trail in the Northwest Territories similarly expanded the initial research design from a survey of traditional sites and documentation of Dogrib place names and narratives to documentation of sacred sites, travel using traditional methods, and development of a training program in archaeological methods and recording of oral traditions for Dogrib youth (Andrews and Zoe 1997:8–10). In the resulting six-category classification of sacred sites, elders recognized five categories but not a sixth, which represented identifications

7/ Paallirmiut drum dancing in traditional clothing at Arviat Heritage Day, near the community of Arviat, Nunavut.

of significance from outside their culture (Andrews et al. 1998:307–8). Recent research projects submitted to the HSMBC have consistently and actively included involvement and consultation of local communities, including elders.

Recently Designated Aboriginal Cultural Landscapes, 1995–2000

Since 1990, the Historic Sites and Monuments Board of Canada has considered a number of Aboriginal cultural landscapes. As early as 1991, Hatzic Rock, now known as Xá:ytem, in British Columbia presented not only archaeological evidence of potential national significance, but also the importance of this transformer site in terms of Aboriginal cultural values. Drawing directly on Gordon Mohs' research on the Stó:lō people, it demonstrated the cosmological relationships that underpinned its role as a sacred site (Lee and Henderson 1992; Mohs 1994). An agreement under the National Cost-Sharing Programme recommended in 1998, following consultation with the Stó:lõ people, endorsed the board's acceptance of the exceptional national significance of sites valued primarily for their spiritual importance to Aboriginal peoples.

The inland Kazan River Fall Caribou Crossing site and the coastal island of Arvia'juaq with the adjacent point Qikiqtaarjuk in the Eastern Arctic, designated in 1995, provide exceptional illustrations of the integrated economic, social, and spiritual values of Aboriginal cultural landscapes (Fig. 7). Chosen respectively by the communities of Baker Lake and Arviat to conserve and depict Inuit history and culture in this area, these areas "speak eloquently to the cultural, spiritual, and economic life of the Inuit in the Keewatin region . . . and as sites of particular significance to the respective communities" (HSMBC Minutes July 1995). The results of

—Earlier archaeological investigations,

—Mapping using a global positioning system,

—On-site visits with elders,

—Oral interviews with other knowledgeable Inuit informants in the communities,

—Recording of traditional stories associated with the areas

identified the traditional Aboriginal values and the scientific values associated with these places (Keith 1995; Henderson 1995). The approved commemorative plaque texts articulate the associative and physical values of these cultural landscapes:

> For centuries, the fall caribou crossing on the Kazan River was essential to the inland Inuit, providing them the necessities of daily life and the means to survive the long winter. Once in the water, the caribou were vulnerable to hunters in *qajaqs* who caught and lanced as many as possible. The Inuit cherished and cared for the land at crossing areas in accordance with traditional beliefs and practices to ensure the caribou returned each year during their southward migration. To inland Inuit, the caribou was the essence of life. All parts were valuable for food, fuel, tools, clothing, and shelter (in Harvaqtuuq 1997:2.3).

> For centuries, the Inuit returned here each summer to camp and harvest the abundant marine resources. These gatherings also provided an opportunity to teach the young, celebrate life, and affirm and renew Inuit society. The oral histories, traditional knowledge, and archaeological sites at Arvia'juaq and Qikiqtaarjuk provide a cultural and historical foundation for future ge-nerations. These sites continue to be centers to celebrate, practise, and rejuvenate Inuit culture in the Arviat area (in Arviat 1997:2.3).

Building on the 1990–91 Northern Native History initiative, the Keewatin area project and the Déline fishery study (see below), in 1996 Christopher C. Hanks extended the articulation of "the elemental link between . . . culture and the land" (Hanks 1996a:887) as the core basis for understanding the cultural landscape of Grizzly Bear Mountain and Scented Grass Hills (Sahyoue/Edacho) in the western Northwest Territories. With a firm base in both local traditional knowledge and the relevant scientific and academic literature, the background paper he prepared on behalf of the Sahtu Dene identified three bases for national historical significance:

> —These people had lived on that land since time immemorial;

> —They had evolved there as a distinct people;

> —The interplay of place names and traditional narratives in Grizzly Bear Mountain and Scented Grass Hills has characterized their relationship to the land (ibid.:885, 888).

Drawing on broad archaeological and ethnographic literature of the subarctic, as well as on extensive oral histories of the Great Bear Lake region, Hanks judiciously presented selected narratives in relation to specific landscape features and larger landscape meanings. The narratives play important roles in sustaining Sahtu Dene culture by transmitting language, prescribing behavior, and identifying sacred sites from generation to generation through the association of place and story. By linking places, names, and narratives, he successfully mapped them on topographical representations of the Great Bear Lake region. Five broad periods provided a time frame that served to group the narratives

8/ *Nagwichoonjik, the Mackenzie River, Northwest Territories, homeland of the Gwichya Gwich'in of Tsiigehtchic.*

thematically. Dene Elder George Blondin, whose own narratives of the region are widely read (Blondin1997), concurred in the framework while at the same time recognizing it did not come from within his culture. Hanks himself notes that for the Dene, "thematic connections of spiritual power and relationships with animals are more significant than time" (1996a:906). The rich historical associations between traditional Sahtu Dene narratives and the "homes" of those stories on two of the four headlands that physically divide the arms of Great Bear Lake show "the land is alive with stories which blend the natural and supernatural worlds, defining [the Sahtu Dene] as people in relationship to the earth" (ibid.:886, 888).

In 1997 the Gwichya Gwich'in of Tsiigehtchic in the western Northwest Territories presented for commemoration, protection, and presentation the segment of the Mackenzie River (Nagwichoonjik) from Thunder River to Point Separation (Fig. 8), which they identified as the most significant area of their traditional homeland. Following Hanks' approach closely, a series of oral narratives of Raven, Atachukaii, Nagaii, Ahts'an Veh, and others were closely tied to the identified land and its defining features (Gwich'in Social and Cultural Institute 1997). The superimposed five period time grouping of the stories served to develop a

> holistic understanding of history, encompassing the whole of the land and assigning the river its meaningful place within it . . .[;] the stories of their history *and* the experiences of their lives on the land . . . [are the] fundamental cultural themes [that demonstrate] the important place the river occupies in Gwichya Gwich'in culture (Gwich'in Social and Cultural Institute 1997:824).

The majority of new national historic sites designated for historic values identified through traditional knowledge and consultation with associated communities have been in the North. However, Apitipik in Lake Abitibi, Quebec, designated in 1996, is the center of the traditional territory of the Abitibiwinni and of the water routes they used to travel through vast areas. Their summer gathering and trading place for centuries, with archaeological evidences of 6,000 years of use at Pointe Abitibi, it is also a sacred site to the Abitibiwinni (Société Matcite8eia 1996).

Yuquot in Nootka Sound, British Columbia, designated in 1997, is the center of the Mowachaht world. Here the Mowachaht-Muchalaht First Nations have lived since the beginning of time. They have hosted travelers since eighteenth century imperial exploration, developed whaling power of which the Whalers' Washing House is the physical encapsulation, and have deep spiritual bonds to the "immense natural power and beauty" of the environment (Mowachaht-Muchalaht, 1997). The 1997 designation responded to the request of the Mowachaht-Muchalaht First Nations that "earlier designations be corrected so that our place in history is clear and accurate" and that "a single commemoration of our area [be made] which will bring all of the history together under the name of Yuquot" (HSMBC Minutes June 1997).

The 1990s study of the history of Nunavut from an Inuit perspective was based on community consultations and elders' judgments and was prepared under the guidance of an Inuit steering committee with staff and knowledgeable scholars' inputs. It represents an alternative approach to the commemoration of the history of Aboriginal peoples. Rather than beginning with the identification of places, it has established a historical and cultural framework for identifying places of principal importance to the Inuit. Three principles express the thematic priorities: enduring use, Inuit culture and Inuit identity, and regional variation. All center on the "close traditional relationship between culture and land use. Many traditional dwelling sites, travel routes, resource harvesting sites, and sacred places have a rich complex of associative values, combining economic, social, and spiritual purposes in a sequence of annual movements from place to place, with people gathering in greater or smaller numbers according to their needs and opportunities" (Goldring 1998).

Concurrent with the "Inuit Traditions" study in Nunavut, the Métis Heritage Association of the Northwest Territories played a leading role in the definition and development of eleven themes related to their history. Community-based oral histories in addition to Euro-Canadian accounts incorporated the traditions of both the Aboriginal and the Euro-Canadian cultures of Métis heritage. "Picking Up the Threads" documents traditional history and land use to assist in identifying places significant to the Métis along the Mackenzie River since the eighteenth century (Payment 1999).

National Historic Sites with Potential Aboriginal Cultural Landscape Values

A number of national historic sites designated before 1990 for their archaeological, scientific, or historical values have characteristics that identify their potential for recognition as evolved or associative cultural landscapes. Commemorated primarily for their capacity through archaeological resources to represent the significant contribution of Aboriginal peoples to Canada over an extended period of time, places such as World Heritage Site Head-Smashed-In Buffalo Jump (*Estipah skikikini kots*), Alberta (National Historic Site [NHS] 1968; World Heritage Site [WHS] 1981) are recognized and endorsed by Aboriginal peoples in association with their cultural heritage. These sites are almost exclusively located in southern Canada (Buggey 1999: 24–5). In the 1990s, however, the approach was extended to a few northern sites, such as The Hay River Mission Sites on the Hay River Indian Reserve, NWT (NHS 1992). Comprising St. Peter's Anglican Church, St. Anne's Roman Catholic Church and Rectory, and the two church cemeteries with their numerous spirit houses, they were designated for "their close association with a critical period in Dene /Euro-Canadian relations" (HSMBC Minutes June 1992). Valued by local Dene for their spiritual role, they may be seen as part of the larger cultural landscape of the community. More recently, the Déline Traditional Fishery and Old Fort Franklin (Fig. 9), NWT (NHS 1996), identified for its significant historical associations, was designated as a place that "speak[s] eloquently to the relationship which evolved in the nineteenth century between Aboriginal people in the north

9/ *Déline fishery, a centuries-old food source of the Sahtu Dene and Métis, at the mouth of the Great Bear River, Northwest Territories.*

and those Euro-Canadian parties who were determined to explore it," to "the support and assistance of the Dene and Métis people" to Sir John Franklin's second expedition, and to the impact of Franklin's and later expeditions on the Aboriginal people of the region, particularly in contributing "to the emergence of the Sahtu Dene as a distinctive cultural group." Also, "the Sahtu Dene see the fishery at Déline as being of particular cultural significance to their occupation of the region" (Hanks 1996b; HSMBC Minutes November 1996). The Sahtu Dene's request for protection and presentation of the site emphasizes the importance of place as expression of Aboriginal history.

Relict Landscapes

A significant number of other national historic sites are also designated on the basis of archaeological values to commemorate the history of Aboriginal peoples that may possess cultural landscape values and that associated peoples might choose to identify as, or within,

Aboriginal cultural landscapes in the context of their heritage. In addition to the Inuksuit at Enusko Point in Nunavut, these include relict village sites, other habitation sites, pictograph and petroglyph sites, tipi rings, burial places, and resource sites, such as quarries. Some or all of the nine abandoned Haida, Gitksan, and Tsimshian villages in British Columbia, designated NHS in 1971–72, for example, may have Aboriginal heritage values similar to those identified by the hereditary chiefs at Nan Sdins (NHS 1981; WHS 1981). Pictograph and petroglyph sites, widely designated both federally and provincially across the country, may be significant features in larger cultural landscapes, such as their examination at Kejimkujik demonstrated. Tipi rings are likewise part of broader cultural landscapes, and designated burial sites could be sacred sites within Aboriginal cultural landscapes. Aboriginal peoples could choose to identify as Aboriginal cultural landscapes some existing national historic sites designated for other values, as was done by the Mowachaht-Muchalaht in reclaiming Nootka Sound for their own history at Yuquot (Mowachaht-Muchalaht 1997). Equally, they might see existing designations of national historic significance currently related to events, such as battles, or Aboriginal cultures, as part of their heritage that would be more effectively commemorated through cultural landscapes.

Some landscapes related to the history of Aboriginal peoples and recognizably of historic value are not currently identified with a specific people. At Grasslands National Park in Saskatchewan, for example, archaeological analysis of the cultural remains provides evidence of the diverse activities of occupation spanning 10,000 years, but one that ended in the past; currently no people claim a direct association with the park area (Gary Adams, pers. comm. 1998). Such landscapes might be addressed as relict landscapes, where the cultural evolution ended in the past but strong material evidences remain, rather than as Aboriginal cultural landscapes, which involve the participation of associated people(s). This division between places associated with living communities and those known only by their scientific evidences of the past would be consistent with Australia's separation of "indigenous heritage places of archaeological significance" and "indigenous places important to the heritage of living cultures" for the identification of environmental indicators for natural and cultural heritage (Pearson et al. 1998:15–19, 57–76).

Guidelines for the Identification of Aboriginal Cultural Landscapes of National Historic Significance

How should national significance in Aboriginal cultural landscapes be identified? What does "national significance" mean in the history of Aboriginal peoples? The HSMBC recognized that its conventional criteria, structure, and framework for evaluation did not adequately respond to the values inherent in the history of Aboriginal people. While the Minister of Canadian Heritage has already designated a number of Aboriginal cultural landscapes, as discussed above, the search

for an appropriate framework to examine significant places related to the history of Aboriginal peoples continued. Whether Aboriginal peoples are identified by First Nation, language group, or traditional territory, it is widely recognized that experiences with the land vary enormously from place to place in Canada. Historical experiences also differ, as do languages. Beliefs and practices have forms and traditions specific to individual groups. The *Report on the Royal Commission on Aboriginal Peoples* identified about sixty distinct groups in Canada (fifty-six First Nations, four Inuit, and the Métis), based primarily on language. This grouping provides one approach to establishing a comparative context within which to evaluate places of national historic significance. Using language group as a field for determining national historic significance is evidently complex. For example, the extensive movements of many Aboriginal groups through time requires understanding the distinctions between peoples within groups, such as the Malecite of New Brunswick and the Malecite of Quebec. The HSMBC also initiated discussion about using "the traditional territory of an Aboriginal nation . . . as the comparative universe for the site proposed for commemoration or designation" (Federal Archaeology Office 1998a:21). Some pilot projects are underway using the concept of Aboriginal nation as a comparative framework (Lee 2000:5). To date, while both language group and traditional territory are required aspects of background papers submitted to the HSMBC, decisions on national historic significance have been made primarily at the level of the individual First Nation, where language, territory, and history all come together. Aboriginal cultural landscapes are compatible with these directions.

Guidelines for Aboriginal Cultural Landscapes

In the context of the HSMBC's criteria for national historic significance (HSMBC 1999), a designated Aboriginal cultural landscape "will illustrate a nationally important aspect of Canadian history." The history of Aboriginal peoples is recognized to be such "a nationally important aspect of Canadian history." As a place designated by virtue of its "explicit and meaningful association" with this aspect, an Aboriginal cultural landscape will "illustrate or symbolize in whole or in part a cultural tradition, a way of life, or ideas important in the development of Canada." The identified elements indicating integrity of a place, except setting, will not normally be essential to understand the significance of an Aboriginal cultural landscape, and will not, therefore, generally apply.

The following specific guidelines form the basis for the HSMBC's examination of the national significance of Aboriginal cultural landscapes (Buggey 1999:29–31).

> 1. The long associated Aboriginal group or groups have participated in the identification of the place and its significance, concur in the selection of the place, and support designation.

This guideline derives from the HSMBC's consistent direction since 1990 that Aboriginal peoples will be consulted, involved, and participating in the identification of frameworks and sites related to their history. It is consistent with the established consultation process for Aboriginal heritage sites and the Statement of Principles and Best Practices for Commemorating Aboriginal History (Federal Archaeology Office 1999). It is likewise consistent with recommendation 1.7.2 of the *Report on the Royal Commission on Aboriginal Peoples* (Canada 1996).

> 2. Spiritual, cultural, economic, social, and environmental aspects of the group's association with the identified place, including continuity and traditions, illustrate its historical significance.

This guideline focuses on the identification of national historic significance through the associated group's long attachment to the territory, its enduring use and activities, its social and kinship relationships, its intimate knowledge of the area, and its spiritual affiliation with it.

> 3. The interrelated cultural and natural attributes of the identified place make it a significant cultural landscape.

This guideline recognizes the integrated nature of Aboriginal relationship to place, including the inseparability of cultural and natural values. Identified places, which will likely be of widely diverse types, will illustrate this core interrelationship of cultural and natural forces that characterizes cultural landscapes. The guideline anticipates that the identification will incorporate diverse aspects of the group's association extended through time. Tangible evidences may be largely absent, with the attributes rooted primarily in oral and spiritual traditions and in activities related to the place. There may also be tangible attributes, such as natural resources, archaeological sites, graves, material culture, and written or oral records. The guideline foresees that the identification of attributes will recognize such physical components as ecosystem, climate, geology, topography, water, soils, viewsheds, and dominant and culturally significant fauna and flora in the context of the associated Aboriginal people's relationship to the place. The Aboriginal expression of these aspects may occur in animal or other natural metaphors.

> 4. The cultural and natural attributes that embody the significance of the place are identified through traditional knowledge of the associated Aboriginal group(s).

This guideline anticipates that the traditional knowledge, including traditional environmental knowledge, will likely encompass narratives, place-names, language, traditional uses, rituals, and behavior related to the identified place. It recognizes that some knowledge cannot be shared, but available knowledge must be sufficient to demonstrate the significance of the place in the culture of the associated group.

> 5. The cultural and natural attributes that embody the significance of the place additionally may be comprehended by results of academic scholarship.

This guideline recognizes the contribution that academic scholarship makes to the understanding of place. History, including oral history and ethnohistory, archaeology, anthropology, and environmental sciences are the most likely, but not the only, relevant disciplines.

Size, Scale, and Boundaries

Identification of Aboriginal cultural landscapes involves not only understanding the historic value of the place to be designated, but also specifying the boundaries of the designated place. The size and scale of these challenge both Aboriginal people and Parks Canada because of their very differing contexts and views. Aboriginal worldviews focus on land rather than landscape features, although specific sites certainly have associated cultural significance and oral traditions related to history. However, given the holistic relationship of Aboriginal people and the land, such places are seen primarily not as isolated spots, but as parts of larger landscapes. Identifiable landscapes may equally be only parts of still larger cultural landscapes. The Dogrib sacred sites identified along the Idaà Trail (Fig. 10) illustrate this relationship of sites with the larger landscape, while the Trail itself is part of the Dogrib cultural landscape comprising 100,000 square miles. The situation in the Canadian North is little different from the context of the Navajo Nation regarding this relationship: "the artificial isolation of important places from the whole landscape of which they are an integral part often violates the very cultural principles that make certain places culturally significant to begin with" (Downer and Roberts 1993:12).

How then are boundaries to be drawn? Aboriginal cultural landscapes might draw on experience elsewhere with protected area management. Canada's national parks use a zoning system to identify park areas requiring different levels of protection and to guide their management use (Parks Canada 1994a: II.2.2). Biosphere reserves also apply a zoning approach that provides for a core area, a buffer zone, and a transition zone, focused on different levels of protection and intervention (UNESCO 1996b: 4). The emergence of bio-regional planning in protected area management, applicable to enormous areas such as the 2,000-mile Yellowstone to Yukon corridor (http://www.Y2Y.net), may offer some potential applicability for Aboriginal cultural landscapes. Downer and Roberts, who are working with the Navajo Nation in the United States, consider the

> "broader context . . . based on landscapes or ecosystems rather than artificially-defined impact zones . . . is emerging from various disciplines in environmental planning. We are convinced that this is the only realistic approach to meaningful consideration of traditional cultural properties and the cultural landscapes of which they are integral part" (Downer and Roberts 1993:14).

Such planning frameworks and co-management approaches (Collings 1997) may provide opportunities for developing mechanisms to ensure commemorative integrity of cultural landscapes such as the designated area of Nagwichoonjik (Mackenzie River).

In Australia, many Aboriginal sites are discrete areas separated by long distances, but interconnected by trading routes or the paths of ancestors; they are most clearly understood when they are recognized as parts of a network, rather than individual components (Bridgewater and Hooy 1995:168). "Anangu, whose political system is egalitarian and uncentralised, visualise places in the landscape as nodes in a network of ancestral tracks. The Anangu landscape is not susceptible to division into discrete areas" (Layton and Titchen 1995:178). The American "Trail of Tears" National Historic Trail, a multi-route and multi-site network that commemorates the forced removal, march overland, and resettlement of the Cherokee (Ani'Yun' wiya) from Georgia, Alabama, and so on, to Oklahoma in 1838–39, is a partnership of diverse groups and diverse sites with linked interpretive programs in nine states. Historian John Johnston, exploring the adaptation of this concept of nodes to the commemoration of Aboriginal history in Canada, notes that it applies to "places that tell an inter-connected story extending over time and place," such as trails and water routes associated with seasonal movements for food (Johnston 1993). Nodes within a network, each of identified importance, could be focal points of protection and presentation in a recognized larger cultural landscape.

Noting that there is "sometimes no obviously cor-

10/ *Kwikati or "Fence Narrows Lake," on the Idaà Trail, Northwest Territories. Dogrib hunters would erect a fence on the spring lake ice to lead migratory caribou to an ambush location, seen at the bottom of the photograph.*

rect boundary," the U.S. National Park Service indicates that the selection of boundaries for traditional cultural properties should be based on the characteristics of the historic place, specifically how the place is used and why the place is important (King and Townsend n.d.). In several respects, the American approach can be recognized in existing national historic site designations of Aboriginal cultural landscapes in Canada. At Kejimkujik, for example, the existing national park boundaries defined a sufficiently large and appropriate area of traditional Mi'kmaq occupancy to represent the larger Mi'kmaq landscape. While in this case administrative convenience provided the basis for accepted boundaries, it is not a recommended selection approach. At Arvia'juaq and Qikiqtaarjuk, clearly defined geographical features—an island and a point— with strong spiritual, social, economic, and archaeological values related to the Caribou Inuit culture, identified the boundaries. Given the importance of the ad-

jacent waters to the cultural significance, future consideration might be given to defining site boundaries that include the key water areas. At Sahyoue/ Edacho (Grizzly Bear Mountain and Scented Grass Hills; Fig. 11), where the designated sites are also two clearly defined land areas related to water, the site analysis and discussion of values effectively articulate the significant cultural relationships of the larger Great Bear Lake landscape. Also, the historic values of the viewsheds at this site are particularly significant in the identification of objectives for the "health" of the site. While discrete geographical features can be very useful in identifying boundaries, it is evident that the values for which the place is to be designated must dominate in establishing appropriate boundaries.

The scale of Aboriginal cultural landscapes and the definition of their boundaries provide significant challenges to the approach of commemorative integrity, which underlies Parks Canada's national historic sites commemorative program. Securing the "health or wholeness" of these vast areas may require close examination of the current understanding of the concept as it applies to historic place, historic values, and objectives for large cultural landscapes.

Protection for Aboriginal Cultural Landscapes

Protection of cultural landscapes in Canada's North begins with respect for the values, uses, and behaviors associated with the landscape so that enduring relationships with the land continue. Integrating management of the cultural landscape into the life of the community and using community traditions and practices for protection and presentation are essential to the long-term "health" of the cultural landscape. The increased role of communities in influencing how lands, waters and resources are managed relates decision-making about places more closely to those whose lives and livelihoods are integrated with them. Land claim agreements provide powers and structures which can be applied to cultural landscapes. Co-management, a well-established approach to renewable resources, can apply equally to cultural heritage, while long-practiced economic activities such as traditional harvesting should be actively encouraged. Conservation and presentation objectives must be integrated with community priorities, community issues, and community structures. Protection for Aboriginal cultural landscapes needs to be integrated with local planning, economic development, tourism initiatives, and their associated funding sources.

Documentation and identification are important tools for protecting cultural landscapes. Where legislation exists, it tends to be enabling rather than prescriptive and to separate natural and cultural resources in a manner inconsistent with the values of the cultural landscape. When direct threats to the cultural landscape occur, the time frame is too short to carry out the research necessary to respond to them. Without docu-

mentation and identification derived from long-term recording of traditional knowledge and inventory of sites, the information base needed to apply existing tools available within planning and environmental assessment processes is missing. Designation of a National Historic Site recognizes and commemorates the historic value of a place, but it does not carry any legal or protective measures for the designated place. Designation may provide access to financial and technical assistance, such as the National Cost-Sharing Program, however, and it may carry moral suasion which builds public recognition and support and opens access to the resources of granting agencies. Traditionally, the most common protection technique for National Historic Sites was transfer of land to the federal crown, in the name of Parks Canada, under the National Parks Act; this approach is now extremely rare. In the absence of specific protective mechanisms, a number of planning tools may be applied to the conservation of places of recognized historic value, and management approaches which protect the character of a cultural landscape may be supported through various planning processes.

One direct protective measure, which has recently been applied to Sahyoue/Edacho (Grizzly Bear Mountain and Scented Grass Hills), is land withdrawal for conservation purposes under a federal Order in Council. In 2000 strongly focused Sahtu Dene community action at Déline, with coordinated activity by environmental organizations such as the Canadian Parks and Wilderness Society (CPAWS) and the World Wildlife Fund Canada (WWF), pushed the Minister of Canadian Heritage and the Minister of Indian and Northern Affairs to withdraw land at Sahyoue/Edacho from development. This status was accorded in February 2001 for a period of five years to provide a period of protection while stakeholders determine the most effective mechanism for long-term protection of the site. The interim mechanism addresses the ever-present threat to landscape integrity from mining development by including sur-

11/ *A campsite at Sahyoue (Grizzly Bear Mountain), a sacred site rich in traditional narrative to the Sahtu Dene, overlooking the western end of Great Bear Lake, Northwest Territories.*

face and subsurface rights in the portion of the site that is federal crown land and subsurface rights in the portion of the site owned by the Sahtu Dene First Nation, currently not covered by the Sahtu Dene and Métis Comprehensive Land Claim Agreement. The interim land withdrawal implements the Protected Areas Strategy for the Northwest Territories, which provides for analysis and assessment of options as basis for decision-making (CPAWS 2001; Canada 2001). This process should result in identification and implementation of how the two peninsulas will be managed for long-term protection.

Recent land claim agreements in the North provide for various integrated management structures for decision-making related to heritage places. Cooperative management boards, regional boards, territorial heri-

tage boards, parks planning and management boards for national parks, and joint working groups are identified mechanisms for achieving participation (Lee 1997). Chapters on Special Management Areas (Ch.10) and Heritage (Ch.13) in the Council for Yukon First Nations' Umbrella Final Agreement (1993) and subsequent individual Yukon First Nations' Final Agreements provide for designation, management planning, and economic opportunities in sites valued by the respective peoples. All incorporate the values of Yukon First Nations People, the equitable involvement of Yukon First Nations and Government, and First Nations' ownership as key components in managing places related to their culture and history within Settlement Land. Some agreements include joint management of specific sites, some provide for the withdrawal of prospecting, mining, petroleum exploration, and coal rights at specified sites, and some identify culturally valued heritage areas (Canada 1993: Ch.10, 13). The Sahtu Heritage Places and Sites Joint Working Group, established under the Sahtu Dene and Metis Comprehensive Land Claim Agreement (1993) to consider and make recommendations to appropriate governments and the Sahtu Tribal Council on Sahtu heritage places, resulted directly from the land claim agreement (Sahtu 2000:11; see Andrews, this volume). In Nunavut, following from the Nunavut Land Claims Agreement (1993), Inuit Impact and Benefit Agreements ensure integration of the regional economy and Inuit culture in all planning and development, including national parks.

Land use planning direction and related decisions that affect cultural landscapes can be key components of a protection strategy. Opportunities may lie in provisions of the Yukon First Nations Final Agreements:

> To identify and mitigate the impact of development upon Heritage Resources through integrated resource development including land use planning and development assessment processes. . . . [And] to ensure that social, cultural, economic and environmental policies are applied to the management, protection and use of land, water and resources in an integrated and coordinated manner so as to ensure Sustainable Development.

Some agreements specify that the cultural and heritage significance of an identified list of trails, caribou fences, fishing holes, gathering places, and spiritual sites, and any impacts upon them, will be taken into consideration in land use planning and development assessment (Canada 1993: Ch.11, 13). These resources are largely identified as specific features rather than cultural landscapes, and some agreements are explicit that there is no commitment by any of the parties to maintaining them or to guaranteeing their continued existence in their current state. Tr'ochëk Heritage Site on the Yukon River, identified for its cultural significance in the Tr'ondëk Hwëch'in Final Agreement (1998), however, was designated a national historic site in 2002 on the basis of its value as an Aboriginal cultural landscape, and its management plan was completed in 2003 (Tr'ochëk 2001, 2002; Neufeld 2001).

At the Fall Caribou Crossing and Arvia'juaq National Historic Sites, the Conservation and Presentation Reports and associated data were delivered to the Nunavut Planning Commission to ensure that information about the importance, values and objectives of the sites was available for use in planning processes. Inuktitut place-names, oral traditions, and archaeological sites have been recorded and entered into geographical information systems (GIS); the Nunavut Planning Commission will maintain GIS data bases for both sites. Provisions were introduced into the Keewatin Regional Land Use Plan to provide protection from development in the historic site area in accordance with the objective that "low impact land use is practised including the absence of permanent structures". The Hamlet Councils of Baker Lake and Arviat, the Baker Lake Hunters and Trappers, and the Kivalliq Inuit Association all supported the prohibition of new permanent structures to avoid damaging archaeological resources and disturbing movement of caribou (Harvaqtuuq 1997:7.12,7.13; Arviat 1997:7.12,7.13). A copy of the Conservation and Presentation Report for the Fall Caribou Crossing was also sent to the Nunavut Water Board because of concern about developments that might adversely affect the water quality and water levels of the Kazan River (Harvaqtuuq 1997:7.20; also Fig. 12). For the Déline fishery, a water and fisheries management plan was recommended (Sahtu 2000:38). In British Columbia a program of traditional use studies in the Aboriginal Affairs Branch of the Ministry of Forests had provided assistance to First Nations to investigate, record and develop data bases of traditional knowledge and places that enable First Nations to respond to planning enquiries and threats to traditional use sites on an informed basis (British Columbia 1996).

Aboriginal communities can also develop certain protective mechanisms for cultural landscapes within existing authorities such as land management pow-

12/ *The Kazan River at Piqqiq, a fall hunting camp in the land of the Harvaqtuurmiut, Nunavut.*

ers. As Brian Reeves reports for Ninaistákis (Chief Mountain), regulating non-traditional visitor activities, stopping non-traditional resource use, guaranteeing freedom of use for traditional religious practices, completing biophysical and cultural inventories, fixing the trail system, and coordinating land use regulation with neighbouring authorities are among the strategies that may be applied (Reeves 1994:285–8). Canada can continue to learn about protective mechanisms for Aboriginal cultural landscapes from Australia's long experience such as the Northern Territory's Aboriginal Sacred Sites Act (1989), which provides blanket protection for sacred sites, and its Aboriginal Areas Protection Authority, which is required to inventory any area, if requested, to identify the existence of sacred sites in the vicinity of proposed capital works (Ritchie 1994:239).

Conservation planning tools may also help to protect cultural landscapes. Based on principles rather than prescriptive actions, they can be rooted in community values and encompass community practices. In 1996

the Harvaqtuuq Historic Site Committee and the Harvaqtuurmiut (Kazan River) Elders, with Parks Canada, developed a Commemorative Integrity Statement (CIS) for the Fall Caribou Crossing National Historic Site. A CIS describes the historic values and management objectives and, subsequently, directs the core development of a management plan for the designated place. The CIS for the Fall Caribou Crossing NHS identified a number of values and measures to determine whether the historic place and its components are unimpaired or not under threat: Inuit traditional beliefs and practices are respected and the wishes of the elders are respected in their treatment; oral histories and traditions are recorded, interpreted and transmitted to future generations; archaeological remains are undisturbed by human intervention unless related to research; low impact land use is practised including the absence of permanent structures; and the health of the Kaminuriak caribou herd and of the Kazan River is properly monitored (Harvaqtuuq 1996:C.2.0–2.5). A management plan will elaborate how such objectives are to be achieved. The *Plan of Management* for Uluru-Kata Tjuta National Park in Australia offers a model for managing a site based on the values of the traditional owners. A joint management board of Anangu people and other Australians with relevant knowledge and expertise co-manage the site in accordance with Tjukurpa, "the Law which governs all aspects of Anangu life." The Tjukurpa provides the core direction for management objectives and management commitments and is integrated in all aspects of park decision-making (Uluru 1991, 2000). While the operational scale of Uluru-Kata Tjuta is very different from cultural landscapes in Canada's North, the principles of its management plan, which roots park management in the values of the Anangu people, and the detailed translation of those principles into objectives and actions, may prove useful for extending the directions of the Fall Caribou Crossing site's Conservation and Presentation Report and for management planning for Aboriginal cultural landscapes in Canada.

The 1997 Conservation and Presentation Report, prepared for a Cost-Sharing Agreement between the Harvaqtuuq Historic Site Committee of Baker Lake and Parks Canada for the Fall Caribou Crossing NHS, illustrates the attributes essential to the protection of Aboriginal cultural landscapes (Harvaqtuuq 1997). Its strategy for protecting the cultural landscape identifies goals and actions for oral traditions, archaeological sites, artifact collections, place-names, landscape, the river, and the Kaminuriak caribou herd. It likewise addresses coordination of heritage activity and cultural tourism potential for the remote site. The agreement, now in effect, provides resources for implementing specific aspects of the strategy. Limited funding in the face of numerous demands for assistance under the National Cost-Sharing Program is, however, a severe constraint on its accessibility and effectiveness for protecting Aboriginal cultural landscapes.

Long term integrity of cultural landscapes may be aided by careful evaluation within established environmental assessment processes of the impacts of proposed development on the values of the place. The Canadian Environmental Assessment Act (CEAA) appears to offer some opportunities for protection relevant to Aboriginal cultural landscapes. In the definition of environmental effect, the act includes:

> any change that the project may cause in the environment, including any effects of such change . . . on physical and cultural heritage, on the current use of lands and resources for traditional purposes by aboriginal persons, or on any structure, site or thing that is of historical, archaeological, paleontological or architectural significance (Sec.2[1]).

Given the integrated nature of natural and cultural values in cultural landscapes, inclusion of traditional knowledge in the evaluation process will be critical to the integrity of the landscape and to the determination of actions to prevent or mitigate impacts of exploration, extraction, and harvesting activities. Most recent land claims agreements provide for joint federal, provincial and territorial environmental assessment processes as do federal-provincial harmonization agreements (Canadian Environmental Assessment Agency 1996).

Monitoring can be a useful strategy for protection of the Aboriginal cultural landscape. At the Fall Caribou Crossing National Historic Site, a Guardian Monitoring Program carried out by community members reports on significant changes, threats or looting to the site observed during occasional visits, including the river, the caribou, and archaeological sites. Traditional techniques for monitoring natural resources can also be useful for recognizing and identifying certain changes in Aboriginal cultural landscapes. Australia's State of the Environment Reporting includes indicators for monitoring indigenous places important to the heritage of living cultures which concentrate on "the recognition of the expertise of Indigenous people in managing and conserving their heritage places and objects and their right to be active participants in the interpretation and management of these places and objects" (Pearson et al. 1998:72).

Critical to protection of Aboriginal cultural landscapes is the continued recording of Elders' experience of the land, of its names and places, of its sacred sites, of the traditional narratives of the culture, and the transfer of the Elders' knowledge to youth. The importance of the people associated with the place being active in the interpretation program and in telling their stories in their own voices is also integral to protection of the cultural landscape and its meaning.

Looking Forward

The measures described above are all soft actions for protecting landscapes in the North. In recent years, there has been increasing public dismay and Ministerial concern that federal designation does not imply any legal protection for national historic sites or any on-going Parks Canada involvement in protection and presentation of the site. The Historic Places Initiative, an undertaking of Parks Canada's National Historic Sites program and the Department of Canadian Heritage with provincial and territorial partners, is developing a strategy with multi-purpose tools for preservation of historic places, including consultation with Aboriginal groups and tools for Aboriginal engagement (Canadian Heritage 2003). The Report of the Sahtu Heritage Places and Sites Joint Working Group observes that existing protective legislation in the Northwest Territories is almost all devoted to protecting natural landscapes and features. Although the sites identified through the Group's research all include natural landscapes or features, the primary value of these sites is their cultural significance. The report urges the federal and territorial governments to develop legislation "which will commemorate and protect cultural landscapes" (Sahtu 2000:25). The Government of the Northwest Territories has now begun to explore a new heritage policy and revisions to the Historical Resources Act.

The approach outlined in this paper represents work in progress, part of a much larger and on-going dialogue involving many people. This continuing exploration of documentation, identification, designation,

protection, presentation, and management focuses upon the symbiotic relationship that Aboriginal people have with the land. These places are not relicts but living landscapes: the cosmological, mythological, and spiritual world of a people who have lived with them in the enduring seasonal round of day-to-day activities where nature and culture are inseparable. Bequeathed through oral tradition from generation to generation, Aboriginal traditional knowledge connects these spiritual relationships through narratives, place names, sacred sites, rituals, and behaviour patterns that are tied to the spirits of the land.

Protection of Aboriginal cultural landscapes even where there is broad agreement on significance remains a challenge. The complex interaction of natural, cultural and spiritual values that characterizes these landscapes lies outside most established conservation frameworks. Recent changes are, however, beginning to broaden these processes from "islands" to "networks". Identifying places people value, documenting them, defining their significance, and managing them in accordance with those values and significance are key steps toward their protection. The powers of land claim agreements and the emergence of collaborative processes such as the Protected Areas Strategy for the Northwest Territories to provide tools for community-based action offer opportunities for broader use of existing frameworks, such as planning processes, to manage and protect Aboriginal cultural landscapes.

Acknowledgments

This paper draws substantially on a study prepared for Parks Canada to assist the Historic Sites and Monuments Board of Canada in recognizing place as an integral focus of its approach to the commemoration of the history of Aboriginal peoples. I am grateful to the numerous people in many programs and organizations who generously shared their knowledge, perspectives, and experiences on various aspects of this subject. I would like particularly to acknowledge insights shared in conversations and writings by Thomas D. Andrews,

Christopher Hanks, Joann Latremouille, Ellen Lee, George MacDonald, Isabel McBryde, Sheryl Smith, and Josie Weninger.

References

Andrews, Thomas D.
1990   *Yamoria's Arrows: Stories, Place-Names and the Land in Dene Oral Tradition.* On file with Canadian Parks Service, National Historic Parks and Sites, Northern Initiatives, contract no. 1632/89-177.

Andrews, Thomas D., and John B. Zoe
1997   The Idaà Trail: Archaeology and the Dogrib Cultural Landscape, Northwest Territories, Canada. In *At a Crossroads: Archaeology and First Peoples in Canada*, George P. Nicholas and Thomas D. Andrews, ed., pp. 160-77. Burnaby, BC: Archaeology Press, Department of Archaeology, Simon Fraser University.

Andrews, Thomas, John Zoe, and Aaron Herter
1998   On Yamòzhah's Trail: Dogrib Sacred Sites and the Anthropology of Travel. In *Aboriginal World Views, Claims, and Conflicts*, Jill Oakes et al., ed., pp. 305-20. *Canadian Circumpolar Institute, Occasional Publication* 43. Edmonton: University of Alberta.

Arviat Historical Society and Parks Canada
1997   *Arvia'juaq National Historic Site Conservation and Presentation Report.* On file with Parks Canada.

Australia ICOMOS
1995   The Asia-Pacific Regional Workshop on Associative Cultural Landscapes: A Report to the World Heritage Committee, April 1995. http://whc.unesco.org/archive/1995/whc-95-conf203-inf9e.pdf

Blondin, George
1997   *Yamoria the Lawmaker. Stories of the Dene.* Edmonton: NeWest Publishers Inc.

Bridgewater, Peter, and Theo Hooy
1995   Outstanding Cultural Landscapes in Australia, New Zealand and the Pacific: the Footprint of Man in the Wilderness. In *Cultural Landscapes of Universal Value: Components of a Global Strategy*, Bernd von Droste, et al., eds., pp. 162-9. Jena: Gustav Fischer Verlag in cooperation with UNESCO.

British Columbia, Ministry of Forests, Aboriginal Affairs Branch
1996   *Traditional Use Study Program Guidelines.* Victoria: Aboriginal Affairs Branch.

Buggey, Susan
1999   *An Approach to Aboriginal Cultural Landscapes.* HSMBC agenda paper #1999-10. http://www.pc.gc.ca/docs/r/pca-acl/index_e.asp

Canada. Privy Council Office
1996   *Report on the Royal Commission on Aboriginal Peoples*, vol. IV. Ottawa: Privy Council Office.

Canadian Environmental Assessment Agency
1996   *The Canadian Environmental Assessment Act Reference Guide on Physical and Cultural Heritage Resources.* Ottawa: Minister of Supply and Services Canada.

Canadian Heritage
2003   *Towards a New Act: Protecting Canada's Historic Places.* http://www.pch.gc.ca/progs/ieh-hpi/pubs/0-622-66831-6/00_e.cfm

Collings, Peter
1997   The Cultural Context of Wildlife Management in the Canadian North. In *Contested Arctic: Indigenous Peoples, Industrial States, and the Circumpolar Environment*, Eric Alden Smith and Joan McCarter, eds., pp. 13-40. Seattle: University of Washington and University of Washington Press.

Craik, Brian, and Bill Namagoose
1992   Environment and Heritage. The Point-of-View of the Crees of Quebec. *ICOMOS Canada Bulletin*, 1(1):17-22.

Dick, Lyle, and Barbara Wilson
n.p.   Presentation, 20 April 1998 in Cultural Landscapes course, HA 489G, University of Victoria.

Downer, Alan S., and Alexandra Roberts
1993   Traditional Cultural Properties, Cultural Resources Management and Environmental Planning. In *Traditional Cultural Properties*, Patricia L. Parker, ed., pp 12-15. *CRM* 16. Washington D.C.: National Park Service.

Federal Archaeology Office [Parks Canada]
1998a   *Commemorating National Historic Sites with Aboriginal Peoples' History: An Issue Analysis.* HSMBC Agenda Papers, #1998-A01. Copies available from National Historic Sites Directorate, Parks Canada.
1999   *Update on 'Commemorating National Historic Sites Associated with Aboriginal Peoples' History: An Issue Analysis.* HSMBC Agenda Papers, #1999-11. Copies available from National Historic Sites Directorate, Parks Canada.

Goldring, P.
1998   *Inuit Traditions: A history of Nunavut for the Historic Sites and Monuments Board of Canada and the People of Nunavut.* HSMBC Agenda Papers, #1998-OB1. Copies available from National Historic Sites Directorate, Parks Canada.

Goldring, P., and C. Hanks
1991   *Commemoration of Northern Native History.* HSMBC Report to the Cultural Pluralism Committee, #1991-13. Copies available from National Historic Sites Directorate, Parks Canada.

Gwich'in Social and Cultural Institute
1997   *"That River, It's Like a Highway for Us": The Mackenzie River through Gwichya Gwich'in History and Culture.* HSMBC Agenda Papers, #1997-30. Copies available from National Historic Sites Directorate, Parks Canada.

Hanks, Christopher C.

1996a   *Narrative and Landscape: Grizzly Bear Mountain and Scented Grass Hills as Repositories of Sahtu Dene Culture.* HSMBC Agenda Papers, #1996-61. Copies available from National Historic Sites Directorate, Parks Canada.

1996b   *The 1825-26 Wintering Place of Sir John Franklin's Second Expedition: A Dene Perspective.* HSMBC Agenda Papers,# 1996-24. Copies available from National Historic Sites Directorate, Parks Canada.

1993   Bear Rock, Red Dog Mountain, and the Windy Island to Shelton Lake Trail: Proposals for the commemoration of the cultural heritage of Denendeh, and the history of the Shu'tagot'ine. Canadian Parks Service, National Historic Sites Directorate, contract no. 1632-929220.

Hanks, Christopher C., and David L. Pokotylo

1989   The Mackenzie Basin: An Alternative Approach to Dene and Metis Archaeology. *Arctic* 42(2):139-47.

Harvaqtuuq Historic Site Committee and Parks Canada

1997   *Fall Caribou Crossing National Historic Site Conservation and Presentation Report.* On file with Parks Canada

Henderson, Lyle

1995   *Arviaq and Qikiqtaarjuk.* HSMBC Agenda Papers, #1995-29. Copies available from National Historic Sites Directorate, Parks Canada.

Historic Sites and Monuments Board of Canada (HMSBC)

n.p.   *Criteria for National Historic Significance.* http://crm.cr.nps.gov/issue.cfm?volume=16 &number=SI

Johnson, Martha

1995   Documenting Traditional Environmental Knowledge: the Dene, Canada. In *Listening for a Change: Oral Testimony and Community Development,* Hugo Slim and Paul Thompson, et al., eds., pp. 116-25. Philadelphia PA and Gabriola Island BC: New Society Publishers.

Johnston, A.J.B.

n.p.   Partnerships and Linkage in Native History Interpretation: Examples from the United States. Report to Historical Services Branch, National Historic Sites Directorate, Parks Canada.

Keith, Darren

1995   *The Fall Caribou Crossing Hunt, Kazan River, Northwest Territories.* HSMBC Agenda Papers, #1995-28. Copies available from National Historic Sites Directorate, Parks Canada.

King, Thomas F., and Jan Townsend, writers and compilers

n.d.   *Through the Generations: Identifying and Protecting Traditional Cultural Places,* Ed Dalheim in association with Pavlik and Associates, video producers.

Available from National Park Service.

Layton, Robert, and Sarah Titchen

1995   Uluru: An Outstanding Australian Aboriginal Cultural Landscape. In *Cultural Landscapes of Universal Value: Components of a Global Strategy,* Bernd von Droste, et al., eds., pp. 174-81. Jena: Gustav Fischer Verlag in cooperation with UNESCO.

Lee, Ellen

2000   Cultural Connections to Land: A Canadian Example. *Parks* 10(2):3-12.

n.p.   Aboriginal Heritage Issues in Canadian Land Claims Negotiations. Paper presented at the Fulbright Symposium *Aboriginal Cultures in an Interconnected World,* Darwin, Australia, 1997.

Lee, Ellen, and Lyle Henderson

1992   *Hatzic Rock Comparative Report.* HSMBC Agenda Papers, #1992-04. Copies available from National Historic Sites Directorate, Parks Canada.

McNeely, Jeffrey A.

1995   Coping with Change: People, Forests, and Biodiversity. *The George Wright Forum* 12(3):57-73.

Mi'kmaq Elders and Parks Canada

1994   *Mi'kmaq Culture History, Kejimkujik National Park, Nova Scotia.* HSMBC Agenda Papers, #1994-36. Copies available from National Historic Sites Directorate, Parks Canada.

Mohs, Gordon

1994   St:olo Sacred Ground. In *Sacred Sites, Sacred Places.* David L. Carmichael et al., eds., pp. 184-208. *One World Archaeology* 23. London and New York: Routledge.

Mowachaht-Muchalaht First Nations

1997   *Yuquot.* HSMBC Agenda Papers, #1997-31. Copies available from National Historic Sites Directorate, Parks Canada.

Parks Canada

1995   *Guidelines for the Preparation of Commemorative Integrity Statements.* Ottawa: National Historic Sites Directorate.

1994a   *Guiding Principles and Operational Policies.* Ottawa: Department of Canadian Heritage.

1994b   *National Workshop on the History of Aboriginal Peoples in Canada, Draft Report of Proceedings.* On file with Parks Canada

Parks Canada in association with the Harvaqtuuq Historic Site Committee and the Harvaqtuurmiut (Kazan River) Elders

n.p.   Fall Caribou Crossing National Historic Site Commemorative Integrity Statement (draft).

Payment, Diane P.

1999.   Executive Summary of *Picking Up the Threads: Métis History in the Mackenzie Basin* ([Yellowknife NWT]: Métis Heritage Association of the Northwest Territories and Parks Canada, 313p., 1998), HSMBC agenda paper #1999-49. Copies available from National Historic Sites Directorate, Parks Canada.

Pearson, M., D. Johnston, J. Lennon, I. McBryde, D. Marshall, D. Nash, and B. Wellington

1998   *Environmental Indicators for National State of the Environment Reporting: Natural and Cultural Heritage.* Environment Indicator Reports. Canberra, Australia: State of the Environment.

Reeves, Brian

1994   Ninaistákis: the Nitsitapii's Sacred Mountain. Traditional Native Religious Activities and Land Use/Tourism Conflicts. In *Sacred Sites, Sacred Places.* David L. Carmichael et al., eds., pp. 265–95. *One World Archaeology* 23. London and New York: Routledge.

Ridington, Robin

1990   *Little Bit Know Something: Stories in a Language of Anthropology.* Vancouver: Douglas & McIntyre.

Ritchie, David

1994   Principles and Practice of Site Protection Laws in Australia. In *Sacred Sites, Sacred Places.* David L. Carmichael et al. eds., pp. 227–44. *One World Archaeology* 23. London and New York: Routledge.

Sahtu Heritage Places and Sites Joint Working Group

2000   *Rakekée Gok'é Godi: Places We Take Care Of. Report of the Sahtu Heritage Places and Sites Working Group* (Yellowknife NWT). http://pwnhc.learnnet. nt.ca/research/Places/execsum.html

Société Matcite8eia and the Community of Pikogan

1996   *Abitibi.* HSMBC Agenda Papers, #1996-64. Copies available from National Historic Sites Directorate, Parks Canada.

Stoddard, N.,

1969   *Inukshuks, Likenesses of Men.* HSMBC Agenda Papers, #1969-60. Copies available from National Historic Sites Directorate, Parks Canada.

Uluru-Kata Tjuta Board of Management and Parks Australia

2000   *Tjukurpa Katutja Ngarantja. Uluru-Kata Tjuta National Park Plan of Management.* http://www.deh.gov.au/parks/publications/uluru-pom.html

Uluru-Kata Tjuta Board of Management and Australian National Parks and Wildlife Service

1991   *Uluru (Ayers Rock-Mount Olga) National Park Plan of Management.* Canberra: Uluru-Kata Tjuta Management, ANPWS

UNESCO

1996a   Clauses 23–42. *World Heritage Convention Operational Guidelines.* http://whc.unesco.org/archive/out/guide96.htm

1996b   *Biosphere Reserves: The Seville Strategy and the Statutory Framework of the World Network.* Paris: UNESCO.

Appendix 1

Recommendations by the Historic Sites and Monuments Board of Canada Related to Designated Aboriginal Cultural Landscapes (As of 1999)

Abitibi, Quebec [Abitibiwinni] (November,1996)

> "Both a traditional summering area and a sacred place for the Algonquin;
>
> importance not only to the Pikogan community, whose origins predate the meeting of the Abitibi and the French in the 17th century, but also by the Wahgoshing community of Ontario;
>
> vestiges of various periods of occupation by the Abitibi Algonquin dating as far back as 6,000 years. . .numerous trading posts which operated there from the 17th century onward."

Arvia'juaq and Qikiqtaarjuk, Nunavut [Inuit] (July,1995)

> "Speaks eloquently to the cultural, spiritual, and economic life of the Inuit in the Keewatin region . . . focusing on . . . coastal activities carried out by the communit[y] of Arviat . . .site of particular significance to the community."

Fall Caribou Crossing Hunt site, Kazan River, Nunavut [Inuit] (July, 1995)

> "Speaks eloquently to the cultural, spiritual, and economic life of the Inuit in the Keewatin region . . . focusing on the inland or caribou hunt . . . carried out by the communit[y] of Baker Lake . . . site of particular significance to the community."

Grizzly Bear Mountain and Scented Grass Hills, Northwest Territories [Sahtu Dene] (November, 1996)

> "Associative cultural landscapes of national historic significance;
>
> cultural values expressed through the interrelationship between the landscape, oral histories, graves, and cultural resources, such as trails and cabins, help to explain and contribute to an understanding of the origin, spiritual values, lifestyle and land-use of the Sahtu Dene."

Mi'kmaq Cultural Landscape of Kejimkujik National Park, Nova Scotia [Mi'kmaq] (November, 1994)

"The cultural landscape of Kejimkujik National Park which attests to 4000 years of Mi'kmaq occupancy of this area, and which includes petroglyph sites, habitation sites, habitation sites, fishing sites, hunting territories, travel routes, and burials."

Nagwichoonjik [Mackenzie River] from Thunder River to Point Separation, Northwest Territories [Gwichya Gwich'in] (June, 1997)

"Its prominent position within the Gwichya Gwich'in cultural landscape;

flows through Gwichya Gwich'in traditional homeland, and is culturally, socially, and spiritually significant to the people;

importance of the river through their oral histories, which trace important events from the beginning of the land to the present...names given along the river, stories associated with these areas, and the experience drawn from these stories;

transportation route, allowing Gwichya Gwich'in to gather in large numbers . . . during the summer;

archaeological evidence . . . extensive precontact fisheries and stone quarries, ensuring Gwichya Gwich'in survival through the centuries."

Xá:ytem (Hatzic Rock), British Columbia [Stó:lō First Nation] (November 1997; February, 1992)

Cost-sharing recommended

"The age of the Hatzic Rock site and its close association to a transformer site of clear importance to the Stó:lō people."

Yuquot, British Columbia [Mowachaht-Muchalaht First Nations] (June, 1997)

"The ancestral home of the Mowachaht and the centre of their social, political and economic world;

continuously occupied for over 4,300 years, the village became the capital for all 17 tribes of the Nootka Sound region;

also the area where Nuu-chah-nulth whaling originated and developed and the site of the Whaler's Washing House, the most significant monument associated with Nuu-chah-nulth whaling;

"focal point of diplomatic and trading activity of Canada's west coast in late 18th century."

Appendix 2

Recommendations by the Historic Sites and Monuments Board of Canada Related to Potential Aboriginal Cultural Landscapes (As of 1999)

Déline Traditional Fishery and Old Fort Franklin, Northwest Territories [Sahtu Dene] (1996)

"The traditional Dene fishery at Déline...its use over time and the long history of sharing its resources, as well as the remains of Fort Franklin, the wintering quarters of Sir John Franklin's second expedition;

they speak eloquently to the relationship which evolved in the 19th century between Aboriginal people in the north and those Euro-Canadian parties who were determined to explore it;

impact of the Franklin expedition and those which were to follow on the Aboriginal people of the region contributed to the emergence of the Sahtu Dene as a distinctive cultural group and the Sahtu Dene see the fishery at Déline as being of particular cultural significance to their occupation of the region."

Hay River Mission Sites, Hay River Indian Reserve, Northwest Territories (1992)

"Close association with a critical period in Dene/Euro-Canadian relations;

two churches, rectory and two cemeteries with numerous spirit houses—significant features in a cultural landscape, rather than the landscape itself."

Head-Smashed-In Buffalo Jump [Estipah skikikini kots], Alberta [Niitsitapi/Blackfoot]

World Heritage Site (1981);

"Bison jump representing communal way of hunting for thousands of years (1968)."

Appendix 3

Designations/Other Recognitions by Territorial Governments Related to Aboriginal Cultural Landscapes (As of 1999)

British Columbia

No designations of Aboriginal cultural landscapes as such;

multi-agency Land Use Coordination Office plays coordinating role for protected areas, including strategy, communications, land use planning;

provincial parks created with historical importance to Aboriginal groups; some co-managed through planning processes;

program of traditional use studies under the Aboriginal Affairs Branch of the Ministry of Forests; no designation, but inventory and recording activities of traditional knowledge and places that enable First Nations to develop information bases from which to respond to planning inquiries and threats to traditional use sites.

Newfoundland and Labrador

No designations or commemorations of cultural landscapes where the heritage values are primarily associated with Aboriginal peoples.

Northwest Territories/Nunavut

No designations of Aboriginal cultural landscapes as such;

extensive inventory and mapping programs have recorded locations and traditional knowledge related to places of significance to Aboriginal peoples;

Sahtu Heritage Places and Sites Joint Working Group established under Sahtu Déné and Métis Comprehensive Land Claim Agreement, sec. 26.4, to consider and make recommendations to the appropriate governments and the Sahtu Tribal Council on Sahtu heritage places; report *Rakekée Gok'é Godi: Places We Take Care of* (2000);

Prince of Wales Northern Heritage Centre website with school programs focused on traditional knowledge and an 11,000-entry geographical names database (http://pwnhc.learnnet.nt.ca).

Quebec

No designations of Aboriginal cultural landscapes as such;

113 archaeological sites classified under the *Loi*

sur les biens culturels have at least one occupation by Aboriginal people; most (84) are identified in category 3 (site, bien ou monument historique ou archéologique) with many (24) in category 5 (dans un arrondissement historique);

provincial law provides for designations and protection under municipal rather than provincial jurisdiction; federal ownership precludes provincial designation on reserve lands;

White Mountain, Lake Mistassini was classified as an archaeological site under the provincial law when it was first in effect; designation and protection apply to the whole mountain, and the cultural value of the area as a sacred place is acknowledged although the classification applies specifically to archaeological significance;

other places, such as the sacred mountain in Monterégie, are known to have significance to Aboriginal peoples;

Yukon

No designations of Aboriginal cultural landscapes as such;

authority exists under the Yukon Historic Resources Act;

identification of Special Management Areas under the Yukon Land Claim, such as Old Crow Flats and Fishing Branch (Vuntut Gwich'in) or Scottie Creek wetlands (White River First Nation), answer in part the need to recognize landscape areas that are in need of special protection/ management by virtue of their historical/cultural and present significance to a First Nation;

First Nations have identified trails to be of heritage interest; awareness also exists of some other landscapes of particular significance to Aboriginal peoples, e.g. Dalton Trail, Beaver House Mountain on the Dempster Highway;

land use planning and development awareness review may address development, land use, or other planning issues that involve landscapes of significance to First Nations.

Protecting Ethnographic Landscapes in Alaska:
U.S. Policies and Practices

RACHEL MASON

Alaska, the "Last Frontier" according to its state motto, is a special case in the United States perspective on ethnographic landscapes. Alaska is different from other states, both in the ways people are tied to the land and in the laws and policies affecting land uses. Three themes unique to Alaska characterize the contrasting perspectives on its landscape: subsistence, wilderness, and frontier opportunity.

Subsistence, in Alaska, refers to the traditional harvest, processing, and distribution of wild plants and animals, activities with cultural significance beyond their nutritional value. The older generation passes down traditional knowledge about subsistence to younger people, including geographic information about locations of animals and their migration routes. Native Alaskan subsistence activities began thousands of years before Western contact.

Frontier opportunities were launched when the first Europeans came to Alaska. Beginning with the establishment of a Russian fur-trading colony in the eighteenth century, non-Native people have rushed to Alaska to reap profit from its abundant natural resources. In addition to fur harvests, other extractive industries have included fishing, mining, timber, and oil development.

Non-Natives have also come to Alaska to enjoy recreational adventures such as fishing, hunting, kayaking, or hiking in its vast wilderness. The scale and remoteness of the Alaska landscape continue to awe visitors and faraway admirers. The Western concept of wilderness is related to the idea of the frontier, since both are considered untouched, uncharted territories. The difference is that wilderness is to be appreciated in its pristine state, while a frontier must be conquered.

Denali Landscapes

Denali National Park and Preserve (NPP), the state's most popular tourist attraction, illustrates both the appeal of Alaska's large-scale landscapes and the complex problems of protecting and managing them. The different uses of the Denali landscape evoke the three themes of the Alaska landscape—subsistence, wilderness, and frontier opportunity (Fig. 13). The park, centered on the highest peak in the Alaska Range, until 1980 was called Mt. McKinley National Park.

Alaska Natives traditionally used the park area for many subsistence activities. They concentrated on moose and caribou hunting on the lower elevations of the region and did not usually have a reason to climb the big mountain now called Mt. McKinley. Archaeological evidence shows that the Dry Creek site, northwest of the park near the present-day community of Healy, was a specialized sheep, bison, and elk hunting camp as much as 11,000 years ago (Brown 1991:4). Like the original users of this site, Athapaskans in the historical period traveled in small family groups in summer, and gathered in larger bands in winter. Their economic unit was a two-family household, and the local band was made up of two to five such households. Fishing was secondary to hunting in their seasonal

45

round. Moose became more important than caribou in the late precontact period (Brown 1991:8–10).

Speakers of five Athapaskan languages used the park: Tanana, Koyukon, Upper Kuskokwim (Kolchan), Ahtna, and Dena'ina. Koyukon Athapaskans lived in the northwest part of the area. Tanana Athapaskans inhabited the northern part of what is now the park; the park's mountains were the southern limit of their traditional hunting areas. An Upper Kuskokwim subgroup traveled in the Lake Minchumina and Kantishna River areas to the west of the park. Ahtna and Dena'ina use areas were south of the park.

The Athapaskans who lived in the region did not have much reason to climb the big mountain, although they did hunt on its lower parts and on other mountains. When Judge James Wickersham attempted to ascend Mt. McKinley in 1903, he encountered a group of Tanana people hunting in the foothills. The Tanana hunters shared fresh meat with Wickersham's party and showed them how to get to the base of the mountain. Another group of Athapaskans showed the explorers how to get to the glaciers below Mt. McKinley's summit (Brown 1991:32–3).

Before the park was founded in 1917, the Mt. McKinley area experienced a brief gold rush. After gold was discovered in the Kantishna Hills, prospectors began to work there in 1905. Later in the same year stampeders from outside Alaska arrived by boat and dog sled. Most became discouraged enough to leave by early 1906. Like other frontier profit seekers, miners had no particular attachment to the land they were working and moved on when the hope of profit was gone (Catton 1997:103, 96).

During the same period big game hunters began a campaign to set aside a national park to preserve Mt. McKinley's remarkable hunting opportunities. A report on the first official exploration of the mountain in 1902 interpreted the abundant bear, sheep, moose, and caribou populations there to be a result of the area's inaccessibility. The sport-hunter-conservationists who promoted the park thought that northern animals, such as

those around Mt. McKinley, were of mythically large proportions. Although they objected more to market hunting than to subsistence hunting, the sport hunters lumped both together as "pot hunters." They despised those who looked for the easiest and most efficient way to hunt, and thought pot hunters selfishly ignored the long-term effects of their hunting on animal populations (Catton 1997:90–4).

The supporters of establishing Mt. McKinley National Park wanted it to be a sportsman's hunting paradise, but they also sought to protect the area's thriving animal populations. They did not want masses of visitors each year. They testified before Congress in 1916 that the park would benefit from its proximity to the Alaska Railroad, but they had to admit the park was thirty miles away from the railroad. The sport hunters had to explain to the Senate committee why they wanted to protect the park's wildlife while only a few miners would have access to hunting there (Catton 1997:104). Finally, with the National Park Service (NPS) director's backing, Congress created the park in 1917, although it would be four years before the NPS hired the first supervisor (Brown 1991:135).

Most of the non-Natives who hunted in the newly established Mt. McKinley National Park were miners. In 1921, new park regulations required that hunters keep records of the game they killed and obtain permits in order to kill game for dog food (Brown 1991:147). The miners' strong dependence on wild meat for food justified their "pot hunting" (Catton 1997:98) in the sport hunter's eyes. Presumably, Athapaskans' hunting for food was also acceptable.

At first the sport hunters who supported the park believed the presence of gold miners was compatible with conserving the area's abundant game. Poaching—by miners, railroad workers, and construction crews—became a terrible problem in the park's early days (Sellars 1998:71). Soon, the park lobbied to ban miners from living within its borders (Catton 1997:117). Nevertheless, some miners still pursue claims today.

Prospectors, Native Alaskans, and wild animals were

13/ *View of Denali Mountain (Mt. McKinley), in Denali National Park and Preserve.*

all part of the popular image of America's Last Frontier. The long controversy over the wolf populations of Mt. McKinley is relevant to landscapes because it shows contrasting perceptions of humans' role in nature. The sport hunters' desire to engineer better hunting opportunities, and the conservationists' reluctance to control wolf populations, have seemed in turn compatible and incompatible. Athapaskans' traditional hunting was not even part of the picture. Plainly, visitor enjoyment conflicted with upholding conservation principles (Sellars 1998:155-9).

The NPS wanted to build roads to attract visitors in automobiles. Some early supporters of wilderness thought the NPS was too enthusiastic about building roads in parks because of the lure of tourist dollars at park concessions (Catton 1997:144). After the NPS lobbied aggressively, construction of the Mt. McKinley Park Road began in 1923 (Sellars 1998:107). It was not completed until 1938. While it did provide access to the mines at Kantishna, it was built primarily for the benefit

of park administration and visitors. The park wanted to give visitors to Mt. McKinley NP a frontier experience, but they also wanted to make it easier for them to visit. Even the first hardy visitors began to demand more refined accommodations than tents and platforms. The NPS preserved the feel of the frontier by constructing rustic-looking log buildings at the park headquarters.

The construction of the Alaska Highway in the 1940s made it possible to drive from the contiguous forty-eight states through Canada to Alaska. Automobile tourism was even more encouraged under the NPS's Mission 66, a ten-year (1956–1966) national campaign to improve park infrastructure. At Mt. McKinley NP, Mission 66 projects included a visitor center, campgrounds, interpretive waysides, and scenic pullouts. The most controversial project was a plan to widen and pave the road into the park. National conservation groups, such as the Sierra Club, fought against road improvement because they believed this would destroy the wilderness character of the park. The compromise solution was to "telescope" the road (Fig. 14), paving the first few miles but keeping the upper portion of the road unimproved—a "wilderness road," as the NPS director called it (Sellars 1998:192).

Today, unlike most of the National Parks in Alaska, Denali National Park—renamed at the same time it was expanded under the 1980 Alaska National Interest Lands Conservation Act—is accessible by road. Motorhomes or RV campers carrying summer travelers are common sights along the Parks Highway to Denali. The north-south railroad between Seward and Fairbanks also goes through the park. Since 1972, visitors have not been allowed to drive beyond the end of the paved road into the park, except with special-use limited permits. They must schedule a time to be shuttled up and down the road in shuttle or camper buses, stopping briefly to watch any wild animals that appear. The buses take their passengers to Eilson Visitor Center (eleven hours

14/ Eilson Road in Denali National Park and Preserve.

round-trip) or farther along the dirt and gravel road to Wonder Lake (eight hours round-trip) for up to an hour stop, then turn back toward the visitor center in the entrance area of the park.

Contemporary park visitors see very little of its aboriginal residents, some of whom have now settled in villages outside the boundaries of the park. In the past, the Athapaskan people who lived in the park area traveled over a broad territory. Small bands separated into families during the summer for subsistence pursuits and came together during the long cold winters (Fig. 15). Potlatches, ceremonial occasions for feasting and gift-giving, also included several days of singing, dancing, speeches, and storytelling.

Athapaskans were expert storytellers and enthusiastic listeners to stories. If the listeners did not seem appreciative enough, the teller might punish them by telling a pointless story (de Laguna 1995:286). Other stories, however, offered moral lessons about proper behavior in a spiritual world that included both humans and animals. Experienced storytellers usually knew intimately the places and animals they mentioned and added their own experiences to the narratives.

A popular kind of story among interior Athapaskan groups was the "Traveler" cycle, such as the Koyukon "The One Who Paddled Among the People and Animals" (Attla 1990; Thompson 1990). These stories center around a culture hero who starts by building a canoe, then goes from place to place and adventure to adventure, encountering people and animals from mythical and modern times. In different versions of the Tanana story, "The Man Who Went Through Everything," the traveler visits Otter, Wolverine, Rabbit, the Gnats, Frog, Mouse Woman, and the Giant, among other characters (de Laguna 1995:96-104, 121-34, 326-33).

The Athapaskan storytellers contrast with the contemporary interpreters hired to tell non-Native bus passengers about the Denali wildlife. Interpreters are typically seasonal employees from outside Alaska, hired not for their knowledge of the park's flora and fauna, but because they are able to establish good rapport with visitors and maintain a fairly knowledgeable patter. The buses migrate up and down the road, as visitors peer out the windows for glimpses of the "Big Five" species: bear, caribou, moose, sheep, or wolf (Pratt 2002). While almost all the visitors see wildlife at some point in their round-trip journey to the visitor center, considerably fewer get to see the mountain during their visit through the clouds obscuring it.

Mount McKinley, at 20,320 feet (6,194 meters) the highest peak in North America, is a favorite objective for expert climbers. It symbolizes the difficulties of the frontier. Each year during the brief spring climbing season, expert climbers from all over the world attempt to reach the top. Many failed ascents have ended in rescue or the climbers' deaths. Non-Native visitors and Alaska residents alike are awed by the difficult ordeal of climbing to its top.

The mountain, however, has different meanings for the Alaska Natives who lived in its shadow. The mountain named after President McKinley was called Denali, "the tall one" by the Koyukon. Athapaskans rarely name landmarks after people. They treat the tall mountain with reverence and avoid talking about it (Kari 1999:7). They would not climb Denali or other high peaks for recreation or competition. In the far northern part of the park, Chitsia Mountain, named for its resemblance to a moose heart, is the site of a Tanana origin myth (Brown 1991:33).

Denali NPP is just one example of the intersections and clashes between understandings of cultural landscapes. Today, Alaska's federal policies are the subject of continuous struggle among subsistence, wilderness, and commercial resource extraction. Advocates of each of these views and practices worry that the other two may override their interests. The situation comes under the purview of federal managers in Alaska because so much of the land is publicly owned.

Subsistence management in Alaska has been contentious for decades. The Federal Subsistence Management Program was instituted in 1991 to regulate subsistence uses of wildlife in Alaska on federal public lands. The federal takeover occurred after the landmark 1989 McDowell decision in the 9th District Court declared that the State of Alaska's failure to provide a hunting priority to rural subsistence users was out of compliance with federal law. Following the 1995 Katie John decision[1] with its subsequent appeals and delays, and the ensuing failure of the State of Alaska to enact legislation that gave subsistence priority to rural residents, the federal government also assumed management of Alaska subsistence fisheries in 1999.

Unlike "subsistence," the term "wilderness" resonates strongly outside Alaska. Despite the popular Western view that wilderness represents untouched nature, the opposite of culture, the concept of wilderness is itself a Western cultural construct. It is perhaps more important to visitors and outsiders than it is to Alaska residents, particularly Alaska Natives, to preserve nature in a pristine condition. Toward that goal, wilderness advocates may prefer non-consumptive recreational pursuits such as catch-and-release fishing to subsistence uses. While some wilderness supporters can accept subsistence uses of natural resources as "hunting to live," few can accept commercial development at the expense of untrammeled wilderness.

Commercial development began in Alaska with the Russian colony's lucrative trade in sea otter furs. Later, gold prospectors, fish processors, and oil developers, among others, flocked to Alaska for a series of extractive industry booms. Like the idea of wilderness, the concept of development comes from outside Alaska, although many Alaskans have embraced one or the other of these concepts. The frontier developers had no intrinsic ties to the land itself. They appreciated the vastness of the landscape, but largely in terms of the vast potential profits that could be reaped from the land and sea.

Laws and Policies Affecting Ethnographic Landscapes

In the U.S.

Cultural landscapes are a relatively new concept in United States resource management. Ethnographic landscapes are newer still, so it is no surprise that government agencies disagree about what they are, how they relate to cultural landscapes, and how they should be protected. The NPS, the lead government agency in cultural resource protection and preservation, initiated its Cultural Landscapes Program in 1990 after several decades of work on historic landscapes. The NPS's Applied Ethnography Program, which coordinates cultural anthropology work in regions throughout the United States, began only a few years earlier, in 1981. Both NPS programs take interest in "ethnographic landscapes," yet the two programs define these phenomena differently. This is partly because while the Cultural Landscapes Program operates under historical preservation laws, the Ethnography Program has no similar constraint.

NPS policies define a cultural landscape as "a geographic area, including both cultural and natural resources and the wildlife or domestic animals therein, associated with a historic event, activity, or person, or exhibiting other cultural or esthetic values" (NPS 2001:129). Ethnographic landscapes are one of four overlapping types of cultural landscape in the NPS classification (NPS 1997:88):

—Historic designed landscapes, deliberate artistic creations reflecting recognized styles. Engineers may also design them. Examples in Alaska are Denali NP's historical headquarters district, created as an attempt to provide visitors with a frontier experience, or the Denali road corridor.

—Historic vernacular landscapes, which illustrate peoples' values and attitudes toward the land and reflect patterns of settlement, use, and development through time. They can evolve independently of deliberate human design. Alaska historical vernacular landscapes include the Kennecott Mine complex in Wrangell-St. Elias NPP, as well as other mines. Seward's red light district, researched for Kenai Fjords NP as part of a historical compliance study for a new visitor center, is another example.

—Historic sites, significant for their association with important events, activities, and people. The Moore homestead, at Klondike Gold Rush National Historical Park, is a rare Alaska example of the type of historic site normally found outside the state. The new Aleutian World War II National Historic Area is another example, although its scale is larger than what is typically called a "site."

—Ethnographic landscapes, which have contemporary salience to groups the NPS calls traditionally associated people, those who continue to use the landscapes in the present day. Typically, these landscapes are used or valued in traditional ways. Iyat (Serpentine Hot Springs) in Northwest Alaska is a sacred and therapeutic site for Inupiaq residents of the area. In Southeast Alaska, Dundas Bay contains both prehistoric and historic remains and is a seasonal subsistence site for Tlingits from the village of Hoonah. Bartlett Cove, also in Southeast Alaska and part of Glacier Bay NPP, has mythical significance because of its connection to the Hoonah Tlingits' creation myth.

Unlike other kinds of cultural landscapes, ethnographic landscapes typically contain both natural and cultural resources (Hardesty 2000:169), possibly including plants, animals, structures, and geological features, as well as human structures and artifacts. Those who use and value landscapes may consider them purely natural, when in fact there is a strong cultural component. The cultural modification of the natural landscape may be symbolic rather than material. Moreover, there may be competing cultural interpretations of the same landscapes: in California, for example, the Timbisha Shoshone traditionally associated with Death Valley NP object to the portrayal of their vital homeland as bleak and dead (Hardesty 2000:178-9, citing Fowler et al. 1995's original research).

Many people may believe their very survival as a

15/ Chief Deaphon and his band, 1919. This Athapaskan group was one of those traditionally associated with Denali National Park and Preserve.

group depends on the continued vitality of ethnographic landscapes. This applies, for example, to the cultural values Alaska Native peoples associate with subsistence hunting and fishing. Many feel that the survival of their culture is predicated upon their continued opportunities to harvest, process, and share wild foods. Non-Native supporters of the wilderness also feel strongly about their attachment to the land. They might, however, think of the entire human race as a reference group, or a beleaguered ecosystem, rather than a single cultural group.

Nationwide, the NPS Cultural Landscapes Program has focused primarily on historic preservation of non-indigenous peoples' structures and activities. Examples of NPS-recognized cultural landscapes include presidential homes and historic ranches, old mines and dams, missions, roads, prisons, and even tenement buildings. The developers of the NPS Cultural Landscapes Program have taken more inspiration from archaeology than from ethnography, perhaps because archaeologists and historical architects share an interest in struc-

tures, material remains, and the past. Many NPS historic landscape projects include a prehistoric component, but fewer encompass contemporary activities. In the United States, as elsewhere, historical sites designated because of archaeological evidence tend to be treated as a set of discrete entities, rather than as part of an integrated landscape (Buggey, this volume).

On the national level, United States government policies toward ethnographic landscapes come from several important laws designed to protect cultural resources. Most of these laws require consultation with the associated peoples affected by management decisions. The National Environmental Policy Act (NEPA) of 1969, which requires an environmental impact statement or environmental assessment for any proposed work with potential environmental effects, was enacted to protect both natural and cultural resources.

The National Historical Preservation Act (NHPA) of 1966, as amended in 1992, requires that places significant to Native Americans be conserved with other culturally significant sites that are part of a diverse national heritage. The NHPA criteria that determine eligibility for the National Register of Historic Places are:

—The quality of significance in American history, architecture, archaeology, engineering, and culture present in districts, sites, buildings, structures, and objects that possess integrity of location, design, setting, materials, workmanship, feeling, and association, and:

—that are associated with events that have made a significant contribution to the broad patterns of our history; or

—that are associated with the lives of significant people, present or past; or

—that embody the distinctive characteristics of a type, period, or method of construction, or that represent the work of a master, or that possess high artistic values, or that represent a significant and distinguishable entity whose components may lack individual distinction; or

—that have yielded or may be likely to yield, information important in history or prehistory (NPS 1997:2).

Clearly, these restrictions eliminate many culturally significant ethnographic landscapes used in contemporary times. A property less than fifty years old meets the criteria only if it is deemed extraordinarily important. Moreover, no cemetery, birthplace, grave, commemorative property, religious property, structure moved from its original location, or reconstructed historic building is ordinarily eligible for the National Register. The NHPA focuses on structures and other alterations of the landscape, rather than on the ways people interpret it. Because an ethnographic landscape may lack material artifacts or written documentation, its value for preservation can be more difficult to determine than a historical structure (Evans and Roberts 1999).

To address this gap, the NPS has taken steps to make Traditional Cultural Properties (TCPs) eligible for the National Register. The NPS developed a bulletin in 1994 to help archeologists and ethnographers identify and interpret TCPs (NPS 1994). While this has been an effective way to recognize individual properties, it has been less helpful in understanding the interrelationship of sites within a landscape.

Another area of legislation affecting ethnographic landscapes deals with protection of and access to sacred sites. Over the past twenty-five years, the United States has built up a unique "legislative package" directly related to Native Americans' freedom to practice traditional religion. The American Indian Religious Freedom Act of 1978 (AIRFA) affirms Native Americans' rights to worship; but it does not have any implementing regulations; and therefore relies primarily on the goodwill of landowners or managers to grant worshippers access to sacred sites. However, a later Executive Order (13007), issued in 1996, more explicitly protects Native Americans' access to sacred sites. Less directly relevant to ceremonial uses, the Archaeological Resources Protection Act of 1979 (ARPA) requires federal land managers to determine whether potential excavation sites have cultural significance to associated peoples. The Native American Graves Protection and Repatriation Act of 1990 (NAGPRA) requires that human remains and funerary items discovered on federal lands be repatriated to associated tribes (Hardesty 2000:182). These laws, special to Native Americans, all protect specific components of ethnographic landscapes.

In Alaska

Government management regimes frequently conflict with indigenous people's ties to the land, and Alaska has been no exception. Before Western contact, Native Alaskans managed the land and its resources according to their own practices and requirements. Today, harvests of wild foods are subject to a complex set of formal regulations that include both federal and state authorities in different contexts, since more than half of all lands in the state are federally managed (Fig. 16). Subsistence uses—hunting, fishing, and gathering wild resources for personal and family consumption and distribution—also co-exist and compete with commercial, recreational, and wildlife conservation uses of land.

Until recently, most NPS cultural landscape projects in Alaska did not focus on subsistence landscapes, but on historical structures and non-Natives' activities. The current focus on ethnographic landscapes sets NPS cultural landscapes work in Alaska apart from the other regions. Some examples of such work in Alaska are:

—Chilkoot Trail and the Dyea Townsite Cultural Landscape Inventories (NPS 1999a and 1999b). Both sites are located in Klondike Gold Rush National Historical Park—headquartered in Skagway, Alaska, near the Canadian boarder—and relate to the routes taken by non-Native stampeders headed north to the Yukon territory in the 1898 Gold Rush. They describe the Native groups who lived in the area and refer to their participation in historical events, but do not address the contemporary importance of the sites [see Horton, this volume].

—The cultural landscapes report for Kennecott Mill Town in Wrangell-St. Elias National Park and Preserve (Gilbert et al. 2001). Kennecott was a non-Native community that grew up around a copper mine in the early twentieth century. It is now abandoned. The report emphasizes developing plans

to restore and preserve the historic buildings and structures at the site.

The ethnographic landscape report is one of the NPS Applied Ethnography Program's standard types of reports:[2]

This is a limited field survey to identify and describe the names, locations, distributions, and meanings of ethnographic landscape features. . . . Community members will be involved in site visits and ethnographic interviewing. Studies will be coordinated with the cultural landscape program, which has primary responsibility for cultural landscape identification and management (http://www.cr.nps. gov/aad/ studies.htm).

At the time of this writing, the Alaska region of NPS has not produced any ethnographic landscape reports. However, many earlier ethnographies are eloquent state-

16/ *Federal lands in Alaska. Shaded areas are federal public lands.*

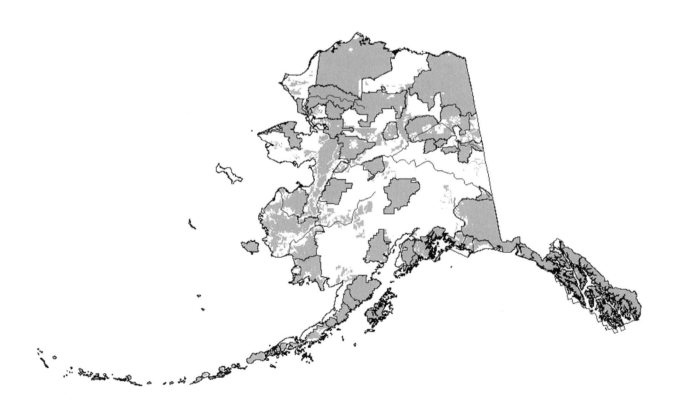

ments of Alaska Natives' attachments to place (e.g., de Laguna 1972; Nelson 1969, 1983; Ellanna and Balluta 1992; Burch 1981, 1994, 1999; Goldschmidt and Haas 1998). Recent examples of NPS-contracted work that focus on ethnographic landscapes of specific value to Native Alaskans include:

—The Shared Beringian Heritage Program's study of Ublasaun, a past reindeer herding community and subsistence settlement near the village of Shishmaref in Northwest Alaska was published in 1996 (Schaaf 1996). Other NPS-sponsored studies of the same region include Simon and Gerlach (1991) and Fair and Ningeulook (1994). The abandoned settlement at Ublasaun is a "memory landscape," a once-vital place that remains in people's hearts and minds (Fair, this volume).

—Place-names studies around Denali National Park and Preserve (Gudgel-Holmes 1991; Kari 1999). These reports are based on linguistic and oral history work with Athapaskan language speakers.

Special circumstances in Alaska affect NPS and other federal agencies. Indirectly, they affect ethnographers'

interests. The Alaskan ethnographers' focus on subsistence harvests, use areas, means of access and place names derives in part from the 1971 Alaska Native Claims Settlement Act (ANCSA),[3] but most importantly from the 1980 Alaska National Interest Lands and Conservation Act (ANILCA).[4] ANCSA and ANILCA set guidelines for managing federal lands in Alaska and set the standard for government recognition of ethnographic landscapes there.

ANCSA, by creating thirteen regional Native corporations and allotting certain lands to shareholders, superimposed Western property and business concepts, along with political territories, upon Alaska Natives' ties to the land. An indirect product of ANCSA was the Bureau of Indian Affairs' 14(h)(1) Program,[5] an office of the agency which oversaw the collection of more than 2,500 taped or written interviews with Alaska Natives about significant sites throughout Alaska (Pratt 2002). The records, stored in the BIA office in Anchorage, represent an important archive of Alaska Native traditional knowledge.

17/ Game Management Units in Alaska. The Alaska Department of Fish and Game divided the state into 26 geographical units to facilitate management of hunting and trapping.

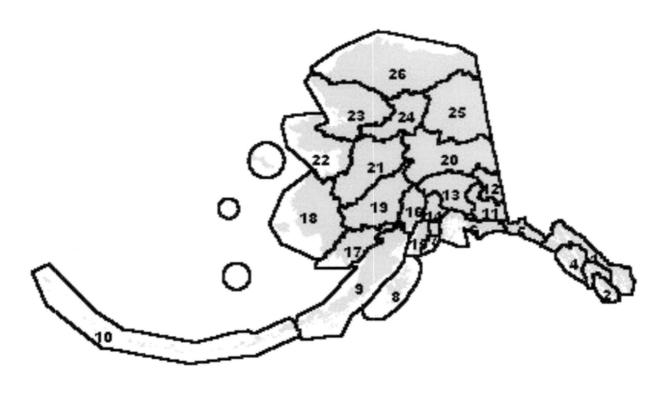

The impetus for settling Alaska Native claims in 1971 came from the biggest frontier opportunity of all, the discovery of oil at Prudhoe Bay. ANCSA extinguished all current Native claims, but it left the door open for ANILCA to establish priority for subsistence harvesting for qualified users. Originally, Title VIII of ANILCA gave subsistence hunting priority to Native rural residents. As a last-minute compromise with the State of Alaska's interests, however, Congress approved a version of ANILCA that gave subsistence priority to all qualified rural residents, both Native and non-Native. Other portions of ANILCA set aside 32.4 million acres (131,118 square kilometers) of land in Alaska as wilderness, not to be touched for development.

ANILCA focused more directly than ANCSA on land conservation. ANILCA created six new national parks, along with several monuments, preserves, wildlife refuges, and wild and scenic rivers. This new law also brought the lands used by Alaska Native corporations created under ANCSA, under federal management and protection (Hardesty 2000:182). ANILCA was groundbreaking legislation because it also created a new management model for protected lands that recognized contemporary subsistence uses by living Native cultures. Robert Arnberger (2001:1-2), NPS Alaska Regional Director, wrote that because of ANILCA, "Alaska is serving as a laboratory of how indigenous peoples and their cultures remain and are joined with the landscape—inseparable from it."

By creating a subsistence priority for rural residents on federal public lands, Title VIII of ANILCA eventually led to the establishment of the Federal Subsistence Management Program in 1991. This interagency program includes representatives of five federal agencies. The U.S. Fish and Wildlife Service is the lead agency; the others are the National Park Service, the Forest Service, the Bureau of Land Management, and the Bureau of Indian Affairs.

Government management of subsistence focuses more on uses of particular resources than on reading the landscape. Established in 1978, the State of Alaska's subsistence research branch, the Alaska De-

18/ The ten Alaskan regions represented by Federal Subsistence Regional Advisory Councils. The geographical regions are roughly separated along cultural lines.

partment of Fish and Game Division of Subsistence has documented subsistence harvests and mapped traditional use areas.[6] Because of the practical need to resolve management concerns, the government agency perspective also de-emphasizes the cognitive aspects of the cultural landscape. State and federal management of resources for subsistence, commercial, and recreational uses cut up the landscape in peculiar ways, by creating several conflicting networks of management units.

Dual management by state and federal subsistence programs further re-organized the Alaska landscape in a new and foreign way. To minimize confusion, the federal program adopted the state's system of twenty-six Game Management Units, designating them "Wildlife Management Units" (Fig.17). Game or wildlife management units are not traditional territories, any more than it is traditional for Native Alaskans to have harvest seasons and catch limits. In addition, the federal program established ten federal subsistence regional advisory councils (Fig. 18). The composition of the regional councils, whose members are appointed by the secretaries of interior and agriculture, is intended to reflect the cultural groups and the different interests of subsistence users in each rural area. Both Natives and non-Natives are eligible to be on the councils, in keeping with ANILCA's insistence on including non-Native subsistence users.[7]

The 1999 addition of fisheries to the federal subsistence management of wildlife heightened subsistence users' interest in the landscapes created by rivers. Athapaskan groups living in Interior Alaska have a particular focus on rivers. Some Athapaskan languages render directions as "upriver" or "downriver" (Kari 2000), in addition to "toward the water" or "away from the water" (Tilley 1994:57), instead of using the Western cardinal directions. At a fall 1999 meeting of the federal Southcentral Regional Advisory Council, an Ahtna Athapaskan resident of the area proposed that wildlife management units be replaced by river drainages as the main units for subsistence fisheries management.

Such a focus would be closer to the traditional management already in use in rural Southcentral Alaska. Although the regional council found the suggestion appealing, this practical and culturally appropriate suggestion did not advance any further in the regulatory channels than that discussion.

Subsistence management regimes in Alaska have contributed to two significant recent developments in scientific research and natural resource management. One is the need to treat traditional ecological knowledge on an equal footing with Western science. Along with scholars' heightened interest in traditional knowledge, scientific research has become more of a collaboration between Western scholars and tribal groups. Traditional ecological knowledge frequently centers on landscapes. Landscapes are an integral part of traditional worldviews (Buggey, this volume) where animals and humans belong to the same spiritual world. Geographic features may also play a part. In Southeast Alaska, for example, some Tlingit clans are named after nearby mountains. Kawagley's study of world-views of the Yup'ik people of Western Alaska begins with a creation myth about humans emerging at the Yukon-Kuskokwim delta (1995:13). Many other Alaska Native creation myths tell how the first humans were placed in their landscape.

The second and related development, influenced by progress toward shared power in resource management decision making in Canada, is the movement in United States government agencies toward co-management by stakeholders, including users and managers. Both in Canada and the U.S., efforts to institute co-management regimes have focused on specific natural resources, not landscape preservation. In both countries, however, indigenous people have become more involved in managing historical or cultural sites (Buggey, this volume). Research involving Native peoples or their lands must now be conducted in consultation with and with formal approval of tribal entities.

Since its inception in 1991, the Federal Subsistence Management Program has made progress toward co-management, in the sense that subsistence users participate meaningfully in wildlife management decisions affecting them. The Federal Subsistence Board is obligated to follow the recommendations of the Regional Advisory Councils, except under special circumstances. Community residents participate and have influence in Regional Council meetings, which are often held in rural Alaska. Other examples of shared decision making include the development of user-manager groups to make regulatory decisions on caribou hunting and the introduction of community quotas for caribou in the Southern Alaska Peninsula herd. In areas outside the purview of the Federal Subsistence Program, legislation affecting oversight of marine mammal and migratory bird hunting has made specific allowances for local users' involvement in management.

In Alaska as elsewhere in the U.S., government management agencies and their scientific advisors have begun to pay more attention to local knowledge and concerns. Despite the movement toward co-management, by their very existence land managing government agencies represent the dominant non-Native culture, not the indigenous people. The concept of land management imposes a legal and political system that may contradict indigenous views of land use rights.

Ethnographic Landscapes

In the U.S.

In the United States, much of land management agencies' interest in attachment to place, and hence in ethnographic landscapes, comes from efforts to protect Native Americans' sacred places (Evans and Roberts 1999:1). Federal land policies, intended to prevent or restrict access to public lands, have incidentally prevented Native Americans and others from visiting sacred or meaningful sites (Hardesty 2000:180). On the other hand, Native Americans may wish to prevent outsiders from disturbing sacred sites or visiting them during ceremonies.

Those accustomed to Western religious concepts may not easily understand why Native Americans view some sites as sacred. Instead of recognizing a few discrete sacred shrines, Native Americans may imbue a more broadly defined landscape with meaning. The journey itself may be more sacred than the landmarks along the way. Sacredness can also be temporary; a site's sacredness may not outlive a specific use.

There is a connection between sacred sites and those important for subsistence uses. Hunting and gathering have spiritual as well as economic and political aspects. Research on the social impacts of the 1989 *Exxon Valdez* Oil Spill showed significant differences between Alaska Natives and non-Natives in the spiritual meanings attached to the environment (Callaway, this volume; Jorgenson 1995). The value non-Natives placed on their favorite hunting and fishing sites differed from the culturally based spiritual significance Natives identified.

Place-names are another arena of conflict between indigenous people and politically dominant managers. Ethnographic landscapes, as constructed by the people who use them, may clash with the dominant group's vision of the same area. Fair (this volume) reviews the literature on toponymy in Alaska and outside the state. In Alaska, substantial NPS ethnographic work focuses on Native attachment to place (Gudgel-Holmes 1991; Kari 1999; Fair and Ningeulook 1994; Fair 1996). Collecting this knowledge adds critical detail to ethnographic documentation of a world-view. For example, indigenous place-names in Denali NPP grow scarcer as one travels upland, since Atha-paskans had little reason to hunt in the snowy mountains (Kari 1999:16). Alaska Native people's efforts to return to place-names previously used (e.g., changing Mt. McKinley's name to Denali) recognize that naming the landscape expresses sovereignty and identity.

Some anthropologists and historical architects working in federal agencies have experienced institutional pressure to develop inventories of sites. In the NPS, for example, all programs have been tasked to develop measurable goals and to document progress toward meeting them. The Ethnographic Resource Inventory

(ERI), Archaeological Sites Management Information System (ASMIS), and the Cultural Landscapes Inventory (CLI) databases were created with that charge in mind. All carry the potential danger of merely listing sites, instead of explaining the relationships between them.

The Ethnographic Resource Inventory is still, in 2004, in its initial stages and not yet fully operational. The only nationwide ethnographic goal in the NPS Performance Management Data System[8] measures the number of ethnographic resources parks add to the ERI each year. The ERI is expected to become the main measure of work accomplished in the agency's Applied Ethnography Program. Eventually, it is hoped, the ERI will produce much more information than a list of resources.[9] At present, however, the ERI does not adequately convey the relationships between ethnographic resources. The Archaeological Sites Management Information System, which serves the NPS archaeology program, has similar problems. The Cultural Landscapes Inventory has the advantage of listing whole landscapes instead of individual resources and of documenting landscape as a process (Horton, this volume). However, inventories have a way of making things concrete and discrete that might better be considered continuous. As Smith and Burke (this volume) point out in reference to Australian indigenous views on time and space, ethnographic landscapes are not a collection of dots but the connections between the dots.

Another approach to U.S. natural and cultural resource management is the ecosystem model embraced in the last decade by some federal programs, including the Fish and Wildlife Service and the Forest Service. The Bureau of Land Management has not so explicitly supported the ecosystem concept, but has adopted some of its features. These steps reflect not only an interest in the interrelated parts of ecosystems, but an admission that humans are part of the natural landscape. Unfortunately, each agency has encountered some difficulties using the ecosystem model. Biologists who favor species-by-species analysis and management have opposed the ecosystem approach. Other problems relate to the bottom-up decision making and focus on partnerships that accompany ecosystem management initiatives. It is not easy to change an agency's hierarchical power structure.

In Alaska

Ethnographic landscapes are not static; they eventually change across a geographical area. Cultural groups need varying amounts of space to make full use of their landscapes. In the past, some Alaskan hunters and gatherers followed migrating animals and traveled seasonally within the designated group territory. Sedentary groups had intimate knowledge of a broad territory because of their journeys for trade or warfare.

Today some Alaska Native groups continue to honor "traveling landscapes." Athapaskan, in particular, are very mobile people and have many travel stories (Mishler 1995). Dena'ina Athapaskan living around Cook Inlet used and traveled over a wide-ranging territory (Kari and Fall 1987). As noted above in the discussion of Denali NPP, some Athapaskan stories focus on a character named Traveler, who dreamed in advance about the places he would visit (de Laguna 1995:330). Nelson (1983:242–3) describes how Koyukon people view the human imprint on the environment:

> This imprint can be illustrated by describing the cultural and personal means with which Koyukon people vest places on the landscape. Some of these are founded in the domain of recent human events; others are ancient and more spiritual than human. Traveling through the wildland, a Koyukon person constantly passes by these places, and the flow of land becomes also a flow of the mind.

Ahtna Athapaskans, too, often tell travel narratives. They describe remembered hunting and fishing journeys, emphasizing survival in the face of hardship. Upper Ahtna travel stories also demonstrate kinship connections across regions (Kari 1986:153–215).

Iñupiat people in Northwest Alaska share stories

19/ Telida, an Upper Kuskokwim Athapaskan village and a Subsistence Residence Zone communtiy for Denali National Park and Preserve.

of traveling, some of them about journeys by sea or along the coast (Fair and Ningeulook 1994). In regard to social dimensions of land use in Point Hope, an Iñupiaq community, Burch (1981) tells of individuals' mobility between settlements, as well as movements of whole settlements. Both supernatural factors (particularly fear of ghosts) and practical quests for ease of access influenced settlement choices.

The sea dominated the landscape on Alaska's southern coastlines, and Aleut and Alutiiq people were fearless travelers by water. They also traveled over land and knew every landmark of certain trails. On Kodiak Island, at the beginning of the twentieth century, it was common for men from the village of Akhiok to undertake a walk of several days to Karluk, on the island's west side (Rostad 1988).

In addition to their geographic aspect, the temporal dimension of traveling landscapes marks a difference between Western and non-Western ways of thinking. While this is often seen as the contrast between linear

and cyclical thinking, non-Western temporal views of the landscape may be more accurately described as "the past living in the present" (Horton 2002, this volume). The Australian Dreamtime famously exemplifies a view of moving landscapes, since some Australian Indigenous people see a group's totemic history embodied in landmarks. Alaska Native traveling stories also show how past deeds and adventures still exist in today's landscape.

Before Western contact, Alaska indigenous people developed complex economies built upon sophisticated exploitation of local plant and animal resources. No group was isolated from other groups; all were traders and travelers who knew varied landscapes by water, coast or on land. It is not too surprising that Alaska Natives find it difficult to accept an imposed Western landscape, or that Western managers would fail to recognize the ethnographic landscapes that co-exist with management regimes.

Nationwide, the NPS formally acknowledges some

traveling landscapes in the form of routes, rivers, and conceptual units, such as the Underground Railroad, the Cherokee Trail of Tears, and Historic Route 66. These monuments or historical trails honor travel and movement instead of discrete sites. The Underground Railroad represents the network of helpers runaway African-American slaves encountered as they traveled north to freedom. The Cherokee Trail of Tears recognizes the forced relocation of Cherokees from their homeland in the Southeastern U.S. to Oklahoma. Historic Route 66 commemorates the route Dust Bowl farmers took from the Central Plains to California during the Great Depression in the 1930s.

For non-Native Americans, preserved historical landscapes tend to celebrate the conquest of nature (Melnick 2000:26). This adds to the ongoing alienation of Native American values from the existing system of historical landscape management. At Alaska's Klondike Gold Rush National Historical Park, for example, visitors are shown the travails of Gold Rush prospectors as they navigated the Chilkoot Trail. Native Americans, however, were not until recently a significant part of the NPS interpretation of the Klondike story.

Native American ethnographic landscapes tend to be more inclusive and more geographically widespread than those defined by NPS cultural landscape guidelines. A landscapes approach is a better way to show how cultural sites and resources are interrelated than the Traditional Cultural Properties approach, which looks at landmarks in a piecemeal fashion (Stoffle and Evans 1990). Unfortunately, cultural resource managers continue to be skeptical of Native Americans' statements about holistic conservation and their attachments to sacred places and activities.

Policy Implications

To explore the implications for policy, we now return to the originally posed three-way struggle among subsistence, wilderness, and frontier opportunities. From the government management standpoint, all three categories represent competing user groups. There tends

to be little interest in overlapping views, despite recognition that there is much overlap between them.

Land and resource managers tend to assume that indigenous foragers had minimal effect on the landscape. For both the early conservation movement and for more recent conservationists, the opposite of wilderness was development (Sellars 1998:211). Both government agencies and conservationists viewed Euro-American management as the only form of management (Callaway, this volume). Native Americans' uses of the landscape were not part of the equation. Today, while a particular site or area may seem to non-Native visitors and scientists to preserve nature or commemorate historical events, it may also represent a homeland to Native people (Buggey, this volume).

Cultural resource managers have embraced the conservation goal of preserving the integrity of the natural landscape and have applied this goal to preserving historical landscapes (Howett 2000). Indeed, integrity is an important criterion for National Register of Historic Places eligibility. Resource managers have not so wholeheartedly supported preserving the integrity of ethnographic landscapes. They tend to manage each species separately, rather than preserve an entire landscape and the activities it incorporates.

An area's designation as wilderness confounds subsistence users as much as do the artificial boundaries of the federal or state game management unit system. In non-Native understanding, wilderness land is uninhabited, unused, and untouched. Indigenous people's subsistence uses are tolerated or ignored largely as long as they do not seem to modify the landscape. Consumptive human uses, even for subsistence or for religious ceremonies, threaten the integrity of non-Natives' perceived wilderness.

NPS examples of ethnographic landscapes in Alaska are mainly those used by Native Alaskans, just as ethnography in Alaska has focused upon the aboriginal inhabitants of the state. In Alaska, ethnographic landscapes tend to remain hidden from public view, while the cultural landscape exemplified in historical monuments and artifacts left by Western culture is widely displayed and interpreted to visitors. Western historical landscapes are also actively promoted to encourage tourism, public awareness, and commercial revenues coming from increased visitorship. Therefore, the spiritual values Native Alaskans attach to their landscape are neither presented nor properly understood by most of the non-Native residents and visitors.

Most current ethnographic research in Alaska, including landscape studies, involves collaboration between Western scholars and Alaska Natives (e.g., Kari 1986; Fair and Ningeulook 1994; Mishler 1995; Ellanna and Balluta 1992). Anthropologists' heightened interest in traditional ecological knowledge has a parallel in historical architects' growing interest in the cognitive aspects of landscape. The significant disciplinary difference may be methodological: anthropologists learn about ethnographic landscapes using the methods of face-to-face interviews and participant observation, while landscape architects look at features of landscape—particularly man-made structures—before interpreting the values embedded in cultural resources.

NPS study of ethnographic landscapes is still in beginning stages, but it has progressed further than in other government agencies. Recognition of diverse contemporary cultural views of the landscape, and of values placed on landscapes, is gradually making its way through the layers of the U.S. federal land management system. The Forest Service and the Fish and Wildlife Service have both regarded landscape diversity as axiomatic to the ecosystem approach they have embraced. Consequently, these agencies have come closer to appreciating the cultural context of ethnographic landscape and have moved away from a species-by-species or site-by-site approach to biota and landscapes. The Forest Service has taken special interest in past human roles in altering landscapes, particularly Native Americans' past practices of purposely setting fires to control the landscape (MacCleary 1994). The Fish and Wildlife Service also acknowledges that humans are active participants in ecosystem change.

The Bureau of Land Management and the Minerals Management Service, both in the U.S. Department of Interior, have developed programs to manage visual landscapes for the protection of scenic values. The Department of Interior agencies and the Forest Service in the Department of Agriculture have all endeavored to incorporate traditional knowledge along with data collected by the methods of Western science in federal decision making (Burwell 2001).

Traditional knowledge is typically tied to a specific place or locality. An important policy implication is that managers must reconcile their need to find broad, one-size-fits-all management (for efficiency, enforcement, or personnel training purposes) with the goals of co-management and use of local knowledge. While many in the NPS believe that landscape protection is best accomplished by the people who use the land, the NPS and other federal agencies also have a national and international constituency. Political pressures on the management agencies may prevent them from wholeheartedly adopting local knowledge as a guide.

Conclusions

United States government policies to designate and protect cultural landscapes are primarily driven by historic preservation laws, particularly the 1966 National Historical Preservation Act. In NPS usage, ethnographic landscapes are a specific type of cultural landscapes, incorporating both natural and cultural elements. They are significant to contemporary, traditionally associated peoples. The American Indian Religious Freedom Act (1978) and Executive Order 30007 (1996), which protect Native Americans' access to sacred sites, and National Register Bulletin 38 (1994), providing guidelines for documenting Traditional Cultural Properties have, to a lesser extent, also influenced management of ethnographic landscapes.

Both the Cultural Landscapes Program and ethnographers in the NPS have had to contend with an institutional interest in considering distinct sites rather than ethnographic landscapes as a whole. Pressure on government agencies to produce measurable results contributes to a practice of merely listing sites, rather than describing their interconnectedness. The common goal of seeing landscape as a process, or a work-in-progress, instead of just buildings or trees, is a reason for agencies and programs to work together.

Until now, government-sponsored ethnographic or cultural landscape work in Alaska has had little explicit reference to ethnographic landscapes. Implicitly, however, ethnography and cultural landscape work in this region has done much to address Alaska Native peoples' attachment to landscape. In state and federal land management regimes, management deliberations and decisions impose a Western regulatory vision upon the indigenous system of land use. Government agencies' increased reliance on traditional ecological knowledge, along with increased support for co-management regimes, brings resource managers closer to understanding and working with indigenous worldviews.

Acknowledgments

Janet Cohen, Tonia Horton, Igor Krupnik, and James Mason provided helpful comments on a draft of this paper. Cari Goettcheus and the late Miki Crespi kindly sent an early paper they wrote together addressing collaboration between the NPS Applied Ethnography and Cultural Landscapes programs.

Notes

1. Katie John, an A[   ] Athapaskan elder from the village of Mentasta, A[   ]ka, was one of the plaintiffs in the *John v. Stat[   ]   ka* case. She and her co-plaintiffs sued for [   ]   fish for subsistence at her family's site.

2. The others are Rapid Ethnographic Assessment Procedure, Ethnographic Overview and Assessment, Traditional Use, Cultural Affiliation, Ethnohistory, and Ethnographic Oral and Life Histories (http://www.cr.nps.gov/aad/appeth.htm).

3. ANCSA's goal was to extinguish aboriginal land claims in Alaska. The discovery of oil reserves in Alaska, and the federal freeze on state land se-

lections, made it more urgent to find a quick resolution to Native land claims (Case 1984:14).

4. Following up on certain provisions of ANCSA regarding unreserved lands, ANILCA enabled the U.S. Department of Interior to withdraw and classify lands in the public interest (Case 1984:298).

5. This program takes its name from the section of the Alaska Native Claims Settlement Act, which authorizes the Secretary of the Interior to withdraw unreserved and unappropriated Native cemetery sites and historical places located on public lands, and to convey them to regional corporations.

6. A list of technical reports, and abstracts from the reports, are listed on the Alaska Department of Fish and Game website: http://www.state.ak.us/local/akpages/fishgame/subsistence/geninfo/publictns/subabs.htm.

7. By the terms of ANILCA, the NPS manages subsistence uses on its lands a little differently from the other federal landholding agencies in Alaska. In certain Alaska parks, such as Glacier Bay National Park, subsistence uses are not allowed. ANILCA established a Subsistence Resources Commission, comprised of local rural residents, for each park that allows subsistence activities. It makes recommendations to park managers and works with the NPS to develop a comprensive subsistence management plan for the park. Under NPS regulations, a person is eligible to harvest subsistence resources in a park if he lives in a designated Resident Zone Community for that park or has an individual subsistence eligibility permit.

8. This goal is optional for national parks.

9. Ethnographic resources are "subsistence and ceremonial locales and sites, structures, objects, and rural and urban landscapes assigned cultural significance by traditional users" (NPS 1997:160).

References

Attla, Catherine
1990   *K'etetaalkkaanee: The One Who Paddled Among the People and Animals.* Eliza Jones, translator. Fairbanks: Yukon-Koyukuk School District and Alaska Native Language Center.
Arnberger, Robert
2001   Living Cultures, Living Parks in Alaska. Paper prepared for the World Wilderness Conference in South Africa, October 2001. Anchorage: National Park Service, Alaska Regional Office.
Brown, William E.

1991   A History of the Denali-Mount McKinley Region, Alaska: Historic Resource Study of Denali National Park and Preserve. Vol. 1—Historical Narratives. Santa Fe: National Park Service, Southwest Regional Office.

Burch, Ernest S., Jr.

1981   The Traditional Eskimo Hunters of Point Hope, Alaska 1800-1875. Barrow: North Slope Borough.

1994   The Cultural and Natural Heritage of Northwest Alaska. Volume V—The Iñupiaq Nations of Northwest Alaska. Anchorage: National Park Service, Alaska Regional Office and Kotzebue: NANA Museum of the Arctic.

1999   International Affairs of the Iñupiaq Nations of Northwest Alaska. Anchorage: National Park Service, Alaska Regional Office.

Burwell, Michael

2001   Minerals Management Service, Alaska OCS Region - Traditional Knowledge. http://www.mms.gov/alaska/native/tradknow/tk_mms2.htm. Updated 6/5/01.

Case, David S.

1984   Alaska Natives and American Laws. Fairbanks: University of Alaska Press.

Catton, Theodore

1997   Inhabited Wilderness: Indians, Eskimos, and National Parks in Alaska. Albuquerque: University of New Mexico Press.

Crespi, Muriel (Miki), and Cari Goettcheus

2000   Ethnography and Cultural Landscapes: the case for collaboration. Paper prepared for the 2000 Annual Meeting of the Society for Applied Anthropology, Merida, Mexico.

De Laguna, Frederica

1972   Under Mount St. Elias: The History and Culture of the Yakutat Tlingit. Smithsonian Contributions to Anthropology 7. Washington, DC: Smithsonian Institution Press.

1995   Tales from the Dena: Indian Stories from the Tanana, Koyukuk, and Yukon Rivers. Seattle: University of Washington Press.

Ellanna, Linda J., and Andrew Balluta

1992   Nuvendaltin Quht'ana: The People of Nondalton. Washington, DC: Smithsonian Institution Press.

Evans, Michael J., and Alexa Roberts

1999   Ethnographic landscapes. Paper presented at the 59th annual meeting of the Society for Applied Anthropology, Tucson, Arizona, April 1999.

Fair, Susan W.

1996   Tales and Places, Toponyms and Heroes. In Ublasaun: First Light.-Iñupiaq Hunters and Herders in the Early Twentieth Century, Northern Seward Peninsula, Alaska. J. Schaaf, ed., pp. 110-25. Anchorage: National Park Service, Alaska Regional Office.

Fair, Susan W., and Edgar N. Ningeulook

1994   Qamani: Up the Coast in My mind, in My Heart. Manuscript on file Alaska Regional Office, National Park Service, Anchorage.

Fowler, Catherine S., Molly Dufort, Mary Rusco, and the Historic Preservation Committee, Timbisha Shoshone Tribe

1995   Residence Without Reservation: Ethnographic Overview and Traditional Land Use Study, Timbisha Shoshone, Death Valley National Park, California. Death Valley, CA: National Park Service.

Gilbert, Cathy, Paul White, and Anne Worthington

2001   Kennecott Mill Town Cultural Landscape Report. Wrangell-St. Elias National Park and Preserve: National Park Service, Alaska Region.

Goldschmidt, Walter R, and Theodore H. Haas

1998   Haa Aaní, Our Land: Tlingit and Haida Land Rights and Use. Seattle: University of Washington Press.

Gudgel-Holmes, Dianne, ed.

1991   Native Place Names of the Kantishna Drainage, Alaska: Kantishna Oral History Project. Denali National Park and Preserve: National Park Service, Alaska Regional Office.

1997   Kantishna Oral History Project, Phase II, Part 1: Interviews with Native Elders. Denali National Park and Preserve: National Park Service, Alaska Office.

Hardesty, Donald L.

2000   Ethnographic Landscapes: Transforming Nature into Culture. In Preserving Cultural Landscapes in America, A. Alanen and R. Melnick, eds., pp. 169-85. Baltimore: Johns Hopkins University Press.

Howett, Catherine

2000   Integrity as a value in cultural landscape preservation. In Preserving Cultural Landscapes in America, A. Alanen and R. Melnick, eds., pp.186-207. Baltimore: Johns Hopkins University Press.

Jorgenson, Joseph G.

1995   Ethnicity, Not Culture? Obfuscating Social Science in the Exxon Valdez Oil Spill Case. American Indian Culture and Research Journal 19(4):1-124.

Kari, James, ed.

1986   Tatl'ahwt'aenn Nenn': The Headwaters People's Country. Fairbanks: Alaska Native Language Center.

Kari, James

1999   Draft Final Report of Native Place Names Mapping in Denali National Park. Denali National Park and Preserve: National Park Service and Fairbanks: University of Alaska, Polar Regions Department.

2000   Some Implications of Three Athabascan Ethnographic Narratives of Nick Kolyaha (of Iliamna), Jane Tansy (of Cantwell), and Jim McKinley (of Copper Center). Presentation at NPS Cultural Resources meeting, Anchorage, Alaska, November 2000.

Kari, James, and Fall, James

1987   Shem Pete's Alaska: The Territory of the Upper

Cook Inlet Dena'ina. Fairbanks: Alaska Native Language Center.

Kawagley, Oscar

1995   *A Yupiaq World View: A Pathway to Ecology and Spirit.* New York: Waveland Press.

King, Thomas F.

1997   *Cultural Resource Laws and Practice: An Introductory Guide.* Walnut Creek, CA: AltaMira Press.

MacCleary, Doug

1994   Understanding the role the human dimension has played in shaping America's forest and grassland landscapes: Is there an archaeologist in the house? *Eco-watch Discussion Site*, 22/10/94, http://www.fs.fed.us/eco/eco-watch/ew940210.htm.

Melnick, Robert Z.

2000   Considering nature and culture in historic landscape preservation. In *Preserving Cultural Landscapes in America*, A. Alanen and R. Melnick, eds., pp. 22–43. Baltimore: Johns Hopkins University Press.

Mishler, Craig, ed.

1994   *Neerihiinjik—We Traveled from Place to Place.* Fairbanks: Alaska Native Language Center.

Morseth, Michele

1998   *Puyulek Pu'irtuq! The People of the Volcanoes: Aniakchak National Monument and Preserve Ethnographic Overview and Assessment.* Anchorage: National Park Service.

National Park Service

1993   *National Register Bulletin 38: Guidelines for Evaluating and Documenting Traditional Cultural Properties.* Patricia L. Parker and Thomas F. King, eds. Washington, DC: National Park Service.

1997   *National Register Bulletin 15: How to Apply the National Register Criteria for Evaluation.* Washington, DC: National Park Service.

1998   *Director's Order NPS-28: Cultural Resource Management Guideline.* Release No. 5 (Final).

2001   *2001 Management Policies.*

National Park Service, Alaska Regional Office

1999a   *Chilkoot Trail, Klondike Gold Rush National Historical Park: CLI Coordinator Review Report.* On file in the Cultural Landscapes Inventory.

1999b   *Dyea Historic Townsite, Klondike Gold Rush National Historical Park: CLI Coordinator Review Report.* On file in the Cultural Landscapes Inventory.

Nelson, Richard K.

1969   *Hunters of the Northern Ice.* Chicago: University of Chicago Press.

1983   *Make Prayers to the Raven: A Koyukon View of the Northern Forest.* Chicago: University of Chicago Press.

Pratt, Kenneth

2002   Director, ANCSA 14(h)1 Office, Bureau of Indian Affairs, Anchorage. Personal communication, May 31 and August 6.

Rostad, Michael

1988   *Time to Dance: Life of an Alaska Native.* Anchorage: A.T. Publishing.

Sauer, Carl O.

1963 (1925) The morphology of landscape. In *Land and Life: A Selection from the Writings of Carl Ortwin Sauer*, John Leighly, ed., pp. 315–50. Berkeley, CA: University of California Press.

Schaaf, Jeanne, ed.

1996   *Ublasaun: First Light: Iñupiaq Hunters and Herders in the Early Twentieth Century, Northern Seward Peninsula, Alaska.* Anchorage: National Park Service, Alaska System Support Office.

Sellars, Richard West

1997   *Preserving Nature in the National Parks: A History.* New Haven: Yale University Press.

Simon, James J.K., and Craig Gerlach

1991   *Reindeer Herding Subsistence and Alaska Land Use in the Bering Land Bridge National Preserve, Northern Seward Peninsula, Alaska.* Anchorage: National Park Service.

Stoffle, R., and M. Evans

1990   Holistic Conservation and Cultural Triage: American Indian Perspectives on Cultural Resources. *Human Organization* 49:91–9.

Thompson, Chad

1990   *K'etetaalkkaanee, The One Who Paddled Among the People and Animals: An Analytical Companion Volume.* Fairbanks: Yukon Koyukuk School District and Alaska Native Language Center.

Tilley, Christopher

1994   *A Phenomenology of Landscape: Places, Paths, and Monuments.* Oxford/Providence: Berg Publishers.

Writing Ethnographic History:
Historic Preservation, Cultural Landscapes, and Traditional Cultural Properties

TONIA WOODS HORTON

In a report released in July 2001, the National Park Advisory Board articulated its concerns that the national parks "actively acknowledge the connections between native cultures and the parks, and assure that no relevant chapter in the American heritage experience remains unopened" with this recommendation:

> [T]he National Park Service should help conserve the irreplaceable connections that ancestral and indigenous people have with the parks. . . . Parks should become sanctuaries for expressing and reclaiming ancient feelings of place. Efforts should be made to connect these peoples with parks and other areas of special significance to strengthen their living cultures (National Park Service 2001:3,8).

Reinforcing this idea, the report asserted, "America's national parks were places of human feeling long before they became parks. They are *ancestral homelands*" (ibid.:8, emphasis added). Without referring to Native Americans in particular, this seemingly commonsensical observation actually presents a formidable challenge to ways in which park histories are written and interpreted. It also highlights the cultural parallax in which the issue of heritage production resides: the differences in knowledge between parks as homelands and as uninhabited places in which historical significance is imposed and interpreted "from the outside," the institutional framework of the National Park Service (NPS). Although the use of the word "homelands" is an enormous advance in policy rhetoric, the implications for heritage construction as well as the subsequent implementation and management of these "sanctuaries" are much less clear.

From the Braudelian perspective of the *longue durée,* the "long view," this brief statement is a tentative overture toward accepting the contingent and provisional nature of the past as an accretion of many layers, physical and symbolic, illustrating human interaction with the landscapes that are now parks. The act of writing history as an interpretation of the past, then, becomes both text and texture for an alternative knowledge of place, a middle ground where the view from within tempers the view from without, negotiating uncertain terrain. Embedding this imperfect and arguably subjective model of history within a landscape is even more challenging: there is no stasis, historical or ecological, possible in a dynamically evolving environment. Landscapes are, at their most essential, compositions of perpetual change.

The historical imperative for parks to include "people with long and deep connections with our parklands and cultural landscapes" suggests, in effect, a reordering of heritage preservation priorities to evoke and interpret the lived experience and cultural association with American lands as they have been inhabited and shaped rather than from the perspective of the visitor, "discoverer," or scientist. The invisible tracery of ideological paradigms has negated, misrepresented, or ignored the complexity of Native American history, obscuring not only their landscape presence, but their very cultural survival. If "history is the essence of the idea of place," then the translation of history into heritage is indelibly etched with the cultural conservation of place (Glassie 1982:664).

Writing history and constructing heritage from this vantage point will be an arduous and painstaking task occurring at a number of levels. It entails, necessarily, the confluence of social and environmental histories, of multiple stories, of mosaics of belief and practice that shift, like a kaleidoscope, depending on the individual and communal experiences in these landscapes called parks. As a result, writing history in the landscape vein is profoundly ethnographic in method; it is culture inscribed, nature adapted. One without the other is incomplete. And nowhere is this potential to understand and interpret "ancestral homelands" more integral than in the NPS' attempt to document and preserve the "ethnographic landscape," defined as a distinctive resource environment representing the heritage values associated with a historical cultural group.[1]

By examining the National Park Service's institutional approach to historic preservation and cultural landscapes—particularly ethnographic landscapes—this essay examines the rather convoluted process of documenting and preserving landscapes through the National Register of Historic Places administered by the NPS. This exploration is important because it begins to illuminate the shortcomings of a historical paradigm applied not only to cultural groups, such as Native Americans, but to cultural landscapes as a whole genre of heritage. The essay concludes with a reflection on how a recovery of landscape as a language and critical practice can transform heritage production. It hints at a sweeping revision that holds promise for not only the ways in which Native American histories of place are written but, in the larger context, for a more sophisticated and integrated interpretation of national parks as landscapes of heritage.

An Uneasy Fit: The National Register and Emerging Cultural Landscape Methodology

In her compelling argument, Anne Whiston Spirn (1998:16, 22) eloquently articulates the profound relationship between humans and land as an active process in which "reading" and "speaking" landscape as a landscape inherently associates people with place. Most importantly, Spirn's description of landscape as an evolutionary process—one developed, lost, recovered, reshaped, or forgotten through time—is intrinsically linked to cultural survival: "The language of landscape uncovers the dynamic connection between place and those who live there." Learning to read landscapes is "relearning the language that holds life in place." Thus, a dialogue between people and place is intimate and revealing; conversely, a "loss of fluency in the language of landscape . . . limits our celebration of landscape as a partnership" (Spirn 1998:16,22).

Thus defined, landscape is essentially a dialogue between humans and place, articulated in multiple realms: the artful shaping of land, the active use and management of resources, the embeddedness of creation stories, and the shapes of enduring heritage. Landscapes are synthetic, integrative, encompassing processes of evolution, mind-boggling in scale. But can the concept of landscape be institutionalized as a way of seeing, of reading land and place in ways that continue traditions of land protection and ensure cultural conservation? How can it transform static histories of place into a vibrant heritage that not only reflects the past, but also the future, as a model of cultural knowledge?

In its role as the steward of heritage places, the National Park Service's responsibility is, first of all, to comprehend, or read, its own landscapes as complex historical and ecological entities in which valuable resources are to be protected. This, of course, is far easier said than done, in part due to the complicated history of the NPS as an institution whose sense of heritage, a common past, is splintered between an array of departments charged with resource protection along the problematic faultlines of "natural" and "cultural." Chief among these departments are the various divisions of cultural resource management, including archaeology, history, ethnography, historic architecture, and cultural landscapes. Segregated from this mix is the division of interpretation, a key element in bridging the gap between documented histories and the articulation of places as repositories of heritage. Additionally, the separation of natural resource management into its own heritage and conservation model adds to the compartmentalization of landscape values, by now bereft of their cultural origins.[2]

The inception of the cultural landscape paradigm in the NPS gathered momentum beginning in 1981 with the recognition that parks were composed of landscapes, a resource type to be inventoried and preserved as part of the agency's mission. This acknowledgment proved to be not only a major definitional shift for the parks, but an ideological and operational one as well. Before implementing the cultural landscapes program, cultural resource studies and management policies in the NPS were constructed along disciplinary lines: history, historic architecture, and archaeology. In the process, the legibility of the historic landscape and its critical role in shaping the nature of its embedded resources (such as structures and archaeological sites) often fell through the cracks. Certain landscape characteristics, such as land use, topography, and vegetation, were generally noted, but not seen as essential determinants for the historic scene. Archaeological relics and monuments, battlefields and sites, were not located in an active field of engagement, but rather seen as static tableaux that preserved and interpreted physical vestiges related to central themes of American nationalism.

The ideological framework for identifying historic resources for preservation relied on museum-dominated theories of American material culture embodied in the

original impetus for historic preservation on a national scale, the Historic Sites Act of 1935. This critical piece of legislation capped years of active lobbying and negotiation by the NPS, especially under the leadership of Horace Albright and, later, the new chief of the History Branch, Verne Chatelain, to move beyond the early twentieth century legacy of preserved public lands focused on archaeological ruins (almost exclusively Native American, such as Casa Grande and Mesa Verde) and battlefield sites designated under the auspices of the Antiquities Act and the Department of War mandates.[3]

The language of the Historic Sites Act focused on "historic sites, buildings, and objects" that illustrated a thematic American history through physical preservation akin to outdoor museums. It also instituted a census approach toward identifying historic properties worthy of preservation, implying a process that was both curatorial and prescriptive, and most importantly, defined by federal standards. With the consolidation of archaeological sites and battlefields, Director Albright's vision that NPS would "go rather heavily into the historical park field" and that it was "in business" as a dominant force in historic preservation set the agenda for the agency as the heritage institution of the nation.[4] More than thirty years later, the creation of the National Register of Historic Places within the provisions of the National Historic Preservation Act (1966) further institutionalized national preservation planning by structuring historic pasts according to strictly defined artifactual typologies within broad thematic definitions of American history, namely the National Register for Historic Places.[5]

Continuing the initial Historic Sites Act's emphasis on guiding a national survey of "sites, buildings, and objects," the National Register reinforced the idea of interpreting a national history through identifying, documenting, and preserving discrete resources, the "historic properties," as artifacts. As the locus of heritage construction at its broadest scale, e.g., the federal government, the National Register continues to represent the dominant historical paradigm in American historic preservation, dramatically influencing how "cultural" resources are defined, and subsequently included in or excluded from, the histories, interpretation, and management of parks as heritage places.

The impress of the National Register, its ability to express a unique character of place in terms of cultural association is highly subject to the degree of fit between its fixed template of themes, contexts, and recognizable (largely tangible) relics of the past. As a "national census of historic properties," the National Register functions as the prime arbiter of the historical value of resources ranging in scale from "objects" to "districts." Its conception of the historical "significance" and material "integrity" of these resources viewed as "property types" relies on an evaluation process consisting of various levels of scrutiny, which in turn reflects critical relationships that must be addressed in order for a property to be considered eligible for listing. First, the property must be designated as a property type, whether object, structure, building, site, or district. The property type relates directly to a prescribed thematic context, which sets up a determination of historical significance due to the property's association with historical events, personages, styles, or its ability to potentially yield meaningful research or information, factors otherwise known as "criteria for evaluation" (National Register 1997).

Within the National Register system, then, constructing the history of a site or district depends on a particular codification of the three-dimensional world as history that:

—Patterns the physical environment into preconceived categories of form;

—Adheres to a typological hierarchy of historical events and individuals; and

—Most importantly, determines its future by assigning heritage values.

As a result of its function as a census, the Register's necessity to draw tight boundaries and strict interpretations are more the exception than the rule. Eschewing the unique process of evolution that characterizes the history of particular landscapes, the essential foci of the National Register are physical vestiges, the artifactual remains, a limitation that obscures, in many ways, the real efficacy of landscapes as heritage resources (especially in the case of homelands and cultural memory).

Discrete themes, bounded sites, and periods of significance with prescribed beginning and end dates augur to some unavoidable consequences when considering cultural landscapes. Before the emergence of a cultural landscape framework in the past few decades, historic preservation professionals in the NPS faced the dilemma of defining historic resources through the formulaic rigor of the National Register, thus distilling historic character and values to discrete entities, the artifacts, supporting a thematic national history. While helpful in identifying elements of historic fabric, this approach rendered the larger context, the cultural landscape, unrecognizable, if not altogether invisible. Particularly absent was the interconnection with the natural environment in which these historic resources not only resided, but by which they were shaped, sited, constructed, and influenced through time. The problem of nature, particularly ecological relationships, constitutes a virtually insurmountable obstacle in the National Register's static view of history (cf. Cook 1995).

The establishment of the NPS cultural landscapes program was a response to the inadequacies of national preservation policies and laws in acknowledging the totality of resource environments within park lands. Building on a legacy of cultural landscape discourse originating with Carl Sauer, and incorporating the vernacular perspectives of landscape historians such as J.B. Jackson, the NPS now defines a cultural landscape as "a geographic area, including both cultural and natural resources and the wildlife or domestic animals therein, associated with a historic event, activity, or person or exhibiting other cultural or aesthetic values" (Birnbaum 1994:1). Cultural landscapes are identified and documented as resources integral to park planning and management. Their importance, according to federal law and NPS Management Policies, lies in the statement that:

> [A]ll cultural landscapes are to be managed as cultural resources, regardless of the type or level of significance. Cultural landscape management focuses on preserving a landscape's physical attributes, biotic systems, and use that contributes to its historical significance. Research, planning, and stewardship are the framework for the program (National Park Service 1998:97).

A genuine handicap for cultural landscapes as an institutionally defined category of resource is the fact that they are subject to the criteria of the National Register, an administrative decision that is apparently irrevocable.[6]

The process by which cultural landscapes are identified, documented, analyzed, and evaluated—literally, how their history is written as *landscapes*—has wide-ranging consequences for their interpretation and management.[7] In a fairly prescribed path, NPS landscape histories focus on an interdisciplinary account of the landscape's natural processes and built forms and their evolution through time, including a thorough documentation of existing conditions. They conclude with an analysis and evaluation based on "landscape characteristics," largely tangible elements ranging in scale from natural systems and features defining a river corridor to small-scale site features such as stone steps.[8] A glaring disjuncture exists in the relegation of "cultural traditions" and "ethnographic information" to the level of a definable characteristic, in deference to National Register typological description. In reality, these are the bulwarks of interpreting landscapes as cultural in the first place (Page 1998:53).

However flexible and adaptive the documentation process may be according to the historical circumstances, its analysis and evaluation rest on a common theme: the level of change and disruption between a determined "period of significance" based on the legibility

of "contributing" or "non-contributing" resources with the landscape's present "condition." According to the National Register, a particular landscape's physical history is primarily a linear chronology in which a period of significance is established as the benchmark by which all landscape change can be measured. This evaluation of the degree and level of change between a landscape's period of significance and its present condition culminates in a determination of "integrity," or its ability to reflect historical values through the surviving physical resources, and thus its viability in National Register terms. This, in turn, leads to a statement of significance setting forth heritage values based on an interpretation that may or may not fully correspond to the panoply of meanings in any particular landscape.

In spite of the philosophical questions posed by the cultural landscape paradigm to the National Register's template of American history, the artifactual underpinnings of this methodology remain, begging the still unanswered question: how relevant is a determination of national significance when cast in a largely predetermined structure of census? In many respects, this institutional process creates its own alternative landscape history, one that represents an artificial, externally driven typology.

This tethering of cultural landscape work in the national parks to the rigid methodology of the National Register has distinct implications for understanding landscapes as heritage, particularly those with deep ties to Native American history. It presents, at best, a frail compromise between incorporating some themes of Native American history (in terms of archaeology, Euro-American settlement contact, and battlefields) and not including them at all. What the National Register has not provided is a framework within which Native American history is not only actively written, but commemorated in terms of associated peoples' homelands, memory-places, and as fields of encounter where landscape is ethnographically constructed as cultural place—in a word, heritage. This cumbersome alliance creates and represents histories of place to fit a physical template that is inherently unequal and incomplete in its understanding of the processes (read: worldviews) of non-Euro-American cultures and their landscapes. Despite the policy that all cultural landscapes are to be managed as cultural resources, regardless of significance, programmatic ties between the cultural landscapes program and the National Register heavily influence the way that landscapes are perceived in the National Park Service. It is an uneasy fit, primarily because of the juxtaposition between the National Register standards and the fluid complexity of landscapes as evolutionary processes.

Despite the restrictive conventions, however, deciphering cultural landscapes in the national parks has broadened the scope of the National Register. While there is gradual acceptance of cultural landscapes in the Register formats, the ambiguities inherent in a multidimensional resource, such as a landscape, present substantial challenges to a typological construction of history and place; change is slow in coming.[9] As an example, the inclusion of landscape characteristics in National Register terminology, however peripheral, does begin to contextualize cultural landscapes as assemblages of artifacts, especially at the scales of land use and spatial arrangement. In other ways, elements such as circulation and vegetation, and topography now describe and document salient aspects of physical landscapes alongside more traditionally associated material features such as archaeological sites, buildings, and structures. Clearly, the construction of heritage shaped by cultural landscapes is one in which newer definitions of landscape as cultural process, for example, can play a larger role. But, such definitions clearly threaten the ideological structure of the National Register as a heritage department because of their very nature as ambiguous, subjective, and contingent.

The difficulty ensues in the latitude of interpretation and the hierarchy of importance with which certain characteristics may possess integrity, while others, such as cultural traditions and ethnographic features, which clearly continue to have an influence over the contemporary landscape, do not. Characteristics such as topography and natural systems can be only documented to a certain degree during the various periods of any landscape history, especially when pictorial evidence, such as aerial photographs, are unavailable. However, the rate and scale of change in these characteristics is far different than for a set of buildings or, for that matter, the cultural traditions associated with land use. How, then, is a standard of integrity for these characteristics to be measured in a period of significance and beyond, when incredibly differing sets of variables are in play? The Register's delineation of property types as "object," "site," or "district" do not reflect basic landscape processes, which are more appropriately defined in an ecological context of patch, edge, corridor, and mosaic (Dramstad et al. 1996:14–6). This is even more the case when dealing with the processes of cultural formation, identity, and belonging, and how they shape landscapes in terms of heritage and commemoration, issues that cannot be simply reduced to a few bulleted paragraphs.

In other words, what may be significant in the historic value structure of the National Register is more than likely not as significant when considering the inherent, site-specific qualities of cultural landscapes. Codification of heritage values in the National Register plays an important role in the protection of historic properties, but as a method by which history is written, its internal semantics and syntax do not reflect the diverse richness and the interpretive opportunities, a literacy if you will, that a less culturally exclusive reading of landscapes can offer. The recalling of history in memory-places, whether in mythic or linear terms, reshapes each landscape in a distinctly cultural footprint depending on who is telling the story, and how it is told. Battlefields and territorial trails become the loci of wildly variant cultural interpretations: conquest or defeat, survival or extinction, sustenance or loss. All are heritage.

Consider, for instance, a definition of landscape as a mosaic of ecosystems reflecting different degrees of anthropogenic change, one that critically alters the historical perception of place as it is contextually explored at different scales and with different vocabularies. The inherent morphology of landscapes is the one historical constant that we can potentially discern; how it affects the course of history is a matter open for interpretation. Utilizing environmental history as the medium in which a site history is forged, for example, radically changes the landscape story of historic and cultural events. In this scenario, battlefields become ecotones, where the patterns of open fields and woodlots, hedgerows and an internal rhythm of irrigation ditches heavily influence the strategies and outcomes of battlefields. In other places, wildernesses are hunting grounds, berry-picking patches, sacred healing sites reflecting a millennial occupation and accretion of ecological knowledge.

This recognition is particularly salient when considering the potential of cultural landscapes methodology to address ethnographic—in this case Native American—histories of place in the national parks. The case of Glacier Bay National Park explored later in this volume (see Horton, part 3) reflects the vulnerability of Euro-American worldviews that frame and interpret landscapes as consensual heritage. Challenging current interpretation of the park as a wilderness, the landscape history of Glacier Bay reveals the persistence of traditional knowledge, association, and use of these lands as homelands and places of cultural significance.

As with much of the landscape history research tied to the National Register, the transposition of a generally perceived Eastern mindset (e.g., design-oriented) to the Alaska and the American West is problematic because of the scale and dispersed settlement patterns in these vast landscapes. Adding to this complex brew is the general bias against acknowledging cultural landscapes in which the material cultural remains are barely legible, if at all, in physical terms, a prejudicial conse-

quence of the dominance of artifactual typology. This discrepancy is especially telling in the case of most historic Native American cultures that were predominantly nomadic or non-agrarian, again particularly relevant to Alaska Natives. Their landscape histories are ones of cyclic movements in large subsistence territories, thus affording little opportunity or need for creating permanent settlements and cultural traces typical of Euro-American landscapes. It also diminishes the importance and interconnectedness of traditional sites considered integral to cultural maintenance and survival, such as sacred and mythological places within an overall territorial landscape.

But map is not territory, or not at least, as Wendell Berry opined, "the territory underfoot" (Ryden 1993:208). Landscape history, although speciously articulated through generic templates defining, analyzing, and evaluating somewhat discrete characteristics, has a greater potential than the conventional documentation proponents will admit at present. What is needed is a contextual reading of landscape dimensions that have remained heretofore virtually invisible, uncovering the patterned complexities, site-specific configurations that direct our perception of landscape as a repository of heritage-in-process, rather than the flawed static history of an artifact assemblage.

As we have seen, part of the problem is definitional in character. The greatest vulnerability of cultural landscapes lies in the institutional mandate to articulate and preserve "resources," in this case, environments dramatically different in scale and composition from the more architecturally and archaeologically derived "sites, buildings, and objects." In delineating the "four general types of cultural landscapes," as "not mutually exclusive . . . historic sites, historic designed landscapes, historic vernacular landscapes, and ethnographic landscapes" (Birnbaum 1994:1), the fundamental difficulties in defining landscapes by external categories are clear. One cultural landscape, potentially, could be perceived as a historic site, a historic vernacular landscape, and an ethnographic landscape depending on how the landscape context was developed from tangible, and sometimes intangible, resources. In many respects, the least ambiguous cultural landscape type is that of the historic designed landscape, one in which intention and execution of a formalized plan can be pegged, without much ado, to a time period, style, master designer, and craftsmen. Historic sites and vernacular landscapes are, by contrast, subject to a greater range of interpretation, especially when considering multiple periods of significance in the case of long periods of settlement history, for example.

The idea of the "ethnographic landscape" in this range of landscape definitions is much more complicated. Defined as "a landscape containing a variety of natural and cultural resources that associated people define as heritage resources," this type of landscape is also within the purview of the NPS ethnography program. The key distinguishing element between the two programs is often explained as the determination of historical significance according to National Register standards and criteria, as opposed to the more purely ethnographic conception of landscape intrinsically tied to a particular culture's association, practices, and recognition of valuable resources. In addition, the mandate that all cultural landscapes are to be managed as cultural resources *regardless of significance* is a complication that is rarely argued within the cultural landscapes program itself. Without the ability to identify and document landscapes as ethnographic in Alaska, for instance, many cultural landscapes in its national parks would be overlooked, and silences in the historical record multiplied.

In truth, it is difficult to argue the difference between "ethnographic" and "cultural" when applied to a more holistic and evolving concept of landscape rather than the staid institutional definitions (Spirn 1998:16; Corner 1999:5). Regardless of the semantic baggage, the inclusion of ethnographic landscapes as a unique venue of study is critical to the cultural landscapes program and to the parks as a whole. It portends recognition, ethnographically conceived in a

landscape model, of the traditional values and associations of a particular community for a certain place. In the case of the national parks, notably many in the Southwest and Alaska regions, ethnographic landscapes are most commonly associated with Native American people; however, the range of ethnographic designations is not limited to indigenous groups.[10] The key question here is whether or not the definition of ethnographic landscapes reflects a viable portrait of landscape as heritage from the "bottom up." The sheer weight of Native American historical involvement with the lands that are now national parks speaks to the exigency in understanding these landscapes as cultural places, especially when considering the matter of "ancestral homelands" (National Park Service 2001:8).

Even with the antiquarian context of the National Register and its implications for writing histories of place, the documentation and management of park lands as cultural landscapes is central, albeit imperfectly defined, to the mission of heritage preservation. The cultural landscape paradigm continues to prove elusive of quantification primarily because it represents a resource base in flux. The implications for landscape as heritage, then, depend on how the landscape is perceived as a dialogical process between people and environment, its internal discourse revealed through stories not bound by external strictures. The more inclusive and interdisciplinary the landscape history, the more complicated and richly embroidered the cultural stories told and preserved. In attempting to reveal the scale and complexity of heritage resources in the resilient landscape paradigm, however, it becomes clear that history, apparently, is a messy business.

Traditional Cultural Properties: The Promise of Ethnographic Landscape Histories

If National Register property types and criteria for evaluating significance prove an uneasy fit with cultural landscape preservation in general, the typological miscasting is even more apparent when considering ethnographic landscapes, especially those generally associated with Native Americans. In the NPS, the differing objectives of the cultural landscapes and ethnography programs with respect to ethnographic landscapes can hinge not only on the identification of these landscapes and the construction and significance of their histories, but also on the means by which they can be preserved. While National Register eligibility is a thorny issue for both programs, one aspect is clear: it provides some degree of accountability, i.e., legal protection from adverse impacts, in the typological recognition of certain ethnographic landscapes as "Traditional Cultural Properties," commonly referred to as TCPs.[11]

In an attempt to increase the diversity of historic property types, the National Register developed the designation of traditional cultural property, a category in cultural associations are "(1) rooted in the history of a community, and (2) important to maintaining the continuity of that community" (Parker 1993:1). The goal was to expand the definition of significance to include "traditional cultural significance," thereby setting the stage for recognition of ethnographic landscapes as protected heritage resources. By the National Register definition, the term "traditional" was not meant to be evocative, but rather to refer to a body of knowledge specific to a contemporary culture:

> "Traditional" in this context refers to those beliefs, customs, and practices of a living community of people that have been passed down through the generations, usually orally or through practice. The traditional cultural significance of a historic property, then, is significance derived from the role the property plays in a community's historically rooted beliefs, customs, and practices (National Register 1994:1).

Thus, the central determinant of a property's heritage value, the assertion of significance, shifted from an externally driven paradigm (e.g., formulas of theme and context) to one that is communally based, providing

the initial guidance for historic preservation professionals to acknowledge alternative versions and constructions of history and its importance as heritage. For example, privileging oral history as evidence, concepts of traditional time and chronologies of events, and the authentication of place value from within a traditional community's perspective all represent distinctly different methodologies from the standard National Register process.

Perhaps the most striking difference between the National Register's approach toward traditional cultural properties and other historic properties centers on a reformulation of the concept of historic significance with relationship to time. The significance of a traditional cultural property is predicated on its association with a community that maintains traditional knowledge. In other words, that knowledge is integral to the preservation of a unique identity, its heritage, in which the past, present, and future are all inextricably bound through stories, songs, genealogy, and most importantly, *places*.

This condition of continuity and association with a contemporary culture is essential. It allows the property to be identified, documented, analyzed and evaluated, ostensibly, from the consensual perspective of the community, or an emic perspective that conflates the categories of past and present. Here, the past is never really past, but part of the present. While some have described this difference as one between linear and cyclic conceptions of time, it is probably more the case that, instead of a concatenation of events spread through time, a traditional community is more apt to view the present as a series of layers in which primordial time and everyday, quotidian reality are indistinguishable, defying David Lowenthal's (1988) description of the past as a "foreign country." Using J.B. Jackson's analogy, there is no Golden Age period of significance or linear chronology in which resources must reside (Jackson 1980:100–1). Instead, the resources are as integral today as they were at any point in the past. In a traditional cultural property, at least theoretically, the past and present converge in the awareness that heritage is an active process of construction. The maintenance and preservation of traditional cultural properties ensure the survival of essential knowledge. Without them, the community's history would be impoverished and cultural survival in jeopardy.

And while this represents a significant advance in broadening the scope of protection afforded to cultural places, in many ways it creates more questions than it answers. Analogous to the uneasy fit between landscapes and National Register property types, contexts, criteria, and significance evaluations, the arguments for the creation of TCPs are also convoluted, limited by terminology, and not fully expressive of the heritage values at stake.[12] Take, for example, the idea of place embodied in an ethnographic landscape. First, the place must be defined as a physical "property." For many traditional cultures, the definition of an important place is a measure of its significance in bringing the present world into being, a compelling difference from mere physical description. Place history cannot be described solely by geomorphology, natural systems, land use patterns, or, even less, its dates of discovery, exploration, and settlement. In other words, the sense of history in traditional terms seen through landscape is a radically different model of the past; its definition of authority, time, and space flies at odds with an arguably antiquarian definition of national heritage embodied by the National Register (cf. Griffiths 1996:1–2).

In the case of traditional cultural properties, the term "traditional history" is particularly appropriate, suggesting that "the history that members of an ethnic or other community tell about themselves in their own terms" is not only associative—in effect, its claim by a contemporary community—but historically legitimate as well. However, the implications of a traditional history entail a sweeping revision, or at least a restructuring, of historical values and, ultimately, heritage construction when fully explored:

A traditional history can encompass beings, acts, and events that are (in an analytic sense) plainly mythical or legendary, as well as oral tradition, oral history, and conventional history. The test of validity of a traditional history is not whether the recounting of events is accurate when taken literally. . . but whether a particular reconstruction is culturally valid and accurate. If a society accepts the mythic and legendary elements either literally or symbolically and the reconstruction is culturally valid (that is, consistent with appropriate cultural standards), then it must be accepted as a valid reconstruction of the past, no matter what literally impossible or fantastic beings or events it incorporates (Downer et al. 1994:42–3).

This entails a heady mix of tangible and intangible elements which begins to turn the neatly prescribed world of the National Register on its head. Writing a history of place as landscape always involves a cultural reconstruction. In the case of ethnographic landscapes or traditional cultural properties, however, generally accepted categories of definition become suspect. Who determines the "integrity" or critical mass of tangible and intangible resources and associated values that can be materially ascribed to a cultural place so that it can be read as distinctive? Who, in essence, has the authority, the authentic voice to write this history, construct this heritage among groups competing for ownership of a particular landscape? Traditional history, as defined above, relies on a completely different historiography, a genealogy of place with origins in both physical and spiritual worlds that inform its significance.

What, for instance, constitutes a "property"? How are its boundaries drawn? More often than not, a sweep of the hand while a story is being told, rather than a line drawn on a map, is more indicative of the cultural delimitations of a traditional place. Mainstream landscape histories rely heavily on the legal concept of property ownership based on survey and deed, seen as an objective, quantifiable standard of measurement. This is not to say that ideas of property did not exist in the traditional worldview. In fact, acknowledged territorial rights were key to the functioning of resource procurement regions and large trade networks, and the source of centuries of war among tribes throughout much of indigenous America. However, attempting to determine where an ethnographic landscape, as a traditional cultural property, begins and ends can be the grounds for serious contention and divergent interpretations.

How is the concept of "integrity" applied to traditional knowledge of place? The matrix of natural and cultural resources—the interconnectedness of landforms, watersheds, corridors, habitats and ecosystems with the cultural evolution of a people—is, in many ways, a distillation of the core of cultural ways of knowing and experiencing place as homelands. It involves preservation of larger narratives, of languages and customs, embodied in the physical container of landscape, not just those resources that reflect a certain period of historical time and that have survived to an appropriate degree of recognition.

And, ultimately, issues of information, confidentiality, and intellectual property become paramount in the identification of traditional cultural properties. If sites are identified as sacred, for example, this becomes a matter of public record. The access to and release of information, even with the goal of protecting traditional values in a community's heritage is often, if not more than likely, at odds with the very public act of designation to the National Register.

Questions abound. In the case of ethnographic landscapes, how is an evolutionary dialogue of people and place captured in a template such as a TCP nomination? Is the character of the place itself, as defined by the "associated people," revealed in this process, ensuring that an appropriate definition of "heritage resources"? Are the standards of the National Register and NPS management policy elastic enough to address the sophisticated, alternative visions of history and significance that emerge from the perspectives of associated peoples? Is there a common ground for understanding parks as negotiated terrain in which the layers of a particular cultural landscape can be integrated rather than juxtaposed as mutually exclusive?

Landscape as Heritage

Certainly one of the most impressive international efforts to deal with the documentation and commemoration of ethnographic landscapes is that of Parks Canada (Buggey 1999, see also Buggey, this volume). Potential applications of the Parks Canada model within the National Park Service and the National Register of Historic Places would advance the emerging issues of Native American homelands and the significance of writing their landscape histories from an ethnographic perspective.

Tackling the complex issues of aboriginal worldviews and landscape values from an interdisciplinary perspective, Buggey's landmark study (1999) was not an academic exercise, but a pragmatic advance in heritage discourse. As a prototype, the study incorporated international efforts underway to recognize indigenous history and heritage by reiterating the indivisibility of natural and cultural place significance. In other words, places recognized for natural significance were also significant in terms of the process of cultural association and identification, not relying on static physical remains as the prime determinant.

Buggey proposed the designation of "aboriginal cultural landscapes" as a way of conceiving indigenous heritage that could be rigorously documented, evaluated, and protected in terms of culture-specific values while contributing to Canadian history as a whole:

> An Aboriginal cultural landscape is a place valued by an Aboriginal group (or groups) because of their long and complex relationship with that land. It expresses their unity with the natural and spiritual environment. It embodies their traditional knowledge of spirits, places, land uses, and ecology. Material remains of the association may be prominent, but will often be minimal or absent (Buggey 1999:35).

The language bears some similarity to the National Register's designation of Traditional Cultural Property and the NPS definition of ethnographic landscapes; but the underlying argument represented a major change toward constructing heritage from a landscape perspective, with or without the critical matrix of physical remains. In doing so, it reformed preservation discourse by emphasizing the intangible basis of an emplaced cultural identity. The idea of aboriginal cultural landscapes rested on the crucible of a sense of belonging, whether in memory of historic events or in evoking homelands, as a result of longstanding ties to particular environments regardless of their protected status as parks. The concept of aboriginal cultural landscapes recontextualized the production of history as heritage. It expanded the parameters of how history is constructed, its cultural authenticity, and its physical location in a landscape, portraying a highly unique geography of time, formation, and belief.

Implicit in this reformulation is the process by which landscapes would be evaluated for their historical significance in terms of aboriginal history's ability to "illustrate or symbolize in whole or in part a cultural tradition, a way of life, or ideas important in the development of Canada," including their cartographic determination ("boundaries") and the interrelated character of the heritage values, natural and cultural. Perhaps the most dramatic change toward a landscape-based heritage was the assertion that the concept of "integrity," the lynchpin for a site's eligibility for the American model of a National Register of Historic Places based on physical resources, "will not normally be essential to understand the significance of an Aboriginal cultural landscape, and will not therefore generally apply" (ibid.:38). The implications of this deconstruction of integrity are enormous.

By developing the concept of the "aboriginal cultural landscape" as distinct from other commemorative landscapes related to Euro-American history, the uniqueness and applicability of this model cannot be understated. While the process may appear, on the surface, as a reassembling of bureaucratic definitions, the implications of the new guidelines proposed for Canada's aboriginal cultural landscapes are, in real-

ity, point toward a radical departure from the ways in which history is constructed as heritage in national parks based on the American model of preservation. Quite simply, the concept of aboriginal cultural landscapes as proposed by Parks Canada holds great promise for a new model in the National Park Service, one that would institute a more sophisticated historical sensibility with respect to Traditional Cultural Properties. In their current delineation, the TCPs still respond to the National Register's overall ideological framework of integrity-based significance resting predominantly on physical evidence recognized with categorical distinctions. Specifically, the ability to determine the historical significance of these indigenous landscapes suggested by the Parks Canada definitions, either in parks or as commemorative sites in themselves, represents a critical leap in thinking because it acknowledges the legitimacy of alternative history, the ability of the landscape paradigm to represent that history as heritage, and by implication, the need to develop preservation and conservation mandates to protect this unique heritage.

This restructuring of heritage domains suggested by Parks Canada and its potential for the TCP nominations in the NPS and its National Register process is no mean feat. It holds incredibly rich prospects for understanding the process of landscape as both text and texture constructed by the people for whom it holds historical meaning, the essence of the idea of homelands. It is also a cultural project directed toward the preservation of place knowledge by incorporating indigenous values into the federal purview of preservation in several key ways. First, the proposal of commemorating history by designating "aboriginal cultural landscapes" eliminates the rather vague conceptual application across ill-defined and indeterminate cultural groups suggested by the NPS cultural landscape version of "ethnographic landscapes." The designation of "aboriginal cultural landscape" focuses specifically on the heritage of First Nations (Native Americans), the repatriation of cultural knowledge and its validation of indigenous worldviews of a given landscape as, for example, a homelands or memory-place. A new emphasis that establishes Native American cultural landscapes as distinctive will profoundly influence the ways in which this heritage is documented, preserved, and interpreted as integral to its institutional mission. This is particularly crucial at a time when new park units are created to commemorate Native American history, such as Washita and Sand Creek battlefields, as well as the emerging recapitulation of long-standing ideologies of exclusion at places like Mesa Verde and Little Bighorn. In addition, pitched legal battles over resource use are increasing the need for histories to reveal the rich associations and legacy of Native American ironically enough, because indigenous traditional ecological knowledge may be the keystone bolstering legal arguments for natural resource protection in the parks. If the recent Environmental Impact Statement addressing vessel quotas in Glacier Bay National Park is any indication, the controversies endemic to a conflict of interest between the "pleasuring grounds" of national parks and the stewardship of the vital resources are far from resolution (National Park Service 2003).

Secondly, writing traditional histories of Native American cultural landscapes accords the oral traditions, stories, and beliefs held by associated communities as the standards by which these landscapes are deemed significant. This methodology relies on intimate familiarity with forms of traditional knowledge about landscapes, reestablishing cultural geographies and their implicit values regardless of park boundaries or visible traces of cultural association. The authenticity of landscape histories, from this perspective, could influence park planning and management decisions on the ground floor. Examples could include, for instance, a new understanding of the integrity of ecological processes (such as the maintenance of previously off-limits natural resource areas as cultural grounds of resource harvesting, e.g., the Tlingit berrying grounds at Dundas Bay—see Horton, this volume), redefining individual

archaeological properties within a larger landscape context, revising wilderness designations in places where cultural associations clearly indicate traditional habitation and use, and transforming definitions of historic "property" and "boundary" into a matrix of interpenetrating zones of interaction and encounter that shift eventually, such as tribal and clan territories. The commemoration of Native American history adds a palpable richness and depth to the visited landscapes, opening an experiential realm that strengthens a sense of place, even in its most contentious and conflicted manifestation.

And finally, the transformation of the existing ethnographic landscape definition and National Register paradigm within NPS requires the revision of an artifactual model of historic preservation to one that incorporates a more fluid construction of heritage as cultural difference. Analogous to the recasting of museums as active "keeping places" rather than collection centers with culture on display, abandoning the object-based curation of a historical landscape creates the opportunity to understand parks as critical proving grounds (Griffiths 1996:219–36). And resonating the policy statements in "Parks for the 21st Century," this transformation embodies an imperative of cultural conservation by restoration in the truest sense of the word, re-storying place with seamless histories of environment and people, nature and culture.

Notes

1. The NPS defines an ethnographic landscape as "a landscape containing a variety of natural and cultural resources that associated people define as heritage resources. Examples are contemporary settlements, religious sacred sites and massive geological structures. Small plant communities, animals, subsistence and ceremonial grounds are often components" (Birnbaum 1994:2). Similarly, the NPS ethnography program defines ethnographic landscapes as "a relatively contiguous area of interrelated places that contemporary cultural groups define as meaningful because it is inextricably and traditionally linked to their own local or regional histories, cul-

tural identities, beliefs and behaviors. Present-day social factors such as a people's class, ethnicity, and gender may result in the assignment of diverse meanings to a landscape and its component places" (Evans and Roberts 1999:7).

2. Examples include the idea of "wilderness" and "wilderness planning" along with "habitat restoration." Such paradigms often insist upon their scientific rationale as a proof validating management approaches, disallowing their own historicity as theories of nature which have, themselves, been subject to change (Griffiths 1996; Nelson 1998; Reich 2001).

3. The use of the Antiquities Act waned after its heyday in the years of the New Deal, but its utility as a way of designating heritage areas continues to the present day. In 2000, President Bill Clinton invoked the Antiquities Act to create the Canyons of the Ancients National Monument in southwest Colorado, consisting of 164,000 acres of the highest known archaeological site density in the United States, www.co.blm/gov/canm/html.

4. A number of battlefields, mostly related to the Civil War, were transferred from the War Department to the Department of the Interior in 1933.

5. "The National Register is the official Federal list of districts, sites, buildings, structures, and objects significant in American history, architecture, archaeology, engineering, and culture. These contribute to an understanding of the historical and cultural foundations of the Nation. The National Register includes: All prehistoric and historic units of the National Park System; National Historic Landmarks, which are properties recognized by the Secretary of the Interior as possessing national significance; and Properties significant in American, State, or local prehistory and history that have been nominated by State Historic Preservation Officers, Federal agencies, and others, and have been approved for listing by the National Park Service" (National Register 1991:i). See also Murtagh 1997; Tomlan 1997.

6. NPS policy on the relationship of cultural landscapes to the National Register of Historic Places, and the enforcement of Register standards and criteria for these landscapes is outlined in *Director's Order 28*. The administrative conflict of interest between the Cultural Landscapes Program and the Ethnography Program's joint interest in

documenting ethnographic landscapes is underplayed in the discussion of their separate roles and responsibilities (National Park Service 1998:87–91, 160–70).

7. The two basic research avenues for cultural landscape study within NPS are the Cultural Landscape Inventory (CLI) and Cultural Landscape Reports (CLR). Both develop landscape histories to differing degrees. The basic difference between the CLI and CLR is that the Inventory is used as baseline identification and evaluation of the cultural landscape as it can be documented. Utilizing much of the same data and process, the CLR is a management document intensively geared toward preservation treatment in light of resource degradation, loss, threat, or proposed changes to the landscape fabric.

8. Landscape characteristics specific to cultural landscape histories in NPS include spatial organization, land use, cultural traditions, cluster arrangement, circulation, topography, vegetation, buildings and structures, views and vistas, constructed water features, small-scale features, and archaeological sites (Page 1998:53).

9. For the National Register's institutional responses to defining landscapes as historic resources eligible for listing see National Register 1984, 1987, 1992a, 1992b, 1992c.

10. The term "ethnographic landscapes" typically refers to a wide range of cultural landscapes of regional origin, including places associated with African American slave culture, urban Chinese settlements in Los Angeles and San Francisco, nineteenth-century European immigrant farmsteads in the mid-West, and Puerto Rican barrios on the East Coast (see Alanen and Melnick 2000; Hardesty 2000).

11. By the terms of the National Historic Preservation Act, Section 106 in regard to Traditional Cultural Properties, "federal agencies, State Historic Preservation Offices, and others who conduct activities pursuant to environmental and historic preservation legislation are responsible for identifying, documenting, and evaluating them [TCPs] in planning" (cf. Parker 1993:3).

12. Consistent with the National Register designations, the guidance in *NRB 38, Traditional Cultural Properties*, does not recognize landscapes as a property type, much less ethnographic landscapes.

In fact, the word "landscape" does not appear in the entire document (ibid.:1–22).

References

Alanen, Arnold, and Robert Melnick, eds.
2000   *Preserving Cultural Landscapes in America.* Baltimore: Johns Hopkins University Press.

Birnbaum, Charles
1994   *Protecting Cultural Landscapes: Planning, Treatment and Management of Historic Landscapes.* Preservation Brief 36. Washington, DC: National Park Service.

Buggey, Susan
1999   *An Approach to Aboriginal Cultural Landscapes.* Ottawa: Historic Sites and Monuments Board of Canada, Parks Canada.

Cook, Robert
1995   *Is Landscape Preservation an Oxymoron?* Paper delivered at the National Park Service conference, *Balancing Natural and Cultural Issues in the Preservation of Historic Landscapes.* http://www.icls.harvard.edu/ecology/cook2.html.

Corner, James, ed.
1995   *Recovering Landscape: Essays in Contemporary Landscape Architecture.* New York: Princeton University Press.

Downer, Alan, Alexandra Roberts, Harris Francis, and Klara B. Kelley
1994   Traditional History and Alternative Conceptions of the Past. In *Conserving Culture: A New Discourse on Heritage.* Mary Hufford, ed., pp. 39–55. Urbana: University of Illinois Press.

Dramstad, Wenche, James D. Olson, and Richard T. T. Forman
1996   *Landscape Ecology Principles in Landscape Architecture and Land-Use Planning.* Washington, DC: Island Press.

Evans, Michael, and Alexa Roberts
1999   Ethnographic Landscapes. Unpublished paper delivered at the 59th Annual Meeting of the Society for Applied Anthropology. Tucson, Arizona.

Glassie, Henry
1982   *Passing the Time in Ballymenone: Culture and History of an Ulster Community.* Philadelphia: University of Pennsylvania Press, 1982.

Griffiths, Tom
1996   *Hunters and Collectors: The Antiquarian Imagination in Australia.* New York: Cambridge University Press.

Hardesty, Donald L.
2000   Ethnographic Landscapes. Transforming Nature into Culture. In *Preserving Cultural Landscapes in America.* A.R. Alanen and R.Z. Melnick, eds., pp. 169–185. Baltimore and London: John Hopkins University Press

Hosmer, Charles
1981   *Preservation Comes of Age.* Charlottesville: University Press of Virginia.

Jackson, J.B.
1980   *The Necessity for Ruins, and Other Topics.* Amherst: University of Massachusetts Press.

Lowenthal, David
1988   *The Past is a Foreign Country.* Cambridge, UK: Cambridge University Press

Murtagh, William
1997   *Keeping Time: The History and Theory of Preservation in America.* New York: John Wiley & Sons, Preservation Press.

National Park Service
1998   *Director's Order 28: Cultural Resource Management Guidelines.* Washington, DC: National Park Service.

2001   Rethinking the National Parks for the 21st Century. National Park System Advisory Board. http://www.nps.gov/policy/report.htm,

2003   *Glacier Bay National Park and Preserve Environmental Impact Study.* Anchorage:National Park Service.

National Register
1984   Guidelines for Evaluating and Documenting Rural Historic Landscapes. *National Register Bulletin* 30. Washington, DC: National Park Service.

1987   How to Evaluate and Nominate Designed Historic Landscapes. *National Register Bulletin* 18. Washington, DC: National Park Service.

1991   How to Complete the National Register Registration Form. *National Register Bulletin* 16A. Washington, DC: National Park Service.

1992a   Guidelines for Identifying, Evaluating, and Registering America's Historic Battlefields. *National Register Bulletin* 40. Washington, DC: National Park Service.

1992b   Guidelines for Evaluating and Registering Cemeteries and Burial Places. *National Register Bulletin* 41. Washington, DC: National Park Service.

1992c   Guidelines for Identifying, Evaluating, and Registering Historic Mining Properties *National Register Bulletin* 42. Washington, DC: National Park Service.

1994   Guidelines for Evaluating and Documenting Traditional Cultural Properties. *National Register Bulletin* 38. Washington, DC: National Park Service.

1997   How to Apply the National Register Criteria for Evaluation. *National Register Bulletin* 15. Washington, DC: National Park Service.

Nelson, Michael P.

1998   An Amalgamation of Wilderness Preservation Arguments. In *The Great New Wilderness Debate.* J. Baird Callicott and Michael P. Nelson, eds. Pp. 154–98. Athens: University of Georgia Press.

Page, Robert

1998   *A Guide to Cultural Landscape Reports: Contents, Process, Technique.* Washington, DC: National Park Service.

Parker, Patricia

1993   Traditional Cultural Properties: What You Do and How We Think. *Cultural Resource Management* 16. Washington, DC: National Park Service.

Reich, Justin

2001   Re-Creating the Wilderness. *Environmental History* 6(1):95–117.

Ryden, Kent C. Ryden

1993   *Mapping the Invisible Landscapes: Folklore, Writing, and the Sense of Place.* Iowa City: University of Iowa Press.

Spirn, Anne Whiston

1998   *The Language of Landscape.* Cambridge: MIT Press.

Tomlan, Michael A., ed.

1997   *Preservation of What, For Whom? A Critical Look at Significance.* Ithaca: National Council for Preservation Education.

Managing the Saami Cultural Heritage in Norway:

The Legal Landscape

INGEGERD HOLAND

Like many, perhaps even most, other countries, Norway has over the last ten-to-fifteen years tried to implement a cultural heritage management system that preserves not only objects, but also their contexts. This includes cultural landscapes where no single object may deserve preservation on its own, but where the whole landscape does. The theoretical criteria for considering landscape preservation are very much the same as those used by other countries. Since these are presented in some detail by other contributors to this publication, this article will concentrate on how such principles have been incorporated into Norwegian cultural heritage legislation and to what extent this has changed practices, with special regard to the Sámi cultural heritage.

The Sámi [also spelled as Saami, Sami, or Same] have, since 1990, been recognized as an indigenous people within the state of Norway. The estimated number of Sámi in Norway and elsewhere today varies from publication to publication. Aarseth et al. (1990) assume that there are about 30 to 40,000 Sámi living in Norway, while another 17,000 live in Sweden, about 5,700 in Finland and about 2,000 in North-Western Russia. Most of the Norwegian Sámi live in the two northernmost counties, Finnmark (25, 000) and Troms (12,000), but there are also more or less distinct pockets of Sámi settlements further south, in the counties of Nordland, Nord- and Sør-Trøndelag, and even in Hedmark in Southern Norway (Fig. 20). Historically, these should probably be seen as the remnants of a more continuous Sámi settlement and population, that has either been integrated into the majority Norwegian culture or left to occupy niches that were of little interest to a predominantly agricultural Norwegian population.

Linguistically, the Sámi speak a Finno-Ugric language, or rather, several varieties of such a language. These are usually called dialects, but the differences between the southernmost and north-easternmost dialects are, in fact, so great that their speakers do not understand each other, and they ought therefore to be classified as different languages. This also probably indicates that they became separated a long time ago.

The Norwegian cultural heritage management system

Organizational Framework

Organizationally, the present Norwegian heritage management system is based on a three-tier administrative structure, consisting of national, regional, and local authorities. The national level consists of the Ministry of the Environment, which is responsible for defining and issuing national policies and guidelines concerning heritage protection and management, as well as providing the legal framework.

Some of the goals of Norwegian cultural heritage management, as laid down by the Ministry, are that:

—The distinctive character and variety of cultural monuments, environments and landscapes (be protected), to ensure that information about them is collected, safeguarded and disseminated,

81

—Cultural monuments and cultural environments are safeguarded as a resource and basis for experiencing historical continuity, cultural history and architectural diversity, recognition and belonging in everyday life in keeping with sustainable development.

The practical implementation of these policies is the primary task of the Directorate for Cultural Heritage (*Riksantikvaren*), which is the executive arm of the Ministry. The Directorate is thus responsible for the management of all protected archaeological and architectural monuments and sites, including those that are part of valuable cultural environments, in accordance with the relevant legislation. The work includes

—the practical implementation of the objectives laid down by the Norwegian Parliament and the Ministry of the Environment,

—advising the Ministry as well as other parts of the cultural heritage management system, the public and industry on matters relating to cultural heritage management and protection,

—ensuring that cultural heritage considerations are taken into account in all planning processes,

—that the interests of cultural heritage are safeguarded at all levels in the same way as the interests of society as a whole,

—that a representative selection of monuments and sites is preserved for present and future generations,

—and helping to increase awareness among the general public of the value of their cultural heritage.

The regional level consists of county heritage officers dealing with Norwegian remains, while the Department of Environmental and Cultural Heritage within the Sámi Parliament is responsible for Sámi remains. This department has four sub-offices, covering all parts of the country with a Sámi population. The regional level is the main level for supervising and controlling the day-to-day interaction between developments of all sorts and the principles of the cultural heritage laws.

Finally, the local level consists of the municipalities, which have the main responsibility for planning and structuring developments in such a way that the principles of the Cultural Heritage Act are followed. They also have the opportunities and means to implement protection orders according to other laws, in particular the Planning and Building Act (see below).

Norwegian Cultural Heritage Legislation: A Historical Overview

Before concentrating on the present legislation, a brief overview of the history of cultural heritage legislation in Norway will serve to put the existing Cultural Heritage Act into context. The earliest law protecting Norwegian cultural remains was the Church and Churchyard Act, which was introduced in 1897. In 1903–04, the discovery and excavation of the Oseberg Viking ship and the fact that the Norwegian authorities had to negotiate a deal with the landowner in order to buy and secure this important archaeological find for the nation, highlighted the problem of the existing private ownership of cultural remains on somebody's land. In 1905, which was also the year when the political union between Sweden and Norway came to an end and Norway regained national independence, the first Norwegian Ancient Monuments Act was passed. This Act provided automatic legal protection for cultural remains older than the Reformation, i.e. 1537 A.D., and was primarily intended to protect grave mounds. It was, however, not the monuments themselves that were the main concern of the Act, but rather the objects they contained; in fact, work that necessitated excavations of interesting grave mounds should not be prevented.

The Act also applied to publicly owned medieval buildings, but neither to those that were privately owned, nor to post-Reformation buildings. In 1920, therefore, the Listed Buildings Act was introduced, providing a legal basis for the listing (designation) of buildings and building parts over one-hundred years of age, or even younger. Approximately 1,200 buildings were quickly listed during the 1920s, and they still form the core of Norwegian listed buildings.

In 1951, the two acts were incorporated into a new

and revised Ancient Monuments Act, which provided automatic legal protection for all monuments and buildings older than 1537 A.D., and also the right to designate monuments, historic places, old roads, bridges and other technical remains, irrespective of age. In addition, it introduced the concept of "disfiguring" (i.e., developments having a negative visual impact on monuments), and gave the authorities the right to schedule an area of land around any monument in order to protect its visual impact in the landscape.

In 1963, boats and ships over 100 years old were included in the Act as the property of the Norwegian state and, in 1965, a new Planning Act was introduced, which simplified the inclusion of conservation areas in public planning, in order to protect valuable building environments.

None of these early laws addressed the question of Sámi remains separately from the Norwegian ones. However, with the changing political climate of the

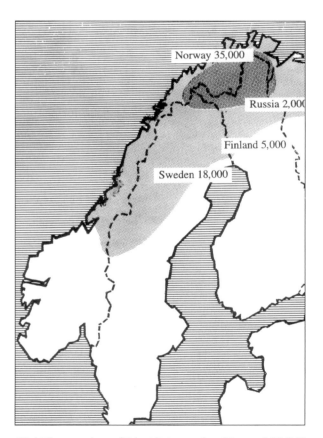

20/ The number of Sámi living today (Hætta 1996:6)
The darker area represent the densest concentration of Sámi settlements.

1950s and 1960s came a greater awareness and acceptance of minority rights and state duties toward minority populations. Among the international conventions that Norway signed in this period, and which also had an impact on the national cultural heritage legislation, was the UN Covenant on Civil and Political Rights, 1966 Article 27:

> In those States in which ethnic, religious or linguistic minorities exist, persons belonging to such minorities shall not be denied the right . . . to enjoy their own culture, to profess and practice their own religion, or to use their own language.

It was incorporated into Norwegian legislation in 1988 through Amendment 110a to the Norwegian Constitution:

> It is the responsibility of the Norwegian state to ensure favorable conditions to enable the Sámi people to maintain and develop its language, culture and social structures.

In the late 1960s, another revision of the Ancient Monuments and Building Acts was initiated, resulting in recommendations in 1970–71, from the committees on ancient monuments and buildings respectively, for a new and revised law. It took until 1978, however, before the current Cultural Heritage Act was introduced, and with it came the first specific legal protection of Sámi cultural remains in Norway. The Act has since been amended several times, a new version was, for instance, introduced on January 1, 2001, but the basic provisions have remained unchanged.

Since 1978, Norway has also ratified several international treaties relating particularly to the recognition of minorities and indigenous peoples, thereby accepting the basic principles laid down in these with regard to the protection of minority cultures. The most important of these international treaties are:

> —ILO Convention No. 169 concerning indigenous and tribal peoples in independent countries, 1989, ratified by Norway on June 20th, 1990, Article 2:

> > Governments shall have the responsibility for developing . . . measures [which promote] the full realization of the social,

economic and cultural rights of these peoples with respect for their social and cultural identity, their customs and traditions and their institutions.

—Agenda 21 from the World Conference on Environment and Development, Brazil 1992: Chapter 26.3, Objectives:

(a) Establishment of a process to empower indigenous people and their communities through measures that include (ii) Recognition that the lands of indigenous people and their communities should be protected from activities that are environmentally unsound or that the indigenous people concerned consider to be socially and culturally inappropriate.

—Convention on Biological Diversity, 1992, ratified by Norway on July 9, 1993, Article 8(j):

Subject to its national legislation, respect, preserve and maintain knowledge, innovations and practices of indigenous and local communities embodying traditional lifestyles relevant for the conservation and sustainable use of biological diversity and promote their wider application with the approval and involvement of the holders of such knowledge, innovations and practices and encourage the equitable sharing of the benefits arising from the utilization of such knowledge, innovations and practices.

—The Council of Europe's Framework Convention for the Protection of National Minorities, 1995, ratified by Norway on June 18th, 1998, Article 5.1:

The Parties undertake to promote the conditions necessary for persons belonging to national minorities to maintain and develop their culture, and to preserve the essential elements of their identity, namely their religion, language, traditions and cultural heritage.

Norwegian Cultural Heritage Legislation: The Present Legal Framework

Today, there are three main groups of Norwegian laws and regulations that govern the work of the local, regional and national agencies and authorities that deal with cultural heritage management in Norway. Each group contains a number of different laws covering specific areas, the main ones being:

—Specialized cultural heritage management legislation, including The Cultural Heritage Act (1978) with later amendments.

—Planning legislation of importance to cultural heritage management, including The Planning and Building Act (1985) with later amendments.

—Legislation regulating the conduct of state agencies and the rights of the public, including The Public Agency (or Administration) Act (Forvaltningsloven) (1967/83), and The Freedom of Information Act (Offentlighetsloven) (1970/89).

The first two groups contain a number of regulations and more specialised laws, which have not been included here. The Cultural Heritage Act, however, is the most important piece of legislation, in that it sets out the basic goals and means of Norwegian cultural heritage legislation. The Planning and Building Act functions as the main tool for reaching some of those goals through active use of planning regulations at the local level, while the last group lays down the formal rules for how the work is conducted, as well as the rights of the public to access any relevant information.

In addition to the national legislation, Norway is also a signatory to a number of international conventions and recommendations that provide a general legal basis for the protection of cultural heritage. Among them are for instance:

—The European Convention on the Protection of the Archaeological Heritage (revised), La Valette, 1992 which states:

[The member States of the Council of Europe acknowledge] that the European archaeological heritage, which provides evidence of ancient history, is seriously threatened with deterioration because of the increasing number of major planning schemes, natural risks, clandestine or unscientific excavations and insufficient public awareness.

—The European Landscape Convention, 2000, which states:

The member States of the Council of Europe [are] aware that the landscape contributes to the formation of local cultures and that it is a basic component of the European natural and cultural heritage, contributing to human well-being and consolidation of the European identity.

The 1978 Cultural Heritage Act and its Provisions

The main principles behind the present Cultural Heritage Act are the concepts of jurisdiction and age; that is, the Act applies to monuments of a certain age within Norwegian territory. The general age limit is the year 1537 A. D., the year of the Protestant Reformation, which historically marks the end of the Middle Ages in Norway.

The same principles also apply to Sámi remains. However, since the minority Sámi culture was perceived as being more vulnerable than the majority Norwegian one, and also perceived to have gone through a different set of chronological changes, the line was drawn at 100 years, at the time meaning about 1880, instead of 1537. This distinction, however, also necessitated the introduction of a third principle into the law, i.e. the concept of ethnicity, since only Sámi remains dating to between 1537 and 1880 were to be automatically legally protected. In other words, all monuments from this period had to be ethnically defined as Sámi in order to be automatically protected by the Act.

The purpose of the Cultural Heritage Act as stated in Section 1 is:

> To protect archaeological and architectural monuments and sites, and cultural environments in all their variety and detail, both as part of our cultural heritage and identity and as an element in the overall environment and resource management. . . . It is [seen as] a national responsibility to safeguard these resources as scientific source material [in particular] and as a permanent basis for the experience, self-awareness, enjoyment and activities of present and future generations.

Monuments and sites are defined as "all traces of human activity in our physical environment, including places associated with historical events, beliefs or traditions." This means that both material remains of human activity, as well as natural features and places with an associated oral or written tradition, are automatically protected if they fulfil the age criterion. Beliefs and traditions will usually be of a religious or mythological nature, which means that, for instance, Sámi holy sites and landscapes are covered by the Act.

The automatic legal protection means that, "no person shall . . . initiate any measure which is liable to damage, destroy, excavate, move, change, cover, conceal or in any other way unduly disfigure any monument or site that is automatically protected by law or to cause risk of this happening" (Sec. 3).

Consequently, when any public or large private development is being planned, "the person or administrative agency in charge of the project is under obligation to find out whether it will affect an automatically protected monument or site in the manner described in Section 3" (Sec. 9). This means submitting the plan to the relevant authority, i.e. the Department for Environmental and Cultural Heritage within the Sámi Parliament for Sámi remains and the county heritage officers for Norwegian remains. If the authority finds that the plan will affect legally protected monuments or sites, but the developer still decides to proceed with the plan, the developer must apply to the Directorate for Cultural Heritage, which decides "whether and, if so, in what way the measures may be carried out" (Sec. 8), for instance whether the monument(s) may be removed by excavation, and how extensive such excavations should be. Excavations have to be carried out by one of five authorised archaeological museums or one particular research institute for medieval remains of certain kinds.

The costs involved at all levels "in investigating automatically protected monuments or sites or in implementing special protective measures on account of projects as described in Sections 8 and 9 shall be borne by the initiator of the project" (Sec. 10), i.e. the "user or polluter pays" principle. Only investigation costs incurred for minor private projects are covered fully or partly by the authorities.

The provisions described above give automatic legal protection to certain monuments, when found either alone or in smaller groups. They are, in other words, primarily object-centered. In addition, however, the Act allows the designation of larger areas by one of two different procedures. Since 1978, Section 19 of the Act gives the Ministry of the Environment the right to

> protect an area around a protected monument or site . . . insofar as this is necessary to preserve the effect of the monument in the environment or to safeguard scientific interests associated with it.

Section 20 of the Act allows "a cultural environment [to] be protected by the King in order to preserve its value to cultural history." Cultural environments are defined as "any area where a monument or site forms part of a larger entity or context" and is thus analogous to the term "cultural landscapes" as used by the U.S. National Park Service (Evans et al. 2001:53). The provision to schedule such landscapes has only been contained in the Act since 1992 (Miljøvernde-partementet 1992a, b).

In practical terms, the outcome of using the two paragraphs may seem much the same, in that they give the authorities the right to "prohibit or otherwise regulate any activity or traffic within the protected area which may run counter to the purpose of the protection. The same applies to dividing the land or leasing it out for the purpose of such activity." However, the underlying legal principles, as well as the legal procedures, are very different. Protection after Section 19 is in reality based on the existence of objects that are already protected by other paragraphs of the Act and is applied in order to preserve their surroundings from disturbing elements (Finne and Holme 2001:168). It is a protection order that can be implemented relatively easily by the Ministry of the Environment, either to an area with archaeological remains or to a built environment. The level of restrictions applying to objects within the area follows either from the Act itself, for those that are automatically protected by other paragraphs of the

Act, or they are laid down by the Directorate for other objects (ibid.:172).

Section 20 preservation of "Cultural Environments," on the other hand, is not dependent on already protected objects within the area, although such objects may exist, but may be introduced in order to protect a landscape that is seen as eligible for protection because of its overall impact and value (ibid.:173). This means that its value must be thoroughly documented and defined, while the scheduling procedure itself is slow and complicated, including thorough consultations with landowners, local authorities and state agencies, and leading eventually to a preservation order being confirmed by the King, i.e. the Norwegian government. The procedure means that preservation according to Section 20 is normally only afforded to landscapes considered to be of national importance and, so far, only four landscapes in Norway have been preserved in this way.[1] The purpose of the restrictions imposed is to preserve the overall qualities of the area that led to its scheduling in the first place.

For both types of preservation, an administrative authority is appointed according to already existing legal regulations. The role of the authority is to uphold the restrictions imposed by the scheduling order, to deal with future maintenance and presentation of the area, as well as with applications for developments or changes of any sort within the area. This authority will be either the county heritage officer (for Norwegian remains) or the Sámi Parliament (for Sámi remains).

While these are the only two procedures for protecting cultural landscapes contained in the Cultural Heritage Act, there are other Norwegian laws that offer opportunities for landscape protection. The Planning and Building Act gives local municipalities the means for protecting valuable local environments if they so wish (Verdifulle kulturlandskap:114), while the Nature Conservancy Act also allows the preservation of valuable cultural landscapes, even if valuable in this context primarily means "biologically valuable" (ibid: 116). However, since cultural landscapes by definition mean landscapes that have developed through the intervention of man, they are also likely to contain material cultural remains of the sort normally dealt with by the cultural heritage authorities. For example, a study conducted in the early 1990s (Direktoratet for naturforvaltning 1994) identified twelve "valuable cultural landscapes" in the County of Finnmark based on biological/botanical as well as culture historical criteria. One of these landscapes was Skoltebyen in Neiden, which in 2000 was scheduled through a Section 20 preservation order, based on the religious and cultural historical importance of the site.[2]

Overall, however, local municipalities are reluctant to apply protection orders to areas of any size, while protection according to the Nature Conservancy Act (for instance, as National Parks) is sometimes vehemently opposed since it places restrictions on traditional use even by local people in order to protect the flora and fauna of the area. Such restrictions may be even more strongly felt in Sámi areas where the use of natural resources in a traditional way is seen as a basis for maintaining the Sámi culture and economy, such as was demonstrated in a couple of recent cases in Northern Norway.

This makes the ongoing work of implementing The European Landscape Convention, which Norway signed on October 20, 2000, as a joint venture between the Directorate for Cultural Heritage and the Directorate for Nature Conservancy, even more important when it comes to future landscape conservation work in Sámi areas. A preliminary strategy document from the two Directorates (Direktoratet for naturforvaltning and Riksantikvaren 2001) was presented on December 1, 2001, marking the start of Norway's participation in a four-year project to implement the Convention in Scandinavia. In it, the two Directorates acknowledge the "need to develop an understanding of the varying cultural importance of the landscape, depending on cultural and social perceptions," and that one of the tasks must be to "contribute to a better understanding locally for a multi-ethnic landscape perception and

importance." This should be done by "developing and implementing procedures and undertakings based on contributions and participation from indigenous and minority groups . . . using for instance experiences from other countries." Acknowledging the need for a multi-cultural approach to landscape preservation in Norway, and hopefully also in Scandinavia as a whole, at such an early stage of implementation, should ensure that these aspects are incorporated into the national and Scandinavian strategies for future work.

Ethnographic Landscapes

The term "ethnographic landscapes" as used by the U.S. National Park Service (Evans et al. 2001:53) has not hitherto been an active part of the legal or management language in Norway. However, it may well be seen to exist as a theoretical concept in the practical work done by the Sámi Parliament when fulfilling its role in the cultural heritage management system of Norway. Unlike the archaeological surveys carried out according to Section 9 of the Cultural Heritage Act by the Norwegian county authorities in order to establish whether developments may interfere with protected cultural remains, the Sámi Parliament and its predecessor, the Sámi Cultural Heritage Council, have always insisted on establishing the broader context of any Sámi remains within a planning area, the Sámi traditions connected with them or the area itself, and the history of any Sámi involvement with the area. This has meant carrying out not only a traditional, visual survey of the area, but also interviewing local people and recording oral traditions and "invisible" knowledge. In this way, many landscapes have probably been defined as "ethnographic landscapes" by the local inhabitants or users, such as the migrating reindeer herders and their flocks. It is as yet not clear how these different narratives are being, or should be, incorporated into the management of both Sámi as well as other cultural remains and landscapes, especially when there are competing narratives constructed by different user groups and even different ethnic groups about the same landscape. The task of safeguarding Sámi remains is formally placed with the Sámi Parliament, albeit in cooperation with the Norwegian authorities both at regional and central level. At present, however, there is probably a tendency towards mutual exclusivity at the regional level when attempting to establish an official narrative about an area, be it small or large. This can be seen to originate from the wording of the law, with its requirement for an ethnic definition of cultural remains and the ensuing division of responsibility between two different authorities. Inevitably, this leads to a certain polarization where any multicultural narrative tends to lose out.

When it comes to divulging traditional knowledge, many Sámi communities prefer to keep such knowledge secret from those who are considered outsiders, and this may well include the central heritage agencies as well as the regional Norwegian ones. The choice of secrecy is made either because the knowledge traditionally has been sacred and therefore available to only a few, or because of fears about the consequences of divulging the location of sites (Husby 2001:179). Although such a view must obviously be respected, it creates its own problems with regard to the legal protection of Sámi remains, since the law, although in theory affording automatic legal protection to all Sámi remains more than one-hundred years old, whether known or unknown, in practice may require monuments to be known in order to successfully prosecute any violation of this protection. For Norwegian remains, this requirement will soon be met by a new national register of both archaeological and architectural monuments, as well as protected areas and landscapes, through work that is currently being finalised by the Directorate for Cultural Heritage. This register will contain information from a number of smaller databases, but access to the information will be graded according to the questioner's status. The fact that a monument is listed in the register will, however, count as making it "known." The Sámi Parliament has so far chosen not to incorporate its own databases for reasons described above.

Protection of Sámi Remains in Particular

The basis of the management of cultural remains in Norway can be seen as a legal landscape, where the articles of the law constitute the physical landscape. In this landscape, the concepts of jurisdiction and age are normally objectively verifiable and thus undisputable. The added provision of ethnicity as a criterion for Sámi remains, however, introduces a cognitive and subjective concept, which the law has difficulties dealing with in an adequate manner. This difficulty is therefore often transferred to those maintaining the law and creates a fertile ground for negotiations and sometimes even conflicts when the legal landscape is perceived in a totally different manner by the Norwegian and Sámi authorities.

In many ways, this situation mirrors the way in which the geographical landscapes of Northern Scandinavia have been seen and described by the different ethnic groups. The Norwegians have tended to see them as wild and untouched landscapes consisting only of geological, botanical and faunal features, which could be mapped and described relatively accurately in scientific terms. For the Sámi living there, however, the same landscapes functioned at a very different level, as an economic as well as a cultural and mythological framework for their life and work. Translating these two opposing perceptions of the same landscapes into an easily applicable legal framework has proved difficult, unless a great degree of pragmatism is exercised when maintaining the principles of the law. This article is an attempt to describe some of these difficulties.

The Norwegian Cultural Heritage Act and Sámi Remains

The Norwegian Cultural Heritage Act is often described as particularly beneficial to the protection of Sámi remains because of the one-hundred year limit for automatic legal protection of such remains, while Norwe-

21/ The old Coastal Saami communities of Sørstraumen (in the foreground) and Nordstraumen in the municipality of Kvænangen, Northern Troms. The landscape contains settlement remains from the Ice Age to the present day, place-names, Saami and Christian religious sites, folklore and stories.

gian remains must be four to five hundred years old in order to benefit from the same sort of protection. The reasons why a limit of one-hundred years was chosen for protected Sámi remains are contained in the original committee recommendations from 1970, which passed more or less unchanged into the new law itself. In the recommendations, the committee described certain Sámi cultural remains, such as sacrificial sites, large pitfall systems for hunting reindeer, burial grounds, etc., as "non-functional" elements in a modern Sámi culture, in the same way as such ancient elements are in the majority Norwegian culture. The difference was that these elements became non-functional at widely differing times, since "the development involving a change to Christian cult, the establishment of Christian cemeteries and the end of the hunting society is greatly retarded in the Sámi areas," as the recommendations put it. In other words, cultural elements that were abandoned in the Middle Ages or even earlier in Norwegian areas were perceived to have survived so long in the

Sámi areas that it was necessary to draw the line at one-hundred years instead of 1537 A.D. in order to protect similar remains.

Later government publications from the 1980s (e.g. Miljøverndepartementet 1987, 1988) expanded on the reasons by describing Sámi remains as

—Representing a different culture and adaptation from that evidenced by Scandinavian archaeology and ethnology,

—Being part of a still living tradition, but perhaps not for much longer,

—Identity markers for a people with a special need for such markers,

—Widespread but modest,

—Prone to being overlooked and destroyed, especially since it takes knowledge of the Sámi culture to recognize them, and since they are mostly located in harsh environments.

The main objectives for Sámi cultural heritage management were therefore seen as 'locating and protecting' Sámi cultural remains; objectives that still remain valid, since our knowledge of where legally protected Sámi remains are located, how many there are, and what state they are in, is still patchy.

However, while the intentions may have been the best, the introduction of the concept of Sámi ethnicity into a legal framework had two consequences:

—Any monument dating between 1537 (in exceptional cases 1650) and the present minus one-hundred years must be defined as Sámi in order to be protected by the Act,

—On the other hand, all monuments older than 1537 are automatically protected irrespective of ethnicity.

This means that only monuments younger than 1537 need the ethnic label "Sámi" in order to be legally protected, and it has more or less unwittingly led to a perception of the term "Sámi" applying only to monuments younger than 1537. The problems are thus how to define monuments as Sámi, and also what to do about the monuments that are not defined as Sámi in the present Sámi areas.

What is a Sámi Monument?

The immediate need—once the 1978 Cultural Heritage Act had been introduced—to define Sámi monuments as such does not seem to have been realized by the law makers, since neither the law, nor the documents associated with it made any serious or stringent attempt at defining what constitutes a Sámi monument, as opposed to the other monuments covered by the Act. For a number of years after the introduction of the Act, Sámi remains and monuments were therefore defined as more or less restricted to those left by the reindeer herding Sámi. On the whole, these remains were younger than 1537, they occurred in areas not occupied by Norwegians or any other non-Sámi ethnic group, they took a form that clearly set them apart from Norwegian remains, and were not of particular interest to Norwegian archaeologists or historians.

It is easy to see, however, that this narrow definition of Sámi remains left scope for an eventual expansion to all sides. As soon as you include the Coastal

Sámi and the Sámi inland farmers in the definition of "Sámi," you literally move into territories which for a long time have been occupied by several ethnic groups: Norwegians, Sámi, and Qvens (Finnish immigrants mainly from the eighteenth century and later). The law, however, treats the remains of these groups very differently, necessitating ethnic labels in order to establish whether a house site is Norwegian (and therefore only protected if it is older than 1537), Sámi (and therefore protected when it is one-hundred years old) or Qven (not protected by the law).

About ten years after the introduction of the Act, the discussion about Sámi cultural heritage management was mainly focussed on administrative problems: how a future dedicated Sámi cultural heritage management system should be organized (e.g. Marstrander 1987); and the required educational and cultural background for those working within the system (Fjellheim 1991; Rauset 1990). Both subjects were, of course, important, but—just like the law itself—the discussion seems to have assumed that a general consensus as to what constituted a Sámi monument existed. For instance, Marstrander (1987:4) defines "ancient monuments" as "stationary monuments which are protected by the law," and includes Sámi monuments in the definition. He then goes on to define Sámi monuments as "material remains left by Sámi ways of life."

By this time, however, the difficulties should perhaps have been realized on the basis of trying to define Sámi in a politically meaningful way. With the establishment of the Sámi Parliament in 1989 and the ensuing elections to choose its members, a formal electoral register had to be established which gave selective voting rights to the Sámi. This meant identifying who the Sámi were, i.e. who would be allowed to register. The accepted definition of a Sámi (Helander 1999) according to the Sámi Act (1987) thus became someone who:

—Speaks Sámi as their first language, or had one parent or grandparent who did so

—Considers himself or herself a Sámi,

22/ Reconstructing the frame for a traditional Saami turf house (gamme) at Nordstraumen in Kvænangen, Northern Troms.

—Lives in entire accordance with the rules of the Sámi society,

—Is recognised by the representative Sámi body as Sámi,

—Has a parent who satisfies these conditions.

The official legal definition of a Sámi thus places the greatest importance on the use of the Sámi language. This, however, is problematic since perhaps half the Norwegian Sámi today do not speak the language any more. The Sámi Act therefore had to acknowledge this historical development by extending the use of the language back to a parent or even a grandparent. Today, approximately 10,000 people have registered for the right to vote in elections to the Sámi Parliament, but any publication on the Sámi will tell you that there are at least as many as 35,000 Sámi in Norway (Aarseth et al. 1990; Hætta 1996), more likely 40 to 45,000 (Helander 1999), or perhaps as many as 60,000 or even 100,000 (Lorenz 1981). The discrepancies be-

tween these figures may also say something about the difficulty of ethnic definitions, be they self-applied (subjective) or imposed (objective).

An example from the municipality of Kvænangen in Northern Troms[3] (Fig. 21) shows the gap between a self-confessed ethnic identity and the unrealized potential resulting from using the criteria above. In the 1891 census, 1,016 people (or 57.4 percent of the population) in Kvænangen identified themselves as Sámi. Nearly one-hundred years later, in 1970, a theoretical calculation based on the language criteria used in the Sámi Act showed that 895 people (42.9 percent) still fulfilled the formal criteria for calling themselves Sámi (Bjørklund 1985:403, Table 44), but only twenty-four people (1.2 percent) did so in the census.

Today, Kvænangen is part of Electoral District 7 for the Sámi Parliament, together with five other municipalities in Northern Troms. The population of these six municipalities totalled 16,759 on January 1, 2003

(Statistisk Sentralbyrå 2004), but only 741 (4.5 percent) of them were registered on the Sámi electoral rolls in 2001, the latest election year (up from 442 at the start in 1989), and only 492 actually voted (Norut NIBR Finnmark 2004). It is difficult to say whether the figures show a general reluctance to register oneself on an ethnic basis, or, more specifically, on the ethnic basis now used for the Sámi electoral rolls, i.e. the language criterion.

Other researchers have tried other definitions of "Sámi-ness." Lorenz (1981:15) says that the simplest definition of a Sámi is "someone born to Sámi parents," but this only defers the definition and raises slightly unpleasant questions about a pure-blooded Sámi or not. What if your mother was Sámi, but your father only half Sámi? Or perhaps an academic study classifies your parents as Sámi, but they themselves do not, having chosen to become Norwegian at a time when being Sámi was a stigma that made life difficult? What does that make you? The same goes for the language criterion. When your mother spoke Sámi as her first language, but now considers herself Norwegian, should that entitle you to claim Sámi ancestry based on her linguistic abilities? [4]

One could also choose occupation as a criterion and say that only those still employed in the traditional Sámi livelihood of reindeer herding qualify as Sámi, as the Swedes have done. In the Swedish case, this means that only 2,700 of Sweden's 17,000 Sámi can officially be classified as such (Aarseth et al. 1990: 14). Reindeer herding is also an industry that is generally portrayed as vital to the survival of the Sámi culture in Norway today. That, however, raises the question of how characteristic it is of the modern Norwegian Sámi. In 1987, only 2,151 people, or about 10 percent or less of the Norwegian Sámi, were employed mainly in the reindeer industry (Aarseth et al. 1990:187), despite it being an industry restricted to the Sámi only. No livelihood figures exist for the rest of the Norwegian Sámi, but studies suggest that a larger proportion of the Sámi than of the Norwegians were employed in

other primary industries, such as agriculture and fisheries, while fewer were employed in the service industries. Many of these non-reindeer herding Sámi, who for hundreds, perhaps even thousands, of years have lived as fishermen and later small farmers, find it difficult to define themselves as Sámi today, when the reindeer herding Sámi are commonly used as the most potent symbol of Sámi ethnicity. This, in turn, may also lead to a narrow view of which parts of prehistory will be defined as Sámi or proto-Sámi.

The Sámi Parliament itself, in its *Samisk kulturminneplan 1998–2001* (Sámi cultural heritage plan 1998–2001), defines monuments as Sámi when

—A living or recorded Sámi tradition is associated with them,

—Local Sámi knowledge associates them with a Sámi cultural context,

—Research results indicate that they document Sámi history and prehistory.

Monuments can also be defined as associated with Sámi prehistory, i.e. they are seen as the physical manifestations of those processes that led to the establishment of the historically known Sámi cultural traits. This means that monuments dating to the earliest prehistory must be seen as the background for both a Sámi and a non-Sámi ethnicity. When they are elements of a present Sámi cultural landscape, the Sámi Parliament finds it natural to treat them as part of the Sámi cultural heritage associated with that landscape. Consequently, the Sámi Parliament defines part of its role within Sámi cultural heritage management as promoting a long-term view of Sámi history within certain areas. They realise, however, that since monuments and landscapes have different meanings to people with different cultural backgrounds living within these areas today, this presents a challenge to the cultural heritage management system.

In a recent and comprehensive work on Norwegian cultural heritage management and its legal basis, Schanche (2001), expressing the views of the Sámi Parliament, defines Sámi monuments as

23/ *The old church at the island of Skorpa in Kvænangen, Northern Troms, one of only three buildings in the municipality to survive World War II. A chapel was built around 1795 as a missionary station for the still pagan Coastal Saami population, while the present building dates back to 1850. The churchyard was established in 1851.*

—Monuments with living or recorded Sámi traditions, be they physical traces or places without any observable human influence,

—Monuments that by general scientific consensus are defined as part of Sámi history and prehistory.

At the same time, she acknowledges that definitions change over time, and become progressively more difficult the further back in time one goes. To Schanche, however, it is natural to include both

—Monuments belonging to those prehistoric roots from which the Sámi culture grew;

—Monuments that are not the result of Sámi activity, but to which Sámi traditions have been attached.

In the same study, Guribye and Holme (2001:55), who represent the Norwegian government position, present a subtly different argument by stressing that a "Sámi" monument must have both an ethnic and a culture historical basis, i.e. a Sámi monument must be physically

located within a present Sámi context or environment in order to be legally recognized as such.

A couple of examples may demonstrate the practical difficulties involved in such ethnic classifications more clearly.

One example concerns standing Sámi buildings over one-hundred years of age which, more or less by default, became legally protected by the 1978 Cultural Heritage Act, Section 4, as discussed above. Reading the original recommendations for the Act today it is doubtful whether an automatic legal protection of all Sámi buildings older than one hundred years was intended. As stated earlier, the recommendations were concerned with "non-functional" elements, but when it comes to buildings, still functional houses and buildings are also covered by the Act, with the often severe restrictions this involves with regard to repairs, modifications, modernizations, etc. This creates the need to define buildings as Sámi, but by which criteria? Does it require being built in a Sámi technique, such as the *gamme* shown in Fig. 22; built by a Sámi; used by a Sámi; or found in a Sámi area? And what about official Norwegian buildings in Sámi areas, such as schools and churches (Fig. 23): should they be regarded as Norwegian or Sámi in this respect? These questions were studied in a three-year project initiated by the Sámi Parliament and supported financially by the Directorate. Although the project final report (Sjølie 2003) lists a number of criteria which can be used to establish the ethnic affiliation of a building, it also leaves some of the questions unresolved, not least those that relate to the establishment of Norwegian central institutions in Sámi areas, such as churches, schools etc.

The same confusion can also be said to apply to the more recent architectural landscapes of Northern Norway. During World War II, the whole of Norway, right up to the border with Russia in the north-east, was occupied by the German army. In 1944, however, the Germans conceded defeat in the north and started retreating south. The retreat was accompanied by so-called "scorched earth" tactics, which meant that the vast majority of buildings in the County of Finnmark and in Northern Troms were burnt down, while the population was forcibly moved to other parts of the country. The devastation coincided with the main Sámi population areas of the country and meant that very little of pre-war material Sámi culture in most of Finnmark and Northern Troms survived the war. After the war, these districts were rebuilt by the Norwegian authorities, using mainly standardized housing, developed by centrally employed architects. Today, it is this post-war architecture that characterises large tracts of Finnmark and Northern Troms, in Norwegian, as well as in Sámi and Qven settlements (Fig. 24). In forty years, therefore, the question will arise whether these standard houses should become automatically legally protected in Sámi areas, but not in Norwegian and Qven settlements. Even the remains of German fortifications in the Sámi areas could end up as protected "Sámi monuments," since they represent a part of history that forever changed Sámi culture in the north.

Yet another example are the Sámi graves in Christian churchyards. Although the Cultural Heritage Act seems to accord automatic legal protection to all Sámi graves more than one-hundred years old, Guribye and Holme (2001:55) claim that this protection only applies when the whole churchyard can be classified as Sámi on cultural historical grounds. In other words, a single Sámi grave in an Oslo churchyard will not be protected—over the years many Sámi have been buried in such Norwegian contexts—while had the same person been buried at the Kautokeino churchyard in the County of Finnmark, the grave would have been legally protected as part of an overall Sámi context. Another project has therefore been undertaken by the Directorate in order to establish which churchyards, and therefore graves, should be defined as Sámi and therefore be legally protected if more than one-hundred years old. So far, the project has carried out surveys in those municipalities in Finnmark and Northern Troms where at least twenty-five percent of the population still called themselves Sámi in the official census around 1900 (Svestad and Barlindhaug 2003; Holand forthcoming). It has located a number of old and abandoned churchyards from the seventeenth, eighteenth and nineteenth centuries, all of them worthy of preservation since they mostly represent the introduction of Christian burial rites in their respective areas. However, only those that are identified as Sámi will, in the end, be afforded the automatic legal protection provided by the Cultural Heritage Act.

One of the most difficult aspects of the law as it stands today, and one which is bound to become even more so in the future, is the definition of remains older than 1537 A.D. as archaeological and thus by default the responsibility of the Norwegian regional and central heritage authorities. This means that all archaeological remains are dealt with by the Norwegian county heritage officers and the Norwegian executive officers for archaeology at the Directorate, even when these

24/ Typical post-World War II farm buildings at Saltnes in Kvænangen, Northern Troms.

remains are located in Sámi areas.

In those parts of the world where Europeans, in particular, arrived late in time, there can be no assumption that the prehistoric remains of that area represent their history. Both Australia and the New World are good examples of this. Norway, however, is different, in that at least two recognized ethnic groups (the Sámi and the Norwegians) both lay claim to the prehistory of the same geographical areas. The Sámi historian Hætta (1996:14) states categorically that the Sámi never immigrated into Northern Scandinavia, but evolved from the Stone Age population of the area and emerged as "Sámi" at least 2,000 years ago (see also Hætta 1980). There is no doubt in his mind that this makes the earlier history of at least Northern Scandinavia Sámi, in the sense that the Stone Age and Bronze Age peoples of the area were the direct ancestors of those people that 2,000 years ago or more were defined or defined themselves as Sámi. Aarseth et al. (1990:20) agree with this view, and the Sámi Parliament, in their website presentation (http://www.samediggi.no) of the Sámi, state that:

The first people arrived in Northern Scandinavia about 11,000 years ago. Whether they were Sámi, we do not know, but we do assume that the Sámi culture emerged and developed from these first inhabitants and up to this day through interaction between people and culture. Because the Sámi are the people who have lived the longest in this area, Norway has ratified ILO Convention No. 169, accepting the Sámi as the indigenous people of Norway. Sweden, Finland and Russia, however, have not yet ratified this convention.

This view, however, is not usually expressed quite as explicitly in general accounts of Norwegian prehistory. The two referred to below are both classic works from the last generation, the one by Professor Anders Hagen of the University of Bergen (1967/77), the other by two eminent South-Norwegian archaeologists, Bente Magnus and Professor Bjørn Myhre (1986). Both accounts should be seen as typical examples of how Norwegian prehistory is commonly presented, not as specific for the authors concerned.

In their account, Magnus and Myhre point to two factors in Norwegian prehistory that would seem to have implications for the interpretation of Sámi prehistory as well:

—The existence of two distinct and different cultural patterns in Norway going back at least to the Early Bronze Age, perhaps as far back as the latter part of the Neolithic, the one being an agricultural culture along the Norwegian coast, perhaps stretching as far north as the County of Troms and with links to continental Europe, the other being a hunting-fishing culture in inland Scandinavia and the northernmost coastal parts of Norway, with links to Eastern cultures.

—The continuity in settlement and subsistence patterns within this latter area, which seems to coincide more or less with the modern settlement areas of the Sámi.

Magnus and Myhre (1986:235, 316) trace the historically known Sámi in Eastern Finnmark back to the last centuries before Christ (the Pre-Roman Iron Age); the Sámi in other parts of Northern Norway to at least the Migration Period (400 A.D. to 550 or 600 A.D.); and even suggest that the cultural border referred to above may point to a proto-Sámi population as far south as the County of Hedmark in Southern Norway already in the Bronze Age (ibid.: 202, 319). This is consistent with the modern extent of Sámi settlements in Norway (see Fig. 20).

A good example of the continuity in settlement and subsistence patterns found in many Sámi areas is the site of Mortensnes in the far northeast of Norway, which is described both by Magnus and Myhre (1986:234–36) and Hagen (1967/77:115). It has an exceptionally large assembly of house sites and graves in particular, dating from the Mesolithic to modern times (K. Schanche 1988; A. Schanche, n.d.). The graves are of a characteristic Sámi type, i.e. located in screes, with some of them dating back more than 2,000 years, and there are also house sites and religious sites within the area that are generally accepted as Sámi (Fig. 25, 26). Furthermore, the site is located in a municipality which even today is considered Sámi, and which had an eighty-four percent Sámi population one-hundred years ago.

Neither Magnus and Myhre nor Hagen contest the fact that most remains within the Mortensnes site must be labelled Sámi at least for the last 2,000 years, possibly even longer. They also seem to accept that the Sámi generally emerged as an ethnic group from the Stone Age and Bronze Age groups that preceded them in any given area. Despite this long Sámi history in many parts of Norway, both Magnus and Myhre and Hagen still prefer not to identify a Sámi or even "proto-Sámi" prehistory beyond the last 2,000 years, i.e. to attach this particular ethnic label to prehistoric remains, and therefore to integrate the Sámi into their account of the prehistory of Norway. Instead, both accounts settle for a few isolated pages here and there on the Sámi. This approach, which is commonly shared by most other publications and scholars in Norwegian history, has the effect of defining the Sámi as different, marginal, and not part of the general historical development of Norway. On the other hand, such a view could be seen to coincide with the present Sámi political wish to establish a Sámi history that is separate and different from that of the surrounding Norwegian society.

Identifying the Sámi as the direct descendants of the Stone Age populations of certain areas of Norway would obviously make innumerable Stone Age settlements and monuments part of Sámi prehistory, in the same way as such monuments are seen as part of Norwegian prehistory. In those parts of Norway that do not have the complications of a multi-ethnic population, there has never been a need to ponder whether Stone Age sites and rock carvings should be seen as potentially ethnically different from the present populations of those areas. However, when dealing with the same sort of remains in the present Sámi or multi-ethnic areas, there are now competing views about whose history they represent: Norwegian? Sámi?,or perhaps just those groups that eventually gave rise to both ethnic communities, but may not have represented different ethnicities in the past.

One example is the World Heritage Site of the Alta rock carvings in Western Finnmark (Helskog 1988; cf. Figs. 26, 27). Professor Knut Helskog from the North-

25/ The sacrificial stone (Graksesteinen) *at Mortensnes in Varanger, County of Finnmark. The stone is surrounded by concentric stone circles.*

Norwegian University of Tromsø, who is the foremost expert on the Alta rock carvings, has discussed the question of their ethnic identity (Helskog 1988: 110). Like the authors mentioned above, he accepts the continuity in settlement and subsistence patterns between the prehistoric populations and the earliest recognised Sámi groups in these northernmost parts of Norway, and that the Sámi emerge as an ethnic group at least 2,000 years ago. This, he suggests, is also the time when the production of rock carvings in Alta comes to an end, perhaps to be replaced by depictions of many of the same motifs on ritual drums similar to those that are known from later Sámi contexts. He is more reluctant, however, to call the rock carvings part of Sámi prehistory.

Even Professor Bjørnar Olsen, also from the University of Tromsø, who has worked specifically with Sámi archaeology in the County of Finnmark, is cautious about applying ethnic labels to the prehistory of that county. In his work on the prehistory of Finnmark (Olsen 1994:139), he suggests instead:

> It may seem that there was not only an ethnic consolidation during this millennium [i.e. the last millennium B.C.], but that many of the formal traits that in historic time have been regarded as typically Sámi, were formed during this period (IH translation).

Another way of dealing with the controversial concept of a Sámi prehistory is to redefine the problem as semantic: "Sámi" becomes the ethnic label for a particular group of people; "Norwegian", on the other hand, just means "within the present borders of Norway" and carries no connotations of ethnicity. Therefore, everything can be labelled Norwegian until proven Sámi! This argument is often used within cultural heritage management, since it avoids the difficulties inherent in a multi-ethnic past.

Archaeology and Ethnicity

The problem of how to define ethnicity archaeologically is not one that is confined to Norway, nor to the relationship between a majority and an indigenous population such as the Norwegians and the Sámi. It is also a theoretical question that is part of archaeological history, and perhaps in particular its relationship to the politics of the day, as demonstrated by Jones (1996, 1997).

In her study, Jones (1997:56) raises the questions "What is ethnicity?" and "How should it be defined?", while pointing out that the word is mostly used without any form of definition, even in scientific studies. As an example, she quotes a study where sixty-five sociological and anthropological studies of ethnicity were surveyed, but only thirteen were found to have some kind of definition of their key subject.

The most common approaches in anthropological studies have been to define ethnicity either in an "objectivist" or a "subjectivist" way. The objectivists regard ethnic groups as "social and cultural entities with distinct boundaries characterized by relative isolation and lack of interaction," while subjectivists see them as "culturally constructed categorizations that inform social interaction and behavior" (Jones 1997:57). In other words, the objectivists define ethnic groups on the basis of the analyst's perception of socio-cultural differentiation (the outsider's view), while the subjectivists see ethnicity as the subjective self-categorizations of the people being studied (the insider's view). Although Jones does not necessarily draw such a conclusion, this could also be perceived as an expression of the slightly condescending viewpoint that researchers are normally objective, whereas the objects of their studies are not.

It is, however, the latter, subjectivist, view that has prevailed since the 1960s, based to a large extent on Barth's theoretical model of ethnicity, as developed in his *Ethnic Groups and Boundaries* (1969). This view has also permeated legislation and policy dealing with indigenous groups—as an example Jones (1997:60) mentions the definition of Australian Aboriginal groups. It is not, however, an entirely unproblematic definition,

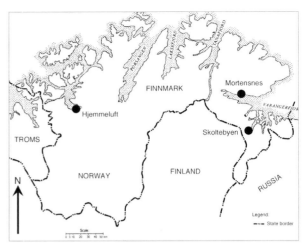

26/ Location of sites in Northern Norway discussed in the text.

as exemplified by the question of how to differentiate between ethnic groups and other self-defining groups, if self-definition becomes the overriding criterion.

It is exactly this tension about the definition of ethnicity generally, coupled with the need for an objective legal definition of Sámi ethnicity, both past and present, which create problems in relation to the Norwegian Cultural Heritage Act. The question is further complicated by the fact that in the case of the Sámi, it is sometimes the researchers that represent the radical view, labelling objects and people as Sámi on an historical basis, while the people themselves do not identify with this label any longer. This not only demonstrates some of the difficulties involved in ethnic labelling, but also shows what Jones (1997:64) calls "the fluid and situational nature of both group boundaries and individual identification."

In order to explore further the concept and perception of ethnicity, as opposed to other group ties, Jones describes another two labels, "the primordial imperative" and "instrumental ethnicities," which have surfaced in ethnicity studies over the last generation. The primordial imperative is a socio-, or perhaps rather, a psycho-biological, approach which sees ethnicity as grounded in "the givens of birth: "blood," language, religion, territory and culture." These "givens" form involuntary primordial attachments with a coerciveness that "transcends the alliances and relationships engen-

27/ The site of Hjemmeluft/Jiebmaluokta in Alta, County of Finnmark.

dered by particular situational interests and social circumstances" (Jones 1997:65). In other words, the individual is born into a set of ties, primarily kinship ties, and values that will define that person's self-identification. The approach has been criticized for romanticizing and mystifying ethnic identity, as well as portraying it as "involuntary and coercive" (ibid:69), thereby defining it as "an abstract natural phenomenon," while overlooking the "historical and social grounding of particular ethnicities" (ibid.:70). The approach, developed in the late 1950s, also carries some unpleasant echoes of earlier nationalism, the ideology of national identity based on bloodlines and descent (ibid.:71).

More acceptable in academic terms has, therefore, been the concept of "instrumental ethnicities," which came to dominate the debate during the 1970s and 1980s according to Jones (1996:67, 1997:75), and which sees ethnicity as "a dynamic and situational form of

group identity" (1997:72). However, the instrumentalist perception also has its difficulties. One is a tendency towards reductionism (ibid.:76), whereby observed consequences of ethnic behaviour are interpreted as the reasons for it. Thus, ethnicity becomes "the mobilization and politicization of culture in the organization of interest groups" (ibid.:77). This leads easily to "a neglect of the cultural and psychological dimensions of ethnicity." It also presupposes that "human behaviour is essentially rational and directed towards maximising self-interest" (ibid.:79), and, just like the subjectivist approach described above, it makes it difficult to distinguish between ethnic groups and other collective-interest groups.

To a certain extent, one could say that the definition of a Sámi for electoral purposes in Norway (as well as in Sweden and Finland) is based on the primordial imperative way of thinking, using as it does the concepts of kinship and inherited cultural traits, such as language, for a legal definition. Most researchers working with the question of Sámi ethnicity would, however, rather adopt a view of ethnicity as a function of a "them-and-us" situation, using Barth's model and historical developments to explain its emergence and background. It is doubtful, however, that anyone would want to label it rational and self-serving, since this would tend to be seen as negative.

This results in a number of different approaches and definitions which all carry both positive and negative aspects, and which are consequently difficult to subscribe to Jones (1996:67–8, 1997:84) herself suggests yet another definition of ethnicity, based on the theories of Bourdieu (1977) and his concept of "habitus" or those perceptions and practices that guide an individual's self-identification. This definition claims that "ethnic groups are culturally ascribed identity groups, which are based on the expression of a real or assumed shared culture and common descent" (Jones 1997:84). The definition attempts to incorporate those aspects of the others that are seen as positive, while at the same time portraying ethnicity as a social process in which "ethnic categories are reproduced and transformed" continuously, in order to accommodate ever changing historical and social circumstances.

While this may be a useful definition of ethnicity for theoretical academic discussions, it does not, unfortunately, solve many legal disputes. The fluid and porous borders of ethnic groups are reflected in objects that incorporate aspects of more than one ethnic group or move between them, while the situational nature of ethnicity makes it difficult to project modern ethnic labels back in time. This, of course, applies as much to "Norwegian-ness" as to "Sámi-ness," but has much greater consequences for the latter, since Norwegian is also equated with a state and its borders. Although the Sámi refer to certain parts of Scandinavia as *Sábmi* (or *Sápmi*, The Land of the Sámi), this has no legal definition and its borders cross those of four nations: Norway, Sweden, Finland and Russia.

For the time being, therefore, Sámi as a definition of legally protected cultural remains will continue to be the subject of interpretations and negotiations whenever the discussion moves away from the politically promoted core of Sámi-ness, the reindeer owning Sámi. As such, one could say that the legal discussions are part of the ongoing development and negotiation of Sámi ethnicity whereby objects, symbols and opinions fluctuate and change allegiance both in time and space. It is a dynamic way of looking at disagreements, which, however, is not easily incorporated into the task of law implementation.

It also has the effect, as Jones admits (1997:142), of undermining some of those minority claims to land and cultural heritage that have been accepted through, for instance, the adoption of ILO Convention No. 169, which gives the Norwegian Sámi status as an indigenous group. The Sámi, like many other ethnic minorities, may be left with the choice of establishing an undisputable continuity between today's generally accepted Sámi culture and that of a distant past, suggesting that little has changed in Sámi culture over hundreds and even thousands of years. More ironically even, the Sámi may be forced or choose to accept a concept of ethnicity that is closely associated with nationalism. Within this particular framework, "group identities are represented as unified, monolithic wholes, with linear and continuous histories which in turn are used in the legitimation of claims to political autonomy and territory," as Jones (1996:62) puts it. Another choice is to interpret and accept Sámi ethnicity as a process that at different times and places has presented itself in different forms, some of which may not be related to modern concepts of Sámi ethnicity. This latter choice, however, may blur the distinction between Sámi and other ethnicities both in the past and in the present to such an extent that it becomes difficult to claim archaeological remains or cultural landscapes as part of a Sámi history.

At the moment, it seems much easier for all sides to accept a multi-faceted Norwegian past rather than

28/ The Eastern Saami site of Skoltebyen in Neiden, County of Finnmark.

a Sámi one. The latter will normally have to show linear development and strong continuity and resemblance with modern Sámi culture, or at least certain parts of it, in order to be accepted as Sámi. Therefore, while the academic discourse stresses the fluid and situational aspect of ethnicity, practice still prefers a rigid and one-dimensional definition, not least as the basis for legal protection of Sámi cultural heritage. For the time being, the two approaches are negotiated from case to case, but some sort of integrated approach will have to be found and incorporated into law, as well as practice, in the not too distant future.

Protected Sámi Cultural Landscapes

The discussion above acquires more than a theoretical relevance when applied to three protected cultural landscapes in the County of Finnmark (See Fig. 26): *Hjemmeluft/Jiebmaluokta* in the municipality of Alta, *Mortensnes* in Nesseby, and *Neiden* in Sør-Varanger. Hjemmeluft and Mortensnes have been protected using Section19 of the Cultural Heritage Act, Neiden through Section 20, and of these three sites, only Mortensnes and Neiden have been formally defined as Sámi cultural landscapes. Together, they offer different perspectives on the difficulties of ethnic classifications,

from the purely archaeological to the purely Sámi.

Hjemmeluft, Alta municipality. The site contains the World Heritage Site of the Alta Rock Carvings (Fig. 27), and its surrounding municipality today is mainly Norwegian. It is formally classified as purely archaeological, and its administrative authority is therefore the Norwegian county heritage officer in Finnmark. Historically, however, the Alta area is commonly seen as a Coastal Sámi area at least from the Middle Ages, probably for much longer, and one could therefore classify the Stone and Bronze Age populations of the area, who produced the rock carvings, as proto-Sámi. Since the monuments, however, are all prehistoric, the site has been formally designated as "archaeological," with no ethnic affiliation.

Mortensnes, Nesseby municipality. The site (Fig. 25) contains a large number of settlement remains, graves and other religious monuments, dating from the Mesolithic to the nineteenth century. The Nesseby municipality is still considered a primarily Sámi municipality. Nearly all remains within the protected area from the last 2,000 years are also commonly accepted as Sámi, as are some of the older remains. The difficulties arise when considering the Mesolithic and Neolithic remains in the area. When the Mortensnes site was protected in 1988, the University Museum in Tromsø was appointed administrative authority according to the provisions of the Cultural Heritage Act. However, later changes to the Act meant that this authority became divided between the Norwegian county heritage officer for archaeological remains and the Sámi Parliament for Sámi remains. In other words, the site acquired a dual ethnicity entirely due to the letters of the law. Since this was deemed impractical in administrative terms, the Directorate has transferred sole authority to the Sámi Parliament, based on an overall evaluation of the site and its location. This decision met with some criticism from Norwegian archaeologists since it is seen to assign a Sámi ethnicity to the prehistoric remains in the area.

Skoltebyen in Neiden, Sør-Varanger municipality. The Neiden site (Fig. 28) comprises the settlement area of an Eastern Sámi group (*siida*), while the surrounding municipality today has a mixed population of Norwegians, Sámi and Qvens (Finns). The Eastern Sámi often see themselves as a minority within the Sámi minority, having converted to Russian Orthodox Christianity in the sixteenth century. The site was originally one of their seasonal settlements, but when the national borders between Norway, Finland and Russia were drawn in the nineteenth century, the Eastern Sámi, who had until then moved freely between the three states, were forced to settle in one of them. The Neiden *siida* chose to settle at Skoltebyen, their old summer settlement. The site contains a Russian Orthodox chapel from the sixteenth century, a number of Eastern Sámi graves and remains of settlements from the later centuries, as well as modern buildings and businesses, the latter owned by descendants of the Eastern Sámi.

When the site was legally designated in 2000, the Sámi Parliament became sole administrative authority since there are no known Norwegian or archaeological monuments within the area. Ironically, this has met with criticism from some of the local Eastern Sámi, who regard the Sámi Parliament, which is dominated by other Sámi groups, as yet another a colonial power.

Conclusion

The three sites thus exemplify many of the difficulties inherent in the present Norwegian cultural heritage legislation when it comes to defining monuments—and even more so sites and cultural landscapes with a variety of monuments—as Sámi. The difficulties are historical, in the sense that they reflect a heritage management system that has evolved over one-hundred years or more. This system in turn reflected a view of history, which, in the twentieth century, tended to regard the Sámi as immigrants to Norwegian territory, especially in the southern parts of the country, and also to equate "the Sámi" only with today's reindeer herders. Modern research has demonstrated that the Sámi have an equally long history at least in certain parts of the country as the Norwegians have in other parts, but also that there were and are a number of Sámi adaptive strategies, with the modern form of reindeer herding being one, but not the only one.

The obligation to identify cultural remains ethnically in order to decide their legal status has, on the one hand, led to a greater awareness and acceptance of Sámi history generally, but also to a polarization of the debate and a sometimes monolithic view of what constitutes Sámi-ness. In this rather antagonistic legal landscape, perceptions have a tendency to appear either black or white, while promoting the greyscales of the picture often brings wrath from both sides of the debate. This may seem surprising in a modern world where so many people juggle multiple identities on a daily basis, but it is not something that can be resolved through heritage legislation. For now, however, it has been left to the practitioners of the heritage laws, on both the Sámi and the Norwegian sides, to negotiate the borders and consequences of the law, as knowledge, perceptions and aspirations change.

Notes

1. The views expressed in this paper are those of the author and not necessarily those of her employer.

2. These include a medieval monastery and the surrounding farm on an island in South-Western Norway (Utstein in the County of Rogaland), a traditional multi-family farm in Western Norway (Havrå-tunet in the neighbouring County of Hordaland), an Eastern Sámi settlement in North-Eastern Norway (Skoltebyen in Neiden, County of Finnmark), and an old silver mining landscape in South-Eastern Norway (Kongsberg Silver Mines, County of Buskerud). A few more cases are being considered at the moment, none of them in Sámi areas.

3. The author was born at Sørstraumen in Kvænangen and comes from a Coastal Sámi background.

4. The examples have been chosen from the author's own family. The author belongs to the first generation with Norwegian as their first and only language.

References

Aarseth, Bjørn, Einar Niemi, S. Aikio, W. Brenna, and Elina Helander
1990   *Samene, en håndbok* (The Sámi: an introduction). Kautokeino and Karasjok. Sámi Instituhtta and Davvi Girji O.S.,

Barth, Fredrik, ed.
1969   *Ethnic Groups and Boundaries.* Boston: Little and Brown.

Bjørklund, Ivar
1985   *Fjordfolket i Kvænangen. fra samisk samfunn til norsk utkant 1550-1980* (The fjord people of Kvænangen: from Sámi society to Norwegian periphery). Oslo: Universitetsforlaget.

Bourdieu, Pierre
1977   Outline of a Theory of Practice. *Cambridge Studies in Social Anthropology* 16. Cambridge.

Direktoratet for Naturforvaltning
1994   *Verdifulle kulturlandskap i Norge. Mer enn bare landskap!* (Valuable cultural landsapes in Norway. More than just landscape). Part 4. Trondheim: Direktoratet for Naturforvaltning.

Direktoratet for Naturforvaltning and Riksantikvaren
2001   *Strategi for arbeid med landskap DN/RA, 1.12.2001* (Strategy for working with landscapes DN/RA, 1.12.2001). Preliminary report. Trondheim and Oslo: Direktoratet for naturforvalt-ning and Riksantikvaren.

Espeland, Else, and Kåre Sveen
1989   Museums in Norway. Special edition of *Museumsnytt.*

Evans, Michael J., Alexa Roberts, and Peggy Nelson
2001   Ethnographic Landscapes. *Cultural Resource Management* 24(5):53-6.

Finne, Marie and Jørn Holme
2001   Fredning ved enkeltvedtak (Listing by individual resolution). In *Kulturminnevern: Lov, forvaltning, håndhevelse,* J. Holme, ed., Vol. II, pp. 140-79. *Økokrims skriftserie* 12. Oslo: Økokrim.

Fjellheim, Sverre
1991   *Kulturell kompetanse og områdetilhørighet: Metoder, prinsipper og prosesser i samisk kulturminnevernarbeid* (Cultural knowledge and area attachment: methods, principles, and processes in Sámi cultural heritage management). Snåsa: Saemien Sijte.

Guribye, Ragnhild and Jørn Holme
2001   Automatisk Fredete Kulturminner (Automatically Protected Cultural Remains). In *Kulturminnevern: Lov, forvaltning, håndhevelse,* J. Holme, ed., vol. II, pp. 32-101. *Økokrims skriftserie* 12. Oslo: Økokrim.

Hagen, Anders
1967   *Norges Oldtid* (Norway's Prehistory). Oslo: J.W. Cappelens Forlag AS. (Revised, 1977).

Helander, Elina
1999   *The Sami of Norway.* http.//odin.dep.no, Ministry of Foreign Affairs.

Helskog, Knut
1988   *Helleristningene i Alta: Spor etter ritualer og dagligliv i Finnmarks forhistorie* (The rock art of Alta: traces of ritual and daily life in Finnmark's prehistory). Tromsø and Alta.

Holand, Ingegerd
n.d.   *Automatisk fredete samiske kirkegårder* (Automatically Protected Sámi Churchyards). In press.

Holme, Jørn, ed.
2001   Kulturminnevern: Lov, forvaltning, håndhevelse (Cultural heritage management: law, administration, implementation). Vol. I-II. *Økokrims skriftserie* 12. Oslo: Økokrim.

Husby, Ivar
2001   Anmeldelse og etterforskning av kulturminnekriminalitet (Investigation and prosecution of cultural heritage crimes) In *Kulturminnevern: Lov, forvaltning, håndhevelse,* J. Holme, ed., Vol. I, pp. 167-195. *Økokrims skriftserie* 12. Oslo: Økokrim.

Hætta, Odd Mathis
1980   *SameTema II: Fra steinalder til samisk jernalder* (Sámi Issues II: from the Stone Age to the Sámi Iron Age). Alta:Skoledirektøren/Høgskolen i Finnmark.
1996   *The Sami: An Indigenous People of the Arctic.* Translated by O.P. Gurholt. Karasjok: Davvi Girji o.s.

Jones, Sian
1996   Discourses of Identity in the Interpretation of the Past. In *Cultural Identity and Archaeology,* P. Graves-Brown, S. Jones, and C. Gamble, eds., London and New York: Routledge.
1997   *The Archaeology of Ethnicity: Constructing Identities in the Past and Present.* London and New York:

Routledge.

Lorenz, Einhart
1981   *Samefolket i historien* (The Sámi in history). Oslo: Pax Forlag AS.

Magnus, Bente, and Bjørn Myhre
1986   Forhistorien:Fra jegergrupper til høvding-samfunn (Prehistory: from hunting groups to chieftain societies). In *Norges Historie*, K. Mykland, ed., Vol. I. Oslo: J.W. Cappelens Forlag AS.

Marstrander, Lyder, ed.
1987   *Fornminnevern og samisk kulturminnevern i samfunnsplanleggingen: Organisering og arbeidsoppgaver* (The preservation of prehistoric and Sámi cultural remains in planning processes: Organization and Tasks). Utredning fra arbeidsgruppe engasjert av Riksantikvaren   og   med   mandat   fra Miljøverndepartementet gitt i brev av 4. juli 1985. Oslo: Riksantikvaren.

Miljøverndepartementet (Royal Ministry of the Environment)
1987   *St. meld nr. 39 (1986-87): bygnings- og fornminnevernet* (White paper on the protection of buildings and ancient monuments). Oslo: Miljøverndepartementet.

1988   *Innst. S. nr. 135 (1987-88): Innstilling fra kommunal- og miljøvernkomiteen om bygnings- og fornminnevernet* (Recommendation from the municipal and environmental committee on buildings and ancient monuments protection). Oslo: Miljøverndepartementet.

1992a   *Ot.prp. nr. 51 (1991-92): Om lov om endringer i lov av 9. juni 1978 nr. 50 om kulturminner* (Government bill on changes to the Act of 9 June 1978 No. 50 on cultural heritage.) Oslo: Miljøverndepartementet.

1992b   *Innst. O. nr. 73 (1991-92): Innstilling fra kommunal- og miljøvernkomiteen om lov om endringer i lov av 9. juni 1978 nr. 50 om kulturminner* (Recommendation from the municipal and environmental committee on changes to the Act of 9 June 1978 No. 50 on cultural heritage). Ot.prp. nr. 51. Oslo: Miljøverndepartementet.

2000   *Cultural Heritage Act of 9 June 1978 No. 50 concerning Cultural Heritage.* Last amended 3 March 2000 No. 14. Oslo: Miljøverndepartementet.

Norut NIBR Finnmark
2004   Statistikk om Finnmark: Sametingsvalget 2001 (Statistics for Finnmark: Sámi Parliamentary Elections 2001). http://www.fifo.no/finnstat/same_valg_tab1.htm

Olsen, Bjørnar
1994   *Bosetning og samfunn i Finnmarks forhistorie* (Settlement and society in Finnmark's prehistory). Oslo: Universitetsforlaget.

Rauset, Solbjørg, ed.
1990   *Samisk kulturminnevernforskning: Rapport fra seminar i Guovdageaidnu/Kautokeino 22-24 november 1989* (Research on Sámi cultural heritage management: Report from the seminar in Guovdageaidnu/Kautokeino, November 22-24, 1989). Oslo: Norges allmenviten-skapelige forskningsråd.

Samisk kulturminneråd
1999   *Samisk kulturminneplan, 1998-2001* (Plan for Sámi Cultural Heritage, 1998-2001). Varangerbotn and Karasjok: Samisk kulturminneråd and Sametinget.

Schanche, Audhild
n.d.   *Ceavccageadgi/Mortensnes: En kulturhistorisk vandring gjennom 10000 år.* (Ceavccageadghi/Mortensnes: A cultural-historic walk through 10,000 Years). Varangerbotn: Varanger Samiske Museum/Várjjat Sámi Musea.

2001   *Samiske kulturminner* (Sámi cultural remains). In *Kulturminnevern: Lov, forvaltning, håndhevelse*, J. Holme, ed., Vol. I, pp. 56-61. Økokrims skriftserie nr. 12. Oslo: Økokrim.

Schanche, Kjersti
1988   Mortensnes, en boplass i Varanger: en studie av samfunn og materiell kultur gjennom 10.000 år (Mortensnes, a settlement in Varanger: A study of society and material cultural through 10,000 years). Unpubl. mag.art. thesis in archaeology. Tromsø: University of Tromsø.

Sjølie, Randi
2003   *Vern og forvaltning av samiske byggverk: utkast til hovedrapport 2003* (Protection and administration of Sámi buildings: draft for the main report, 2003). Varangerbotn: Sametinget.

Statistisk Sentralbyrå
2004   Folkemengde 1. januar 2003 (Census, January 1, 2003). http://www.ssb.no/emner/02/01/10/folkber/tab-2003-12-18-01.html

Svestad, Asgeir and Barlindhaug, Stine
2003   *Samiske kirkegårder: Registrering av automatisk freda samiske kirkegårder i Nord Troms og Finnmark* (Sámi churchyards: A survey of automatically protected Sámi churchyards in Northern Troms and Finnmark). NIKU Rapport 4. Oslo and Tromsø: NIKU.

Concepts and Practices in Ethnographic Landscape Preservation:

A Russian North Perspective

PAVEL M. SHUL'GIN

The problem of preserving historical and cultural legacies occupies a significant place in the social consciousness of Russia and in contemporary Russian scientific discourse. During the 1990s, radically new concepts were developed and established about this subject. New legislative decrees were adopted, and many practical policies were launched to protect the rich cultural heritage of the Russian Federation. In many ways, these initiatives were linked to the significant political and social changes that had been occurring in Russia since 1985 and, especially, after 1991. This evolution entailed greater freedom and the ability to express diverse social opinions, with the country engaged in a rapid transition from self-imposed ideological seclusion to international cooperation.

Recent Public Attitudes and Their Reflection in Scientific Approaches

Between 1970 and 1990, the conditions for preserving the cultural and natural heritage of the former Soviet Union had deteriorated sharply. The deterioration was related to ever-increasing ideological pressure in the Soviet regime, a drive for unified cultural and social life that was actively promoted "from the top down." The government vigorously promoted its aims to unify individual ethnic cultures and fuse them into a new, quasi-ethnic community labeled "The Soviet People" (i.e., Bromlei 1981:329-55). In that ideological setting, culture was relegated to a secondary—if not insignificant—role, in view of the absolute priority given to industrial development and economics in

general, as the fundamental factors in the country's development.

With industry the center of concentration, development projects with the potential to devastate indigenous homelands and cultures were perceived as perfectly acceptable goals for the nation's economic progress. For example, monumental projects were undertaken for redirecting waters from northern rivers to the south of the Soviet Union to create huge reservoirs (and to flood large agricultural and forest areas in the Russian North and Western Siberia). The reservoirs were considered necessary to provide for the needs of industry and agriculture in the southern regions. Seizure of huge territories inhabited by indigenous minority peoples (such as Khanty, Nenets, and others) for exploring oil and gas fields was common, especially in the eastern and northern regions of the USSR. State-run industries confiscated traditional ethnic areas without compensating local residents or providing adequate, new living conditions.

Social changes occurring in the Soviet Union with the start of perestroika [policy of economic and governmental reform after 1985-1986] could not skirt these problems. It was natural that the issues of ethnic consciousness and protection of the cultures and rights of indigenous peoples and other minority groups became so extraordinarily pressing at the end of the 1980s. The idea of cultural and ethnic unification as the primary path for the country's development was repudiated and replaced by the goal of preserving and reviving the many national cultures in the Russian Federation. Correspondingly, a new crucial task emerged: the identification and documentation of the variety in Russia's ethnic and historical heritage. Public interest in and awareness of one's native land, ethnic origins, religious traditions, and family roots skyrocketed. For a long time, such concerns about heritage had been considered insignificant, had not been encouraged in official Soviet propaganda, and at times, had been openly suppressed.

This trend coincided with the beginning of a powerful and popular environmental movement. Many grassroots environmental groups, organized beginning in the second half of the 1980s, asserted the rights for citizens to live in a clean environment and for complete disclosure to local constituencies of risks associated with existing manufacturing or planned construction projects (Litovka 1989).

It is no accident that one of the more prominent expressions of the 1980s, in fact, a widely shared slogan in the public and scholarly community alike, was the concept of "the ecology of culture," as advanced by the late Academician Dmitrii S. Likhachev (1980; 2000). Having coined this new term, Likhachev—then the most authoritative and popular Russian historian—linked the two central issues of the time. The first concerned the continuity of social consciousness and the role of historical roots in the ongoing transformation of Russia (and of the then-Soviet Union). The second issue was the interaction and spiritual interrelationship of nature and society. Likhachev's concept assumes that the key conditions for the preservation of a culture include not only the protection of its historical treasures, cultural traditions, and cultural education of the public, but also the protection of nature, without which a modern nation cannot exist. According to Likhachev, if preserving the natural environment is a condition for man's biological existence, then preserving the cultural environment is the most important condition for man's moral and spiritual life.

New Trends in Russian Heritage Research

During the perestroika years (1985–1991), new concepts were advanced in Russian cultural politics and scholarship related to the preservation and documentation of cultural heritage. It is important to note the following three basic transitions.

Individual to Diversified:

> The transition from the once-established practice of separate (isolated) research and protection of cultural and natural monuments to preservation of heritage in its integrity and diversity.

This new approach was based on evolution from the protection of individual monuments to the preservation of an entire historical and cultural heritage that subsumes the heritage objects themselves, the environment in which they exist, and people (or better, the local community) as carriers of heritage. This shift was probably the most important trend in Russian scientific and sociocultural practices of the 1990s and would define many other changes for several years to come. Specifically, this type of approach allowed work to begin for preserving the face of the territory's common cultural landscape and its historical environment, instead of protecting a selected individual monument as an object of cultural heritage.

New programs are being formulated—and many are already being implemented—to identify the entire scope of heritage, including not only historical and cultural monuments, but also other, very important elements. Such elements include, but are not limited to, folk culture, traditions, ethnic crafts and trades, the historical urban environment, agricultural development and the system of settlement, the ethnocultural environment, the natural environment, and traditional nature management (subsistence economy). These phenomena are no longer viewed merely as necessary background or conditions for any prominent monument or significant historical phenomenon. They are seen as direct, significant parts of a common ethnic legacy—as special elements that define the originality of the culture of a particular country or region.

The trend toward preservation of heritage in its integrity and diversity initially became visible in new efforts to identify and document historical and cultural monuments. Work to inventory monuments in various parts of the country has intensified, and previously existing lists of cultural or historical monuments now include thousands of new entries. Their numbers include not only prominent archaeological, architectural, and historical sites, as well as monumental art, but also objects that never had been considered in any detail. Public buildings in historical cities, objects of industrial architecture, the entire complex of the historical ensemble, and other objects and structures were among those included under the newly expanded definition of heritage objects.

After the new inventories of historical and cultural heritage were performed in the early 1990s, the number of monuments placed on the government register and under protection in Russia increased exponentially.[1]

In many small historical Russian cities, the number of protected objects increased by virtually an order of magnitude (*Istoricheskii gorod* 1997). This escalation is reflected in the publication of a collection (begun in 1997) of historical and cultural monuments, a kind of Russian "national register of monuments" (*Svod pamiatnikov* 1997; 1998–2001).

Historical and Cultural Context:

The transition toward viewing heritage as a reflection of historical experience in the interaction between man and nature.

This new perspective on cultural/historical heritage as a systemic phenomenon is extremely important. Under the new approach, individual objects of heritage cannot be preserved apart from each other or apart from their environment. Consideration not simply of an individual monument, but of the entire historical and cultural complex in all its variety, offers the best

path to acknowledge the integrity of cultural and natural heritage. This tenet refers both to the situational unity of the monument and the environment in which it was created (and which comprises its natural landscape surroundings and the functional unity of monument and environment). As a rule, every cultural monument is tied by innumerable threads of its functional intent to its surrounding environment, which forms a unique ecological niche for the monument.

Unfortunately, this new, integrated approach has not yet been implemented adequately through specific, conceptually consistent programs for protecting cultural and natural heritage. As in the past, rigid bureaucratic barriers remain between Russia's state cultural institutions and environmental protection agencies. In particular, virtually all functions of the national park network established in Russia as a special form of protection for nature, culture, and ethnic traditions, are limited to environmental protection. To date, most expectations that had been conferred on this integrated network back in the 1980s (Maksakovskii 1998) remain unfulfilled. However, quests for such integration are under way.

Territorial Approach:

The importance of the territorial approach to researching and preserving heritage, when the primary objects of protection are territories.

Prior practice has made it clear that the protection of isolated historical and cultural objects cannot be effective apart from the preservation of their surrounding historical and natural spaces. Preservation of the broader space, or environment, is necessary from the point of view not only of how a monument—whether a natural system, architectural complex, or ethnic community—is perceived, but, most importantly, of its long-term sustainability. Thus, the creation in Russia of historical/cultural and natural protected areas calls for the simultaneous resolution of problems in both the preservation and rational management of historical, cultural, and natural monuments. The status of such protected areas has not yet been clearly defined under Russian legislation. However, their creation has gradually advanced from theoretical discussions to practical implementation. Consequently, several large museum-conservation areas and many national parks have emerged, per se, as territories with single natural-cultural spaces [see Wiget and Balalaeva, this volume].

A "historical-cultural territory" may be defined as "an integral spatial object where several natural, historical, and cultural objects of exceptional value and significance may be found." Such a designation is conferred based on the existence of a local complex of monuments and territories objectively linked by ethnic, economic, historical, or geographical factors. The existence and combination of a complex of memorial, architectural, or archaeological objects determine the territory's uniqueness. Other possible determinants of uniqueness are ethnic traditions and economic activity, folklore and ceremonial ethnic culture, and natural points of interest or historical forms of nature management[2] that represent exceptional value from the point of view of the history and culture of a separate people or of Russia as a whole.

The best examples of such historical-cultural territories may be small, historical cities (home to numerous monuments and architectural structures from the sixteenth through eighteenth centuries), including the surrounding, old villages and natural grounds; old manors or Russian Orthodox monastery complexes, where nature, architecture, and local community make up a single whole; and great historical battlefields. Ethnographic landscapes are related, in particular, to the habitation of minority ethnic groups, and Russia's northern indigenous peoples also fall into this category.

In all these trends, the unity of three factors that are carriers of heritage—historical and cultural heritage, the natural environment, and the inhabitants of these territories—is apparent. It must be stressed that protection and use of heritage are viewed today as organic parts of the modern sociocultural and eco-nomic development of every territory.

It is these new approaches in Russian scientific discourse and practices in heritage preservation that allowed the introduction, in the 1990s, of the pioneering (for Russia) concept of cultural landscape. The closely related concept of "ethnographic landscape" also emerged, and the two terms frequently are discussed together.

The Concept of Cultural Landscape in Russian Heritage Studies

The contemporary understanding of cultural landscape is ambiguous in both international and Russian scientific discourse. Three basic approaches to the interpretation of this term must be distinguished.

The first approach is based on the concept that a cultural landscape is a locale that has been inhabited over a long historical period by a certain group of people who are the carriers of specific cultural values. Minority ethnic groups and/or local communities based on religious traditions (such as Russian Old Believers) are cited often as examples of such groups.

A similar approach to defining a cultural landscape and its study is characteristic of the school of cultural geography established by Carl Sauer (1925/1963; 1927). In this approach, a cultural landscape is an artificial landscape created by the long-term settlement and other interrelated activities of local communities and cultural groups. In this sense, the term "cultural landscape" is virtually equivalent to the term "ethnographic landscape." Moreover, despite the fact that the latter term is practically absent from Sauer's work, much attention is devoted to factors and results associated with the transformation of the natural landscape by various ethnic populations. At the same time, significant attention is devoted to the structure of the settlement, features of land utilization, and local architecture whose creation was influenced by local and other factors (Salter 1971).

In Russian scientific discourse, the concept of the cultural landscape as a modification of the natural landscape developed gradually during the course of the twentieth century. In the nature-centric approach, the geographic landscape is the set of natural phenomena that, ideally, has not been touched or changed by man (Isachenko 1965). Its antithesis is the anthropogenic landscape, which has been changed/transformed by man and, sometimes, even "spoiled" by human intervention. In this latter approach, the cultural landscape is seen as a "good" anthropogenic landscape that has been transformed by human activity, according to a specific program. Such a landscape commonly exhibits high esthetic and functional properties (Mil'kov 1973, 1978).

Still another perspective has become established in Russian landscape research during the past decade and is even more widely accepted. This perspective considers the cultural landscape an integrated, territorially localized set of material components and phenomena formed as the result of interaction between natural processes and diverse human activities. Within this framework, the notion has developed that the results of human action, embodied in objects of material and spiritual culture, are an intrinsic part of the cultural landscape (Vedenin 1997).

The basis of this approach is the notion of the active role played by intellectual and spiritual human activity in the formation of a cultural landscape. In this approach, the role of the intellectual and spiritual component of the landscape is specifically acknowledged. It is stressed that

> spiritual and intellectual values, preserved and passed down from one generation to another in the form of information, not only define the formation and development of a cultural landscape, but are also an integrated part of it and are subject to the influence of other, material components of the landscape (Vedenin 1997; Vedenin and Kuleshova 2001).

This perspective clearly argues that the manifestations of a cultural landscape are not limited to its scenic values; it also emphasizes the aspect of territorial differentiation (spatial diversity) of cultural phenomena. Thus, the results of changes occurring in traditional economics and nature management also become components of every cultural landscape. Such changes usu-

ally interfere with specific ethnocultural features of a local population (such as language, religion, daily and artistic culture, and other factors) as well as with the many forms of "invisible" cultural legacy, such as historical events of great significance and related cultural memory. Through these interactions, the cultural landscape accumulates and manifests the intellectual and spiritual potential of a nation or given regional group.

It is under this third interpretation that cultural landscape becomes the main theoretical concept for development of a new framework for preservation and management of Russia's cultural resources. It is hoped that "cultural landscape" is also destined to become a basic term in practical activities and in the emerging national system of documentation and protection of cultural monuments and historical and cultural territories. A similar approach has been adopted as the basis of activity at the Russian Research Institute for Cultural and Natural Heritage (RRICNH), a research center established in 1992 and named after Dmitrii S. Likhachev (Russian: 'Institut kul'turnogo i prirodnogo naslediia').

The government decree that created RRICNH set forth two main goals for the new state scientific agency:

> —Implementing in Russia the primary provisions of the United Nations Educational, Scientific, and Cultural Organization (UNESCO) convention regarding the protection of cultural and natural heritage;

> —Substantiating and developing regional programs for preservation and management of cultural and natural heritage (for diverse types of regions and local communities).

In its work, RRICNH attempts to address issues related to both methods and management of a unified policy for preserving cultural and natural heritage. Its work has served as the basis for the creation of new museums, museum-conservation areas, and national parks. RRICNH has initiated the development of integrated programs for heritage preservation of historical cities, rural settlements, and territories. The institute participates in numerous research programs on living traditional culture and organizes heritage surveys and research expeditions (Shul'gin and Shtele 1998; Vedenin 2000; Shul'gin 2002; Vedenin 2003).

RRICNH research is based on the cultural-landscape zoning of various regions of Russia. It promotes the establishment of a network of historical and cultural territories as primary objects for development and implementation of heritage preservation projects. One of these territories is the so-called "ethno-ecological area." This term usually refers to the area populated by a minority ethnic group, an indigenous community, or a specific group (subdivision) of a larger ethnic population (Vedenin and Shul'gin 1992; Shul'gin 2000).

The term "ethno-ecological area" was introduced in the Russian scientific discourse in the late 1980s (Ler and Lebedev 1989; Bogoslovskaia 1990), thanks to a few pioneer interdisciplinary studies conducted by Russian biologists and ethnographers. The purpose of the studies was to protect the traditional cultures of minority groups and their unique natural environments. During 1989–1990, proposals were set forth for establishing protected areas in Primorskii Krai and the Chukchi Autonomous Area (Chukotka), so that indigenous nature-management practices, traditional subsistence economies, and customary ways of life would be maintained. Anthropologist Igor Krupnik advanced a closely related term, "ethno-ecosystem," using the example of indigenous sea-mammal hunters and reindeer herders of the Russian Arctic and Subarctic (Krupnik 1989, 1993). According to Krupnik's definition (1989:24), an ethno-ecosystem includes stable ethnic communities (populations) that are linked by their common use of lands, their common labor, and the habitation of a specific territory.

Another influential, integrated approach to the identification of cultural and ethnographic landscapes was advanced by a team of physical and economic geographers from Moscow University (MGU) (Kaganskii and Rodoman 1995; Kalutskov et al. 1998; Turovskii 1998). MGU has held an annual seminar "Cultural Landscape" since 1993. Recently, a spin-off of the seminar, a special lecture course called "Fundamentals of Ethnocultural Landscape Studies," was offered at the Department of Physical Geography and Landscape Studies of the MGU School of Geography (Kalutskov 2000). For several years, field surveys of the ethnographic landscape of the local Russian population have been conducted under this program in the Pinega District of Arkhangelsk Province in the Russian North (Kul'turnyi landshaft 1998).

In the MGU approach, ethno-ecological territories largely are lands inhabited/used by indigenous peoples of the North. Ethno-ecological territories may also include relatively isolated habitations of other, small ethnic communities. In these territories, a traditional culture and a particular system of settlement and manner of colonization have developed. There are traditional economic holdings and holy places. In such cases, a relatively small territory often contains the entire history of an ethnic community or minority nation and, at the same time, is itself the economic and cultural basis for its modern residency. In such territories, many natural objects have a historical or mythological character and an animated significance for the local people. Examples include rivers, lakes, hills, and even individual trees [see Wiget and Balalaeva, this volume].

The preservation of a given historical space, its identification, and its protection from abrupt external disturbances function as a pledged security for preserving the culture and traditional forms of economic, spiritual, and religious distinctions of the local population. This particular kind of territory can receive special status and legislative protection as a guarantee of preserving, as a whole, not only the historical and natural heritage of the given area, but also the ethnic group that inhabits it. For such territories, the related concept of ethnographic landscape is directly applicable.

Ethnographic Landscape Preservation in Russian Legislation

Although Russian heritage studies set forth several new concepts and approaches during the 1990s, the current situation in Russia with regard to protected status for historical and cultural territories, and ethnographic landscapes in particular, is still cause for concern. One important obstacle that prevents implementation of a landscape approach to preservation of historical-cultural heritage (and ethnographic landscapes as its constituent part) is the inadequacy of an appropriate legislative basis. Russian legislative practice does not keep pace with social and economic change. Because of the great inadequacy of legislation to effectively address issues of economic regulation, land ownership, and taxation, new legislation aimed at protecting cultural heritage often is relegated to second place. Some laws introduced for deliberation and legislative approval by the Russian Duma [Federal Parliament] undergo a long period of consideration—sometimes up to six to eight years. For example, a law concerning historical and cultural monuments and culture has been debated in the Russian Duma for more than six years. Several variations of this law have been considered, but none has advanced to the final stage of deliberation, much less to a vote. Passage of this law was put off until 2001, although the first half of year 2000 was used to consider other legislation. Almost the same situation occurred with a law on traditional nature management. The proposed law was discussed for seven years and enacted only in May 2001.

It should be recalled, however, that Russia undertook perhaps the first legislative attempt directly related to preserving ethnographic landscapes of indigenous peoples as early as the nineteenth century. The action was related to passage in 1822 of the Russian Imperial Law entitled "Regulations for the Administration of Aliens" [that is, of the various non-Russian and non-Slavic ethnic communities]. Former governor-general of Siberia and prominent reformer Mikhail M. Speranskii played a leading role in preparing this legislation (Polnoe sobranie 1830). The "Regulations" secured for the indigenous population—especially the Native peoples of Siberia and the Russian North—the traditional territories of their settlements, their forms of

economic activity and of the local self-government. Thus, the issues of sustainable habitation for indigenous peoples and preservation of their environments were addressed under one law nearly 200 years ago.

The pioneering nature of these "Regulations" of 1822 in establishing a new approach and set of relationships between the government and Russia's indigenous peoples has been acknowledged (Murashko 2000). Unfortunately, this law, a nearly ideal legislation for its time, failed—like many other "good laws" in Russia. In addition to being abused by local authorities, the law was eroded by many subsequent legislative initiatives. It should be noted that the legal system that developed in Soviet Russia a century later, in the 1920s, implicitly expressed many provisions that were surprisingly similar to those of the "Regulations" of 1822.

However, by the mid-1930s, a new government policy for industrial development in Siberia and the Russian Arctic was being developed in the USSR. The new policy embodied the principles of a totalitarian administrative approach, which prioritized economic interests over cultural and human values. For indigenous peoples of the North, the mid-1930s and subsequent periods were times of compulsory cultural and social assimilation. Relocations of indigenous populations from their original places of inhabitation were common in the Russian North (as elsewhere), beginning in the 1940s. The closure of hundreds of small Native settlements and forced relocation of their residents to larger communities was practiced on a mass scale. Relocations were related to development of mineral resources, use of forced labor (the infamous GULAG prison system), military construction, and testing of nuclear and other weapons. Such policies led to disturbance of traditional management practices in many areas and degeneration of the cultural landscape, sometimes even to the extent of depopulation.

During those times, efforts to preserve Native ethnic territories could be accomplished through protection of natural sites, usually in the form of nature conservation areas and reserves. Thus, despite the clearly insufficient attention devoted in the USSR to protecting the cultures and traditions of its many indigenous nations, a network of protected natural territories (called nature reserves, Russian: *zapovedniki*) developed steadily between 1930 and 1960. This network included several reserves established across Russia's northern regions. The development of this network established a practice under which attempts at preserving cultural landscapes of indigenous peoples could be channeled exclusively under national legislation for protection of natural areas. This situation remains unchanged to the present day.

The new federal law "On the Status of Protected Natural Areas" (Federal'nyi zakon 1995), adopted in 1995, is marked by a substantially enhanced level of detail compared to other Soviet legislation. The law also allows certain articles and provisions to be used for preservation of traditional management practices and cultural landscapes of indigenous peoples. However, this law focuses on nature conservation, by definition. Thus, protection of indigenous cultural landscapes can be accomplished somewhat under the auspices of Russia's network of national parks and nature parks. Among the many tasks it assigns to these parks, the legislation includes "the preservation of the natural environment and natural objects, and the restoration of disturbed natural and historical and cultural complexes and objects."

Russia's national parks are more strictly protected than nature parks. The former (national parks) are under the federal management system and are financed through the federal budget. This classification includes territories that have national importance because of their unique natural objects, but also have high historical and esthetic value. The latter (nature parks) are administered by local governments of territories that are constituent members of the Russian Federation and financially supported under the local area budgets. This administrative structure allows, to a certain extent, the inclusion of specific local features in management and economic activity. Like national parks, Russia's nature parks are aimed at preservation of natural landscapes that have high ecological and esthetic value. However, these areas are also intended to be used for recreational, sociocultural, and other purposes. Thus, recreation, tourism, and cultural and educational activities are, to a greater extent, permitted and even encouraged in nature parks.

The provisions of the federal law for both national and nature parks, nevertheless, generally do not address traditional management practices of indigenous peoples. Correspondingly, they are not, in any defined way, legally aimed at protection of areas inhabited by minority indigenous nations and ethnic groups. Such issues had not been addressed in Russian legislation for a long time. It was not until the new law, "On the Fundamentals of Government Regulation of Socioeconomic Development in the North of the Russian Federation," was adopted in June 1996 that the actual term "traditional management practices" (of indigenous people) was established in Russian legislation (Glubokovskii 2000).

Thus, the protection of cultural (and ethnographic) landscapes in Russia urgently requires the adoption of new legislation under which preservation of ethnic lands and cultural diversity is combined with support for and revival of ethnic cultures and indigenous economies. A draft proposal for a new law for protection of historical and cultural territories in Russia was introduced in 1990, first within the framework of the Russian Cultural Fund and, later, by the RRICNH (Proekt statusa 1990). This federal law, "On the Objects of Cultural Heritage (Monuments of History and Culture) of the Peoples of the Russian Federation," was finally adopted in 2002. It could be viewed as the most serious attempt thus far to address the problem. However, this and other similar attempts remain unrealized—to date, no follow-up regultaions and policy acts have been developed in Russia for protection of historical and cultural monuments. Instead, an old 1976 law from the Soviet era is more or less still in place and it in no way addresses the new political and social realities of the country.

In light of this evident legal vacuum at the federal level, individual republics and provinces of the Russian Federation have developed some important documents. In this context, several legislative acts (or proposals) that concern historical and cultural territories, including the homelands of minority indigenous and/or local populations of the Russian North, can be cited. Examples include the Republic of Karelia law, "On Unique Historical and Natural Landscape Territories" of 1992 (Zakon Respubliki Kareliia 1994); a regulation by the legislative assembly of Nizhegorod Province on the historically and culturally designated lands associated with Old Believers (1995); and a number of similar, regional acts. These acts assume the protection of specific historical territories, but simultaneously advocate measures for preservation of significant ethnographic (cultural) landscape characteristics of the locale.

Another example is a regulation enacted by the Head of the Administration of Vladimir Province in Central Russia (as of April 1999) on the establishment of a particular type of protected territories, called "historical-landscape complexes." The first such historical-landscape complex was established around the famous Church of the Intercession at Nerl. The landscape, including the church, built in the twelfth century, was named "Bogolyubovo Meadow." To a certain extent, these local legislative decisions are prototypes of future federal actions that are necessary to preserve ethnographic landscapes.

Probably the most far-reaching effort in such local legislation has been undertaken in the recent draft law "On Traditional (Native) Subsistence Management Areas" in Khanty-Mansi Autonomous Area (*Okrug)* in Western Siberia (Bogoslovskaia 2000). This draft law attempts to combine the present-day system of administrative division of the Russian Federation (with three levels: province, area, and district) and the principles of territorial self-government and land and resource management by the indigenous communities.

The adoption of these and other local legislative documents, as well as the growing general awareness of the need to preserve ethnographic landscapes in Russia as a special category of heritage, were remarkable events of the 1990s. These events have helped create conditions that eventually will advance the development of similar legislation at the federal level.

The Current System of Cultural and Natural Landscape Protection: Structure and Resources

It is clear that no legislative regulations concerning preservation of ethnographic landscapes are in place, and, essentially, that no Russian government agency considers these issues directly within its jurisdiction. Under existing legal practice, the best form of protection that ethnographic landscapes may receive in today's Russia exists under nature preservation legislation. The current Russian federal law of 1995, "On the Status of Specially Protected Natural Areas," identifies seven types of protected territories:

—Natural monuments

—Nature conservation areas

—Federal nature reserves

—National parks

—Nature parks

—Dendrological parks and botanical gardens

—Medical health-improvement sites and resorts

In terms of overall size, three of these types of protected territories are most significant: federal nature reserves, national parks, and nature parks. These designated types differ in legal status and functions.

The national system of government-owned conservation areas, called "federal nature reserves" (*zapovedniki*) is rightfully considered the pride of Russia's preservation policy. The first such reserves were established as examples of "undisturbed natural territories" in 1916. As of the beginning of 2000, they comprise an overall area of more than thirty-three million hectares (81.5 million acres), with a network of ninety-nine federal nature reserves under government control.

These conservation areas are strictly protected, and

access is rigidly restricted. Of Russian nature reserves, twenty-two have international status as biosphere reserves and are certified accordingly. There are more than thirty federal nature reserves in the various northern areas of Russia, in both European and Siberian sectors (Gosudarstvennyi doklad 2000). The establishment of nature reserves has led to successful preservation of large territories of "undisturbed" (rather, lightly disturbed) natural environment. In practice, however, their functions and practical activities have little connection with the preservation of ethnographic landscapes.

Two types of protected areas in Russia have the greatest connection to the preservation of ethnographic landscapes: national parks and nature parks.

National Parks

National parks are federally protected areas that include natural complexes and objects of particular ecological, historical, or esthetic value and are intended for environmental preservation, educational, scientific, or cultural purposes and for regulated tourism. Unlike nature reserves, Russia's national park system is a relatively recent phenomenon. The first national parks were established in 1983; by 2000, there were thirty-five. A large number of these were created in the 1990s under newly promulgated post-Soviet social policy. National parks were intended to occupy a different niche from that occupied by government-owned nature reserves and to combine the tasks of nature preservation and cultural heritage protection.

Today, the total combined area of national parks in Russia is nearly seven million hectares, approximately 0.4 percent of the Russian Federation total. Some 4,000 people are employed in the park system. Four national parks have been created in the northern regions of the Russian Federation, all in the European section (Gosudarstvennyi doklad 2000). Until 2000, nearly all national parks were under the control of the Federal Forestry Service of Russia. (Only one national park is under the jurisdiction of the Moscow City government). In 2000, the Federal Forestry Service ceased to exist as a

separate governmental agency, and it now functions as a subdivision of the Ministry of Natural Resources of the Russian Federation. Thus, virtually all protected natural territories of federal significance appear to be concentrated under the control of the Ministry of Natural Resources.

Many Russian national parks, particularly those created during the 1990s, have a clearly recognized ethnographic component and therefore may be viewed as historical or present-day ethnographic landscapes. A good example is Alankhay Park in Aginsk-Buryat Autonomous Area (near Lake Baikal). Established in 1999, this is one of the most recent national parks. The park's greatest point of interest is Alankhay Mountain and its ridges. The park territory is distinguished by richly diverse animal and plant species, hot springs, and various mineral objects related to the geological history of the region. In addition, for hundreds of years, the area has been a place of worship for the indigenous population, the Buryat. The Alankhay Buddhist religious complex, the sixth most important holy place for Buddhists around the world, is located there.

Russia's national parks have not yet become venues for implementing an active policy for preserving ethnographic landscapes. During their former subordination to the Federal Forestry Service, basic problems related to their cultural policies remained virtually unresolved. Many proposals aimed at preservation of cultural and ethnographic heritage under park system jurisdiction never materialized.

Nature Parks

Nature parks have almost the same status as national parks, but have greater possibilities for recreational and economic activities, as well as educational and cultural programs. Commonly, a local department or committee on natural resource management that is part of the provincial or local republic government manages nature parks. By 2000, only thirty such parks had been established (more than half of them in Russia's northern regions), with a combined total area of more than

29/ Ostyak (Khanty) mother and daughter, at their family camp, Salym River, Sivokhrebski Yourts, 1911.

30/ Visiting the Kayukov Family Camp, Salym River, Punsi Yourts, 1999.

twelve million hectares (29.7 million acres). The total number of nature parks seems unduly small, especially because creation of a nature park does not require a federal decision and may be accomplished at a local level (Gosudarstvennyi doklad 2000).

Russia's network of nature parks is still in its initial, formative stage. These parks include some very small, protected areas in cities (for example, some nature parks are located within the City of Moscow), as well as huge territories with areas greater than one million hectares (2.47 million acres) (located mainly in Siberia and the Russian North). Some nature parks have very little connection with ethnographic landscapes; others are directly connected with preservation of areas that have specific cultural and ethnographic value to local populations. The latter include Numto Lake and Konda Lakes nature parks in Khanty-Mansi Autonomous Area. These parks are located in the core homeland areas of the Khanty and Nenets indigenous people. Another ex-

ample, Beringia Nature Park in Chukchi Autonomous Area in the Bering Strait region, even includes the designation "nature-ethnic" in its name, to underscore both its natural and cultural preservation functions.

It is obvious that locally managed nature parks may eventually become one of the primary organizational forms for preserving ethnographic landscapes, particularly across Russia's vast northern areas. However, the current subordination of nature parks to local environmental protection agencies remains one of the obstacles to fulfilling these tasks [see Fedorova, this volume]. The shortage of funding and trained personnel is a permanent problem, and in many regions, the preservation of cultural heritage cannot be addressed directly under the dominant environment protection agenda.

Museum-Conservation Areas

Another type of protected territory that may be instrumental in preserving Russia's ethnographic landscapes is the museum-conservation area (Russian: *Muzei-zapovednik*). Museum-conservation areas are officially listed as "cultural institutions" and are administered by the Ministry of Culture of the Russian Federation. A museum-conservation area differs from a typical museum by virtue of the close connection of the given territory with its historical and memorial legacy or its specific geographic location. Examples of museum-conservation areas are historical battlefields, memorial country estates associated with prominent public figures and cultural celebrities, and the most outstanding architectural complexes or historical cities and settlements.

By 2000 in Russia, there were eighty-eight such museum-conservation areas, managed directly by the Federal Ministry of Culture or by regional cultural agencies and departments of provincial and republic governments in the Russian Federation [see the list of major Russian museum-conservation areas in Vergunov et al. 2000:170–4]. Many museum-conservation areas are rather small. They are often limited to the territory occupied by a historical or architectural monument, a country estate, or a park complex. However, some comprise significant tracts of land. For example, Solovetskii Museum-Conservation Area, on Solovetskii Archipelago in the White Sea, occupies 106,000 hectares (261,820 acres). The existence of a large territory under historical preservation is evidence of both the environmental-protection significance of museum-conservation areas and their ability to protect traditional ethnographic landscapes within their boundaries.

At present, approximately thirty (of eighty-eight) museum-conservation areas may be considered focused somewhat on preservation of cultural or historical landscapes. For some, preserving the cultural landscape is their essential function and the main purpose of their creation. Examples include the site near Moscow where the historic Battle of Borodino was fought in 1812, during the Napoleonic invasion;[3] Mikhailovskoe Museum-Conservation Area, associated with the family estate (and adjacent) of Alexander Pushkin, Russia's most famous poet; and Yasnaya Polyana Museum-Conserva-

tion Area, Leo Tolstoy's family estate. Under a recent proposal advocating the establishment of the Kulikovo Pole Museum-Conservation Area (the site of a historic battle in 1380), the primary objective of activities is the preservation of the historical landscape. (Muzei-zapovednik "Kulikovo pole" 1999).

Most museum-conservation areas are in the center of European Russia, and their activities are related primarily to preserving the legacies of certain historical events and/or prominent personalities. Only a small number of such areas, like the Solovetskii and Kizhi Museum-Conservation Areas, are concerned with preservation of ethnographic landscapes. Both Solovetskii and Kizhi are in northern European Russia (Arkhangelsk Province and the Republic of Karelia, respectively) and thus are possible examples of Russian policies for protecting northern ethnographic landscapes. Neither area, however, has any indigenous/minority population or any objects related to indigenous cultural heritage.

This brief review of major types of protected areas illustrates that preservation of ethnographic landscapes in Russia cannot be resolved under current protective legislation or existing organizational structures. The lack of policy coordination between environmental protection agencies and cultural agencies, both at federal and local levels, further aggravates the situation. A fundamental breakthrough could be achieved by the adoption of new federal legislation that would be focused on specific issues of cultural and ethnographic landscape preservation and management. Until such legislation is developed and adopted, the best venue for sufficiently effective work to preserve individual ethnographic landscapes would be under the status of nature parks. However, such landscapes must be managed (or co-managed) under a joint policy and in close cooperation between and among environmental protection and cultural heritage agencies, and not exclusively under nature conservation management (the most common practice today).

31/ Traditional Khanty storage structures at Aidar Yourts, Salym River, 1911.

32/ Khanty storage structures (ambars) at Punsi Yourts, Salym River, 1999.

Ethnographic Landscapes Protection Programs in the Russian North

Within the specific focus of his review, regional projects for protection of cultural (ethnographic) landscapes in regions of the Russian North are of particular interest. The first pioneering efforts to create such protected territories for northern ethnographic landscapes were launched in the late 1980s and early 1990s. In 1989, a proposal was introduced in Primorskii Krai in the Russian Far East to establish a system of protected natural areas under a new program of general ecological management/conservation. The proposal may be considered a crucial step for many subsequent efforts to follow.

The proposal was developed by a group of natural scientists from the Biology and Soil Institute of the Far East Branch of the then-USSR Academy of Sciences in Vladivostok (Ler and Lebedev 1989). Native ethnographer Yevdokiia A. Gaer assisted environmental specialist L. Ivashchenko, the primary author of the proposal and the leader of a team of ecologists.[4] In addition to advancing pure environmental recommendations urging preservation of natural monuments and valuable natural landscapes of the study area, the proposal expressed great concern about the status of the indigenous population.

For the first time in Russian practice, a goal was set to create a system of protected ethnic territories, with a special management policy for areas of traditional subsistence activities of indigenous people (Ler and Lebedev 1989:33–5). The proposal also advocated strong support for indigenous people of Primorskii Krai, preservation of the environment in their traditional areas of residence, and (among other social and economic measures) restoration of hunting and fishing resources in their traditional subsistence areas. For the latter goal, four zones of primary indigenous subsistence use were identified in the region. The zones consisted of taiga (mountain boreal forest) landscapes and several sections of the marine coastal zone. The overall protected area was intended to be about 50,000 square kilometers (20,000 square miles), or nearly thirty percent of Primorskii Krai.

Unfortunately, those recommendations were not implemented, and no territories for priority subsistence use by local Native people were established—either in terms of the originally designated status (as Native ethnic territories) or of the size of the area to be set aside for protection. Some ideas from this 1989 proposal were considered separately under a later environmental conservation plan adopted by the regional government in the 1990s.

In approximately the same year (1989 or 1990), another Russian biologist, Lyudmila S. Bogoslovskaya (Bogoslovskaia) from the Moscow-based Severtsev Institute of Ecology, advanced a similar proposal. It argued for the establishment of a specially designated, ethnic-ecological territory for the Native people of Chukotka, in the Bering Strait area. This huge, protected natural area, to be named Beringia Park (*Beringiia*), would be created on the Chukchi Peninsula. According to the initial outline, this territory would be designated under international biosphere reserve or national park status and would span both sides of the Bering Strait, one in Chukotka, Russia and the other in Alaska, on the U.S. side (Bogoslovskaia 1990; International Park 1989).

The key purpose in creating a park on both sides of the Bering Strait was to preserve a contiguous ethnic territory (including the land and the coastal marine area) and a traditional resource management system based on sea-mammal hunting and fishing. The proposal strongly advocated revival of the traditional settlement system and repopulation of several abandoned camps and villages of the Chukchi and Yupik (Asiatic Eskimo) indigenous people. The proposal also addressed the issue of restoring family and clan contacts among indigenous residents of the two countries. Such contacts had existed for centuries, until they were interrupted in the 1940s [they remained disconnected between 1948 and 1988], because of the Cold War isolationist policy of the Soviet government.

Bogoslovskaya's proposal, which was worked out by a team of experts in the early 1990s, was one of the soundest attempts formulated for preserving north-ern ethnographic landscapes of indigenous people. Unfortunately, the proposal could not be implemented in those years, because of the lack of appropriate legislation.

Only after the 1995 adoption of the new federal law, "On the Status of Protected Natural Areas," was Beringia Nature-Ethnic Park established in the Chukchi Autonomous Area. This new park, however, is under local, not federal, jurisdiction—unlike the adjacent area across the Bering Strait in the U.S., which is designated as a federal preserve named Bering Land Bridge National Preserve. Since the new, Russian Beringia Nature-Ethnic Park is under the management of local environmental protection agencies of the Chukchi Autonomous Area, few if any ideas from the original 1989 proposal have been implemented there. However, many ideas advanced during the development of the park were used later in similar proposals in other regions of the country and in the formulation of new legislative initiatives.

In the mid-1990s, several new proposals for protection of Native ethnic (ethnographic) territories were developed in the Khanty-Mansi Autonomous Area [see Wiget and Balalaeva, this volume]. The development of new proposals was a by-product of the intensive oil and gas explorations in the area that posed a real threat to the region's natural environment and to the traditional habitation of the Khanty and Mansi indigenous people.[5] The oil- and gas-rich Khanty-Mansi Autonomous Area owns the bulk of Russia's energy resources; it is one of five regions of the country with the largest local budgets. Because of this new source of local funding, the area government is capable of undertaking a large number of its own environmental and cultural protection initiatives.

During the 1990s, the Khanty-Mansi local government supported (albeit rather reluctantly) two new trends in environmental protection policy:

—Gradual expansion of the network of protected natural areas;

33/ Khanty reindeer herders often keep their reindeer in smoky log cabins to protect it from mosquitoes in summer time, such as this one at Salym River, 1999.

—Creation of a system of Native "clan- and community-owned lands" that belong to indigenous inhabitants (Merkushina and Novikov 1998).[6]

The total area occupied by such clan and community lands of indigenous people is estimated to be nearly thirty percent of Khanty-Mansi's overall territory. These lands, as a rule, are territories of priority subsistence use and traditional resource management.

The legal status of such Native-used lands is uncertain, if not precarious. At this writing, no law regarding the ownership of Native lands has been adopted by the local legislative body, the Regional Duma. Two draft versions of such a law are under consideration, and both have been in legislative discussion for a long time. In one version, Native lands are considered under land-law acts only. In the second version (introduced by a team chaired by Lyudmila Bogoslovskaya, now with the Russian Institute of Cultural and Natural Heritage), clan and community lands are considered portions of integral ecosystems, together with traditionally used natural resources. These lands are also regarded as the basis for the social, cultural, and economic well-being of indigenous people who carry on traditional subsistence economy and ways of life

(Obsuzhdenie kontseptsii 1999). In this view, clan and community lands in the Khanty-Mansi Autonomous Area may be considered (to a certain extent) legally established and legislatively approved Native ethnographic landscapes.

In addition, three nature parks were established in 1998 in the Khanty-Mansi Autonomous Area. Of those, Numto Lake Park and Konda Lakes Park are located in traditional subsistence areas of the Khanty and Nenets indigenous people. Those two nature parks may be considered closely associated with ethnographic territories of local Native groups (communities). However, the actual preservation regime in both parks is based almost exclusively on protection of the natural environment; it bears little relevance to the issues of culture and social policy regarding indigenous residents.

A more recent initiative is dedicated to the creation of a new type of protected natural and cultural territory in the Khanty-Mansi Autonomous Area. The area under discussion is in the Bolshoy Salym River basin. Under this new initiative, an attempt was made to combine environmental protection policies with efforts to preserve the traditional management practices and cultural heritage of indigenous people (Figs. 33–

35). The name of the new protected area, Punsi, is taken from the name of a nearby lake and Native settlement; in the local Khanty dialect, the word means "duck down." The size of the area to be designated for protection is about 6,500 square kilometers (2,600 square miles).

Proposals to establish a protected natural area in the Bolshoy Salym River basin were advanced more than ten years ago (in the late 1980s) by wetlands biologists. The area considered is a combination of relatively undisturbed natural landscapes between the Salym and Yugan River valleys that are typical for a mid-taiga (boreal forest) zone. Across Western Siberia, most of these landscapes have been damaged irreparably during the last few decades by the virtually unchecked advance of Russia's oil-and-gas industries. The proposals of the 1980s argued for the creation of a protected natural territory (as a natural conservation area) to preserve undisturbed boreal wetland ecosystems that had unique value. In the original blueprint, the boundaries of the protected areas were to be drawn along the lines of specific river basins. This practice would apportion not only the large section of wetlands, but also the rivers and streams that feed them, as a key condition to the integrated protection of the characteristic boreal forest bog ecotone.

The initial proposal, however, by no means considered this region significant in terms of its unique ethnographic value. Largely unbeknownst to wetland biologists, the traditional boreal forest subsistence economy of the indigenous Khanty people has been fully preserved in this area. About ten traditional family camps and settlements are still used actively (Figs. 31, 32). The local Khanty families have preserved virtually all knowledge and skills related to their traditional way of life, subsistence technologies, and crafts (Salymskii krai 2000). The area also constitutes a unique habitat of Western Siberia's southernmost population of domestic reindeer. Because of these factors, the Salym (and Yugan) River basin offers fertile ground for any attempts to revive the traditional form of indigenous

economic activity, taiga reindeer herding (Fig. 33).[7]

The area also supports sustainable populations of many fur-bearing and game animals, including moose, river otter, and sable, which are critical for the survival of traditional ways of life. Here, a traditional Khanty system of landscape use remains intact through the variety of settlement patterns, and living and utility structures—including family and storage cabins, hunting lodges, fishing cabins and ponds, enclosures for domestic reindeer, traps set for wood grouse (Fig. 34), fishponds, and so on. Each family plot is filled with a system of paths that pass along solid ridge beds and over boggy areas; wood planks support many paths (Fig. 35).[8]

The territory under discussion also has great archaeological value. More than 200 historical sites have been identified there, including old settlements, abandoned ancient sites, Native graveyards, and sacred sites of various ages. This concentration of historical sites and monuments is very high for any given area within the boreal forest zone; thus, the Salym River basin may legitimately be called one of the core areas for the history of the Khanty nation. A large number of the documented archaeological monuments in the area are associated with ancestors of the modern-day Khanty (from the Bronze and Early Iron Ages). Those ancient settlements and sacred sites are often the basis of Khanty myths and legends, many of which can be linked with actual historical events.

The area thus preserves a highly unique concentration of historical and cultural monuments, a distinctive Native local group that has been using the region for several generations, and a highly developed system of nature management built of clan, family, and community lands. This northern ethnographic landscape is exceptional in its naturalness and state of preservation. The combination of unique natural environment and unprecedented sociocultural richness is the primary reason this region should be assigned the status of a protected natural and cultural area. Under existing Russian legislation, and considering

34/ The author explores a Khanty wood grouse trap near Punsi Yourts, Salym River, 1999.

local economic realities, the best way to accomplish this designation may be as a nature park, to be established, financed, and administered by the area government.

Therefore, unlike earlier initiatives, the new proposals for the creation of Punsi Nature Park advocate establishing a specific nature-ethnographic complex (ethnographic landscape) as the primary objective (see Bolota i liudi 2000; Shul'gin 2003:38). This objective must be achieved by protecting the unique natural resources of the area and preserving the rich cultural heritage of the local indigenous people. Several other types of activities should be encouraged as well—for example, scientific research, museum work, and regulated tourism.

The new nature park may also offer a highly valuable contribution to raising the general educational potential of the region. Several special classes and programs that supplement traditional school and college courses can be developed and conducted in the park.

The first of these, of course, should be ecological education, boreal forest ecosystem studies, and study of the local Khanty lore. A summer educational camp for local students could be organized on the park's territory, with courses in ecology and ethnography, as well as field archaeology, as the basic curriculum. Through cooperation with local schools and visiting scientists, the nature park will be able to train its own staff of rangers and workers, with a new sense of dedication toward the ecological and cultural tasks needed to revive their native land.

Organized tourism may also turn out to be an important supplement to activities of the future park. Rather than promoting mass flow of tourists to the area, the new proposals suggest a specialized program of tours for a small number of researchers and people who are interested in studying the unique natural environment or cultures and languages of the indigenous residents, the Khanty. A nature park, with its professional staff, will be able to accommodate these specific requirements and (considering the low numbers of potential visitors) service the participants by using either local Khanty buildings or modern models of traditional dwellings. Such a specialized style of tourism could become an important source of income for the nature park.

Utilizing the richness of potential educational and tourism experiences, of course, would be one of the primary goals of the future park's activities, which suggests the need to preserve the ethnic distinctiveness of its indigenous residents, the Salym River Khanty. This task should be achieved through support for, and even reintroduction of, local forms of nature management such as boreal forest reindeer herding, fishing, moose and bird hunting, and collection of local plants, mushrooms, and berries. In this way, the set of traditional nature management practices and crafts techniques will be introduced as the components of the unique cultural heritage of the area. As a related benefit, a new nature park under such a pioneer design can offer employment opportunities for several local residents; it can also develop economically viable formats for preserving and marketing local products such as mushrooms, berries, and fish.

These and many other ideas about the status and structure of the future park were first addressed in a more general manner at an international seminar on "Wetlands and Archaeology" (1988). A more detailed proposal for a Punsi Natural and Ethnographic Area was prepared nearly ten years later by a team of experts from the RRICNH, in cooperation with other researchers from Nefteyugansk, Moscow, Ekaterinburg, and St. Petersburg (Bolota i liudi 2000). At present, the government of the Khanty-Mansi Autonomous Area is preparing a package of legislative documents for the creation of Punsi Nature Park. It is presumed that developing the park's rather complex functional structure will be a long process. Eventually, the park is to become not only the key agency for local environmental protection, but also a special organization with a strong humanitarian orientation and important social functions in the heavily industrialized Nefteyugansk Region.

The forthcoming creation of Punsi Nature Park as a protected natural and cultural area in Western Siberia is one of a few attempts to jointly preserve natural and ethnographic landscapes across Russia. However, this project may provide a powerful impetus for similar initiatives in other regions. It also may continue to be recognized as an important step in cultural preservation for Russia's indigenous people. Unlike the efforts of the 1980s and even the early 1990s, this project is no longer an isolated venture of a few concerned environmentalists. Active efforts are under way in the Khanty-Mansi and Yamal-Nenets Autonomous Areas within the scope of the newly created Numto Lake and Konda Lakes Nature Parks. New programs have been launched recently in both Khanty-Mansi and Yamal-Nenets areas to document and protect the sacred sites of local indigenous people (Balalaeva 1999; Kharyuchi, this volume). An ambitious program in documentation of historical and sacred sites is being conducted on Vaygach Island off the Russian Arctic coast under the leadership of Peter V. Boiarskii (Boiarskii 1998, 2000).

The staff of Kenozersk National Park is undertaking one of the best-organized efforts in the restoration of traditional northern landscape. This park is in Arkhangelsk Province, in the northern section of European Russia, not far from the ancient Russian city of Kargopol. The associated program for restoring local landscapes is focused on the preservation of traditional land use and management practices of the resident Russian population. The economy is primarily rural, with traditions of maintaining plowlands or arable lands, hayfields, and pastures, as well as fishing grounds. Efforts by Kenozersk National Park include restoration of old roads and residential, agricultural, and religious structures (wooden chapels and crosses). In fact, the park's primary goal is restoration of the traditional ethnographic landscape of Northern Russia. This goal is a significant challenge for a local heritage program, because of recent, drastic depopulation of the territory and a corresponding decrease in the number of remaining rural settlements.

35/ A wooden path (putik) *through the marshes to the family reindeer pastures and fishing sites, Salym River, 1999.*

In recent years, the influential All-Russian Society for Protection of Nature (ARSPN), Russia's oldest non-governmental public association of environmentalists and natural scientists, has similarly been changing its focus. Moving beyond its traditional initiatives for exclusive protection of valuable natural areas and monuments, ARSPN argued recently for the establishment of a network of traditional nature-management areas. The proposed list includes some thirty-four areas that represent specific ethno-ecological zones—natural habitats of compact residences of indigenous peoples and long-time Russian settlers. The areas nominated by ARSPN for special protection are located not only in Siberia and the North, but also in the Northern Caucasus (see Maksakovskii and Nikolaev 1997).

Conclusion

The idea of identifying and protecting ethnographic landscapes—as a key component in preserving the rich-

ness of cultural heritage of Russia—has been under discussion by the Russian scientific community for more than ten years. Russian legislative practices, however, are lagging severely in meeting the practical needs that are essential to build viable mechanisms for protection of the country's unique cultural and natural heritage. Until very recently, the lack of appropriate legislation significantly retarded the implementation of even the best ideas and most advanced local projects. Nevertheless, in recent years, several proposals to protect ethnographic landscapes have been at least partially implemented by taking advantage of provisions in some new Russian laws on the protection of natural areas.

Such a policy is being pursued most actively in the Russian North, within the scope of the most recent efforts (after 1990 and even after 1995) for the creation of new nature and national parks. Many dedicated Russian heritage and environmental scholars are conducting corresponding, vigorous research. The visible, practical results of all these efforts have facilitated several new legislative proposals, on both federal and regional levels, that eventually would help protect ethnographic landscapes, in conjunction with protection of the richness of nature in the Russian Federation.

Acknowledgments

Since the late 1980s, the author has participated in many efforts to preserve cultural, historical, and natural heritage in Russia. This long experience testifies to the impossibility of achieving any kind of success without the close cooperation of many specialists, in social and environmental sciences alike. This article is a definite reflection of such continuous cooperation. The author would like to express special gratitude to professor Iurii (Yuri) A. Vedenin, who made the most helpful contributions as a partner in long-term discussions of the concept of cultural landscape; to Lyudmila S. Bogoslovskaya, for help in the field of traditional management practices and contemporary legislative issues; to N.B. Maksakovskii, for many consultations regarding the protection of natural heritage; to Igor Krupnik, for advancing the idea of this survey article and offering many valuable comments; and to G.P. Vizgalov, who has been the most active advocate for the creation of Punsi Nature Park, and who invited the author to participate in this exciting project. Georgene Sink translated this paper and Igor Krupnik kindly checked the translation against its Russian original.

Notes

1. As of 1999, the total number of cultural monuments under the Register of Protected Cultural Monuments of the Russian Federation was more than 86,000. Of those, 24,192 were listed as historical monuments, 14,974 as archaeological monuments, 22,500 as architectural and urban monuments, and 2,357 as objects of monumental art (Vergunov et al. 2000:163).

2. A very important new trend in heritage research and preservation in the 1980s was the identification and revival of historical techniques and traditional forms of nature management (Danilova and Sokolov 1998). Research into nature management, as a rule, began to be applied in the study of the cultural development of northern indigenous peoples or other minority groups of Russia (Raiony prozhivaniia 1991; Klokov 1997; Zaitseva 1997). Of course, this field of cultural heritage cannot be associated directly with historical and cultural monuments, under their present definition. In many cases, it has not even taken material form as any type of object that could be preserved in museum collections or directly at the locality. However, the sociocultural role of such elements of ethnic heritage is undisputed. In some areas of Russia, especially in its northern and eastern sections, these elements play leading roles.

3. This bloody battle has been memorialized in numerous works of art, including Leo N. Tolstoy's *War and Peace* and Peter I. Tchaikovkii's *1812* Overture, and discussed today on numerous sites on the World Wide Web.

4. In the same year, 1989, Gaer was elected deputy of the Supreme Soviet (federal legislature) of the USSR from the huge Far Eastern legislative district. Gaer is a Native political activist and prominent figure in the indigenous rights movement of Native people of the nearby Amur River region.

5. The development of new proposals probably was connected even more closely with the creation of several local administrative agencies after 1992. Locally tax-based budgets and policies offered increased independence to these agencies and enabled them to address many regional issues.

6. Under present-day Russian legislation, indigenous people "lease" or "use" these lands.

7. Once a widespread practice across the boreal forest zone, reindeer herding today has virtually become a lost art in most other regions of Siberia.

8. On the whole, the system of family land-use in the Salym River basin is very close to the one documented by Andrew Wiget for the nearby Yugan River Khanty families (Wiget 1999; see also Wiget and Balalaeva, this volume).

References

Balalaeva, Olga E.
1999   Sviashchennye mesta khantov Srednei i Nizhnei Obi (Sacred sites of the Khanty of the Middle and Lower Ob River). In *Ocherki istorii traditsionnogo zemlepol'zovaniia khantov (materialy k atlasu)*, A. Wiget, ed., pp. 139–156. Ekaterinburg: Tezis Press.

Bogoslovskaia, Lyudmila S.

1990   Mezhdunarodnyi park v Beringii. Kommentarii spetsialista (International park in the Beringia area: A specialist's commentary). *Poliarnik* August:3.

Bogoslovskaia, Lyudmila S., ed.

2000   *Problemy traditsionnogo prirodopol'zovaniia. Sever, Sibir' i Dal'nii Vostok Rossiiskoi Federatsii* (Problems of traditional nature management: The North, Siberia, and Far East of the Russian Federation). Moscow: Izdanie Gosudarstvennoi Dumy.

Boiarskii, Petr V., ed.

2000   *Ostrov Vaygach. Kul'turnoe i prirodnoe nasledie. Pamiatniki istorii i osvoeniia Arktiki* 1 (Vaygach Island: Cultural and natural heritage—monuments of history and of the Arctic explorations). Moscow: Institut Naslediia.

Bolota i liudi

2000   *Bolota i liudi: materialy mezhdunarodnogo seminara "Bolota i arkheologiia* (Wetlands and people: Proceedings from the international seminar "Wetlands and Archaeology"). Moscow: Institut Naslediia.

Bromlei, Iulian V.

1981   *Sovremennye problemy ethnografii: ocherki teorii i istorii* (Current Issues in ethnography: Essays in theory and history). Moscow: Nauka Publishers.

Danilova L.V., and A.K. Sokolov, ed.

1998   *Traditsionnyi opyt prirodopol'zovaniia v Rosii* (Traditional experience in nature management in Russia). Moscow: Nauka Publishers.

Federal'nyi zakon

1995   *Federal'nyi zakon ot 14-go marta 1995 no. 33-F3 "Ob osobo okhraniaemykh prirodnykh territoriiakh"* (Federal law of March 14, 1995, No. 33-F3, "On the Status of Protected Natural Areas"). *Sobranie zakonodatel'stva Rossiiskoi Federatsii* 12.

Glubokovskii, Mikhail K.

2000   Problemy traditisionnogo prirodopol'zovaniia v Rossii [Issues in traditional nature management in Russia]. In *Problemy traditsionnogo prirodopol'zovaniia. Sever, Sibir' i Dal'nii Vostok Rossiiskoi Federatsii*, L.S. Bogoslovskaia, ed., pp.4–6. Moscow: Izdanie Gosudarstvennoi Dumy.

Gosudarstvennyi doklad

2000   *Gosudarstvennyi doklad "O sostoianii okruzhayushchei prirodnoi sredy Rossiiskoi Federatsii v 1999 godu"* (Government report "On the condition of the natural environment in the Russian Federation in 1999"). Moscow: State Center for Ecological Programs.

International Park Program

1989   *International Park Program "Beringian Heritage". Reconnaissance Study.* U.S. National Park Service. Denver: Denver Service Center.

Isachenko, Alexandr G.

1965   *Osnovy landshaftovedeniia i fiziko-geograficheskoe raionirovanie* (Basic study of landscapes and physico-geographical zoning). Moscow: Nauka.

Istoricheskii gorod

1997   *Istoricheskii gorod Yalutorovsk: materially k programme sokhraneniia i ispol'zovaniia istoriko-kul'turnogo naslediia goroda i ego okruzheniia* (The historical city of Yalutorovsk: Materials and program for preserving and utilizing the historical and cultural and natural heritage of the city and its surroundings). Pavel M. Shul'gin, ed. Moscow: Institut Naslediia.

Kaganskii, Vladimir L., and Boris B. Rodoman

1995   *Landshaft i kul'tura* (Landscape and culture). *Nauki o kul'ture: itogi i perspectivy. Informatsionno-analiticheskii sbornik* 3. Moscow: Russian State Library.

Kalutskov, Vladimir N.

2000   *Osnovy kul'turnogo landshaftovedeniia* (Fundamentals of cultural landscape studies]. Moscow: Moscow State University.

Kalutskov, Vladimir N., Tatiana M. Krasovskaia, V.V. Valebnyi, A.A. Ivanova, Vladimir L. Kaganskii,   and Iuri. G. Simonov

1998   *Kul'turnyi landshaft: voprosy teorii i metodologii* (The cultural landscape: theoretical and methodological issues). Moscow and Smolensk: Smolensk State University.

Klokov, Konstantin B.

1997   Traditsionnoe prirodopol'zovanie narodov Severa: kontseptsiia sokhraneniia i razvitiia (Traditional nature management system of northern peoples: concept for preservation and development). *Etnogeograficheskie i etnoekologicheskie issledovaniia* 5. St. Petersburg: St. Petersburg State University, Institute of Geography.

Krupnik, Igor I.

1989   *Arkticheskaia etnoekologiia. Modeli traditsionnogo prirodopol'zovaniia morskikh okhotnikov i olenevodov Severnoi Evrazii* (Arctic ethno-ecology: models of traditional nature management by maritime hunters and reindeer-herders in Northern Eurasia). Moscow: Nauka. Revised English translation (1993): *Arctic Adaptations. Whalers and Reindeer Herders of Northern Eurasia.* Hanover and London: University Press of New England.

Kul'turnyi landshaft

1998   *Kul'turnyi landshaft Russkogo Severa* (Cultural landscape of the Russian North). Moscow: FBMK Publishers.

Likhachev, Dmitrii S.

1980   Ekologiia kul'tury (Ecology of culture). *Pamiatniki otechestva* 2:10-16. Moscow.

2000   Izbrannoe o kul'turnom i prirodnom nasledii (Selected essays on cultural and natural heritage). In *Ekologiia kul'tury: Al'manakh Instituta Naslediia "Territoriia"*, Iu. L. Mazurov, comp., pp. 11-24. Moscow: Institut Naslediia.

Ler, P.A., and B.I. Lebedev, ed.

1989   *Sistema okhraniaemykh prirodnykh territorii v ekologicheskoi programme Primorskogo kraia* (System of the nature conservation areas under the ecological program of the maritime region). Vladivostok: Far Eastern Branch of the Academy of Sciences.

Litovka, Oleg P., ed.

1989   *Ekologiia-narodonaseleniie-rasseleniie: teoriia i praktika* (Ecology, population, settlement: theory and practice). Leningrad: Geographical Society.

Maksakovskii, Nikolai V.

2000   Ob'ekty vsemirnogo naslediia v Rossii (Monuments of world heritage in Russia). In *Ekologiia kul'tury. Al'manakh Instituta Naslediia "Territoriia"*, Iu. L. Mazurov, comp., pp. 44–56. Moscow: Institut Naslediia.

Maksakovskii, Nikolai V., and S.V. Nikolaev, ed.

1997   *Osobo tsennye territorii prirodnogo i prirodno-istoriko-kul'turnogo naslediia narodov Rossiiskoi Federatsii* (Particularly valuable areas of natural and natural-historical-cultural heritage of the peoples of the Russian Federation). Moscow: Independent International University of Ecology and Political Science Publishers.

Merkushina, T., and V. Novikov

1998   Zapovednykh territorii dolzhno byt' bol'she (There should be more conservation areas). *Yugra: dela i liudi* 2:27–31.

Mil'kov, Fedor N.

1973   *Chelovek i landshafty* (Man and landscapes). Moscow: Mysl' Publishers.

1978   *Rukotvornye landshafty* (Artificial landscapes). Moscow: Mysl' Publishers. Muzei-zapovedniki

Muzei-zapovednik "Kulikovo Pole."

1999   *Muzei-zapovednik "Kulikovo Pole:" kontseptsiia razvitiia* ("Kulikovo Battlefield" museum-conservation area. Development concept). Moscow: Institut Naslediia.

Murashko, Olga A.

2000   Korennye narody Severa Rossii i problemy sokhraneniia i razvitiia traditsionnogo prirodopol'zovaniia (Indigenous people of the Russian North and issues of preserving and developing traditional nature management systems). In *Problemy traditsionnogo prirodopol'zovaniia. Sever, Sibir' i Dal'nii Vostok Rossiiskoi Federatsii*, L.S. Bogoslovskaia, ed., pp. 21–31. Moscow: Izdanie Gosudarstvennoi Dumy.

Obsuzhdeniie

1999   Obsuzhdeniie kontseptsii i proektov zakonov (Discussion of law blueprints and concepts). *Zhivaia Arktika* 1:16–27. Moscow.

Polnoe sobraniie

1830   *Polnoe sobranie zakonov Rossiiskoi imperii* (Complete collection of laws of the Russian Empire). Vol. XXXVIII. St. Petersburg.

Proekt statusa

1990   Proekt statusa unikal'noi istoricheskoi territorii (Project status of an unique historical territory). In *Sbornik materialov 1 Vsesoiuznoi konferentsii po sokhraneniiu i razvitiiu unikal'nykh istoricheskikh territorii*, V. I. Azar, Yu. A. Vedenin, S. Yu. Zhitenev, N. M. Zabelina, N. A. Nikitin, P. M. Shul'gin, and K. M. Yanovskii, comps., n.p. Moscow: SFK Press.

Proekt zakona

2000   Proekt Federal'nogo zakona "O territoriiakh traditsionnogo prirodopol'zovaniia korennykh malochislennykh narodov i inykh malochislennykh etnicheskikh obshchnostei Severa, Sibiri i Dal'nego Vostoka Rossiiskoi Federatsii" (Draft of the federal law on the lands of traditional subsistence usage by the small-numbered native peoples and other minority ethnic groups of the North, Siberia, and the Far East of the Russian Federation). In *Problemy traditsionnogo prirodopol'zovaniia. Sever, Sibir' i Dal'nii Vostok Rossiiskoi Federatsii*, L.S. Bogoslovskaia, ed., pp. 56–66. Moscow: Izdanie Gosudarstvennoi Dumy.

Raiony prozhivaniia

1991   Raiony prozhivaniia malochislennykh narodov Severa (Habitation areas of minority Northern Peoples). A.I. Chistobaev, comp. *Geografiia i khoziaistvo* 4. Leningrad: Geographical Society.

Salter, Christopher L., comp.

1971   *The Cultural Landscape.* Belmont, CA: Duxbury Press.

Salymskii krai

2000   *Salymskii krai* (Salym Region). Ekaterinburg.

Sauer, Carl O.

1963 (1925) The Morphology of Landscape. In *Land and Life: A Selection from the Writings of Carl Ortwin Sauer*, John Leighly, ed., pp. 315–50. Berkeley, CA: University of California Press.

1927   Recent Developments in Cultural Geography. In: *Recent Developments in Social Sciences.* E. C. Hayes, ed. New York.

Shul'gin, Pavel M.

2000   Kul'turnyi factor v regional'noi politike [The Cultural Factor in Regional Politics). In *Ekologiia kul'tury. Al'manakh Instituta Naslediia "Territoriia"*, Iu.L. Mazurov, comp., pp. 35–43. Moscow: Institut Naslediia.

2002   Rabota Instituta Naslediia nad kompleksnymi regional'nymi programmami (Heritage institute works on complex regional programs). In *Nasledie i sovremennost'* 10 (*10 let Institutu Naslediia*), pp.19–43. Moscow: Institut Naslediia.

Shul'gin, Pavel M. and Olga E. Shtele

1998   Institut kul'turnogo i prirodnogo naslediia (Institute of cultural and natural heritage [of Russia]). *Rossia v sovremennom mire* 1:154–61.

Svod pamiatnikov

1997   *Svod pamiatnikov arkhitektury i monumental'nogo iskusstva Rossii: Bryanskaya oblast'* (Register of architectural monuments and objects of monumental art of Russia: Bryansk Province). Moscow: Nauka Publishers.

1998-2001 *Svod pamiatnikov arkhitektury i monumental'nogo iskusstva Rossii: Ivanovskaya oblast'* (Register of architectural monuments and objects of monumental art of Russia: Ivanovo Province). Moscow: Nauka Publishers.

Turovskii, R.F.

1998 *Kul'turnye landshafty Rossii* (Cultural landscapes of Russia). Moscow: Institut Naslediia.

Vedenin, Iurii A.

1997 Ocherki po geografii iskusstv (Studies in the Geography of Art). St. Petersburg: Dmitrii Bulanin Publishers.

2000 Formirovanie novogo kul'turno-ekologicheskogo podkhoda k sokhraneniiu naslediia (Developing a new cultural-ecological approach to heritage preservation: on the history of the creation of the Russian Institute of Cultural and Natural Heritage). In *Ekologiia kul'tury. Al'manakh Instituta Naslediia "Territoriia"*, Iu.L. Mazurov, comp., pp. 25–30. Moscow: Institut Naslediia.

Vedenin, Iurii A., and M.E. Kuleshova

2001 Kul'turnyi landshaft kak ob'ekt kul'turnogo i prirodnogo naslediia (The cultural landscape as an object of cultural and natural heritage). *Izvestiia Akademii Nauk*, (Geography series) 1:7–14.

Vedenin, Iurii A., Olga E. Shtele, and Pavel M. Shul'gin

2003 Problemy sokhranenii istoriko-kulturnykh territorii v Rossii (Issues in the preservation of the historical-cultural areas in Russia). *Orientiry kul'turnoi politiki 7*. Moscow: Ministry of Culture.

Vedenin Iurii, A. and Pavel M. Shul'gin

1992 Novye podkhody k sokhraneniiu i ispol'zovaniiu kul'turnogo i prirodnogo naslediia Rossii (New approaches to the preservation and utilization of the natural heritage in Russia). *Izvestiia Akademii Nauk* (Geography series) 3:90–9.

Vedenin Iurii, A. and Pavel M. Shul'gin, eds.

2002 *Nasledie i sovremennost'. 10 let Institutu Naslediia* (Heritage and modernity. To the 10th anniversary of the (Russian) Heritage Institute). Moscow: Institut Naslediia.

Vergunov, A.P., S.V. Kulinskaia, and Iurii L. Mazurov

2000 Ekologicheskii minitoring kul'turnogo naslediia (Ecological monitoring of the cultural heritage [of Russia]). In *Ekologiia kul'tury. Al'manakh Instituta Naslediia "Territoriia"*, Iu.L. Mazurov, comp., pp. 163–179. Moscow: Institut Naslediia.

Wiget, Andrew, ed.

1999 *Ocherki istorii traditsionnogo zemlepol'zovaniia khantov: materially k atlasy* (Studies in the history of traditional Khanty land usage: atlas materials). Ekaterinburg: Tezis Press.

Zaitseva, Olga. N.

1997 Sravnitel'naia kharakteristika tipov traditsionnogo prirodopol'zovaniia korennogo naseleniia Zabaikal'ia (Comparative characteristics of types of traditional resource management practices of the indigenous people of the Trans-Baikal Region) In *Sovremennye metody geograficheskikh issledovanii*. Irkutsk: Institute of Geography, Russian Academy of Sciences.

Zakon Respubliki Kareliia

1994 Zakon Respubliki Kareliia ob unikal'nykh istoricheskikh prirodno-landshaftnykh territoriakh (The law of the Republic of Karelia on unique historical natural-landscape territories). *Territory* 1:37–8.

36/ Two Yamal Nenets men making sacrifice at the Khagen-Sale sacred site, Yamal, 1928.

part 2

PROTECTING THE "INVISIBLE": STORIES FROM THE ARCTIC ZONE

"To Save the Yugan":
The Saga of the Khanty Cultural Conservation Program

ANDREW WIGET AND OLGA BALALAEVA

Through the vagaries of history and politics, much of the world's land is controlled by states whose majority populations are culturally different from the resident, minority populations whose traditional lands they control. Management regimes, even "conservation" ones, originated in the interests of the dominant culture and often began with the peculiarly Western distinction between nature and culture. In the preservation context, Cultural Resource Management (CRM) emerged from a recognition that culturally significant places and objects both encode and express the body of traditional knowledge and values distinctive of a particular culture. Understanding the nature and role of such cultural resources is important for developing culturally compatible resource-use policies because cultural resources encode the framework of beliefs and values that motivate behavior.

The advantage that the concept of "ethnographic landscape" brings to cultural anthropology, preservation discourse, and CRM is that it invites the dominant culture to understand in local terms the functional and semantic interrelationships among elements that are often understood and managed separately. Adequately translating this concept into practice thus should result in a management program that is not only more equitable, because it is adapted to the needs of both dominant and resident cultures, but one that is more effective, since it accounts for more complex interrelationships that motivate behaviors. The present experience in northern Eurasia, however, suggests that ecological rather than anthropological issues dominate cultural

landscape policies (Dömke and Succow 1998). In the broader conservation vision, what is needed is a means of balancing ecological, historical preservation and cultural conservation priorities.

This paper describes an ongoing effort to strike such a balance by incorporating elements of ethnographic landscape study into a plan to define the boundaries and zonation scheme for a proposed, co-managed protected area in the territory of the Yugan Khanty people of Western Siberia.

The Context for the Khanty Cultural Conservation Program

The Khanty are one of Russia's forty-five northern tribal peoples whose total population is less than 200,000.[1] Some of these tribes, like the Khanty, survive in territory that has been their home for thousands of years since before the Russians came. Khanty culture was born in and is specifically adapted to the forest-and-swamp ecosystem of the West Siberian boreal forest. Western Siberia is dominated by the Ob–Irtysh River system, the third largest river system in the world in terms of volume of water. The limits of the Middle Ob River basin correspond roughly to the northern and southern boundaries of Khanty-Mansi Autonomous Area, or okrug (KMAO; see Fig. 37). Today the low sand hills and higher ridges dotting and edging the floodplain, which, until the 1950s, supported a unique, heavily acculturated Khanty cultural formation, now support most of the area's urban population and the transport and petroleum production infrastructure. From the city of

131

Nizhnevartovsk on the east to the area capital of Khanty-Mansiysk on the west, a distance of approximately 1,000 kilometers (or 650 miles), the Ob River drops only fifty meters (164 feet).

North of the middle Ob River valley, the land slopes gently in a southeasterly direction drained by several major Ob tributaries—the Lyamin, Pim, and Trom-Agan Rivers. Except for birch-dark conifer and aspen-cedar forests along the rivers, most of the landscape between the highlands and the Ob River floodplain consists of lakes, ponds, and muskeg swamps. Perhaps more than fifty percent of the surface area is water. South of the middle Ob, the land slopes gently, dropping less than sixty meters in the 500 kilometers (310 miles) between the highlands and the Ob floodplain. Highland muskeg swamps drain into large river systems—the Bolshoi (Big) and Malyi (Little) Yugan, Salym, and Balyk Rivers. The proportion of higher land and pine-green moss forests to swamp is much greater than in the north. Rapid freezing leads to a winter period of uninterrupted frost for 145 to 155 days, with an average low of -20 to -35˚C. and maximum lows near -55˚C. This is followed by rapid thawing, flooding, and hot summers, heavy with mosquitoes, with average high temperatures around +20˚C and maximum highs around +37˚C. The whole region has permafrost about six meters (twenty feet) below the surface.

Among the 22,000 or so Khanty, three groups—Northern, Southern, and Eastern—can be distinguished by differences in dialect, subsistence patterns, and material culture. Northern Khanty live in the Beloyarsk and Salekhard Districts. The Eastern Khanty, the focus of this project, are located principally in Khanty-Mansi Autonomous Okrug. The Khanty still maintain their clan system and their traditional way of life in widely separated extended family settlements in traditional hunting territories. Everywhere they support themselves through hunting and the trapping of furbearers like sable and fox. Fish constitute a large part of their diet, but reindeer herding is common north of the Ob, hunting moose and wild reindeer south of the Ob River.

Most Khanty are literate in Russian and fluently bilingual, but prefer to speak Khanty. And despite the efforts of the Orthodox Church, which in some areas has gained converts of varying degrees of allegiance, and despite the suppression of Native religion under the Soviets, traditional belief and ritual still flourish. The Khanty believe in a three-zone cosmos with this middle world existing between an upper sky world and an underworld. Each of these is divided into seven levels. The high god, Numi Torum, cannot be approached directly, but only through addressing one or more of his seven sons and seven daughters, each of whom became a patron of some dimension of the natural world: rivers, fish, animals. The youngest son in his human incarnation was elevated to the senior position among the sons, and in his animal incarnation became Bear, the master of the forest. As with many northern peoples, a special Bear Festival is occasionally celebrated to honor a bear that has been killed (Schmidt 1987, 1989).

Because the patrons of the major tributary river systems are also lineage-founding deities, different Khanty clans claim traditional use rights to different river systems tributary to the Ob. Most Khanty extended families live on traditional family hunting territories protected by family gods who are considered offspring of these lineage-founding deities. Khanty thus believe that sacred power has been historically invested in both the landscape and the lineage. These gods are said to live in specific sacred places and often have shrines marking these sites. The gods are worshiped through blood sacrifice (yir) of animals, especially reindeer, and through bloodless sacrifice (pory) of boiled meat. Prayer and sacrifice ensure protection from and healing of disease and injury, long life, tranquility, fertility, and prosperity. A variety of factors contributes to this cultural persistence (Rushforth and Chisholm 1991:16–17), but there continues to be enough acculturative pressures that some are redefining their cultural heritage in ways that have been called neotraditional (Pika 1999).

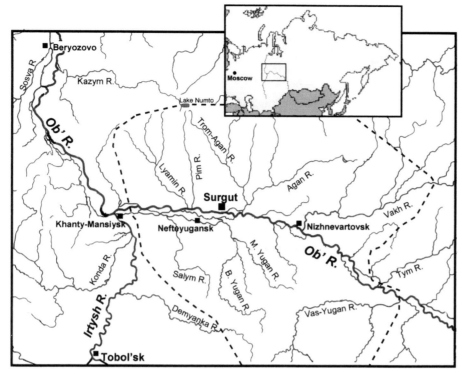

37/ The Middle Ob River Basin. The dotted line marks the area of Eastern Khanty settlement. Their communities are associated with different river systems.

Now, after millennia, Khanty land and culture are threatened with destruction. In the late 1960s, oil was first discovered in West Siberia. At that time, the town of Surgut had less than 10,000 people. By the late 1980s all but a few areas (Kazym River, Yugan River basin) had been seized by the Ministry of Energy and the government oil monopoly, and the region virtually supported a collapsing Soviet economy by providing cheap domestic petroleum and petro-dollars generated from export. Today the Khanty-Mansi Autonomous Area is the site of one of the world's most extensive petroleum developments, Surgut has 280,000 people, and the area's population has swelled to over a million, swamping the less than 10,000 Khanty and Mansi indigenous people (Wiget and Balalaeva 1996).

The process of production during the Soviet period was characterized by a minimal regard for environmental protection, preservation of cultural properties, and effective consultation with indigenous peoples. Khanty families, like those on the Agan River, were forcibly relocated into villages from their tradi-tional family hunting territories, or driven into villages by the destruction of their land's subsistence productivity, as on the lower Pim and Trom-Agan River systems.

However it may be regarded elsewhere, the collapse of the Soviet Union has been devastating socially, culturally, economically, and ecologically for the Eastern Khanty and their land. Profiteering by privatized oil companies coupled with the internal debt crisis has meant that deteriorating pipelines and aging equipment have not been replaced. The low productivity of individual well clusters (some leave more than fifty percent of the oil in the ground) and spillage (more than 3,000 pipeline breaks occur a year) drives the expansion into new territories for production.

Recognizing the extent of the environmental destruction that had resulted from petroleum development, and pressured by Russian environmentalists and scientists, the Soviet government in 1982 authorized the establishment of the Yugan Zapovednik (Nature Preserve) in the territory embraced by the two arms of the Bolshoi and Malyi Yugan Rivers, to preserve some of this magnificent and unique boreal forest ecosystem (Fig. 38). The Khanty families who live along these rivers in more than fifty extended family settlements were compelled to sacrifice their winter hunting territories for the new nature preserve. Nothing addressed the cultural conservation needs of the Yugan Khanty.

At the 1987 meeting of Yugan Khanty hunters and fishermen, Vladimir Kogonchin of Ugut proposed that the community apply to the Supreme Soviet [of the former Soviet Union] to designate the Yugan basin a zone of priority land use, a "green zone." Attempts were made to advance this proposal informally, even at the highest levels; but nothing came of this effort. On May 6, 1990, Khanty representatives to the KMAO Council of People's Deputies worked to pass through the Council of People's Deputies a bill that, building on the "green zone" concept, gave special status to the Khanty family hunting territories and that assigned traditional uses of the land priority over other forms of development, including industrial uses such as petroleum production and timber harvesting. On the Yugan, such a "zone of Khanty living" was defined and a proposal to set aside a zone of special land use was sent to the government, but again nothing came of it.

History of the Khanty Cultural Conservation Program

In 1993 we were asked to review a draft of the environmental impact assessment for the World Bank's Second Oil Rehabilitation Project in Khanty-Mansi Autonomous Okrug. That document claimed there was only one site of any cultural and historical significance in the entire eastern half of Khanty-Mansi Autonomous Okrug. By its silence, the document seemed to proclaim that Eastern Khanty culture, for all practical purposes, was non-existent, not a factor to be seriously calculated in the development equation. Unlike the situation in many densely populated regions of developed countries, where publication of the location of culturally significant places combines with ease of access to hasten looting, vandalism, or destruction of such places; in Siberia it is silence, not publication, that contributes to the destruction of the ethnographic landscape. Because the nature and extent of the Siberian boreal forest is an obstacle to general access, only oil companies and other entities with helicopters and other specialized means of transport can threaten the cultural landscape. And they can do it in the absence of witnesses, appealing disingenuously to the lack of information concerning these places. Our first projects,

therefore, were born from the real need to restore to public consciousness both the historical and the contemporary presence of the Khanty on the land and to create conditions under which deniability is impossible.[2]

The 'Sacred Trust' Project (1994–95) aimed to develop the basic data needed to support any plan for preserving Khanty sacred places and guaranteeing access to them. Given the limitations and unsystematic nature of previous ethnography in the area, we focused on identifying sacred places and determining the criteria by which the Khanty assign religious significance to features of the landscape and river systems. In this, we followed established western models, especially comparable work among Native American tribes (Kelly and Francis 1994; Basso 1996).

A scientific classification of Eastern Khanty sacred places has not yet been developed. Our more modest task has been to formulate a working typology, based on our materials from extensive field surveys, the work of folklore-ethnographic expeditions to the Kazym region from Urals State University, and a review of the ethnographic literature (Balalaeva 1999). On this basis, we can distinguish two main categories of sacred places: (1) unmodified features of the natural landscape, and (2) landscape features modified by the addition of cultural elements. The first type—natural sacred places—can be classified according to their basic elements into two groups, water features and landforms.

Water forms include a variety of phenomena connected with water: lakes, swamps, small rivers, ponds, whirlpools, confluences, rapids, and turns in the river (Fig. 38). Khanty believe that they depend on the spirits living in these places for luck in fishing and good fortune generally, and try to make the spirits more beneficent by throwing offerings of money or dried bread into the water. The size and nature of the offering differ in each case, and the importance of the offering depends on the reasons for making the offering.

Large natural features in this category are lakes, rivers, and swamps. Often the place name of the sacred water reserves includes lexemes such as *yimyng*

38/ Aerial view of the Bolshoi Yugan River basin. The area is a rich forest-riverine environment for which the local Khanty community has spent the last 15 years trying to secure a protected status.

(sacred). On the Yugan River, Lake Larlumkina is considered sacred. According to myth, warrior gods had a fight above this lake. When the local god was wounded, the reindeer drawing his sled dived into the water and now they are there, underneath the lake, two reindeer bulls. The local warrior god flew up into the sky, transformed into thunder, and became the god *Chuv Iki*. When the fishermen set the nets, sometimes the nets are stuck, and the fishermen say that the nets are stuck on the antlers of these reindeer. It is taboo to cross this lake directly; one must make a circle along the shore. The belief that different kinds of spirits live in these lakes is widespread. The basins of Kazym, Vakh, and Yugan Rivers have sacred lakes where, according to local beliefs, water spirits live that look like very big pike with horns. A subgroup of smaller water features includes ponds, as well as whirlpools,

rapids, turns, and confluences of rivers. In the upper part of Malyi Yugan River, above Achimovy settlement, there is also a whirlpool that is connected with mythological legends of *Tondor Iki*, the main deity of this river. According to local beliefs, one should throw two or three pieces of dried bread into this whirlpool. "If one does not throw the dried bread, this god, this Tondor Iki, won't like it; and he might punish you."

Landforms comprise the second major category of natural sacred places. Most prominent here are high places that include hillocks, hills, ridges, and very high hills. Another subgroup consists of promontories and islands, a group including higher, dry places in swamps. A third, smaller group consists of groves, mostly birch, small patches of forest. A fourth group consists of individual sacred trees of unusual shape or rare types and individual stones, also with unusual size or shape.

High places in the Ob River basin are relatively rare. This singularity and the dominating character of such formations naturally predispose the sacralizing, or sanctifying, of these objects. Almost all the distinguished high places have sacred status and, accordingly, ritual and mythological significance. On the Yugan, Trom-Agan, and Pim Rivers, sacred high places are most often called *kot myx*, meaning "earth house." A *kot myx* is a god's house. On Trom-Agan, above the mouth of its tributary, Ai-Trom-Agan, there is a sacred place for all Ob Khanty, a hill called *Torom Yaoun Kot Myx*. Offerings are taken there regularly at the beginning of seasonal activities and sporadically for other reasons. On the top of the hill is a high, distinguished pine tree on which Khanty hang pieces of fabric. The Trom-Agan Khanty say that the mountain with the pine tree is nothing other than the house with the chimney pipe. Newly married Khanty follow custom by going to this place to pray and make an offering at the beginning of their married life. Women are prohibited to go to the top of the hill. In this case, the husband climbs to the top to make the offering, and the new wife stays in the boat by the shore. Also, usually, it is taboo to remove something from a *kot myx*. There is a whole group of stories concerning people who violated this taboo, for example, by breaking a branch of a tree on a *kot myx*, with the result that the offender's arm withered or he died. The owner of a *kot myx* could be not only one of the river patron deities, venerated by the whole community, but also a family spirit. Thus, on Kanterov family land in the Pim River basin, there is sacred *Ochet Vut Mutikh Kot Myx*. This is a Kanterov sacred place where their family *hlung* (spirit) lives. Women of this family take wood from this place for the images they make of their personal protecting spirits.

Kot myx are a particularly threatened group of sacred sites. In the lower part of Bolshoi Yugan, it is said, there was a sacred place for all Ob' Khanty mentioned long ago by Dunin-Gorkavitch (1995:150), Yegutskaya [Evutskaya] Gora. Khanty from different places came here to make offerings. In the 1970s this sacred mountain was in a territory of oil development and almost leveled, but there are still stories devoted to this hill in local oral tradition. On Trom-Agan River a high place dedicated to *Yaoun Imi*, the Old Woman of the River, was destroyed entirely. Now only a large hole in the ground exists where once a hill stood. This is because the hills are made entirely of sand, which is dug up as the material for the roadbed construction throughout Western Siberia (Fig 40).

In the end our fieldwork identified more than seventy-five Khanty sacred places in the Surgut region alone (Balalaeva 1999; Fig. 39). Maps of sacred sites in different Khanty residence areas were produced using Geographic Information System (GIS). This work was the only report on Siberia presented at the UNESCO Conference on Natural Sacred Sites in Paris in September 1998.

The Khanty Traditional Land-Use Atlas Project (1996–98) was a two-year, international collabo-

39/ *Map of sacred sites of the Yugan Khanty area, 1998.*

PROTECTING THE INVISIBLE/ SAVE THE YUGAN

40/*This huge sand pit is all that is left of a sacred hill, Imi Yaoun, Mother of the River, on the Trom-Agan River. The authorities developed the site despite knowing it was a sacred place in active use.*

rative research project in applied social sciences with Russian colleagues from Urals State University in the city of Ekaterinburg (Yekaterinburg) and supported by the then called Ministry of Nationality Affairs and Regional Policy of the Russian Federation.

The project grew out of our increasing concern that petroleum development was threatening Khanty culture by destroying the physical environment to which Khanty subsistence-based culture was specifically adapted (Wiget and Balalaeva 1996; Wiget 1999b). The entire region suffers from soil, water, and air pollution, which degrade the land upon which Khanty subsistence hunters and fishermen depend. One of our informants told us that in spring the Agan River is "just one big oil slick." According to men who formerly worked in the fishing collective on Agan, 200 tons of fish a year were brought out of the river; by the 1980s after the onslaught of oil development, that had dropped to 100 tons a year; in 1995, when we talked

to them, that figure had diminished to only twenty tons. On the middle Trom-Agan River, Khanty report that furbearers (fox, wolverine) and predators (bear, wolf) have virtually fled the area in the last five to eight years as a result of oil development. One woman reported that her son-in-law lost his entire herd of 100 reindeer when they drank polluted water.

To demonstrate the effect of oil development on Khanty life, the Atlas project aimed to provide the first contemporary, broadbased, and integrated documentation of many categories of Khanty traditional land use:

—Traditional and contemporary settlements, both individual extended family settlements and villages;

—Individual family hunting territories;

—Places of cultural significance, including cultic sites, sites with mythical associations, traditional cemeteries;

—Archaeological sites;

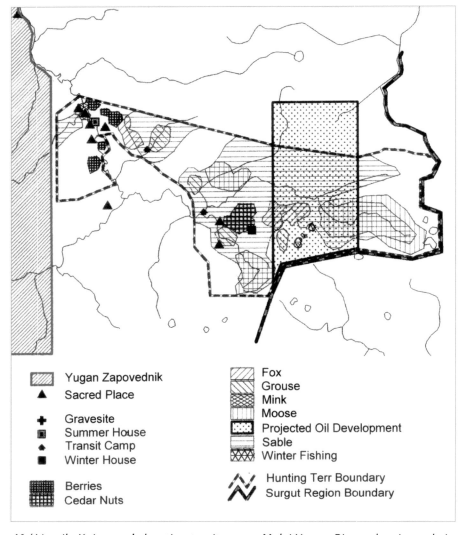

Legend:

Yugan Zapovednik
▲ Sacred Place
✚ Gravesite
🏠 Summer House
♦ Transit Camp
■ Winter House
Berries
Cedar Nuts

Fox
Grouse
Mink
Moose
Projected Oil Development
Sable
Winter Fishing

〜 Hunting Terr Boundary
〜 Surgut Region Boundary

41/ Vassily Kaimysov's hunting territory, on Malyi Yugan River, showing subsistence areas, sacred places, and projected oil license territory.

(a) individual, extended family settlements, and (b) villages;

2) regional traditional religious resources, especially: (a) places of cultic activity, including (a1) sacrificing places and (a2) shrines; (b) landforms with cultural value derived from specific mythological, legendary or historical association; (c) landforms with cultural value derived from association with classes of spirits; (d) cemeteries;

3) regional traditional economic resources, including: (a) boundaries of family hunting territories; (b) hunting, fishing, berry picking, pasturing (reindeer) resources; (c) communal lands; (d) reindeer trails, portages, and other transportation routes;

4) microstudies of traditional land use in six Khanty family hunting territories representing variations in ecosystems, subsistence economy, family size, and proximity to development territories.

—Other land use features, such as reindeer trails, communal hunting lands, fishing, hunting, gathering, and pasturing areas, and so on.

Additional maps highlighted the development of industrialization and infrastructure associated with these lands. All identified sites were accompanied by an ethnohistoric description. All data were compiled into a computerized database integrated with an ArcView GIS computerized mapping program.

The specific objectives of the project were to produce cartographic representations of the many types of data, linked to a comprehensive computerized database, and framed by interpretive, scholarly essays:

1) regional settlement patterns, either archaeological or historic (abandoned or contemporary);

As a complement to these comprehensive area maps of the region, intensive studies of traditional land use were undertaken on six family hunting territories, reflecting the wide regional differences in Khanty cultural patterns (Wiget 1999a). Figure 41 is a resource exploitation map drawn with the help of one large Khanty extended family numbering about thirty people living on the upper reaches of the Malyi Yugan River.[3] The map illustrates the principal types of flora and fauna harvested in the hunting territory, as well as the permanent winter and summer residences and the transitional camps used during the spring and fall movements between the permanent houses. Note that the oil license territory impinges on their main source of winter food, both fish and moose, and harvestable furs. The results of the project were published in 1999, with several family hunting maps attached (Wiget 1999a; Ocherki 1999); the book was distributed without charge to Khanty leaders and regional and area administration officials to serve as a fundamental planning document. It is already playing an important role in support of the efforts to gain a protected area status for the Yugan Khanty community's traditional lands in the Yugan River basin.

At approximately the same time the Sacred Trust Project was being completed and the Atlas project was being prepared, the co-authors, working with the head of the Yugan Khanty community association "Yaoun Yakh" and the staff of the Yugan Zapovednik (Federal Nature Reserve), began to prepare a strategy for preserving the Yugan basin based on the creation of a UNESCO-type Biosphere Reserve. The plan aimed to create a complex, co-managed territory that linked the 600,000-hectare (2,300 square miles) Yugan Zapovednik (an existing Russian Federal Nature Reserve) as a core area to a newly created, federal-status area consisting of the 1.7 million hectares (6,500 square miles) of Yugan Khanty family hunting territories comprising most of the watersheds of the Bolshoi and Malyi Yugan Rivers. Working with local government authorities, leaders in the Khanty community, and Khanty families, we defined reasonable boundaries for the various areas in the proposed biosphere reserve (Fig.42).

Because of a variety of negative consequences that could result from linking the Khanty lands to the Zapovednik, as well as the political unwillingness of the local administration to cede more land to federal government

control, the original plan has been amended. The current plan was worked out in consultation with the Khanty community, the Surgut regional and Khanty-Mansi Autonomous Area administrations, representatives of Ecojuris (a Moscow-based environmental law NGO [non-governmental organization]), and the authors. It abandons the entanglement with federal jurisdiction by avoiding a formal connection with the Yugan Federal Nature Reserve and envisions a two-step process. The first step is the creation of a protected area composed of Khanty family hunting territories along the Bolshoi and Malyi Yugan Rivers (OTTP, Russian - *Okhraniaemaia Territoriia Traditsionnogo Prirodopol'-zovaniia* [Protected Territory of Traditional Land Use]) with protected status awarded by Khanty-Mansi Autonomous Okrug; after establishment, application would be made to UNESCO for international recognition as biosphere reserve (Wiget and Balalaeva 1997, 1998b, 1999).

To provide the scientific data necessary to develop effective co-management policies for the Yugan protected area, we engaged in two projects. The area

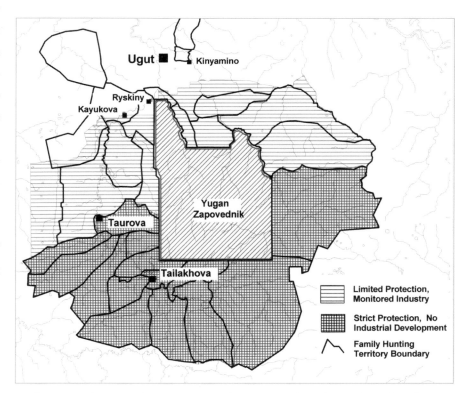

42/ Proposed Yugan Khanty "Protected Territory of Traditional Land Use"

Ethnoecological Survey (1998–99) represented the necessary first step in the transformation of the previously supported scientific research, network building, and community development into concrete strategy to realize the cultural conservation goals of the proposers' prior work among the Eastern Khanty. Extending models of gathering data for the traditional land-use study first piloted for the Khanty Atlas Project, the project developed the ethnographic, socioeconomic, and ecosystemic data necessary to establish baseline parameters for common planning of scientific and community development projects in the proposed Yugan Khanty Biosphere Reserve. As described below, over the course of those two years, we visited every family hunting territory, administering a comprehensive survey instrument and working with the landholding families to map their land use. By 2002, we completed a Cultural Resource Inventory and Assessment of the Proposed Yugan Khanty Biosphere Reserve. This project provides for an inventory and assessment of cultural resources in the Yugan Khanty community necessary to supplement the inventory of traditional economic resources and practices completed in the previous project. Taken together, these two projects offered a comprehensive representation of the cultural and ecological conservation issues that will be the focus of the comanagement plan governing the administration of the proposed protected area. This paper explores these projects and the lessons being learned from them.

Methodology

For our work, we began with the hypothesis, central to ethnographic landscape studies, that all uses of landscape are cultural, that treating traditional land use as something separate from understandings of landscapes will result in false conclusions that undermine attempts to create effective management policies (Brody 1981).

An ethnoecological survey attempts to create an organized body of data on how a traditional cultural community uses the land and resources on which it depends. The necessity for developing such an under-

standing has been confirmed by the practical experience of conservationists around the world who know that, despite popular stereotypes, the conservation practices of indigenous peoples, who do have an interest in sustainable harvest, nevertheless are not always consistent with the best conservation practices of Western science. Insofar as conservation activity impacts resources, economies, and populations, it serves a variety of political interests; and conservationists continually strive to find mechanisms to effectively negotiate "best practice" from among these interests. Moreover, one of the interests against which conservation of the physical environment, its flora, and fauna, must always be balanced is the preservation of cultural practices that contribute to a specific historic and sociocultural community identity.

An ethnoecological survey gathers data on:

—Kinds of natural resources on which a community depends

—Amounts of resources required for a self-identified "acceptable" standard of living in specific types of economy

—Patterns of land use in which individuals are engaged to secure the natural resources they need

—Relationships between fundamental needs such as family size and health, the claim on resources made in the name of these fundamental needs, and the instrumentalities (material base) used to secure satisfaction for these needs.

The kinds of data gathered enable the discovery of broad patterns of behavior that reflect community practice. Although these kinds of data are most economically gathered through an interview instrument that will generate a coherent data set (Table 1), even in the best of circumstances (working with a small village population, for example) confirmation of survey results should come from field observations.

At the same time, because the practices described have a geographic dimension, affecting specific populations in specific ecosystems, it is impossible to understand the data without mapping. Consequently, in

Site Name:	(Khanty) Torum Kur Pur Wethlem Wantvng (English) Where Torom Put His Foot Down
Site Number:	58
Category:	IV, Modified Landscape
Specification:	Landform with *izbushka* [sacred log house]
Location (Decimal degrees):	N 59.15, E 74.21
River System:	Bolshoi Yugan
Extended family settlement:	Kolsomovy
Administrative Unit:	Surgut Region
Village Administration:	Ugut
Keeper:	None. The former keeper passed away. Now access is unregulated, though it is customary to inform Yefim Kolsomov, the owner of the local hunting territory on which the site exists, of the intention to visit the site.
Description: Location	The site is on the west bank of the upper Bolshoi Yugan River, just above Kolsomovy extended family settlement. The site is not visible from the river. One would have to know its location to know where to take the boat to shore. Yefim Kolsomov took me there. The site gets its name from a depression in the skyline formed by the treetops against the background of the western sky.
Description: Access	There is a wide, shallow cove in the west bank of the river. The land slopes gently from the forest edge to the water, a distance of about 20 meters, with tall grass rising out of the sand the entire way, fallen willow saplings, and other flood debris. Once in the forest, there is a very narrow, but visible trail. Still, it is hardly worn. The trail crosses through the forest a distance of no more than 100 meters.
Description: Site	The trail comes to a small izbushka or cabin (see Fig. 44), about 2.5 meters long on its front, short side and 3 meters on its long side. The roof peak is no more than 1.5 meters. A black cloth covers the door opening. Inside is a bare plank floor with a single shaitan, or idol, standing against the back wall. There is also a glass jar in which people have left paper money and coins. Following a trail from the doorway along the left side of the izbushka, behind it into the forest no more than 10 meters, one finds a single "retired" shaitan, left to decompose and return to the forest. About 20 meters north of the clearing where the izbushka sits is a small stream, also a significant feature.
Description: Boundaries	The significant area is a geophysical depression "where Torom put his foot down." The small stream (summary of toponymic legend, below) bound this area on the north, Bolshoi Yugan River on the east side, and by locally elevated heights of land that form the rim of the depressed area on the west and south side.
Significance (Provide Oral, Historical Information, Local Toponymic Legend):	Torom (The Khanty high god) wanted to see how things were on earth. He leaned over from the sky and put one of his feet down, stepping onto the earth. That's how this place was formed and still keeps the shape of Torom's foot. Where Torom stepped down, a stream emerged. People are prohibited from looking at this stream under penalty of being blinded. This is a summary of a toponymic legend, now forgotten. It was compiled from elements provided by Yefim Kolsomov and Pyotr Vassilievich Kurlomkin.
Status:	According to visual evidence of money deposited and oral testimony by Yefim Kolsomov, the site is still being used, especially by families in the upper part of Bolshoi Yugan and by travelers.
Condition:	Good. No vandalism reported.

addition to completing the survey instrument, hunters themselves are asked to mark particular kinds of land-use patterns on maps brought into the field. The statistical data would then be compiled into databases, which would be imported into a GIS and linked to digitized cartography for the purposes of both analyses and representation.

As extensive as the ethnoecological survey was, we understood that it was incomplete in itself. We knew that to understand both Yugan Khanty hunting and conservation practices, we needed a clear sense of their cultural values and how those values are put into play in decision-making and norm-maintenance behaviors. This required on-site documentation of oral traditions, both folkloric and historical, which encode Khanty cultural values and practices; both structured and unstructured interviews; and as well as observation and documentation of seasonal practices. We also needed to complete gathering basic data on other kinds of cultural resources, such as archaeological resources, which were very poorly understood and yet beyond our competency. Trying to accomplish these goals while also gathering the statistical information was simply logistically impossible. We are in the process of integrating this cultural data, although gathered separately, with the ethnoecological survey data, acquiring the necessary base layer satellite imagery to map both ethnoecological and cultural resources in a usable GIS format.

Community Engagement

Often overlooked in community relations is that most of these relationships are formed and sustained in discursive contexts, where key terms like "tribal," "culture," "minority," "ecology," "subsistence," and other less obvious ones like "dependence" and "necessity" and even "science" have been assigned different definitions and values by the parties involved. Three discourses, which have a heightened potency in Russia, have substantially affected the representation and interpretation of our work with ethnographic landscapes and indigenous peoples (Wiget and Balalaeva 1998a).

Perhaps more than any other country in the experience of both co-authors, Russia is committed to the ideology of progress, which, when dealing with its indigenous northern minorities, at best emerges as a willful paternalism and at worst as the most brutal and self-serving kind of rationalization for exploitation. Certainly much of this is rooted in a Marxist ideology of the inevitable succession of economic systems, which consequently views Khanty and others like them as doomed archaisms. More importantly, however, the effects of centralized thinking still linger in bureaucratic

and administrative paternalism: in the preference for industrialization over other forms of development; in the assumption that indigenous peoples ought to be "modernized," though, of course, in as accommodating a manner as possible, because they will be inevitably modernized, in any case; in the legal legacy of state-controlled land. This complex of paternalism and self-justifying fatalism is also reflected in the emergence of Russian populist conservation ideology, in general.

Preservationists might appear to be logical allies, because a strict preservationist philosophy protects historical resources in the territory of potential development. Nevertheless, the opportunities for indigenous peoples to seek protection under Russian historic preservation law is practically limited in several ways. First, as in the West, this protection is extended principally to monuments or structures of cultural and historical significance. The emphasis on the built environment predisposes preservationists to undervalue sites of historical and cultural significance to traditional peoples and which are often unmodified landscape features, —high places, sacred groves of trees, river confluences, sandbars, and so on (Fig.43)—or, if modified, are distinguished by structures without apparent architectural significance. Secondly, for all practical purposes, determination of significance is based on the role of the site in the development of the ethnic Russian cultural formation, the Russian state, and the Russian Orthodox Church, all of which preclude assigning significance to cultural or historical sites of importance to indigenous peoples. Third, the law on protection of places of worship is also almost uniformly interpreted to apply to Orthodox churches and excludes indigenous peoples' concerns.

Environmentalists might seem even more natural allies than preservationists.[4] Although the former Soviet Union adopted very strong nature conservation legislation, which won both internal support (rooted in a peasant society, Russia has a deep historical and cultural ideological investment in nature) and external praise, a series of dramatic and highly visible catastro-

43/ Forested high places in swamps, called 'islands,' are often sacred sites.

the philosophy undergirding what might be called "the compensation model of environmental management" is one of mutually agreed upon absolute sacrifices. This differs considerably from a multiple-use, joint management model based on mechanisms to elicit and manage compromises.

Relationships with the Eastern Khanty

During the course of this work, we established good relationships with several truly representative, effective, and competent Khanty local leaders, and consult regularly with them as they try to develop forms of representative self-government within the legal structures authorized by the statutes of the Russian Federation. We have been closely monitoring the development of this Native leadership as it seeks to form national communities and national corporations, and we have provided them with information about and contacts with Native governments in the U.S. and Canada. To develop their interests and strengthen their competencies in 1995, 1996, and again in 2001, we brought local Khanty leaders to the United States so that they could experience firsthand the structures of self-government within which Native Americans live and manage their lands and resources. In July 1996, after a site visit to the Yugan by a representative of GOSKOMSEVER (State Committee on Northern Development of the Russian Federation) found local support for the concept, we spent many days traveling by boat on both the Bolshoi and Malyi Yugan Rivers, stopping at each family settlement to explain the nature of the biosphere reserve concept and collect signatures to establish one in the Yugan region. Every adult in every family we approached signed eagerly.

phes of centralized planning—the heavy metals pollution of the Lena and Yenesey Rivers, the desiccation of the Aral Sea, the pulp-mill pollution of Lake Baikal, the petroleum horrors of Samotlor, the radioactive waste in Novaya Zemlya—created an activist environmentalist movement. Now Native organizations increasingly are broadcasting their claims to this constituency with the familiar slogans about the economic and cultural connections of Indigenous peoples to the land, of cultural formations specifically adapted to particular environments, of "noble savage" philosophies based on sustainability and mutuality, rather than unilateral exploitative extraction. Nevertheless, efforts to rally support along these rhetorical lines have generally failed. The conservation philosophy, which one hears even from high-placed academicians and bureaucrats, is that the strictest preservation of exemplary instances of key ecosystems must be ensured. Nevertheless, this strategy appears something of a tradeoff, for it was only in 1996 that the Russia Duma adopted environmental management criteria for development projects that met Western standards, and several years later those criteria are still poorly enforced. What goes unsaid in conversations about nature preservation is that that which is not protected will be destroyed. In short,

Relationship with the Yugan Khanty

As our focus on the Yugan Khanty developed, we took steps to establish that relationship more formally. Today we have represented ourselves to the federal, area, and regional governmental officials, NGOs, and other concerned parties as independent scientists providing technical assistance to the Yugan Khanty community association, Yaoun Yakh, working under their formal invitation, with an agenda and itinerary registered by them with the Surgut Region administration and operating under a jointly signed Letter of Agreement, specifying work, resources, and responsibilities of both parties.

Although this level of formality belies the intimacy of personal relationships developed in ten years between the researchers and the Yugan Khanty, it has proven useful in positioning us as "independent," though engaged, in the subsequent political interactions between the Yaoun Yakh Community Association and the officials of the area and regional governments. The formalization of this relationship also had the effect of modeling for them how, in the absence of defined treaty rights, they might nevertheless find other mechanisms to assume control over access to community lands, population, traditional knowledge, and intellectual property. It has also bolstered the political presence of Yaoun Yakh by demonstrating that they have continued access to international audiences and resources. We also facilitated for them a grant application that enabled them to obtain legal counsel from Ecojuris, a Russian environmental law NGO.

Relations with Responsible Government Entities

We have been careful to acknowledge all protocols, required by law or custom, and, within the limits of confidentiality, share results of our research regularly with government officials and NGOs, not only to quiet suspicions concerning the nature of our work, but to raise consciousness and to create conditions under which deniability is impossible. Toward this latter goal, we maintain a website and have occasionally used our access to the Internet to publicize protests from the Yugan Khanty community association, Yaoun Yakh, at the community's request.

Project Implementation

During this project, the co-authors traveled by outboard motorboat along the entire 1,800 kilometer (1,170 mile) combined length of the Bolshoi and Malyi Yugan Rivers to complete an extensive house-to-house, family-to-family survey. We visited every hunting territory, extended family settlement, and Native village or camp. Combining map-assisted structured interviewing with the eight-page questionnaire, the survey has provided data in three major areas—traditional land use; material base and domestic economy; and health and social organization—so that we can begin to establish a baseline against which the impact of development on the Bolshoi Yugan River basin and on the traditional way of life of the Yugan Khanty can be measured. We had planned to survey the Malyi Yugan River and part of the longer Bolshoi Yugan River in 1998, and the reminder of the Bolshoi Yugan in 1999.

As the following summary log of the project suggests, an important logistical constraint for us in this process was the great distance between Yugan Khanty settlements, often four or five hours by boat, and the limited amount of time available for fieldwork. These limitations meant that simply ensuring a thorough, representative, and reliable response to a simple survey instrument became a daunting task in itself. This project also raised two constraints peculiar to the former Soviet Union. First, all maps under 1:500,000 scale, a scale far too big to be useful for our work, are still considered state secrets; sponsorship of our work by the now-defunct State Committee of the North of the Russian Federation (GOSKOMSEVER) enabled us to purchase 1:200,000 scale maps, allowing us to partially overcome this initial obstacle, though even this scale is too large. Ideally, 1:50,000 scale maps should be used. A second constraint is the limitation on the use of handheld GPS (Global Positioning Systems) in Russia, but these, too, we were able to overcome.

1998 Field Season

July 8. We departed for the Yugan, from Chornaya Rechka, the oil industry base, in a helicopter that took us directly to the Kurlomkiny extended family settlement on the upper Bolshoi Yugan River, where we were able to confirm some nineteenth century land use practices described by historical literature.

July 9. We departed by motorboat to Larlumkiny, the highest settlement on Bolshoi Yugan River, about four hours of travel above Kurlomkiny. Larlumkiny is a complex settlement of six families, four of whom are related; its territory is huge. We administered our survey instrument and mapped land use in this hunting territory. We continued on to visit one of the most important Khanty sacred places, two archaeological sites, and a Khanty cemetery near Lake Larlumkina. We returned to Kurlomkiny around 11:30 in the evening.

July 10. We did additional interviewing at Kurlomkiny. At 3 p.m. we flew out by helicopter to Ugut.

July 10-15: Ugut Village. We began by meeting with the local principals involved in the project. We reviewed the plans that we had made for the survey, engaging fully the head of the Yugan Khanty community, Vladimir Kogonchin, and two members of the interviewing team, Igor Kogonchin and Anna Baikalova from the Yugan Zapovednik. Baikalova made useful additions for ecological data to the survey instrument we were using. While arranging for our longer trip on Malyi Yugan River, we made a short motorboat trip on the lower Bolshoi Yugan River near Ugut. This was only partially successful, because at a couple of the extended family settlements at the village of Ryskiny, the residents were drunk, a result of recent cash distribution from the oil company; this is a situation that we have never met with on the middle and upper parts of either Bolshoi or Malyi Yugan Rivers. Both Baikalova and Igor Kogonchin accompanied us on this trip to observe and practice the survey/interview/mapping techniques that we were using for data collecting.

July 15-20: Malyi Yugan River. We left Ugut by motorboat on the morning of 15 July and arrived around midnight at Surlomkiny extended family settlement, the first above Kinyamino. During this first part of the trip, we were able to administer the survey and map land use at one intermediate family settlement. On July16, we administered the survey and mapped land use at Surlomkiny. We continued upriver on 17 July. Between 17-19 July we stopped at every *yurta* (camp) on Malyi Yugan, administering the survey and mapping land use, reaching the highest point, Asmanovy settlement, more than 500 river miles from Ugut. Some of the documentation was accomplished on the way back. We arrived in Ugut at 2 a.m. on 20 July. After finishing up business in Ugut, and arranging with Kogonchin and Baikalova on a work plan for winter, we returned to Surgut on 22 July.

Over the winter, Kogonchin and Baikalova administered the survey at Kinyamino and Ryskiny, both of which could not be done in the summer. Wiget and Balalaeva began GIS data entry and mapping.

1999 Field Season

June 24. We traveled by helicopter to Ugut, staging point for our 1999 field season. There we met with Vladimir Kogonchin, head of the Yugan Khanty community and developed plans for our cooperative work. Our task was to administer the survey to all the Khanty families from Kolsomovy near the top of the river (we had done Kurlomkiny and Larlumkiny settlements the previous year). Because we had with us Konstantin Karacharov, an archaeologist of the Institute of History of the Russian Academy of Science, Urals Branch in Ekaterinburg, whom we had invited to join us to conduct the first archaeological survey of the Yugan basin, we still needed to return to Kurlomkiny and Larlumkiny. The plan was to send us all ahead by helicopter to Kurlomkiny; with local help, we would take care of the archaeological portion of survey work there in a couple of days. By the time we returned from Larlumkiny, Kogonchin would have arrived at Kurlomkiny by motorboat from Ugut, and we ourselves would start down river, continuing the survey. We expected a grueling trip from the uppermost settlement on the river back to Ugut, more than 500 miles by outboard motorboat.

June 26. We arrived at Kurlomkiny. From the very beginning things went well. The archaeological survey of the upper Bolshoi Yugan River was very productive, and we developed an excellent and efficient working relationship with Karacharov. We could anticipate that the data he was providing would assist us immensely in strengthening arguments for preservation of the Yugan for its historical and cultural value.

June 29–July 6. We started down river. The Bolshoi Yugan River differs from Malyi Yugan River in that there are many more Khanty, they live farther apart, and there are several Native villages, in which some Khanty families live permanently though they travel to fishing areas and avail themselves of "common" (unassigned) hunting grounds. We visited, interviewed and did map work with more than twenty families living on fifteen different extended family settlements, as well as interviewing and doing map work with an additional fourteen families living in the villages of Tailakhova, Taurova, and Kayukova. In the larger villages, we worked as two teams, with the co-authors forming one team and Karacharov and Kogonchin the other. Map work and interviews with other residents of Kayukova and Ryskiny had been concluded in 1998, the first season of fieldwork. Along the entire length of the river, while the authors were doing map work and interviews, Karacharov also did interviews, site mapping, and testing, for the preliminary archaeological survey. In the end, he had identified by inspection or report thirty-one sites, including several multilevel complexes of enormous importance, as well as a complex of prehistoric trails and roads. We returned to Ugut very early on the morning of 6 July 1999.

We spent the next several days in Ugut. Additional interviews and map work were done with Khanty families we had missed at their extended family settlements but who were in Ugut to purchase supplies. We also developed with Vladimir Kogonchin a revised draft of the charter for the proposed co-managed Yugan Protected Territory; we were especially concerned about two elements, a zonation scheme that would provide for designations of different kinds of uses and forms of protection, and a usable co-management structure. We met with Anna Baikalova and Konstantin Karacharov, not only to compare preliminary findings, but also to describe the kinds of reports we would need from the Malyi Yugan. Finally, we defined work that remained to be done, especially the few families that we had missed on either river. The interviews and maps were sent to us in the U.S. in November 1999.

Gaining protected area status for the Yugan requires successfully passing through two commissions (regional and okrug). As a result of the authors' previous work as well as the assistance of the Moscow-based legal NGO Ecojuris, the administrations of Surgut Region and Khanty-Mansi Autonomous Okrug are now formally taking up the proposal to establish a legally protected area on the traditional homeland of the Yugan Khanty. This project thus has entered the critical phase.

In August 1999, we accompanied Vladimir Kogonchin, the head of the Yugan Khanty community, to Khanty-Mansiysk, the capital of the okrug, where we met with a number of area officials whose responses to the project varied. Finally, the group met for more than a half-hour with Governor Alexandr Filipenko, who appeared to be generally supportive of the project and invited us to submit materials directly to his office. He had been surprised at the volume and nature of communications he had received from around the world on his office fax machine in support of preserving the Yugan; these resulted from our dissemination of information about the Khanty and the current state of the project on our internet website (http://www/nmsu.edu/~english/hc/hcsiberia.html) In mid-November 1999, we had sent to him an initial packet of materials. While in Khanty-Mansiysk, Balalaeva, Wiget, and Kogonchin briefed Tatiana Gogoleva, the president of *Spasenie Yugry* (Save the Yugra), the major

Khanty cultural association, on the project.

At the regional level, the Surgut regional commission, the formation of which was resisted for so long, was finally called into meeting at the end of 1998. It met only once and briefly, to approve the general idea of establishing some kind of protected territory on the Yugan River. From beginning to end, however, this regional commission process has been heavily biased in favor of administration interests and the history of unilateral administrative decision-making. Thus, for the Khanty community to realize their social and political aims, it is necessary that they compel a dialogue with the administration over the organization, and management of the OTTP. A package of documents that was provided to the okrug officials in mid-November was also sent to the Surgut administration.

The data gathered on these two field trips were combined with ethnographic data gathered previously at selected extended family settlements and with ethnohistoric data compiled from a survey of nineteenth and early twentieth century literature. Confirmation of survey results should come from field observations; but clearly, the same constraints that were factors in administering the survey made direct observation of the relevant behaviors in every household impossible. A second concern, then, was to identify a few representative households with whom we could establish a long-term relationship that permitted direct observation under the relevant conditions. In the Cultural Resources Survey and Assessment now underway, we have identified specific extended family settlements on the Bolshoi and Malyi Yugan Rivers, which our own previous fieldwork or the survey indicated had one or more family members who were known to the community as cultural specialists or who were likely to have a substantial body of knowledge concerning Khanty beliefs and practices associated with the landscape. Especially sought after were oral traditions, especially toponymic and local legends, etiological stories, memorates, and oral historical narratives, from hunt-

44/ At Lake Larlumkina near the top of the Bolshoi Yugan River is a complex cultural heritage site, consisting of an active cemetery, two nearby archaeological sites, and this sacred place with labases which serves as homes for three spirits and their helpers.

ing and traveling to homebuilding, all of which might dramatize Khanty values, beliefs, and practices associated with the landscape.

2000 Field Seasons

The co-authors went to the field twice in 2000, each time identifying a specific extended family settlement for confirming data gathered on the survey and better understanding seasonal uses of the land. In July 2000, the team traveled to the Kuplandeyevy settlement on the middle part of Bolshoi Yugan River, to interview two brothers, both sons of a shaman, and the elder, Nikolai Petrovich, also one of only two remaining singers of Bear Festival songs. We subsequently learned that two months after we had left Nikolai Petrovich, he passed away. In December, we traveled again to Kurlomkiny, this time to observe winter hunting practices, as well as to discuss the findings of our survey. Kurlomkin is the only person on Bolshoi Yugan River beside Kupland-eyev who knows Bear Festival songs.

Findings

All ethnographic findings concerning Khanty values, beliefs, and practices associated with the landscape disclosed so far by the Khanty Cultural Conservation Program have implications for the development of co-management policies for the planned protected area in the Bolshoi Yugan River basin.

Ethnographic Findings

The project has produced a number of findings significant for understanding the West Siberian boreal forest as a Khanty "cognized" landscape. It confirmed our governing hypothesis: Khanty conceive of a complex, but direct and roughly isomorphic connection between the multiple layers of their religious pantheon and the different levels of land use. The relationships are:

(a) The High Gods : Sky, Earth Surface, Underworld generally

(b) Their Children : Major Tributary Rivers

(c) Their Children's Children : Family Hunting Territories

Using toponymic and ethnographic data from our own work and the work of others, we developed a typology of sacred places that distinguishes between unmodified geophysical features—such as lakes, whirlpools, sand bars, high places, and sacred groves—and those geophysical features that have been modified by the addition of constructions. Such sites are "sacred" because a mythological event is associated with them.

We can assert that the Yugan Khanty recognize that some sites that they might not classify as "sacred" are nevertheless seen by them as "culturally significant." This is especially true of some archaeological sites to which oral historical legends are attached.

Fieldwork interviews, archaeological survey, and a review of the ethnohistoric literature all confirm that wide forest trails, marked on contemporary maps as "reindeer roads," are often of great age and of enormous significance to the cognitive map by which Yugan Khanty establish their social and historical connections to Khanty communities on other river systems.

Khanty thoroughly understand ecosystems as fish and game habitats, as well as the concepts of microenvironments and population cycles, and differentially value each of the four major ecosystem types found in the Middle Ob River basin relative to the contribution of their resources to the traditional economy.

While Khanty understand their family hunting territories as bounded entities, that single boundary does not adequately express their appropriation of landscape. Our earlier ethnographic work confirmed that certain traditional practices represented in nineteenth century ethnohistoric literature still pertain: Khanty landholders partition their territory into fractions that they allocate to other family members; they transfer use rights to resources even while retaining claims to the land; and they still permit "hot pursuit" onto their territories of animals chased from neighboring lands. As we found out in our December 2000 trip to the Kurlomkiny settlement, and it is a datum never reported before, Khanty hunters perceive different levels of exclusivity in "holding" their lands: areas for trapping are the exclusive domain of the landholder, known in these circumstances by the Russian-Khanty epithet, *pyt' iki* or "[trap]line man," where trespass is severely approbated, while other areas are less exclusively claimed, and hunting-fishing trespass less approbated.

Yugan Khanty families often hunt beyond their family lands, a historical situation aggravated by the creation of the Yugan Zapovednik. This has meant that Khanty conceptualizations do not coincide with either governmental administrative boundaries or with natural definitions, such as tributary drainage systems.

Policy Implications of Findings

In ethnographic landscape studies, all findings of ethnographic significance will have direct implications for the management of behaviors, lands, and resources, which will often emerge as problem areas highlighting different conceptions of landscape. For example, the development of national or international regimes of legal protection requires generalized categories of sites that can accommodate the dynamic character of tradition. Nevertheless, generalized categories have the potential for missing the site-specific or culture-specific features of a place from which its sacred character derives. One solution might be to generate simple lists or registers of identified sacred places, but such lists require some generalized principles to justify the inclusion of places in the register. They also lack the ability to guide planners in terms of what to consider in the development process and tend to be generated by the development projects that disclose the existence of sacred places at the last minute. This tension between generalized (emic) typologies and culture-specific (etic) typologies is especially felt in developing protection regimes for natural sacred places of indigenous peoples. Our concerns focus on three main areas of confusion.

Problems of Form

It is typical to identify natural sacred sites according to particular elements of landscape. For the Khanty, these would include: lakes, rivers, swamps, uris, whirlpools, rapids, turns, and confluences of rivers, hills, ravines, islands, promontories, sacred groves, individual sacred trees, and stones. Two difficulties emerge with such a simple strategy: the problems of Complexity and Scale.

Complexity. Such a simple model of identification does not consider that natural sacred places may often be composed of several natural elements. On the Yugan, Pim, and Kazym Rivers, for example, the majority of sacred swamps include different kinds of high places: hillocks (Russian: *bugor*), ridges (Russian: *gryady*), "islands" (Russian: *ostrov*), or isolated trees, although there are several examples that indicate that simply swamps themselves can have special status. Sometimes different toponyms point to the same place. Local people call *Iming Soyem* (sacred creek)—located in the Trom-Agan River basin near Yubileinoe village (Russian: Svyatoy Ovrag, Sacred Ravine). The problem is even further complicated when one considers that such natural sacred elements may also include cultural elements, such as constructions to house the spirits. The region of Lake Larlumkina on the Yugan River is considered in its combination of several natural and cultural elements: the lake itself and high places near the lake shore, as well as a three shrines, a cemetery, and two archaeological sites. One very knowledgeable Khanty person suggested that the entire basin of the Pim River is considered by many Khanty to be sacred.

Scale. The complexity of such forms raises the question of what exactly should be protected in a site-based regime of legal protection. This is a matter of both area and access. Area questions have to do with establishing boundaries of sites to be protected; in very large areas, like Larlumkina, this may involve developing zonation strategies. Access questions are raised by the scale of a site as well as its function: Does access require a special route to the site that should be incorporated into a protection plan? Do the functions need to be protected from observers?

Problems of Function

We found it very difficult to strictly categorize sites according to their presumed function. When a place is referred to as *sacred*, what attributes of it are actually being pointed out. Our experience with the Siberian Khanty, as well as reports from several Native American groups (Kelley and Francis 1994), suggests that a place is typically referred to as sacred because of its association with religious belief (myth) and/or cultic practice. Yet, even these terms acquire a certain flexibility as tradition begins to shape itself out of the seeds of an origin long since lost to cultural memory.

Cultic Functions. Because of the high visibility of and anthropology's bias toward cultic activity, sites associated with offerings, sacrifices, or other forms of cultic behavior are often foregrounded in typological systems, in a manner parallel to the foregrounding of sites marked by constructions, as opposed to sacred natural features. This poses several problems, not the least of which is the fact that the sacredness of cultic sites may be reconfigured. Cultic practices may persist even after any memory of the mythic event or association that focused attention on the place has been lost. We have contemporary data that the religious power that once energized recently destroyed sacred places can be communicated to newly revealed sacred places, or, simply, new sacred places, hitherto unknown, may be revealed to the community through dreaming or other culturally sanctioned channels. These places have no mythic associations.

Mnemonic-Iconic Function. As American anthropologist Keith Basso (1996) has demonstrated, the association of place with myth and legend often gives sites a substantive mnemonic function as a culture's beliefs, values, and normative practices are mapped onto a landscape filled with stories. For example, on Bolshoi Yugan River, near Kykalevy settlement, a sacred whirlpool is marked by the following legend:

When people came and began to travel along the Yugan, and the [god's] wife was probably very ill-natured. She began to confuse people to delay them. Later, the grassy bank there, when it dried entirely [after the water lowered later in summer] became like stone. Her husband became angry and kicked her. Below this place appeared a deep, deep whirlpool. 'If you don't want to look at people, then you should live in a deep whirlpool,' [so the husband addressed the wife].

It is important to understand that even if no cultic practice emerges from this association, the association is functional in the strictest sense. Nevertheless, there is as much flexibility with this mnemonic-iconic function as with the cultic function. Religious belief can be enlarged from a mythic association to include associations with legend. An archaeological site, Vosh Vort Pay, on the upper Malyi Yugan River is considered sacred because of its legendary, quasi-mythic associations: To this place sand had been brought to create an island in the middle of the swamp on which a fortress had been built of large, palisaded logs. Other logs were dragged up the slope and stacked for defense; when the enemy attacked, the logs were released to roll down on them. According to legend, people known as *Aryx Yakh*, "The People Sung About" in Khanty epic songs, lived there: "The people were about three meters tall. What was strange about them was that they had no navels. These warrior giants' names were Nyomyl and Toruk." Interestingly, other texts we recorded from different sources say that the gods had no navels.

While many countries have a regime of legal protection for cultic places categorized as places of religious worship, as well as a regime of legal protection for places with a mnemonic-iconic function categorized as places of cultural significance, it is unclear whether the legal systems of most countries comprehend the ambiguity in and linkage between these categories from an indigenous perspective. The result is a scattershot pattern of protection that focuses on some sites highly marked by Western standards, while overlooking the broad and complex network of function-

45/ Khanty caretaker, Yefim Kolsomov at the labas commemorating where the high god Torum stepped down onto the earth. The site is featured in the model documentation presented in Table 1.

ality that links these more visible sites with the other, less-visible ones.

Problems of Participation.

The complex relationship between social structure and indigenous religious belief and practice is also a cause for confusion. We have identified more than 150 sacred sites in the Middle Ob River basin; but the fractions of the population who participate, through knowledge, belief or practice, in the traditions associated with these sites (Fig.45) vary considerably and pose problems for developing both typologies and regimes of legal protection.

Khanty social organization is based on extended families or lineages, with related lineages grouped into clans (Khanty *cir*). While the present settlement pattern has been influenced by migration and forced relocation in the Middle Ob region, evidence from our own fieldwork and the ethnographic record indicates

that different Khanty clans even today claim traditional use rights to different river systems tributary to the Ob River, in part because they believe their lineage was founded by divine ancestors who were also responsible for the creation of the river systems on which the majority of the clan lives (*Pupi* [bear] *cir.* Bolshoi Yugan River; *makh* [beaver] *cir.* Malyi Yugan River). Most Khanty extended families live on traditional family hunting territories, protected by family gods who are considered offspring of the lineage's founding deities. These lineage deities are the seven sons of the high god, each a patron of a major tributary of the Ob River. Roughly speaking, the principal deities are responsible for cosmological-level events, their first-generation offspring for the watersheds of the major tributaries, and the second-generation offspring for individual family lands along each watershed. Traditional Khanty thus believe that sacred power has been historically invested in both the landscape and the lineage.

This, however, creates an apparent and problematic hierarchy of interest. Khanty do distinguish between communal (Russian: *obshchie*) sacred sites, clan sacred sites, and family sacred sites. Nevertheless, because each category is embedded in the one above it, all, even a particular extended family's sacred place, is said to have a bearing on the success and prosperity of the Khanty community as a whole. Consequently, it would be incorrect to view community-wide sites as somehow more significant than the sacred places of individual, extended families.

Recommendations and Conclusions

The definition of familiar cultural resources, such as sacred sites, cemeteries, archaeological sites, and historical monuments, as very narrowly circumscribed locations is inevitably flawed, especially when dealing with the cultural resources of indigenous peoples. In our experience, among indigenous peoples:

—"Site" implies a boundedness or localization of phenomenon that may not obtain,

—"Sacred" is a category of inquiry that is less useful than "cultural significance"

—"Cultural significance" is very locally determined and cannot be presumed without intensive fieldwork

—"Cultural significance" is less likely to be signaled by a preservable characteristic of objects or places than by a set of proscribed human behaviors

Based on our experience, we believe that ethnographic landscape projects should:

—Identify the ways in which local uses of key terms of environmental, preservationist, and other social science discourses differ from the way the terms are used by advocacy and interest groups

—Link "site" and "behavior" through "discourse" by focusing principally on documentation of personal narratives, oral history, and folklore

—Integrate "sites" into networks based on ethnographically determined patterns of human behavior or conceptualization, not on typologies of form

—Combine the documentation of conventionally recognized forms of culturally significant sites with the documentation of social and economic uses of land

—Understand ethnographic landscape as a "layered" not just a "partitioned" complexity

The effort to create a co-managed, protected territory for the Yugan Khanty is ongoing. Our work on the Cultural Resources Survey Project concludes next year; the charter for the Yaoun Yakh Community Association is being redrawn to conform to new laws on community associations. We continue to pursue other legal, social, and scientific approaches to preserving the lands of the Yugan Khanty, such as nominating archeological sites, singly and in networks, for protected status. The effort to save the land and culture of the Yugan Khanty represents an initiative of great importance for Russia. For indigenous people in a country that has no tradition of recognizing indigenous peoples' sovereignty, nor as yet has any laws recognizing the unique status of indigenous people or providing for private, individual or communal land ownership, the proposed protected territory provides a legal basis for local self-government and control of land use in their traditional territory. For conservationists, it represents the first opportunity to effectively monitor with the close cooperation of the local population the human impact on a complex ecosystem and manage with them its sustainable development. Grounding cultural conservation programs among indigenous peoples in policies based on a dynamic model of human ecology, rather than on a static and more easily contested model of historical preservation, has several advantages. It means at once a more comprehensive program, based on the concept of "landscape," rather than "site," and a more effective program, since it manages behaviors ('uses') rather than structures or things. Moreover, under this banner, conservationists can become allies, instead of antagonists of Native interests.

The successful establishment of a protected area for the Yugan Khanty now depends principally on extraordinarily powerful petroleum magnates and on the will of government authorities, who are also responsible for the sale of oil licenses. Though the financial costs of oil production in the Yugan basin are extraordinarily high, to say nothing of the tragic and irreversible human cost to the Khanty, pressure from oil companies continues, and tracts of the Yugan River basin, which the Khanty use to feed their families, are still being sold. Unlike the situation in the West, where local constituencies might find government instruments to exert political pressure on their own, and where the greatest threat to cultural landscapes often comes from trespassers, poachers, and grave robbers, silence is not the best conservator of cultural value. In the political and economic environment of Siberia, the scientific gathering and public dissemination of ethnographic information is essential. First, publication makes deniability impossible for policymakers. Second, it demonstrates the complexity and indispensability of the cultural landscape in ways that expose the weak, exploitative nature of stand-alone cultural programs, such as festivals and museums, sponsored by Russian officialdom. Third, dissemination of information on cultural landscapes can frame an alternative discourse to those of natural resource exploitation and contested rights that may powerfully serve the interests of cultural conservation.

For Russia—a country with many nature reserves but a poor record of protecting the environment and sustaining the internationally acknowledged rights of indigenous peoples—the proposed Yugan Khanty Protected Territory thus represents a unique initiative.

Notes

1. The official listing of these peoples is provided in "O yedinom perechene korennykh malochislennykh narodov Rossiiskoi Federatsii" (On the unified list of indigenous minority peoples of the Russian Federation), 24 March 2000. For overviews of Khanty culture, see Levin and Potapov 1956; Kulemzin 1984; Kulemzin and Lukina 1992; Balzer 1994; and Golovnev 1995. Balzer 1999 is a very valuable ethnohistorical work. Earlier works include Karjalainen 1995 [1922]; Chernetsov 1987 [1927]; and Dunin-Gorkavitch 1995 [1904].

2. The authors thank The John D. and Catherine T. MacArthur Foundation for their support of fieldwork among the Western Siberia Khanty in the mentioned projects. Further information about the projects can be found on the World Wide Web at: http://www/nmsu.edu/~english/hc/hcsiberia.html

3. Data based on authors' fieldwork at the Kaimysovy extended family settlement, Upper Malyi Yugan River, Surgut Region, Khanty-Mansi Autonomous Okrug, June 1996.

4. Alliances between environmental interests and indigenous interests are widely proclaimed in the international arena, but they have a mixed record of success, if measured by amicable cooperation in the pursuit of mutual interests (see Stevens 1997).

References

Balalaeva, Olga
1999   Sviashchennye mesta khantov Srednei I Nizhnei Obi (Khanty sacred places of the middle and lower Ob River). In: *Ocherki istorii traditsionnogo zemlepol'zovaniia Khantov (Materialy k Atlasu)*, pp. 139-56. Ekaterinburg: Tezis.

Balzer, Marjorie Mandelstam
1994   Khanty. In: *Encyclopedia of World Cultures*, Paul Friedrich, ed., pp.89–92. Boston: G. K. Hall.
1999   *The Tenacity of Ethnicity: A Siberian Saga in Global Perspective*. Princeton: Princeton University Press.

Basso, Keith
1996   *Wisdom Sits in Places: Landscape and Language among the Western Apache*. Albuquerque: University of New Mexico Press.

Brody, Hugh
1981   *Maps and Dreams*. Vancouver: Douglas and MacIntyre.

Chernetsov, Valerii N.
1987   *Istochniki po etnografii Zapadnoi Sibiria* (Sources in West Siberian Ethnography). Tomsk: Tomsk University Press.

Dömke, Stephan, and Michael Succow
1998   *Cultural Landscapes and Nature Conservation in Northern Eurasia*. Bonn: Naturschutzbund Deutschland.

Dunin-Gorkavich, A.A.
1995   *Tobolskii Sever: Obshihii obzor' strany, eio estestvennykh bogatstv i promyshlennoi deiatel'nosti naseleniia* (The Tobolsk North: a general survey of the country, it natural wealth, and industrial activity of the population). (Reprint of 1904 edition) Mos-

cow: Libereya.

Golovnev, Andrei V.

1995   *Govoriashchie Kul'tury: Traditsii Samodiitsev i Ugrov* (Talking Cultures: Traditions of Samoyeds and Ugrians). Ekaterinburg: Russian Academy of Science, Urals Branch.

Karjalainen, K.F.

1995   *Religiia Yugorskikh Narodov* (Religion of the Ugrian people), trans. N. V. Lukina. 2 vols. Tomsk: Tomsk University Press. [reprints the first two volumes of 1921-27, *Der Religion der Jugra-Völker*. 3 vols. Folklore Fellows Communications 41, 44, 63. Helsinki-Porvoo: Suomalainen Tiedeakademia].

Kelley, Klara, and Harris Francis

1994   *Navajo Sacred Places*. Bloomington: Indiana University Press.

Kulemzin, Vladislav M.

1984   *Chelovek i priroda v verovaniiakh Khantov* (Man and Nature in Khanty Beliefs). Tomsk: Tomsk University Press.

Kulemzin, Vladislav M., and Nadezhda V. Lukina

1992   *Znakomtes': Khanty* (Meet: Khanty). Novosibirsk: Nauka.

Levin, Maksim G., and Leonid P. Potapov, eds.

1964   *The Peoples of Siberia*. Chicago: University of Chicago Press.

Ocherki Istorii

1999   *Ocherki istorii traditsionnogo zemlepol'zovaniia Khantov (Materialy k Atlasu)* (Essays on Khanty traditional land use and history (materials for an atlas). Ekaterinburg: Tezis.

Pika, Alexander, ed.

1999   Neotraditionalism in the Russian North: Indigenous Peoples and the Legacy of Perestroika. *Circumpolar Research Series* 6. Edmonton and Seattle: Canadian Circumpolar Institute and University of Washington Press.

Rushforth, Scott, and James S. Chisholm

1991   *Cultural Persistence: Continuity in Meaning and Moral Responsibility among the Bearlake Athapaskans.*

Tucson: University of Arizona Press.

Schmidt, Eva

1987   Khanty and Mansi Religion. In: *The Encyclopedia of Religion*, Mircea Eliade, ed., v. 8, pp. 280-88. New York: Macmillan.

1989   Bear Cult and Mythology of Northern Ob' Yugrians. In: *Uralic Mythology and Folklore*, Mihaly Hoppal and Juha Pentakäinen, eds., pp. 187-231. Budapest: Ethnographic Institute, Hungarian Academy of Sciences.

Stevens, Stan, ed.

1997   *Conservation Through Cultural Survival: Indigenous Peoples and Protected Areas*. Washington, D.C.: Island Press.

Wiget, Andrew

1999a   Ekonomika i traditsionnoye zemlepol'zovanie vostochnykh khantov (Economy and traditional land use of the Eastern Khanty). In: *Ocherki istorii traditsionnogo zemlepol'zovaniia Khantov (Materialy k Atlasu)*, pp. 157-200. Ekaterinburg: Tezis.

1999b   Chiornyi Sneg: neft' i vostochnye khanty (Black snow: oil and the Eastern Khanty). In *Ocherki istorii traditsionnogo zemlepol'zovaniia Khantov (Materialy k Atlasu).* pp. 201-14. Ekaterinburg: Tezis.

Wiget, Andrew, and Olga Balalaeva

1996   Black Snow: Oil and the Khanty of Western Siberia. *Cultural Survival Quarterly* 20(4):17-9.

1998a   Siberian Perspectives on Protected Use Areas as a Strategy for Conserving Traditional Indigenous Cultures in the Context of Economic Development. In: *Development in the Arctic: Proceedings of the 7th Nordic Arctic Research Forum Symposium*, Tom Greiffenberg, ed., pp. 88-100. Copenhagen: Danish Polar Center.

1998b   The Siberian Khanty 'Sacred Trust' Project: Emic and Etic Strategies for Creating Fieldwork-Based Typologies of Sacred Places. In *Natural Sacred Sites: Cultural Diversity and Biological Diversity. Proceedings of the First International UNESCO Seminar*. Paris: UNESCO.

Nenets Sacred Sites as Ethnographic Landscape

GALINA P. KHARYUCHI[1]

In the Yamal-Nenets Autonomous Area (*Okrug*) in Northwest Siberia—as in many other regions of arctic Russia—the problem of preserving cultural sites and monuments related to local Native people is quite acute [see Fedorova, this volume]. Environments are changing and many habitats are being broken up under rapid industrial development, mainly for oil and gas, of the indigenous population's lands. The traditional system of wildlife management, subsistence usage, and land preservation is deteriorating. In the near future, development will begin in the northernmost section of the West Siberian tundra and may even include the High Arctic coastland and offshore grounds, where proven oil and gas deposits exist. In conditions of such rapid industrial development, the preservation, registration, and governmental protection of ritual sites as monuments of the ethno-cultural heritage of indigenous people are acquiring greater urgency.

In 1990, a new research unit, the Laboratory of Ethnography and Ethnolinguistics, an offshoot of the *Institut Problem Osvoeniia Severa* (IPOS; Institute of Problems of Development in the North), was established in the city of Salekhard, the regional center of the Yamal-Nenets Area. Since 1998, it has been transformed into the "Center for Humanitarian Research on Indigenous Minority Peoples of the North of Yamal-Nenets Autonomous Area" (CHR). Representatives of the region's indigenous peoples—the Nenets, Khanty, and Selkup—became staff researchers and scientific collaborators. One crucial field of CHR activities became the mapping of sacred sites (or "ritual places") of the area's

indigenous people, which was named a key heritage goal by the local Association of Indigenous Minority People of the region, *Yamal—Potomkam!* (Yamal: For Our Descendants!). In 1994, two CHR staff researchers—Leonid Lar and I—began surveys under this program. Lar made a draft map of the Yamal District sacred sites and prepared it for publication (Lar 1995). He later used it for his Ph.D. dissertation, "The Traditional Religious Worldview of the Nenets," which he defended in 2000 (Lar 1999).

As a Native researcher and a Nenets woman born into a nomadic reindeer herding family on the Gydan Peninsula, I was responsible for mapping Nenets sacred sites in my native region, the Gydan Peninsula (Fig. 46), which is territorially a part of the Taz District of the Yamal-Nenets Autonomous Okrug.

Both Lar and I were sharply aware of the scientific importance of this work, and the impacts of industrial development spoke to its practical urgency and value. The immediate task was to identify and document the remaining monuments of spiritual culture for the Nenets people—because the destruction of Nenets sacred sites in areas that had undergone oil and gas development, road construction, and other industrial activities was taking place before our eyes. We did not know how to create a system for protecting sacred sites, but we felt that a special administrative ruling or legislative act was essential to prevent their damage and destruction.

Extensive oil and gas exploration has taken place on the Gydan tundra since the 1970s, and several known Nenets ritual places and sacred sites have already been

155

destroyed during the early geophysical and exploratory surveys. The indigenous tundra residents, the Nenets herders and fishermen, have been powerless against these intruders. The geologists were drilling holes in our land,[2] and were disturbing the peace of the Lower World's inhabitants and the spirits of sacred places. Where possible, Nenets people have restored the damaged sites and conducted ritual "cleaning" of the area. But they did not know how to protect their sacred places.

In December 1994, I first reported on this project at the Third World Archaeological Congress in New Delhi in a paper titled "Mapping Nenets Sacred Sites of Gydan Peninsula" (Kharyuchi and Lipatova 1998). In 1999, I defended a Ph.D. dissertation titled *Traditions and Innovations in the Nenets Ethnic Culture*, later published as a book (Kharyuchi 1999a, 2001). Its second chapter, "The Sacred Sphere of the Traditional Nenets Society," was dedicated to Nenets beliefs and rites related to or performed at sacred sites, and to their modern transformation. The map I made of Nenets sacred places on the Gydan Peninsula (at the scale 1:2,000,000) was attached as an appendix to my dissertation (Kharyuchi 1999b; 2001:216a). Some seventy traditional sacred sites of the Gydan Nenets that still exist and are revered today are designated on the map (Kharyuchi 2001:216–7). For each sacred site, the following information was recorded: traditional site name and its interpretation; origin of the site; events and legends (stories) related to the site; and its modern preservation status (condition). Many Nenets traditional sacred sites in the study area were first documented more than seventy-five years ago by V. Toboliakov, a participant of the Gydan Expedition of the Russian Academy of Sciences in 1926–1927 (Toboliakov 1930). This made it possible to compare the state of preservation, functionality, and changes of various sacred sites over almost eighty years, as well as the preservation of the rites and oral traditions related to them. This chapter discusses my work in surveying and documenting Nenets sacred sites and some of the results.

Sacred Places: a Personal View and Features of the Ethnographer's Work

Beginning my work, I experienced a deep internal emotional conflict. I, a Nenets woman, born and brought up in a traditional family of reindeer herders, knew well the complexity of the task and the challenges I faced. As a Nenets woman, it was difficult for me to collect information about sacred sites, because of the traditional gender roles prescribed from childhood and the many taboos still practiced in the nomadic Nenets society, especially in the sacred sphere. Sacred rituals are still almost exclusively the men's area of knowledge and activities. Women are rarely if ever included and as low-level participants at minor rituals only. All information pertaining the origins, clan and family ownership, and the rites to be performed at sacred places is still strictly controlled by men. Therefore, women, even senior ones, are often quite ignorant about sacred sites and are presumed to be such under traditional system of beliefs.

The initial stage of my survey was especially arduous. During my first field trips, or while on short holiday visits to tundra camps with my relatives—who are practicing reindeer herders—I collected some data, in no way advertising my main interest. I feared the condemnation of the elders among my family and clan people; because of that, I felt that I should address only youths. The young people assisted me with pleasure. As a Nenets woman, I could not ask questions of the elderly men, nor demonstrate any interest in sacred places, much less visit and describe them (except for special female sites). I also faced many special obstacles in approaching the sites, because I had not achieved that advanced age when a [post-menopausal] woman again becomes sacredly pure, and many taboos, including those on a woman visiting ritual sites, no longer apply to her.

It started to change once an elderly shaman from my clan told me that I should "hold the drum in my hands" [that is, could and should practice shaman rituals myself]. I was surprised by his words, more so because this was our first meeting and I was not personally acquainted with him, although he knew about me. I therefore took his words merely as a joke, as I had no extrasensory or other special abilities whatsoever. Most of my adult life had been spent in an urban environment and in another culture. I had graduated from a high school and a teacher's college under the Soviet system of government education and, as an adult, continued to live in the city and communicated less with my people on the tundra.

Probably, in a traditional society, I would have had an unusual destiny. After this memorable meeting with the shaman, it somehow became psychologically easier for me to engage in documenting Nenets sacred sites. It seemed as if I had received a "blessing" and could now approach even elderly men and other senior persons. Not everyone can relate to this theme; maybe, I thought, it means that it is written in my destiny to do this work in the name of protecting Nenets sacred sites and for the sake of my people. And so, although I have not become a *shamanka* [female shaman] myself, I could approach this sacred field from another angle—the scientific.

I belong to the community of tundra Gydan Nenets, a special ethno-territorial grouping living on Gydan Peninsula (Figs. 46, 47). The Gydan Nenets have a special dialect [of the Nenets language], and they live sepa-

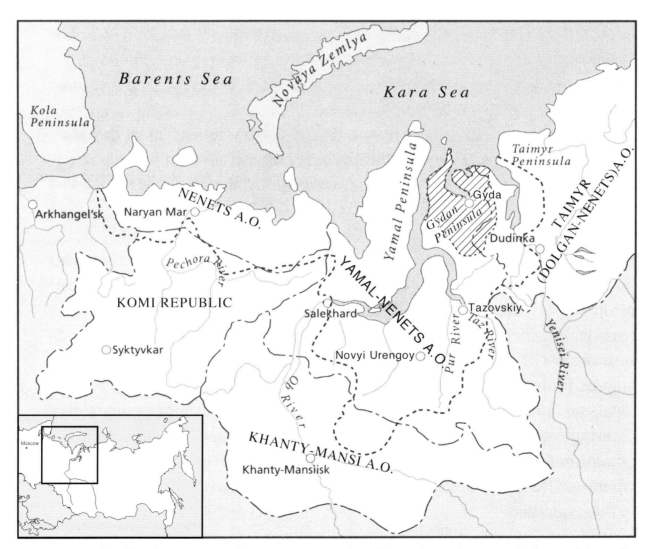

46/ *Area populated by the Nenets people in Arctic Russia (dotted line). The study region, the home of the Gydan tundra Nenets on the Gydan Peninsula, is shown by a diagonal pattern.*

rately from other groups of tundra reindeer Nenets by virtue of our land's remoteness. My parents were reindeer herders employed by the Gydan State Fisheries Processing Plant. Throughout their life, they cared for a large herd of government-owned reindeer, and upon retirement, they became private reindeer herders. The family herding operation is carried on now by my brothers, who live in a tundra camp; they inherited my parents' reindeer together with our family guardian spirits. I, to the contrary, left the tundra at an early age, gradu-

ated from Tyumen University, worked for many years as a schoolteacher, became engaged in anthropological research, and defended a dissertation on the history and culture of my people. Although I live in Salekhard, I try to visit my relatives on the tundra every year, to spend some time in my native environment and with my community. As an anthropologist (ethnographer), I am supposed to take a detached view of my native tradition, observe changes in the lifestyle and spiritual culture of my people, and to gather field data, from which I have to make conclusions and write scientific papers. This is a challenging path. I am especially interested in today's changes to Nenets spiritual culture, and in the attitudes of modern young people toward family relics and ritual sites, and their own performance of ceremonies and rituals.

It is not easy to get to my native "roots." First, I fly from Salekhard, to the city of Novyi Urengoy, and from there, to the district center, the town of Tazovskskiy. From Tazovskskiy, I fly by helicopter to the small northern town of Gyda (in Nenets: *Nedya*—a pen for wild reindeer). I leave town on a reindeer sled, traveling with my brothers on a long trek across the tundra to our family camp. Forty kilometers (25 miles) from the town of Gyda is the *Khekhe khan soteya* site, literally "hill of the sacred sled." Sacred sleds with ritual objects [images of guardian spirits] are left at this sacred site after the death of their life-long owners. Two such sleds have been left on *Khekhe khan soteya*. One of them belonged to the father of my fellow countryman Port Salinder (1917–1998). A former re-

47/ Galina Kharyuchi (center) during a winter field survey.

PROTECTING THE INVISIBLE/ NENETS SACRED SITES

48/ Active Nenets sacred site in Southern Yamal, 1996.

indeer herder and chair of the herders' collective farm in the 1950s, he moved to town upon his retirement, lived there until the end of his life, and had no reindeer of his own. He could not keep his family ritual objects in a wooden house that was considered spiritually "unclean." After his death, his son brought his father's old sled with all his guardian spirits to this sacred site, where it remained until recently.

In addition to sacred sleds, antlers and heads [old skulls] of sacrificed reindeer are left at this place, as well as traces of "bloodless" sacrifices, such as offerings of food and other gifts (Fig. 48). We stop so that the reindeer can rest, and we rub our numb arms and legs. My brothers walk up the hill and leave their offerings at the site. They sip and then pour a drop of vodka on the ground—regaling the spirit of the site—then leave the bottle there, placing it among the antlers of sacrificed reindeer. Aloud or mentally, they talk with the site's spirit, asking for clear weather and a safe road. I always stay below: a woman cannot go up to this sacred site.

We travel farther on our reindeer sled across the snow-covered white tundra. Coming toward us along this route are other herders from their family camps, going for supplies or picking up their children in town. They have been traveling for twenty-four hours or more. We stop, greet each other, exchange news, and go our separate ways. Their sled reindeer are tired, but ours are anxious to head home. But any time they pass the *Khekhe khan soteya* site, all Nenets stop their sleds without fail and conduct an offering ceremony. Once I tried to photograph the site from a distance, but this particular shot failed. So, I do not know what it looks like in detail and have no recorded image of the site.

A legend about the genesis of this ritual site exists. Once, a large caravan of reindeer sleds (in Nenets, *myud*) was moving across the tundra from north to south. The day was clear. The leaders of this long caravan had already reached the hill that designated a watershed. Suddenly the sky darkened, the wind rose, and a whirlwind of snow began to spin. The reindeer were falling and fighting about the sleds; the people were ready to drop. Then they began to ask *Num* (the Nenets supreme deity)[3] to save them, sacrificing a white bull reindeer as a symbol of the white whirlwind. But the weather did not calm down; *Num* had not heard the people's supplication.

Then an old Nenets, the head of this clan, having loosened a sacred sled from the reindeer and sleds, began to drag it toward the north, from whence the blizzard was blowing. But it was hard for him; he was old. Suddenly from out of the snowstorm his small grandson appeared. The two of them dragged the clan's sacred sled to the hilltop. Before their eyes, the hill began to grow toward the sky, thus lifting the sacred sled. Having risen to the height of a medium-sized *khorey* [a wooden pole for driving reindeer, three to four meters long], the hill seemed to stop moving. At that very moment, the weather changed, as though there had been no snowstorm. Like partridges, the people began to shake off the snow. Having collected the rest of their reindeer and belongings, they sacrificed three bull reindeer. The people stood the heads and antlers of the sacrificial reindeer on the hill near the clan's sacred sled. The caravan moved off. For a long time, in the distance, people saw the clan's sacred sled that had been left behind.

I heard this legend in the early 1990s from Boris G. Shushakov, who is close to me in age. Born in 1950, he lives in the town of Gyda and was about forty years old at the time. The knowledge of traditional stories connected with the history and spirits of a certain site, even among the town residents, is evidence of the reverence for sacred places that is held by modern Nenets people of middle and even quite young age.

I happened by this site two more times. In the summer of 1997, after my father's funeral, we moved deep into the tundra with the family herd and set up our family herders' tents not far from this sacred place. Our family was in mourning, and for an entire year, none of us could visit sacred places. I was surprised that even

the reindeer and dogs did not go very close to that place. The next time was in the summer of 2000. I had arrived at my family camp in the middle of July to make a map of sacred sites. A neighbor from another family at our camp, coming from the Salinder clan, made a sacrifice to the sacred sled and ancestral spirits. Nenets people of the Salinder clan are called *khabi* and are considered of Khanty origin. In the middle of summer, they usually make a sacrifice to ancestral spirits. Inhabitants of all neighboring tents must come without an invitation and participate in the feasting, together with the spirits. I had my own professional interest in the ceremony; besides the fact that, as a guest, it was mandatory that I show respect to the ancestral spirits. The host of the ritual was a private reindeer herder who had graduated from an agricultural institute. At one time, he had worked as a veterinary expert with the collective farm herd. Now there are many such private reindeer herders on the Gydan tundra, with high school and even higher education, who have their own herds with up to 500 to 800 reindeer.

Having moved our family camp from the site closer to the village, we set up our tents near an abandoned oil rig (Fig. 49), which was in the middle of the beautiful, blossoming tundra. Remains of the rig's metal construction, sticks, boards, and torn bags from cement and some unknown powder were sticking out of the ground; this place carried a stench. However, a lot of good wood suitable for making sled parts was available. On the tundra, only dwarf birch and rose willow grow, and the only available wood is driftwood from the shores of the great rivers and the Ob Bay. During free shifts from herd watch, our men spent time at the abandoned rig and made sled parts. I photographed this terrible place and asked a few general questions about tundra sacred sites. Work on my map could only be done fitfully, as the men were busy with the reindeer and were going to the rig. But my main informant, sixty-year-old Khatibi Ivanovich Yabtunai, came for me as soon as he had free time and said, "Let's play map."

49/ Nenets children at an abandoned oil rig site.

We went to the back part of a tent, and I spread a map on the ground and started to mark and write on it. The other herders came over in stages, and everyone who knew sacred sites identified them, and told stories about them.

Traditional Nenets Views of Spirits and Sacred Sites

In Nenets views, the earth (the ground) is alive, and each hillock, hill, river, lake, and sea has a custodial spirit. All spirits, regardless of their function, are valued as forces that unite the Nenets people. This has been noted by many authors as a characteristic not only of the Nenets—both tundra- and forest-dwelling—but also of their neighbors, the Khanty people [Wiget and Balalaeva, this volume]. A place inhabited by a spirit was visited not only by the social group to which the given spirit "belonged" (or was guardian of), but also by many of their neighbors, sometimes from very remote areas. Native informants assert that the presence of sacred sites is an indication of an area belonging to a given people forever. Among the Khanty, the desecration or destruction of any ritual structures was considered a trespass on one's clan territory (Kulemzin 1995:70). Although this statement was made in connection with the Khanty people, the concept is fully applicable to the Nenets as well.

On the tundra, elders frequently warn young people about adopting a respectful attitude to the earth and any hill or lake that has its own guardian spirit. In winter, in the white silence of the tundra, especially in gloomy weather or on a sunny spring day when the horizon merges with the ground, these places orient travelers. They are visible from afar and seem to point the way. The same purposes are served by a burial ground or cemetery in a high place. If it is the burial location of an older person, it is often said that "my grandfather or grandmother has shown me the way."

Places that are sacred in their own right—*Khebidya ya* (literally, sacred ground: *khebidya* means sacred, *ya* means the ground)—are marked by the highest sacred importance. Nenets place names signifying sacred sites frequently contain direct information about the sacredness of a certain land feature. *Khebidya ya* is added to common place name-formants, such as *ngo* (an island), *to* (lake), *soti/suti* (a plateau with a wide base and gentle slopes), *syeda* (a hill), *yakha* (a river), *sokho* (a high-peaked hill with a wide base). Apparently, natural features that contain spirits make up the most basic category of Nenets ritual sites.

Sacred sites have no precisely established borders and no marked transitions into the nearby non-sacred landscape. Usually such sites are located in noticeable places, near a stone of some special shape, on top of a hill, or on the shore of lake (Fig. 50). A lake, too, can be sacred; and, therefore, people are forbidden to fish in it, or it is mandatory that the first catch be sacrificed to the spirit of the sacred lake. A shaman determined when a sacred site should be revered by everyone or by a particular clan or family, as well as what needed to be placed there or was considered *khekhe* (spirit). The shaman also determined which image this spirit—the custodian of the given sacred place—has.

Thus, sacred places are actively used cultural sites. They are usually located in the areas where reindeer herders live continuously and use for their economic activities, although particularly practices, such as herding, fishing or trapping, are traditionally limited or often completely forbidden at or near the site. This clearly puts Native sacred sites to the category of "monuments of spiritual culture." They accumulate significance through a long history and are characterized by a conservatism of form and ways of practicing/performing certain ritual activities. Such functions allow us to define a ritual site as a nomadic people's equivalent to a temple. Actually, northern sacred sites are true open-air temples for my people. Here one can find all major spatial and spiritual components of a temple, such as a strict layout of the sacred space; a sculpture or an object of religious significance; the developed attributes of a ritual at the site focused on this central object or sculpture; specified norms and rules of behavior for participants; and a sustained tradition about the for-

mation and reasons for emergence of the given sacred site. The basic difference between a sacred place and a temple, characteristic of major world religions, is the obvious esoteric nature of the ritual site (Gemuev 1990; Gemuev and Sagalaev 1986:154); that is, its visitation, and even knowledge of it, is open only to a small circle of devoted or chosen persons.

As other peoples go to pray in a temple, for the Nenets, such sacred places are temples: "special places delineated in oral tradition or legends, having a special sacred value, and possessing power over the people who belong to a traditional community" (Balalaeva 1999:142). As Balalaeva has noted (ibid.), these places are sacred in the broadest sense: they connect the traditional way of life of a people with sacred myths, the most ancient cosmological planes of mythology, and religious ritual.

Sacred islands are given special importance by the Nenets. As ethnographer Andrei Golovnev has pointed out,

> [I]n contrast with the major world religions, under the Nenets religious beliefs, the most important temple is not considered the one that people visit most often, but that (place) that is nearly inaccessible or is accessible only to the chosen few (2000:208).

And as Nenets elder Avvo Vanuito has stated (Golovnev 2000:232), "the major gods live at the ends of the Earth." Sacred islands are difficult to access, and this circumstance begets the appearance of new customs. Sometimes there is a transfer from the island to the mainland, to the continental coast adjacent to the island, not of the sacred place itself, but of all the intended special rituals to be performed there. Thus, another sacred site for carrying out a ritual appears on the mainland, and the coast adjoining the island should also be protected. For example, the *Ngoya-khebidya-ya* site has already been "transferred" in such a manner from Shokalskyi Island in the Kara Sea to the mainland, and the *Yarongon khantalba* sacred site has been similarly transferred from the nearby Sibiryakov Island.

Restoration of Nenets sacred sites destroyed by

50/ Nenets sacred site at Cape Tiutey-Sale ("Walrus Cape"), Northwestern Yamal, 1928.

surveyors and geological prospectors is becoming another new phenomenon. The Nenets people place scattered sacrificial antlers, animal skulls, stones, and other objects on the original location. In the Nenets' views of the spirit world, a magic force exists in features that have an unusual appearance. If a stone sits on a given place, a shaman could "recognize" that this stone is none other than one of the forms into which the spirit has become manifest. When I was twelve years old, I once went with the children to cut tundra grass, which is used as insoles for footwear and for mats. A fog came up unexpectedly, and we lost the way to our tents. We were lost for a long time, but behaved quietly and did not panic. We became tired and decided to rest on a hill. On this place, we saw a stone that looked similar to a seated person. While sitting around it, we decided that this was not an ordinary stone, but the spirit of this hill. While we were resting, the fog passed, and we easily found the way to the tents. We took the stone with us, and our father put it [with other sacred objects] on the sacred family sled.

The Survey Area

Gydan Peninsula is the northeastern-most extension of the West Siberian plain, roughly between 68°N and 73°N and between the mouths of Taz and Ob Bays on the west and Yenisey Bay in the east. A large part of the peninsula is related administratively to the Taz District of Yamal-Nenets Autonomous Okrug. The district also includes the northern part of neighboring Taz Peninsula, which is washed on the north and east by the waters of Taz Bay. The total area of Taz District is 173,4000 square kilometers (66,950 square miles); its administrative center is the town of Tazovskiy—in Nenets, *Khalmer-sede,* which means "Dead Men's Cape."

Three large Native communities, the towns of Gyda, Antipayuta, and Nakhodka, are in the district territory. Also on Gydan Peninsula proper are several small villages and trading posts: Matyuy-sale, Yesya-yakha, Khalmervonga, Yuribey, Razvilka, Mongatolyang, Nyakhar-yakha, and Tanamo. The area under the Gydan Town Council authority has more than 3,000 residents (3,279 as of January 1, 2004), mostly Nenets, including several hundred nomadic families living in tundra camps.

By decision of the Yamal-Nenets Okrug administration, and with the consent of Russian federal agencies, Gydan Peninsula was given the status of a "specially protected ethno-natural territory," in which only traditional subsistence activities such as reindeer herding, hunting, and fishing are allowed.

Surveys and ethnographic research focused on drafting a map of traditional Nenets sacred sites and adjoining areas are regarded as critical components to creating an appropriate legislative base for their future protection, which is an ultimate goal of our work. This should solve several problems. The legislative actions will protect the homeland of the Northern indigenous peoples, and thus will facilitate the preservation of an ancient civilization of nomadic reindeer herders. The actions will create additional protected areas for preserving the flora and fauna of northern regions, which will facilitate the continuity of natural landscapes and sustainable development of the North.

In the territory of the Gydan Peninsula, several "specially protected natural areas" have been established by various legislative actions during the last few decades.

—Gydan Federal Nature Reserve (*Gydanskii gosudarstvennyi zapovednik*)

> 878,174 hectares (3,390 square miles) in area, this reserve of national significance was established by Decree No. 167 of the Government of the Russian Federation on October 7, 1996. Its purpose was "the preservation of genetic stock of the plant and animal species, discrete types and communities of plants and animals, and the typical and unique ecological systems of the North."

—Yamal State Wildlife Preserve, (*Yamal'skii prirodnyi zakaznik*)

> Of regional significance, the Gydan site, 162,000 hectares (625 square miles) in area, was established by Resolution No. 322 of the Tyumen Regional Executive Committee on May 19, 1977, for a period of ten years. A ruling (No. 66) by the governor of the Yamal-Nenets Area on February 11, 1997, extended its validity until 2006. Its purpose was "[t]he maintenance of the in-

tegrity of natural communities; preservation, reproduction and restoration of disappearing species of animals and birds; and preservation of their habitats, flora, and fauna."

—Gydoyamovskiy State Nature Preserve (*Gydoyamovskiy prirodnyi zakaznik*)

> Of regional significance, this 765,000 hectares area (2,954 square miles), is also being planned for a large section of the peninsula. According to the preserve's prospectus, it is designated as a "zoological-botanical" site; that is, it preserves the arctic flora and fauna.

In the district territory, the creation of two more preserves has been proposed, the status of which will be specified during the design phase:

—Taz Bay Fishery Preserve

> Encompasing Taz Bay, including the mouth and lower watercourse of the Taz River, a 300,000 hectares area (1,158 square miles), its goal is preservation of a valuable fishing basin. Prospecting, exploration, and commercial drilling for oil and gas will be prohibited.

—Messoyakha Preserve

> In the middle and lower courses of the Messoyakha River, 5,000 hectares in area (20 square miles), its goals are the same as listed for the Taz Bay Preserve.

Besides the existing and planned natural preserves,[4] the Taz District features two smaller "natural monuments":

—*Nyamboy*, a forest "islet" on the arctic tundra, considered "a botanical monument"

—*Messoyakha*, 600 hectares (1,482 acres) in area, in the Lake Lysukai-to area. Renowned for numerous discoveries of fossilized animals: mammoths, musk oxen, and so on, it has been designated as a "paleontological natural monument."

The Russian federal "Regulation for Natural Preserves" also established an additional two-kilometer secure zone, extending outward from the established border of protected areas.

Several Nenets sacred sites exist on the Yavay (Evay-Sale), Oleniy, and Mammoth Peninsulas; on Sibiriakov, Shokalskiy, and Oleniy Islands, which are part of the

Gydanskiy Federal Reserve, on the Gydan site of the Yamal State Nature Preserve, and on the projected Gydoyamovskiy Preserve. In accordance with the official Russian designation of protected areas (nature preserves, monuments, and parks—see Shul'gin, this volume), geological exploration, construction, and other industrial activities are forbidden or strictly limited within their boundaries; but the traditional subsistence activity of the indigenous population is allowed.

Several large fields of fuel and energy deposits have been mapped and explored in the territory governed by the Gydan Town Council:

—*Shtormovoye* (Storm) field, 24,000 hectares (93 square miles) in size, with gas and gas condensate deposits

—*Utrenn'ee* (Morning) field,122,000 hectares (471 square miles) in size, with gas, gas condensate, and oil

—*Gydanskoye* (Gydan) field, 65,000 hectares (251 square miles) in size, with gas and gas condensate.

Legislative Basis for the Protection of Nenets Sacred Places

In April 2001, the Federal Duma of the Russian Federation enacted the federal law "On the Lands of Traditional Subsistence-Use of the Indigenous Minority Peoples of the North, Siberia, and the Russian Far East," which had been discussed by the Russian Federal Duma (Parliament) for many years. According to this law, priority areas used for traditional subsistence are designated to provide conditions for the preservation and development of "historically established" economies that are the basis for the daily activities and spiritual culture of Northern indigenous peoples. Priority subsistence use areas include reindeer pastures, clan and ancestral hunting-and-fishing grounds, natural monuments, and ritual-cultural places. In the neighboring Khanty-Mansi Autonomous Okrug [to the south of the Yamal-Nenets Okrug], where the majority of the Native lands are under industrial development, it has been proposed that a part of the lands now under industrial development be withdrawn and designated as priority

subsistence-use areas of the Native population [see Wiget and Balalaeva, this volume]. A paradoxical situation thus arose: it is necessary to "withdraw" ancestral Native lands from industrialists and oil companies in order to return them to their owners.

According to the enacted laws, "priority subsistence-use areas" in the North are to be secured for registered "enterprises" of traditional economy(ies)—that is, Native family or clan herding and fishing cooperatives, communities or other economic institutions employing Native people. In the area under consideration, which is administered by the Gydan Town Council, no new registered community or family "enterprises" have been created by or of local residents as yet. Therefore, Gydan local authorities or the management of the Gydan State Fisheries Processing Plant allocate pastures and assign reindeer migration paths to individual reindeer herders or families who graze public reindeer herds (herds owned by Okrug and local agencies).

In Yamal-Nenets Okrug, the local legislative and executive authorities think that the actual economic life-sustaining base of these people is the land in the so-called "traditional subsistence-use areas." The total area of these lands in the Yamal-Nenets Okrug is 76,925,000 hectares (297,000 square miles). It is essential to secure traditional subsistence-use lands for local residents before any active industrial development takes place so that the lands do not need to be withdrawn later, as has been recently proposed for the neighboring Khanty-Mansi Okrug.

On October 1, 1997, a law was enacted in the Yamal-Nenets Autonomous Okrug titled "About the Regulation of Land Use in Places of Residence and Traditional Economic Activity by Indigenous Minority Peoples of the North on Lands of Yamal-Nenets Autonomous Okrug." The creation of communities and the securing of ancestral lands are being carried out based on the recently enacted (July 2000) Russian federal law, "About General Principles for Establishing Communities of Indigenous Minority Peoples of the North, Siberia, and the Russian Far East," and Chapter 6 of the

Yamal-Nenets Autonomous Okrug Law, "About Local Self-Management in Yamal-Nenets Autonomous Okrug," which is titled "The Form of Providing for the Local Self-Management of Indigenous Minority Peoples of the North in the Areas of Their Compact Residence." This law was enacted in December 1996.

The version of the "specially protected natural areas" that is known as "Ethno-Natural Parks" is another form of protection for the indigenous population's lands in the Russian North [Shul'gin, this volume]. The legal basis for establishing ethno-natural parks is found in Section 1U, "On Natural Parks," of the Russian federal law (No. 33-F3) of March 14, 1995, "About Specially Protected Natural Territories." In the Yamal-Nenets Okrug, a law titled, "About Specially Protected Natural Territories of the Yamal-Nenets Autonomous Okrug," also was enacted on October 14, 1997. A federal law titled "About the Bases for Government Regulation of the Social and Economic Development of the North of the Russian Federation" (Article 12) was enacted June 19, 1996. Another important legislative act is the Yamal-Nenets Autonomous Okrug Law of October 21, 1998, titled, "On Reindeer Herding." This law establishes the legal, economic, environmental, and social bases by nominating reindeer herding as one of the key traditional economic activities for Northern indigenous peoples. It also created conditions for support of effective economic practices of Native herders and for the preservation of their traditional lifestyle and culture (*Sbornik zakonov* 1999:493). The federal version of the same law pertaining to the reindeer herding activities of the indigenous peoples of Siberia and the Russian North is still under deliberation by the Russian Federal Duma (as of 2004).

Presently in the Yamal-Nenets Okrug, lands under heavy industrial (oil and gas) development are, for the most part, located in the Pur, Yamal, and Nadym Districts, and in the southern section of Taz District, where major oil and gas deposits have been under exploration and industrial exploitation since the 1970s. In these areas, the traditional habitat of the indigenous peoples

is being severely damaged, and several measures are being taken for restoring traditional economic sectors, for example, by creating clan- and family-based Native "communities" [cooperatives or other economic units]. Establishing such communities and registering them as economic units is one form of securing traditional-use lands for individual families or clan- and territorial-based groups. However, by 2001, in the entire Yamal-Nenets Okrug's territory, only five "indigenous communities" had been registered, with a total population of 1,251. Of those communities, four were in the Pur District and one was in Priural'sk District. That is why adoption of the Russian federal law "About the Traditional Use Lands of Indigenous Minority Peoples of the North" is so essential for resolving problems related to the land rights and land ownership of the Russian indigenous peoples. By the year 2004, the number of registered "indigenous communities" in the Yamal-Nenets Okrug grew to twenty-seven, but they still constitute the minority of the okrug's Native population.

Matters are more favorable in my native area, on the Gydan Peninsula. The development of oil and gas deposits there has been put on hold since the early 1990s, and at this time the industry has no visible impact on the daily life and the economy of local indigenous people. Both public sector Native employees of the municipal enterprise "Gydan State Fisheries" and individual nomadic families are engaged primarily in traditional economic activities, such as reindeer herding, fisheries, trapping, and so on. On January 1, 2003, there were 1,050 Native nomadic families in the entire Taz District (with a combined population of 5,188); of those, 787 nomadic families, with a combined population of 2,373, are under the jurisdiction of the Gydan Town Council. As of January 1, 2004, the total number of domestic reindeer in the Gydan Peninsula is about 92,000, of which but 4,000 are owned and managed by the Gydan State Fisheries Processing Plant [which is a holdover from the old Soviet economic system] and about 88,000 belong to individual families of Nenets private reindeer herders.

The Program "Cultural Heritage of Indigenous People of the Yamal-Nenets Okrug": Some Preliminary Results

However, the days will eventually come when prospectors and company workers will return to our lands to resume the aborted industrial exploitation of the Storm, Morning, and Gydan oil and gas fields, where dozens of active sacred sites and cultural monuments of the Gydan Nenets are located. We are aware that such a development may be resumed at any time, and we should be prepared in the future to face this challenge to our traditional economies, lifestyles, and culture.

Preserving the historical heritage of Northern people, including their reindeer-herding culture and way of life, is a complicated problem for which the governmental agencies, scientific institutions, and public organizations of Russia should bear (and share) responsibility. Many new federal and local laws support these purposes. Under these new Russian laws, direct responsibility for preserving sacred sites lies with the companies and organizations that explore and develop the areas where indigenous peoples reside.

Northern sacred sites symbolize both the unique core and the most important component of cultural heritage of the Nenets, Khanty, Selkup, and other Native people. This core can be easily damaged and even destroyed by industrial development if left unchecked and without special means for preservation. Therefore, the system of protected natural areas that exists now in Russia should include both natural protected areas and sacred sites of the Native population. Unfortunately, in Russia in general and in the Yamal-Nenets Okrug in particular, very few people are engaged in the study and documentation of Native sacred sites, much less in their protection; and current efforts in this field are utterly insufficient [see Fedorova, this volume].

The protection of sacred sites in Russia and the designation of special status for them were discussed publicly for the first time in the mid-1990s only. The issue was raised repeatedly by representatives of public organizations, leaders of Native communities, and heads of the Russian Associations of Indigenous Minority Peoples of the North (RAIPON). In 1998, at the Eighth General Assembly of the Inuit Circumpolar Conference (Nuuk, Greenland; July 29, 1998), the President of RAIPON, Sergei N. Kharyuchi, argued for the need to include sacred sites and ritual places of Northern indigenous peoples in the system of protected areas (Kharyuchi 1998, 1999:69–72). Sergei N. Kharyuchi, as do I, comes from a Nenets herding family from the Taz District. Soon Kharyuchi approached the governor of the Yamal-Nenets okrug, Mr. Iurii Ne'elov, with a request for the assistance of the okrug administration in documenting and protecting these sacred sites. In reply, in 1999 Governor Ne'elov signed a special regulation in this regard (see below).

Until then, only two programs for documenting the sacred sites of indigenous people had been in operation across the entire northern section of Russia: on Vaygach Island in the Barents Sea—by a group from the Institute of Cultural and Natural Heritage of Russia, under the direction of Petr Boiarskii (Boiarskii and Liutyi 1999; Boiarskii and Stoliarov 2000)—and, in the Surgut District of Khanty-Mansi Autonomous Okrug [Balalaeva 1999; see also Wiget and Balalaeva, this volume]. On Vaygach Island, where the Native population is virtually absent and there are hardly any tourists or geologists, the preservation of Nenets sacred sites is probably not threatening to anyone. In Khanty-Mansi okrug, the situation is much worse, and despite a large amount of work on documenting sacred sites and Native ritual places, the protection of these places has not yet been legislated.

In the Yamal-Nenets Okrug, the official documentation of sacred sites for their preservation was started; but in the most recent years, Governor Iurii Ne'elov issued the special regulation, "About the Creation of a Historical-Ethnographic and Scientific Research Center for Indigenous Minority Peoples of the North" (No. 786,

December 20, 1999). Under that regulation, provisions were made, in particular, for financing the construction of historical-ethnographic and scientific research center (or "complex") in the city of Salekhard. The Scientific Center for Humanitarian Research on Indigenous Minority Peoples of the Yamal-Nenets Autonomous Okrug (CHR), an ethnographic museum with collections on Native peoples, an exhibition hall, souvenir workshops, and a store, would be housed in its building. Simultaneously, the Department of Affairs of Indigenous Minority Peoples under the Okrug administration was tasked with drafting a Yamal-Nenets Okrug law titled, "About the Ritual and Religious Places of the Indigenous Minority Peoples in Yamal-Nenets Autonomous Area." Together with the CHR, the department was tasked to prepare a map of Native sacred sites to be included in the list of cultural and historical monuments located on the Okrug territory [see also Fedorova, this volume]. In the year 2000, a new research and survey program, "The Cultural Heritage of Indigenous Minority Peoples of Yamal-Nenets Autonomous Okrug" was launched, which developed and implemented special measures for protecting cultural heritage monuments, including traditional sacred sites and ritual places.

For this purpose, it was necessary to produce detailed maps of Native sacred sites. In 2000, preliminary surveys for identifying and researching Nenets sacred sites on the Yamal and Gydan peninsulas were conducted, under a contract with the okrug administration. I was put in charge of the surveys on the Gydan Peninsula, and Leonid Lar was named the principal investigator for the Yamal District. At first, we used available handwritten and published schematic maps, which both Lar and I made during our previous research and in preparation for our Ph.D. dissertations (Kharyuchi 1999, 2001; Lar 2000). These first maps of sacred sites were incomplete, as they were executed in fits and starts in the course of other field trips and short-term visits or vacations. For the starter, I used the small-scale maps from my dissertation and the initial text from the section devoted to traditions and innovations in the sa-

cred sphere of the Nenets (Kharyuchi 1999, 2001:81–101). Lar also relied on his own materials, including his sketchy map of Nenets sacred places on the Yamal Peninsula published in 1995 (Lar 1995:167). Only thirty-eight sacred sites on the entire Yamal Peninsula were featured on this earlier map, accompanied by a short text, although Lar has been collecting materials on sacred sites since 1986 (Lar 2000:166). Since 1995, Lar collected more extensive field data and made a much more complete map of sacred places. He personally surveyed many sacred sites featured on the map, whereas others have been documented from the words of his Nenets informants who live nearby. In total, Lar has identified more than fifty Nenets sacred sites in the Yamal District, with detailed descriptions, site name identifications, and analysis of their modern conditions.

For the 2000 program, new tasks were formulated, more sophisticated methods for sacred sites documentation were determined, and the first annual report was composed in 2001. All our field reports and materials were submitted to the Department of Affairs of Indigenous Peoples of the Yamal-Nenets Autonomous Okrug, which sponsored this program. As soon as financing was available in July 2000, I left for the first field trip in the Taz District. It was necessary to work onsite with the local Nenets assistants who had critical information about the sacred sites. Information about why these maps were being made was disseminated widely; therefore, the charting of maps and recording of data on sacred sites involved the nomadic Nenets population for the first time in the process of state-sponsored protection of places of cultural significance and lands of traditional subsistence (Fig. 51). We hope that, in the future, local residents will be able to participate directly in land management (security measures) and development of traditional land use. This is especially important in light of any future actions on the development of the oil-and-gas industry on Gydan Peninsula and in northern Yamal.

The maps of Nenets sacred sites that Lar and I are developing will be submitted to the register of cultural

51/ Nenets herders work on the map of traditional sacred sites, summer 2001.

and historical monuments of the Yamal-Nenets Autonomous Okrug. The final stage will be preparing a research report and creating a map titled "Sacred Sites of Gydan Peninsula" as a classified document "for agency use." It is worth mentioning that no modern topographic maps were given to us for the project and each of us worked with old maps that we had scrambled together on various occasions in Salekhard. I used an old map of the Gydan Peninsula produced in 1960, with a scale of 1:300,000 (1 centimeter = 3 kilometers), which featured several incorrectly located rivers and lakes, as my informants indicated. During trips and work in herders' tents, the map became scuffed and torn. Unfortunately, I had neither more detailed maps nor any other modern equipment on these trips [such as GPS and/or satellite and air imagery]. In December 2000, when the preliminary maps of sacred sites were delivered together with the report, they registered some 125 sacred sites, possibly less than half of all the existing ritual sites of the Gydan Nenets. The revision and up-

date of the materials collected under the program was reserved for the 2001 field season. My map of sacred sites, with the attached descriptive materials, is to be submitted "for agency use" only; Lar plans to publish his data eventually as a monograph.

Final maps of sacred sites will be delivered to the okrug administration and to the Inspectorate on Protection and Use of Monuments of History and Culture (created in January 2000). Additional copies of maps will be submitted to municipal agencies of the Taz and Yamal Districts, and, through them, to local village administrations, and to the oil-and-gas and other enterprises working in the two districts.

The program "Preservation of the Cultural Heritage of Indigenous Peoples of Yamal-Nenets Autonomous Okrug" has been the first positive experience in collaboration among the Okrug administration, local researchers, and indigenous people. For the first time professional ethnographers—natives to their districts and members of the very same indigenous communities (Fig. 52) who are interested in and worried about the preservation of their people's heritage—have been involved in this work. Knowledge of Native language and traditional culture is helping us observe ethical and moral standards while gathering materials on the delicate topic of sacred sites, their modern uses, and the preservation of ritual traditions connected with them.

Of course, the results of the one-year program were limited, considering the modest funding. In 2000–2001, the okrug administration allocated just 40,000 rubles [about $1400 USD] to Leonid Lar and me for our surveys; we were able to accomplish little for this amount. In my plans, I had outlined continuing the surveys and searching for additional or new financing. But our research unexpectedly received international support. In April 2001, a seminar took place in Moscow with the participation of representatives of the International Secretariat of Indigenous Peoples, and an agreement for a new pilot project was signed, called "The Significance of Protecting Sacred Sites of the Indigenous Population of the Arctic: Sociological Research in the North of Russia." The project was supported by the Russian Association of Indigenous Peoples of the North (RAIPON), the Danish Environmental Preservation Agency (DEPA), the program "Conservation of Arctic Flora and Fauna" (CAFF), and the Indigenous Peoples' Secretariat (IPS). For the 2001 surveys, a small amount of funding was allocated to the Taz District of Yamal-Nenets Autonomous Okrug, as having some experience in such studies. Additional funding was given to surveys in the Olyutorsk District in the Koryak Autonomous Okrug in the north of Kamchatka.

This joint international project emphasized that sacred sites of northern indigenous peoples are often located in areas where the preservation of nature is also important. Therefore, preservation of such sites would promote protection of the environment as a whole. Great attention was given to the ecological value of indigenous peoples' traditional knowledge about sacred sites. In the course of the project, the biological characteristics that make a site "sacred" to local people were to be established.

With the 2001 funding, some sociological research was also conducted and over seventy local residents—Native reindeer herders, hunters, and fishermen—were interviewed. Plans were made to extend the existing maps of Nenets sacred sites for the entire Gydan Peninsula that includes Gydan and Antipayuta tundra. My former student, Michael Okotetto, of the reindeer Nenets origin, was appointed as the lead researcher for the project. Michael used to work as an inspector for the protection division of the *Nesey* farming enterprise of private reindeer herders in his native Seyakha River region in the Yamal District. Today he is a staff researcher of the CHR and he is also the head of the herders' cooperative (*obshchina*) called *Ilebts*, which means "giving life" in the Nenets language. His knowledge of English was one of the selection criteria for participating in the project. I became his advisor and regional supervisor for the fieldwork in the Taz District. Together we composed a sociological questionnaire for interviewing local residents. Our fieldwork was conducted until September 2001; then we analyzed the collected materials, questionnaires, and site reports. By that time, dozens of local residents were involved in one way or another in reporting information on sacred sites through our survey; and, simultaneously, we informed local people about our tasks and disseminated materials on our previous work. Altogether, some 260 Native sacred sites have been mapped and documented within the study area, including data on the current status of the sites; its origins; associated traditional rites; natural environment (such as, physical landscape, vegetation, etc.). Our preliminary project report was produced in 2003, in both Russian and English versions, and it will be published shortly. Brief results of our 2001 survey were also published elsewhere (Kharyuchi 2002a, 2002b, 2003).

Conclusion

In summary, I want to share some personal considerations about the results of my work in the documenta-

52/ *Nenets reindeer herders from the Gydan Peninsula, 2000. These men, now mostly in their 30s and 40s, are the keepers of the life style and cultural traditions of their ancestors.*

tion of Nenets sacred sites in the Yamal-Nenets Okrug for more than a decade. In my view, personal characteristics of a given researcher are very important to this type of work. Male ethnographers have a much wider access in studying rituals, traditions, and stories related to sacred places (and even more information may be open to a Native artist, such as my colleague Leonid Lar). What is most important is the ability to visit sacred sites and (engage in) the graphical documentation and identification of the ritual objects located there. Certainly, even to a Native researcher who grew up in a traditional family, it is hard, both physically and psychologically, to visit each and every known sacred site, even for the sake of science; it is less possible (even for a male Native researcher), to make sketches and measurements, and take photographs there. Such actions at sacred sites usually elicit condemnation from local people, especially from elders.

According to traditional norms, no woman, including a female Native ethnographer, can visit a sacred site, except for female sites and those that are accessible to everyone. Even today, this taboo is still applied strictly, even to Native scientists of local origins. In addition to the restrictions on visiting, there are restrictions on the specific questions a woman can pose to men, especially to elders. Naturally, the old men did not share with me what I could not ask them about. Also, the attitude toward scientists even from indigenous peoples has a dichotomy of "ours / not ours," "from our region or an outsider," which has great importance. For example, in my case, my long and enduring connections with my native region have helped my research on Nenets sacred places on the Gydan tundra. In my native district, most of the people in their forties and fifties ("the middle generation"), that is, my contemporaries, know me well—from the boarding school, teaching college, and/or my earlier work as a teacher. Youths and children of school age know my name from the curriculum. Elderly people refer to my father's memory respectfully; and they esteem my mother, who raised my brothers and sisters, who are also well known and respected people in the district. The kind memory of my husband's late father, Nikolai Maximovich Kharyuchi, who worked during World War II as the head of the Red Tent Brigade on the Gydan Peninsula [educational and medical teams that offered services to the nomadic families before the establishment of local hospitals and schools], is still alive. His sons are now well-known people in the district; and, they are my relatives.[5] This also facilitated my access and worked greatly to the success of my surveys of sacred sites.

In our tundra district, no one, especially of the Nenets origin, has ever collected information about Native sacred places, even during earlier campaigns aimed at the persecution of shamans [in the 1930s, 1940s, and 1950s]. In our area, the attitude toward visiting ethnographers has always been positive and a little bit indulgent because, from the Nenets viewpoint, they usually are interested in "funny (if not foolish) questions and things;" but no harm has ever been seen from them. Leonid Lar, ethnographer, artist, and my partner in the documentation of traditional sacred places, has talked about how Nenets women laughed at him when he asked them to show their needlework pouches so that he could make sketches.

It is sometimes believed that more can be told to a "foreign" researcher—that is, to a visitor, an outsider (i.e., Zen'ko 2000)—than to one of "our own," particularly if such a researcher is a woman, and especially if a visiting ethnographer is going to pose some delicate, even intimate (personal) questions about which "one of us" would never dare to inquire directly. But most likely, vague and often incorrect information would be given to such an outside researcher, simply to be rid of him. We find references to such obviously incorrect information even in many solid scientific publications.

Of course, the most negative attitude of the local population is toward oil and gas workers and geological prospectors. Nenets elders are afraid of these newly arrived, inconsiderate people and of their evil acts in relation to the tundra and its inhabitants. At the same time, they think with pity about "those who do not know sin" and believe that these people will someday be punished for their desecration of Nenets sacred places and defiance to their spirits. However, I also think with some apprehension of the archaeologists preparing to engage in describing and studying Nenets sacred sites and burial places (Fedorova 2000:11–2; Kharyuchi 2000:78). It is difficult to say whether the tundra people will understand and cooperate with them.

As a Nenets woman, I have a responsibility to follow my native traditions that prescribe certain rules of behavior (as well as certain restrictions and taboos on the possession and distribution of sacred knowledge). But I also recognize my huge responsibility to my people. Frequently doubt arises about whether I am, in fact, doing the right thing by being so actively engaged in this work on documenting sacred sites and traditional ritual places. Will this some day hurt me and my family, my children or even my grandchildren? Have the spirits of these places become enraged? Still, I believe that this work has to be performed in this time; it happened that this mission fell to me as a Native ethnographer. And how else could we protect the most sacred cultural property of my people? Any deliberate policy of hiding information on sacred sites, of withdrawing it from outsiders (such as confidential databases, confidential information only "for our own people" and so on) is possible on reservations or on tribal lands. There, people are entitled with the rights to their land; they control to whom and how access to their territory is given. In our Yamal-Nenets Okrug and everywhere in Siberia, there is none of this, which means that anyone can come to our land (without asking our permission) and destroy our monuments, pleading their "ignorance."

Under traditional Nenets society, there was no need for special protection of sacred sites: people lived by the customs of their ancestors and did not visit sacred places without a special purpose [such as to make ritu-

53/ Traditional Nenets sacred site on Yamal Peninsula, 1928.

als and offerings]. People from other groups who lived in the villages or traveled through the tundra feared these places and avoided them altogether; there was never an incident of defilement or vandalism on their part. Native people still strictly follow these rules today. But times have changed: geologists, gas, and oil workers have arrived; and we are not alone in our lands. In the boundless tundra, we cannot put a protective plaque at each and every sacred place (Fig. 53). Thus, local residents themselves must protect their sites, should put up notices, and must actively protest if their sacred places are exposed to destruction. However, many local people are still passive or shy with the authorities. When they see that their sacred sites are pilfered from, damaged, or destroyed by the new arrivals, all the tundra people can do is to rely on those who are more educated, literate, and who are more skilled in talking to the officials. Many of my rural kinsmen still view such educated Native professionals as the only defenders of their culture and way of life.

This means that some system of governmental protection for Native sacred places and other ritual sites is absolutely necessary. In principle, those Native sacred sites that are located on the lands of federal nature reserves or local preserves (and there are quite a few of them in our region) fall under some protection, inasmuch as access to such areas is strictly limited. At any rate, that is what is written in federal and okrug regulations about protected natural areas. Accordingly, it is essential that the regulations on security measures and limited access to sacred sites be applied widely and more strictly. To put such sites under governmental protection, it is important to identify them as sacred places, position them on a map, and document the navigational/positioning coordinates. A survey should confirm whether the site is located within the borders of a specially protected natural area (preserve, reserve, biosphere reserve, etc.), and determine its dimensions and biological characteristics (such as landscape, type of vegetation, and so on).

All other information about sacred places is identified and recorded exclusively in accordance with the wishes and with the full consent of the local Native population. For example, the keeper (owner) of a family or clan sacred site has his full right to withhold certain information from recording and to share only the portion he considers necessary. I believe that there must be some sort of classified information for the preservation of sacred knowledge and of Native cultural tradition.

The recent survey and documentation of Nenets sacred sites on the Vaygach Island [in the Barents Sea] conducted by the Marine Arctic Interdisciplinary Expedition of the Institute of Cultural and Natural Heritage of Russia can be cited as a model for such an approach. A mockup map of sacred places on Vaygach Island has been prepared and a catalogue/directory of local cultural monuments has already been published (Boiarskii and Liutyi 1999; Boiarskii and Stoliarov 2000). Altogether, some 150 natural monuments and more than 230 monuments of local history and traditional Nenets culture are shown on the map and described in the catalogue. The significance of Vaygach Island, which is sacred to the Nenets and is referred to in the Nenets language as *Khekhe ngo* (Island of idols), is that this island has had no permanent Native residents during the last few centuries. At the same time, this was the main location of several important Nenets sacred sites that were visited periodically. The sacred sites of Vaygach Island held a critical place in the hierarchy of ritual centers of the Nenets' sacred world. According to Nenets tradition, the island was the place where the key Nenets spirits (ancestors or major gods) used to live and the figures or effigies (wooden sculptures) of these main spirits were once located.

In 1827, these wooden images were destroyed (burned) by Russian Orthodox missionaries; on Vaygach Island alone, more than 400 wooden and twenty stone idols were destroyed (Lekhtisalo 1998:64–6; Veniyamin 1855:125). The Nenets believe that after the images of the main Nenets gods were destroyed, their "spirit

children" flew off the island and settled in many places throughout the areas of Nenets migrations, from the Kola Peninsula to the Yenisey River. Many legends exist related to this dispersal of the Nenets spirits from the island and across the Nenets area. In the beginning, two stones—idols of *Vaigach-Vesako* (Old Man) and - *Khadako* (Old Woman)—were venerated. They had four sons, "who dispersed to various places on the tundra." *Nyu-khekhe* (Son-idol / Son-spirit) remained as a small rock on the Vaygach Island. *Minisey* was a peak of the Polar Ural Mountain Range; *Ya mal khekhe* moved to the western side of the Ob Bay; and *Khar Pod* was a larch glade or Kozmin Coppice in the Kanin tundra along the White Sea shore (Veniyamin 1855:125). In 1983, Vaygach Island, with adjoining small islands and a three-kilometer offshore area, was declared "Vaygach State Hunting Preserve" of regional value (total area 333,000 hectares or 1,285 square miles).[6]

Sacred sites that are not located in the specially designated natural preservation areas [such as in federal and local nature preserves, parks, etc.] and, in general, all sacred places and burial sites of indigenous peoples, should be protected as highly valued monuments of cultural heritage. Here the mechanism of protection is *knowledge* about their special status and value to indigenous peoples, that is, education and cultivation of respect for heritage monuments and for others' cultural tradition(s). This is especially crucial in areas of active industrial development and oil and gas explorations, where there are many visitors, and, frequently, transient people coming in large groups, such as geological parties and exploration and rig crews. Both ways of protecting our heritage monuments—either by restricting access to the lands designated under some natural protection status or via dissemination of knowledge, public education, and cultivation of respect to Native heritage—should be effective and should supplement each other.

Notes

1. Translated by Georgene Sink. Edited by Igor

Krupnik and Cara Seitchek. Krupnik's editorial comments are added in brackets.

2. According to Nenets traditional beliefs, the surface of the ground is a thin border between "this" and the Lower World. Therefore, to the Nenets, it was strictly forbidden to dig, excavate, drill or simply pick at the ground – ed.

3. *"Num"* also means "sky" and "weather."

4. As of 2004, there were altogether 15 areas under various forms (regimes) of federal or local preservation in the Yamal-Nenets Okrug, including the two recently established units, *Kharbey* "geological monument" and *Syn-Voykar* "ethnic territory," with its special land-use status. Several more units are currently under planning or preparation, including the Taz Bay Fishery Preserve, Gydoyamovskiy State Nature Preserve (both in the Taz District), and National Park "Yuribey" in the central portion of the Yamal Peninsula, Yamal District.

5. Galina Kharyuchi's husband, Sergei Nikolayevich Kharyuchi, is the president of the Association of Indigenous Peoples of the North, Siberia, and the Russian Far East (RAIPON), and also the Chairman of the Duma (local legislative body) of the Yamal-Nenets Area.

6. Nevertheless, the proposed measures for protecting Nenets ritual monuments on Vaygach Island, and especially for development of limited tourism on the island, aroused alarm among the local residents and protests by the Yasavey Association, which represents the Native population of the Nenets Autonomous Okrug — ed.

References

Balalaeva, Olga E.

1999   Sviashchennye mesta khantov Nizhnei i Srednei Obi (Khanty Sacred Sites along the Middle and Lower Ob River). In *Ocherki traditsionnogo prirodopol'zovaniia khantov (Materialy k atlasu)*. A. Wiget, ed., pp. 140–56. Ekaterinburg.

Boiarskii, Petr V., and A.A. Liutyi, eds.

1999   *Ostrov Vaigach. Kheibidia ya – sviashchennyi ostrov nenetskogo naroda* (Vaigach Island Khebidya ya - Sacred Island of the Nenets People). Cultural and Natural Heritage. Indexes, explanatory text to a map, reference data. Moscow: Russian Institute of Cultural and Natural Heritage.

Boiarskii, Petr V., and V.P. Stoliarov, eds.

2000   *Ostrov Vaigach. Kul'turnoe i prirodnoe nasledie* (Vaigach Island. Cultural and Natural Heritage).Vol. 1. Moscow: Russian Institute of Cultural and Natural Heritage.

Fedorova, Natalia V.

2000   Sem' let Yamal'skoi arkheologicheskoi ekspeditsii: proshlye rezul'taty i zadachi na budushchee (Seven Years of the Yamal Archaeological Expedition: Past Results and Tasks for the Future). *Nauchnyi vestnik* 3:4–12. Salekhard.

Gemuev, Izmail N.

1990   *Mirovozzrenie man'si: dom i kosmos* (The Mansy Worldview: Home and Cosmos). Novosibirsk: Nauka Publisher.

Gemuev, Izmail N., and A.M. Sagalaev.

1986   *Religiia naroda man'si. Kul'tovye mesta (XIX-nachalo XX vv.)* (Religion of the Mansi People. Sacred Sites, 19th Century and the Beginning of the 20th Century). Novosibirsk: Nauka Publishers.

Golovnev, Andrei V.

2000   Put' k semi chumam (A Journey to Seven Tents). *Drevnosti Yamala* 1:208–36. Yekaterinburg and Salekhard.

Kharyuchi, Galina, P.

1999a   *Traditsii i innovatsii v kul'ture nenetskogo etnosa (vtoraia polovina 20 v.)* (Traditions and Innovations in the Ethnic Culture of the Nenets, Second Half of the 20th Century). Summary of the Ph.D. Dissertation. The author's abstract of a dissertation as a Candidate of Historical Sciences. Tomsk: Tomsk University.

1999b   *Traditsii i innovatsii v kul'ture nenetskogo etnosa (vtoraia polovina 20 v.)* (Traditions and Innovations in the Ethnic Culture of the Nenets, Second Half of the 20th Century). Unpublished Ph.D. dissertation manuscript. Appendix 3: List of Sacred sites of Gydan Peninsula. Salekhard: author's personal archive.

2000   Nenetskie sviatilishcha i ikh klassifikatsiia (Nenets Sacred Sites and their Classification). *Nauchnyi vestnik* 3:77–9. Salekhard.

2001   *Traditsii i innovatsii v kul'ture nenetskogo etnosa (vtoraia polovina 20 v.)* (Traditions and Innovations in the Ethnic Culture of the Nenets, Second Half of the 20th Century). Tomsk: Tomsk University.

2002a   Zhertvennyi kompleks kul'tovykh mest (Sacrificial Complex of (Native) Ritual Sites). *Nauchnyi vestnik* 11:48–51. Salekhard.

2002b   Kul'tovye mesta nentsev: sviashchennye landshafty (Nenets Ritual Sites: Sacred Landscapes). In *Severnyi Arkheologicheskii Kongress: Tezisy dokladov*, pp. 157–8. Yekaterinburg and Khanty-Mansiisk: Nauka.

2003   Ob izuchenii nenetskikh sviatilishch (On the Study of Nenets Sacred Sites). In *V Kongress etnografov i arkheologov Rossii. Tezisy dokladov*. V. Tishkov, ed., pp. 315–6. Moscow: Institute of Ethnology and Anthropology.

Kharyuchi, Galina, and Lyudmila Lipatova

1998   Traditional Beliefs, Sacred Sites, and Sacrificial Rituals of the Nenets of Gydan Peninsula in the

Modern Context. In *The Archaeology and Anthropology of Landscape. Shaping Your Landscape*, P.J. Ucko and R. Layotn, eds., pp. 284-97. *One World Archaeology* 30. London and New York: Routledge.

Kharyuchi, Sergei N.

1998   The Necessity of Governmental Protection of Sacred Places and Ritual Sites of the Indigenous Peoples of the North. Paper presented at the 8th General Assembly of the Inuit Circumpolar Conference. Nuuk, July 26, 1998.

1999   *Sovremennye problemy korennykh narodov Severa (Doklady i vystupleniia)* (Contemporary Problems of the Indigenous Peoples of the North. Reports and Public Presentations). Tomsk: Tomsk University.

Kulemzin, Vladislav M.

1995   Mirovozzrencheskie aspekty okhoty i rybolovstva (The Worldview Aspects of Hunting and Fishing) In *Istoriia i kul'tura khantov*, N.V. Lukina, ed., pp. 65-76. Tomsk: Tomsk University.

Lar, Leonid I.

1995   Bogi i shamany nentsev Iamala (Gods and Shamans of the Yamal Nenets). *Narody Severo-Zapadnoi Sibiri* 2:161-71. Tomsk: Tomsk University.

1999   *Traditsionnoe religioznoe mirovozzrenie nentsev* (Nenets Traditional Religious Worldview and Beliefs). Summary of the unpublished Ph.D. Dissertation. St. Petersburg: Peter the Great Museum of Anthropology and Ethnography (Kunstkamera).

2000   Sviashchennye mesta nentsev. In *Problemy vzaimodeistviia cheloveka i prirodnoi sredy* 1:66-71. Tyumen: Institute of the Problems of Northern Development.

Lekhtisalo, Toivo

1998   *Mifologiia iurako-samoiedov (nentsev)* (Mythology of the Yurak Samoyed (Nenets). Translated from German edition by N.V. Lukina. Tomsk: Tomsk University.

Rezolutsiia

2000   Rezolutsiia nauchno-prakticheskoi konferentsii po itogam polevykh arkheologicheskikh i etnograficheskikh issledovanii (Resolution of the Scientific and Applied Conference on Results of Field Archaeological and Ethnological Research). *Nauchnyi vestnik* 3:94-5. Salekhard.

Sbornik zakonov

1998   *Sbornik zakonov Yamalo-Nenetskogo okruga (s sentiabria 1995 g. po iun' 1998 g.)* (Collection of Laws and Legal Documents of the Yamal-Nenets Autonomous Area. From September 1995 through June 1998). St. Petersburg: Publication of the State Duma of the Yamal-Nenets Autonomous Area.

1999   *Sbornik zakonov Yamalo-Nenetskogo okruga (s sentiabria 1998 g. po dekabr' 1999 g.)* (Collection of Laws and Legal Documents of the Yamal-Nenets Autonomous Area. From September 1998 through December 1999). St. Petersburg: Publication of the State Duma of the Yamal-Nenets Autonomous Area.

Toboliakov, V.T.

1930   *K verkhoviiam ischeznuvshei reki* (To the Upper Reaches of a Disappearing River). Sverdlovsk.

Veniyamin, Archimandrite (Smirnov)

1855   Samoedy mezenskie (The Mezen Samoyed). *Vestnik Russkogo Geograficheskogo obshchestva* 14. St. Petersburg.

Zen'ko, Aleksei P.

2000   Traditsionnaia dukhovnaia kul'tura iamal'skikh nentsev v sovremennykh usloviiakh (iz polevykh materialov) (Contemporary Status of the Yamal Nenets Traditional Spiritual Culture. From Field Observations). *Nauchnyi vestnik* 3:83-6. Salekhard.

Landscapes of Tradition, Landscapes of Resistance

DONALD G. CALLAWAY

Fifteen years ago, in mid-winter, I took a taxi ride from Bethel south to Napaskiak. The taxi left down the boat landing near the Alaska Commercial Company store in Bethel, drove up an intangibly marked ice road formed by the frozen Kuskokwim River, and ended by driving up a bluff into Napaskiak. Halfway through this ride I chanced to look south and was jolted by a panoramic view of a layered landscape. The greenish gray of the Kuskokwim ice, the off white snow on the river-banks, the nearly black vegetation on the tundra, and the light buff slice of the sky's horizon pushed down by gunmetal clouds are all indelible in my memory. I suspect that almost anyone from any culture would share the emotional impact of viewing similar landscapes with such layered contrasts (Fig. 54).

It would be difficult to find a cultural heritage that views the rivers, streams, and mountains of their environment as a simple inanimate backdrop for biological processes and cultural activity. Admittedly, variation exists within any society. Many individuals in our society have a primarily instrumental view of the environment, valuing natural resources primarily for their commercial potential (Fisher 2001:264). Others have developed a complex aesthetic with deep roots in our cultural history. In fact, many philosophers of environmental ethics imbue the landscape with picturesque, sublime, and scientific values (e.g. Carlson 2000).

However, despite the widespread aesthetic experiences that bind us all to landscapes, there are divergent perspectives, resulting from differing cultural values, that are contested in contemporary regulatory

regimes that manage human relationships with their environment. This chapter describes conflicts between two different cultural resource management traditions, forced by history and circumstance, to occupy the same landscape. It will focus on Alaska and will contrast indigenous perceptions and management regimes with those of Western government agencies.

The concept of "landscape" has manifold interpretations. Mason (this volume) considers some of the definitions codified in the U.S. National Park Service (NPS) policy. For example, the NPS uses two generic, but not necessarily mutually exclusive, types of landscape concepts—cultural and ethnographic landscapes. This chapter borrows from both in defining a landscape as a geographic area that includes cultural and natural resources. These landscapes can exhibit cultural and aesthetic values and can be associated with historic events or with traditionally associated people or other actors (e.g., Western resource managers). In addition, our consideration of landscape attempts to understand the relationship between man and "animal,' as well as the spiritual and ethical connection these entities have with and in landscapes. While we do not attempt an exhaustive typology of landscapes, our working definition includes the relationship of humans to geomorphic features, biological domains, and other human agents.

Indigenous Alaskans' perceptions and experience of landscape contrast with the Western tradition of defining and managing landscapes. Both cultures' positions are *landscapes of tradition*, albeit very different traditions. The political reality that empowers the tradition of Western resource managers to make the rules creates the context for *landscapes of resistance*. In Alaska, as among indigenous groups throughout the world (cf. Guha 1990; Scott 1985), a landscape of resistance is frequently characterized by a conscious failure of Alaska Natives to comply with the regulations of Western management regimes.

This chapter describes how indigenous communities (Iñupiaq, Yup'ik, and Athapaskan) name their landscape, articulate their relationships to animals (animal/persons), and express spiritual values and attitudes. Local cultural processes form the ethical and epistemological basis for landscape management. Our comparison of Native and non-Native values and attitudes concentrates, perhaps unfairly, on non-Native resource managers in government agencies. The competing views can be reconciled, not necessarily in the sense of concurrence, but in the sense of an agreement to work together, an accommodation generous enough to respect and encompass multiple views. While some may regard these overlapping areas of agreement to be an incomplete, perhaps even unsatisfactory compromise (Soule 1995), these partial areas of agreement do allow for the maintenance and support of the underlying objectives that sustain both worldviews—the respect for and conservation of the natural resources that sustain us all.

A major caveat is required here at the beginning of this narrative. Constraints on chapter size, coupled with a lack of comprehensive information, will by necessity force the offering of assertions and generalizations as if there is a homogenous ethnic and cultural attachment to landscape. It is essential to realize that values and attitudes vary not only between cultures but also within cultures. Gender, age, life experience, education, income, and "role" all influence perceptions, attitudes, and values about the landscape from an indigenous or Western perspective.

One empirical study, to be described below, shows significant differences in knowledge, attachment to place

and commodity, versus spiritual values of the land found in a sample of indigenous community residents, long-term non-Native residents of Alaska, and non-Native newcomers. Thus, while there are statistically significant differences in measures between cultures, there is also considerable variability among individuals within the same culture.

Subsistence as more than an Economic Endeavor

It is helpful to briefly discuss the underlying political and legal structures that frame the "subsistence" issue in Alaska. The 1980 Alaska National Interest Lands Conservation Act (ANILCA) provides the most important parts of that structure. Title VIII of ANILCA, Subsistence Management and Use, details the federal government's regulatory regime. Section 803 of Title VIII defines subsistence use as:

> [T]he customary and traditional use in Alaska of fish, wildlife and other renewable resources for direct personal or family consumption, for the making and selling of handicraft articles from the non-edible by-products of fish and wildlife taken for direct personal or family consumption and for customary trade, barter, or sharing for personal or family consumption.

This bureaucratic definition focuses on economic processes. Subsistence resources do provide sustenance and are a major portion of the diet, especially in small communities where the costs of shipping store-bought foods are prohibitive. However, numerous research efforts show that from the (predominantly Native) local actors' point of view, the harvest of subsistence resources does more than supply nutrition.

Collective subsistence activities, whether gathering clams, processing fish at a fish camp, or seal hunting with a father or brother, often provide the most basic memories in an individual's life. These activities define the sense of family and community. They teach how to identify and harvest resources and how to process them efficiently and without waste into a variety

54/ *Sunset on the Yukon River.*

of food items. Distribution of resources promotes the most basic values of Native and rural culture: generosity, respect for the knowledge of elders, self-esteem for a successful harvest, and public appreciation for sharing the harvest. No other set of activities provides a similar moral foundation for continuity between generations.

Moreover, food preferences are the most conservative behaviors in any culture. The unique preparation and special taste of foods children encounter as they grow up stays with them forever. Years later, the taste and smell of certain foods evoke memories of family and belonging. The preservation of subsistence as a valued cultural activity depends on the continued transmission of knowledge about the landscape: where to find resources and how to ethically obtain them, process them, and share them with others.

An Athapaskan Sense of Place

Keith Basso, who has worked for many years with the Cibecue Apache[1], concludes that "Apache constructions of place reach deeply into other cultural spheres, including conceptions of wisdom, notions of morality, politeness and tact in forms of spoken discourse, and certain conventional ways of imagining and interpreting the Apache tribal past" (Basso 1996:xv). Similarly, Athapaskan groups in Alaska have distinct constructions of place.

Tanana

Howard Luke, an Athapaskan elder, is originally from the Tanana River town of Nenana. In 1937 he lived in the small community of Chena Village just southwest of the contemporary city of Fairbanks. Howard has written a book, *My Own Trail* (1998), a personal history of his family and community in the Tanana Valley. It contains a map of place names and stories of the region. As William Schneider (1998:100) writes in his Afterword,

> The map is also a natural history of old channels, good fishing eddies and Howard's

record of changes in vegetation and animal populations. Glimpses and images from this historical spectrum are the subject of his stories and the setting for his lessons of how to take care of the land and water.

About Toghoteelee, a hill just north of Nenana, Howard says, "If warm weather is coming they could tell, you could hear it on top of that hill. That used to be their weather report right there." With reference to the Chena River that runs through Fairbanks, he notes:

Chena River used to be a wide river, high water, at one time. Water never did drop. We don't respect the water and that's the reason we're losing it. At that time people respect the water and water just stayed right there (Luke 1998:103).

These examples provide a small sense of how place-names are more than mere geographical markers. Places provide information about or note changes in the environment, changes that may be caused by failures in ethical behavior. Ray Barnhardt (1998:xii) observes:

The Athabascan people, who have occupied the Interior region for well over 10,000 years, have developed a sense of place that is deeply rooted in cultural traditional and spiritual ties linked to the natural environment on which they have always depended for their livelihood and their life. The hills, creeks, bogs, and sloughs that show up under English names on the USGS maps of the area, take on new names and significance when referred to in the stories by Athabascan elders.

Dena'ina

The Dena'ina, Athapaskan speakers of the Cook Inlet region, live a couple of hundred miles south of Fairbanks and the Tanana River. The city of Anchorage, with about a quarter of a million people (over half of Alaska's population) is located on Upper Cook Inlet. Most of the territory described in the book, *Shem Pete's Alaska: The Territory of the Upper Cook Inlet Dena'ina* (Kari and Fall 1987), is no longer used by the Dena'ina people. It is ironic that most Alaskans who live on a landscape of their own contemporary construction have little awareness of previous occupation or use. The book contains maps, stories, songs, and

about 720 Native place-names. One of the authors, James Kari, notes that:

The names and commentary presented here convey important information about the traditional economy, population centers, transportation, and beliefs of the Dena'ina . . . place names and the stories associated with geographic features are fine examples of the Dena'inas' rich and varied oral heritage. . . . Here, in the south-facing basin beneath the tallest mountains in North America, the Dena'ina can demonstrate that they have used virtually all lakes with food fisheries, all the major stream basins, all of the most accessible passes through the Alaska range, and all lands below 5,000 or 6,000 feet in elevation (Kari and Fall 1987:4).

The last speakers of the Upper Cook Inlet dialect of Dena'ina learned place-names while traveling on the landscape or by hearing the oral traditions of their elders. The Dena'ina speakers reported the place-names with affection, noting their associations with ancestors and the land (Kari and Fall 1987:29). The country Shem Pete knew covered about 26,500 square miles.

The section below compares place-names from *Shem Pete's Alaska* with selected entries from Orth's *Dictionary of Alaska Place Names* (1971). To facilitate comparison between these two naming traditions the following typology was developed, although it is not exhaustive nor does it contain mutually exclusive taxa:

—Place-names describing geological features;

—Place-names associated with subsistence activities;

—Place-names that mark an event that happened in the past;

—Place-names indicating mineral deposits;

—Place-names that act as trail guides or maps;

—Places that reflect non-edible wildlife;

—Place-names associated with spiritual aspects of the landscape;

Kari (1999) notes some underlying contrasts between the Athapaskan and Western naming conventions. For example, Athapaskans virtually never name places after people. In addition, while no peak in the magnificent Alaska Range lacks an English name, Athapaskan place-names dwindle in number as altitude increases because seldom-used areas are rarely given names. Athapaskan place-names define important use areas and provide an evocative topological index to their cultural history. For the sake of brevity we will illustrate the typology mentioned above with only one example (out of many) for each of the taxa.

Place-names describing geological features

—Dena'ina (Shem Pete 1987:41): *Nadudiltnu Li'a*, Glacier of River That Streams Join' [McArthur Glacier]

—Western (Orth 1971): Mushroom Reef (on Kodiak Island), named by USC&GC in 1929 "because of the mushroom shape of the reef." [Note: Like other English "mushroom" places this is more indicative of the shape of the structure rather than a guide to good eating.]

Place-names associated with subsistence activities

—Dena'ina (Shem Pete 1987:44): *Ch'k'e'ula Betnu*, 'River Where We Chew Something (waterfowl)' [Chuitkilnachna Creek, prime waterfowl hunting area.]

—Western: Orth (1971) lists no less than 35 "Fish Creeks" and 19 "Fish Lakes" in addition to 17 "Salmon Creeks" across Alaska.

However, many of those 'Fish Creeks' have little or no reference to fish or fishing, like the one on the Aleutian Islands that received an arbitrary name beginning with "F" to correspond to "F" grid by the U.S. Army for tactical purposes during World War II (as published on a 1954 Army Map Service map).

Place-names that mark an event of the past

—Dena'ina (Shem Pete 1987:42) *Tach'nach'ninchett*, 'Where Someone Put a Man's Head Underwater [south fork of Cottonwood Slough]. This name derives from a story about a fight between two men over a single fish.

—Western (Orth, 1971): Murder Cove (Admiralty Island). Named in 1869 because "traders occasionally anchor here and one small party, while asleep on the beach, were murdered by natives, their boat rifled and bodies left to be destroyed by wild animals."

Place-names indicating mineral deposits

—Dena'ina (Shem Pete 1987: 128): *Chish T'el'iht*, 'Where Ochre (cinnabar) is gathered,' [Three mile creek].

—Western (Orth 1971): Cinnabar Creek [SW of Sleetmute "stone people" "people of the whetstone people"]. Local name reported in 1944 by USGS; name derived from the deposits of cinnabar, a mercury ore, which were found there.

Place-names that act as trail guides or maps

—Dena'ina (Shem Pete 1987:41) *Tubughnen Nuch'utdali*, 'Let's go back to Tyonek.' A sled trail follows this stream between Tyonek and the base of the Alaska Range.

—Western (Orth 1971): none

A thorough perusal of Orth (1971) could not provide examples of Western "trail guide" place-names in Alaska, suggesting a major difference in the linguistic and conceptual construction of the landscape between indigenous and Western actors.[2] The contrast is illustrated by an oral history I conducted in spring of 1998 with Alex Tallekpalek in Levelock, a Yup'ik-speaking community on the Alaska Peninsula. Alex was a gracious host and out of many memories from that discussion two stand out: the seriousness of mind and purpose that is required to find, harvest, and consume food; and the absolute requirement to always know where you are. Alex, speaking of the training he received from his grandfather in the 1930s, constantly underscored the survival lessons of knowing where you are:

> Oh, I started from ten, when I was ten years old. He used to tell me to, 'You go ahead and go. I'll watch you while you go. And then give you help. I'll time you, see how far you travel. And make sure when you, when you go, you remember that tree over there. You mark it, and you go somewhere remember that tree, that little hill, you mark that, too. That's your, your marker where you, where you travel. So when you come back, you, you know where, where you go. And steady your hand. Your mountains, your trees, your creeks and all that. He teach me all them things, you know. Every time you travel with dogs and come up on top of the hill, you stop. Look around. And you look

where you came, your landmarks, don't forget. That creek you came across, don't forget that. . . . I never did forget . . . but when we travel, oh, every time I travel with him he always tell me, 'Where are we now? Did you study your landmarks?' I [just say] 'Oh yeah, I remember that little house, that creek right there.' 'You're right.'

A couple of hundred miles northeast of Levelock, several Athapaskan groups—Koyukon, Lower Tanana, Upper Kuskokwim, Dena'ina and Ahtna—have shared boundaries in what is now Denali National Park. Kari's (1999) work on place-names in this area identifies 1650 features from the five Alaska Native groups who used the park area. He describes numerous rule-driven features of Athapaskan place-names. In many names, prefixes and suffixes systematically orient the speaker's and the listener's positions on the landscape. A prefix might indicate the headwaters of a river, canyon, mouth of a stream, and so forth. Suffixes might indicate upstream, downstream, or either bank. Kari shows how Athapaskan place-names, functioning as signs on a mental map, are vital for orientation in the band's large land use area. The names cluster around stream drainage systems and a few prominent features (Kari 1999:11).

Place-names that reflect non-edible wildlife

—Dena'ina (Shem Pete 1987:284): *Yuditnu* 'Golden Eagle Creek,'[creek on north shore of Eklutna Lake]. There were few entries in this category, for reasons that can only be speculated upon. First, the Dena'ina considered almost all animals to be edible. Ravens, eagles, coyotes, and wolves were all probably in the non-edible category. The absence of such names may represent a sampling artifact, reluctance to name features after creatures with great spiritual power, or simply disinterest in naming features after animals with little utility.

—Western (Orth 1971): Eagle Bluff [near Eagle, Alaska]. Local name given in the late 1890s; so named because of eagles nesting there (Henning, 1965:204).

Place-names associated with spiritual aspects of the landscape

The spiritual aspects of landscape reside most uniquely with individual cultural values and attributes. This section amplifies the concepts of Dena'ina place-names with material from the Han, an Athapaskan group now residing north of Alaska's second largest metropolitan area, Fairbanks. Interestingly, Athapaskan place-names that reflect spiritual aspects of landscape can be readily found in the literature, but this category of place-names is substantially underrepresented in Western landscapes. While spiritual construction of the landscape, through concepts of wilderness or sacred ground (e.g., battlefields, cemeteries, and memorials), can be found in the histories of various landscapes, they are not easily obtainable from the Western place-name vernacular.

—Dena'ina (Shem Pete 1987:57): *Ch'chihi Ken*, 'Ridge Where We Cry, [sloping ridge south of Mt. Susitna]:

> That big ridge going downriver from Dghelishla [Mount Suisan] all the way to Beluga, they call Ch'chihi Ken. They would sit down there. Everything is in view. They can see their whole country. Everything is just right under them. They think about their brothers and their fathers and mothers. They remember that, and they just sit down there and cry. That's the place we cry all the time, 'cause everything just show up plain (Kari and Kari 1982:1).

—Han (Mishler and Simeone 2004): Eagle Bluff, near the village of Eagle (Fig. 55) is known to Han as *Tthee Tawdlenn* or "water hitting right in to it."

In contrast to Western painterly or scientific values the Han, who live on the upper reaches of the Yukon River, view the landscape as animated with spiritual presence. Mishler and Simeone (2004:36) explain that this name conveys more than a physiographic description. Sarah Malcolm, a Han woman, recalled that the chief "always said lots of things about the bluff," especially in speeches; he would even say he was chief of Eagle Bluff. The authors speculate that these recollections fit into a common Athapaskan practice where established

PROTECTING THE INVISIBLE/ LANDSCAPES OF SURVIVAL

55/ Eagle Bluff, known to the Han as "Water hitting right in to it."

settlements are associated with hills that are named and honored in potlatch songs and oratory as "grandfather's face":

> As dominant features on the landscape, these hills were symbolic of the strength and wisdom of the old chiefs or leaders. The people were said to live beneath or under these hills as they would live under the guidance of a strong and moral leader. The hill, like a good leader, is there to stand as an example or reminder to people of how they should conduct their lives (De Laguna 1975:91).

—Western (Orth, 1971): A Western sense of the metaphysical nature of place is conveyed by Lonely Lake, in the Brooks Range, so named in 1966 by Mr. and Mrs. Gilbert F. Staender because when they set up a base camp at this lake they were completely isolated.

No Athapaskan place-name that I have come across provides a sense of abandonment or isolation. This difference between being on and being of the landscape is nicely illustrated in Desperation Lake, a place-

name in the Brooks Range Orth obtained in 1956. Orth thought wolf hunters probably named it in the 1940s. In contrast, the Iñupiaq (Eskimo) name for the same place is *Tupichalik*, meaning "new tent" in reference to camping along the lake's dry gravel beach.

Non-Indigenous Spiritual Views of the Landscape

Cemeteries, battlefields, and memorials all have significance as sacred and spiritual landscapes in American culture. We all have memories of locations visited on family vacation and the places where we grew up may have special and perhaps spiritual importance. In addition, farm families may have a strong spiritual connection to the landscape they have tilled for generations.

Of course, it is no surprise that America, the benchmark of world capitalism, has numerous commodity values for American landscapes. In addition, from certain perspectives even spiritual values may be cynically regarded as being thinly disguised commodity "fetishes." For non-Native New Age spiritualists, the land resonates with newfound animism that some view with skepticism (Lippard 1997:147). One Western spiritual view of the landscape, however, has a direct feed into landscapes of resistance: wilderness.

Wilderness

Ansel Adams' photographs present a closely cropped view of landscape as the sublime.[3] For some, the beauties of landscapes represent "the last trace of the religious experience left in materialistic America." (Jussim and Lindquist-Cock 1988, quoted in Lippard 1997:179). One might suspect that for wilderness advocates Ansel Adams pictures capture, in a visual form, those transcendental qualities of landscape often encountered in the writings of Emerson, Thoreau, and Muir. As Callicott notes:

> The first notable American thinkers to insist, a century and a half ago, that wild nature might serve "higher" human spiritual values as well as supply raw materials for meeting our more mundane physical needs. Nature can be a temple Emerson (1989) enthused, in which to draw near and to commune with God. Too much civilized refinement, Thoreau argued, can over-ripen the human spirit; ... [building on their philosophy]. John Muir (1901) spearheaded a national, morally charged campaign for public appreciation and preservation of wilderness. People going to forest groves, mountain scenery, and meandering streams for religious transcendence, aesthetic contemplation, and healing rest (1998:340).

Whatever its etiology, it seems reasonable to consider this construction of the wilderness landscape as having spiritual underpinnings.

One problem with the currently received view of wilderness is its ethnocentrism; it ignores the presence of indigenous people (Callicott 1998:348). Some critics of wilderness consider the idea "museumized nature" (Talbot 1998). From another point of view, implementation of the wilderness ideal displaces indigenous people from rezoned "wilderness areas" or restricts their access to resources in such areas (Guha in Callicott

1998). A subtler outcome of excluding humans from the landscape, but perhaps more devastating in the long run, is the alienation of local people who can be crucial to the conservation process. Their exclusion, if their situation is desperate enough, can lead to resistance as they actively poach "protected" resources (Talbot 1998:339–40).

Although the situation has not reached an impasse in Alaska, there is considerable potential for conflict. The federal government manages nearly two-thirds of all lands while Native entities now occupy only about ten percent of their former land base. Lands controlled by indigenous entities now represent less than two-thirds of all the wilderness acreage in Alaska (Tables 2 and 3).

Thus, there is a palpable tension as to what are the attributes of a "wilderness landscape" in Alaska. Considerable finesse is required of land managers as they seek a compromise between the wilderness advocates' and local communities' concepts of spirituality and the landscape. Wilderness advocates are especially concerned about the potential aesthetic impacts to the landscape from the technologies (e.g., all terrain vehicles, or ATVs) rural residents use as they harvest wildlife resources (Fig. 56).

The National Park Service, ATVs, and "Natural" Landscapes

Most of the Alaska wilderness areas designated by ANILCA provide for continued access for rural populations:

> The Secretary shall ensure that rural residents engaged in subsistence uses shall have reasonable access to subsistence resources on the public lands. (Section 811(a) of ANILCA). . . .The Secretary shall permit on the public lands appropriate use for subsistence purposes of snowmobiles, motorboats, and other means of surface transportation traditionally employed for such purposes by local residents, subject to reasonable regulation. (Section 811(b) of ANILCA)

The section-by-section analysis of the title further

56/ An ATV trail through a meadow in bloom.

Table 2/ Ownership of Land in Alaska

OWNER	MILLIONS OF ACERS
Bureau of Land Management	85.0
Fish & Wildlife Service	72.4
National Park Service	52.9
Forest Service	22.5
Department of Defense and other Federal lands	2.3
State of Alaska	90.3
Native corporations	37.4
Other Private Lands	2.7
Total acreage in Alaska	**365.5**

Table 3/ Alaskan "Wilderness" Status Land

AGENCY	MILLIONS OF ACRES	% OF AGENCY TOTAL U.S. ACREAGE
Fish & Wildlife Service	18.7	97
National Park Service	33.5	91
Forest Service	5.8	17
Total	**58.0**	

amplifies the intent of the phrases "other means of surface transportation" and "traditionally employed" to include the

> [U]se of new, as yet unidentified means of surface transportation, so long as such means are subject to reasonable regulation necessary to prevent waste or damage to fish, wildlife or terrain (ANILCA Chapter VII:275).

The National Park Service may apply additional restrictions with respect to access to its lands. Only specified "resident zone communities" or residents with special permits are allowed to harvest park resources. The designations are usually liberal enough to incorporate most of the active hunters. The NPS may also restrict the types of technology used to harvest subsistence resources.

ATVs are an efficient and convenient form of transportation for harvesting resources, but they can also create trails of denuded vegetation. Those trails provide little threat to conservation of nature resources. However, with respect to aesthetics—and being un-

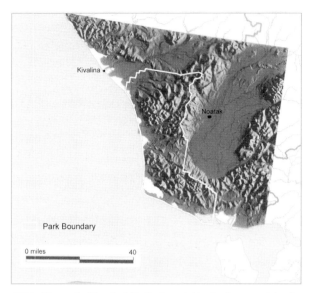

Kivalina •

Noatak •

Park Boundary

0 miles   40

57/ Noatak Shaded Relief and Hydrology, with the imposed boundaries of the Cape Krusenstern National Monument. Western land managers often draw boundaries across watersheds and other geomorphic features. These boundaries may have little overlap with traditional land use.

questionable evidence of man's presence—they can create considerable conflicts about what a landscape can or should contain.

The trails are anathema to Western visitors who want to have a "wilderness" experience in a national park. To traditional subsistence users, who consider themselves participants in the landscape, the trails are a small price for doing business. Although subsistence users evince discomfort when the issue is formulated in the context of respect for the land, their misgivings are usually set aside when balanced against practicalities. In essence, as one man noted, "We are not going back to carrying these loads out by foot."

This is especially true in the contemporary context where people live in sedentary communities and the distances involved are much greater. Seasonal camps once located near available resources no longer exist. Nor are subsistence users much swayed by preservationist arguments, for in many cases their extensive current use of ATVs is occasioned by sports hunting pressures on local resources that were formerly obtained adjacent to their home use area. Most local hunters would be happy for shorter ATV trips if the

resources could be obtained nearby.

Neither side condones damage to the landscape, although one side views humans and their technology as an impairment of the landscape's spiritual qualities while the other sees humans (and their pragmatic use of efficient harvest technology) as an integral part of the spiritual landscape. Part of this conflict lies in the divergent perspectives both sides have on human-animal interactions. Wilderness advocates assume that land managers need to prevent human interference with the "natural" animal populations. In fact, the total exclusion of a human presence is illogical, illegal, and impractical.

It is illogical because most wilderness advocates are themselves at least temporary consumers of the wilderness landscape. It is illegal in that ANILCA guarantees reasonable access to these lands for subsistence purposes, effectively modifying the Wilderness Act in Alaska's wilderness areas. Finally, it is impractical because wilderness areas are not islands. Caribou migrate on and off such designated areas, and most bird species in these areas are neotropical migrants who leave for the winter. Pollution, climate change, and the invasion of exotic species are all impacts on wilderness areas. In the absence and perhaps impossibility of strong enforcement, local communities resist the imposition of outside management in a variety of ways. Much of what Western land management personnel perceive as resource management is really management of a virtual landscape.

Geographic Information Systems (GIS), a Western "Resource" Management Tool

Federal and state land managers in Alaska use a variety of tools in their regulatory process. The tools structure and constrain how they perceive Alaska landscapes. In this chapter landscape is loosely defined to include physical features, biological populations (flora and fauna), and the cultural definitions of the relationships between the physical, biological and human. Interestingly, indigenous perspectives often truncate this typology by not drawing a distinction between animals (or even geological features) and consciousness. Thus, animals are aggregated with the social, sentient decisions often relegated only to humans in the Western perspective.

In contrast, federal and state land managers separate landscape components into geological, biological, and cultural components. This disaggregation can be illustrated by considering the GIS themes used by land managers in Alaska. These layers include topography (Fig. 57), river and stream systems, roads, boundaries of conservation units (Fig. 58), boundaries of game management units, vegetation maps, and ecozones.

For some regions of Alaska, social and cultural information is also plotted using GIS technology, e.g., community traditional harvest areas for a variety of species (e.g., moose, caribou, bear, fish, berries), or use areas during different time periods. Such information is critical for documenting customary and traditional uses for eligibility and access decisions. Despite the tremendous amount of information that GIS can convey, traditional indigenous views of the landscape are only weakly reflected in use area and place name data (Fig. 59). Instead, the data is abstracted and transformed to meet the decision context, comfort levels, and expectations of Western

land managers. One kind of information that westerners often overlook is the indigenous values related to animals and animal-persons.

The Yup'ik Landscape of Human—"Animal-person" Relationships

Central to indigenous traditional views of the landscape is the issue of human relationships with the resources they depend upon. Some of the best descriptions of these values come from the Yup'ik speakers of the Yukon/Kuskokwim region of West Alaska (Fienup-Riordan 1990). Yup'ik cultural values prescribe the proper treatment of "animal-persons" and the consequences of violating these rules. Animal souls are infinite, and what humans' harvest are only their "clothes." In fact many Yup'ik believe that when animal-persons offer themselves in great numbers, it is clear that humans are fulfilling their side of the bargain by showing respect. The Yup'ik belief that there is no relationship between a decline in an animal population and over-harvesting is in dramatic contrast with Western concepts of game management.

In fact many Yup'ik hunters face a difficult decision when they come across any animal (Morrow and Hensel 1992:40). A Yup'ik hunter who is out looking for caribou, but comes across an older male moose out of season is required by Yup'ik belief to harvest that animal. Failure to avail oneself of the gift presented is a profound

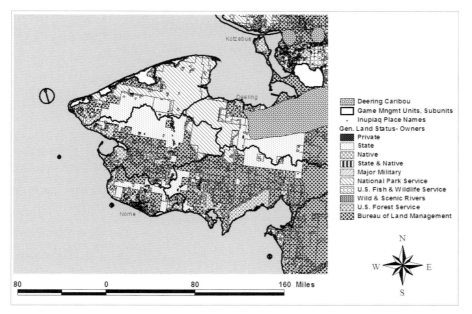

58/ Present-day land-status owners, Seward Peninsula, Alaska. Traditional subsistence users are confronted with a bewildering variety of land statuses, each with their own regulatory framework. For example, the community of Deering's traditional caribou harvest area now extends across federal, state, and Native lands.

Deering Caribou
Game Mngmt Units, Subunits
Inupiaq Place Names
Gen. Land Status- Owners
Private
State
Native
State & Native
Major Military
National Park Service
U.S. Fish & Wildlife Service
Wild & Scenic Rivers
U.S. Forest Service
Bureau of Land Management

mark of disrespect that will be noted by the animal–person and communicated to other animal–persons. It may lead to the unavailability of that species in the future. Thus, under Western precepts, to harvest the moose is to put pressure on the moose population and ensure its continual decline. Under traditional Yup'ik precepts, *failure to harvest* the moose leads to the same outcome.

Yup'ik are also taught that if they "play" with fish, the fish will not return the following year. These beliefs have led to serious friction with catch-and-release fishermen. By the Western conservation model, catch-and-release fishing ensures the survival of the fish stocks. Local Yup'ik believe that this disrespectful practice will lead to the eventual disappearance of the fish, after the fish tell their relatives how they were treated and discourage them from making the same journey.

Traditional Yup'ik elders believe that the more you harvest, the more that will return. However, the pre-

cept to harvest resources that present themselves is overridden by a stronger sanction: harvest no more than you need. One must exhibit respectful behavior after the ultimate gift is bestowed, but checks and balances are also present in the Yup'ik traditional management regime. Thus, the hunter who comes across a moose, mentioned in the example above, would not harvest the moose if he felt the meat would go to waste.

Fienup-Riordan's (1990) depiction of the Yup'ik worldview presents a problem of idealization and compression of these dynamic beliefs. In one household that I talked with in the Yukon/Kuskokwim region of Alaska, the senior members held (in the main) to traditional values, the middle-aged and younger adults respected but did not necessarily practice them or agree with them, and the teenagers and younger members hardly reflected upon them.

To avoid generalizing one set of values and beliefs about the landscape to a whole community, we turn to the results of a formal social science survey with a large sample, controlling for differences in age, gender, ethnicity, and some facets of personal history. Such an empirical and representative picture of peoples' behaviors and values, while less in depth, suffers less from idealization

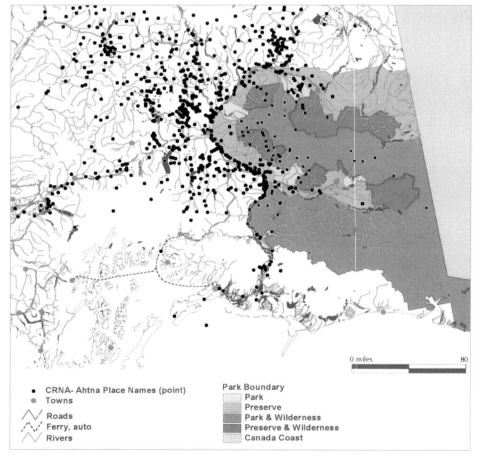

59/ Ahtna Place-Names Each black dot represents an Ahtna place name, and black dots in park-shaded areas indicates the traditional use of park resources. GIS projections such as this are used in the regulatory process as evidence in decisions that grant eligibility to conduct subsistence activities on park lands.

- CRNA- Ahtna Place Names (point)
- Towns

/\/ Roads
/\,\/ Ferry, auto
/\/ Rivers

Park Boundary
- Park
- Preserve
- Park & Wilderness
- Preserve & Wilderness
- Canada Coast

0 miles   80

PROTECTING THE INVISIBLE/ LANDSCAPES OF SURVIVAL

and compression.

Knowledge of the Environment

A multi-method research methodology designed to study the social and cultural impacts of the Exxon Valdez oil spill (EVOS) involved interviewing 2,728 residents of communities in the Gulf of Alaska.[4] This research indicated that personal, psychological, and community impacts resulting from the EVOS varied dramatically with the values imputed to the landscape. And while these values cannot simply be explained by Native/non-Native differences, it is clear that significant differences in degree occur between these groups. Jorgensen's (1995) analysis of the consequences of the EVOS demonstrates that Natives' and non-Natives' ideas, sentiments, and acts were organized quite differently concerning environmental and other ethics. These differences had an important effect on how the outcomes of the spill were perceived. Jorgensen (1995) notes that in the same environment Natives know more about wildlife resources than non-Natives; that Natives more frequently identify spiritual values rather than commodity values as the preeminent attribute of the environment (Table 4); and that Natives more frequently report that places in the environment have special meanings for them and their relatives (Table 5).

Sixty-nine percent of the 388 key informants in the EVOS survey were non-Native and thirty-one percent were Native. Each was asked to identify seventy-seven natural resources (including marine and land mammals, fish, marine invertebrates, birds, and plants) in the areas that person used. Researchers asked which species were available locally in sufficient numbers. Ninety-five percent of Natives responded to all seventy-seven questions about resource sufficiency, but not one non-Native responded to all seventy-seven questions.

The survey research results clearly showed that nearly half the Native respondents viewed the landscape as possessing only spiritual values whereas less than six percent of non-Natives felt the same way (Table 4). When these findings were presented to a Yukon/Kuskokwim elder and spokesman, he indicated that in his region three-quarters, not half, of respondents would assert only spiritual and no commodity values to the landscape. His assertion is based on the perceptive insight that indigenous communities in the EVOS region have a longer history of repression of traditional values and the forced introduction of other behaviors—e.g., commercial fur harvests.

Another question asked whether the respondent had memories about special places in his area. As Table 5 shows, both Natives and non-Natives have strong symbolic attachments to the landscape, but Natives accumulate many more such symbols. Jorgensen's multivariate analysis seems to indicate that long-term non-Native residents and high-income Native residents seemed to have borrowed more heavily from the other culture's repertoire.

Landscapes of Resistance

Both Guha (1990) and Scott (1985) have used the phrase "landscapes of resistance" in the context of indigenous resistance to exploitation and management of their traditional resources. Guha, writing about peasant resistance in the Himalayas, believes that interpersonal relationships and the organization of economic activities are intimately linked to the ecological attributes of the landscape—plants, animals, topography, climate, and habitat. He hypothesizes that as ecosystems change, social and production relationships will also change. In Guha's account colonial powers forced concepts of individual land ownership to replace the communally oriented land tenure practices of local inhabitants. Indigenous communities who were denied access to forest resources responded with a variety of forms of resistance, including labor slowdowns, destroying commercial stockpiles, and ignoring a variety of regulations. Largely because of the resistance, the Western forestry principle of "sustained yield," a continuous profitable harvest of forest products, was never achieved.

After Indian independence from Great Britain, Guha documents how these historical underpinnings gave rise to the Chipko (Hugging the Trees) movement, which in 1980 forced the Indian government to agree to a fifteen year ban on commercial forestry in the area. The Chipko movement also inspired many other indigenous communities to resist large dam projects and commercial use of forests throughout the world.

Guha concludes that an indigenous ideology (like Chipko) that articulates a traditional view of the landscape can forestall commodity uses of natural resources. In addition, any outside interest (commodity or conservation driven) that fails to take into account the "moral economy" of traditional landscapes (and the traditional rights embedded in such landscapes) are also bound to fail.

In Alaska, traditional views of the landscape—including knowledge of place, communal use of resources, ethical tenets as to the reciprocal nature of human/animal relationships, and the spiritual sense of topography—have been challenged by a dominant outside perspective that claimed power to manage and interpret the landscape. This outside perspective saw the land as property and "animal–persons" as commodities lacking sentience. The dominant culture that did impute spiritual attributes to the landscape thus excluded humans as a feature. These opposing perspectives led to local resistance to Western management practices.

In my research experience in more than fifty rural Alaska communities, I have always been struck by the contrast between the formal regulatory regime of Western land managing agencies and actual behavior evinced by local communities. Western managers depend on seasons (when a species may be harvested) and bag limits (how many and what type, e.g., young males only) to accomplish their conservation goals. These management procedures rely on the willing compliance of local communities or an effective threat of law enforcement. For example, Morrow and Hensel note that:

> Enforcement of waterfowl hunting laws has always been sporadic, with local resistance

Table 4/ Spiritual vs Commodity Values Associated with the Environment (from Jorgensen 1998:95)

ETHICS AND SIGNIFICANT SYMBOLS ATTACHED TO ENVIRONMENT	NATIVES (%)	NON-NATIVE (%)
1. The environment, or features of it (rivers, forests, coal seams, oil deposits, fish, sea mammals, etc.) are viewed as commodities, that is, items whose values are established in the marketplace and are available for purchase or sale.	0	31
2. Combination of commodity and spiritual views.	54	60
3. The environment, or features of it, are viewed as being endowed with spirits to which significant cutural symbols are attached (e.g., helpfulness). The general environment is not conceptualized as a commodity.	46	6

Table 5/ Special Meanings Associated with the Environment (from Jorgensen 1998:94)

SIGNIFICANT SYMBOLS ATTACHED TO PLACES IN LOCAL ENVIRONMENT	NATIVES (%)	NON-NATIVE (%)
1. None	4	7
2. A Few	24	44
3. Many	28	44
4. Many, which have accumulated over two or more generations	44	5

sometimes effectively thwarting agents' efforts. The most famous incident was the Barrow Duck-In of 1961. When several native men including a state legislator were arrested for spring bird hunting [banned by regulation at that time – D.C.] 300 Inupiat (138 of them holding dead eider ducks which they claimed were taken illegally), gathered in the community hall (Chance 1990:146–47). Faced with arresting much of the community, enforcement agents backed down.

Yupiit remember past repression [by law enforcement officers that fine individual hunters and confiscate subsistence technology – D.C.] and are discreet about swan harvesting. The legacy of repression is also kept alive in a large repertoire of told narratives about acts of "civil disobedience" such as armed stand-offs with authorities. One ubiquitous story concerns shooting holes in the floats of a Fish and Wildlife sea-plane so that it is unable to land and arrest offenders

MONTH	Jan	Feb	Mar	April	May	June	July	Aug	Sept	Oct.	Nov.	Dec.
Caribou												
Moose												
Sheep												
Bear												
Rabbit												
Beaver and Muskrat												
Pike and Whitefish												
Ptarmigan and Grouse												
Fur Trapping												

▓▓▓ **Traditional Tetlin Harvest Cycle**   ▬▬▬ **Contemporary Tetlin Harvest Cycle**

60/ Contemporary and Historic Annual Cycle for the Community of Tetlin, Alaska. This graph shows that traditional times of harvest for a variety of species in historic time (shaded area) has an imperfect overlap with the regulatory seasons of the contemporary Western management regime (Halpin 1987:31; Guedon 1974: 43, 45). Note: Sheep are not included in the contempory annual cycle regulations.

(with disabled floats, the agents can only fly home, since they must beach the plane after a single landing). Such tales are told with pride and humor in the vein of "Robin Hood vs. the Sheriff's men." (1992:44)

The Western regulatory regime requires valid and representative data on the status of wildlife stocks and the current harvest levels of those stocks. To establish bag limits, biologists estimate the current population and then, using a variety of statistical models, determine some level of sustainable harvest. However, the underlying data supports for both these processes are often questionable. The lack of reliable resource population data is compounded by the fact that self-reporting mechanisms for harvest levels are also unreliable. When anthropologists collect harvest information in face-to-face interviews, under promise of anonymity, and compare these results with reported tag and permit data, actual harvest levels are often ten times higher than the official estimates.

As will be detailed below, official seasons, especially in areas away from road-connected communities, are followed insofar as they overlap with traditional behaviors. Usually, employing the efficiencies required of subsistence pursuits, animals are harvested when they are available (or when they present themselves) and in quantities linked to need and processing capabilities and not to an existing bag limit (Fig. 60).

Federal and state regulatory structures are the principal connection between local hunters and government land managers. Regulations concerning bag limits, seasons, and harvest reporting are the primary means by which land managers and their biologist advisors seek to conserve and manage wildlife populations. Spaeder et al. (2001) document a history of considerable conflict between customary practice and government regulation in Northwest Alaska. They show that throughout this history a significant number of regulations were incompatible with traditional practices; despite the fact the traditional practices were non-wasteful and posed no threat to the conservation of the resource. The wildlife regulations applied to Alaska Native hunters were inappropriately imported from another context where they were used to regulate sport hunters.

A brief example (drawn from Moore 1984:10) illustrates the illogic and the impracticality of game regulations in the face of customary and traditional views and behaviors. Only twice a year, for a short period, do caribou migrations normally bring animals within range of a local village (Fig. 61). During the spring migration the animals have little body fat left after the long winter and are considered undesirable by local hunters. If the official harvest season for caribou does not coincide with the fall migration (when the animals are in prime shape for harvesting) then that community, which may derive half its nutrition from caribou, is out of luck. Naturally, under these circumstances the community ignores the seasonal restrictions.

Hunters from rural communities actually see the caribou on the landscape and note its availability and condition. Western perspectives of the landscape do not see the tundra or the caribou; they see a stochastic model that they believe allows them to predict and conserve the ongoing caribou population. Currently (since the herd now numbers 500,000) seasonal restrictions are liberal but bag limits could become a source of conflict. Bag limits are fifteen caribou per day. However, caribou are usually at some distance from a community, and it is expensive to locate and transport the harvested animals. Customarily hunters take what they need for their household and to redistribute in the community. Thus, when they chance upon a herd they may take twenty to forty animals and return to the community immediately to prevent spoilage. Although they could take a hundred animals in a week without any impact on the health of the herd, they can only legally take fifteen animals per day. Because such a restriction is completely impractical given their circumstances, they violate bag limits by taking what they need when the animals are available.

A number of potential violations are created in this harvest scenario. It violates game laws to give away harvested meat, completely in contradiction to traditional values that demand hunters redistribute and share their harvest with their extended family, elders and community members in need. Nor can extended family members pay for the gas used by the hunter without committing a violation. Almost none of the few hunters who obtain a hunting license actually carry it with them. Customary practices such as driving animals toward a waiting (and hidden) hunter are illegal. Few hunters send in harvest reports. It is not surprising that a hunter ignores, resists, and resents Western management regulations when his traditionally efficient practices may net him thirty citations on any given hunt. These cita-

tions can result in the confiscation of his snowmachine, his rifle, and hunting equipment and several hundred dollars in fines.

Although only a limited number of pages apply to any specific community, villagers rarely read the state (112 pages) or the federal (172 pages) booklets on game regulations. Many villagers are unaware that common sense practices such as shooting beaver (they can only be trapped under current regulations) or chasing game with a snowmachine violate the law. A survey of twenty-seven Kiana residents concluded that no one in the community, except the Alaska Department of Fish and Game (ADFG) license vendors, understood the hunting and trapping regulations (Regulation Review 1989:22). In another study, a Kotzebue resident said: "Local people have a hard time sifting out the important regulations from the unimportant ones" (Spaeder et al. 2001:33). The large number of regulations, a lack of English language or reading skills, and the fact that regulations are rarely enforced by either state or federal officials provide little incentive for traditional hunters to learn or follow game regulations. Compliance with Western management regimes most often occurs when regulations are consistent with customary practice.

Non-compliance also has the potential for serious friction in the community, as newcomers, such as non-Native teachers, have reported season or bag limit violations. However, for many younger subsistence hunters, non-compliance has become a norm and signifies, among other things, a resistance to outside attempts to control their perceptions of traditional landscapes. A number of analysts have suggested self-regulation and local enforcement as a possible solution to this conflict. Several Kiana residents called for a revitalization of traditional elder-based authority entities. In a sense land managers would have to delegate some of their authority to allow misdemeanor violations to be heard and ruled on by local leaders. One Kiana respondent who advocated this approach stated, "I would rather face the game warden than the elders if I wasted

61/ *Alaska Native caribou hunt.*

game (Spaeder et al. 2001:39). This solution omits any mention of the Western management practices of seasons, bag limits, or reporting requirements, and instead focuses on violations committed against a shared view of the traditional landscape (i.e., the overarching prohibition on waste). In an important sense, this commitment to avoid waste is at the heart of all conservation efforts, Western or traditional, although it may have little to recommend it to many wilderness advocates.

Landscapes Reduced to Biological Models

The literature on statistical modeling of biological (and geological) processes is enormous. We focus on the models provided by biologists and ecologists because it is their advice that land managers seek in constructing resource management plans. Biologists often, but not exclusively, base their advice on the outcomes of their modeling efforts. One form of statistical model is termed "density dependent." As Pimm (1991:359)

notes, "Perhaps no other topic dominates traditional population ecology more than does the discussion of whether density changes are density dependent."[5]

Two simple examples will illustrate the uses of this type of statistical model. The first comes from a debate begun in the 1940s about modeling halibut populations. Essentially one side believes that changes in population density can be solely ascribed to fishing pressures. In this density dependent model, the number of halibut recruited each year to the halibut population is directly related to how many halibut fishermen catch. From a management perspective, decreasing the catch will increase the halibut population. Burkenroad's competing "density independent" model states that for any particular year fishing pressures play only a small part in halibut recruitment and that the major impact on the increase or decrease in halibut numbers is due to "climate forcing." Climate forcing links changes in the ecosystem to variation in ocean currents and water temperature (Hare n.d.). These

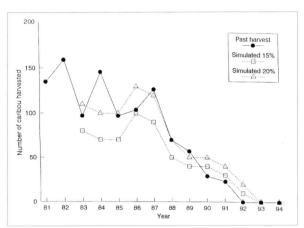

62/ Mentasta Caribou Herd Density Dependent Model. A density dependent model comparing actual harvest with simulated harvest levels that would have occurred had the cooperative management protocol been in force at that time.

changes range from annual or seasonal, interannual (El Niño) to interdecadal (Pacific Decadal Oscillation). Recent evidence suggests that decade-long oscillations in temperature are related to zooplankton biomass bloom (i.e. increases in the amount of zooplankton available) that may, in turn, increase halibut larvae survival as larvae and juveniles feed in near surface waters.

The second example deals with a critical management problem related to the Mentasta Caribou Herd, part of whose range intersects Wrangell-St. Elias National Park and Preserve. The herd decreased from 3,100 animals in 1985 to fewer than 900 in 1994. In a cooperative agreement to allow some subsistence harvest, a simple density dependent model (Fig. 62) was used to calculate herd size with harvest through time. The model provided a decision tree for establishing harvest levels: If the two-year mean fall calf recruitment (number of calves surviving into the fall) was greater than eighty, a hunt could occur, while a recruitment of less than eighty would eliminate any hunting. Other provisos included limiting the hunt to bulls only if the past two-year mean bull to cow ratio was greater than 35:100 (Mentasta Caribou Plan 1995).

Interestingly, as in the halibut example, a density dependent model that works for the Mentasta Herd would not be appropriate when applied to the much larger Western Arctic Caribou Herd (WACH). Now num-

bering over half a million animals, the WACH fluctuates in size from fewer than 75,000 animals to the current maximum in cycles that span decades. However, research in Canada and other areas indicates this boom and bust cycle has nothing to do with levels of human or other predation, and is more directly linked to climate change. In this case, precipitation and snow cover influence the caribou's access to the lichen they depend on for food.

In both these examples, resource managers view the landscape as abstract and in a sense a virtual landscape. When indigenous views of the landscape conflict with model outcomes, a contested landscape begins to occur. A typical outcome is a complete rejection of the resource agencies' landscape, reinforcement of traditional perspectives, and the creation of a landscape of resistance.

In the case of the WACH, local harvesters' reactions to what ADFG biologists believed was a precipitous decline of the herd in the mid-1970s provides an important example of the difficulties of managing wildlife when harvesters and managers have divergent perceptions of how many animals populate the landscape. In the 1970s caribou were counted using aerial surveys without the benefit of recent enumeration techniques such as radio collars or photo census. Agency managers and biologists believed that the herd had declined because of human and animal (especially wolf) predation (Fall 1976).

Working from this density dependent model of the landscape, biologists responded to what they believed to be a crashing population by severely restricting harvest. Managers were faced with attempting to set a regional harvest quota on the basis of what little harvest data they could obtain from local residents (some of whom they paid fifty dollars a month to act as village reporters), or assessments from pilots. After harvest by humans was determined to be approximately 25,000 caribou per year between 1952–1973, the Board of Game abruptly limited harvest from the WACH, a herd that had had no seasons or bag limits for seventeen years,

194

to 3,000 bull caribou for the 1976–1977 hunting season (Davis and Valkenburg 1978).

Soon after these restrictions were in place, relations between harvesters and the ADFG reached a crisis point. Local people did not believe the biologists' assertion that caribou had sharply declined, because many of them saw large numbers of caribou on the landscape, even passing through their village (Davis 1976). To this day, most local residents do not believe that a significant caribou decline occurred during that period. A recent survey in the area showed that seventy-eight percent of villagers believed the caribou population had *not* declined since 1970, while seventy-seven percent of managers believed that the herd had declined (Man and the Biosphere 1995).

Despite new regulations and the threat of arrest, the local harvest of caribou during that crisis period probably exceeded the quota established by the Alaska Board of Game. The majority of harvesters simply did not comply with "compulsory" harvest reporting provisions. In 1977, ADFG reported that for the entire range of the herd, only nineteen percent of the hunters had returned permits as required by law (ADFG 1977). This is the landscape of resistance through noncompliance.

It is not completely clear to what degree the 1970s caribou crash reflected a precipitous decline of the magnitude asserted by ADFG or whether it resulted from incomplete surveys that omitted a significant portion of the herd. However, in 1978, ADFG biologists found 106,000 caribou in the herd, almost twice the number of animals that agency biologists had believed were present two years before (Kruse 1995). Since it is unlikely that the herd size would double in two years, it appears that inaccurate data manipulated in an inappropriate model lead to a distorted perception of what was happening on the landscape.

Most of Spaeder's respondents did not view harvest by humans as a key factor controlling the overall size and distribution of a wildlife species. They widely believed that if local people harvest only to meet their needs, without waste, animal populations would be maintained. In Table 6, Spaeder (2001:66) summarizes differences between Western and indigenous knowledge as it relates to "management" practices.

When Differing "Traditional" Views of the Landscape Meet: A Case Study from Bethel, Alaska

In the traditional view of the landscape, animals are sentient, respect requires the remains of animal–persons be returned to the water or land, practices conform to the seasons of the landscape, and words have power. In the Western view, resources are commodities, animals and the landscape are acted upon, not with, and bureaucratic rules and statistical models serve as the basis for conservation efforts. One of the best examples of the meeting of different constructions of the landscape leading to frustration and resistance is found in Morrow and Hensel (1992:47–9). Using transcripts from public fisheries meetings held in Bethel in the early 1990s, the study clarifies opaque exchanges between regulators and local Native fishermen. Western land managers seem unaware of the nature of traditional landscapes. Whereas the fisheries biologists are very concerned about fish returns and are actively considering closing the fishery, Native elders, based on years of observation and experience, counsel that it is an ill-considered decision.

Elders attending the public meetings tried to explain salmon behavior to the regulators. They noted that there were clear signs of abundant fish, based on local people's long experience and observations. They said weir counts were low because the sentient fish avoid low water conditions. One elder pointed out that on another system where water levels were higher, fish were ascending normally (ibid.:47). The meeting transcripts reveal the biologists' patronizing dismissal of the elders' observations. The outcome of this subsistence closure was dramatic. The salmon harvest, which forms up to seventy percent of the wildlife diet in these riverine communities, was lost. The small amount of income gained from the commercial fishery—income that households depended on for cash to purchase boats, motors, fuel, and nets—was also lost.

Part of this distressing interaction comes from different conceptions about how the environment works. For the Yup'ik, conservation requires practices that signify respect for the environment. Animals possess sentience and intent. Their absence is by conscious decision, usually affected by human behaviors that breach reciprocal trust and respect. Changing weather patterns, reduced fish stocks, and absent game are all attributed to a human failure to respect nature. By contrast, non-Native scientists assume that resource decline is caused by overharvesting, habitat destruction, or climate change.

Even the way one speaks about the land and its resources has a dramatic impact on relationships. Yup'ik speak of the absence of fish as a temporary consequence of conditions such as wind direction or water level. Non-Yup'ik managers, on the other hand, explicitly voice their concerns in terms of declining fish populations. The Yup'ik, who believe fish can hear and understand human speech, are understandably nervous that the biologists' assertions would become a self-fulfilling prophecy. In the transcripts Yup'ik speakers were careful not to say there were not enough fish. Resource managers thought the Yup'ik response was predictable given their economic and nutritional investment in keeping the fishery open. Fisheries managers wanted local fishermen to admit, given sonar and weir counts, that the fish were not returning. This in turn increased the anxiety of local people who felt that such an admission was tantamount to guaranteeing the outcome.

In his concluding remarks to the fishery manager, the elder tried to communicate the consequences, from his view, of a fisheries closure,

the fish are coming in response to people's need. When they come, they must be taken: a decision to close the fishery will allow them to pass and they may be offended and not return in future" (ibid.:49).

This edited quote points out the most important stricture on human/"animal–person" relations. Not to harvest an animal that has consciously decided to present itself is a profound breach of respect that may lead to the animal and all its congeners deciding never to return. What wildlife biologists saw as a conservation measure, was seen by Yup'ik as a disrespectful act that could lead to catastrophe.

Developing a Shared View of the Landscape

The question of whether to conserve ethnographic landscapes seems poorly formed. Views of the landscape vary between and within cultures. However, as Table 6 indicates, all the landscape views considered in this chapter share a commitment to the conservation and continued utilization of wildlife (albeit in a non-consumptive mode for wilderness advocates). The art in achieving this objective is not to insist on the priority of any view in toto. With respect to the issues discussed in this chapter, a number of processes have been identified that allow selective overlap or acceptance of multiple viewpoints. Cooperative management techniques lead these mechanisms. If we break resource management regimes down into four generic activities:

—Research

—Allocation

—Enforcement

—Regulation

one can show how combining multiple views of the landscape can lead to a shared (or at least agreed upon) perspective.

Table 6/ Characteristics of Scientific and Traditional Knowledge Systems

Knowledge System Characteristic	Western Resource Management Science	Traditional (Local) Knowledge
Mode of data collection	·Based on experimentation and systematic direct and indirect observations. Knowledge base and management framework seen to be	·Based on less systematic ground-based observations. Ecological knowledge linked to myths and place-based narratives.
Temporal Scale of knowledge	·Short-term populations surveys providing a synchronic perspective.	·Long-term observation coupled with intergenerational knowledge providing a diachronic perspective.
Spatial Scale of knowledge	·Large scale (i.e., for moose, entire watershed; for caribou, herd range)	·Smaller scale (i.e. traditional subsistence harvesting zones; for some big game species, large portions of a watershed)
Locus of knowledge	·Knowledge held by wildlife professionals. Management system hierarchically organized.	·Knowledge diffuses, seen to be increasing with harvesting experience.
Goal of knowledge base	·Establish generalized principles explaining and predicting the status and behavior of wildlife.	·Understand the dynamics and behavior of wildlife in the local area.
Assumptions about system dynamics	·Populations can be maintained at or around a stable equilibrium point. Populations can be controlled by harvest, predation and habitat enhancement. (Population models emphasize density dependent variables.)	·Many species seen to have population cycles. Harvest and predation can affect populations, though animal population dynamics remain largely autonomous.
Goal of management and harvesting activities	·Species manipulated or controlled to achieve sustainable yield.	·Goal is to respond and adapt to system surprise (uncertainty).
Ecological systems structured by:	·Bio-physical forces	·Bio-physical forces and unseen super-natural forces
Preferred conservation strategies	·Regulate uses, control of means, methods, seasons and bag limits; access open to all user groups.	·Control (limit) access to traditional use territories.

Spaeder et al 2001:66. Table adapted from Berkes 1995; DeWalt 1994; Feit 1988; Usher 1986; Usher and Wenzel 1987.

Research

As discussed above, a determined effort is underway to establish a cooperative management board for the Western Arctic Caribou Herd (Western Arctic Caribou Herd 2003). One management function that all parties have agreed on is in the area of research. To overcome the impasse between land managers and local communities about the size of the WACH, a number of cooperative research arrangements have been put into place. Two efforts stand out. First, caribou surveys are now carried out with local hunters on board the planes. Before the current agreement, indigenous hunters regularly complained that observer planes missed pockets of caribou. Local hunters, who have carefully monitored the migration of the caribou in their area, now fly with the observers. Both sides benefit from this process: biologists attain more valid estimates of herd size, and local hunters are more likely to believe the estimates when their input is an integral part of the process.

In addition, biologists are now recruiting hunters to collect a series of measurements on each caribou they kill, including proportion of body fat, condition of bone marrow, presence of parasites, and gross body weight. Local hunters use traditional knowledge to maintain a dialogue with the biologists (who put these measurements into a variety of models) as they jointly assess the health of the herd. Efforts such as these tend to lead to convergence on estimates on herd size and the health of the herd, although the sides may still diverge substantially as to why and how these outcomes have occurred.

Allocation

The Kilbuck Herd, numbering about 7,000 caribou, ranges mainly in the Yukon-Delta National Wildlife Refuge in Western Alaska. In 1990, the Kilbuck Caribou Herd Co-Management Regime was jointly established. The participants included eighteen Yup'ik Eskimo villages, the U.S. Fish and Wildlife Service, and the Alaska Department of Fish and Game (Spaeder 1995). Using a density dependent model of herd dynamics (an appropriate model given the small herd size), the working group agreed to a permit-based, bulls-only harvest, limited to five percent of the total herd. The group next addressed the potentially difficult issue of how to divide the initial annual harvest quota of 125 animals among eighteen villages, which varied in community size (70–550 people), proximity to the herd, and customary use of the resource.

Once the allocation limit was established, the task of distributing permits was delegated to the Native members of the group. Instead of arguing about need ("our community is larger and needs more permits") or precedence ("our community has harvested these animals for hundreds of years and you never hunted them"), these representatives decided to divide the permits equally among the eighteen communities. This egalitarian solution reflected the Yup'ik view of the landscape. For example, interviews with Native respondents suggest that this decision ex-

presses the Yup'ik value of sharing.

> Respondents stated that they felt it was important to share things over which one cannot extend ownership, such as big game. No one "owns" the caribou, respondents asserted, just as one cannot own the fish in the ocean. This decision also serves as an example of one way that native groups attempt, where possible, to embed their own values within a regime whose character and structure is decidedly non-Native (Spaeder 1995:24).

The Mentasta Caribou Herd, mentioned above, provides another interesting example of the allocation issue. When fewer than thirty caribou are available to harvest under the management plan, permits for these caribou were given to elders in the most traditional and long-established communities. Designated hunters were allowed to harvest the caribou and provide them to the elders. During one year, only one caribou was harvested because hunters did not make extraordinary efforts to meet the harvest quota as the herd was relatively inaccessible during the year. This fits with the traditional practice of harvesting only those resources that can be efficiently obtained.

A compromise landscape emerges in both these examples. The communities' decision to restrict their harvests goes along with but does not necessarily agree with the biologist's view of how caribou operate on the landscape. In return, the biologists allow the community to allocate how the caribou are obtained and distributed without necessarily agreeing with the view of reciprocity between humans and animal–persons.

Enforcement

Non-compliance with resource management is a basic mechanism of resistance for local people. Despite the fact that several models of cooperative enforcement exist in Alaska, most land managers believe that enforcement cannot be delegated to local or tribal entities. In addition, law enforcement personnel tend to have a very circumscribed view of the landscape linked to regulation and violations of seasons and bag limits.

Given the vast expanses of Alaska landscapes and the limited number of enforcement personnel, however, most village residents' behavior is based on their own tenets and values. Enforcement prosecution, including fines and confiscation of hunting equipment, seem to be counterproductive in the long run (e.g., the 1961 Barrow Duck-In).

Regulation

ANILCA mandates the implementation of Regional Advisory Councils, composed of local subsistence users, who develop proposals to the Federal Subsistence Board on hunting eligibility, seasons, and harvest limits. The councils' recommendations on their proposals carry considerable weight with the Federal Subsistence Board. In fact, the board may only reject the councils' recommendations on proposals for a few circumscribed reasons, such as potential harm to the resource. Thus, ANILCA provides for the incorporation of local experience and perspective of the landscape into Western management practices.

While the text of ANILCA assumes that local rural residents know a lot about local fish and wildlife populations, it also seems to imply that the absence of a Western resource management regime is the absence of *any* management regime. This common misconception results in Western land managers' anxiety that without the strong hand of bureaucratic organization, local communities, now armed with Western technology, will over-harvest wildlife resources and threaten their viability.

This fear is both a product of ignorance, failing to be aware of indigenous conservation practices, and the classic error of affirming the consequence with respect to the premise. In this case Western conservationists invent a concept, i.e., "the tragedy of the commons," and then project this circumstance into any situation that lacks armed enforcement officers. Recent historical research has called into question the formulation of this concept. Resources held in common in seventeenth century Europe often had informal checks and balances. In addition, numerous anthropological treatises have documented the existence of formal and complex indigenous management regimes (Brightman 1993).

Despite these problems, the Regional Advisory Councils have provided a forum where divergent views of "landscape relations" have been able to co-exist. None of the constituencies have abandoned their views; rather they have expanded their awareness to admit that other perspectives exist. Biologists still use statistical models and eschew the sentience of animals; traditional harvesters still believe that landscapes are animate, that one must engage in reciprocal practices with animal–persons, and that statistical models are suspect when they conflict with their own experiences on the land. A cooperative approach that leads to a general agreement about the size and health of "resource" populations provides the trust or "social capital" that allows both sides to ignore the different processes that lead to similar conclusions.

Postmodern arguments trumpet the demise of a privileged perspective, however, at the same time; actors do not have to agree on the "true" nature of the landscape to respect one another. Co-management and cooperative endeavors require not the same view but an agreed upon vision. Such shared visions are reciprocal gifts, where both sides sacrifice their clothes to share the same spiritual journey. I hope this paper has shown that the imposition of one's cultural view of the landscape on other actors is, in the end, self-defeating. Active awareness of other perceptions of the landscape will most effectively allow land managers to achieve their conservation objectives.

Notes

1. Southern congeners of Alaska's interior Athapaskan communities. Apache and Alaska Athapaskan languages while mutually unintelligible, are closely related and form part of the same language family

2. This is not to say that current indigenous practices do not incorporate the latest western GPS technology in their subsistence practices.

3. Although Lippard (1997:179) characterizes his pictures as "tranquilizing" and "misleading."

4. The survey was done in 1987-1991 under a contract to the United States Department of Interior, Minerals Management Service, Anchorage, Alaska

5. Although we decline to discuss the applicability of these density dependent models, in general we agree with Pimm when he states, "And yet, as a community ecologist, I find the usual discussions of these issues incredibly circumscribed." (Pimm 1991:359)

References

Alaska Department of Fish and Game
1977   Results of the Fall 1977 Western Arctic Herd Permit Hunt. Juneau: Alaska Department of Fish and Game, Division of Wildlife Conservation.

Barnhardt, Ray
1998   Introduction. In *My Own Trail*, by Luke Howard, pp. xi-xiii. Fairbanks: Alaska Native Knowledge Network.

Basso Keith
1996   *Wisdom Sits in Places*. Albuquerque: University of New Mexico Press.

Berkes, Fikret
1995   Indigenous Knowledge and Resource Management Systems: A Native Canadian Case Study from James Bay. In *Property Rights in a Social and Ecological Context: Case Studies and Design Application*. S. Hanna and M. Munasinghe, eds. pp.99-109. Washington, DC: Beijer International Institute of Ecological Economics and the World Bank.

Brightman, Robert
1993   *Grateful Prey, Rock Cree Human-Animal Relationships*. Berkeley: University of California Press.

Callicott, J. Baird
1998   The Wilderness Idea Revisited. In *The Great New Wilderness Debate*. J.Baird Calicott and Michael P. Nelsonl, eds., pp. 337-66. Athens: University of Georgia Press.

Carlson, Allen C.
2000   *Aesthetics and the Environment: The Appreciation of Nature, Art and Architecture*. London: Routledge.

Chance, Norman
1990   *The Iñupiat and Arctic Alaska: An Ethnography of Development*. San Francisco: Holt, Rinehart, and Winston.

Clark, W.G., S.R. Hare, A.M. Parma, P.J.Sullivan and R.J. Trumble
1999   Decadal Changes in Growth and Recruitment of Pacific Halibut (*Hippoglossus stenolepis*). *Canadian Journal of Aquatic Science* 56:173-83.

Davis, D. and C. Grauvogel
1976   *The Western Arctic Caribou Herd*. Staff Report to the Alaska Board of Game. Juneau: Alaska Department of Fish and Game, Division of Wildlife Conservation.

Davis, J., and P. Valkenburg
1978   *Western Arctic Caribou Herd Studies*. Final Report. Juneau: Alaska Department of Fish and Game, Federal Aid in Wildlife Restoration.

De Laguna, Frederica
1975   Matrilineal Kin Groups in Northwestern North America. In *Northern Athapaskan Conference. Proceedings*, Vol.1, A. McFadyen Clark, ed., pp. 17-145. *National Museum of Man, Mercury Series. Canadian Ethnology Service Paper* 27. Ottawa.

DeWalt, B.R.
1994   Using Indigenous Knowledge to Improve Agriculture and Natural Resource Management. *Human Organization* 53(2):123-31.

Emerson, Ralph W.
1876   *Nature*. Boston: J. R. Osgood [reprint 1989 Boston: Beacon Press].

Fall, James
1976   *Wildlife Information Leaflet* 3. Juneau: Alaska Department of Fish and Game, Division of Game.

Feit, Harvey
1988   Self-Management and State Management: Forms of Knowing and Managing Northern Wildlife. In *Traditional Knowledge and Renewable Resource Management*. M.M.R. Freeman and L.N. Carbyn, eds., pp.92-104. Edmonton: Boreal Institute for Northern Studies.

Fienup-Riordan, Ann
1990   *Eskimo Essays. Yup'ik Lives and How We See Them*. New Brunswick and London: Rutgers University Press.

Fisher, John Andrew
2001   Aesthetics. In *A Companion to Environmental Philosophy*, Dale Jamieson, comp., pp. 264-76. Malden: Blackwell Publishers.

Guha, Ramachandra
1990   *The Unquiet Woods: Ecological Change and Peasant Resistance in the Himalayas*. Berkeley: University of California Press.

Henning, Robert
1965   *The Milepost. Alaska Highway Guidebook*. 17th Revised Edition. Juneau: Alaska Northwest Publishing Company.

Jorgensen, Joseph G.

1995   Ethnicity, not Culture? Obfuscating Social Science in the Exxon Valdez Oil Spill Case. *American Indian Culture and Research Journal* 19(4):1–124.

Jussim, Estelle and Elizabeth Lindquist-Cock

1988   *Landscape as Photography.* New Haven: Yale University Press..

Kari, James

1999   *Dena'inaq'titaztun, Native Place Names Mapping in Denali National Park and Preserve.* Draft Final Report. National Park Service, Denali National Park and Preserve. Contract # 337662. Fairbanks: University of Alaska, Fairbanks.

Kari, James and James Fall

1987   *Shem Pete's Alaska: The Territory of the Upper Cook Inlet Dena'ina.* Fairbanks: Alaska Native Language Center and the CIRI Foundation, University of Alaska, Fairbanks.

Kari, James and Priscilla Russell Kari

1982   *Dena'ina Elnena: Tanaina Country.* Fairbanks: Alaska Native Language Center, University of Alaska Fairbanks.

Kruse, Jack, Dave Klein, Steve Braund, Lisa Moorehead, and Bill Simeone

1998   Co-management of Natural Resources: A Comparison of Two Caribou Management Systems. *Human Organization* 57(4):447–58

Lippard, Lucy R.

1997   *Lure of the Local: Senses of Place in a Multicentered Society.* New York: W.W. Norton & Co.

Luke, Howard

1998   *My Own Trail.* Fairbanks: Alaska Native Knowledge Network.

Mentasta Caribou Herd

1995   *Mentasta Caribou Herd Cooperative Management Plan.* Final Version, revised March 1995. Glennallen: Wrangell-St. Elias National Park and Preserve.

Mishler, Craig and William E. Simeone

2004   *Han, People of the River.* Fairbanks: University of Alaska Press.

Moore, G.

1984   A Review of Game Management in Northwest Alaska. Self Published in Kotzebue.

Morrow, Phyllis, and Chase Hensel

1992   Hidden Dissension: Minority-Majority Relationships and the Use of Contested Terminology. *Arctic Anthropology* 29(1):38–53.

Muir, John

1901   *Our National Parks.* Boston: Houghton Mifflin.

Nash, Roderick

1982   *Wilderness and the American Mind.* New Haven: Yale University Press.

Orth, Donald J.

1971   Dictionary of Alaska Place Names. *U.S. Geological Survey Professional Paper* 567. Washington, DC: U.S. Government Printing Office.

Pimm, Stuart L.

1991   *The Balance of Nature, Ecological Issues in the Conservation of Species and Communities.* Chicago: University of Chicago Press.

Regulation Review Working Group

1989   Kotzebue Sound Regulation Review: Results of Village Interviews. On file, Alaska Department of Fish and Game, Division of Subsistence, Juneau.

Schneider, William

1998   Afterword. In *My Own Trail*, by Luke Howard. Pp. 99–103. Fairbanks: Alaska Native Knowledge Network.

Scott, James C.

1985   *Weapons of the Weak, Everyday Forms of Peasant Resistance.* New Haven: Yale University Press.

Sheldon, Charles

1908   The Cook Inlet Aborigines. In *To the Top of the Continent.* Frederick Cook. Pp. 269–77, Appendix C. New York: Doubleday, Page, and Company.

Soule, Michael E. and Gary Lease, eds.

1995   *Reinventing Nature?: Responses to Postmodern Deconstruction.* Washington D.C. and Covelo, CA: Island Press.

Spaeder, Joseph

1995   *The Qavilnguut (Kilbuck) Caribou Herd: An Alaskan Example of Cooperative Management.* Report to the Eighteen Participating Yup'ik Villages and Alaska Department of Fish and Game. Juneau: Alaska Department of Fish and Game and U.S. Fish and Wildlife Service.

Spaeder, Joseph, Donald G. Callaway, and Darryll Johnson

2001   The Western Arctic Caribou Herd, Barriers and Bridges to Cooperative Management. *National Park Service Technical Paper, Cooperative Ecological Studies Unit*, pp. 1–100. Seattle: University of Washington.

Talbot, Carl

1998   Wilderness Narrative and Capitalism. In *The Great New Wilderness Debate.* J. Baird, Callicott, and Michael P. Nelson, eds., pp. 325–36. Athens: University of Georgia Press, Athens.

Usher, Peter J.

1986   *The Devolution of Wildlife Management and the Prospects for Wildlife Conservation in the Northwest Territories.* Ottawa: Canadian Arctic Resources Committee.

Usher, Peter J., and George Wenzel
1987   Native Harvest Surveys and Statistics: A Critique of Their Construction and Use. *Arctic* 40(2):145-60.
Western Arctic Caribou Herd

2003   Western Arctic Caribou Herd Working Group. Western Arctic Caribou Herd Cooperative Management Plan. Nome, Alaska, 33 pp. http://www.wildlife.alaska.gov/management/planning/Caribou_web.pdf

"The Whole Story of Our Land":

Ethnographic Landscapes in Gambell, St. Lawrence Island, Alaska

IGOR KRUPNIK

As cultural change and modernization has overtaken many Indigenous settlements across the North, one of the most visible signs is the profound transformation of the physical landscape. When old teachers' reports, elders' memories, and historical photographs are matched against today's local settings, time and again it looks as if events separated by a few decades took place in a different physical and social space—in terms of the general look of Native communities, their social composition, dwelling type, and relation to and the use of the surrounding area.

Other changes related to the way(s) people mentally organize their environment are invisible but, nevertheless, profound. An anthropologist checking early accounts or comparing notes of the same community some ten, twenty, or thirty years later, would easily recognize the difference in types and number of local place names, nature of stories about the area, set of local features used as spiritual and identity markers, and others. Such shifts in socially recognized and culturally organized environment, the "ethnographic landscape," may progress even faster than the real physical transformation of a given place. Often, such mental projections of the same physical landscape can be surprisingly disconnected, if not worlds apart, particularly in the cases of population or language shift, rapid acculturation, and/or other breaches in cultural continuity. Because of that, various chronological phases of the local "ethnographic landscape"—if not clearly distinct "landscapes" (in plural)—may be identified or construed at one physical location. Similarly, archaeologists rec-ognize subsequent cultural phases of an ancient village and/or independent local settlements via stratified site excavation. Unlike archaeologists, who uncover physical traces of ancient sites from the ground, it remains to cultural anthropologists and local historians to retrieve and recreate such old mental constructions, former ethnographic landscapes, from people's memories and written records.

This paper is an attempt at construing a 200-year history of the changing ethnographic landscape(s) of one Native Alaskan community, the village of Sivuqaq/ Gambell on St. Lawrence Island. Sivuqaq/Gambell is by no means unique in undergoing a dramatic physical and social transition through the centuries. Unlike other Native Alaskan communities, however, it enjoys one of the best-documented records of change in its historical environment. This record was accumulated through extensive archaeological excavations at nearby ancient sites, and through several recent oral history and educational programs undertaken by community members, often in cooperation with anthropologists (*Akuzilleput Igaqullghet* 2002; Crowell 1985; *Sivuqam Nangaghnegha* 1985–89; Silook 1976; *Yupik Language* 1989). Voluminous narratives, archival documentation, and historical photographs produced by early visitors to St. Lawrence Island are also available. The present synopsis of the changing ethnographic landscape at Sivuqaq/Gambell is based on such a survey of existing records; it has been made possible thanks to the dedicated collaboration of many of today's elders, who shared their knowledge and historical memories of their Native village (see below, Acknowledgments).

This paper is also an effort in "applied preservation ethnography." As new types of dwellings replaced old ones, and the main village site expanded across its traditional location, huge portions of local heritage were all but abraded, both physically and mentally. Some sections of the old village are currently under water; others have been dramatically transformed by new construction. Many more were lost through neglect, abandonment, insensitivity of new construction projects, and thinning of the once thriving cultural tradition.

In this respect, Sivuqaq/Gambell is hardly different from any other historic town, whose rich cultural heritage is threatened by population growth, modernization, and new living standards. Hundreds of such historic settlements in the U.S. and elsewhere have witnessed their old houses being replaced by modern apartment buildings, and their cobblestone streets transformed into parking lots and strip malls. As in Sivuqaq/Gambell, it is often left to fragile human memory to be the sole guardian of the vanished local scenery otherwise preserved in old museum photographs, paintings, and historical records. This paper discusses some modern strategies in heritage documentation and the appropriate community policies that may be applied to preserve the legacy of the long-gone ethnographic landscapes in a living Arctic town.

The Setting

The community of Sivuqaq/Gambell (population *ca.* 650) is located on a flat gravel spit attached to the rocky Cape Chibukak, the northwestern tip of St. Lawrence Island, on the Bering Sea coast (Fig. 63). The island has been American territory since 1867, although the village is situated much closer to Asia than to North America (mainland Alaska). Barely forty miles of water separates it from nearby Chukchi Peninsula, Siberia, and the tops of the Siberian mountains are visible from the village on a clear day. Local residents, with the exception of a handful of contract schoolteachers, are mostly

Native Yupik Eskimo. They call their village (and the whole island) Sivuqaq and themselves Sivuqaghhmiit, when speaking in their language, Yupik. The official name of the town, Gambell, was designated in 1899 to honor its first white missionary-teacher who drowned in 1898. Native residents use both town names, although "Gambell" is commonly preferred when talking and writing in English.

The late anthropologist Charles Hughes produced an emotional image of dramatic changes that were twisting and shaping the old village of Sivuqaq/Gambell. On his first visit in the summer of 1954, he called the landscape he observed "the torn grass:"

> Evidence of significant shifts in the Gambell Eskimos' way of life presented itself even before we have reached the village on the mile-long journey from the point of landing. . . . Fourteen years earlier [i.e., in 1940] the entire gravel spit stretching from Mt. Chibukak out to the sea was covered with grasses and other plants, making a thin matting of vegetation over the loose pebble underneath. . . . Nothing marred the smoothness of this green plain except the two or three archaeological sites—remains of old villages—in which the Eskimos dug for specimens. . . . But now most of the covering was gone, turned over and churned under by tractors of the construction crews and military bases. . . .The destruction of the thin edge of green on the seaworn pebbles was merely a symbol of a much larger set of circumstances, which had come to Gambell in the (last) fourteen years. Now hundreds of empty oil drums, rusted and filigreed by the rains, snows, and sea spray, dotted the gravel spit. . . . As we approached closer to the village, we came across twisted and bent sections of steel matting, intended, a couple of years before, for an airplane runway to link Gambell regularly with the outside world (Hughes 1960:16, 20).

Today the oil drums and metal debris have been cleaned up, and scattered patches of meager grass covering the spit can be seen again. No visible signs remain of the old military sites and installations that marred the landscape and epitomized the harsh image of change as observed in 1954 (Mobley 2001). But the once-"pristine" gravel spit is now covered with a sprawling

63/ Aerial view of Cape Sivuqaq with the Sivuqaq (Gambell) Mountain, Troutman Lake, and the village of Gambell at the bottom right end of the spit.

modern town of some five hundred residents, inhabiting dozens of new family houses, public and store buildings, and an impressive new schoolhouse. The gravel cover is again turned over and churned under—this time, by the tracks of the Honda four-wheelers that serve as major transportation in the community. In fifty years, the whole village has literally been on the move: not only in time, but also in space. Only a handful of older buildings remain at the former village site a half mile away.

The present-day town of Sivuqaq/Gambell is split into two distinct parts about a half mile apart. The "new village," of several dozen modern residential houses and many modern public buildings and warehouses, is located on the flat gravel plain between the lake and the northern shore of the cape (see maps and description in: Callaway and Pilyasov 1993; Crowell 1985; Jolles 2002; Jorgensen 1990:26, 28-9; Mobley 2001:10-12, 18-19). The "old village" made of more traditional houses sits on top of a small ridge that descends to the western shore. The "new village" was established in the mid-

1970s; before then, all residents lived at the "old" site.

Judging from several C-14 dates obtained from the ruins of old dwellings and abandoned ancient sites, the area has been populated for the last 2,000 years, if not longer. Ancient people lived here very much like the present-day residents, primarily by hunting walruses, seals, whales, and other marine mammals, and by fishing, hunting birds, and collecting greens and berries. They traded actively with other communities on the island and with the villages on the Siberian (and later Alaska) mainland (Ackerman 1984:108-13; Mason 1998:260-5). The overall shape of the inhabited area at Cape Chibukak (Sivuqaq), however, has changed substantially over the last 2,000 years, as the flat gravel plain or foreland attached to the rocky cape (Sevuokuk Mountain) has been gradually expanding to the west and to the north.

Physical Changes in the Sivuqaq/Gambell Landscape

Henry B. Collins, Smithsonian archaeologist who conducted excavations at and around Sivuqaq/Gambell in

1929–1930, produced the first outlines of "historical landscapes" of the area, based on his surveys of local ancient sites (Fig. 64):

> Immediately to the south of the present village [today's "old site"] are the pits of earlier houses of wood and whale bones, some of which were occupied until the end of the last century. Sunken caches or meat cellars, built entirely of whale bones, are well preserved, some, in fact, being still in use. Near the head of the lake the ruins of this recently abandoned site merge imperceptibly into those of an older and more extensive site, known to the Eskimos as Seklow-aghyaget [Siqluwaghyaaget], "many caches." About half a mile to the northeast a grass-covered midden, marking the site of another old village, rises conspicuously from the gravel plain; this site the Eskimos call Ievoghiyuoq [Ayveghyaget], "place of the walrus," from its resemblance to a herd of walrus lying on the ice. Some 200 yards south of Ievoghiyoq, and at the foot of the plateau, is still another old site known to the Eskimos as Miyowagh [Mayughaaq], "the climbing up place" (1937:33).

According to Collins, these ancient sites were, in fact, the landmarks of the changing shape of Cape Chibukak, as the series of successively younger beach ridges were built by the retreating surf zone and shore currents, so that the old village sites had to be moved repeatedly to remain closer to the beach. Thus, the Mayughaaq site and another ancient settlement, Hillside, higher up above the slope of the Sevuokuk Mountain, were the oldest in the area. The site of Ayveghyaget, located some 200 yards closer to the present-day northern shore and separated from Mayughaaq by four beach lines, should be dated from a later period. The site at Siqluwaghyaaget was populated next and was inhabited until the end of the pre-contact period (i.e., about AD 1700), when people relocated the village closer to the expanding western shore. About 100 to 120 years later, they moved again to build a precursor of the historic village on a higher ridge. Since then, the village moved several hundred yards farther northward along the western shore, as all the historical houses of the late 1800s and early 1900s were located north of

the abandoned underground dwellings (Collins 1937:33–4, 1940:546). These settlement shifts might have caused substantial reconfiguration of the local ethnographic landscape(s), even if people continued to exploit the same area, with more or less the same type of economy.

It is hard to say whether the old sites at and around Sivuqaq/Gambell were occupied by one residential population or by distinct communities that moved from one place to another through the centuries, as the land was physically changing under people's feet. It is quite likely that, at least, the three latest settlements—Siqluwaghyaaget, Collins' "old section" (sometimes named Mangiighmiit by today's elders), and what is known today as Gambell "old site" (i.e., historic village of the 1900s)—were inhabited by related communities. The sheer proximity of three sites argues for their continuity. The connection between the "old section" and the historic village of the late 1800s and of the 1900s is also supported by local oral tradition.[1]

According to Collins, at some point during the eighteenth century, people started to build semi-subterranean dwellings at the "old section" site, to the south of the historic village, along the elevated gravel bar between the lake and the sea (Collins 1937:189; Fig. 50). Today's residents call this type of house *nenglu* in Yupik, and igloo when speaking in English. Collins argued that the houses at that "old village" site were abandoned "some forty or fifty years" before his visit, that is, before 1880 (Collins 1937:190, 261). Today's elders remember these houses from "grandfathers' stories" only:

> My grandfather also told me about the old underground houses, *nenglu*. They used to live in these *nenglu*s when they were young. I think he was born in a *nenglu* house. They used to make roofing of whalebones and they put walrus hides on top but particularly very big pieces of ground (sod). It was very warm, just like a good roofing. They put many whalebones on top, so that it could keep these big pieces of ground (sod) on the ceiling. (Who lived in this house?) I think, his parents used to live there, *Temkeruu*'s

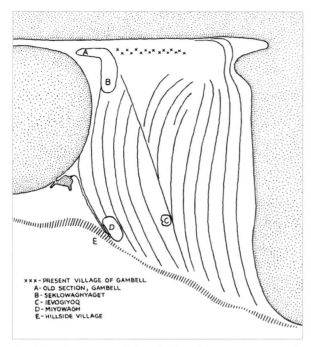

64/ *Outline map of Gambell and vicinity, at north-west end of St. Lawrence Island (Collins 1937:189).*

[grandfather's] parents; maybe, also their brothers and family. . . . Maybe, they once lived in one *nenglu* but as far as I remember, they always had different (separate) living quarters—two or maybe three (residencies) in one *nenglu*. They called it *saaygu*. They got a door and they somehow separated this *nenglu* into (family) living quarters. They used clay lamps, number of them for light and heating.

(Have you ever seen such a house?) Yes, in the camp *Tapghuq* there was a *nenglu* that used to be of my father's side grandfather's relatives. It was *Aymergen*'s *nenglu*. It was not ruined yet when I first saw it. They used to stay at the *Tapghuq* camp along with my grandfather and family. . . . But *Aymergen*'s old *nenglu* was still staying there, although it was probably many years ago when they used to stay [to live] there (Avalak/Beda Slwooko 1999; *Akuzilleput* 2002:409).

At some point about the mid-1800s, the semi-subterranean winter sod-houses at Gambell were swiftly replaced by a new type of above-ground winter dwelling, *mangteghapik*, with an inner chamber made of walrus and reindeer skins (see descriptions in: Jackson 1903:28; Geist and Rainey 1936:12–13; Moore 1923:346–9; *Sivuqam* 1989:100–5). According to archaeologists (Collins 1937:261; Geist and Rainey 1936:12), this type of winter house was introduced from Siberian Yupik

villages across the Bering Strait, presumably because of increased contacts. Most of the present-day elders age seventy and older were born in such houses and remember it well. This shift obviously made a great impact on the overall appearance and the general configuration of the village. As the underground sod-dwellings at the "old site" were abandoned, people were building new skin-covered houses farther north, along the beach ridge. Hence, the whole village was gradually moving northward.

This village landscape of dome-shaped, skin-covered houses surrounded by smaller tents or frame cabins, vertical whalebone rafters, boat-racks, and meat cellars is depicted in many early photographs of Sivuqaq/Gambell from the 1880s and until the 1930s. Unfortunately, no photographs or good accounts of the village exist before 1881.

The most significant event in the recent history of St. Lawrence Island occurred in the winter of 1878–1879, when a terrible famine, probably coupled with an epidemic, wiped out more than half of the island's population. Several villages were completely destroyed, and many communities barely endured with few survivors. With the death of so many people, the pre-famine social geography of the island made up of several settlements, clans, and tribes, was almost obliterated.

The village of Sivuqaq was less affected by the tragedy than, probably, all other large communities on the island (see contemporary reports and estimates in Doty 1899:187, 217; Hooper 1881:10; Muir 1917:108; Krupnik, 1994; Mudar and Speaker 2003). A portion of its population survived, preserving some cultural continuity with the earlier residential community. Many survivors from other settlements hit by the famine moved to the area. They were joined by several Yupik families from Siberia, eager to leave their mainland villages because of a similar combination of bad weather, poor harvest, and mass starvation. These people brought with them their specific customs and group names, as well as memories of distant places and landscapes. This mixture of local and introduced traditions was the foundation on which the present-day community of Sivuqaq/Gambell, and its culturally organized environment, "ethnographic landscape," was created.

Construction of the government school-building in 1891 and the arrival of residential white teachers in September 1894 marked the second major documented event to reconfigure the historic village of Sivuqaq/Gambell. Carpenters from the ship that transported the lumber from San Francisco (Gambell 1910:3; Jackson 1903:29; *Akuzilleput* 2002:267) erected the school building ("a strong, plain structure, forty feet in length by twenty in width") in 1891. From 1894, with the arrival of the first teachers, and for decades thereafter, it served as the only public building in the village, combining the functions of schoolhouse, teachers' residence, Presbyterian mission, and community hall.

Vene Gambell, the first teacher, claimed that the schoolhouse was built "on the outskirts" of the village (Gambell 1910:3); one of his photographs in 1897 depicts a large empty space at one side of the school (Jackson 1898:36). The practice of the time was to place schoolhouses (and the teachers) some distance apart from the Native residential area. Today's elders, however, remember the old school building of the 1920s and 1930s located at the center of the community, surrounded from all sides by Native houses. That suggests that the village of the late 1800s was made of several dispersed house clusters or neighborhoods, with plenty of free space in between (Fig. 65).

The next significant event in village history was the "big flood" of 1914 (or 1913). Several accounts of the "big storm" of 1914 were first recorded by anthropologists Alexander and Dorothea Leighton in 1940; many of today's elders recount similar stories they heard from their parents (Leighton 1940; see *Akuzilleput* 2002). The storm reportedly created a huge wave that flooded a whole section of the historic village. It wiped out several houses and an entire small neighborhood located at or close to today's beach. That forced the residents to move out and to rebuild their houses on higher ground in the central portion of the village, close to

the school building. As a result, the former spatial structure of the village, made of several separate neighborhoods was dramatically transformed:

> There were a lot of houses made of walrus hide (in Gambell). Some of them are under the sea now, especially two of them that I know belonged to the Tungiyan's and Anangti's. . . . Our house was where the boat racks are now. To the north was Temkeru's. Farther north from Temkeru's was Kaningok's and to the west of the meat racks was Nemayak's. These three houses were also located where the boat racks are now.

> At that time the beach was farther down and there was no erosive waves back then. At least the waves did not go beyond the banks of the beach.

> Back in those days when the waves started getting bigger than normal, we (also) moved from our original place to where we are now. The waves weren't really that big but everybody decided to move (Lloyd Oovi in *Sivuqam* 1985:10–17).

As some families were forced to move their dwellings to the center, those who lived at the southern end decided to leave for good. Shortly after the storm of 1914, they moved to reindeer herders' camps in the interior of St. Lawrence Island. Eventually, they settled at the new village of Savoonga, forty-five miles from Gambell.

Anthropologist Riley Moore, who visited the village in 1912, shortly before the "big flood," reported that some families were already using lumber frame houses during the summer months "but they (the residents) move into Native houses built of [walrus] hides and driftwood as soon as cold weather begins" (Moore 1923:350). It was the prohibitive cost of imported lumber that kept the number of frame houses low. By the 1930s, however, the transition to lumber houses was almost complete and the last traditional skin-covered dwelling was dismantled in the summer of 1940 (Hughes 1960:16). Still, an old tradition of using two types of residences during the year—a winter house and a summer skin tent (*guigu*)—persisted, as almost every family kept separate lumber structures for its summer and winter occupation. This combination of wooden

65/ *St Lawrence Island Yupik women and children in front of a traditional semi-subterranean house,* nenglu, 1889, *one of the earliest historical photographs of Sivuaqaq/Gambell, showing the very dispersed nature of the old village, with plenty of empty space in between the house clusters.*

structures, boat-racks, scattered whalebones, and vertical jaw-poles made a picturesque image of the village, as seen from many photographs (Fig. 66) and visitors' accounts:

> As approached from the direction of the sea, the village was seen as a cluster of wooden houses arranged roughly in three straggling rows running parallel to the western beach. In front of the houses and typical of practically all Eskimo settlements were the many whalebone racks within easy reach of the water, onto which whaleboats and skin-covered Native craft were lashed.

> The center of the village was clearly the square bounded by the newly constructed schoolhouse and teachers' quarters, the community store, the nurse's residence and dispensary, and the Presbyterian mission, the oldest building in the village and the first permanent white construction, which dated from the late 1890s and for many years served as church, school, and community meeting hall. The fifty or so Eskimo houses were constructed of lumber imported from the mainland, and they could be grouped by a casual glance into two types. . . . The first type of house was typically the summer dwelling place, and the second was the

structure in which a family spent the winter. Most families had a house of each kind (Hughes 1960:15–16).

In the 1930s, some lumber houses were transformed into winter dwellings, with old-style sleeping places of reindeer skins (*agra*) built inside. Families stopped using seal-oil lamps for heating and cooking, and switched to coal and oil fuel stoves. Then, the skin-covered sleeping places were dismantled as described in *Akuzilleput* (2002:412):

> I was born in 1926, and our old (winter) house was still there. Then my uncle *Waamquun* built another house of a similar shape to the old winter home. The whole frame-house, but with this (round-shape) front, like the old winter-home. And he put the same *agra* inside. But soon after that it was gone, when they put the heater inside. And after that they just moved to their summer house year-round.

> I was probably five or six years old, when my uncle built this new house and put the *agra* inside. But later on there was no more *agra*. They made a full room and a little door, so that we could go in and out. And we started to use kerosene heater or other heater to heat

the room. And stopped using seal-oil lamps. I was probably ten years old, when it happened [1935 to 1938]" (Anaggun/Ralph Apatiki, Sr., 1999).

We did the same thing at about the same time, in the later part of the (19)30s. But our family was using a wood stove. And also kerosene lamp for the light, until we finally got electricity here. It happened about 1940 (Akulki/Conrad Oozeva, 1999).

Then all people remodeled their homes. They changed their inner rooms, they put lumber instead of fur (wall covers) inside. And also made doors and windows instead of these reindeer skins we used to go under. They made the same winter houses but just put lumber on the outside instead of the walrus hides with ropes (Kepelgu/Willis Walunga, 1999).

The 1940s to the 1960s also witnessed several major construction projects run by outsiders at or close to the historic village. First, the new housing section for the personnel of the Civil Aeronautics Administration (CAA) was built a short distance from the village, beginning in 1943. After World War II, two U.S. military bases operated near Gambell between 1948 and 1958 (Hughes 1960:295-304, 351-3; Mobley 2001:8-10). A small airstrip appeared to the south of the historic village in 1940, which was expanded during World War II. Several old pits, meat-cellars, and whole sections of the "old site" were destroyed by this construction. Finally, during the 1960s, a huge new schoolhouse was built in the middle of the village near the central public place. The historic school building erected in 1891 and later transformed into a Presbyterian church, was torn down, marking a symbolic end to the era started in 1891 to 1894.

A far more radical shift happened during the 1970s, when new state and governmental funding became available in Alaska due to increased oil and gas tax revenues. Between 1972 and 1982, a new town was built on the exposed gravel spit between the lake and northern shore, about half a mile (500-1,000 meters) from the old village. Some fifty new family houses were constructed, accompanied by several public buildings (Jorgensen 1990:154-7). These buildings were erected

in regularly arranged rows, with no linear connection to the main axis of the old village. Some families, nevertheless, chose to stay in their old houses close to the western beach. As a result, the overall area now occupied by the community has increased almost tenfold. The system of the "old" and "new" village sites (almost thirty years old now) is likely to be preserved for years, since several family houses in the "old village" have been remodeled and even upgraded for continuous occupation.

The Social Construction of Landscape

As change swept through the village of Sivuqaq/ Gambell, outside visitors and Native residents kept remarkably different images of the same site. To outsiders, it was a chaotic conglomerate of clumsy skin-houses, lumber cabins, and boat-racks arranged in irregular groupings and "straggling rows." For the residents, their village was a highly organized universe, a network of well-defined and tightly knit units and neighborhoods that influenced every form of subsistence and social activity. In analyzing historical narratives, one has to grasp and reconcile those two different mental constructions. Unfortunately, early visitors left few references to the spatial composition of the traditional community, whereas the residents' perspective on the organization of their village was not documented until recently. The first Native account of life in Sivuqaq/ Gambell in the early 1900s was published in 1985 (*Sivuqam* 1985:10-17, Lloyd Oovi's narrative and map), while another critical resource, a village census and map made by Paul Silook in 1930, remained virtually unknown until few years ago (see *Akuzilleput* 2002:383-97).

Outsiders until the early 1900s (Moore 1923) did not recognize the core element of the village social order, the patrilineal clans (*ramket*). Otto Geist made some vague references to "sections," into which the traditional village of Sivuqaq/Gambell was divided; these "sections" were reportedly occupied by families "[that were] closely related by blood or by communal

66/ Gambell's landscape as of summer 1930, with a modernized lumber house, drying racks, boats, and remains of a bowhead whale hunt in the foreground.

interests" (Geist and Rainey 1936:11). Today's elders remember such clusters of houses occupied by related families as the way their community was organized spatially and socially in their childhood years *(Akuzilleput* 2002:400, 407–8):

> The relatives, the clans used to live close together all the time, from the old days. *Pugughileghmiit* tried to stay together and *Sanighmelnguut* on the other side" (Kepelgu/ Willis Walunga, 1999).

> As far as I remember, we lived together with my grandparents from my mother's side. My grandfather's name was *Temkeruu.* . . . The nearest house to us was (that of) *Aatghilnguq*, my grandfather's younger brother, and his family close-by. And another nearby house was of other close relative, *Qanenguq*. And *Mangtaquli*, another close relative, was close-by too. But *Aatghilnguq*, my grandfather's younger brother and family, was the most close to us (Avalak/Beda Slwooko, 1999).

> I think, most of the families, the clans tried to stick together. But after this big storm, when many houses were destroyed, they started moving their houses to the higher grounds. Since that time, it somehow started to be taken apart [the close kin residencies]

(Akulki/Conrad Oozeva, 1999).

The spatial position of residential kin neighborhoods was not documented until the exact location of most of the family houses revealed in Paul Silook's and Lloyd Oovi's maps had been checked against village censuses of 1910, 1920, and 1930. In the early 1900s, the village consisted of at least six such neighborhoods. At the southern end, there was a group of skin-houses belonging to the Qiwaaghmiit clan, originally from Siberia. Slightly to the north of the Qiwaaghmiit, families from two villages abandoned after the famine of 1878–80, Nasqaq [Nasqaghmiit] and Nangu-pagaq [Nangupagaghmiit], formed their own tiny neighborhood. When the Qiwaaghmiit moved to reindeer camps following the flood of 1914, the site occupied by the Nasqaghmiit and the Nangupagaghmiit became the "new" southern end of the village.

Members of the Pugughileghmiit clan built at least two more separated house clusters closer to the old beach area and farther north of the Nangupagaghmiit-Nasqaghmiit residences. Both clusters were abandoned after 1914, when several houses were washed away by storms. The Pugughileghmiit then moved their houses to the central area near the school building. The area to the north of the old schoolhouse was occupied by a large neighborhood of the Sanighmelnguut clan, also from Siberia. Finally, the northern end of the historic village was the residential area of the small Uwaaliit clan (literally, "the northernmost people"). A few smaller house groups belonging to other clans created additional tiny neighborhoods.

Similar clan-based residential neighborhoods existed in many Yupik communities in Siberia, from which several Gambell clans had originated. In the Siberian Yupik villages, clans or clan sub-sections (close family groups or lineages) exerted substantial territorial control over many components of the village landscape (Krupnik and Chlenov 1997). These included the boat-racks area; sites for underground meat storages, boat launching, and landing at the beach; areas for clan and family/lineage rituals off the main village; places where sled dogs were kept; and lineage and/or clan sections in village graveyards. Such a spatial organization probably existed in a similarly organized community of Sivuqaq/Gambell during the late 1800s and early 1900s. It could be reconstructed from today elders' memories and stories passed from older generations.

There is surprisingly little indication in the early records of any higher form(s) of socio-territorial division in the community, other than clan and kin residential neighborhoods. William F. Doty, the schoolteacher in 1898–1900, made a brief reference to two "factions" in the village, one which was affiliated by marriage with the "Indian Point Natives," or the people from the Yupik village of Ungaziq on the Siberian mainland. These two factions, reportedly, "two or three years ago [were] on the verge of fighting, but at present appear to respect a truce" (Doty 1900:189). The lack of evidence is even more puzzling, as present-day elders have strong memories of two former "halves" of their old village, the *Akingaghmiit* (people of the southern side) and the *Uwatangaghmiit* (people of the "farther," or northern side)

that existed during the early- and mid-1900s (*Akuzilleput* 2002:404).

> The side to the north of the old school building, of the central place was called *Uwatanga*, *uwatangaghmii*, and the other side, the southern side was called *Akinga, akingaghmii. Uwatangaghmiit—Akingaghmiit.* Our family was from the *Akingaghmiit*, from the southern side (Anaggun/Ralph Apatiki, Sr., 1999).

> That was how we remembered the old village [of Gambell]... They probably made this division between the north and the south side to make it easier to describe (the village), to understand. Otherwise, it would be one whole big village (Akulki/ Conrad Oozeva, 1999).

> Because the old schoolhouse was so small, every time they had to bring people together, one half of the village goes in one hour and then another side, the southern side (of the village) goes in another hour. Our family was included into the "northern side" (Kepelgu/ Willis Walunga, 1999).

Such a "south-north" opposition created a well-balanced spatial system, similar to the one that existed in the largest Siberian Yupik communities, Ungaziq (Chaplino, Indian Point) and Nevuqaq (Naukan—see Krupnik and Chlenov 1997). The space "in between" thus made the ideal spatial center, the most logical village public space. This central place in historic Sivuqaq/Gambell was indeed the favorite community site for wrestling, racing, and other athletic competitions (Fig. 67); it was called *Qellineq* ("something that gets packed down from pressure"). In *Akuzilleput* (2002:406) it is described thus:

> In the middle of the (old) village, somewhere in this area, there was a place called *Qellineq*. It was the place where they all got together for wrestling, weight-lifting, running. There were rocks for lifting. But this place is gone now, all gone (Kepelgu/Willis Walunga, 1999).

> We lived very close to the center of the village, to the old school building. They used to have a place there, it is "old" new houses now. . . . where the young people used to build their muscles. It had a lot of big-size rocks and also a big circle where they used to run. This place was something like an annex near the old school building. . . . And many other people in these old days, they wake up

67/ Two men wrestle, while other villagers watch nearby, at Qellineq, *the traditional village public space near the "old school" building in Sivuqaq/Gambell, St. Lawrence Island, 1912.*

early in the morning and run to that central area, every morning. Just to watch younger people running or wrestling or doing something (else) (Avalak/Beda Slwooko, 1999).

One of the most favored men's pastimes at the *qellineq* ground, beyond wrestling and racing around a special running circle (*aqfaquq*), was rock-lifting. A set of huge round-shaped boulders used as lifting stones was once a remarkable social feature of Gambell landscape (Moore, 1923:365; *Akuzilleput*, 2002:194):

> The traditional recreation area (*Qellineq*) used to be where the elementary school is now located. There were a lot of big round-shaped rocks (*uyghaget*). These rocks each weighed from 60 to 400 pounds each. Maybe even more. These rocks were brought there by only one man, Neghqun. He must have been very strong because the rocks he carried were huge (Lloyd Oovi in *Sivuqam* 1985:12–13).

Reconstructing Other Components of Sivuqaq Ethnographic Landscape

Other landmarks in and beyond the historic village site were parts of shared ethnographic landscape created by the community over the years. The beach and the surf zone was always the key component of the village area, as men launched their hunting boats almost every morning and brought the animals they killed to butcher, process, and to share the food. The beaches off the historic village have different names: *Aywaa* or *Paamna*, on the northern side, and *Uughqa* or *Saamna* (literally "south side, one down below"), along the western shore. The storage racks for skin-boats (*Angyilghat*) were built both to the west and north of the tip of the cape called *Singikrak*. Three names were used for sections of the beach area: *Imun*, the lower zone behind the first beach ridge that flooded during the high storms only; *Aatneq*, the surf area where children played; and *Qaasqaq*, the highest portion of the beach (pers. com., Kepelgu/Willis Walunga 2001; Fig. 68). The boat-rack area was also used for special spring offering ceremonies, *eghqwaaq*, performed separately by each kin-based boat crew (*Sivuqam* 1989:162–3).

The beach was the main focus of community daily life for most of the year, but other areas were used farther away from shore. Children needed a place to play, and women always looked for places to gather water, collect grass, greens, and berries, and discard refuse. The dead had to be buried. Many family and clan rituals were performed outdoors, often at a significant distance from the village. Finally, there was a need for both physical and social place for community entertainment, sport events, and meetings with visitors and guests. In the "old times," there was the never-ending need for community defense against raids from other island villages and from nearby Siberia, requiring a system of look-outs and fortified positions in case of enemy attack, and protected shelters for defense. Additional "defense perimeter" was created by dog-sled teams carefully positioned on the village outskirts, so that the main community area was literally encircled by the guarding ears of the sled dogs (pers. com., Branson Tungiyan 2001).

The site of the old underground houses (*Nenglulluget*) south of the village was famous for its tall grass, picked in summer by women and girls and used as insulation inside the roofs and walls of skin winter houses (*Sivuqam* 1989:102–4). Farther south, and at some distance from the historic village, lies a former meeting place for the *Pugughileghmiit*, people who lived in the village of Pugughileq, at Southwest Cape. William F. Doty (1900:206, 231) described witnessing a complicated ceremony of greeting the visiting *Pugughileghmiit* in the fall of 1898. A special place used for community ball games was once located "in back of the village." There, men would play against men with a wooden ball, and girls against boys using a softball (ibid.:193; Silook 1976:24; *Sivuqam* 1985:22–3). When visitors from Siberia arrived at Gambell, ball games usually occurred in three locations: at the southern end of the west beach (*akingan qaasqaa*), north beach (*uwatangan qaasqaa*), and east of the village (*tunutangani* [the back area]; *Sivuqam* 1987:138–9). Other sites for wrestling and racing competitions were located at the western beach, at the central area (*Qellineq*), and along the northern shore. The circular route for foot-racing, *Kilgaaqu*, nearly

two miles long, was an important component of the local landscape. During the summer, "often parties of fifteen to thirty [men and youth] may be seen running upon this track" (Moore 1923:364).

There was a special place for arrow-shooting practice, off the "old village" site (*Nenglulluget*) called *Pitegseghaghvik* (pers. com., Kepelgu/Willis Walunga 2001). Collins referred to "three rows of jumping stones" (*nanghiissat*) located on top of the Gambell Mountain, about two miles from the village. According to his Yupik assistants, those stones were once used by young men while training to become runners or strong warriors (Collins 1937:354–5). A documentary made in 1930 and preserved at the National Anthropological Archives, Smithsonian Institution, shows Collins' assistants duly demonstrating such training practices.

Little information exists on the location of the communal graveyard before the move to the historic village. Gambell, the first teacher between 1894 and 1897, claimed that

> formerly the dead were interred near the houses; later they were placed in a cave(?) or an old house, of which there are three or more now partly filled with bones. Now when a death occurs, ... four to ten men drag the body over the ground about a mile to a rocky bluff 600 feet high. Children are placed at the foot and important persons near the top, while those of low degree are stationed midway (Gambell 1898:143).

Geist reported the same distribution of individual burial sites along the mountain slope during the 1920s (Geist and Rainey 1936:30). The present-day community graveyard is located at the same place, about one-and-a-half miles from the historic village, on the rocky slope of the Sevu-okuk Mountain. There is even a reference to the special "suicide place" east of the village, where people used to end their life near a big rock, brought from the mountain by a strong man, *Neghqun* (*Sivuqam* 1989:167).

Otto Geist, who spent the winter of 1928–1929 in Gambell, referred to

> several places of worship . . . located at

many places between the cape mountain and the village, particularly near the shore of the lake. All had small fireplaces often containing freshly charred wood. Offerings [to the deceased ancestors] were put under large rocks, with several reindeer skulls and antlers from Siberia and polar bear skulls left at these places by worshippers (Geist and Rainey 1936:30).

Such family or, more often, lineage ritual sites were used for the fall memorial ceremonies, *Aghqesaghtuq*. In Siberia, each Yupik village had several family sites or a whole area with many sites located close by (Krupnik 2001b: 307-15). These sites were still in use in Sivuqaq/Gambell during the 1930s (Fig. 69), as seen

from the following story:

> Ataayaghhaq would often go to offer sacrifices (*aghqesaghtutuuq*) down [from the old village] where the new housing is now (about 150 yards north of Troutman Lake). The altar [ritual site (*aghqesaghtughvik*)] was along the lake shore somewhere between where Anangiq's and Kegyuuqen's houses are now. Ataayaghhaq never used matches to start a fire at his altar. . . .Ataayaghhaq would let us know when he was going to be doing these things. He would call only youngsters to come along on his sacrificing trips. Our family place of sacrifice was around Tapeghaq [a site by the lake] (Nuughnaq/ Ruby Rookok, 1984; *Sivuqam* 1987:145-7).

Evidence of the ancient fortifications and defense structures was seen in the remains of old whale jaws "jutting out from the sand between the sea and the lake" east of the historic village. These bones were reportedly the few surviving remnants of many such jaws erected as a barricade for protection in case of invasion by the Siberian people (Geist and Rainey 1936:26). Another old defensive structure noted by Collins (n.p.) was made of whale jaws to the south from the village (*Akuzilleput* 2002:227). Today's residents still remember stories heard from elders about an old "fortress" of whale jaw bones (*maniitet*)—now completely destroyed—that was once built near the lake, so as not be seen from the beach. It was reportedly surrounded with

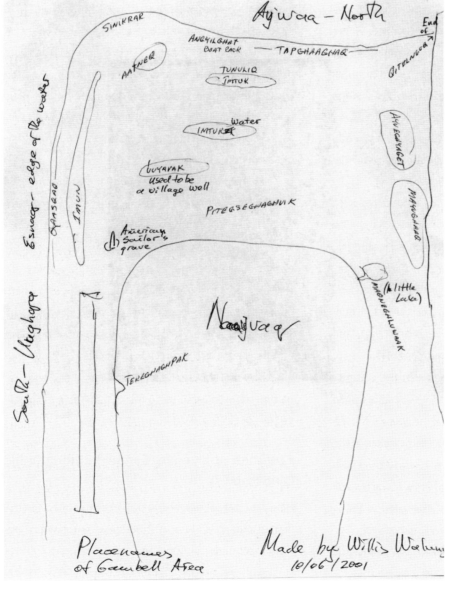

68/ Map of Sivuqaq/Gambell area, with major local place names, drawn by Willis Walunga, 2001.

stone walls and used as a shelter in case of an attack from the sea (*Eskimo Heritage Program* 1979). Stories about such raids by boatloads of warriors from Siberia figure prominently in the folklore of the *Sivuqaghhmiit*, the people of Gambell (Silook 1976:4, 113-4).

A network of historic trails was another important component of the local ethnographic landscape. Although most transportation was done by boat (in summer) and dogsled (in winter), there were several established traditional trails, some with special names that connected the village of Gambell with the nearby settlements (see *Sivuqam*1989:176-9).

The adjacent seascape—with its system of shore currents, tides, ice leads, and established hunting areas—featured prominently in both physical and cultural environment. The sea and ice off Gambell, where major subsistence hunting occurred, was watched constantly; and it was the focus of daily talks, community concerns, valued cultural expertise, and knowledge transmission. Dozens of local terms identified every variation in sea, ice, and weather conditions, including many terms for types of shore ice and beach ice formations (*Sikumengllu Eslamengllu* 2004).

Local ethnographic landscape and seascapes were also filled with dozens of personal and place names, as well as with innumerable stories and shared memories. Such an oral tradition—the body of transmitted stories, memories, names, and images—was the "core" of every documented cultural environment built through generations of human occupation, use, storytelling, and spiritual affiliation. Transmitted via shared narratives, it helped maintain a strong bond between the community and its utilized space (Fair 1999:29). Several dozen old place names, stories about the origins of the village of Sivuqaq/Gambell, and other historic sites in the area have been recorded (*Sivuqam* 1985,1987, 1989; *Akuzilleput* 2002; *Yupik Language* 1989). Many are still recalled by today's elders and are now used in Yupik cultural curriculum at the Gambell village school.

Finally, every successive ethnographic landscape was always but a segment of a larger cognized space —physical, social, and spiritual—in the minds of its residents. Before 1878, when St. Lawrence Island was densely populated, earlier ethnographic landscapes had been obviously construed as a network of smaller spaces belonging to individual villages. Of those, Sivuqaq/Gambell and its nearby communities, such as Meregta, Nangupagaq, Nasqaq, as well as more distant villages like Kukulek, Pugughileq, were the key elements of the islanders' cultural universe. The situation changed dramatically after all other settlements on the islands were abandoned after 1880. That left the area around today's Gambell as the only viable social landscape on the island. Nevertheless, the tradition related to the old sites survived, and many abandoned villages were quickly restored as family hunting and fishing camps. Subsequently, these "other places" were reincorporated into the village ethnographic landscape of the late 1800s and early 1900s. They remained the sites of family and clan origins and identity; the focus of constant longing, personal attachment, detailed local knowledge, and of innumerable narratives transmitted over generations.

That traditional ethnographic landscape changed dramatically when the Yupik people of St. Lawrence Island, once followers of traditional shamanistic worldviews, became devoted Presbyterian Christians, mainly during the 1920s and 1930s (Jolles 2002). There are few references to those earlier spiritual landscapes where humans shared the land and the sea with various game spirits, "site masters," malignant spirits, *tughneghat*, and other supernatural beings. One can draw certain parallels with the way(s) the Yupik people in Siberia regarded their universe up to the 1950s and even in the 1980s (Krupnik and Vakhtin 1997:243).

Evolution of Sivuqaq/Gambell Ethnographic Landscape(s)

Henry B. Collins, a Smithsonian archaeologist, was the first to outline an almost 2,000-year sequence of ancient occupational sites and major related cultural stages at and around Gambell (Collins 1931:138-42,

69/ Traditional sacrificial site at the outskirts of Sivuqaq/Gambell, St. Lawrence Island, 1930.

1937:32–5). Collins' approach may be used to build a similar framework in the evolution of local ethnographic landscape(s) that followed transition in cultural/occupational stages. Of course, such a synopsis of changes in local ethnographic landscape is a product of many guesses. The main challenge here is to find the way and proper justification for one to identify contiguous stages in an age-long transition versus what may be regarded as separate (independent) landscapes. This issue will be addressed at the very end of this section.

Whatever scenario may seem plausible to an outsider ethnohistorian, it would never be the only version available, as the saga of village history has—and probably always had—several interpretations. Some gaps between the scientists' records and the narratives shared by today's residents of Sivuqaq/Gambell (only a small portion of which is written down and available in English) can be bridged. Other discrepancies, particularly with regard to absolute dates, the size of the pre-contact island population, and the links between

ancient and more recent communities would be harder to accommodate. Likewise, the story of the "early days" in Sivuqaq/Gambell area and of people's relations to the surrounding landscape remains a work in progress in the minds of its residents and in anthropologists' writing alike.

Old "Prehistoric" Sites (Mayughaaq, Ayveghyaget)

The people of Sivuqaq evidently preserved some historical tradition related to many abandoned ancient sites in the area by the time both Collins and Geist started their work in 1927–1930. Ancient sites' names were quickly recorded and a few stories related to the old villages were documented (e.g., Geist and Rainey 1936:12). Those ancient sites are still featured in some narratives related to the origins of the community of Sivuqaq/Gambell (*Sivuqam* 1989:178–9). The site names, however, are recent rather than age-old place names and are clearly based on words from the present-day St. Lawrence Island Yupik language. Similarly, no present-day clan traces its origins to those ancient sites; nor have any former associated clan names been reported. The continuity gap notwithstanding, the ruins of ancient sites around Sevuokuk Mountain and stories related to them were somehow (re)incorporated into the local ethnographic landscape of the late 1800s and early 1900s—as they obviously are today.

The Siqluwaghyaget Village (1500 to 1700)

Surprisingly, no similar stories have been recorded regarding the later village site near the Nayvaaq (Troutman) Lake that was reportedly populated until the 1500s–1700s (cf. Collins 1937:189). No present clan or family on the island traces its origins to former residents of the village. Evidently, no viable oral tradition related to the Siqluwaghyaget community was around even seventy years ago, when both Collins and Geist searched for stories about early area settlements. This is the most stunning gap in the area's continuity; save any focused effort by today's elders to retrieve stories they once heard from their forefathers, that old ethnographic landscape is lost.

The "Old Site"(1700s to the 1850s)

Very little is remembered of the later community known as Manighmiit that resided in several underground houses closer to the beach and south of the historic village of the 1900s. The only observation of that community belonged to a Russian Navy captain, Otto von Kotzebue (1817), offering hardly any clue to the physical and social setting of the time (Kotzebue 1821:195–6, cited in Collins 1937:21). Still, some elders of today claim that their grandparents or great-grandparents were born at the "old site" with the underground dwellings, Nenglulluget, and, hopefully, some memories of that old landscape may still be recorded.

The Pre-famine "Historic Village" (before 1878)

We know some general facts about the size, physical shape, and the composition of the pre-famine community and of its landscape. The village was then quite big and located slightly more to the south, compared to the village of the 1900s. It was already composed of several clans and clan residential neighborhoods, and was undergoing a rapid transition from semi-subterranean houses (*nenglu*) to surface skin-covered dwellings (*mangteghapik*). Thanks to increased contacts with whaling ships after 1850, lumber was brought in, so that the first wooden constructions appeared.

The most important transformation was probably a spreading-out and a gradual northward advance of the more compact earlier settlement. It was advanced by the arrival of several distinct clan groups, such as the *Pugughileghmiit*, "people from Pugughileq" at the Southwest Cape, and the *Aymaramket* clan from Siberia. Both groups obviously built their separate clan neighborhoods away from the earlier "old site."

There is little chance, however, that we can reconstruct the pre-famine ethnographic landscape in any detail, unless some yet unknown documentary records are available. We know almost nothing about the way the village was organized before the famine and where the houses of those who perished and of those who survived have been located. Elders of today are reluctant to share the old "famine stories," reportedly, because their parents and grandparents were unwilling to talk to them about that tragic experience.

The "Pre-school" Village (1880 to 1894)

There are many more general references and little specific data about the village landscape during the short period between the famine and the arrival of the first teachers in 1894. Many old houses and several sections of the early "historic village" might have been abandoned, as their residents perished during the famine. New houses were built and new clan neighborhoods were established by survivors from other island villages and by Siberian migrants. Based on today's fragmentary narratives, the post-famine village was more a combination of isolated kin (clan) hamlets than

70/ Beach area in Sivuqaq/Gambell in 1889, with summer tents, storage racks, and winter wooden houses, with their skin roofs removed for summer drying of the floor area.

the coherent settlement known from the later days. The northernmost group, the *Uwaliit*, lived almost one kilometer apart from the southernmost cluster of houses at the opposite end of the village area. Many empty spaces were available (Fig. 70), which were readily occupied by the incoming clans, with each group trying to create the network of subsistence, storage, ritual, and burial areas of its own.

The "Skin-house" Village (1894 to 1914)

This is the first ethnographic landscape of the past for which several records exist, including narratives of early schoolteachers, historical photographs, village censuses with personal names (of 1900 and 1910), and elders' memories. The village of Gambell around 1905 had at least three main residential neighborhoods or big house clusters standing quite apart from each other (*Sivuqam* 1985:10–25). Most probably, the new schoolhouse erected close to the central area (*Qellineq*) gradually emerged as a center of social gravity and community integration. As more and more winter skin-dwellings were built closer to this new core area, the community started to look more like an integrated village.

Overall, the landscape of the early 1900s can be reconstructed with substantial details, including personal stories related to activities and events at specific areas. The stories are still shared by today's elders, despite the fact that many sections of the early-1900s village were destroyed through the flood of 1914, beach erosion, and house relocation.

The "Early Lumber-house" Village (1914 to 1935)

This is presently the core ethnographic landscape of the so-called "historic village" that is solidly documented in many photographs, village censuses, and elders' narratives. Its basic spatial feature was the bipolar and almost linear structure of the village, with the schoolhouse and the community area, *Qellineq*, at its center. Several new houses had been built at and around this central public area, so that by the late 1920s there was no visible gap between the *Uwatangaghmiit* (northern) and *Akingaghmiit* (southern) sections of the village. Both sections consisted of several clans and family/lineage groups.

Several areas and structures outside the main village were critical elements of this ethnographic land-scape, such as the village cemetery, racing and meeting places, sacrificial sites, trails, and various public spaces (see above). Whereas many of these features have been physically destroyed, the virtual landscape is still remembered in exquisite detail by many today's elders, born during the early 1900s.

The Lumber-house Village (1935 to1948)

That village is similarly well remembered by an even greater number of today's seniors. Some evidence exists that its social landscape became more simplified, as fewer traditional rituals in and particularly out of the village have been performed (*Sivuqam* 1985:52–3). Racing, wrestling, and other traditional athletic competitions became less common, replaced by church ceremonies and July Fourth public celebrations. The end of regular summer visits from Siberia eliminated another key element of village communal life, together with the sites and areas used for it.

Modernized "Old Village" (1940s to early 1970s)

This was another short-lived landscape that underwent rapid transformation. The construction of new housing for the Civil Aeronautics Administration (CAA), a permanent airstrip, and two military camps outside the village introduced some new and alien components to the local setting.

Despite that, the village of the 1950s and 1960s still had a general look of a traditional Native community (see pictures in Hughes 1960; Bandi 1984; Wicker 1993), although parts of its traditional landscape were quickly eroding. Construction of the new schoolhouse created a major dent in the center of the historic village site, as the old schoolhouse was torn down and the central public space, *Qellineq*, destroyed. The former wrestling and racing area was also taken away by the new school building, and the huge lifting stones were dumped outside the village. The elders reportedly kept gathering at the old public space;

but little by little, this practice ceased as did daily athletic competitions, wrestling, and other traditional open-air activities.

During that era, at least one traditional-like component was added to the local landscape at the beach and boat-rack area (*Qaasqaq*). When tractors and other heavy equipment became available in the 1950s, local whaling captains started to pull the heads of killed bowhead whales (skulls with jaw bones and baleen) onto the beach in front of their houses. There are currently eight groups of skulls and/or individual skulls with jawbones along the boat-rack area. Each is remembered by the name (or family) of the captain who killed the whale. The skulls were left as "trophies," and no rituals were reportedly performed at their placements (*Akuzilleput* 2002:422).

"New Village" (1970 to present)

Finally, construction of the "new village" on the gravel spit plain to the east of the historic village began in the 1970s. This created an entirely new ethnographic landscape. Most of the village's public activities were relocated to a new communal space, *Qerngughvik*, near the new IRA building. The "new village," with its regular lines of modular housing units, made the former community division of the *Akingaghmiit* and the *Uwatangaghmiit* obsolete. Some of the new houses were built right at or very close to the old family ritual sites (*Aghqesaghtughviget*) near the lake. Many former subsistence areas were abandoned, like collecting tall grass for house insulation. The underground meat-cellars went unused, and four-wheelers and snowmachines replaced dog teams. Yet, the community preserves its traditional beach and boat-rack area outside the historic village and the old graveyard on top of Sevuokuk Mountain. Several families also maintain residence or keep up their old houses at the "historic" site (Fig. 71).

Discussion: Preserving Sivuqaq/Gambell Ethnographic Landscapes

Such a multi-layer historical "stratigraphy" of the

71/ Section of the "old village" of Sivuqaq/Gambell, 2001.

Sivuqaq/Gambell area offers certain guidelines, upon which the overall succession of its ethnographic landscapes could be construed. If the continuity in communal life, in shared memories, and in people's identity is to be taken as the main criterion, the sequence of the post-1880, or the "pre-school," "pre-flood," "lumber-house," and the "modernized" village settings represent stages in one "ethnographic landscape." That landscape, nevertheless, had incorporated elements of several earlier settings, including those from the ancient communities that once lived at the Mayughaaq, Ayveghyaget, and Siqluwaghyaget sites, with which the later residents of Sivuqaq/Gambell had hardly any direct ties. These old village sites represent remnants of the previous ancient landscapes. Of those, nothing but modern names, some physical traces, and a few related stories remain.

Enough evidence exists to argue that a gruesome population loss during the famine of 1878–1880 caused a huge gap in local landscape continuity. Al-

though the community itself was quickly restored, it preserved but a fraction of the old residential population; the survivors were then mixed with and culturally incorporated by the various groups of migrants, who built a new social system (cf. Krupnik 1994). One sign of the new spatial order was the move of the village graveyard to a place some 1.5 miles away, to the slopes of the Sevuokuk Mountain. The emerging linear shape and the "South-North" (*Akingaghmiit-Uwatangaghmiit*) division of the village site was another sign of a profound landscape reorganization caused by the famine. A similar break in landscape continuity took place almost a hundred years later, when the "new village" was constructed at its present site, almost a mile away from the "old village."

As newer types of dwellings gradually replaced older ones and the main village site moved several times over the centuries, many components of the earlier ethnographic landscapes were all but abraded, both physically and mentally. In this respect, the village of

Sivuqaq/Gambell is hardly different from many historic towns and villages that weathered dramatic cultural change and historically insensitive development wrapped as "modernization." Scores of such communities made great progress in protecting their legacy via preservation efforts—restoring old buildings; bringing new residents and tourists to the once emptied streets. It is much harder, though, to recreate the mental or memory framework of the old landscape. Here, few protective or economic measures would suffice; rather a combination of policies is needed that will match preservation with cultural revitalization, education, and other public programs. The story of today's Sivuqaq/Gambell is quite instructive in this regard.

First, the village of Sivuqaq/Gambell, and St. Lawrence Island in general, underwent substantial changes in its legal status over the last thirty to fifty years. Once a Native territory, it came under the *de facto* U.S. Coast Guard supervision in the 1880s and became a government reindeer reservation in 1903. The first system of local government, the IRA council (under the Indian Reorganization Act [IRA] of 1934) was established in 1939; the locally elected City Council (since 1963) and Native Corporation supplemented it (since 1971, see Callaway and Pilyasov 1993:27; Little and Robbins 1984: 53–8). Today, Sivuqaq/Gambell is, again, a self-administered community, with almost all its land, surface, and subsurface resources administered by the local Native corporation owned by Native shareholders.

Second, the physical connection of the community to its traditional village and the surrounding landscape remains basically unbroken. Most of today's residents cross the old village site every day when they go out hunting or come from the beach area. Several families continue to live at the "old village" permanently. Third, the present-day community is blessed by a very strong and dedicated group of elders, who are the guardians of local knowledge, cultural heritage, and of a thriving tradition of storytelling. Narratives about the "old village" are duly recalled; they are commonly shared, retold in public, and taught at the local school under the

Yupik language curriculum program (see below). Those stories remain a critical channel for community coherence and continuity. Fourth, the modern community of Sivuqaq/Gambell generally maintains the old social system on which it was founded, the clan and extended kin network. Several clan and family groups still identify certain areas in the old village, or across the nearby landscape, as places of special value to their tradition. Thus, the old landscape contains not only a past heritage, but it persists as a fully functional terrain for today's living community.

This view of local ethnographic landscape as a contemporary functional cultural terrain is critical in designing any strategy for its preservation. Traditionally, attention has been focused on the protection of Gambell's unique archaeological sites. Native residents, visiting diggers, and professional archaeologists in search of old artifacts and fossil ivory have long exploited those ancient sites. By 1980, most archaeological sites around Sivuqaq/Gambell were badly damaged by generations of excavations and unregulated digging (Crowell 1985, 1987). In 1988, five prehistoric sites at or around Gambell had lost their national landmark status, because their archaeological and historic value had essentially been destroyed by artifact digging activities. They are still listed on the National Register of Historic Places (Mobley 2001:2).

Little can stop "subsistence digging," as the islanders' excavation of ancient sites is often called (Staley 1993:348; Mobley 2001:2). All land on St. Lawrence Island is privately owned by the village corporations of Gambell and Savoonga, and no current federal or state antiquities laws apply to protect the island's archaeological resources. Many elders acknowledge that unregulated digging is destroying the most valuable component of cultural heritage (Fig. 72); but no solution is in sight unless other sources of income become available, as the sale of archaeological artifacts provides critical income to many families (Crowell 1987:2; Jorgensen 1990:172; Staley 1993:349). Competition over old artifacts and ivory also explains people's re-

72/ View of the former Siqluwaghyaghet *site, now almost destroyed by "subsistence digging," 2001.*

sistance to any heritage regulations that may limit access to and freedom of excavation at the ancient sites.

The preservation of the historic ethnographic landscape is, however, a different story. No commercial value has been identified for the old village site and no outside body challenges the Sivuqaq/Gambell village corporation's control over the land management in this area. Hence, the village corporation, in cooperation with the IRA council and the mayor's office, could establish a regime aimed at protecting the old site. Today, the corporation has no protection strategy for the historic village area; nor is there a shared recognition of its special cultural value. The shortage of funds, coupled with the elders' aversion to new construction, has saved the historic village from a large-scale renovation so far. Smaller efforts, however, are eagerly supported, like the recent initiative in digging for old whalebones for resale to commercial artists and souvenir shops on the mainland. Some land is also owned by agencies other than the village corporation, such as the airstrip area at the southern edge of the historic

village, which are under the control of the Department of Transportation (Federal Aviation Administration). Plans exist to expand the village airstrip to make it suitable for bigger planes, but this construction would threaten the large section of the "old site" with remains of semi-subterranean houses near the lake.

Beyond site protection, several other strategies may be used in historical landscape preservation at the "old town" of Sivuqaq/Gambell, such as: education; historical documentation; community re-creation; creation of a local museum and/or cultural center; and regulated tourism. Even in a small town of 650 residents, this creates a challenging need for coordination, if not consensus, among many different local players.

For example, cultural education is the prime responsibility of the Gambell village school system. It combines local elementary, middle, and high school; but it is placed under the overall supervision of the Bering Straits School District administration located some 500 miles away, in the mainland town of Unalakleet. Since 1987-89, the Gambell school has established the Yupik

Language and Culture Curriculum (Grades K-12) developed by local educators. A highly knowledgeable and enthusiastic Yupik teacher, Christopher Koonooka, is currently teaching a Grade-9 course named "The History of St. Lawrence Island" (including the history of *Sivuqaq*/Gambell), in one class per week. Unfortunately, no visual materials, such as historical photographs and old maps are used, and no teacher's guide is available. When talking to students, it is obvious that a few hours of classes hardly suffice to project elders' stories onto today's terrain and into the minds of those born in the very different setting of the modern village site.

Many local programs, such as the Yupik Language and Culture Curriculum at the Gambell High School, the Eskimo Heritage Program of the Kawerak Inc. in Nome, and the regional Elders' Conferences could address documentation of the Sivuqaq/Gambell ethnographic landscape history. Some outside efforts may be helpful; individual scholarly research projects have much to contribute, too. As this chapter illustrates, there is no shortage of both written and oral resources to document the local ethnographic landscape history, but no special brochure, catalog, or illustrated guidebook is available. Pending adequate funding, a popular history of local ethnographic landscape can be produced. It may be formatted as a regional heritage report; illustrated community sourcebook; a bilingual collection of elders' stories; Native heritage curriculum; site-survey report; area ethnohistory; catalog of local place names—or any combination of the above (e.g., *Akuzilleput* 2002; Burch 1981; Fair this volume; Koutsky 1981; *Sivuqam* 1985; *Ublasaun* 1996; *Yupik Language* 1989).

A re-creation (both physical and mental) of certain historic spaces and related activities is another established strategy to strengthen people's connection to their former cultural environment. The residents of Sivuqaq/Gambell had a successful experience in such a re-creation: in 1976, as a part of the U.S. Bicentennial

activities, they erected a modern replica of the *mangteghapik*, winter skin-house, and *nenglu*, old semi-subterranean house, at the southern end of the village. Both buildings were not maintained properly and eventually went into disrepair.

At present, the town of Sivuqaq/Gambell has neither a local museum nor a cultural center to display its history and heritage, save a small exhibit of traditional ethnographic objects in glass cases at the village high school and an even smaller private display of archeological artifacts at the main corporation building. Neither is open on a regular basis, and neither feature old photographs or other images of the former historical landscape. Discussions about building a small local museum or a community cultural center continue; but shortage of funds is prohibitive. With some imagination and local initiative, alternative strategies could be explored. A few abandoned winter houses of the 1930s are still standing at the historic village site. The interiors can be restored and filled with traditional daily objects and historical photographs, perhaps hosting a display on the former ways of village life, a small tourist center (see below), or an educational facility for the history classes under the Yupik Language Curriculum.

Finally, regulated commercial tourism could make a substantial contribution, by bringing needed funds, professional expertise, and public attention to the preservation of the local ethnographic landscape. Since the early 1990s, Gambell has been put on the route of many Arctic boat cruises; each year one or more tourist ships visit the town and unload dozens, sometimes, hundreds of tourists onto its streets. Usually, the tourists are taken to the public meeting place, *Qerngughvik*, at the "new village," where they are entertained by the village dancing team, often followed by a spontaneous trade in ivory carvings and other craft souvenirs, and by the tour to the old site, offered by local residents. The town, however, has no brochure or historical booklet to offer to its visitors; nor is there a program for guide training, established historical tours, or consistent tour narrative. The village corporation is the prime agency to manage tourist activities and to authorize further investment to make better use of local historical resources. So far, very little groundwork has been done, and no assistance has been sought from the National Park Service and many individual researchers, who happened to work in the community.

Conclusions

The village of Sivuqaq/Gambell on St. Lawrence Island offers a remarkable set of ancient and recent ethnographic landscapes in various stages of preservation. It has rich archaeological resources, with a 2,000-year record of culture change that is backed by solid scientific excavation and thoroughly documented museum collections. It enjoys abundant historical photography and is home to a thriving Native community, one that is strong in its cultural roots and in knowledgeable elders. For the first time in decades, this community is now in control of its land and has the rights to protect and to manage its historical resources.

At the same time, the village of Sivuqaq/Gambell offers an excellent testing ground in what could be done to preserve Native ethnographic landscapes across the North; how this could be done; and why very little has been done so far to advance such preservation. Because of the island's specific legal status, no state and federal heritage protection regime is in place to exert outside pressure. It remains for the local community to take full responsibility and install the system of heritage efforts it deems desirable.

Today, the people of Sivuqaq/Gambell possess the legal rights, cultural knowledge, and the awareness they need for such a mission. It is almost like a "blank check" to be invested in community heritage preservation; but it will not be valid for a long time. Whereas governmental agencies are looking for strategies to protect local ethnographic landscapes, it is the story in Sivuqaq/Gambell—and in many other Native communities across the North—that really matters. Whether this is going to be a story of community success or failure, it is worth recording.

Acknowledgments

This reconstruction of Sivuqaq/Gambell's ethnographic landscapes is based on an approach developed during an earlier ethnohistorical survey of traditional Yupik communities in Siberia (1975–1987), undertaken with anthropologist Michael Chlenov. I also received encouragement and inspiration from Ernest S. Burch Jr., who has proved that 200-year-old Native cultural landscapes could be successfully reconstrued via painstaking examination of ethnohistorical records and elders' narratives (Burch 1981;1998). The study of Gambell landscapes emerged as an outgrowth of an earlier cooperative heritage project (1998–2000), sponsored by the National Science Foundation (OPP #9812981). I owe special gratitude to Willis Walunga/*Kepelgu* of Gambell, who introduced me to the riches of his community's history and who was my major source of local expertise ever since. I also want to thank many current and former residents of Gambell—Stephen Aningayou/*Kiistivik*, Ralph Apatiki Sr.,/*Anagguri*, Ora Gologerngen/*Ayuqi*, Clarence Irrigoo/*Miinglu*, Hansen Irrigoo/*Pulaaghuri*, Winfred James/*Kuulu*, Conrad Oozeva/*Akulki*, Raymond Oozevuseuk/*Awetaq*, Beda Slwooko/*Avalak*, and Branson Tungiyan/*Unguqti*. They were very generous in sharing their historical knowledge and personal memories. My colleagues, Aron Crowell, William Fitzhugh, Ingegerd Holand, Tonia Horton, Rachel Mason, Charles Mobley, and Cara Seitchek offered valuable comments and criticism. The study was accomplished thanks to the support of the Arctic Studies Center, Smithsonian Institution; Gambell IRA Council; and Western Arctic National Parklands office of the National Park Service in Nome.

Note

1. This paper was written in 2000–2001 as a follow-up to the St. Lawrence Island Yupik Heritage project (Akuzilleput 2002). More discussions of Gambell's history and social system may be found in several recent publications, including Blumer 2002, Jolles 2002, Mason 1998, Mason and Barber 2003, Mudar and Speaker 2003.

References

Akuzilleput Igaqullghet
2002   *Akuzilleput Igaqullghet. Our Words Put to Paper. Sourcebook in St. Lawrence Island Yupik Heritage and History.* Igor Krupnik and Lars Krutak, comp.; Igor Krupnik, Willis Walunga and Vera Metcalf, ed. *Contributions to Circumpolar Anthropology* 3. Washington, DC: Arctic Studies Center, Smithsonian Institution.

Bandi, Hans-Georg
1984   Algemeine Einführung und Gräberfunde bei Gambell am Nordwestkap der St. Lorenz Insel, Alaska. *Academica Helvetica. St. Lorenz Insel-Studien* 1. Bern and Stuttgart: Verlag Paul Haupt.

Blumer Reto,
2002   Radiochronological Assessment of Neo-Eskimo Occupations on St. Lawrence Island, Alaska. Pp. 61 –99, in: Archaeology in the Bering Strait Region. Research on Two Continents. Don E. Dumond and Richard L. Bland, eds. *University of Oregon Anthropological papers* 59.

Burch, Ernest S., Jr.
1981   The Traditional Eskimo Hunters of Point Hope, Alaska: 1800-1875. North Slope Borough.

1998   *The Iñupiat Eskimo Nations of Northwestern Alaska.* Fairbanks: University of Alaska Press.

Burgess, Stephen M.
1974   *The St. Lawrence Islanders of the Northwest Cape: Patterns of Resource Utilization.* Unpublished Ph.D. Dissertation, University of Alaska Fairbanks.

Callaway, Donald G., and Alexander Pilyasov
1993   A Comparative Analysis of the Settlements of Novoye Chaplino and Gambell. *Polar Record* 29(168):25–36.

Collins, Henry B.
n.p.   Field Notes from 1930 Fieldwork. Filed at the Arctic Studies Center archives, Smithsonian Institution.

1931   Ancient Culture of St. Lawrence Island, Alaska. *Explorations and Field-Work of the Smithsonian Institution in 1930.* Publication 111. Washington, D.C.: **[publisher?]** pp.135–44.

1937   *Archeology of St. Lawrence Island, Alaska.* Smithsonian Miscellaneous Collections 96(1). Washington: Smithsonian Institution.

1940   Outline of Eskimo Prehistory. *Smithsonian Miscellaneous Collection* 100:533–92. Washington: Smithsonian Institution.

Crowell, Aron L.
1985   Archaeological survey and site composition assessment of St. Lawrence Island, Alaska, August 1984. Unpublished report contributed to the Department of Anthropology, Smithsonian Institution and Sivuqaq, Inc., Gambell, p. 122.

1987   The Economics of Site Destruction on St. Lawrence Island. *The Northern Raven*, n.s. 6(3):1–3. Wolcott, Vt.

Doty, William F.
1900   The Eskimo on St. Lawrence Island, Alaska. *Ninth Annual Report on Introduction of Domestic Reindeer into Alaska 1899,* pp.186–223. Washington: Government Printing Office.

Eskimo Heritage Program
1979   *Eskimo Heritage Program. Proceedings of Elders Conference.* Tape EC-SL-79-19 (transcript). Nome: Eskimo Heritage Program.

Fair, Susan W.
1999   Place-Name Studies from the Saniq Coast. Shishmaref to Ikpek, Alaska. *Arctic Research of the United States* 13 (Spring-Summer):25–32.

Gambell, Vene C.
1898   Notes with Regard to the St. Lawrence Island Eskimo. *(8th Annual) Report on Introduction of Domestic Reindeer into Alaska*: 141-4. Washington: Government Printing Office.

1910   *The Schoolhouse Farthest West. St. Lawrence Island, Alaska.* New York: Woman's Board of Home Missions of the Presbyterian Church.

Geist, Otto W., and Froelich G. Rainey
1936   *Archaeological Excavations at Kukulik, St. Lawrence Island, Alaska.* University of Alaska Miscellaneous Publication 2. Washington, DC: Government Printing Office.

Hooper, C.L.
1881   *Report of the Cruise of the U.S. Revenue-Steamer Corwin in the Arctic Ocean.* Washington, DC.

Hughes, Charles C.
1960   An Eskimo Village in the Modern World. Ithaca: Cornell University Press.

1984   St. Lawrence Island Eskimo. *Handbook of North American Indians,* Vol.5, Arctic. D. Damas, ed., pp.262–77. Washington: Smithsonian Institution.

Jackson, Sheldon
1903   *Facts about Alaska. Its People, Villages, Missions, Schools.* New York: Woman's Board of Home Missions of the Presbyterian Church.

Jackson, Sheldon, comp.
1898   *(Seventh Annual) Report on Introduction of Domestic Reindeer into Alaska, 1897.* Washington: Government Printing Office.

Jolles, Carol Zane, with Elinor Oozeva
2002   *Faith, Food, and Family in a Yupik Whaling Community.* Seattle: University of Washington Press.

Jorgensen, Joseph J.
1990   *Oil Age Eskimos.* Berkeley: University of California Press.

Koutsky, Kathryn
1981   Early Days on Norton Sound and Bering Strait.

An Overview of Historic Sites in the BSNC Region. *Anthropology and Historic Preservation, Occasional Papers* 29. Fairbanks: University of Alaska Fairbanks, Cooperative Park Studies Unit, Vols. 1–8.

Krupnik, Igor

1994 'Siberians' in Alaska: The Siberian Eskimo Contribution to Alaskan Population Recoveries, 1880–1940. *Ètudes/Inuit/Studies* 18(1–2):49–80.

2001a Beringia Yupik "Knowledge Repatriation" Project Completed. Some Team Member's reflections. *ASC Newsletter* 9:27–9.

2001b *Pust' govoriat nashi stariki. Rasskazy aziatskikh eskimosov-yupik. Zapisi 1975–1987* (Let Our Elders Speak. Siberian Yupik Oral Stories, Recorded in 1975–1985). Moscow: Institute of Cultural and Natural Heritage of Russia.

Krupnik, Igor, and Michael Chlenov

1997 Survival in Contact: Yupik (Asiatic Eskimo) Transitions, 1900–1990. Unpublished manuscript.

Krupnik, Igor, and Nikolay Vakhtin

1997 Indigenous Knowledge in Modern Culture: Siberian Yupik Ecological Legacy in Transition. *Arctic Anthropology* 34(1):236–52.

Little, Ronald L., and Lynn A. Robbins

1984 Effect of Renewable Resource Harvest Disruptions on Socioeconomic and Sociocultural Systems: St. Lawrence Island. *Alaska Outer Continental Shelf Office. Socioeconomic Studies Program, Technical Report* 89. Anchorage.

Mason, Owen K.

1998 The Contest between the Ipiutak, Old Bering Sea, and Birnirk Polities and the Origin of Whaling during the First Millenium A.D. along Bering Strait. *Journal of Anthropological Archaeology* 17:240–335.

Mason, Owen K., and Valerie Barber

2003 A Paleo-Geographic Preface to the Origins of Whaling: Cold Is Better. In: *Indigenous Ways to the Present. Native Whaling in the Western Arctic.* Allen P. McCartney, ed. Pp.69–107. *Studies in Whaling* 6; *Occasional Publication / Canadian Circumpolar Institute Press* 54. Edmonton and Salt Lake City.

Mobley, Charles M.

2001 *Archaeological Monitoring of Military Debris Removal from Gambell, St. Lawrence Island, Alaska.* Anchorage: Charles Mobley & Associates.

Moore, Riley D.

1923 Social Life of the Eskimo of St. Lawrence Island. *American Anthropologist* 25(3):339–75.

Mudar, Karen and Stuart Speaker

2003 Natural Catastrophes in Arctic Populations: The 1878–1880 Famine on St. Lawrence Island, Alaska. *Journal of Anthropological Archaeology* 22:75–104.

Muir, John

1917 *The Cruise of the Corwin. Journal of the Arctic Expedition of 1881 in search of De Long and the Jeannette.* Boston and New York: Houghton Mifflin.

Porter, Robert P.

1893 *Report on Population and Resources of Alaska at the Eleventh Census, 1890.* Washington: Government Printing Office.

Silook, Roger S.

1976 *Seevookuk: Stories the Old People Told on St. Lawrence Island.* Anchorage.

Sikumengllu Eslamengllu

2004 *Sikumengllu Eslamengllu Esghapalleghput – Watching Ice and Weather Our Way.* Conrad Oozeva, Chester Noongwook, George Noongwook, Christina Alowa, and Igor Krupnik. Washington DC: Arctic Studies Center, Smithsonian Institution.

Sivuqam Nangaghnegha

1985 *Sivuqam Nangaghnegha.* Lore of St. Lawrence Island. Echoes of Our Eskimo Elders. Vol. 1: Gambell. Anders Apassingok, Willis Walunga, and Edward Tennant, ed. Unalakleet: Bering Strait School District.

1987 *Sivuqam Nangaghnegha.* Lore of St. Lawrence Island. Echoes of Our Eskimo Elders. Vol. 2: Savoonga. Anders Apassingok, Willis Walunga, Raymond Oozevaseuk, and Edward Tennant, ed. Unalakleet: Bering Strait School District.

1989 *Sivuqam Nangaghnegha.* Lore of St. Lawrence Island. Echoes of Our Eskimo Elders. Vol. 3: Southwest Cape. Anders Apassingok, Willis Walunga, Raymond Oozevaseuk, Jessie Ugloowok, and Edward Tennant, ed. Unalakleet: Bering Strait School District.

Staley, David P.

1993 St. Lawrence Island's Subsistence Diggers: A New Perspective on Human Effects on Archaeological Sites. *Journal of Field Archaeology* 20(3):347–55.

Ublasaun

1996 *Ublasaun.* First Light. Inupiaq Hunters and Herders in the Early Twentieth Century, Northern Seward Peninsula, Alaska. J. Schaaf, content editor. Anchorage: National Park Service.

Wicker, Hans-Rudolf

1993 Die Inuit der St. Lorenz-Insel. Eine ethnologische Analyse ökonomishcher und verwandtschaftlicher Structuren. (The Inuit of St. Lawrence Island: An Ethnological Analysis of it Economic Structure). *St. Lorenz Insel-Studien* 3. *Academica helvetica* 5. Bern: Verlag Paul Haupt.

Yupik Language

1989 *The St. Lawrence Island Yupik Language and Culture Curriculum. Grades K-12.* Anders Apassingok, Project Director. Unalakleet: Bering Strait School District.

Susan Wilhite Fair (1948–2003) in Tribute

HERBERT ANUNGAZUK

The field of anthropology harbors a cluster of many interests. It is a field that attracts many disciplines deeper into the depths of additional learning otherwise unforeseen in the societies they represent. Anthropology has had its foot inside the mesh of arctic study for the last century, but it seems that only within the last four decades has a new generation of anthropologists begun to pave the road to human sciences that is proper to the culture and heritage of arctic people. There is always exceptional time involved in working with the Indigenous community; but the time spent will have formed lasting friendships that are rarely severed in the lifetime of a person. It is always a sad time when one is asked to produce a tribute about someone you have worked with, especially in a field that probes into the depths of your being and your culture.

Sadness was certainly felt by many when word was received that Susan Wilhite Fair was no longer a part of the world that has been created in the universal effort to learn and understand northern cultures. I had not expected to work in depth with Sue, but I began working with her following the unexpected passing in 1997 of her able colleague, Edgar Nunageak Ningeulook of Shishmaref, Alaska, a lifelong student of the culture and heritage of his people. Several of Sue's papers contain information that is intimate to the people of Shishmaref. Her early work as a manager in an art co-operative may have formed an interest to pursue studies in folklore because from art begins a story, and from this Sue may have formed a solid interest to study the ways of northern people. In my understanding of Sue Fair, one of her greatest interests was in the place-names of the land that reverberated into realness in any land. The place-names were christened upon the land before time became numbers, and in the thoughts of the generations who know the names, they continue to sing the gift to the people who knew that the land would provide for them. Thus, Sue knew and understood that the people had a special meaning with place.

Sue blended herself well into her work. She understood the stories of the land that the people told during her work with people who are of the land (Fig. 73). She noted the statement of Edgar's mother, Hattie Ningeulook, when she included "These kinds of stories they always tell, our parents and grandparents. They say that in those days past, the earth possesses them." Her note in what may be her final essay in "Eskimo Drawings" that "the comparison of written records with oral traditions is one of the most rewarding and painstaking jobs of the folklorist and historian" is a lasting statement to anyone.

Sue's work included other subjects that are also recognized as a part of the people among the people of the Bering Strait. In our existence, she saw that the effort to continue surviving in such a harsh land was a reality that the people continue to face, despite the new reality that the people are facing today. Sue had projects that are not finished; so some of the work that she began before her passing may never be completed.

I saw Sue for the final time during the celebration and presentation of the *Eskimo Drawings* exhibit in May 2003. Sue, and I, and many distinguished participants had been approached by Dr. Suzi Jones of the Anchorage Museum of History and Art to provide a paper that would enforce the forthcoming publication that was to follow.

Sue's experiences in the art world were extensive, and they include being the guest curator in several installations throughout Alaska. She was especially proud of her work in the Maniilaq Health Center in Kotzebue that was completed in 1998, and the art and ethnographic displays in the Yukon-Kuskokwim Health Center in Bethel.

Sue was born in the nation's capitol, Washington, D.C., on June 22, 1948. We found in the celebration of her life that her early education began in "southern Indiana public schools." She received her B.A. in Anthropology later in life than most from the University of Alaska in Anchorage, and she furthered her studies non-stop until she received her doctorate after completing graduate studies in Folklore and Folklife at the University of Pennsylvania in 1994. Her dissertation was *Native Art in the Public Eye: The Affirmation of Tradition*, which was in press in 2002 as *Alaska Native Art: Tradition, Innovation, Continuity*. Sue served as adjunct or half-time professor of anthropology and art history in several locations with the University of Alaska. She most recently held a joint appointment with the English Department, Southwest Center at the University of Arizona in Tucson.

Dr. Susan Wilhite Fair passed away in Tucson, Arizona, on June 1, 2003. She is survived by one child, Michael Louis Kaputak Fair.

73/ Susan Fair and Edgar Ningeulook (Susie's collaborator, also deceased) interviewing Gideon Barr.

Names of Places, Other Times:

Remembering and Documenting Lands and Landscapes near Shishmaref, Alaska

SUSAN W. FAIR

> These kinds of stories they always tell, our parents and grandparents. They say that in those days past, the earth possesses them.
> (Hattie Ningeulook, Shishmaref, 1981)

The accurate, contextual, and comprehensive collection of place-names (toponyms) and the enormously rich varieties of data associated with them must be a key force in the long-term preservation of Native ethnographic landscapes, for the northern cultural, linguistic, and physical landscape is steadily changing, as it has always done. In the Iñupiaq village of Shishmaref in Northern Alaska, many young people do not know the old toponyms, although some are inventing new place-names. Place-name study and resulting publications (and maps) may ultimately serve to bond younger people with these lands, now within the boundaries of the Bering Land Bridge National Preserve, an area of roughly two and three-quarter million acres managed by the U.S. National Park Service. Also, the barrier island upon which Shishmaref is located is rapidly being lost to the sea. Residents have voted to move. In a generation or two, the village itself may be a "memory landscape" preserved only in names and stories.

This essay follows several previously published works written about place-naming around Shishmaref, Alaska (also referred to here as *Kigiqtaq* and the *Saniq-Saniniq* coast). I discuss here how our community-based collaborative Shishmaref research was conceived, how we conducted the work, and what, ultimately, will be produced with these data. During this project, we referenced many scholars who have collected and inter-

preted place-names in various ways in the last century. While the information in most of those books and essays remains classic, informative material, it includes only a fragment of the audiotaped and field-gathered information actually collected by their authors. Existing popular and scholarly literature on place-naming illuminates the importance of such studies, and the finest examples illustrate the way in which members of these groups—insiders and residents—perceive the land. Most of this literature, however, is not written for Native audiences.

Early in the history of anthropology and folklore, scholars recognized the central importance of place to Native American peoples. Boas' "The Study of Geography" (1887), his research in Baffin Land and Hudson Bay (1901-1907), and his work among the Kwakiutl (Kwakwaka'wakw) (1934) broke ground for subsequent research. Waterman followed with a study among the Yurok (1920), as did Kroeber for the entire State of California (1916; also 1939). Kniffen's "Pomo Geography" (1939) was another milestone. More recently, the compilation and analysis of place-names has been transformed by Basso's work with the Western Apache (1996, 1988, 1986, 1983) and Gelo's writing on Comanche narrative (1994).

In the North, Brody's 1982 *Maps and Dreams* is considered a classic. Cruikshank's essays on Athabaskan place names (1990, 1991) are superb Canadian community-based works. Rankama's 1993 work with the Sámi exemplifies Scandinavian research. Alaska place-name scholars include Thornton, working with

230

the Tlingit of southeast Alaska (1995; 2000) and Kari and Fall, with *Shem Pete's Alaska*, on Dena'ina Athapaskan (1987).

Few Native American scholars or authors have written about their own perceptions of land, about naming, or about toponyms, however, although they often speak (orally) about the topics with great eloquence.[1] Native writers of fiction and Native poets discuss the land more frequently, perhaps because lyrical works are more suitably read aloud, just as a place-name and its sociocultural context are customarily told, not written. These important works underscore Native links between traditional (past and present) emic expression, family, folk belief, and the natural world.

In the Shishmaref area (Fig. 74), Iñupiaq place-names like Tapqaq and their translations ("sandy shore") were first recorded by Russian explorer and trader Ivan Kobelev in the 1790s, who worked in the service of the Billings expedition (Ray 1975:6). Dorothy Jean Ray's (1983 [1964]) studies of northwest Alaska place-names were amplified by elder Morris Kiyutelluk of Shishmaref, working with Kathryn Koutsky to collect data in support of the Alaska Native Claims Settlement Act of 1971 (Koutsky 1981). What resulted were lists of names included in more comprehensive ethnographic works. Koutsky and Kiyutelluk's research was followed by Bureau of Indian Affairs (BIA) interviews with Gideon/Kahlook Barr Sr. and other local collaborators in 1988, then with Jeanne Schaaf's interviews for the National Park Service's Shared Beringian Heritage Program (Schaaf 1996). Place-names are imbedded in most of these interviews. My work with Edgar/Nunageak Ningeulook, sponsored by the National Park Service and the National Science Foundation, followed in 1993 and later.

This discussion focuses on how Iñupiaq people in Shishmaref name, feel about, and function within the landscapes where they live and travel, hunt and gather. Naming, effect, performance, competence, and history are intertwined dynamically here in the act of place-naming and in the retelling of toponyms. These pro-cesses are explicit and creative, and in the high context environment of a Native village, much of the creative process is shared. This is just as true of place-naming as it is of storytelling and the production of art. Our goal has been to look at toponyms as both vehicle and symbol of cultural ideology, while recognizing them as cultural artifacts within the ethnographic landscape.

The transmission (and retention) of place-names and the accompanying preservation of local data associated with them remains an important part of daily life in Shishmaref. Local tales and anecdotes are anchored in landscapes known intimately to their tellers; all contain references to specific sites and, often, to personal names. Yet the transmission of this information is usually casual and unremarkable, as the days when young men gathered in the more formal social environment of the *qazgri* (men's house) to listen to such tales are long past and the morals of the tales are often lost on today's youth. A trip up the Saniq coast toward Cape Espenberg mirrored this reality for us. As wind and water thrashed our boat, Captain Harvey Pootoogooluk narrated the shape and history of the land to Edgar/Nunageak Ningeulook. He spoke continuously, although it was difficult to talk or hear. His words were not for amusement, but spoken as traditional lessons. Each named site, even if it has disappeared into the sea, was reiterated as a holistic conglomerate of present-day activities, Inupiaq history, associated genealogy, traditional beliefs, and moral lessons.

The Function of Place-names in the Iñupiaq Landscape

Iñupiaq toponyms and associated folktales underscore human ties with the Earth, local landscape, and destiny, providing predictive models of what it means to be Iñupiaq. During traditional times, place-names were preserved and transmitted orally in community and extended family contexts because the information imbedded in them was essential to daily life. In Alaska, as modernity encroaches upon and in many ways is wel-

231

comed by rural Native peoples, the physical landscape of many villages and towns has changed dramatically along with the cultural landscape. Yet, knowledge of the land and sea remains paramount to both literal and psychological survival. Although Native villages have been transformed and ancient social networks modified, the core Iñupiaq values of living in close interdependence with land and sea, and of using these great resources wisely and with moral understanding, continue.

The Iñupiat and their lands are inseparable. Brown defines this relationship as one of kinship—Earth is a relative: "A dominant theme in all Native American cultures is that of relationship, or a series of relationships that are always reaching further and further out" (1989:11). Shishmaref elder Hattie Ningeulook spoke of land in Iñupiaq terms by saying "the earth possessed" her people (1981). She meant, literally, that the Iñupiat could not be separated from earth or sea without a profound loss of identity. Like other Northern Native peoples, Iñupiat commonly identify individuals and communities by their connection with landscapes and localities, general and specific. Identity is configured in several ways: individually, around extended family kin groups, and communally, as people who inhabit an entire region (Schweitzer and Golovko 1994:51). Continued preservation of traditional familial and regional identity remains very important, especially for people who have resettled during historic or recent times (either voluntarily or through forced cultural change) into hub-communities like Shishmaref. Documenting place-names and associated data is a way to preserve this identity and to keep a people's historical landscapes alive.

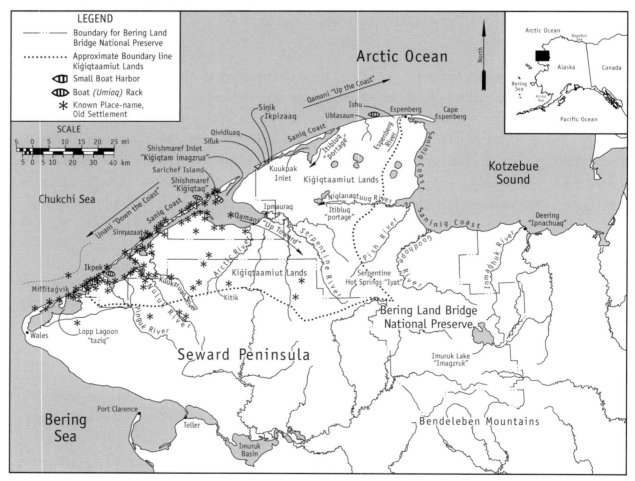

74/ Northwestern shore of Seward Peninsula, Alaska (the Saniq-Saniniq coastline), showing major traditional communities and Native place-names, documented from the present-day Iñupiaq elders.

Communities throughout this area are adjacent to lands managed by the U.S. National Park Service (NPS); residents use NPS lands—places they or their ancestors have named—for subsistence hunting, gathering, and fishing. The majority of residents here are Iñupiat, although the region is now designated for "multiple use" by (mainly) non-Native administrators. A "wilderness suitability review" conducted when the preserve was established concluded that all federal lands in the preserve were eligible for wilderness designation (NPS 1985). But "wilderness" is an invented concept that Iñupiat do not necessarily support. Leopold stated unequivocally to conservation-minded Western idealists that "raw wilderness gives definition and meaning to the human enterprise" (1966[1949]:279). Conversely, E. Estyn Evans calls the concept of natural environment "an abstraction" for many cultures (1972:518). Certainly "raw wilderness" is neither a reality nor an ideal for Iñupiat—nor for most Native Americans. The Iñupiat and their ancestors walked, used, named, and lost these lands to the sea for thousands of years.

At the village, town, regional, and national levels, knowledge of names and place continues to renew and maintain a deep sense of self and community. Gathering information toward this end was an important goal of this study. A profound example of this process occurred on September 11, 2001, as all Americans—Iñupiat and other Native Americans among them—reacted to a tragic event, to history being made. Now, there is a particular urban landscape named "Ground Zero." Ground Zero is a young toponym that provides a large lesson in evaluating the worth and meaning of a place-name (which may sometimes seem small or remote) and its associated context, consequences, and meanings. Perhaps non-Natives should look to Ground Zero for a model of how much a toponym can mean, of the enormous weight a place-name can bear as they research the histories of other groups and manage their lands.

In the Iñupiaq village of Shishmaref, as among other Native American communities, the naming of specific sites, localities, and general regions is one of the most important ways in which people transfer communal history, recall significant family events and heroic indi-

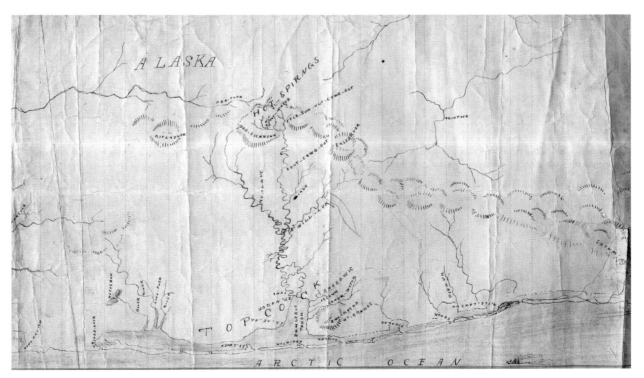

75/ Hand-drawn map of the Saniq area, produced by one of Tom and Ellen Lopp's Iñupiat herder apprentice students, probably by Thomas Sokweena (Sokeinna) or James Keok in Wales, Alaska, 1902.

viduals, convey moral lessons, and underscore societal rules. Throughout Alaska, toponyms also serve to preserve language, annotate boundaries (those of dialect and ethnicity), and draw attention to particular geographic features, which in turn refer to extended family, safety, and subsistence. The landscape is a text, patterned culturally in particular ways. Knowledge about it is transmitted traditionally through oral history, generally related while at the place itself.

These ancient patterns of sociocultural transmission have changed considerably in the twentieth century.[2] This study began at a time when many knowledgeable elders—those who saw the turn of the nineteenth to the twentieth century—are passing away. With each of their deaths, traditional knowledge of the landscape diminishes. Thomas Thornton, working among the Tlingit, notes that the documentation of toponyms has resulted in the revitalization of some names in Southeast Alaska. Likewise, Herbert Anungazuk acknowledges that young Saniq-Saniniq area Iñupiat know less about the land and its names than they once did, but expects a "surge of interest" in this knowledge as this and other projects progress.

People of the Shishmaref Area

> Arctic River, there is always someone there too, so they call those people Agugvigmiut. . . . Each area had an old site and there are always some people that's been living there. *The people are called by the landmark's name* (Gideon Kahlook Barr Sr., Shishmaref, 1987; emphasis added).

Shishmaref elders, like many Native Americans, call themselves and their kinsmen "real people." When telling stories about the region, some Iñupiaq collaborators say that select narratives were handed down from the *Iñupiapiat*, "first people," or "genuine real people" of the region. Traditional settlements along the Saniq-Saniniq coasts from Wales to Shishmaref, on to Cape Espenberg, and beyond to present-day Deering were scattered at regular intervals at resource-rich locations, occupied by extended family groups. In times past,

these people did not think of themselves as one society; small local communities, in fact, sometimes feuded bitterly. Families of the Saniq-Saniniq region, like all Iñupiat, referred to themselves as belonging to their winter settlement: *Qividluamiut* (of Qividluaq) or *Kigiqtaamiut* (from Old Shishmaref). These semi-permanent winter "family tree settlements," as Shishmaref elder Charley Okpowruk called them, served as base locations while families moved seasonally for subsistence purposes. An extraordinary hunter (*umialiq*) and his family, living in close proximity to his brothers, other male relatives and their families, dominated each community. Most of those men served as crew members during the *ugzruk* (bearded seal) hunt and continue to do so. Later, some were employed as reindeer herders and apprentices.

Shishmaref area residents speak several Iñupiaq sub-dialects. In present-day Shishmaref, speakers of the Ikpikmiut, Kigiqtaamiut, Qividluamiut, and Pitaamiut (Pimiuli) dialects can still be identified. Dialectical differences in the region are often very subtle, but they are important in understanding the lay of landscape and the nature of the sea, as well as one's identity and origins. A misinterpretation of a name's meaning in an unfamiliar geographic area may disorient a traveler. Along the Shishmaref area coast, for example, the term Saniniq refers to a sandy beach, translating as "land between two points." The coastline from Cape Espenberg to Deering is also called Saniniq, but in the Pimiuli dialect of that area, the term translates more accurately as "shallow ocean," indicating that the coastline must be known well and traveled with care (Barr 1991; Burch 1994:395).

Geographic and societal identities were virtually inseparable for the Iñupiat (pers. comm., Charles Lucier, November 28, 1996); thus, river drainages and discrete landscapes often functioned as societal boundaries. Individuals and family members would have been interchangeable, in a sense, with particular sites, place-names, and even landscapes and ecosystems. During this project, village collaborators divided mapping and analysis into three major areas defined by drainages and by proximity to other Iñupiaq nations:

—The Saniq coast and interior west of Shishmaref nearly to Wales, a village historically allied to Kigiqtaq;

—Serpentine Flats and the interior upland regions; and

—The coast eastward to Cape Espenberg.

The latter includes some of the Saniniq coast toward Deering, as well as mountainous areas and portages leading into the Inmachuk and Niqlanaqtuuq ("place with brants") river drainages.

The first non-Native credited for visiting Kigiqtaq was Otto Von Kotzebue, during his voyage of 1816–7 on the *Rurik* (Van Stone 1960:145). Observing the coastal lowland, Kotzebue remarked that the local- and extended-family settlements that Kobelev had tentatively mapped along the coast indicated "a numerous habitation" (Koutsky 1981a:40). The term *Tapqaq*, first recorded by Kobelev as the name for this coastline, described

"lakes, ponds, and pondlets thrown down like pieces of a gigantic jigsaw puzzle along the lonely *tapqaq* (sandy strand) between Shishmaref and Cape Espenberg" (Ray 1975:6). Local inhabitants were called *Tapkakmiut* and the best-known "people of the sandy shoreline" were the residents of the Shishmaref area, though the term *tapqaq* also applied to several other Seward Peninsula locations (Ray 1983:233–4).[3]

Along the western Saniq coast, the focus of our National Science Foundation study, the largest traditional communities were Kigiqtaq, Sinnazaat, Ikpek, and Milletagvik, at one time each with fifty to eighty residents. There were no major inland settlements in this region, except for Ipnauraq ("small bluff," "rocky wall," or "little bank") near the mouth of the Serpentine River. The village was abandoned after many residents ate tainted fish and perished, although some contemporary residents still attribute the incident to witchcraft, for a shaman's charm could cause incidents like this (pers. comm. Edgar Ningeulook, 6/94; Koutsky 1981:22;

76/ Watercolor of the Messenger Feast, or Wolf Dance, by Headman E-too'-ach-in-na (sic) of Ipnauraq, near present day Shishmaref. One of a series of painting of festivals and susbsistence life created for Nome's Judge Wickersham in 1902, it is unclear if this particular event took place in Ipnauraq or in a neighboring village where E-too'-ach-in-na may have visited.

Ray 1983:213; D. Ningeulook 1997). Today, Ipnauraq is a popular fish camp and winter landmark for those traveling by dogsled across the ice to and from Shishmaref. Charley Okpowruk said that Ipnauraq once held Messenger Feasts (Wolf Dances; Fig. 76) to which Old Shishmaref residents were invited for exchange feasts: "Our elders that we caught, they say Wolf Dance is not a fun [secular] dance. . . . Their *kalukaq* (box drum) was heard nearly twenty miles from here." (C. Okpowruk 1998; also Fienup-Riordan 1996:38–41; Fair 2001). This would indicate that Ipnauraq was a large village suitable for archaeological investigation.

Each of these now abandoned communities was thus located in a landscape replete with names and infused with kinship relations of critical importance to its members. Old Shishmaref/Kigiqtaq was partially destroyed during historic times by Kauwermiut warriors from Mary's Igloo as residents clustered inside *qazgriit,* enjoying winter festivities. Milletagvik, which served as a mission and reindeer herding station overseen by Sokeinna and his wife Elubwok, both from Wales, was affected by the 1918 global influenza epidemic; and nearby Wales was devastated. Residents of Sinnazaat, which may have had as many as twenty homes during historic times, perished long ago from eating tainted Beluga whale meat, as elders recall. During Ningeulook's boyhood there was a graveyard at Sinnazaat with many traditional burials: "The site is no more because erosion has taken it away. Erosion occurred from both the lagoon and ocean sides. There is not a trace left of all the graves, either. . . . Some of the graves were so dense that they had to be piled on top of one another. These were all above-ground burials" (D. Ningeulook 1997).[4]

Ikpek, home of the Olanna family, was spared such a tragedy, and was occupied year-round by a few residents as late as the 1950s, although a government school had been established in Shishmaref in the 1920s. Ikpek was the last traditional Saniq community to resist modernization. Families there lobbied for a school, but it was never built; many Ikpekmiut chose to keep their children at home on a seasonal basis while they hunted and trapped. Itinerant missionaries traveling the Saniq coast converted many Ikpek residents from traditional practices to the Christian faith, however, and Ikpekmiut were drawn to Shishmaref by the Lutheran Church. Ultimately, Ikpek was converted to a seasonal camp and Native allotment site, albeit a significant one, and its residents moved out to Brevig Mission and Shishmaref.

Consequently, Shishmaref became the hub village for the northern Seward Peninsula Saniq coast and Serpentine Flats. Former coastal residents brought with them Iñupiaq dialects and sub-dialects as well as affiliations with settlements that had not always been friendly with Kigiqtaq. They also circulated distinctive origin stories, folktales, personal narratives and memories, as well as graphic arts featuring their home landscapes, in addition to toponyms. Now, residents who tire of the size and faster pace of Shishmaref, or who marry outside the village, often move to Brevig Mission, Wales, or Deering.

Geographic Context: The Saniq and Saniniq Coasts, Serpentine Flats, and Uplands

Long strands of windswept barrier islands, saltwater lagoon systems, and beaches lace the northern Seward Peninsula coast of the Bering Strait and the Chukchi Sea for more than 100 miles from Cape Prince of Wales northeast to Cape Espenberg. Contemporary Shishmaref is situated on Sarichef Island (a.k.a. Kigiqtaq, literally, "island"). Barrier islands are by nature narrow, fragile, and transitory. Neither Sarichef Island nor any other area coastal, island, or bluff mainland locations have ever been stable enough to support major communities (especially with large infrastructures) for long periods of time, although today, Shishmaref has grown to more than 600 residents. Historic photographs of Shishmaref illustrate the gentle appearance of sod homes arranged in two rows down the length of Kigiqtaq in the center of the island, grassy paths leading between. By the early 1920s, a few rectangular

77/ *The village of Shishmaref, late 1920s, showing a lumber house with sod buttresses in the center, traditional* iglu *homes (grassy hummocks) throughout, its safe oceanside beach to the north (right), and the white frame government school and quarters in the central background.*

"lumber houses" were interspersed. These frame homes were coveted, although they were less efficient than traditional dwellings and many were buttressed with sod for insulation (Fig. 77).

Across the many lagoons that separate these islands from the mainland, the coastal lowlands undulate gently, sparkling with tundra lakes and string bogs. Each low rise gives navigational guidance or bears meaning for Iñupiaq travelers—some of these toponyms very likely have been in continuous use since before Kotzebue's 1816 contact. Several large rivers along the Saniq coast drain into the Chukchi Sea or into the lagoons, including the Nuluk, various branches of the Serpentine, Aaghuqviiq (Arctic), and Espenberg.[5] Beyond Cape Espenberg along the shores of Kotzebue Sound, the Saniniq coast, major drainages include an estuary formed by the Niqlanaqtuuq River, as well as the Goodhope, Pish, and Inmachuk Rivers. These waterways, all used by Shishmaref and Deering residents, provide freshwater fish and anadromous salmon, and serve as transportation routes into the interior.

The repertoire of the late Gideon/Kahlook Barr Sr. included a traditional tale about Itivyaaq, one of the tributaries near Cape Espenberg in his home region, which illustrates the use of such waterways, portages, and corridors.[6] Allusions to the competitiveness of Iñupiaq boat captains (*umialiit* or "big men"), as well as illustrations of the flexibility and diverse use of animal skins are enmeshed in this narrative (Fair n.d.). Specific geographic references and practical hints in the narrative may assist someone traveling the same route today, for the old portage is used regularly as a snowmachine trail between Shishmaref and Goodhope Bay (NANA 1992). Barr's comments about his father, Makaiqtaq, demonstrate that use of the land as well as the social role of skin boat captains was changing even at the turn of the nineteenth to twentieth century:

"There's a story behind this Itivyaaq River, how it's used," he said.

One time there were two skin boats returning from Kotzebue where the big Eskimo trading center is. Coming back from Kotzebue, they have to go through Kotzebue Sound because of the weather conditions (on open seas). And while they were camping at the mouth in two boats, well—One decided to go through Itivyaaq.

To go overland, as you follow this Itivyaaq River, you go a ways, and you have to go overland [by portage] to another river that goes out to Shishmaref Lagoon. . . . They call it North Fork or East Fork, that is part of the Serpentine River. . . . And they only have to go less than a mile to drag their skin boat from Itivyaaq on into what they call Kialiik. And then, from there on down the river, on the North Fork River—what we call Kialiik. No problem, it's deep.

The further you go out, the narrower it gets, and on to Itivyaaq going up. The closer you get to the overland portage [itibliq] when the weather is dry, the water would be low. But when the weather is wet, wet with rain, there is no problem getting up to the area where they go overland to North Fork River. When the water is a little too low, they even have to carve the side of the riverbank. In order for the skin boat to go through—just in the tight spots only. That's the way boats were used in the early days.

So these two captains (umialiqs), well—One makes up his mind to go overland. To go through Itivyaaq and go out through North Fork. So, the other one decides to go around on the ocean side, alright. When the weather calms down, one boat is gonna go through the ocean coast side . . .

And then they left together. And alright, the last time they talked together, they wondered which one of them will get to Shishmaref first. So, when they both took off, one goes up the river, Niqlanaqtuuq River, on to Itivyaaq. And when they arrive in Shishmaref, that other boat had not arrived yet. And it was almost twenty-four hours later, when that other boat arrived in Shishmaref.

That's an old [oral] record of that: How these two captains get together and argue, sort of argue over which is closest. This man said it's real close, as long as you have to go overland—It's a real shortcut. But the other guy didn't believe it. So he just goes on the ocean coast side while the other boat goes overland river.

That's the way it was used. Either way, from Shishmaref or from Serpentine side, on up to Niqlanaqtuuq. Whenever they wanted to

make a shortcut it was used in those days. But even in my father's time, nobody had used it so far, according to my father. He said they talk about it—but they never tried (Gideon/Kahlook Barr Sr., Shishmaref, 1988).

The entire Saniq coastline is extremely dynamic, while the Saniniq side is protected somewhat from the open ocean, as Barr's narrative indicates. Because the barrier islands have almost no vertical relief, there is nothing to moderate arctic winds; the sands are moved, redeposited, and built up intermittently by intense and repetitive wave action (NPS 1985). Particularly forceful storms sometimes roll in from north and west, bringing devastating floods that erode shoreline cliffs, sweep away the ruins of old settlements, and threaten modern villages with devastation or relocation, as in the cases of both Shishmaref and Kivalina. During the fall of 1993, 1997, 2001, and 2002, Shishmaref was pummeled by dramatic storms that endangered many houses and eradicated traditional foods (qigniq) stored in underground caches called sigluaq (Fig. 78). Although a few elders resisted, several homes were relocated to the old airport at the outskirts of town, the Lutheran Church donated lots, and some homes were abandoned. In the near future, commercial and government buildings, airport, boat landings, and the school will also be in jeopardy, and villagers have already voted to relocate (Verrengia 2002). These lands shift perpetually; and although the Iñupiaq are accustomed to adaptation, the size of the village and its infrastructure make the move difficult and expensive to contemplate, plan, and execute. Meanwhile, a particularly harsh fall storm could destroy the main part of Shishmaref.

Overall, four distinct biological-geographical terrain types are represented on the Seward Peninsula: Shishmaref Lowlands, Uplands, Kuzitrin River Basin, and Imuruk Lava Flow (Eisler 1978:3). The entire region is a part of the intermontane plateau system dominated by an alpine tundra ecosystem based atop deep permafrost (Koutsky 1981). Although the area is located in the Subarctic, Shishmaref weather is harsh and unpredictable. Less than two feet of snow falls here in the average year, but winters are long and sometimes, snow drifts to the eaves of homes, businesses, and the school in the central area. The summits and flanks of nearby mountains are often used for game spotting and weather prediction. The late elder Charley Okpowruk gave such an example of the uses of Ear Mountain (*Inigagik*, translates as "place of beseechment") (also Keithahn 1962:73; Koutsky 1981:14–5; C. Weyiouanna 1997). Okpowruk prefaced his story with an explanation of the function and meaning of Iñupiaq folk-tales, differentiating between "true stories" and apocryphal tales that demonstrate Iñupiaq history and worldview:[7]

> *True stories, what we call them is* ikomorauq . . . *they actually happened—like guiding the person's actual true way of life. The true way of dealing with the other generation or the other person. . . . I would call it true culture to the younger generation.*

The man's way is protection of the young person in terms of hunting and traveling on the ocean. And a lot of that is knowing prediction on the weather, too. When I grew up, they didn't have any barometer or anything, or radio. The prediction of the wind and wind direction comes from our area here, especially on that Ear Mountain, where it's kind of windy. By looking at the cloud conditions up there and the cloud conditions on the horizon, we can tell [Fig. 79].

When we go to have a north wind in springtime, those thunderclouds always form up. . . . That's where the north wind is going to be. And the clouds on the stratus—you always see them, called stratus. They always say the wind won't go though the tunnel of those, it has to go sideways. And all that mountain up there, there are clouds that form certain ways on that Ear Mountain. . . .

Ear Mountain tells the weather condition, tells about it. Sometimes it doesn't have any clouds, or clouds form up on that deal on the halfway mark there. When clouds form up on the middle in a real narrow strip, that's one of the wind directions. . . . And when it's completely cloudy, just only on the top, that's when we're going to have a north wind. If the clouds started coming up on top there, from the other side . . . it has to mean a south wind. . . .

Also, Ear Mountain has two big rocks there,

78/ *A west-end Shishmaref home hangs precariously over the oceanside bluff created by a severe September 1997 storm.*

and Eskimos got another name for those two rocks—*kummuk*. It's a body louse or hair louse. This might be true, long ago. A couple of people got so much body lice that these lice got their wings and just flew them up there. That's how they turned into rocks.

> *I really don't know if that part is true or not.*
> (Charley Okpowruk, Shishmaref, 1991)

Goals of the Shishmaref Place-Name Project

The project discussed here was a team study conducted in cooperation with the Shishmaref IRA Village Council and the Shishmaref Native Corporation in 1997–1998. While the importance of place-names emerged naturally during the initial project, sponsored by the National Park Service, the subsequent community-based NSF project was defined by several goals. Most of all, villagers wanted to see continued documentation and analysis of local place-names and associated information to the fullest extent possible. They also requested that a high-quality, well-designed educational map be produced for classroom use.

A key goal was thus the systematic mapping and recording of place-names and associated oral histories about names and landscapes, as well as the documentation of travel, migration, and subsistence routes throughout the area. These data would ultimately be tied to extended family settlements (and associated dialects), demonstrating the range of influence and land-use patterns of specific local families. Life histories are one way of obtaining such information. Genealogies of key collaborators were the first step, expanding to their relationships with other families. Residence patterns, marriage alliances, the proprietary use of landscape, and the avoidance of certain areas would emerge from the initial genealogical family studies. We also collected and examined restrictions and taboos associated with landscapes and place-names.

We intended to demonstrate the way in which toponyms continue to be added to the local repertoire (or do not) and how they change with time, underscoring that Iñupiaq time and traditions are interlocked in a fluid historical process. Initial research indicated that changes in place-names appear to result from a combination of factors, such as language loss and difficulty in pronouncing ancient names. We sought to identify processes by which local place-names transformed as new groups migrated in and out of the area, land use changed, and elders passed away. Toponyms are invented or changed as new incidents occur at specific sites (Boas 1901; Burch 1995).

Several examples of such place-name change were evident at Shishmaref. One ethnonymic transformation noted in earlier research is the creation of "ghost forms," words (in this case toponyms) that previously did not exist and may "obliterate genuine archaic features" of the name (cf. Goddard 1984:98–99). In the Shishmaref area, an example of this phenomenon is the place-name Nuizhaakpak, "to come into view" or "big cloud." This site has an Iñupiaq nickname, the root word *nuyaq*. It is also often called "New York," because the original

toponym is difficult for local non-Iñupiaq speakers to pronounce; consequently, it has become an abbreviated or completely different form, a ghost of the original. Translations of Nuizhaakpak collected at different times may refer to folktales that are now lost, for the root word connotes caution about potential harm. More specifically, it means "to naturally take caution in approaching a known inhabited area, in this case, Shishmaref" (pers. comm. Herbert Anungazuk, 1998). This indicates strained relations between Iñupiaq (and other) groups. Stories about Yakpatakgaq, a site near the mouth of Nuluk River, provide clues. "Big clouds" are a motif in Yakpatakgaq stories and other local folktales, in which shamans create bad weather or poor visibility so villagers (or enemies) cannot be seen and attacked. Oral history associated with the now-abandoned village tells how a dense fog created by a Siberian shaman (Koutsky 1981:23, 32), facilitated a surprise summer attack by Siberians.

An unrealized goal of this project was to achieve an *understanding of the human experience of landscape through linguistic analyses of place naming patterns* (syntactic and semantic). In the past, residents of the region—through trading, traveling, warring, courting, and establishing kin—came into contact with a wide variety of other people and needed to communicate with them. An open-coding linguistic system appears to have prevailed, and code-switching between languages and dialects may have affected place-name assignation and preservation. Dialectical differences for topo-nyms will obviously be linked to particular informants—it is very important not to subsume these differences in translation and transcription.

Project Methodology

Oral histories collected in years past, especially those recorded in Iñupiaq, are rich with toponyms and imbedded with other information that demonstrate the many ways the landscape is used and perceived by locals. In Shishmaref, however, as in much of Alaska, such archival material has rarely been analyzed in terms

79/ *Several Shishmaref boaters, including the late Melvin/Asitona Olanna and his crew, gather on the open Chuckhi Sea while hunting* ugzruk *during the May 1987 spring hunt, with Ear Mountain, used by villages for weather prediction and assistance in navtigation, clearly in the distant background.*

of its inherent window into the Native view of land. Also, information of this type has seldom been viewed as a guide to how such lands might better be managed. Native people "managed" their lands for millennia by knowing them intimately, walking and hunting them extensively, sharing resources, protecting lands from intruders while making alliances with those whom they wished to know, and by telling stories about the landscape in animated ways. Now, traditional stories are told less often as elders pass away, and technology changes, so new methods of place-name transmission— narrative, videotape, and map—must occur if this information is to be preserved.

In this respect, audiotaped interviews accompanied by intensive mapping sessions provide the best way of obtaining place-name data when this is combined with a thorough review of previously written and taped information. Working closely with an astute local Iñupiaq historian, the late Edgar/Nunageak Ningeulook,

the project approach became a blend of methodology from folklore, anthropology, and cultural geography combined with various topics local interviewers added while speaking in Iñupiaq. Therefore, the transcriptions sometimes contained surprises. Existing audiotapes (including folktales) previously recorded in the Shishmaref locality or conducted with former Shishmaref residents living in Nome and Anchorage were also important to the study; most contained place-names as well as more generalized references to landscapes.[8]

In the early to mid-1980s, an important body of oral history was collected on St. Lawrence Island and in numerous other places, including Shishmaref, for the Eskimo Heritage Program, sponsored by the National Endowment for the Humanities (NEH) and based out of Nome. Those transcripts provided massive amounts of information about Native landscapes.[9] Translation and transcription of this material by local scholars (nearly twenty years later) is still underway in Shishmaref under the guidance of Kawerak, Inc. and the National Park Service.

At the beginning of the research, comprehensive ethnohistoric research uncovered many toponyms buried in writings both scholarly and popular, most without rich context. Historic archival photographs (including some family photos) were used; one large group, the Edward L. Keithahn collection (Fig. 80), was brought to the National Park Service, Shishmaref Native Corporation, and ultimately, the Alaska State Library (Historical Collections). Whenever possible, ethnographic still photographers were brought in to record research efforts, particular events, and daily life.

Topographic maps were shown to elders and other knowledgeable local residents selected by team leaders, the Council, and Corporation board members. During previous NPS research, elder Gideon/ Kahlook Barr Sr. had been interviewed intensively, so it was natural to begin with and add to Barr's narratives, which focus mainly to the east of Shish-maref toward Cape Espenberg. Later, with NSF funding, Davey Ningeulook—eldest hunter in the village—was chosen as the first person from whom we would collect a life history. Ningeulook's geographic knowledge most intimately spans territories from present-day Shishmaref to Milletagvik. He and his wife Frieda Eningowuk Ningeulook worked on mapping with us. All of this information was simply color-coded to each informant (with colored pencils) as we mapped and talked with other residents.

Proper orthography is a consistent problem in most Native place-name and landscape studies. Older studies of place-names often used the rather antiquated approach of collecting place-names as objects, usually resulting in lists of names out of context. Differences in pronunciation and orthography between dialects were often ignored. There are many names in the literature, but most of them are spelled out phonetically (thus misspelled) and, often, duplicated.[10]

Ningeulook and I developed a rather formulaic layout of place-name information. The same type of entry, though slightly less elaborate, can also be seen in Kari and Fall's *Shem Pete's Alaska* (1987). When published in book form, this information will be layered more heavily with folktales, personal narrative, historic and contemporary photographs, and illustrations of contemporary art and artifacts. Entries are designed primarily to be useful to Shishmaref readers because of the depth and breadth of information included in them, while contributing to the scholarly literature as well. First, we number the Iñupiaq toponym and add the place-name in English when appropriate. This information is followed by the dialect used for spelling the name with its translation when available. We then list the sources of these translations followed by references or numbers assigned to the place-name on various published or existing maps (see Appendix).[11]

We also include citations like "Edgar Ningeulook 6/94," which mean that Ningeulook (or others) commented personally on orthography and translations of place-names during the course of the research. Such bibliographic entries are included with more formal citations, all including entry numbers from other maps when applicable, for BIA, Bering Straits Native Corporation, National Park Service, and other place-name research and cartography that have been conducted in this region, much of which is presently unpublished. Then, more contextual information is given along with each Native contributor's name and date. Such entries may be descriptive, anecdotal, or may include entire folktales pertaining to place-name or local landscape. When more than one person was interviewed, comments are generally given in order of familiarity with the area and length of contribution. It was obviously important to work with people who know a site or region well: and it is quickly apparent where their knowledge drops off geographically, both on the map and in their narratives. Information from scholarly and historical references follows. Then each entry lists every spelling that we have encountered for

80/ Members of the traditional "city council", several of whom helped save the village of Shismaref from the influenza epidemic of 1918, in a photograph taken in 1923 by Edward Keithahn and now in the NPS collections.

the toponym, a policy inspired by the work of Dorothy Jean Ray. An elaborate example of our place-name layout is the entry for Qividluaq included in the appendix. Today, Qividluaq is in ruins, and its former residents (*Qividluamiut*) live primarily in Shishmaref. Where they will be in the future will be the choice of individuals, families, and the community, as the sea forces them to leave Sarichef Island for good (Fig. 81).

We worked closely with AutoCAD experts at Mc-Clintock Land Associates to create a map of the study area, but numbers and names are so numerous that an overlay system may have to be used during publication. We now have enough information for three volumes on Shishmaref area place-names, more than 250 sites (there are no doubt many more) that fall naturally into the three ecological and cultural niches discussed previously. Our first volume works west from Shishmaref and Sarichef Island to Milletagvik. As we worked on this project, the Shishmaref Native Corporation began formal ANCSA land allotment surveys, which are now nearly complete. This information might enrich

the place-name study or may be used to launch other projects. There were various discussions about using GPS to pinpoint sites precisely on our maps, but most local people felt that it was not in their best interests to have outsiders know exactly where someone could fly in to a site, perhaps plundering it.

Most Shishmaref residents we worked with thought a book was the appropriate way to present information about cultural and ethnographic landscapes. Many also wanted to see a documentary film produced that would include elders talking about the land and telling associated stories on-site. Obviously, the classic way of receiving this information is in the context of the place where a particular activity is being conducted. Elders and other storytellers still commonly do this at camp; so young people on the hunt, at a berry picking site, or waiting for sourdough pancakes in the morning may be treated to such tales in context. At home in the village, children are more likely to be on the computer, studying, carving, or working, for life is fast-paced in Shishmaref today. The desire for books about local toponyms was confirmed by the title the village corporation gave our first volume: *Nunaptigun Ilisaituat: We're Learning About Our Land*. This name underscores the fact that each local resident does not know commensurate information about the local landscape and nearby seas, nor is each one acquainted intimately with the same areas.

Land as Iñupiaq Text

The concept of land as other than a commodity is unfamiliar and perhaps uncomfortable to many non-Natives. The Western capitalist viewpoint is that land (like labor) is a commodity that can be bought, sold, and speculated upon without regard for the future impact of such actions on other human beings or on the land itself. Nonetheless, American literature and history romanticize and laud an "unspoiled" landscape. Despite encroachment by Western land use practices, the 1971 establishment of the Alaska Native Claims Settlement Act (ANCSA), and the resulting transfer of money and lands (Berger 1985; Rude 1996), however, many Iñupiat continue to use the land much as they did in the nineteenth century. The essence of Iñupiaq worldview regarding land is one of stewardship, not private ownership; lands are held in honor of generations past and for future generations. Traditionally, no single individual can alter this circumstance.

Toponyms reveal how the Iñupiat regard their landscape, as it functions as a text for those who have been taught to read it. Reading the landscape depends on knowing the names attached to places and the information associated with those names. Such information is transferred verbally and is usually contained within extended families. Among the Iñupiaq, place-names are most often metonymic; that is, they point to the attributes of a site rather than assigning metaphor to it. Metaphors are of dubious use to a people who must know precisely the texture and quality of ice or the moment when the *ugzruk* have arrived.

Place-name texts bolster family and community solidarity by reaffirming former boundaries of dialect and extended family. In addition, they record important events in local and regional Iñupiaq history and identify uses of the landscape, including proprietary usage. Many historical tales associated with place in the region refer to migrations, wars, abductions, and famines. Such disruptions would undoubtedly have affected the acts of remembering or discarding certain toponyms. Some scholars state that there may have been no truly traditional societies remaining intact in northwest Alaska after 1850 (Burch 1975:10). If this is the case, place-names serve to remind people today what it was like to be Iñupiaq in historic (and perhaps prehistoric) times.

The present research indicates that land, for the Iñupiat, is an entity much like a person—a distinctly animistic viewpoint. The Earth itself can speak. One of the ways it has spoken and continues to narrate Iñupiaq landscape and worldview is through the act of place-naming. A number of tales collected from this region refer to persons actually traveling through or being in the land, rather than existing on it or seeing it as a resource. The fact that most *Kigiqtaamiut* are now devout and enthusiastic Lutherans does not diminish traditional beliefs about the nature of land or their relationship to it. When Iñupiaq persons talk, they sometimes refer to places that speak and to their own conversations with animals.

Non-Natives depart from the commodity view of land when they refer to land as "sacred" or designate it as wilderness. If one employs usual Western definitions of the term sacred, however, land and sea used by Shishmaref residents are neither "consecrated, holy, or set apart especially for the service or worship of God." Secondary definitions, less rigid, come closer to the Iñupiaq view and include "hallowed by religious association" and "held in reverence"[12] for personal and ritual actions by Native peoples. Certainly, when they regard the land with great care, it has deeply spiritual dimensions. For this reason, "sacred" is probably the easiest way to describe this state of being as it applies to the land.[13]

81/ *Shishmaref, 1983, viewed here from the Lutheran Church steeple looking east, with the curve of Sarichef Island noticeable in the distance.*

In the Shishmaref area, Katizrvik is a place used for gathering and can refer to a gathering of human beings at a particular site. Likewise, *katimawik* is a "place for a meeting" and is used for land-based sites, but more commonly, for a church structure—in Shishmaref, the beloved Lutheran Church. The interchangeability of the root word *katit-* implies a comparison between the act of gathering together on the land and gathering together in a church. The word can also be used in Iñupiaq for "come together, as in marriage," or "join" (Anungazuk 1997).

Patterns associated with place-naming also appear to be affiliated closely with the following themes: geography, subsistence hunting and gathering, kinship and social structure, local history, personal experience, and beliefs. There has been some disagreement as to whether a place could have been named after a personal Iñupiaq name during traditional times. In one view, such a practice would have conflicted with the person's name soul (Ray 1983[1971]:254), while an-

other asserts that many places on the Seward Peninsula and elsewhere in northwest Alaska were "explicitly named after individuals (as opposed to accidentally having the same name)" (Burch 1994:419). The latter appears to be the case in the Shishmaref area. One of project collaborator Edgar Ningeulook's Iñupiaq names, for example, was Nunageak; he was named after a small river near Cape Espenberg.

Place-Name Classifications in Shishmaref

> The place where I will start is an old igloo site at Cape Espenberg. This man's name, Ilaganiq, it's the story. Just from the story I inherit from my grandparents. His home was right at the tip of Espenberg, just a few hundred yards away from the lighthouse. (Gideon/Kahlook Barr Sr., Shishmaref, 1988).

Several types of Shishmaref area place-names have begun to emerge during this research. Place-name classifications identified to this point include descriptive or geographic toponyms associated almost entirely with a geographic feature (Thornton 1995:152–64) as well as a number of generic descriptive toponyms affiliated with areas like portages, mud flats, caribou drive areas, and cliffs. Closely related to the descriptive geographic toponym is the activity toponym, associated with endeavors conducted at a particular site. While this type of toponym may reflect geography, activity, or both, what it usually signifies for a local person is a seasonal performance (usually a traditional economic pursuit) or historic event associated with the site. *Nunivliq* refers to any productive berry-picking place (Fig. 82), for example, although such a place may also bear another site-specific toponym (Fair 1997). Other generic terms that refer to topographic features include *taziq*, for any lagoon and *kitik*, for sites where a "stone used for tanning hides" can be found.

Survival narratives are a popular and instructive type of tale usually told by Iñupiaq men. Harvey Pootoogooluk tells the story of Ishu, for example, which involves an incident that occurred long before his birth. This family text, an ancient survival narrative that has legendary attributes, served to bond him with his adoptive family and their proprietary locality by pointing up a brave adoptive ancestor. Pootoogooluk and other adult Shishmaref men regularly tell survival stories and hunting narratives about their experiences with weather and animals, providing windows into the worlds of typical Iñupiaq hunters. These stories usually link directly to a place-name and serve as teaching tools for younger people. Sometimes, they are humorous anecdotes about the dangers of not paying close attention to one's surroundings.

Because many actual named sites are now abandoned or lost to the sea, associated toponyms and tales sometimes substitute for the landscape itself. Such a place-name remains alive, tied to and perpetuating Iñupiaq morals and beliefs. Abandonment of a site does not usually result in functional deletion of a toponym from the local repertoire, although place-names associated with the loss of tales known only to specific persons or kin groups may result in the extinction of such names. Toponyms for sites and landscapes that have

disappeared may be called memory names, related to the kind of place-name change associated with ghost places, although in this case they have actual names and are not ghost forms of the original toponym. As Gideon/Kahlook Barr Sr. said of one such place: "It's no longer a river anymore in these days. So, it's just an old site—which becomes just a story" (1988). River, site, place-name, story, memory—a continuum emerges, a mental stratigraphy of place.

Ikpizaaq (a place where you make clear a space for games) is an example of a memory name. It refers to a productive spring hunting camp on the Kalik River, once a large village used for fall festivals. Ikpizaaq was said to have had two *qazgriit*, traditional communal houses. After subsistence activities were completed, travelers from different regions gathered there for competitive games and other activities (Koutsky 1981:17). A particularly memorable historic event at Ikpizaaq involved the tragic drowning of many villagers during a football game (similar to ice hockey) on weak ice (Burch 1980: 270). The loss of a number of active hunters and youths threatened the survival of the entire community and might have led to its demise; thus, this memory name serves as a cautionary device (ibid). Gideon\Kahlook Barr Sr. and others tell Ikpizaaq stories:

> Today's time, it looks as if there was no one [that] has been living there. All the old houses are covered with a sandstorm from the beachside during the summer. . . . If people don't believe this story concerning this old village igloo site, they can go ahead and dig [Ikpizaaq] up, and approve this story I am telling. (Gideon/Kahlook Barr, 1988)

Another type of activity toponym is associated with traditional taboos, especially with those about not disturbing gravesites or homes where a death is known to have occurred. Some landscapes are affiliated with supernatural occurrences and shamanic activity, and some such areas were avoided while others were not. In the last few decades, however, many archaeological sites have been under the increasing threat of recreational (and income-producing) digging for artifacts. With the

82/ The fish and berry-picking camp of Harvey and Bertha Pootoogooluk, on a branch of the Serpentine River near Shishmaref, 1998.

establishment of Bering Land Bridge National Preserve, considerable information about the protection of sites was disseminated in Shishmaref, and some residents participated in archaeological field and lab research. This resulted in a somewhat broader understanding of the impacts of disturbing sites and of the legal implications of "pot hunting."

Some Shishmaref elders now use narratives about the disturbance of ethnographic materials to illustrate the way in which contact with places that have been inhabited may result in illness, misfortune, or even death. Shishmaref elder Fannie/Kigrook Barr says that digging for artifacts is a recent practice, and perhaps a dangerous one: "We scarcely look around for 'old-timers' [artifacts] long ago. Because some of them are scary, scary digging, you know."

She relates how one of her children found "some kind of carving in the other side of our house [at Espenberg] on the point across there. . . . They say, all sweat—his body's always wet—after only one night"

(Barr and Barr 1993). Her husband, Gideon/Kahlook Barr Sr., added to this conversation that

> as much as he wanted to keep it, he had to bring it back from where he found it. . . . Still, what [the person] own, it still had power in it, evil power. . . . In earlier days, graves, and human bones—they'd have their beadwork and all of their property buried with them right there. When somebody picks it up . . . some people died from it right away (ibid).

Both geographic place-names and activity toponyms are closely associated with Iñupiaq national structure as well as extended family ties when they are remembered and told. In the local family, tales were and still are told by individuals about their ancestral localities. The stories define particular families as shaped by specific and intimate places. Toponyms of this kind are family texts, often related as personal narratives or memorates. There are several types of family texts. Tales of a particular heroic ancestor, those that draw attention to an important event in family history, memorates regarding incidents in the life of a single family member (ancestor or contemporary resident), and those that tie specific families to mythological beings and their activities. Some tales serve as broader creation texts, bolstering the identity of many people. These names are mnemonic devices for remembering now-fragmented Iñupiaq nations and family groups as well as differentiating members from outsiders. The lines here between myth (the origin stories of both people and landforms) and tales that contain known historical truth are blurred, as they are in most cultures.

The *Ilaganiq* tales, for example, are a corpus of stories that Gideon/Kahlook Barr Sr., his sister Bessie Barr Cross, and a few other individuals learned from their relatives and ancestors at Cape Espenberg: "The place where I will start is an old *iglu* site (homesite or small community) at Cape Espenberg. This man's name, Ilaganiq, it's the story. His home was right at the tip of Espenberg." As told by Barr, the protagonist of the Ilaganiq creation story is a strongman (an institutionalized Iñupiaq male role) related to the Barr family far back in time. Ilaganiq, a robust and aggressive young man, remained at home to care for female relatives as his brothers traveled. But he began to terrorize area hunters, probably somewhere near present-day Deering. On hunting and trading trips north, he repeatedly forced neighbors to relinquish all of their hard-won caribou skins. They finally ended their subservience by stuffing Ilaganiq and the skins into his departing kayak so tightly that he couldn't maneuver, and then killed him.

Ilaganiq's mother was enraged to hear of her son's death. She took her mitten and reshaped the Cape, making the shoals so shallow that hunters from other areas would no longer be successful there (Gideon/Kahlook Barr Sr. 1987). A large whale skull marking the family homesite has been moved several times by Barr ancestor-curators, and more recently, by Shishmaref residents and NPS personnel, to save it from encroaching seas. The mythological aspects of this creation text tie Barr's ancestors to the beginnings of their landscape and to superhuman kinsmen and women. The legendary components of place-naming at the Cape refer to Ilaganiq, who is at once strongman (an admirable type of man), hero (one who can support many), and badman (one who does not share). Ilaganiq was human. The message of the tale to today's Inupiaq listeners is to emulate Ilaganiq's good qualities and powerful bearing while remembering the character flaws that resulted in his death (Schaaf 1996; Fair 1996:113).

Conclusions: How Our Work Can be Used

> People always look for lots of berries, that's why they always go further up and further all the way to Ikpek and, ah, 'cause someplace not many berries but always go further. Look for more berries. My Native allotment is at Apquagaagzruk, right here right on this side and right up here someplace other one. I chose that area 'cause it got more berries sometimes. . . . That place, I find it myself. (Davey Ningeulook, Shishmaref, 1997)

Place-names and associations with landscape are intimately imbedded in *Kigiqtaamiut* life and worldview. Just as the land itself has distinctive form, these place-names, tales, and histories provide cultural contour and context to what cultural geographers have referred to as the "occupied Earth" (Evans 1972) and folklorists would surely see as the texts and texture of a people and their chosen ancestral place (Dundes 1980).

Toponyms cluster on the landscape and on our maps, drawing attention to complex connections between themselves and features of the landscape. Family texts, descriptive-geographic names, activity names, creation texts, and memory toponyms all serve multiple purposes. They reflect Iñupiaq residence and land-use patterns, language and dialect (including slang), social relationships, the transmission of information by gender, economic practices, local beliefs, history, morals, and other traditional knowledge. More recently, they demonstrate creative interplay of old-style naming processes with modern ANCSA initiated land survey and allotment. If the land is a text for Saniq-Saniniq residents, then the loss of traditional knowledge that would be transmitted in place-names and associated stories means that many young Iñupiat no longer hear or can "read" this text.

Native peoples and Western scholars are improving their communication about the important ties between local landscape and traditional knowledge. In this respect, Shishmaref and other place-name research helps bridge the gap between old-style, typically natural and spontaneous Iñupiaq oral transmission of history about place and new ways of recording and relating such information about the Iñupiaq landscape. Traditional talk about place still occurs each day in most Alaska Native communities, but as elders pass away and modernization encroaches, Native youths take less time to participate in traditional activities and to listen actively in context. And, as it always has been, some individuals (elders or not) are better historians than others, more determined to pass such knowledge on. These are the performers, the eloquent historians, and it is essential to identify and work with them.

As Shishmaref loses ground to the sea and residents contemplate a move to a mainland location, it may be instructive and comforting to look to a place-name for precedent. Up and down the coast, once populous villages are gone, yet the words of elders echoed in our research give the old ethnographic landscapes renewed life and underscore their timeless importance. Thus, in the words of Shishmaref elder and master polar bear hunter, Davey Ningeulook:

> The land has names, be it on the coast or inland, but we are beginning to forget these names. The days are here when we are starting to forget the names of the land; the period of forgetting the names has already begun. . . . Many do not know the place-names that we [elders] know. . . . Before, a person might not know place-names in a certain area, but a person who does know them would add to the knowledge. . . . Many people have forgotten the place-names of the land and, also, erosion has removed many of these sites to where you can no longer see them. Sites along the coast with names are no longer there. . . . When we do cite place-names of those removed by erosion, *we still mention the name of the sites, even though they are no longer there* (Davey Ningeulook, 1997; emphasis added).

During this project, we gathered place-names, genealogies, family and community stories, migration and subsistence routes, as well as folktales and other traditional forms of oral historic preservation. As in any field endeavor, it was critical to record as much information as possible, as quickly as was realistic and with a variety of approaches. Ultimately, an important goal of the project has been to generate a broader general understanding of Saniq-Saniniq peoples' great love and knowledge of their land and their abiding relationship with it. Final analysis of these data will also result in scholarly cross-cultural comparisons of Inupiaq place-naming with similar endeavors in other areas, including many distant from the Arctic. Whether remembered and orally transmitted, audio-taped, mapped, photographed, filmed, or written, such records will be critical to the management and protection of lands where Native peoples have lived and will continue to be.

Acknowledgments

This essay is drawn closely from several other previously published pieces and works in progress (Fair 1996, 1997, 1999; Fair and Ningeulook 1995). My work with the late Edgar/Nunageak Ningeulook (1949–1997) on Shishmaref area toponyms was first funded by the National Park Service, Department of Cultural Resources, Alaska Regional Office, Shared Beringian Heritage Program (CA 9910-6-9035). Jeanne Schaaf, Herbert Anungazuk, and Tim Cochrane of the National Park Service, as well as Luci Eningowuk, then-president of the Shishmaref IRA Village Council, all gave support and assistance. The NPS research formed the bedrock of an in-depth collaborative planning grant funded by the National Science Foundation (OPP-9708443) in collaboration with Shishmaref Native Corporation. Percy Nayokpuk, president of SNC, Clifford Weyiouanna, and all members and officers, as well as Karen Sinnok, then-president of the IRA Council, and Darlene Turner, current president, are the kind of Iñupiaq movers, thinkers, and contributors who make research of this kind possible. John Sinnok painstakingly transcribed most of our audiotapes. Ningeulook died unexpectedly in July 1997, and though our work faltered as a result, Herbert Anungazuk stepped in as lead Iñupiaq scholar. We are indebted to Ernest S. Burch Jr., Dorothy Jean Ray, and Charles Lucier for their pioneering ethnographic work in northwest Alaska. This essay is dedicated to the elders of Shishmaref in memory of Melvin/Asitona Olanna, Gideon/ Kahlook Barr Sr., Inez/Ningeulook Nayokpuk, Edgar/ Nunageak Ningeulook, Charley Okpowruk, Reila Okpowruk, Walter Nayokpuk, and Elsie Weyiouanna. It is written with special thanks to Morris Kiyutelluk, Percy Nayokpuk, Davey and Frieda Ningeulook, Harvey and Bertha Pootoogooluk, Molly and Vincent Tocktoo, and Alex Weyiouanna for the stories, places, life lessons, and friendship they have been willing to share.

Notes

1. Exceptions to this are Momaday 1976a and 1976b, as well as Silko 1990.

2. As an example, I used to receive occasional letters from Shishmaref about place-names, which almost always included information about hunting, weather, and daily village life and deaths.

3. This was not a local or emic designation. In general, the people of this area called themselves either Kigiqtaamiut or by the name of their winter settlement. The map illustration drawn by a turn of the century Wales artist shows the outsider designation Tapkak (sic). See Fig. 75.

4. Local residents are told "never to bring home what is alongside of or found in a grave because the spirit of the deceased person is intact even after death." Objects placed on a grave are considered owned and belong at the site, while the grave itself is considered by Iñupiaq to be inhabited. People buried at this place would be referred to as *Situwaashuwaat* (Anungazuk 1997).

5. Not all Iñupiaq place-names for these rivers were available at this writing.

6. *Itibliq* is the generic Qividluamiut term for a portage or "place for traversing."

7. Okpowruk gave a classic framework or introduction to his narrative, which is why I have italicized the beginning and end. Gideon Barr's earlier tale about the portage does not identify the tale type, but indicates that his story contains historic truth as well. Most societies differentiate between myths, legends, folktales, and other forms of narrative (Dégh and Vázsonyi 1976 [1981]. In this case, Okpowruk carefully identified what scholars might call a legend with a preface indicating that the story can be taken in part as historic fact, while ending with the comment that he does not believe all parts of the legend .

8. Some of them had been taped to facilitate implementation of the Alaska Native Claims Settlement Act (ANCSA) after 1971 and are located with BIA. I contributed interviews conducted in Shishmaref on my earlier projects (1982, 1991), as did Edgar Ningeulook.

9. The NEH research was initiated by Suzi Jones, then Folk Arts Coordinator at Alaska State Council on the Arts. Each of the villages identified for the study by Kawerak, Inc., hired local Native historians and translators to do the work. These data remain in village archives, with Kawerak, and with some of the interviewers. In Shishmaref, Edgar Ningeulook was the primary fieldworker and coordinator.

10. I regret that my early publications may actually contribute to this problem. We find new spellings continuously, and I have been corrected on some earlier spellings. Orthography for the place-name volumes for Shishmaref will be guided and checked by local Iñupiaq scholars and by Lawrence Kaplan of Alaska Native Language Center.

12. Some of these maps are more accessible to the general public than others. It was our intention to consolidate this information into one published source for the benefit of Inupiaq readers in Shishmaref, as well as for scholars.

13. *Webster's Encyclopedic Edition*, Lexicon Publications, Inc., New York, 1989 Edition.

14. Gulliford (2000:67) discusses these cross-cultural issues by quoting Hawk Little John, a Cherokee: "It is difficult to verbalize in another language, for another culture, exactly what makes a place sacred."

References

Anungazuk, Herbert
1997   Personal communication to the author.
Arctic Environmental Information and Data Center (AEIDC)
1975   *Alaska Regional Profiles: Northwest Region*, Lidia

Selkregg, ed. University of Alaska, Office of the Governor, and Joint Federal State Land Use Planning Commission for Alaska. Salt Lake City: Wheelwright Lithographic Co.

Barr, Gideon Kahlook Sr.

1987   Three audiotaped interviews by Jeanne Schaaf. Transcribed by Mary Ann Roddy, edited by Herbert O. Anungazuk, May 15–16. Nome. National Park Service, Alaska Region, Shared Beringian Heritage Program, Anchorage.

1988   Gideon K. Barr Sr.'s, Place-names, Espenberg. Self-audiotaped interview, possibly in Nome, AK. Transcriber, location, and date unidentified. Bureau of Indian Affairs (BIA) ANCSA audiotape 88-ESP-005 to 88-ESP-011, Anchorage.

1991   Audiotaped interview by James Simon and Jeanne Schaaf. Transcribed by Herbert O. Anungazuk, September 21. Shishmaref. National Park Service, Alaska Region, Shared Beringian Heritage Program, Anchorage.

Barr, Fanny Kigrook, and Gideon K. Barr Sr.

1993   Audiotaped interview by Susan W. Fair and Edgar Ningeulook. Transcribed and translated from Inupiaq by Fred Tocktoo and Edgar Ningeulook. August 4, Shishmaref. National Park Service, Alaska Region, Anchorage.

Basso, Keith

1983   Western Apache Place-Name Hierarchies. In *Naming Systems*, 1980 Proceedings of the American Ethnological Society, Harold Conklin, ed., pp. 78–94. Washington, DC: American Ethnological Society.

1986   Stalking with Stories: Names, Places, and Moral Narratives among the Western Apache. *Antaeus* 57:95–116.

1988   "Speaking with Names": Language and Landscape among the Western Apache. *Cultural Anthropology* 3(2):99–130.

1996   *Wisdom Sits in Places*. Albuquerque, NM: University of New Mexico Press.

Berger, Thomas R

1985   *Village Journey: The Report of the Alaska Native Review Commission*. New York: Hill and Wang.

Boas, Franz

1887   The Study of Geography. *Science* 9(210):137–41.

1901–1907 The Eskimo of Baffin Land and Hudson Bay. *Bulletin of the American Museum of Natural History* 15, Pts 1 and 2. New York: American Museum of Natural History.

1934   Geographical Names of the Kwakiutl Indians. *Columbia University Contributions to Anthropology* 20. New York: Columbia University Press.

Brody, Hugh

1982   *Maps and Dreams*. New York: Pantheon Books.

Burch, Ernest S. Jr.

1971   The Nonempirical Environment of the Arctic Alaskan Eskimos. *Southwestern Journal of Anthropology* 27:148–65.

1975   Eskimo Kinsmen: Changing Family Relationships in Northwest Alaska. *Monographs of the American Ethnological Society* 59. St. Paul.

1980   Traditional Eskimo Societies in Northwest Alaska. In *Alaska Native Culture and History*, Y. Kotani and William B. Workman, eds. Senri Ethnological Studies 4. Osaka, Japan: National Museum of Ethnology.

n.d.   Place-name data from Gideon Barr, unpublished working notes, July 11, 1991.

1994   *The Cultural and Natural Heritage of Northwest Alaska Vol. V: The Iñupiaq Nations of Northwest Alaska*. Kotzebue, AK: NANA Museum of the Arctic and National Park Service, Alaska Region.

Carpenter, Edmund S

1955   Space Concepts of the Aivilik Eskimos. *Explorations: Studies in Culture and Communication* 5:131–45.

Cruikshank, Julie

1990   Getting the Words Right: Perspectives on Naming and Places in Athapaskan Oral History. *Arctic Anthropology* 27(1):52–65.

1991   *Reading Voices: Oral and Written Interpretations of the Yukon's Past*. Vancouver: Douglas & McIntyre.

Degh, Linda, and Andrew Vazsonyi

1976 [1981]   Legend and Belief. In *Folklore Genres*, Dan Ben-Amos, ed. Austin: University of Texas Press.

Dundes, Alan

1980   Texture, Text, and Context. In *Interpreting Folklore*, Alan Dundes, ed., pp. 20–32. Bloomington, IN: Indiana University Press.

Eisler, David C

1978   *Subsistence Activities in the Proposed Bering Land Bridge National Reserve*. Fairbanks, AK: Anthropology and Historic Preservation, Cooperative Park Studies Unit, University of Alaska Fairbanks.

Evans, E. Estyn

1972   The Cultural Geographer and Folklife Research. In *Folklore and Folklife: An Introduction*, Richard M. Dorson, ed., pp. 497–532. Chicago: University of Chicago Press.

Fair, Susan W.

1996   Tales and Places, Toponyms and Heroes. In *Ublasaun: First Light*, J. Schaaf, ed., pp. 110–4. Anchorage: National Park Service.

1997   Iñupiaq Naming and Community History: The Tapqaq and Saniniq Coasts Near Shishmaref, Alaska. *Professional Geographer* 49(4):466–80.

1999   Place-Name Studies from the Saniq Coast: Shishmaref to Ikpek, Alaska. *Arctic Research of the United States* 13(Spring-Summer):25–32.

2001   The Iñupiaq Eskimo Messenger Feast: Celebration, Demise, and Possibility. *Journal of American Folklore* 117(Spring):466–80.

2002   Shishmaref: Whalebone Carving in a Northern Village. *American Indian Art*, 54–65, 80–1.

n. d.   The Northern *Umiaq*—Shelter, Boundary, Identity. *Perspectives in Vernacular Architecture*, IX. Alison K. Hoagland and Kenneth Breisch, eds. Nashville, TN: University of Tennessee Press. (in press).

Fair, Susan W., and Edgar Ningeulook

1995   *Qamani: Up the Coast, in My Mind, in My Heart.* On File at the National Park Service, Division of Cultural Resources, Anchorage, AK.

Fienup-Riordan Ann

1996   *The Living Tradition of Yup'ik Masks. Agayuliyararput: Our Way of Making Prayer.* Seattle: University of Washington Press, Anchorage: Anchorage Museum of History and Art.

Gelo, Daniel J

1994   Recalling the Past in Creating the Present: Topographic References to Comanche Narrative. *Western Folklore* 53:295–312.

Goddard, Ives

1984   The Study of Native North American Ethnonymy. In *Naming Systems. 1980 Proceedings of the American Ethnological Society.* E. Tooker, ed., pp.95–107. Washington, DC: American Ethnological Society.

Gulliford, Andrew

2000   *Sacred Objects and Sacred Places, Preserving Tribal Traditions.* Boulder: University Press of Colorado.

Kari, James M., and James A. Fall

1987   *Shem Pete's Alaska: The Territory of the Upper Cook Inlet Dena'ina.* Fairbanks: Alaska Native Language Center, University of Alaska Fairbanks.

Keithahn, Edward

1923   *Eskimo Adventure: Another Journey into the Primitive.* Seattle: Superior Publishing Co.

Kniffen, Fred

1939   Pomo Geography. *University of California Publications in American Archaeology and Ethnology* 36 (7): 353–480.

Koutsky, Kathryn

1981   *Early Days on Norton Sound and Bering Strait: An Overview of Historic Sites in the BSNC Region. I: The Shishmaref Area.* Occasional Paper 29. Fairbanks: University of Alaska, Cooperative Park Studies Unit.

Kroeber, Alfred

1916   California Place-Names of Indian Origin. *University of California Publications in American Archeology and Ethnology* 12 (XII):31–69.

1939   Cultural and Natural Areas of Native North America. *University of California Publications in American Archeology and Ethnology* 38. Berkeley, CA: Unversity of California.

Leopold, Aldo

1949   *A Sand County Almanac.* New York. Sierra Club/ Ballantine Books.

Lopp, William T

1892   A Year Alone in Alaska. *American Missionary* 45:357–68.

Momaday, N. Scott

1976a   *The Names.* Tucson: University of Arizona Press.

1976b   Native American Attitudes to the Environment. In *Seeing with a Native Eye: Essays on Native American Religion,* W. Capps, ed., pp. 79–85. New York: Harper and Row.

NANA Regional Corporation, Inc

1992   *Iñupiat place-names in the Nana Region.* Compiled by NANA elders and staff (with the cooperation of the National Park Service). On File at the Board of Geographic Place-names.

National Park Service

1985   *Bering Land Bridge National Preserve/Alaska.* Draft of the General Management Plan/Environmental Assessment Land Protection Plan/ Wilderness Suitability Review. On File at the National Park Service, Alaska Region, Anchorage, AK.

1994   *Siulipta Paitaat: Our Ancestor's Heritage.* Video, 29 min. Produced by Alaska Region, Shared Beringian Heritage Program, Anchorage, AK.

Nelson, Edward William

1899   *The Eskimo about Bering Strait.* Eighteenth Annual Report of the Bureau of American Ethnology, 1896–1897. Part 1. Washington, DC: Smithsonian Institution, U.S. Government Printing Office. (Reprinted in 1983 by the Smithsonian Institution Press.)

Ningeulook, Davey

1997   Audiotaped interview, life history, with Edgar/ Nunageak Ningeulook and Amy Craver. Shishmaref, AK. April 12, 1997. Shishmaref: Shishmaref IRA Village Council and Anchorage: National Park Service, Cultural Resources Division (CA 9910-6-9035).

Ningeulook, Hattie

1981   *The Man Who Became a Caribou.* Audiotaped interview with Edgar Ningeulook, translated and transcribed by Edgar Ningeulook, July 2, 1981, Shishmaref.

Ningeulook, Jack Herman

1983   *The Blown-Away People..* Audiotaped interview translated and transcribed by Edgar Ningeulook, Shishmaref, AK. Eskimo Heritage Project, SH/EN-83-006-T4. Nome, AK. Kawerak, Inc.

Ningeulook, Ray

1967   Personal communication (oral history) to Edgar Ningeulook at Kuukpak, AK.September.

Okpowruk, Charley

1991   Audiotaped interview (in English) by Susan W. Fair, Shishmaref, Alaska, tape 1 of 5, January 28, 1991.

Pootoogooluk, Bertha

1993   Personal communication to Susan W. Fair and Edgar Ningeulook. August 4, 1993. Shishmaref.

Pootoogooluk, Harvey

1993 Audiotaped interview (in Inupiaq) by Edgar Ningeulook and Susan W. Fair. Transcribed and translated by Fred Tocktoo and Edgar Ningeulook, August 4, Shishmaref. National Park Service, Alaska Region, Shared Beringian Heritage Program.

Rankama, Tuija

1993 Managing the Landscape: A Study of Sámi place-names in Utsjoki, Finnish Lapland. *Etudes/Inuit/Studies* 17:47-69.

Ray, Dorothy Jean

1971 Eskimo Place-names in Bering Strait and Vicinity. *Names* 19(1):1-33.

1975 *The Eskimo of Bering Strait, 1650-1898.* Seattle, WA: University of Washington Press.

1977 *Eskimo Art: Tradition and Innovation in North Alaska.* Seattle, WA: University of Washington Press.

1983 Ethnohistory in the Arctic: The Bering Strait Eskimo. *Alaska History* 23. Kingston: Limestone Press.

Rude, Robert W

1996 *An Act of Deception.* Anchorage: Salmon Run Press.

Schaaf, Jeanne

1988 *The Bering Land Bridge National Preserve: An Archeological Survey.* Vol. II, Site Descriptions. Report AR-14. Anchorage: National Park Service, Alaska Region.

1994 Cooperative Research and Resource Management in Protected Areas: A Case Study in the Proposed Beringian Heritage International Park. Paper presented at the *Human Ecology and Global Climate Change Conference: The Role of Parks and Protected Areas Workshop*, October 18-21, 1993.

Schaaf, Jeanne, ed.

1996 *Ublasaun: First Light. Inupiaq Hunters and Herders int he Early Twentieth Century, Northern Seward Peninsula, Alaska.* Anchorage, AK: National Park Service, Shared Beringian Heritage Program.

Schweitzer, Peter P., and Evgenii V. Golovko

1995 *Contacts Across Bering Strait, 1898-1948 (Traveling Between Continents, Phases One and Two).* Report Prepared for the U.S. National Park Service, Alaska Regional Office.

Silko, Leslie Marmon

1990 Landscape, History, and the Pueblo Imagination. In *The Norton Book of Nature Writing*, R. Finch and J. Elder, eds., pp. 883-94. New York: W. W. Norton.

Thornton, Thomas Fox

1995 *Place and being among the Tlingit.* Ph.D. dissertation, Department of Anthropology, University of Washington. Ann Arbor, MI: UMI Dissertation Services.

2000 Person and Place: Lessons from Tlingit Teachers. In *Celebration 2000*, S. Fair and R. Worl, eds., pp. 79-86. Juneau, AK: Sealaska Heritage Foundation.

VanStone, James W.

1960 An Early Nineteenth-century Artist in Alaska: Louis Choris and the First Kotzebue Expedition. *Pacific Northwest Quarterly* 50(2):145-58.

Verrengia, Joseph B

2002 Rising Seas Imperil Alaska Town. *Arizona Daily Star*, September 15, p. A10.

Waterman, Thomas T

1920 Yurok Geography. *University of California Publications in American Archaeology and Ethnology* 16(5):177-314.

Appendix

"Qividluaq" : Example of Place-Name Entry Data

Qividluaq (Qividluamiut); translation: "a place where there is a lagoon behind and a beach coast outside" or "small bank" (BIA-14; Koutsky, 1981; Edgar Ningeulook, 6/94; BSNC-104; KTZ-009; NANA, 1992:3/17).

[According to] Gideon Kahlook Barr Sr.:

> Ancient sod houses at *Qividluaq*, once a large community, have eroded into the ocean, and only one house and a "warehouse," or cache, remain. The cache belonged to William *Ukaaniq* and his wife *Piyula* (Beulah), who died in the 1940s. Shishmaref sculptor Harvey Pootoogooluk was raised at *Qividluaq* after his adoption by the elderly couple. Barr, whose family lived at *Qividluaq* in 1918 when he was an infant, describes the *Saniq* coast as "more likely an island all the way across and down to Shishmaref." He adds that between *Qividluaq* and Shishmaref at present, it looks as though the coast was uninhabited, "because all the old sites, igloo sites, have eroded away from the big storms we had in earlier days" (Barr, 1988).

Edgar/Nunageak Ningeulook related the following tale about *Qividluaq*, which he learned in 1984 from Jack Herman Ningeulook, his paternal uncle:

> There are many ghosts in this community. At one time, a husband and wife were traveling to another settlement and planned to overnight in one of the sod houses at *Qividluaq*. Upon entering the house, they noticed that the inhabitants, a couple, were dead. Their faces were very distorted. The travelers were terribly frightened. They could not sleep that night, so they turned back, returning to their original point of origin. Upon their return, both husband and wife died instantly because they had been exposed to the evil spirits at *Qividluaq*:. This

area was thought to have had many evil spirits that might claim people. But when a lone traveler slept there overnight, he would not be bothered by the spirits.

Harvey Pootoogooluk tells many stories about *Qividluaq*. The story of *Ishu*, "really deep lake" or "the one with a devil [in it]" which follows is both family text and memorate handed down about Agnaaniq, his father's elder brother, who once killed a stranger who attacked him as he was hunting. This tale would have served to bolster his attachment to his adopted family as well as familiarizing him with the area:

> The man had a knife and ran after him. When the other man ran toward him, when this other man tried to use a knife on him—When he did so, he ran over willow thickets, *qiliknausraq*. . . .When he did not get the intruder, he went back to where he left the rifle. When he found the gun, he went back to where the intruder was last seen. . . . *Agnaaniq* waited for him to come closer. He was in front of the intruder. The intruder had a good rifle—But *Agnaaniq* shot him here, while the intruder was looking around for something. . . . *Agnaaniq* tied the [man's] rifle to his victim, and sank him in the lake called *Ishu*. It is called "deep lake" because it is a deep lake . . . . The intruder, his victim, had on fish mukluks, king salmon mukluks. He was from away from here, far away from here. He was an Indian, from a place called *Igaluwik*. (Harvey Pootoogooluk, Shishmaref, 1993)

References: See Burch (1971:154-5) for a discussion of the visible forms taken by ghosts. Koutsky writes that the name of the village was Salliniq, referring to the barrier island strand itself, which probably actually refers back to the term Saniniq (1981:17-8). Residents of Qividluaq spoke a distinctive dialect and referred to themselves as Qividluamiut according to Morris Kiyutelluk (1976) and Edgar Ningeulook (1994). Key local families at Qividluaq included Ningeulook, Eningowuk, Kiyutelluk, Pootoogooluk, Walluk, and Barr.

The Komanaseak and Nagozruk families of Wales also originated from this locality. Nagozruk family members including Kate/Ataseaq, and her brothers Sockpick, Adams, and Eningowuk migrated to Wales during a famine, probably some time in the late 1800s (McClintock, 1995).

Ray links the village closely with Sinik, across the lagoon, noting that Qividluaq was said to have had seven houses and possibly one *qazgri* in 1892 (Ray 1983:214; Jackson 1895:97). She also notes that the village was called Chibamech on Kobelev's original 1779 map (1983:230). Qividluaq residents went to the Niqlanaqtuuq River on the Saniniq coast for fall fishing and sealing during traditional times (ibid.). The site was indeed once well populated; recent National Park Service archaeological research notes "two intact house depressions, three associated cache depressions, and a large rectangular depression" which may be the *qazgri* at one location. Nearby, another site contains nine house depressions and 13 caches, and still another has 11 houses and 26 cache remains (Schaaf 1988:120). The remains of Harvey Pootoogooluk's boyhood home, the raised cache mentioned above, a grave, and scattered parts from boats are nearby (ibid.). Some of the houses were constructed with materials scavenged from shipwrecks. There is another *Sinik* on the *Saniniq* coast, the spit at Elephant Point, according to Charles Lucier's collaborator, Jessie Ralph. Qividluaq residents and their descendants now live in Shishmaref.

Also known as or spelled: *Kivaluaq, Kivalluaq, Kividluk, Kevalooauk, Kividlo, Kevedlok, Kivuklouk, Qivaluaq, Qivaluq, Qipalut, Chibamech.*

Medieval Tales, Modern Tourists:

Exploring the Njal's Saga Landscape of Southern Iceland

ELISABETH I. WARD AND
ARTHUR BJORGVIN BOLLASON

The subarctic North Atlantic island of Iceland has an austere physical landscape; treeless rolling hills, large lava fields, barren glaciers, active volcanoes, tumbling waterfalls, steaming springs, and towering cliffs commingle in surprising ways. Before the arrival of the Vikings to Iceland in 874 A.D., the island was an uninhabited, wild place. Since that time, succeeding generations directly descendent from those first settlers have acculturated the land, turning it from wilderness into settled areas. The process of settling the land created an ordered society, complete with laws, property rights, inheritance claims, and so on (Hunt and Gilman, 1998; Hann, 1998). And yet there are few if any physical markers of these old land divisions visible on the landscape. Areas in the mountains are shared by entire communities, and fences—once extremely rare—are even today sparingly employed, allowing the horses and sheep to roam freely.

Iceland's population is today slightly over a quarter of a million people. Before the 1950s, Iceland's peak population had been around 70,000 people, a number reached by 1250 A.D. Thereafter, famine, disease, and low birth rates had reduced Iceland's population at times to precariously low numbers, in an area of more than 103,000 square kilometers (40,000 square miles). This low population density meant that the landscape was not altered heavily by man-made projects. Perhaps the most dramatic human action was the quick clearing, within the first one-hundred years of human habitation,

of the shrub-like dwarf birch trees that covered much of the island (Vesteinsson 2000: 165). Thereafter, Iceland became virtually treeless.

Because of the poor quality—and later absolute scarcity—of trees, the early settlers in Iceland modified their traditional timber-dependent house construction techniques, and instead began building houses out of turf and rock, a practice that continued into the 1940s. Only fifty years after abandonment, such houses quickly become indistinguishable from the surrounding landscape. Combined with the dearth of trees, fences, or obvious man-made projects, the lack of old buildings gives Iceland's landscape an unparalleled sense of openness. This encourages broad outlooks across vast distances, as any glance at photographs of Iceland will quickly confirm (Fig. 83). From the roadside, one takes in entire valleys, regions, and mountains many miles away.

Landscape in a Cultural Context

To outsiders, the *openness* of the Icelandic landscape can easily be interpreted as the *emptiness* of that landscape (see Callaway, this volume). But to make this assumption is to overlook a fundamental aspect of the Icelandic culture. For Icelanders, the efforts of their ancestors to claim and settle this island are of supreme importance, on both a practical and symbolic level. Land ownership claims are dependent upon it, while at the same time, their sense of human agency is heightened by reflecting on that process of making the wild civilized. Far from being a simple physical entity, as it might be for a modern Western city dweller, land is a hotly contested and central part of Icelandic culture. The Farmer's Party is the strongest party in Icelandic politics, and laws exist banning foreigners from owning land, especially in the countryside. The foremost Icelandic artists are all landscape painters, and today photography books of Icelandic landscapes—though partially intended for tourist consumption—are extremely common.

Beyond economics, politics, and art, Icelanders also give the landscape meaning through their storytelling in both oral and written form. By remembering, retelling, and writing stories about the original settlers, of later medieval saints and sinners, and of recent notable figures, they retain knowledge of the culture-history of the land. An example illustrates how widespread this knowledge is: a professor from the University of Reykjavík regularly took his students on a field trip to southern Iceland as part of a course on Icelandic history and literature. He always stopped the bus at a certain spring, and told the students the story of Gudmund the Good, Bishop of Iceland in the thirteenth century. This bishop took as his holy duty the blessing of cliffs, springs, and islands. Once special evocation was said over a particular spring; all that washed their face in it afterward would be cleansed of all sins. Every year, as the professor would stop beside this spring near the roadside and tell the students this was the famous spring blessed by Gudmund, a local farmer would stand nearby and listen. But after the professor left with his students, the local farmer would inform any passerby that again the professor had gotten it wrong. According to the farmer, the actual spring blessed by the bishop was a few hundred yards to the east of the one pointed out by the professor.

This local knowledge of the landscape is retained mostly by the elderly farmers who take pride in knowing the names, stories, and places of importance in their immediate area. They grew up at a time when Iceland-

ers lived in the same area their whole lives, as had their family for generations before, and stories about the landscape were common at family gatherings or in conversations with neighbors. Today's Icelanders have a different experience; many families have left the countryside to reap the benefits of the education, jobs, and health care provided in the capitol. American popular culture—first introduced when an American base was established in Iceland just after World War II—offered new entertainment choices. But one aspect of Icelandic culture has coincidentally safeguarded against these changes obliterating generations of accumulated stories: a love of the written word.

Books About the Land

Icelanders are proud that their population is one-hundred percent literate, and reading and writing have been the purview of subsistence farmers almost as commonly as priests and other members of the upper class since the thirteenth century. According to Halldor Laxness, "Icelanders have always had a fascination with the written word." However, knowledge gained from books is not automatically given precedence over traditional folklore. Farmers whose shelves are filled with books also maintain a vibrant cultural belief in supernatural beings such as little people (even diverting the course of a major construction project so as not to disturb a purported "little people" settlement). For non-Icelanders (útlendingar, literally out-landers), the lack of distinction between oral and written knowledge in Icelandic culture can be difficult to grasp, but the two coexist as complementary epistemological systems. Neither is automatically granted an air of authenticity, and both are considered reliable.

Beginning in the 1920s, the Travel Association of Iceland began producing annual books about Iceland for Icelanders that cover specific regions and districts. These books often incorporate the knowledge of local farmers, or were written by the farmers themselves and seamlessly blend knowledge from various sources into a single document about a region (for example,

83/ *Iceland's treeless landscape allows for expansive views of the landscape, such as this one towards Thrihyrning (threehorned)* Mountain.

Godasteinn, a yearbook about the Rangar region in southern Iceland). Traditional stories, facts about geographic formations, names of specific farms and landscape features, and family histories are all included.

The regional books mimic one of the first books ever written in Icelandic, called *Landnámabók,* which chronicles the lives and adventures of the first settlers, the regions in which they settled, and the place-names they set upon the geographic features. Iceland was uninhabited when the first Viking seafarers voyaged across the North Atlantic (Vesteinsson 2000), save for a few recluse Irish monks who quickly left. The first settlers were therefore free to name the features of land after themselves (Hjorleif's Hill, Ingolf's Mountain); after the resources they found important (Salmon River, Forested Hill); and also according to their physical appearance (White River, Smokey Bay). Though many of these place-names were established more than 1,000 years ago, they are still intelligible to Icelanders today because of the conservative nature of the Icelandic language. By simply parsing the place-names, Icelanders have a ready mnemonic to remind them of the people and stories that inspired the place-names.

In the 1960s, the tradition of remembering regional histories and narratives found expression in an unillustrated, two-volume set called *Landid Thitt* (your land), which features extensive histories on selected places of interest. At times, the same pages of the book reference a saga hero, a medieval priest, a seventeenth century merchant, and a modern painter, as long as they all had a connection with the same landscape area. In 1978, a few years after the opening of the first road linking all the settlements of Iceland (called the Ring Road), a single illustrated volume entitled *Islenska Vega Handbókin* (Icelandic roadtravel handbook) came out. Organized by region and road number, it keys detailed maps to numbered paragraphs that provide information ranging from geological factoids to medieval saga excerpts to nineteenth century folk beliefs. The *Vega Handbókin* has been a best seller since that time through many revisions and has been translated into English and German. It is a common experience—including for the authors of this paper—that no drive into the countryside is made without this "road bible" as a constant companion. In essence, it fills the relatively featureless Ice-landic landscape with culturally relevant pieces of information, making each drive a pilgrimage through the Icelandic storehouse of narratives. There is little concern that the cultural landscape knowledge is in danger of disappearing, especially since government support exists to increase that knowledge through ar-chaeological surveys and historic research (Ragnheidar Traustadóttir, coordinator of the National Museum of Iceland Regional Survey, pers. comm. to E.W., 2002).

The Cultural Centrality of Sagas

While several books testify to the long tradition of re-taining local histories, they tend to elide the cultural preference for one type of narrative, the *sagas*. Begin-ning in the twelfth century, Icelanders began writing on calfskin in their native tongue stories that had been passed down orally, some for over three hundred years. Called *sogur* (sing. *saga*) from the verb "to say"—it also has the meaning "history" or simply "story"—sagas are at once sophisticated literature and living folktales. Most sagas are believed to have been first composed orally and then written down in much the same way they were spoken, though this point is under constant schol-arly debate (see Olason 1998; Sigurdsson 2004 for sum-maries). Since the thirteenth century, the written books have been recopied, incorporating new elements of the stories as the folktales changed, until a huge cor-pus accumulated. Each retelling incorporates new thoughts and new knowledge, blurring the line between literature and folklore. Because each builds on some-thing that had existed before, there is no acknowledged "author" as such; most sagas are anonymous works of literature. This might indicate that they were so well known, common, and retold so often that they were considered the property of the culture rather than any one person. Though philologists have made careful comparisons between different versions to uncover changes in the stories, which have been used as evi-dence of authorial intent (Hastrup 1985; Palsson 1992), these are often changes that reflect the political reality of the author's own day, as would be expected of any living folkloric tradition.

The sagas are classified by academics into different types according to subject matter. Many stories are about bishops, saints, or priests; several books are devoted to the kings of Norway and Denmark; and in the fifteenth century, romantic tales from foreign lands were trans-lated into Icelandic. The preservation of many of these books (and the obvious signs of use) suggests that they were highly valued in their day; the sagas contin-ued to be recopied by hand until the nineteenth cen-tury. While all forms have value, by far the largest body of written stories—called the *Sagas of the Icelanders*—is about the first settlers and their descendants as they struggled to create an ordered society out of scratch in a newly inhabited land. As the "origin myth" for the Iceland nation, the *Sagas of the Icelanders* are the best-known and most-loved stories (Kellogg 1997). Since the eighteenth century, they have been printed, trans-lated, and sold en masse around the world, especially in Scandinavia, the British Isles, and the United States. Also, these tales have received the greatest level of attention from scholars at universities around Northern Europe and North America for the last one-hundred years. In the remainder of this paper, when the term saga is used, it should be understood to refer to *Sagas of the Icelanders*.

Once, when Vigdis Finnbogadóttir, then President of Iceland, was giving a talk in Germany, she discussed how the European landscape is dominated by medi-eval castles. By contrast, she noted that in Iceland, there are no such monuments to the works of man, but there are "castles hidden in the landscape. We call them the *Sagas of Icelanders*" (pers. comm. to A.B., 1986). In this analogy, the history of kings or saints or priests would be cottages, while the sagas are given the sta-tus of castles. Though saga place names are recogniz-able in the farms that still bear those names today, it is not those particular farms themselves that are the castles. Rather, those farms are reminders of stories "hidden"—or situated—in a landscape, and that entire landscape is culturally meaningful.

Sagas in Icelandic Daily Life

The literary fecundity of the sagas is clearly demonstrative of cultural worth and effort, but the sagas are more than books to sit on a shelf: they are a part of the daily consciousness of Icelanders. Beginning in the sixteenth century, poems about saga characters circulated around Iceland, and were extremely popular. One poem from the eighteenth century by a well-known poet, Sigurd Breidfjord, about the main female villain of *Njál's Saga*, Hallgerd, cast her in a favorable light. An indignant farmer, couched in the traditional view of Hallgerd as the perpetrator of evil against the main hero in the saga, countered with another poem, which was quickly passed around (Sveinnson 1958). Such was the potency of the saga narratives more than 800 years after the events they recount.

Today, the sagas are not only taught in the schools formally, but they are commonly discussed informally at home, especially in the rural districts. Linguistic phrases and clichés spring from events in the sagas:

—*ad lyfta Grettis taki* would be the English equivalent to "lifting a heavy load" of biblical reference, but the Icelandic phrase makes particular reference to a saga hero, Grettir, who was able to lift an incredibly heavy rock.

—When young children are caught doing something wrong, their guardians will often use a phrase from *Njál's Saga*, "*Tekid haf jeg hvolpa tvo, hval skal vil tha gera*, " meaning, "I've captured two puppies, what should I do with them?" a tacit threat by one of the more ferocious Viking warriors, Skarphedinn from *Njál´s Saga*.

—*Dyr mundi Haflidi allir* ("expensive would it be to pay for all of Halflid's life") is a phrase sometimes used when an expensive price is quoted for merchandise, for example, since in *Sturlunga Saga*, the family of a slain warrior (Halflid) is awarded an absurdly high compensation amount.

The most famous quotes from the sagas are known to all, even if they have never read the sagas, including

84/ This rendering of the meeting between dapper Gunnar and his beautiful future wife Hallgerd by A. Bloch was reproduced as a postcard, 1929.

the final statement by the main female in *Laxdala Saga*, "*Theim var eg verst, er eg unni mest,*" (he I treated worst, I loved/valued the most).

Mass media including newspapers, film, television and radio programs also do their part to popularize the saga characters (Fig. 84). Several recent debates about saga characters that played themselves out in the national papers, and sometimes the nightly news, included: the sexual preference of Njál; the sexual problems of Hrutur; Egil's drinking habits; Gunnar and Hallgerd's marriage problems and the national affiliation of Leif Eriksson. The sagas also are inescapably part of the daily life of Icelanders living in Reykjavík, who drive on Gunnarsbraut (Gunnar's road, named after the saga character Gunnar) or along the other streets named after saga characters (Helgason 1998).

Through these public debates, Icelanders are participating in a group performance of their identity. They are demonstrating what they have in common with each other: a shared heritage originating in the time of settlement as remembered in the sagas. Each debate in the paper, each cliché used in conversation, and each quote from a saga is simultaneously an outgrowth of that cultural heritage and a performative assurance of its continued cultural validity. It is a testament to the stability of Icelandic culture, despite being under foreign rule of Denmark and Norway for almost 800 years, that this connection to events and people who lived more than 1,000 years ago is still deeply felt.

The Saga of Burnt Njál

Though the Icelandic sagas as a body of literature have received much academic interest abroad and continue to elicit common cultural interest in Iceland, a few works do stand out as more highly valued for various reasons, including their breadth of coverage (*Heimskringla*); historical import (the *Vinland Sagas*); or narrative structure (*Laxadala Saga*). For the purposes of this paper, we will be examining one saga of that latter category, *The Saga of Burnt Njál*, or simply *Njál's Saga*. It is an especially carefully constructed saga, with common novelistic elements such as foreshadowing, a spiraling complexity in events, and a dramatic final climax. Unlike most sagas, it is simply too long for one to imagine it was recited orally, and might therefore have been originally composed as a written work. The *Saga of Burnt Njál* contains 159 chapters, and a recent English translation occupies 219 pages (Hreinsson 1997a). But even in this case, where authorial effort in weaving an intricate tapestry by combining elements from perhaps several folktales to create one epic story is obvious, the author's name is unknown.

In very brief form, the saga focuses around a hero named Gunnar and his wise friend Njál. Conflicts arise during each one's relationships with women, their children, their neighbors, and their rivals in other parts of the country and abroad. In typical fashion for sagas, these conflicts result in one party killing a member of the other party. The case is then brought before the appropriate legal body (the first Icelanders established a parliament and law court in 930 A.D.), where monetary or legal compensation (in the form of banishment) is sought. Though the saga is called the *Saga of Burnt Njál*, a great many of these conflicts actually revolve around Gunnar, with Njál supplying astute and sometimes tricky legal advice to Gunnar that often angers the other party, thus provoking further conflict. Gunnar dies after being attacked at his home by over thirty men (and betrayed by his problematic though beautiful wife) near the middle of the story, and then the course of events continues to play out with Njál's sons inheriting Gunnar's conflicts and some of their own. Near the end of the story, Njál's home is also ambushed, and as his enemies guard the doors, he, his wife, two daughters, three sons and one grandson are burned alive inside the house. His son-in-law, Kari, manages to escape, and finally avenges this terrible deed.

This adventurous tale, complex story line, and wonderfully drawn characters have supplied much fodder for debate among Icelanders and foreign academics. It has been taught in school in Iceland since the turn of the century, and many university courses have been developed around it. George Dascent did the first English translation in 1861, and from this sprung a series of alternative translations stretching to the present day. German and Scandinavian translations have been no less prolific since the late nineteenth century. In prefaces to many of these translations, *Njál's Saga* is described as the greatest work of literature in the Icelandic Saga tradition (Magnusson and Palsson 1960).

Njál's Saga and the Icelandic Landscape

What is less noted in these academic discussions is the relationship between this saga and the Icelandic landscape, especially the landscape of southern Iceland where most, though not all, of the saga action takes place (Fig. 85). Specific local details in *Njál's Saga* allow for the residents of the area to feel a personal connection to the story and the characters. The saga writers used the sense of wide vistas and landscape perspectives described above in creating their tales (Kaalund 1877). For instance, the scene just before the famous burning of Njál's farm, as his enemies gather, is set up through this horseback ride through the landscape:

> Then they mounted their horses and rode up into the mountains and on to Fiskivotn and on to the west of these, and then headed due west for Maelifellssand, with the Eyjafjallajokul to their left, and then down to Godaland and from there to Markarfljot. At mid afternoon they came to Thrihyrning and waited there until early evening. By that time everyone had arrived except Ingjald of Keldur, and the Sigfussons condemned him strongly, but Flosi told them not to blame Ingjald while he was not there—"we will settle with him later." (Hreinsson 1997a:152).

The knowledge of the land conveyed in this quote begins to hint at how intricately tied narrative is to landscape in Icelandic folkloric saga tradition.[1] As the all-knowing saga narrator sets up the characters and their conflicts, scenes shift between farms, some in other districts far away, if not in fact in foreign lands. But the sagas almost invariably describe the specific routes taken, and verify this by listing the number of days the character took in getting from place to place. The narrator does not simply skip from one locale to another, but rather takes his reader (or listeners) through a mental journey across the landscape, pointing out landmarks along the way. For this reason, familiarity with the Icelandic sagas tends to breed familiarity with the Icelandic landscape.

Njál's Saga is certainly no exception to this, whether one follows along with Gunnar as he goes to settle with his cousin's ex-husband's father on the east coast, or along with Kari as he avenges his family members in Norway. It was perhaps this sense of movement across the landscape that first inspired English visitors to Iceland in the nineteenth century to try to physically re-

85/ Map of Iceland showing the range of territory covered by characters in Njal's Saga. *The location of the Saga Centre is between Hlidarendi and Bergthorshvol on the southern coast.*

trace the narrative story line scene by scene. While not always taken in strictly chronological order, visitors in Reykjavík would head eastward, across the mountains, as had Gunnar after divorcing his first wife, back to the land of his childhood, Hlidarendi in Flotshlid. Such pilgrimages to the saga sites were once popular for academics and elites from the U.K., where translations of *Njál's Saga* were especially common. The well-respected historical painter, W.G. Collingwood, visited Iceland in the 1890s, and his paintings of the saga landscapes as well as his travel book describing his journey undoubtedly contributed to this phenomenon (Collingwood and Stefansson 1899).

It should be noted that in some cases, in their enthusiasm and as a reflection of how closely tied the sagas seem to be to the landscape, scholars and historians in the nineteenth and twentieth centuries either named or renamed places with saga related-names, according to their own interpretations (Fridriksson 1994). This has led to multiple places with the same saga-inspired place-name, and discussions about which place-name is more legitimate are ongoing. This suggests to some—especially archaeologists relying on place-name data when conducting surveys and determining where to dig—that the saga place-names are unreliable. Research at the Icelandic Cultural Ministry (*Örnefastofnu*) suggests there is considerable continuity of place names, at least from the seventeenth century (Gudrun Gudmansdóttir, pers. comm. to E.W.). The authors of this paper offer that where renaming has taken place, especially by the local population, it can be taken as a sign of the living tradition of Iceland's saga landscapes.

To date, numerous books have been published describing saga sites and the probable routes taken across landscape, the newest publication being a book titled *Njáluslodir,* where Bjarnason (1999) lists and describes all the sites mentioned in *Njál´s Saga.*

It is not just in the general route that the sagas relate geographic details. Understanding the action described in certain scenes depends on a more in-depth knowledge of the landscape. For instance, in one battle scene, Gunnar's physical prowess is well demonstrated by his ability to ward off thirty attackers, but his mental quickness in diverting his route, when he sensed an ambush, to take him to a uniquely defendable place (a large rock near a swift moving river; Fig. 86) is perhaps the more important part of the narrative. In both general outline and in specific scenes and action sequences, the sagas are tied to knowledge of the land.

Local Identity and Njál's Saga

The international renown of *Njál's Saga* has certainly been a point of pride for the entire Icelandic nation—small and isolated as it is—and cited often at academic conferences and in political speeches as evidence of Icelandic skill with the written word. But beyond its literary recognition, *Njál's Saga* also has a more concrete, local value. According to the saga, the main character Njál lived at a certain farm called Bergthorshvol, and a farm of that same name still exists on the same piece of land in the south of Iceland, on the coast opposite the Vestman Islands. The main hero, Gunnar, is called Gunnar of Hlidarendi because he owned a farm named Hlidarendi in the hilly district (Fljotshlid, the river hillside) inland from Njál's farm. Hlidarendi also exists today as a working farm, and the entire Fljotshlid area is still a major farming area in southern Iceland. Though few local residents claim direct ancestry from Njál or Gunnar, all Icelanders are descendants of those early settlers.

For the local residents of the area where the characters in *Njál's Saga* lived, the saga is far more than a great work of literature. It is their own regional story, as well as their own personal history. It is, in other words, part of their identity. If debates about the sagas are common in the national newspapers, debates about the *Njál's Saga* characters for residents of this district of Iceland are codified performative moments of that identity in the form of conversations on almost a daily basis (Hymes 1983). One amusing example comes from a recluse farmer, who rarely interacted socially with his

86/ Gunnarsstein (Gunnar's stone), *believed by the locals to be the location where Gunnar and two others lodged a successful defense against thirty armed men.*

neighbors. But after reading a flyer put out by the women's committee announcing an event on August 23, 2001 to commemorate the burning of Njál's farm, he had to speak up. After taking several stiff drinks, he called up the event organizer, and announced that there was a terrible problem. You see, he had spent many years reading *Njál's Saga* carefully, and by looking at clues in the story about the ripeness of the hay and the care given to the sheep, he had determined beyond a shadow of a doubt that the burning had actually taken place on August 21. He advised the commemoration be moved two days earlier, accordingly.

This is but one of dozens of examples of how common discussions of *Njál's Saga* are for the residents of the area. Such a situation is not unique to southern Iceland; most districts of Iceland have a saga that took place in their area (Hreinsson 1997b:388–90). Because of this, sagas landscapes—landscapes tied to specific saga narratives—are a defining characteristics of much of the Icelandic landscape.

The Saga Centre in Hvollsvollur

The preceeding argument has outlined the extent to which Iceland's cultural landscapes, particularly saga landscapes, have been continually preserved and made meaningful within Icelandic culture. But that culture has undergone tremendous change in the last fifty years, and the question arises as to how the tradition of saga landscapes can be incorporated into modern realities. One community, Hvollsvollur, in the region of southern Iceland where *Njál's Saga* mostly took place, has undertaken a unique experiment to see whether or not the Icelandic sense of a voyage through a narrative-rich saga landscape can become a commodity within a capitalist economic system; in so doing, they have also posed the broader question of whether or not a landscape which is essentially sacred in one culture can be interpreted and presented in such a way that it becomes meaningful to foreign tourists who do not share that cultural background.

In the late 1990s, when the southern part of Iceland (more specifically, the regional administrative unit Rangarvallasysla) was facing a huge economic slow down as the younger generation stopped farming and the fishing market bottomed out, the district representatives wanted to find a quick way to increase revenue. The only industry at that time that was doing well in Iceland was tourism. Tourism has been a booming industry since the 1970s, thanks in no small part to Icelandair, the only commercial airline servicing Iceland (until late, when it has partnered with SAS). It has heavily promoted travel to Iceland in both the U.S. and Europe by offering discounted fares and special weekend trips. Often these include tours to the natural wonders of Iceland: Gullfoss, a magnificent waterfall that tumbles more than ninety feet, or to Sneafellsjokull, the most westerly glacier. The austere beauty of these sites is well conveyed in the glossy brochures given out at every hotel. Buses depart on regularly scheduled tours from both the airport and various hotels for these natural wonders. Tour companies rely on the innate allure of such destinations, and this approach has successfully made tourism the second largest national industry, after fishing. A recent Gallup poll found that there were as many tourists to Iceland in the summer of 2000 as there are Icelanders (280,000).

The local governmental officials in southern Iceland understandably wanted "a piece of that action." But there are few if any outstanding natural wonders in this region; mostly there are broad plains, pleasant rivers, and comely rolling hillsides. It is not a place to inspire awe, but rather to foster feelings of comfort. A nearby forest is one of the few in Iceland, which makes it popular with Icelanders, but it is not what visitors from places with real forests—like the Black Forest in Germany or the Redwood Forest in California—would make a special effort to see. And as in all of Iceland, there are no large buildings or other outstanding manmade wonders to behold in southern Iceland.

What southern Iceland does have is *Njál's Saga*. As described above, a select class of tourists from England and Scandinavia had been coming to this part of Ice-

land specifically because of *Njál's Saga* since the late nineteenth century. Travel books about Iceland (i.e. Russel 1914) had always highlighted this region as *Njáluslod*, the area where *Njál's Saga* took place (Fig. 87, see below also). Although only sixty of two-hundred of the place-names mentioned in Njál's Saga are found in this area (Bjarnason 1999), no other district has a greater concentration. Most importantly, the two main characters, Gunnar and Njál, lived in this area. Thus, it was quite logical that the district representatives decided to gamble on encouraging tourists to visit Rangarvallasysla because of *Njál's Saga*. For these locals, the landscape was naturally filled with stories of saga heroes and exciting events, thanks to the unknown author of *Njál's Saga*. An Icelander does not look at Gunnar's farm at Hlidarend without associating it with the hero of *Njál's Saga* and his wife Hallgerd. And the mountain Thrihyrning (see Fig. 83), in the mind of an Icelandic traveler, is connected with the story of Flosi, who hid in a valley at the top of that mountain after the dramatic fire at Bergthorshvol. The Icelanders and foreigners who know *Njál's Saga* look at the landscape and see not just the physical features: a fast-running river or a low, green hill. Instead, these natural features lead Icelanders to think about the exciting and important events that happened here more than 1,000 years ago. This shared, imagined cultural landscape was tangible enough to the local community leaders that they believed they could make a tourist attraction around it, the Saga Centre. Because this tourist attraction relies on the pre-existing cultural landscape of southern Iceland, created primarily through a specific saga narrative, it is an appropriate focus in seeking to understand saga landscapes in their modern manifestation. What this analysis suggests is that the existence of the Saga Centre not only serves to preserve the cultural landscape, it also is a transformative agent of that landscape, giving it new meaning.

Beginning of the Saga Centre
Beginning in 1996, community leaders from the ten

87/ *A sign along the main highway indicating the boundary of the community of Fljotshlid* (Fljótshliðarhreppur), *a part of the larger Njaluslod* (Njáluslóð) *region.*

towns that make up Ragnarvallasysla had meetings to discuss a proposal to create a special tour of the places mentioned in *Njál's Saga.* Six of the ten communities allocated funds from their annual budgets toward the development of this idea, and the mayors of each contributing town appointed a board. Early on, the tour was envisioned as a two-day trip with a night in a hotel, and brochures were printed, describing this tour. It was quickly determined that a building would be necessary as a specific destination in what is otherwise an amorphous areal destination, and it could also serve as a starting point from which the tours could depart. In the building, several components were included: a tourist center with leaflets about area attractions, a sales shop, some office space, an exhibition hall, and a Viking style dinning area.[2] For the first two years, there were few bookings for the tour.

In late 1996, the board hired a designer and purchased a building, calling it "The Saga Centre". The building was located in Hvollsvollur, which is centrally located within the Rangarvallasysla and happens to be the hometown of one of the strongest proponents of the idea, a dentist and community leader. A designer was hired, Bjorn G. Bjornsson, one of the most experienced exhibition creators in Iceland. In going about his job of designing the center, he traveled to many international Viking exhibitions and sites, including the Jorvik Center in York, the Dublin National Museum, L'Anse aux Meadows in Newfoundland, and museums in Scandinavia.

The exhibition reflects the influence of established Viking exhibitions in that it contains a broad discussion about the Vikings and the Viking Age, which takes up approximately a third of the floor space. Another section focuses on the history of saga writing in Iceland, discussing such personages as the famous historian and explainer of saga poetry, Snorri Sturlusson. The remainder of the exhibition, slightly less than half

ELISABETH I. WARD AND ARTHUR B. BOLLASON

the floor space, focuses on *Njál's Saga* itself. In one of the letters from the designer to the Viking Adventure and Feast in Dublin (Sept. 13, 1996), the designer commented that the sagas are an underutilized asset in Icelandic tourism, and it seems indeed he had few examples from which to model this exhibition. To "exhibiting" the saga, a personality profile of the main characters and a brief overview of the main action scenes in each section—primarily through extensive quotes on the wall and historic paintings inspired by the saga action—is attempted. No photographs of the landscapes are used, and there are no artifacts in the exhibition, save modern recreations. While the exhibition is an important part of the visitor's understanding of the saga, the main focus seems to have been on creating an exhibition that would meet international standards for a Viking exhibition, coupled with what might be called an uncertainty as to how to handle the exhibition of the narrative of the saga itself.

Changes and Successes

In other ways as well, the Saga Centre, though locally inspired and locally funded, has attempted in its development to be internationally savvy. In 1999, it hired Arthur Bjorgvin Bollason, a foreign radio correspondent, television personality, and tour guide to be its director. His knowledge of tourism in Iceland and good contacts in the media were seen as special assets from the point of view of the local magistrates. Since becoming director, he has instituted a number of changes, all intended to make the Saga Centre more palatable to an international audience by focusing less on the narrative details of the saga and more on the individual characters in the saga. The tours were shortened from two days to several hours and divided into tours for Icelanders and tours for tourists. A dining hall with Viking-style wooden benches was completed in 2001, allowing the Saga Centre to begin offering traditional meals to participants in the bus tours, which makes visiting the Saga Centre a day-long excursion. Some groups forgo the bus tour and come only for the enter-

tainment offered on weekend nights. Friday night has a one-hour musical play based on nineteenth century songs about the *Njál's Saga* characters. On Saturday, a play is shown about Gunnar and his notorious wife Hallgerd—she refused to give him strands of her long hair when his bowstring broke, thus leaving her husband unable to defend himself against an onslaught of his enemies. Both are told in Icelandic with English text as a handout, and they are very popular with Icelanders and foreigners, and convenient for those for whom the bus tour is physically difficult. Everyone who works at the Saga Centre, including the men who sing in the musical, are locals from the area, except the director (A.B.B.).[3] In this way, though offering a variety of options to visitors, the Saga Centre has maintained a strong connection to the local community. This has been accomplished in the face of a markedly more visible profile. Newspaper articles about the newly added entertainment has encouraged Icelandic visitors, while tour companies adding the Saga Centre as a destination choice for bus and cruise ship groups has greatly increased international visitorship.

Visitor Profile

All of this has combined to make the Saga Centre one of the most visited cultural tourist destinations in Iceland. In the summer of 2001,[4] only visiting the site of the original parliament, which is also a beautiful national park in a tremendous natural setting, was more popular. The fact that Hvollsvollur, a small and rather nondescript farming community that is a 100 kilometer (60 miles) drive from the capitol of Reykjavík, has become so well visited, and profitable,[5] is remarkable.

Visitors to the Saga Centre have been a surprising mix of foreigners and Icelanders. The original target audience was foreigners, though certainly given the manner in which Icelanders like to explore their own landscapes, it was assumed Icelanders would come as well. During the summer of 2001, more than 17,000 visitors came, sixty-five percent Icelanders, and thirty-five percent foreigners. Most are over fifty years of

88/ The first stop on the tour, Hof, where visitors must visualize several farms that used to be located in the area.

age, but there are also large student groups in the autumn and the spring. The visitors are extremely diverse and cross gender and class divisions: during one Saturday, there were two groups taking the tour simultaneously, one of professors from the teachers' training school, and the other group was the crew from a fishing trawling company.

Defining *Njáluslóð*

While all of the activities at the Saga Centre are interesting from a museological and tourist industry point of view, of primary concern for this paper is the Saga Centre's function as the starting and ending point for journeys through the saga landscape.

The tours are designed to extend that sense of a narrative-filled landscape to those who may be less familiar with *Njál's Saga*. It consists of either vans or buses that are filled with groups, both foreign and Icelandic, led by Saga Centre guides. The groups often arrive together to the Saga Centre. If they have announced their plans ahead of time (which most groups

do), they are met and led through the exhibition by the director. After that overview, a knowledgeable local guide joins them on the bus, and the tour begins. The buses take a particular route through the landscape, stopping at places that are described and mentioned in *Njál's Saga* (see below). At each stop, the guides retell or reread the portion of the saga that is relevant to that spot, and answer tourists' questions. The stops typically last fifteen minutes or so, with the guide saying a few words, including reading from the saga, and then tourist taking photographs, walking around and asking questions, before returning to the van (Fig. 88).

Given the nature of the saga, which includes scenes set on the west coast of Iceland, at the National Assembly site near Lake Thingvellir, and scenes in Norway and England, choices needed to be made about what to include and what to exclude in the bus tours. The political motivation to get people to come to this particular region surely influenced the choice of sites, limiting it to those sites within the boundaries of the six communities that contributed funds toward the creation of the Saga Centre. These communities, and indeed perhaps others, have considered themselves part of the Njáluslod (*Njáluslóð*) area since the eighteenth century, when this area name was first coined. The name itself is broadly understood: a compound of the name of Njál, the main character in the saga, in possessive form (Njálu), and the noun *slod* (*slóð*), which is a geographic term suggesting an area subject to common forces, as would be used for run-off plains for a particular river, and so on. In the same manner that the glacial rivers and sand erosion have through the centuries changed the face of the land in the *Njál's Saga* region, the unknown author of the saga, and all the generations who have retold the story since, have managed to "change" the landscape by giving it new meaning. But the boundaries of this influence are amorphous; *Njáluslod* is the entire landscape region rather than a specific place. The bus tour is essential in actively defining what the linguistic term *Njáluslod* means. By physically circumscribing a specific geographic area, that area becomes *Njáluslod* in the minds of the participants.

Simultaneously, the physical area determines and limits the narrative elements of the saga that are included. Kari's avenging actions in England—the satisfying conclusion to the saga—are not mentioned, because they cannot be demonstrated through reference to the local landscape. Conversely, a rather minor character, the uncle of Njál's illegitimate son,[6] is given full airing because his farm is still in existence today, including, as is appropriate for a Viking Age farm, escape tunnels. Through the agency of the Saga Centre, the inter-relatedness of the saga and the landscape is further reinforced and mutually developed, such that the one defines the other. The understanding of what *Njál's Saga* is and what it means has, therefore, been transformed through the Saga Centre's existence. Because Icelanders do not consider the sagas stale literary texts, but rather an integral part of their daily lives, such an evolution of its purpose and meaning to fit current needs is not beyond their expectations.

Saga Bus Tours

The flexible relationship between the saga and the physical landscape allows for the content of the tour, and therefore the amount of the saga discussed, to be determined on a case-by-case basis as appropriate, depending on the audience. For foreigners, the bus tour is shorter, and includes fewer sites. Usually, the foreigner tours take approximately two hours and include about five stops. In comparison, the Icelandic tours take at least three hours, and include seven or eight stops. The number, duration, and choice of stop is somewhat dependent on the weather and the size and interest of the group; but the two basic tours begin in much the same way, by heading west from the Saga Centre along the main paved road.

The first stop is the farm of Hof, with a view of the farm Vollur, where *Njál's Saga* begins. This is located about fifteen minutes up the road from the Saga Centre, in a rather sparsely populated plain that is far less fertile than it was 1,000 years ago (Fig. 88). Hof was where the family that caused much hardship for Gunnar and Njál lived, and the eldest son on this farm started the fight that eventually led to Njál's being burned alive inside his home. There is no farm there today, though a herd of Icelandic horses occupies one fenced in portion. Usually, the guide will use this stop to introduce the main characters and will read the opening few paragraphs plus a few other appropriate selections, as the group gathers around him. The guide will normally point to the locations of two other farms that are mentioned in the saga and that can be seen in clear weather from Hof, though there are no old buildings at any of these places today. Within the framework of the saga narrative, they are not mentioned until later in the story, which may be one reason the guide does not read particular passages about these farms, or it may be because it is somewhat unclear for the visitor exactly where the farms stood. One of these two farms, Kirkju-baer, was the farm that Gunnar's wife had one of her slaves break into as retribution for an insult the farmer levied at Gunnar, which is a com-

89/ A tour guide (l) relates the story of the death of Gunnar the Hero while standing at Gunnar's farm, Hlidarendi.

pelling story that the guides usually relate.

Proceeding into the interior along a dirt road, the tour bus turns toward the mountains. Keldur, a still inhabited farm with intact, older buildings of traditional sod construction, is the next stop. Here Ingjaldur, a relation of Njál's who almost joined with the vigilante party for the slaying of Njál, lived. As a minor character in the saga, his farm does not need to be included in the saga tour. However, since it is an authentic, traditional farm type, it allows the guide to explain a few things about Icelandic farming. Also, two escape tunnels that lead from the house to a nearby riverbank are especially evocative of the dangerous rivalries of the Viking Age and later. The guide does not usually read an excerpt from the saga at this point but rather talks generally about Icelandic daily life. The farm derives its name from the naturally warm spring (rather than hot spring) that flows nearby.

Farther into the interior, the bus meets up with the Ranga River and proceeds along its western bank. This section is completely deserted, having been turned into an arctic desert by the successive eruptions of Mount Hekla. After a few bumpy kilometers, the guide points out a large stone sitting by the side of the river. Though not specifically named in the saga as such, this stone has been called in local folklore "Gunnars-stein," meaning Gunnar's Stone (see Fig. 86). *Njál's Saga* includes a dramatic episode where Gunnar and two companions made a defense against thirty armed men and were victorious, though one of the three, Gunnar's brother Hjortur, was killed. Because the saga relates that Gunnar took up a defensive position along the river at a place he knew well, locals have reasoned that this large stone would have provided sufficient defense for a skilled archer to mount a defense. Depending on time available to do so, the guide will read this battle scene excerpt from the saga as he sits on the stone itself. Excavations in the area have revealed

ELISABETH I. WARD AND ARTHUR B. BOLLASON

archaeological pieces that may have been associated with archery,[7] as well as human remains, so this has added credence to the name Gunnarsstein and to this as the location of the battle.

Heading southeast over the hills at the base of the mountains, the guide points out a few sites along the way from the window of the bus, including especially the "Three Horned" Mountain (see Fig. 83) . According to the saga, a farmer with several sons and who raised champion horses lived at the base of this mountain, though the location of their farm is uncertain (ruins of four or five farms have been identified). The sons challenged Gunnar to a horse duel, and this led to a rivalry that eventually contributed to Gunnar's death. Between two of the tops of this mountain is a natural valley or gully, into which the attackers of Njál are thought to have hidden after the burning.

Winding along this mountainous terrain, the bus eventually links again with the paved road, and heads northeast along the Markarfljot River toward the glaciers. The Fljotshlid (river hillside) district, a rich agricultural area, lines this stretch of road. At one farm on these hills, named Hlidarendi, lived the main hero of the saga, Gunnar. The bus stops at this location (Fig. 89), and the guide will normally relate a number of stories, including those about the nineteenth century church on the property and a twentieth century artist who lived nearby, but then the guide will read about the death of Gunnar. This is dramatic for a number of reasons, not the least of which is the fact that, as Gunnar was struggling to ward off forty men, he asked his wife for strands of her long, thick hair to use as replacements for his broken bow string. She coyly replied, "Does anything depend on it?" and then refused him his wish, as retribution for a slap she received many years earlier from him. Most tour members are appalled at this story of betrayal, but the guide will often relate the debates about this scene, including one recent theory that the husband and wife were just enjoying a nice give and take as a final farewell. There are no physical remains from Gunnar's farm, and in fact the

exact location of the house on the hill itself is unknown, though the boundaries of the farm lot are well established. From this vantage point, one looks south across the plain of the Markarfljot River, toward the Vestman Islands. For the foreign tourists, this is the last stop on the tour. The guide therefore uses this vista to point out a few other places included in the saga. Njál's farm, Bergthorshvol, was on the plain of the Markarfljot River, so the guide will normally point in its direction and tell the story of the burning of Njál, since the foreign tour does not go to this site. Instead, it returns up the paved road to the Saga Centre. This route takes approximately two hours.

The Icelandic tour proceeds from Hlidarendi south across the plain of the Markarfljot River. It stops at Dimon, a large hill that has not been eroded, as has the other land in the area (Fig. 90). Here the story is told of the bravado of Skarpedinn, one of Njál's sons, who had skid across a nearby river when it was frozen, brandishing an axe and killing several men, while escaping unharmed himself. This location is also where the guide often reads from a poem composed about a different event in the saga. When Gunnar was supposed to leave Iceland as punishment for a killing, he was riding his horse south across this plain. His horse stumbled, and as Gunnar landed on the ground, he turned to face Hlidarendi to the north. Then he said how beautiful Fljotshlid looked and that he would not leave. This led to his enemies' finding him and killing him in his house. Both of these stories are usually related at Dimon, though neither of these events was supposed to have taken place exactly at that location. Rather, it provides a dramatic setting to tell these two stories—separate from each other in terms of the saga narrative—which took place nearby.

The final stop of the Icelandic language tour is Bergthorshvol, the farm of Njál. This farm lies due west of Dimon, also in the Markarfljot River plain. Today, a farm still exists that is called Berthoshvol. On the farm property are several mounds, which were likely the refuse piles from previous farmhouses (Fig. 91). Njál's

90/ Dimon, a dramatic rise on an otherwise flat plain, provides a convenient location for an Icelandic tour group and guide (center, white jacket) to contemplate scenes from Njal's Saga.

house is believed to have stood on one of these hill-ocks. The bus stops at this farm, and everyone files out. The guide stands atop one mound, and tells the story of the burning of Njál, pointing north across the plain to the Three Horned mountain from whence his enemies emerged (normally commenting on the un-likelihood that Njál would not have noticed a large group of men coming at him from such a distance). He then relates the dramatic tale of Njál and his wife, and one young grandson, agreeing to die together, although their enemies offered the women and children a chance to leave. This simultaneously violent and touching epi-sode is very near the chronological end of the saga narrative itself, so it is a fitting last stop for the tour. The bus then returns to the Saga Centre by heading north and then slightly east. The Icelandic tour normally takes about three and a half to four hours.

Often the guests stay for a traditional meal and the live entertainment offered on Friday and Saturday nights before heading back to their abodes for the evening.

Guides

The guides themselves are obviously an important com-ponent in the tenure and content of the tour. There is neither a formal application nor training process for the guides; rather, local people with knowledge of the saga, a knack for public speaking, and available time are informally recruited through the community network. Though there is a prescribed route and agreed-upon stops, the guides are otherwise free to discuss what they know and interests them. Besides the difference in physical route and duration, the infor-mation presented in the foreign versus Icelandic tours is therefore somewhat different. During the summer of 2001, there were four main guides: an elderly local farmer, Magnus; two priests, Gunnar and Sigurd; and the Saga Center director himself.[8] Magnus' lack of bi-lingualism necessitates that he be the guide for only the Icelandic tours, and he has developed a particular flair for his work. As the longest serving guide, and a local resident of the area whose grandfather used to tell him the story of Njál and Gunnar, Magnus conducted more than thirty-six tours during the summer of 2001. Despite his in-depth knowledge of the saga, he tended to discuss all the interesting stories of the landscape in the tradition of the Icelandic road books described above, rather than just those stories related to *Njál's Saga*. As he said, "History is always happening. Today's stories are not so different from the saga times [stories]" (pers. comm., August 2001, translation E.W.). Some visitors find this lack of focus disappointing since they came specifically to the Saga Centre because of *Njáls Saga*, while others, especially those less familiar with the saga, are relieved to have a more diverse range of stories discussed. Unfortunately, due to ailing health, he has had to cut back on his tours recently, and since a replacement has not yet been found, the number of tours offered has been curtailed.

The other guides can and certainly do conduct the longer Icelandic tours, but they also lead the foreign groups. For foreign visitors, the guides stick more closely to the saga narrative, though natural history facts concerning volcanic eruptions, changes in the course of the rivers, and so on, are also discussed. This focus lends a certain performative formality to the foreign tours, which complements the fact that the foreign visitors often know each other far less well than the Icelandic groups that come to the Saga Center and spend less time together on the tour itself. It is less of a social event for the foreign tour participants, conversely more focused on the guide as the common binding element of the group.

For foreign groups especially, a guide—as performer of the saga, embodiment of the saga narrative—is required. For Icelanders and specialist tourists, *Njál's Saga* itself is innately interesting. But for the average tourist, who came to Iceland lured by images of a wild land, *Njál's Saga* has to be *made* interesting. By focusing on the common human elements of the characters, such as Gunnar as a husband with a difficult wife, the narrative is made more accessible. Making the stories enter-

taining for foreign visitors is also the job of the guides. The two live plays held on weekend evenings at the Saga Center extend the knowledge of the narratives told in *Njál's Saga*, and are attended both by visitors who take the tours and those that do not.

The presentation of the saga to foreigners in this entertaining and lively way is one more way that the concept of *Njál's Saga* is delimited through the agency of the Saga Centre. The saga is therefore being translated more than just linguistically. It is being culturally translated to suit modern tastes and interests, shortened to match the average visitor's limited knowledge of the saga and to fit in the comfortable time period of a bus ride, and to coincide with the physical boundaries of the landscape through which the bus travels. This translating fits within a wider pattern of the Icelandic approach to the sagas as a living tradition; the Saga Centre is simply giving *Njál's Saga* new currency.

Working the Imagination

The setup, route taken, schedule, and words of the guides are all deliberate actions intended for a specific outcome: to fill the *Njálaslod* landscape with a saga narrative. But since the Saga Center is the first and only saga interpretive site with guided tours in Iceland, the effect these actions would have on the visitors was uncertain. The bus tours are a physical group tour into the imaginary, a ride through the countryside to *see* that which no longer exists, where a group of adults crowd into the middle of a grass field, "looking" at something that cannot be seen (see Figs. 88,89).

In this situation, the human power of imagination needs to take over, enabling people who have no previous knowledge of the saga to "see" the events that took place 1,000 years ago in the landscape. The landscape itself, which exists in front of their eyes, can serve as a mental trigger for these events. With the help of the imagination, it seems tourists can recreate the story in the mind, reanimating the characters of the saga and making them alive in the landscape. The land-

91/ *Bergthorshvol, the site where Njal and his family were burned alive, is the last stop on the Icelandic tour; it has no obvious physical remains from the saga time period.*

scape becomes a "frame", which the visitor has to fill with his or her own painting of the saga events. With the help of the guide, the traveler thus creates his own story, his own vision of what happened in *Njáluslod* centuries ago.

Because the tour relies so heavily on the imagination of the visitor, and because there is so little to be seen physically, such a tour is even meaningful for those without vision. In the summer of 2000, a group of blind Icelandic adults booked the tour. They had with them a trained assistant who described the physical landscape to them, and they had the Saga Centre guide telling them the saga. Thus, despite the logistic problems such a guided tour faces (such as finding enough qualified and available guides), the format itself has proven capable of conveying a powerful message about the relationship between landscape and saga narratives in Icelandic culture.

An informal survey of visitors[9] suggests that the tours were mostly effective at encouraging visitors to work their imagination. Icelanders, especially those familiar with the saga, found it pleasurable to "see" the

saga events and to visit (or revisit) this saga landscape. However, some foreign visitors commented that they would like to have a map or understand more exactly where the guide was pointing. Even the foreigners who admitted to taking the tour only because they wanted a chance to be outside, to see the Icelandic landscape, expressed an appreciation for the stories. One visitor, who was familiar with *Njáls Saga* from college, said that he came to learn about Icelandic culture, and felt there was no better way than getting a sense of how important these stories are to Icelanders.

Conclusion

The majority of tourism campaigns about Iceland, such as the slogan of the 1990s that dubed Iceland "The Land of Fire and Ice," foster and project an image of a wild, uninhabited land, devoid of the works of man. While brochures might mention Iceland as the land of the sagas or of the Vikings, the beautiful and mysterious physical landscape and raw natural beauty are touted as the primary attractions. This tacitly implies the land is solely there for the enjoyment of outsiders, and in-

ELISABETH I. WARD AND ARTHUR B. BOLLASON

deed the major activities offered are glacier snowmobile rides, hikes to untamed waterfalls, and horseback tours through the uninhabited interior.

Such a view of the landscape is directly at odds with the well-documented tradition Icelanders themselves have of filling their landscape with stories. When Icelanders look at a scenery or take a country drive, their perception is influenced by a storehouse of narratives. For Icelanders, it is the places tied to specific people and historic events which are of interest. The other geographic features may be beautiful, but they carry little, if any, cultural meaning. At the Saga Centre, the guides and the locals who work in the sales shop and kitchen, or act in the Saga Centre plays on the weekends, are telling people about something that is particularly meaningful: a saga landscape. As described by one of the local magistrates involved in the creation of the center

> Tourists who come to a foreign land want to have interesting information about the people and the land that they are visiting. . . . [I]f they do not receive such information . . . they will not be intrigued despite the fact that the land is beautiful and the sun is shining. In this nation live the people, and they must acquaint them with a wider perspective. The people and the land have their stories and the land has meaning (Letter to Board of Trustees, 21 July 1998).

As in no other tourist spot in Iceland, the Saga Centre acts as a host, inviting tourists into Icelanders' symbolic home, a culturally meaningful landscape. Just as a polite host leads a guest through the home, pointing out which objects in the home have special meaning, the guides on the bus tours make tourists feel welcome and a part of the wider cultural milieu by sharing with them meaningful stories. For a brief moment, the tourist can try to see the land through the eyes of an Icelander. And then they are offered home-cooked meals and told a story in a welcoming room by more locals. This means that foreigners who come to the Saga Centre have a great deal more interaction with local people than they will have in other tourist sites in Iceland. The

Saga Centre, as a nexus for local-international interaction, has skillfully utilized this opportunity, and it seems foreign visitors do come away with an understanding of this region's saga landscape.

For Icelanders, the Saga Centre has other import. Here their national identity as Icelanders interacts with a particular local form, whether they go on the tours or only come for the evening entertainment. Going to the Saga Centre thus becomes an enactment of their *Icelandic-ness*, the shared cultural heritage common to all Icelanders, just as the debates in the paper or the common clichés do; perhaps even more so. Like a pilgrimage in the Roman Catholic world, it is simultaneously a mental and physical act, demonstrating that cultural affiliation and buttressing the importance of the sagas in Icelandic culture. With every footstep, and each turn of the wheel of bus, Icelanders are making that preexisting cultural landscape meaningful again.

Maintaining the meanings associated with saga landscapes faces a number of challenges. Iceland has undergone tremendous social and economic change in the last fifty years. The rural population has been encouraged, via tax incentives and the existence of good schools and hospitals, to move to urban centers, particularly the capitol of Reykjavík. Though young people still learn about the sagas through various means, these uniquely Icelandic stories must now compete with satelite television, the Internet, and other forms of popular entertainment. Once an agrarian economy, the Icelandic economy is now a modern, capitalist economy. By demonstrating that cultural heritage can become a viable source of economic gain, the Saga Centre offers Icelanders a model for how to bridge the gap between the past and the present. Unlike other Northern peoples described in this volume who are currently documenting their cultural landscapes, Iceland's ethnographic landscapes have been documented for eight hundred years, beginning with the efforts of the anonymous saga writers. What is required is a means to encourage young Icelanders to continue to honor that heritage.

The Saga Centre offers one such means, and a timely one at that. The number of tourists coming to Iceland has begun to eclipse the size of Iceland's population itself, and a moment of cultural crisis, like those experienced by small Caribbean nation-states, may be on the horizon (Shimany et al. 1994). The number of Icelanders who have visited the Saga Centre suggests a proactive response. In the face of an onslaught of tourists—many of whom come with no appreciation of the history or culture of the land, and expect to see an exotic wilderness—Icelanders are attempting to shift the focus to that which is meaningful to them, their Icelandic saga landscapes. They face an uphill battle, as tour companies and promoters try to package the Saga Centre as a more traditional tourist stop; some book groups only for the dinner or musical play, and not for the bus tour itself. As the Saga Centre continues to evolve into an increasingly popular foreign tourist destination, it is unclear what role the original focus of the center, the bus tours through the landscape, will have. In the meantime, this small farming village in southern Iceland will continue to be the unlikely spot where local attempts to transmit and maintain an Icelandic sense of the landscape compete with the needs and expectations of foreign tourists.

Acknowledgments

While perhaps the greatest thanks belong to the many, unnamed tour participants who kindly became subjects of our study, a few named individuals also deserve thanks. Ambassadors Einar Benediktsson and Jon Baldvin Hannibalsson facilitated introduction of the co-authors, Gunnar Jonsson of Icelandair generously provided airfare, and the Ladies Club of Flotshlid extended use of their summer cottage. Thanks to Ted Birkedal of the U.S. National Park Service for encouraging the inclusion of an Icelandic component in this northern ethnographic landscape volume and to the volume editors for their careful and thoughtful feedback. John Steinberg of UCLA also provided critical commentary which strengthened the paper, and Gisli Sigurdsson of the Arni Magnusson Institute assisted with illustration suggestions. But we reserve our final thanks to the anonymous author of *Njál's Saga*, whose careful crafting of the tale has inspired generations and enriched the landscape immeasurably.

Notes

1. This aspect of saga literature has not been extensively studied, though Adalsteinsson 1996, Overing and Osborn 1994, and Petersson 1981 make use of the continuity in saga placenames and descriptions of the landscape in their respective arguments. One author (E.W.) will be focusing on the relationship between sagas and the landscape for her dissertation research.

2. A Viking dining hall in a community near Reykjavík has been a popular tourist destination since the early '90s. So they were hoping to recreate that, but soon found forming the cadre of 15 performers needed for such a Viking re-enactment hall impossibly complicated.

3. One of the authors of this paper, Arthur B. Bollason, was director of the Saga Centre from 1999 until fall 2003.

4. The bulk of this paper is based upon data from the summer of 2001, when Arthur Bollason hosted Elisabeth Ward at the Saga Centre. Comments pertaining to visitors' experience are based on several ride-alongs Elisabeth made with various tour groups and interviews with participants. Other information regarding the background of tour groups comes from Arthur's reservation system.

5. The Saga Centre began to break even two years ahead of schedule.

6. Children born out of wedlock were not and are not openly biased against in Icelandic culture, though they may not have completely equal access to inherit land and money.

7. One of the pieces found at this site is a bone ring likely used to protect the index finger while drawing back a bowstring. Of considerable interest to some saga enthusiasts, this piece is decorated with a stag design, and the name of Gunnar's brother, who died at the attack, means stag. Lay people therefore speculate this was the

exact piece used by Gunnar's brother.

8. Gunnar the Priest transferred parishes in early 2002 and is no longer conducting tours.

9. Conducted by E. Ward, August 13–19, 2001.

References

Adalsteinsson, Jon Hnefill
1996 Eftirhreytur um Freyfaxahamar (Reverberations off Freyfax's rockface). *Mulaping* 23:67–89.

Bjarnason, B.
1999 *Njáluslodir* (The region associated with Njál). Reykjavík: Mal og Menning.

Collingwood, W.G. (William Gershom), and Jon Stefansson
1899 *A Pilgrimage to the Saga-Steads of Iceland.* Ulverston: W. Holmes. 1899. Reprinted 1988 as *Fegurð Íslands og fornir sögustaðir: svipmyndir og sendibréf úr Íslandsför W.G.Collingwoods 1897 with a forward by Haraldur Hannesson, Björn Th. Björnsson and Janet B. Collingwood Gnosspelius.* Reykjavík: Örn og Örlygur.

Fridriksson, Adolf
1994 *Sagas and Popular Antiquarianism in Icelandic Archaeology.* Aldershot: Avebury.

Hann, C.M., ed.
1998 *Property Relations: Renewing the Anthropological Tradition.* Cambridge: Cambridge University Press.

Hastrup, Kirsten
1985 *Culture and History in Medieval Iceland: An Anthropological Analysis of Structure and Change.* Oxford: Clarendon Press; New York: Oxford University Press.

Helgason, J.K.
1998 *Hetjan og höfundurinn* (Heroes and the authors) Reykjavík: Mal og Menning.

Hreinsson, Vidar, ed.
1997a Njál's Saga. In *The Complete Sagas of Icelanders. Vol. 3: Epic—Champions and Rogues*, pp. 1–220, tran. Robert Cook. Reykjavík: Leifur Eiriksson Publishing.
1997b *The Complete Sagas of the Icelanders. Vol. 5: Epic—Wealth and Power.* Reykjavík: Leifur Eiriksson Publishing.

Hunt, Robert C., and Antonio Gilman, eds.
1998 Property in Economic Context. *Monographs in Economic Anthropology* 14. Lanham, MD: University Press of America.

Hymes, Dell H.
1983 *Essays in the Hstory of Linguistic Anthropology.* Philadelphia: J. Benjamins.

Kaalund, K.
1877 *Bidrag til en historisk-topogarafisk Beskrivelse af Island* (Towards an historic-topographic description of Iceland). Copenhagen: Gyldenalske boghadel.

Kellogg, Robert
1997 Introduction. In *The Complete Sagas of Icelanders, Vol. 1: Vinland—Warriors and Poets*, V. Hreinsson, ed., pp. xxix–liii. Reykjavík: Leifur Eiriksson Publishing.

Magnusson, Magnus, and Hermann Palsson
1960 *Njál's Saga.* London: Penguin Books.

Olason, Vesteinn
1998 *Dialogues with the Viking Age: Narration and Representation in the Saga of the Icelanders.* Reykjavík: Heimskringla.

Overing, Gillian R. and Marijane Osborn
1994 *Landscape of Desire: Partial Stories of the Medieval Scandinavian World.* Minneapolis: University of Minnesota Press.

Petursson, Halldor
1981 Söguslodir á Úthéraði (Saga regions in the rural areas). *Mulaping* 11:91–103.

Russell, W.S.C.
1914 *Iceland: Horseback Tours in Saga Land.* Boston: Richard G. Badger and Toronto: The Copp Clark Co., Ltd.

Schimany, Peter, Volker Grabowsky, and Andreas Roser
1994 *Aspekte der Moderne: negative Dialektik, Nationalismus, Tourismus* (Aspects of modernity: negative dialectics, nationalism and tourism). Egelsbach, Germany; Washington, DC: Hänsel Hohenhausen.

Sigurdsson, Gisli
2004 *The Medieval Icelandic Saga Tradition and Oral Tradition: A Discourse on Method.* Publications of the Milman Parry Collection of Oral Literature 2. Cambridge: Harvard University. Translation of *Túlkun Íslendingasagna í Ljósi Munnlegrar Hefðar: Tilgáta um Aðferð.* Reykjavík: Stonfun Árna Magnússonar Á Íslandi, 2002.

Sveinsson, Gunnar
1959 *Matthias Johannessen: Njála í íslenskum skaldskap* (Matthias Johannesse: Njál in Icelandic poetry) Reykjavík: Skirnir.

Vesteinsson, Orri
2000 The Archeaology of *Landnám*: Early Settlement in Iceland. In *Vikings: The North Atlantic Saga*, William Fitzhugh and Elisabeth Ward, eds., pp. 164–74. Washington, DC: Smithsonian Institution Press.

Cultural Seascapes

Preserving Local Fishermen's Knowledge in Northern Norway

ANITA MAURSTAD

The word "landscape" was first used in the late six-teenth century (Oxford English Dictionary). The term "seascape" did not come into use until 200 years later, and it is usually simply translated as "pictures of the sea." However, seascapes have other values beyond the picturesque that I will focus on in this article. I could make a systematic comparison of seascapes with landscapes and list their basic differences. Some are quite obvious. The land holds footprints and paths—traces of human occupancy that often date back thou-sands of years. Water is fluid and ever changing. The traces of a boat moving through a seascape last only a few minutes. The land impresses with its mountains, green valleys, and rivers. In some areas fences also stand out to mark borders of property. At sea there are no such visible marks. Regional, national and interna-tional borders are ink on paper conventions and charts while fishermen's perceptions of local common-rights are imprinted in their minds. The sea has mountains and valleys though, but they are invisible, hidden un-der the surface. The surface may also hide strong cur-rents. The sea is dangerous. It can produce violent storms that easily crush human-made entities, like boats and buildings. People drown at sea. Dying on land, people are normally found and given a specific place to rest. The sea holds no such place and we talk of the sea as we talk of the Lord; it gives and it takes.

The sea is also mysterious in other aspects; it repre-sents the unknown and is surrounded by folklore and myths. *Draugen* is the Norwegian name for a monstrous sea spirit who sails the sea and takes other vessels down. He is more cruel and intelligent than the land trolls that humans can outsmart. Humans can lure land trolls into sunlight where they are turned into stone, a common theme in many fairy tales. The different char-acter of Draugen and land trolls can symbolize the human degree of control with seascape and landscape, respectively. Draugen also directs his viciousness to-ward men only and the character may, as suggested by Hauan (1995), tell about men's mastering of their ac-tivities at sea.

Comparing land and sea, the seascape appears as an opposition to land. But to its daily users the sea is much more. It is movement, action, purpose, and inter-action—between people *and* the sea as well as among the people *at* the sea. The conceptualizations of both landscapes and seascapes are experiential and con-ceptual constructs, as cultural experience and percep-tions form their descriptions. The concept "seascape" and the cultural elements it contains, however, are highly invisible and scarcely described. In Norwegian we talk of landscapes (*landskap*) but do not have an equiva-lent term for seascapes (ie: *sjøskap*). "Seascape" is also rarely used in the scientific discourse, to say nothing about heritage- and land-preservation literature. With the growth of the sport diving industry in the 1950s grew the Norwegian concern for the submerged mari-time cultural history as the divers brought several valu-able items on shore, as well as made important discov-eries that were later excavated by marine archaeolo-gists (Nævestad 1992). Cultural history, however, even maritime, does not capture the cultural elements of the seascape that I will address here. Borrowing from the growing body of literature focusing on cultural or ethnographic landscapes (see most recent reviews: Buggey 1999; 2000; this volume), I will look at seascapes in terms of the *everyday practice* of small-scale fishermen. Buggey (2000) proposes a definition for Aboriginal cultural landscapes as places "valued by an Aboriginal group (or groups) because of their long and complex relationship with that land. . . . It embodies their traditional knowledge of spirits, places, land uses and ecology." Rather than focusing on archaeological sites in the seascape, and seeing the seascape only as an opposition to the landscape, I will conceptualize the seascape as I have learned it from my study of small-scale fishing practices in the north of Norway.

Cultural seascapes make up a large part of the human environment, particularly in northern areas, where many groups traditionally made and still make their living by fishing and/or marine hunting. There are different perceptions of landscapes and, similarly, there are many varying visions of seascapes. Since I have studied small-scale fisheries I will focus on the knowledge of the seascape that local small-scale fishermen use in their daily activities. I will present various characteristics of a cultural seascape, as it functions in the minds and daily life of small-scale fishery experts in Northern Norway. More specifically, I will focus on cultural seascapes created and maintained by the small-scale, shore-based, traditional fisheries in Troms and Finnmark, the two northernmost counties of Norway (see map in Holand, this volume). By small-scale fishery, I refer to those fishermen using vessels less than thirteen meters (about forty-three feet) long. These characteristics form the point of departure for my following discussion on how northern seascapes could be managed in the present Norwegian resource management framework.

The data used in this paper were collected during several long-term studies of small-scale coastal fishing in Troms and Finnmark conducted over a twelve-year period. These counties hold around forty percent of the nation's small-scale fishing vessels (Maurstad 1997). The data were collected intermittently since 1989 through participant observation and unstructured open-ended interviews with fishermen, in addition to my personal first-hand experience in small-scale commercial fishing for a full year (see Acknowledgements, below).

Basic Features of Northern Norway Seascape

Finnmark and Troms counties cover an area of 75,000 square kilometers (30,000 square miles) and have a combined population of 225,000. Most people live on the coast in small towns and shore villages, as the area has few cities (the biggest local city, Tromsø, had a population of 60,000 in the year 2000). The fishing villages in Northern Norway are mostly scattered along the coast and on offshore islands. In some places, the distance between neighboring villages is quite large; in others, one can find five villages within a range of 150 kilometers (93 miles). Some villages have five active fishermen; others have twenty. Very few are larger.

Although Northern Norway coastal seascapes are located above the Arctic Circle (between 68° N and 71°N), the warm Gulf Stream maintains a water temperature that supports extremely rich marine resources. Also surface temperatures along the coast are quite mild: -2° C (28.4° F) is an average for the winter months. Besides the traditional two or three winter storms, winds normally range between the strengths of a gale and a breeze. A gale of twelve knots or more makes fishing difficult, and local fishermen normally do not fish in such weather conditions.

The topographic conditions of the area favor fishing. The coastal seascape consists of open waters off the barren, mostly rocky, coast. Small bays, numerous islands and islets, and large and small fjords often break several miles into the country. The water of the coastal seascape can be as deep as 500 meters (270 fathoms). Some fish species stay in the area year round whereas others migrate for a certain season for spawning or feed-

92/ The fishing village Kjøllefjord, Finnmark, northern Norway, is an important bay for small scale fishermen from all over Norway traveling to the seasonal cod-fishery in spring.

ing. Both the fjords and the open coast are used for fishing. Fishing depths depend on the species and the gear at hand, and can take place in shallow waters with a depth of twenty meters (65 feet) or more, as well as in the very deepest waters.

The northeast arctic cod stock, which migrates to the coast twice a year, is the basis of the coastal fisheries' sustainability in northern Norway. In early winter months, the bigger cod comes from the Barents Sea to spawn. The bulk of the cod swims for the spawning grounds off Lofoten Islands, providing fishermen along its main migration route, as well as in Lofoten, with good fishing opportunities. In early spring, a smaller sized cod arrives at its feeding grounds off the coast of Finnmark. Many small-scale fishermen fish in their home waters throughout the year, but some travel to the Lofoten Islands fisheries in early winter, or to the more northerly Finnmark fisheries in spring (Fig. 92). This pattern follows a traditional cycle of seasonal movement and activities that has long been followed in peasant coastal fisheries off northern Norway. Other migrat-

ing resources include haddock, saithe, and herring; these also provide local fishermen with good seasonal opportunities. In addition there are smaller local cod stocks and other local resources, such as halibut, flounder, redfish, cusk, monkfish, wolf-fish, and lumpfish.

Although rich, the ecology of the northern Norway seascape has changed during the last fifty years. While my mother and older cousins could once sit on a rock on the shore and catch fish using a bent needle and some sewing thread, there is neither the same amount of fish along the shore, nor is it that easy to catch anymore. The basic technology is still simple: gill netting, jigging, and baited long lines form the three most common traditional gear types. Newer fishing gear, such as purse seining, is increasing rapidly, particularly after the catch quotas were introduced in 1990. As quotas are maximum allowances, time has become a critical factor and many see the purse seine as the most efficient method in getting the quota on board the vessel quickly (Maurstad 2000a).

Fishing sometimes takes place in near shore waters, almost at people's doorsteps (Fig. 93). In the fjords, one can often fish fifty to one-hundred meters (160 to 325 feet) from the shore. Along the open coast, small boats usually fish farther away, four to six nautical miles off the coast. In a few places, the shore-based fishing extends up to twelve nautical miles. Larger vessels occasionally use these waters as well; so, conflicts arise from time to time. Small-scale fishermen usually insist that since larger vessels are capable of using more distant offshore waters, they should do so and leave the inshore waters to the local fishermen.

The smaller vessels are also very efficient and capable. Most full-time fishermen now operate fully equipped vessels with modern technology such as Global Positioning System (GPS), radars, echo sounders, and jigging machines. Today, an experienced person can easily master a fishing vessel of thirty-five feet; and if the fishery is good, the vessel can very well provide a living for two. In recent years, quotas have pushed fishermen more towards individually operated boats. It is the boat that holds the catch quota and sharing it with a crew has become economically unfavorable (Maurstad 2000a).

It is the men who catch the fish. Of the total Norwegian fishermen population of 20,000, only two percent are women. Women who are engaged in fishing do it either with their male relatives, usually husbands or fathers, in small boats, or as factory workers on board larger fishing vessels (Munk-Madsen 1998).

No official Norwegian statistics cover small-scale fishermen; but according to my estimates (Maurstad 1997), the total Norwegian small-scale fleet in 1996 consisted of some 5,600 boats. These small vessels are most numerous along the northern shore. They make up eighty percent of the total Norwegian cod fishing fleet by number, and they catch around twenty percent of commercially important cod species. The Troms and Finnmark small-scale fleet counted 2,200 vessels in 1996; those caught around 30,000 tons of cod that year.

As for training, no school has taught the fishermen their knowledge. Like the common practice among previous generations, today's fishermen learn their craft from each other, mostly from their fathers and uncles. Through growing up in a fishing culture, boys normally acquire skills in navigation and dealing with the sea through their play. Young boys are often taken on an occasional fishing trip at the age of ten and even younger, and they become full-time fishermen in their early teens. Of course, this is mostly true for the senior generation of today's fishermen. Present-day children now attend school until age sixteen or mostly eighteen with their schoolwork occupying more of their time. Recently, some type of formal education in the form of craft certificates has been established, but very few local fishermen have these certificates. Hence, the training to become a fisherman is still first and foremost informal.

Fishermen's Knowledge of the Seascape

Fishermen need basic knowledge on where and how to find fish, how to get there and come back safely, what tools to use, and how to use them. This has to be done in a safe manner, as the sea is a moving floor and every operation has to be carefully performed. The complex knowledge surrounding this particular use of the seascape is hard to comprehend and visualize. If we were to follow a fisherman on a fishing trip with a silent movie camera we would understand only a small portion of what fishermen do to make their living. We would see a fisherman leave his house around three or four in the morning, board his ship, and sail out to sea. At some point he would cut back his engine. We would see him remove a buoy from the sea and start hauling his nets or his longline. Hauling the gear, he would pick off the fish as it enters the boat. When done, he would run the engine for a while, then suddenly stop it, and throw the gear back into the sea. Then he would start the same procedure at another buoy in a different place. If he were jigging, the same procedures occur; the only difference is that there would be no buoy to mark where to start.

93/ *Small-scale fishing in the near-shore seascape of Lyngenfjord, northern Norway.*

This silent movie is quite illustrative to an outsider's perspective on what fishermen do. What I aim at here is to "subtitle" the silent movie, that is, focus on aspects that represent critical components of fishermen's knowledge of the seascape. I will organize my description as follows: First, I will talk of the *vertical* and *horizontal* dimensions in space as fishermen's knowledge relates both to what is located under the water surface and how to move across that surface. Furthermore, there is a *time* dimension that organizes activities as well as *regional* and *local* dimensions, since fishermen use various sections of the sea at various times during the year. As both competition and cooperation characterize the fishery, and as fishermen acquire knowledge from each other, the *relational* dimension is another important component of the seascape. Finally, since it is mostly men who fish, I will also talk of a *gender* dimension in the cultural seascape.

Vertical Dimension: Catching Fish

When the fisherman sets his gear into the sea, the assumption is that the gear will catch the fish. Actually, when it comes to the gear used by small-scale fishermen, it is the other way around. Gill nets, long lines, and various hook-and-line devices are all called "passive gear," since their success in fishing depends on the fish finding the gear at the right time and in the right place. Using passive gears implies that the fisherman must know how to *make* the fish find his gear. In other words, he must know precisely (more or less) the location of the fish he is after on every trip.

The fisherman knows a lot about the sea floor, as well as the many characteristics of the body of salt water between the sea floor and his vessel. The sea floor is basically flat ground, a depth or a slope, and its shape is often expressed in the fishermen's names of places in the seascape. There are flat grounds such as

Ole-Nilsa-grunnen, Paalsgrunnen—compounds from people's first names plus the word floor—and *Lodde-grunnen*, and *Nisegrunnen*—compounds refering to certain species that inhabit the sea, capelin and porpoise respectively. There are rocky grounds such as *Rakkenes-skallen* and *Steinskolten; Rakkenes* is a common place-name, and often place-names at sea have their counter-parts ashore—the fishing site's location is in relation to known land marks. There are depths known as *Søyla* and slopes known as *Leitbakken*. The names *Stein* and *Søyla* describe physical features of the bottom: it is rocky and/or shaped as a gauge, respectively. The meaning of *Leitbakken* refers to the technology commonly used at this fishing site; *leit* means search, so here jig-ging—searching the sea for fish with a hook and line—is implied (Hovda 1961).

As with landscapes, there are far more local names in the oral history of places than there are to be found on charts. Although the use of GPS, a satellite-based system that can pinpoint the exact location of its owner by coordinates of latitude and longitude, has become more common, fishermen still know and use the sea-scape place-names. As they start fishing, they learn not only the place-names, but also their location by land-scape coordinates. Thus, fishing places are embedded in a rich cultural history of the area, where one has to know the names of mountains, valleys, points, or other special characteristics of the landscape in order to orient oneself in the seascape. One fisherman ex-plained to me that he realized the relevance of this knowledge only when he tried to teach his brother-in-law some good fishing sites. As his brother-in-law had grown up elsewhere, he first had to learn the names of the mountains in the new area before learning the names of the fishing places, thus making the teaching process last longer than usual. The fisherman also com-plained about other fishermen's increasingly using GPS-coordinates instead of names. He himself was operat-ing a vessel without this technology; and when he asked where other fishermen had been that day, they re-sponded by citing their GPS-positions. "Give me a break,"

he said, "use the names of the places. I don't know where 69.48.389 N and 017.40.211 E is!"

There are more good reasons for fishermen to keep using the place-names, as many names are valuable concepts that hold information about different species. Different fish species stay at different places at sea. Hence, the name *Karibakken* (the slope of Kari) tells that this is a slope where cod is likely to stay. Redfish stays in the depths; cod stays along the slopes to shal-lower depths during the spawning season; and the fast-moving saithe tends to accumulate in places character-ized by strong currents, like around the points. But whether he knows the names or not, the fisherman who enters a seascape unknown to him can assess the sea-scape for good sites of saithe, cod, redfish, lumpfish, and so on by a variety of different approaches:

> He can look at the sea chart to check the depth conditions;
>
> He can check the coastal landscape in search of any points where the fish is likely to occur;
>
> He can listen to the boat radio to hear where other boats are fishing;
>
> He can talk to friends in the fishery in order to learn what they have caught at various places;
>
> He can gain personal experience, that is, drop his gear into the sea, following the assessment men-tioned above and, thus, get more information about the place.

Most fishermen, however, use areas they know and fish in places that are known to provide certain resources. In those areas they do not use maps, as they fish in places that they have used throughout their long fish-ing career and/or have learned about from their fa-thers.

A wealth of accumulated ecological knowledge is used in the fishery. For many species, fishermen know their local migration routes. Fishermen from any par-ticular fjord, for instance, can describe how the cod enters the fjord some time in March, swims in on the eastern side of the fjord, and that it takes three weeks for the cod to come to the village where they live. Then, they would be able to fish it for another two weeks, until it spawns and swims out.

An example of other local knowledge is that in the cusk (of the codfish family) fishery fishermen say that they cannot use one area for longer than, perhaps, two weeks in a row. The fish "fishes itself up," they say, and the area needs to rest for a while. Fishermen then exploit another place for a couple of weeks before returning to the first site again, after the fish has recovered. This local ecological dynamic was argued by local coastal fishermen as imperative to understanding the effect of automatic long-line boats' exploitation of the local areas. The fishermen maintained that after the long-liners' use, it took a month or more before the fish stock recovered; sometimes the season was off completely for the small-scale fishermen afterwards. The reason for the long-liners' longer exploitation of the area is that they have very effective gear; they can stay in the area with a lower profit rate than the small-scale fishermen could afford. The latter usually left when the return fell below seventy kilos (155 pounds) per tub of line, thus leaving the field at a higher fish concentration than did the automatic long-liners.

Another example of fishermen's ecological expertise is their knowledge about the nature of the sea floor. Not all places that hold fish are good fishing sites. Some places hold "slime eel" (Atlantic hagfish) that will eat fish trapped on gill nets and long-lines. The sea bottom also sets limits for gears: if it is rocky, gill nets will be damaged. This does not mean that the fishermen run home after their discovery, in order to change gear. Usually, the fishermen tend to use the gear they like the most. If they prefer gill netting, they develop their knowledge about favorable places for that kind of gear and vice versa. It does mean, however, that fishermen always benefit from an intricate knowledge of local seascapes. One fisherman claimed, for instance, that when the weather was bad and he could not go off the coast, he knew a small place where seven tubs of long-line could fit. This was also a site no large vessel could use or be able to find. It would be hard to access, because of its closeness to the shore;

and was not considered profitable for large vessels.

As such, fishermen have well-developed knowledge of local ecology, which in many aspects goes way beyond what scientists know (Maurstad and Sundet 1998). This should not come as a surprise as coastal resources have not been subject to detailed stock assessment research until recently. Concerning local cod, fishermen's knowledge has proved especially valuable. Norwegian cod stock assessments are based on the studies of two types of cod: the northeast arctic cod and the coastal cod. My interviews with fishermen, however, have supported recent research that argues that there are several local stocks of cod. This is important management knowledge. Local stock health may be different from that of the northeast arctic and the coastal cod stocks, thus implying the need for other, if not locally adapted, protective measures.

Fishermen themselves have for a long time talked of different types of cod, according to the specifics of cod's habitat, status, and age. Eythórsson (1993:136) discusses the local Sámi taxonomy in Lille Lerresfjord, Finnmark. Here fishermen talk of three fjord types of cod that are different from the northeast arctic cod: *tararunuk, vuotnaguolli* and *buoiddesguolli* (sea tangle cod, fjord cod and migrating cod). Fishermen that I interviewed had Norwegian names for the first two fjord types of cod, *taretorsk* and *fjord-torsk*. In addition, they talked of *blankfesk*, referring to the shiny look of a migratory cod. Some other categories included *gotfesk* (cod with roe), *gjeldfesk* (immature cod), *nikolaifesk* (cod that Nikolai used to fish in this territory), and *berlevågtorsk* (the local cod that is present near the community of Berlevåg, Finnmark).

A final comment concerning vertical aspects of fishermen's knowledge of seascape relates to technology. Fishermen know what technology to use for various areas, species, and seasons. As mentioned earlier, they often tend to favor one gear type over another; they often explain their choice of gear with reference to individual preferences. "I am not a hook and long-line guy" they say, or "I do not have a stomach for that tool." By this expression they mean that in jigging one has to move from place to place or have patience to wait at one place. While using gill nets or long-lines, they put the gear into the sea and haul it later. Temperament, experience, and skills developed with the use of one tool seem to decide what gear fishermen prefer. I should add here, however, that these choices were more relevant before the quota system was introduced in 1990. The quotas have changed many characteristics of the fishery, most importantly by forcing the fishermen to speed up their efforts (Maurstad 2000a). As quotas are maximum allowances, and as it is important to catch out one's quota in order to be allowed a quota for the next year, the fishermen's choice of gear is now more a result of what is seen as profitable. For many this means continuing to operate tools they are most skilled at; but as new incentives are introduced, more and more fishermen see purse seining as an effective small-scale gear.

Horizontal Dimension: Traveling to a Fishing Site

Knowing the seascape, fishermen seldom use maps when they travel to their fishing places. Rather, they rely upon the seascape's three-dimensional, more visually complete counterpart, the coastal landscape. Mountains, valleys and other characteristics are navigational points as well as location signs marking where to go and where to fish. Although the use of GPS has become more common, the coastal landscape has not lost its critical value in marking the route. First, place-names that are parts of the landscape can be remembered better than just numbers. Second, moving through a coastal landscape gives you a sequence of the real journey: when you reach *Silda* (the Herring) you know you have come this far and that you have the long *Sørøysundet* (South Island Sound) to pass. Some time thereafter come the heavy streams of *Magerøysundet* (Meagre Island Sound). All the names along the route enable the fishermen to remember the trip and also some of its important characteristics, like the location of underwater reefs and sunken rocks. Although

sea charts are quite detailed, not all of the sunken rocks are marked. As a part of the knowledge I acquired while fishing from Tromsø to Finnmark, I still remember, some fifteen years later, several routes I once traveled. For example, as you enter the Meagre Island Sound, when the currents run strongly against you, by holding hard to the right side of the sound you would be able to run with a good current. But then you must beware of a sunken rock fifteen minutes or so into the sound. I would never have remembered that these events would occur in that sequence if they were presented as a configuration of numbers of the GPS locations. On the other hand, had I had a GPS at that time, I could have marked the places and stored it forever electronically. The GPS is therefore a good support, but rarely a full substitute to the fishermen's highly sensitive knowledge of places in the coastal land- and seascape.

To highlight more aspects of "horizontal" knowledge of the seascape, one has to remember that fishermen often travel by way of shortcuts. They know how to navigate between islands and sunken reefs on routes that the map does not mark. Newcomers have to travel the long way when they come on their own. When one follows a local fisherman, the trip to the shore may be considerably shorter.

Such shortcuts are especially good to know when the weather changes, since this can let you reach the harbor much faster. Knowledge of weather and how the various winds affect the local land- and seascape are also part of the fishermen's local expertise. A weather report on gales, for instance, may still enable fishing. The southeastern winds are often tamed by the landscape, thus enabling the fisherman to find places to fish, or find refuge if that is necessary (Fig. 94).

While speaking of safety, I should also mention that fishermen often travel across a seascape with a partner. "Comrade-vessels" is an established concept and comrade-vessels often go together for longer distances, for example, to and from the fishing areas of Lofoten Islands or Finnmark. They often also fish to-

94/ Sudden weather changes challenges the fisherman, though intricate knowledge on wind performance in the local seascape may still provide the fisherman with fishing opportunities.

gether, providing safety by looking out for each other. Other safety issues, such as the careful handling of machinery, apply to many professions besides fishermen. What is special in dealing with the seascape is that it provides a moving floor for the operations. Accidents do happen. If the fisherman slips while pulling the nets, he can get caught in the capstan. That may lead to a broken arm or, in the worst case, to one being stuck, and having no way to get to the radio and call for help.

Another dangerous operation is when the fishing gear and lines go overboard. The fisherman may get trapped in a loop, an event that will throw him overboard immediately. To avoid this the fisherman must be alert, always, of where his feet are. He should try to plant them down safely before setting the gear and not move them before the operation is over.

Naturally, there are safety issues related to weather. The stronger the wind, the more stress is put on a fisherman to be careful and on alert. The wind is but one aspect of the fishing trip. Currents are as important both for setting the gear and for moving through the seascape. There are areas that are quite strenuous to pass if the wind and currents run against each other. But currents can also help one to move. Small-scale vessels normally run at a speed of seven to ten nautical miles per hour; and running with the tide will make a difference of, perhaps, one mile an hour. Traveling from Tromsø to the seasonal Finnmark fishery, on a trip that normally takes a day and a night, a fisherman's local knowledge tells him that departing when the high water mark has sunk one foot in Tromsø provides a good current for the first part of the trip.

As such, fishermen share a vast body of knowledge on the routes between areas of the seascape. Weather conditions, underwater stones and rocks, special currents, and so on, form the image of the seascape and are the imprints that fishermen store in their memory. Having traveled the route before or traveling with a comrade-vessel, they can memorize the whole trip, they can plan when to be alert or when they may have time to boil coffee. Traveling from Tromsø to the Finnmark fishery, for instance, there is a rough bit of sea some six to seven hours after one's departure that lasts for an hour or so. Then all loose equipment on the vessel should be fully secured. Thereafter comes some four hours of shielded sea, where one can turn on the autopilot and make pots of coffee or even dinner as one wishes.

Regional/Local Dimension: Multiple Seascapes

Another critical feature of fishermen's knowledge of the seascape is that fishermen normally know many seascapes. Of course, they know best the area they fish, and that may not necessarily be in their home area. As most of the fishermen also partake in fisheries in Lofoten and Finnmark, they usually develop detailed knowledge of the seascapes that are far from their hometowns. One man I interviewed had used the same Lofoten fishing area for fifty years. He had an extremely detailed knowledge of this area, as well as of the area where he had grown up.

Fishermen's knowledge is, thus, both regional and local. There are general aspects in the fishermen's knowledge that apply everywhere—like which gear to use and how. Such knowledge refers to depths, grounds, and slopes all over the North. Experience acquired from years of fishing on a small boat also has a fairly universal application. But there are aspects of seascape knowledge that apply only in a local setting, like the above-mentioned story of a local fisherman who could fit seven tubs of long-lines at a particular site, where no other gear could be used.

Time Dimension

Currents vary with time, that is, with the tide; and fishermen travel in sync with currents and tides. As mentioned, the tide will help to increase the speed of the journey as well as to make the journey less troublesome or dangerous, as there are areas at sea that can be quite unpleasant if the wind and the current work against each other.

Time is also important in deciding when to fish. If the currents run strong one could be at the right location, but the gear may not be effective when it reaches the bottom. It could be tangled due to the heavy current, or the meshes could be folded together, thus preventing the fish from entering the net. Therefore, not only does the fisherman have to know the strength of the current, but he also has to know its direction to ensure good placement of the fishing gear at sea.

Fish behavior also varies with time, as the stock goes through various cycles during the year. Fish feed and spawn in different seasons, and their presence in local waters depends on these cycles. A combination of moon phases and tides is of special importance. For herring, especially, the moon cycles are critical to follow, as the herring fishery is reportedly the best around the full moon. For other species, fishermen also refer to how the fishery fluctuates with the moon cycles. They also know what biology and biological changes occur throughout the year, so that they can record the distribution of various species in time and space for almost every month. They also know how to exploit those species, the most efficient gear types to employ, and the best species to fish in a certain season or month of the year.

Relational Dimension

I have already mentioned how the fishermen acquire their knowledge. Usually, they learn from male mentors, such as fathers and uncles, through both play and direct teaching. They also learn continuously from each other. They talk by radio on their vessels, in the harbor when they deliver their catch, and at home by calling each other on the phone. Although fishermen talk constantly about fishing, this is not a free flow of information. Knowledge of good fishing sites is an important production asset, and thus it often remains confidential to individual fishermen or within the local community of fishermen. Fishermen share information in a rather selective way. Newcomers often complain that coming to a new place and asking local fishermen where to go produces few clear answers. Only after they fish in the harbor for a while, proving themselves as "worthy," will the door to local knowledge open. The notion "worthy" is mine, but it encompasses certain personal qualities that fishermen value among themselves, such as being good at catching fish and being knowledgeable and respectful with regard to informal rules and regulations.

This way of communication can be ascribed to the fact that fishing is both a competition and involves cooperation (Bjørnå 1993). Fishermen need each other as colleagues both for the purpose of information and in case they need help. They also compete over resources and space, so that they would like to know more about a competitor before dealing with him in any close manner.

Thus, informal codes of conduct shape the rules of behavior in the seascape. There are also access regulations to abide by. Local fishermen tend to be the prime users of the home area. A newcomer who tries to access the best local sites will meet sanctions, such as having his gill nets or other gear damaged. Most newcomers know this; when accessing a new area, they normally exploit places that locals do not use (Maurstad 1997).

Newcomers often have some sort of relation to the locals before entering a new area, especially a fjord or a small fishing village involved in gill netting. Knowledge of people is a prerequisite in the use of the seascape and people usually know each other over long distances. Fishermen may talk about how they know

so and so, when they prepare to go to a new place to fish. The relationship to people in the area will help one be accepted among local fishermen, as well as learn something about the local fishing sites. As this knowledge is not found in any book, one must talk to people in order to learn about a new area. Being granted access to the local knowledge network is always easier when there are friend or family bonds to activate.

Another relational element operating in the seascape is that fishing crews often consist of relatives, such as brothers, brother-in-laws, or fathers and sons. Relatives are considered worthy of sharing competitive advantages, such as production secrets on fishing sites. Kin-based organization of crews also offers certain economic advantages. A father—who usually has low debts based on his long work experience and age—may leave the vessel for part of the year when fishing is not as good, thus allowing his sons to share the income. The sharing of the catch is regulated by standards set by the Fishermen's Association; but often these standards are not followed strictly when close relatives man the vessel.

Gender Dimension

It is mostly men who work the coastal waters of northern Norway, and therefore the knowledge related to the seascape is mostly a male knowledge. The seascape is a man's world, a part of men's culture, whereas women spend more of their time in the cultural *landscape*. The village looks different to men and women. Men usually see it twice a day from the sea, when going to and coming from fishing. Women, although they sometimes go out with their men, mostly see the village from within, by walking the ground in the course of their daily activities. Similarly, they see the sea from the village, while men see it from *being* on it. This provides unequal frames of reference for the perception of the seascape by men and women.

But men and women do share each other's worlds. Several researchers have referred to the valuable work that women do in relation to the fishery (Davis and

Nadel-Klein 1988). Gerrard (1983) names women as the "ground crew" of the fishing vessels. Their ground crew tasks include equipping the vessel, taking care of the fishermen's clothes, cleaning, baiting longlines, and so on. Although women still perform such jobs, today it has become common that women have their own careers. That leaves less time for women to provide ground support to the men in the fisheries (Jentoft 1989). Davis's recent work in Newfoundland illustrates that although women's roles are changing in ways that undermine the harmony of gender relations, women still remain committed to raising their families in coastal communities (Davis 2000).

Gender perspectives are also relevant with regard to the socialization of children in coastal villages. Boys and girls live and grow up in different worlds. They obtain different perspectives on the seascape very early. On visiting a fishing harbor, one may often find boys playing in racing speedboats with outboard engines. Few girls do this, and those who do take on the status of a "tomboy." Feminist researchers have advocated that many women want to fish, but that they face institutional and cultural barriers. Overcoming those barriers by providing, for instance, easier access to the fishing quotas for women is seen as one way to include more women in the seascape (Munk-Madsen 1998). Today girls, more than boys, tend to leave their villages for schools. Stimulating women to enter the fishery is also thought to help recruitment to the remote fishing villages.

A Jack of all Trades

By focusing on the fishermen's knowledge, I have thus far reviewed some issues that are directly linked to the use of the seascape. A full description of the fishermen's knowledge, however, should include a much broader range of issues and activities that are crucial to the fishermen's success. Fishing is a multi-faceted task, and every fisherman performs many other jobs that are not directly related to fishing. Administrative work is one such aspect, as a fisherman has to administer his boat,

his crew, the shares, and so on. He also markets his fish: while the boat is at the fishing site, a fish buyer calls with a request for a certain species and a deal is set. While going to and from the site, he cooks breakfast and dinner. Hence, the fisherman is a cook. There is also constant education. As the fisherman listens to the radio and talks with others on the mobile phone, he constantly educates himself, as well as plans the next set of operations. While at sea, things may break down; so, the fisherman must do maintenance, repair machinery and so on. Finally, there is personnel management, security management, and political work, not to forget being a family man. Often while at sea, the fisherman talks with his wife and family.

The fisherman is definitely a jack-of-all-trades; and many aspects of his activities, though not related directly, are nevertheless important components of cultural seascapes. It is this manifold nature of seascape that holds all other activities together.

Current Status of Coastal Fisheries in Northern Norway

Coastal fishermen in Norway have been politically strong, especially during the last century, when considerable institutional protection was built to preserve their way of living. For example, as the trawler technology developed in the late nineteenth century, England, Scotland, and Germany had some 1,500-steam trawlers at the turn of the nineteenth to twentieth century (Christensen 1991). But in Norway, as in Canada, the coastal fishermen's opposition halted the development of the trawler technology (Apostle et al. 1998). The Norwegian authorities passed several acts in support of the coastal fishermen's interests. As a result, as late as the 1920s and 1930s, when the international trawler fleet had expanded tremendously, Norwegian trawlers still counted less than twenty (Sagdahl 1982).

After World War II, however, freezing technology and industrialization were seen as having a promising future. A process of modernization and industrialization for the Norwegian northern fisheries was started, this time initiated by the government authorities. Eventually, the Norwegian trawler fleet expanded, but not as much as the authorities wanted it to. Coastal fishermen rejected working on the trawlers, and they did not follow resettlement programs advanced by the Norwegian government after World War II. Upon its retreat from northern Norway, the German Army burned to the ground nearly all houses and public buildings in Northern Troms and Finnmark counties. In rebuilding the region, the Norwegian authorities aimed to relocate people from their traditional coastal communities. They wanted to centralize the settlement, but people rejected such a development. Local residents just wanted to rebuild their individual houses in remote coastal areas and on the islands (Brox 1966).

Thus, the post-World War II modernization programs did not succeed as planned. Instead, an extensive local infrastructure of roads, electricity, and public services was built around Norwegian coastal fisheries. Even though this infrastructure is now scaled down, the coastal fishing culture is still living side by side with the industrial fishing culture. Coastal fisheries do enjoy political support. They are seen as the social and economic backbone of the many coastal communities, whereas employment and settlement in the North are still considered national political goals. But coastal fishermen face harder conditions since the introduction of individual catch quotas and new access rules in 1990. As a result, there has been a steady decline in the number of active fishermen during the last decade. In 1986, there were 3,500 small-scale cod-fishing vessels in Troms and Finnmark counties altogether; only 2,200 were in business in 1996, ten years later (a reduction of thirty-seven percent). In terms of the overall catch, however, the reduction was only eleven percent. The reduction of the catch is probably moderated by the fact that the total Norwegian catch was thirty percent larger in 1996 compared to 1986. But another factor is as important: the new regulations provided the fishermen with new incentives to expand. As fishermen must fish their quota to be assigned future fishing rights, fisher-

men can no longer let individual needs decide their efforts. Rather, small-scale fishermen catches, which used to show great variation, are now more homogenous. One can say that while fishermen used to fish cod, they now strive to fish quotas (Maurstad 2000a).

Small-scale fishermen also compete over space and resources with other interests in the coastal zone. Of particular interest is that Norway is planning a huge increase in its fish farm production. The knowledge in the seascape depends on how it is used, as small-scale fishermen, large scale vessels, fish farming, tourism, and so on, set their different imprints on the seascape. If fishermen no longer use the area, the knowledge I have addressed here cannot be generated by other industries and will be lost.

Loss of knowledge can also result from elderly fishermen passing away, of poor or no recruitment of younger people into the fishery, or of village closure and abandonment. We can assume that a substantial wealth of knowledge on coastal seascapes is already gone, due to these factors. Although shifting modernization projects of the Norwegian governments have been halted by local residents' unwillingness to comply, the projects of the 1950s and 1960s did lead to substantial resettlement. In the latter decades, the national fisheries' infrastructure has also been scaled down. Several fish plants have been closed since the 1980s. Post offices and other public services were also reduced. Many smaller communities have been closed and/or abandoned along the northern coast of Norway. Some of the fishermen who have moved from their former residential places continue, however, to fish the areas off the coast of old villages where they were born. But since there is little recruitment of younger people, the stock of knowledge about local seascapes is decreasing with each year.

The coast is also a shipping lane. In recent years, there have been several shipwrecks in people's back yards, and many wrecked ships and boats are still lying there, causing a loss of the aesthetic value of both the seascape and the coastal landscape. There are plans for increased petroleum activity in northwest Russia, as well as plans to transport nuclear waste for treatment in Russia, causing concern about traditional fishing grounds being lost because of oil spills and nuclear contamination.

As such, there are several threats to the future small-scale fisheries and to the present knowledge of the seascape. The small-scale fishermen may be able to cope with these new challenges, however. Small-scale fishing is an intrinsic part of northern culture (Fig. 95). To many people, it is far more than a job or a seasonal occupation, and it will not disappear quickly and easily. This is its main source of strength. But it has been, and still is, an "invisible" type of activity in the sense that knowledge about small-scale fishing practices is not well disseminated and is poorly protected. The unexpected effects of the new regulations, for instance, must be seen as a result of the authorities' lack of knowledge about the small-scale fishery. Since the main problem the authorities had to deal with was a sudden shortage of fishing resources, it could not have been their intention to increase small-scale fishermen's efforts. Nor was there a need to, as the lack of profitability was not an issue among small-scale fishermen.

Preservation of Cultural Seascapes: Protecting the Invisible

As small-scale fishing practices remain all but invisible to the authorities, the same is even truer with regard to the knowledge related to the seascape. This knowledge is primarily unwritten, maintained through practice, and transferred orally between fishermen. That means that it is very hard for regulating authorities to understand, access, and implement this knowledge in their regulatory practices. More importantly, it means that a particular cultural seascape exists only as long as the particular knowledge about it is maintained within the user's community. When fishermen no longer use the seascape, it will turn back to a "sea wilderness"—an uncultured sea. The same applies to the seashore. When fishermen no longer use mountains and places along

the shore and on the seabed as reference points for their fishing and traveling, the knowledge about place-names, navigation, and local conditions is gone. The shore will become "wilderness" in the same way the unused seascape became the uncultured and unrecognized scenery that we observed earlier through a virtual silent movie camera. The question is, then, how to make the cultural seascape more visible.

Legal and General Framework for Protection of Seascapes

A range of recent international conventions stipulates that states shall codify in their national laws the need for the preservation and maintenance of indigenous and local knowledge that is important for sustainable use (Posey 1994). This is highly relevant to the protection of cultural seascapes; but to my knowledge, these laws and conventions have not been transformed into any specific policies or measures in the protection of the cultural seascape. The UNESCO Convention on the Protection of World Cultural and Natural Heritage of 1972 defines "cultural heritage" as monuments, groups of building or sites (Article 1), and "natural heritage" as areas important from a scientific or aesthetic point of view (Article 2). The proponents of protection of cultural landscapes argue that this current definition of protection neglects important cultural values. As defined by Buggey (2000), Aboriginal cultural landscapes embody traditional knowledge of spirits, places, land uses and ecology. The convention has not integrated these points. It hardly refers to any *knowledge* about the cultural landscape itself, related traditions, stories, myths, and so on. In light of its inadequacy for protecting cultural landscapes, the World Heritage Convention is also insufficient, in its present form, to protect cultural seascapes.

Norwegian laws do take the issue of cultural landscape preservation into account. The Norwegian Conservation Act of 1970 (19 June, No 63), Article 5, allows for preserving "characteristic or beautiful . . . natural or cultural landscapes." By specifically mentioning

95/ Small-scale fishing vessels resting in Tromsø on their way to the Finnmark fishery.

"cultural landscapes," the Norwegian Conservation Act seems to go further in protecting cultural values than the World Heritage Convention. However, most sites that are protected in Norway with reference to the Conservation Act are given their protected status because of their scenic or wilderness value. Bans on hunting formerly overexploited bird populations, such as puffins and eiders, have long been in place. In more recent years, there has been a concerted effort to create coastal marine reserves to protect bird nesting areas. Although it is important to protect the natural resources of the seascape, as well as to see the seascape itself as nature, those are certainly not the most important values to be considered in cultural seascape preservation. Thus, the Norwegian Conservation Act is also an insufficient tool for protecting cultural seascapes.

The Norwegian Cultural Inheritance Act of 1978 (9

June, No. 50) sounds more promising. Cultural inheritance is defined as "all traces of human activity in the physical environment, including places that embed historical happenings, belief or tradition" (Article 2) and some aspects of fishing culture could certainly find protection within these frames. However, the management practice with reference to the Cultural Inheritance Act has been to protect items in the seascape such as sunken vessels, as well as other single findings of archaeological importance. As I have argued, protection of cultural seascapes involves more than protecting monuments and archaeological sites. It involves the protection of immaterial objects such as the knowledge in the everyday practices of fishermen. Should the Cultural Inheritance Act be of use to the protection of cultural seascapes, the awareness of what is the cultural seascape must be broadened. In fact, any protection of cultural seascapes will first and foremost depend on an *awareness* of cultural seascapes. Managers need an image of it first and second a will to manage. This hypothesis applies not only to managers. Fishermen also need a different image of the seascape. They know the sea through their practices, but they do not talk of cultural seascapes. As I mentioned earlier, there is not even a Norwegian word for seascape. No wonder then, that the cultural seascape lacks protection in the existing legal framework. But this situation could be changed.

During the last decade, Norway has demonstrated a growing focus on the planning and regulation of development in the coastal zone. The Planning and Zoning Act of 1985 (14 June, No. 77) was expanded in 1989 to include the sea within the straight base line. So far, this law is used mostly for development: it allows local municipalities to plan the use of the municipal sea-space, such as where to allocate sites for fish farms, recreational areas, industrial effluence, and so on. This law may provide a basis for developing an awareness of the cultural seascape for two reasons:

—The Planning and Zoning Act is in the making. Although established in 1989, planning in the northern coastal zone did not begin until the late 1990s, when Norway decided to increase her fish farm production. Today, there are ongoing debates on the law's future form and practice, and it should be possible to integrate the concept of the cultural seascape within the scope of this act and within the institutionalized practices of managers.

—Under the Planning and Zoning Act, the municipal governments seek knowledge on the current use of and various interests within seascapes under their authority. The law states that affected groups or individuals should be involved early in the planning process; and local fishermen are already invited to map out their fishing practices, especially fishing sites.

Thus, the fishermen, the main users of the seascape, have gotten new arenas for speaking of the seascape, thereby conceptualizing their practice for managers and a broader audience. This user approach in visualizing the seascape is especially important when it comes to managing cul-

tural seascapes, for reasons I will discuss below.

A Management Approach

Recently, scholars in the international resource management studies have taken a greater interest in local fishermen's knowledge. The key issue is whether such knowledge should be or will be integrated into mainstream fishery and biological research. The benefits of doing so are twofold. First, the fishermen's knowledge of local marine environment is supposed to improve scientific biological knowledge, upon which management recommendations are usually constructed. Second, local fishermen are regarded as being able to successfully negotiate the complex nature/culture relationship through their sustainable harvest (Coward et al. 2000; Durrenberger and King 2000; Dyer and McGoodwin 1994; Freeman and Carbyn 1988; Inglis 1993; Maurstad and Sundet 1998; Neis 1992; Neis and Felt 2000; Newell and Ommer 1998; Pinkerton 1989, 1999; Wilson et al. 1994).

In many case studies, fishermen are actively sought as consultants for their knowledge of specific issues that are critical to science and management. Scholars in the field of co-management argue, nevertheless, that fishermen should be more than just "consulted" and that it should be a real power-balance between fishermen and government agencies. Otherwise, fishermen may feel they are being "co-opted into [the] governments' convenience" (Pinkerton 1989:4). The process of co-management may be characterized by symbolic gestures and make-believe (Jentoft 2000); or—as I have argued elsewhere (Maurstad 2000b)—fishermen enter the process of cooperation by anticipating that they will be regarded as the Ph.D.s of the fishing grounds, whereas they are, in fact, treated merely as research assistants to the biologists.

These perspectives are especially relevant when talking about seascapes. As mentioned earlier, the fishermen's knowledge of fishing sites and how to use them may be seen as production secrets. The knowledge held by an individual fisherman may offer him a competitive advantage over other local fishermen. In the same way, the seascape knowledge of one community of fishermen may provide competitive advantages over other neighboring communities. These days, there is no legal protection for such secrets. There exists a vague set of informal rules that guide access to the knowledge and the right to use this knowledge locally. The knowledge is oral, and fishermen disseminate it to others when they find them worthy. Knowledge has a meaning in a certain social context and as a part of a specific social activity. Revealing fishing sites in a book, or in any other written and published form, does have the potential of changing the informal rules of the fishery. This is because the book interferes with the process of transmission of knowledge and with the existing rules of the game. Acquiring fishing knowledge from a book—ready to buy in the bookstore and available to everyone—is a completely new way of gaining local fishing information. One does not have to prove oneself worthy and to perform according to culturally defined standards before reading a book on fishing sites. When knowledge is accessible through the book, the obligations toward those who originally possessed and shared that knowledge may become less strict and valid, and, perhaps, even totally absent (Maurstad 2002).

The consequences of publicizing the fishermen's knowledge pose an obvious dilemma when it comes to visualizing the knowledge of the seascape. In the course of coastal development, various interests need to be clarified and, if fishermen do not speak out, they may become more invisible and peripheral than they are today. If they do decide to speak out, they may lose access to certain fishing sites, as various competitors can use that knowledge to their own advantage. In Maurstad (2002), I discuss the various solutions to the dilemma of documenting valuable knowledge on the seascape and, at the same time, protecting the production assets of individual fishermen. I conclude that the most valuable lesson to learn is that the relationship

between fishermen and managers must change character. Fishermen must be more than consulted. They should be actively engaged in cooperative approaches to management. They should politicize their knowledge and meet in arenas for discussions on first what is their knowledge of the seascape; second on how can it be used; and third, used by whom.

Researchers also play a role. Apart from their general role in understanding, documenting, and describing various aspects of the management process, researchers can help facilitate the process of mapping fishermen's knowledge. As Tobias (2000) illustrates, in citing many mapping projects in Canada, where indigenous people were involved in mapping landscapes as proof of their physical occupation in order to be used as evidence in court cases, good research methods are crucial. Indigenous peoples, when defending their issues in court, have learned that having no data is even better than having poor data. Methodology is also an issue when it comes to presenting knowledge on the seascape. Since there are many users in the coastal zone, conflicts over space abound; and good mapping projects become crucial to the legitimacy of fishermen's rights to and knowledge of the seascape.

Scientists' performance, however, raises a whole set of other debates. Since fishermen's knowledge of the seascape is oral and orally transmitted, moving knowledge from the oral sphere to the written will definitely influence the knowledge in ways we do not know and with consequences we cannot anticipate at the moment (Maurstad 2002). Furthermore, science is not just an objective reporter of knowledge. When science helps in conceptualizing the seascape, it also helps in creating it (Maurstad 2000b; Holm 2003). The cooperative approach mentioned above between fishermen and managers should also include scientists, but it is important that fishermen become more than research assistants to scientists and managers. The problems of defining what is the cultural seascape, who can access the knowledge about it, and how it should be protected will not be solved immediately by empowering fishermen's positions. Nor would we easily gain an understanding of the consequences of writing down oral culture. Integrating fishermen in cooperative approaches to management and knowledge production, would, however, enable more qualified discussion, as well as give fishermen a say in these important issues of their prime concern.

Another consideration when attempting to integrate fishermen into the debate over how to protect the sea is that most local inhabitants, including fishermen, have mixed feelings toward the concept of "protection." Recent Protection plans have advanced various forms of protection of areas and resources that local inhabitants have traditionally exploited. Locals have seen these plans as a ground for cultural conflict; "educated" planners from the south come to the north "to protect the wilderness." Locals complain that the planners do not understand their cultural use of resources and places (Sandersen 1996). Fishermen do consider themselves worthy of protection because of the economic value of their small-scale fisheries, as well as their cultural role in preserving Norwegian folk traditions. They maintain that they protect nature better through their use of nature than when there is *no* use of nature. When they use the landscape (or seascape), they act as its caretakers; but when no caretakers are in place, other interests may rob nature. Thus, local people will most probably meet the idea of protecting seascapes with little enthusiasm. The matter may be different when the issue is the protection of their fishing culture. Thus, including fishermen in the management may facilitate a new approach to the protection of seascape as something that is helpful to the fishermen's own culture.

The Norwegian Planning and Zoning Act of 1985 is a tool that could be developed for such purposes. Its focus is planning the use of—in my terms here—the seascape, and it states that users shall be involved in the process of planning. The important future issue is how the awareness of cultural seascapes develops, as well as where power to make decisions on protection is located. For now the law assigns but a consultant's

role to the users. Even the municipal governments have no real power in managing the sea; they can make plans for allocation of space, but the national and regional fishing authorities make resource management decisions while the national and regional environmental authorities decide what culture needs protection. Because protection of cultural seascapes is so closely linked to fishing activities, there are several dilemmas here. One is the power of local municipalities; currently, many municipalities face severe economic expenses and it is likely that they would hesitate to protect cultural seascapes should the protection involve rejecting development by other industries. Although local municipalities assumingly have the best knowledge of local seascapes, state governments may be a better facilitator of protection—provided of course that they develop the will to protect. The other dilemma relates to the divided sector interests mentioned above. Government agencies do not seem to agree on the issue of use or protection, neither on the national level nor on the regional level. Regarding coastal zone plans, the County Fisheries Director can object to the municipal plans with reference to a range of Norwegian laws besides the Planning and Zoning Act of 1985. So, also, can the County Governor object to their plans. Osland (2001), who has worked in the bureaucracy of managing fish farming for fifteen years, says that the municipalities often feel that the higher government bodies use the planning processes as arenas for their own fights over principles.

Real co-management then—one which balances use and protection, interests of various users and interests of various management bodies—is thus rather hard to accomplish. Regarding the protection of cultural seascapes, the Norwegian Planning and Zoning Act can assist in increasing awareness of cultural seascapes, since discussions on how to use the sea is already going on with reference to the law. In a later stage, when the issue is specifically which law should be responsible for protection of cultural seascapes, the relationship between this law and the Cultural Inheritance Act should be discussed further. In any case, both laws need be broadened: the Cultural Inheritance Act to include contemporary fishing culture and fishermen's knowledge of fishing activities in the seascape; and the Planning and Zoning Act to increase awareness of the cultural seascape.

Conclusion

A vast body of the fishermen's knowledge exists and is linked directly to the use of the sea. Fishermen know how to move through the seascape by way of reference points on the coastal landscape as well as in the seascape. They have knowledge of the sea floor that helps them navigate successfully. They also have knowledge of tides, currents, and winds—all invisible to the outsider or to a non-knowledgeable person.

Contrary to the common view, the value of the seascape is more than that it is picturesque. This is very similar to the role of the landscape, although far more elusive and difficult to document. As is so with landscapes, knowledge of the seascape is maintained almost exclusively via fishing activities, memories and oral stories, that is, via *cultural* modes of transmission. As such, it is priceless. Should the seascape transform into the "uncultured" sea, the knowledge about seascape is gone. Unlike historical landscapes, where certain information on the past can be extracted via archaeological excavations and/or from written sources, there is almost no way to restore the lost knowledge about cultural seascapes.

Moreover, this knowledge is useful far beyond the practical needs of the economy and social welfare of coastal fishing communities. It is also extremely useful to fishery science and management. This is another reason to talk about seascapes. Currently, it is landscapes that can gain protection; when such protected status is given, the preservation of landscape is primarily based upon certain historical, aesthetic, wilderness, or scientific reasons. There is a surprising lack of consciousness about seascapes, and that is especially so concerning *cultural* aspects of both land- and seascapes. Therefore, expanding the concept of -*scape* may increase awareness and help to draw attention to the relationship between human activity and natural environments, be it on the land or at sea.

Protecting seascapes is indeed a big challenge, since it is very much like protecting the invisible. To the majority of people, the special uses and values in the seascape remain unknown. While cultural landscapes are also mostly invisible, cultural seascapes are even more so, as seascapes lack any physical marks of human presence, and exist in human mind, memory, and knowledge only. Increased public consciousness about these parts of the world's cultural heritage is, thus, very important. Although landscapes, and even cultural landscapes, do have some protection under current Norwegian law, the awareness of the meaning of the sea seems to stop at the seashore. The ongoing coastal zone planning holds promise for changing this situation by the fact that it takes place locally, quite near the local seascapes and involves the users directly by allowing them to state their concerns. When these processes have developed more, the hope is that the border of awareness of what is the sea may be expanded.

Acknowledgements

First, I want to thank all the fishermen who willingly shared with me their knowledge of seascapes. They made writing this article possible. I am also grateful to the Norwegian Research Council for providing financial support for my earlier studies of small-scale fisheries in northern Norway. Last, but not least, I thank my colleagues, particularly Igor Krupnik, Terje Brantenberg, and Dona Lee Davis. Igor and Terje inspired me and provided much helpful advice during my research and writing, while Dona offered valuable comments for the final article. I am deeply grateful to these three for their constructive input.

References

Apostle, Richard, Gene Barrett, Petter Holm, Svein Jentoft, Leigh Mazany, Bonnie McCay and Knut Mikalsen
1998   *Community, State, and Market on the North Atlantic Rim: Challenges to Modernity in the Fisheries.* Toronto: University of Toronto Press.

Bjørnå, Hilde
1993   *Fra konkurranse til samarbeid. En studie av samhandling mellom fartøy på fiskefelt* (From competition to cooperation: A study of interactions among fishing vessels at fishing sites). Tromsø: Hovedfagsoppgave i Samfunnsvitenskap, Universitetet i Tromsø.

Brox, Ottar
1966   *Hva skjer i Nord-Norge? En studie i norsk utkantpolitikk* (What's happening in North Norway: A study of Norwegian rural politics). Oslo: Pax Forlag.

Buggey, Susan
1999   An Approach to Aboriginal Cultural Landscapes, HSMBC agenda paper 1999-10. See: *http:// parkscanada.pch.gc.ca/aborig/HSMBC/ hsmbc1_e.htm*
2000   An Approach to Aboriginal Cultural Landscapes, Definition of Aboriginal Cultural Landscapes *http:// parkscanada.pch.gc.ca/aborig/aborig20_e.htm*

Christensen, Pål
1991   En havenes forpester - et kjempestinkdyr. Om trålspørsmålet i Norge før 2. verdenskrig ("An ocean pest, a gigantic skunk": On the trawler issue in Norway before World War II). *Historisk Tidsskrift,* 70(4):622-35.

Coward, Harold, Rosemary Ommer and Tony Pitcher, eds.
2000   *Just Fish: Ethics and Canadian Marine Fisheries.* St. Johns, NF.: Institute of Social and Economic Research, Memorial University of Newfoundland.

Davis, Done Lee
2000   Gendered cultures of conflict and discontent. Living 'the crisis' in a Newfoundland community. *Women's Studies International Forum* 23(3):343-53.

Davis, Dona Lee and Jane Nadel-Klein
1988   To Work and to Weep: Women in Fishing Economies. *Social and Economic Papers* 18. St. John's, NF: Institute of Social and Economic Research, Memorial University of Newfoundland.

Durrenberger E. Paul and Thomas D. King, eds.
2000   *State and Community in Fisheries Management : Power, Policy, and Practice.* London: Bergin & Garvey.

Dyer Christopher L. and James R. McGoodwin, eds.
1994   *Folk Management in the World's Fisheries: Lessons for Modern Fisheries Management.* Boulder: University Press of Colorado.

Eythórsson, Einar
1993   Sami Fjord Fishermen and the State: Traditional Knowledge and Resource Management in Northern Norway. In *Traditional Ecological Knowledge: Concepts and Cases,* J. T. Inglis, ed., pp. 133-42. International Program on Traditional Ecological Knowledge/International Development Research Centre. Ottawa: Canadian Museum of Nature.

Freeman Milton M. R. and Ludwig N. Carbyn, eds.
1988   *Traditional Knowledge and Renewable Resource Management in Northern Regions.* Canadian Circumpolar Institute Occasional Publication No 23. Edmonton: University Of Alberta.

Gerrard, Siri
1983   Kvinner i fiskeridistrikter: Fiskerinæringas "bakkemannskap" (Woman in fishing areas: the "groundcrew" of the fishing industry)? In *Kan fiskerinæringa styres?* B. Hersoug, ed., pp. 217-41. Oslo: Novus Forlag A/S.

Hauan, Marit Anne
1995   Om å kappseile med Draugen. Naturmytiske vesen og mannsrollen i den nordnorske fiskerikulturen (Sailboat racing against Draugen: Mythic-natural creatures and the male role in northern Norwegian fishing culture). In *Mellom sagn og virkelighet,* M. A. Hauan and A. H. Bolstad Skjelbred, eds., pp. 49-61. Stabekk: Vett og Viten A/S, Stabekk.

Holm, Petter
2003   Crossing the Border: On the Relationship between Science and Fishermen's Knowledge in a Resource Management Context. *MAST* 2(1):5-49. Norwegian College of Fishery Science, Tromsø, Norway.

Hovda, Per
1961   *Norske Fiskeméd. Landsoversyn og to gamle médbøker* (Norwegian fishing *méd* [fishing ground identified via reference to landscape features]: National review and two old *méd* books). Stavanger, Oslo, Bergen, Tromsø: Universitetsforlaget.

Inglis, Julian T., ed.
1993   *Traditional Ecological Knowledge: Concepts and Cases.* International Program on Traditional Ecological Knowledge/International Development Research Centre. Ottawa: Canadian Museum of Nature.

Jentoft, Svein
1989   *Mor til rors. Organisering av dagligliv og yrkesaktivitet i fiskerfamilier* (Mother at the oars: Organizing daily life and occupational activity in fishing families). Tromsø: Norges Fiskerihøyskole.
2000   Co-managing the Coastal Zone: Is the Task Too Complex? *Ocean and Coastal Management* 43:527-35.

Maurstad, Anita
1997   *Sjarkfiske og ressursforvaltning: Avhandling for Dr. Scientgraden i Fiskerivitenskap* (Small-scall fishing and resource management:Doctoral Thesis in Fishery science). Tromsø: Norges Fiskerihøgskole, Universitetet i Tromsø.

2000a To Fish or Not to Fish - Small Scale Fishing and Changing Regulations of the Cod Fishery in Northern Norway. *Human Organization* 59(1):37–47.

2000b Trapped in Biology: An Interdisciplinary Attempt to Integrate Fish Harvesters' Knowledge into Norwegian Fisheries Management. In *Finding Our Sea Legs: Linking Fishery People and Their Knowledge with Science and Management.* B. Neis and L. Felt, eds., pp. 135–53. St John's: ISER, Memorial University of Newfoundland.

2002 Fishing in Murky Waters: Ethics and Politics of Research on Fisher Knowledge. *Marine Policy* 26:159–66.

Maurstad, Anita and Jan H. Sundet

1998 The Invisible Cod: Fishermen's and Scientist's Knowledge. In *Commons in Cold Climate: Reindeer Pastoralism and Coastal Fisheries.* S. Jentoft, ed., pp. 167–85. Casterton Hall: Parthenon Publishing.

Munk-Madsen, Eva

1998 The Norwegian Fishing Quota System: Another Patriarchal Construction? *Society and Natural Resources* 11:229–40.

Neis, Barbara

1992 Fishers' Ecological Knowledge and Stock Assessment in Newfoundland. *Newfoundland Studies* 8(2):155–78.

Neis, Barbara and Lawrence Felt, eds.

2000 *Finding Our Sea Legs: Linking Fishery People and their Knowledge with Science and Management.* St John's: ISER, Memorial University of Newfoundland.

Newell, Dianne and Rosemary E. Ommer

1998 *Fishing Places, Fishing People: Traditions and Issues in Canadian Small-Scale Fisheries.* Toronto: University of Toronto Press.

Nævestad, Dag

1992 *Kulturminner under vann* (Cultural heritage under water). FOK-programmets skriftserie nr. 1. Oslo: NAVFs program for forskning om kulturminnevern.

Osland, Anne B.

2001 Integrert kystsoneplanlegging : skjebnefelles-skap eller egnet verktøy for verdiskapning i kystsonen (Integrated coastal zone planning: our shared future, but it is a suitable tool for adding value to the coastal zone)? *Plan* 2:30–44.

Pinkerton, Evelyn, ed.

1989 *Co-operative Management of Local-Fisheries: New Directions for Improved Management and Community Development.* Vancouver: University of British Columbia Press.

1999 Factors in Overcoming Barriers to Implementing Co-management in British Columbia Salmon Fisheries. *Conservation Ecology* 3(2):2 ;[online] URL: *http://www.consecol.org/vol3/iss2/art2*

Posey, Darrell A.

1994 Traditional Resource Rights (TRR): de facto Self-determination for Indigenous Peoples. In *Voices of the Earth:: Indigenous Peoples, New Partners and the Right to Self-determination in Practice,* Leo van der Vlist, ed., pp. 217–40. The Netherlands: Utrecht International Books/The Netherlands Centre for Indigenous Peoples.

Sagdahl, Bjørn

1982 Struktur, organisasjon og innflytelsesforhold i norsk fiskeripolitikk (Structure, organization and influence in Norwegian fishery policy). In *Fiskeripolitikk og forvaltningsorganisasjon,* Knut H. Mikalsen and Bjørn Sagdahl, eds., pp. 15–47. Stavanger, Oslo, Bergen, Tromsø: Universitetsforlaget.

Sandersen, Håkan T.

1996 *Da kommunen gikk på havet – om kommunal planlegging i kystsonen* (When the community went to sea: On municipal planning in the coastal zone). NF-rapport nr.10/96. Bodø: Nordlandsforskning.

Tobias, Terry N.

2000 *Chief Kerry's Moose – a Guidebook to Land Use and Occupancy Mapping, Research Design and Data Collection.* A joint publication of the union of BC Indian Chiefs and Ecotrust Canada, Vancouver.

Wilson, James A., James M. Acheson, Mark Metcalfe and Peter Kleban

1994 Chaos, Complexity and Community Management of Fisheries. *Marine Policy* 18(4):291–305.

96/ Harry Simpson, a Dogrib elder, demonstrates how Dogrib chief Edzo used Big Rock, near Mesa Lake on the barrenlands, in the 1820s to hide his son and brother while he negotiated a lasting peace with Akaitcho, chief of the Yellowknives, their long-term enemies.

part 3

REGIONAL APPROACHES TO DOCUMENTATION AND PROTECTION

"The Land is Like a Book":

Cultural Landscapes Management in the Northwest Territories, Canada

THOMAS D. ANDREWS

To the Indian people our land is really our life. Without our land we . . . could no longer exist as people. (Richard Nerysoo, Fort McPherson, 1976—from Berger 1977:94).

On April 1, 1999, following nearly fifteen years of land claims negotiations, the map of northern Canada changed dramatically with the creation of the new territory of Nunavut. Nunavut—the homeland of Canada's Inuit—represents the transformation of a cultural landscape into a geopolitical landscape, where political self-sufficiency is now in the control of the Inuit themselves. In reality, two new territories were created: the new Nunavut, and a smaller Northwest Territories (NWT), largely forgotten in the glow of media interest in the creation of its newer sibling. If Nunavut represents the transformation of a cultural landscape into a geopolitical one, what is the status of NWT cultural landscapes? Cultural landscapes, still important from the perspective of NWT Aboriginal worldviews, are under pressure from changes and impacts from resource development, which have escalated in the last two decades. What trends, changes, and developments have taken place over the last two decades? How are NWT Aboriginal societies working to preserve and protect northern cultural landscapes? This paper reviews these changes from the perspective of cultural landscape research, with particular emphasis on the recent developments in the Mackenzie River valley of the Northwest Territories.

Cultural Landscapes in the NWT

[I]f we remember the teachings of the legends and live them, if we take the sign set on the land for us as our symbol, we will never have any trouble surviving as a nation. (Stanley Isiah, as told to George Blondin—from Dene Nation 1981:ii)

We kept on traveling, and grandfather . . . kept on talking to me. . . . That was how the grandfathers taught the children (George Blondin, Deline, 1990—from Blondin 1990: 204)

For the Dene, Métis, and Inuvialuit[1] of the Northwest Territories (Fig. 97) the land is indeed a special thing. More than just a space, it is a blanket woven from strands of stories centuries old—a landscape imbued with rivers of meaning. It is a cultural landscape where physical features are used as mnemonic devices to order and help preserve oral narratives, which themselves encode knowledge relative to identity, history, culture, and subsistence. To paraphrase Richard Nerysoo, the land is life.

The mnemonic link between geographic feature, place name, and oral narrative has been well documented in many societies that preserve rich oral traditions (see Buggey, this volume; Andrews et al.1998; Feld and Basso 1996; Hirsch and O'Hanlon 1995). Vast territories known intimately by members of highly mobile societies and codified by names form the basis of a complex ethnogeography, where the physical world is transformed into a social geography in which culture and landscape are fused into a semiotic whole. These cultural landscapes meld natural and cultural values and are often difficult to compare with Western catego-

301

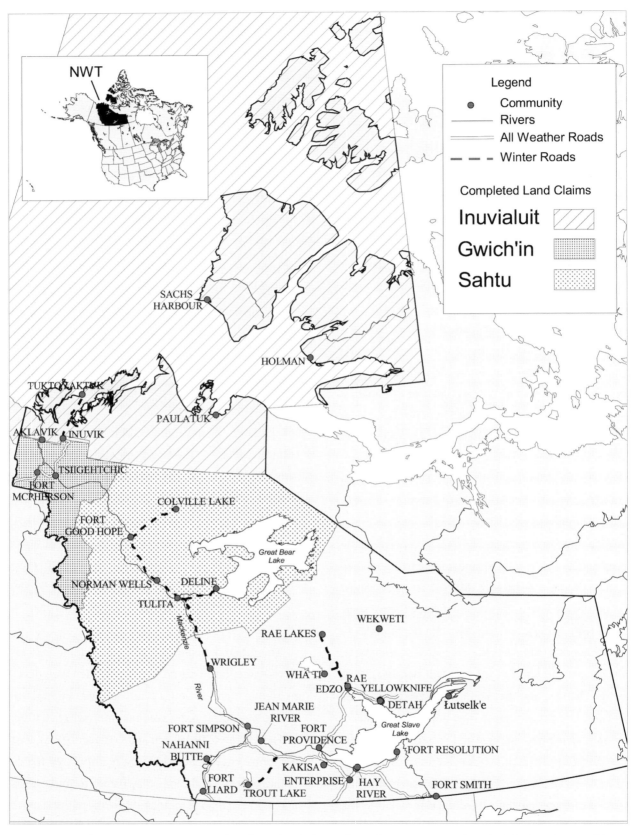

Legend

- Community
- Rivers
- All Weather Roads
- Winter Roads

Completed Land Claims

Inuvialuit
Gwich'in
Sahtu

SACHS HARBOUR

HOLMAN

TUKTOYAKTUK

PAULATUK

AKLAVIK   INUVIK

TSIIGEHTCHIC

FORT MCPHERSON

COLVILLE LAKE

FORT GOOD HOPE

Great Bear Lake

NORMAN WELLS   DELINE

TULITA

WEKWETI

RAE LAKES

WRIGLEY

WHA TI   RAE
EDZO   YELLOWKNIFE

JEAN MARIE RIVER

DETAH   Łutselk'e

FORT SIMPSON

FORT PROVIDENCE

Great Slave Lake

NAHANNI BUTTE

FORT RESOLUTION

KAKISA

FORT LIARD   ENTERPRISE   HAY RIVER   FORT SMITH

TROUT LAKE

Mackenzie River

97/ The Northwest Territories, Canada. Three land claims have been negotiated in the NWT and passed into settlement legislation—for the Inuvialuit, Gwich'in, and Sahtu Dene and Métis. The Dogrib, occupying the region north of Yellowknife, have completed a land claim agreement, but it awaits passage by the Canadian Parliament. The roads represented by dotted lines are usable only in winter.

ries of geographical description. As young people travel with their elders, they are told the names and stories, using geographic features as mnemonic aids, and in this way travel, or mobility, becomes a vehicle for learning. Elders who have worked on the land all their lives, who have visited places of spiritual significance, who have traveled to the edge of the world—and who have learned and recounted the stories about these places— are regarded with great respect because they are very knowledgeable. In this way, knowledge passed down through the ages in stories is mediated through personal experience. Mobility, and the knowledge gained from it, is therefore tied to notions of prestige as well (Andrews et al. 1998:311–13). The ethno-pedagogy of educating and socializing children with the land is an ancient tradition, corroborated by oral tradition and supported by archaeological research (see below).

Though there are many examples to draw upon to illustrate this relationship, the site of Ayonikɩ (Fig. 98) is particularly useful, as it is said that the site witnessed the creation of the Sahtu Dene and their neighbors. The following passage is taken from the Sahtu Heritage Places and Sites Joint Working Group report (T'Seleie et al. 2000:18–20), which is described more fully later in the paper:

> The story takes place at a time in Sahtu history long ago when humans and animals could change form. Sahtu Dene history is divided into two great time periods: the time of the 'Old World,' when animals and humans could change form, and lived together. This was succeeded by the 'New World,' a time when humans and animals took their final form. With the New World, people and animals lived in harmony, abiding by rules of mutual respect and conduct. These are the rules that guide hunters to respect the animals that give themselves for food. We are living in the New World today. As told by an Elder from Colville Lake, the story of Ayonikɩ begins...
>
> In the ancient days everyone lived together— the Inuit, the Gwich'in, and the Dene from this region. The big war that happened at Ayonikɩ happened because of two children that were fighting one another over an owl. Everyone began to fight because of the

children and it is said that the battle was so fierce that there was a lake of blood that formed on that hill. Finally an Elder stood and asked the people to stop fighting. Everyone went their separate ways, and even the languages changed with time. A lone dog wandered toward Gwich'in country and that represents the Gwich'in. A young man wandered to the Arctic coast and that represents the Inuit. That is why the Inuit are so agile. The children ran towards Great Bear Lake; they represent the Neyagot'ine [Délɪne people]. That is why the people of Bear Lake are so energetic. An Elder stayed here, and he represents the people who live here today. That is why the people of this area are so wise.

Generally stories are not interpreted for young people, and are told without the explanation that ends the story of Ayonikɩ, above. The elders say that young people must try to understand the meaning of the story through their own experience, noting that this encourages independent thinking, and provides for a strong future for the youth. As family groups traveled from place to place along the trails that cross the Sahtu landscape, children were told the names of the places and the stories that reside at each. As they grew to adulthood and began telling their own children the same stories, the places themselves became aids for remembering the vast oral tradition in which Sahtu Dene and Metis culture finds its roots (Fig. 99). In this way the land teaches the young their identity, their history, the rules of their society. Experience becomes the catalyst for the acquisition of knowledge. These places are considered sacred, and are important to the future well being of Sahtu Dene and Metis culture.

The link between land and culture in the NWT represents an ancient system that operates in complete harmony with the landscape, where both mental and physical sustenance is sought and found. What remains of this today? Does this system continue to function? With the current pace of change in the North, is this ancient ethno-pedagogy still valid?

The Changing Landscape

> Some young people today claim that the traditional way of life is a thing of the past. I believe that as long as there are Dene, then

we will not abandon the traditional way of life. I tell the young people to listen to what we have to say because then they will be able to benefit from the teachings that we are passing on to them. Our oral tradition, once written, will last as long as this land, and if they retain this information in memory they will gain from it. That is why we are working on the land. (Harry Simpson, Rae Lakes, 1991—from Andrews et al. 1998:317)

Someone once remarked in reference to the pace of change in the NWT that if you are unhappy with the status quo, wait a few days until negotiations change it. Over the last century, both the pace and degree of change have been dramatic, and it has had dramatic impacts on northern indigenous societies. Beginning over two centuries ago with early exploration and the fur trade and continuing today with the prospects of major resource development, the landscape of the NWT has been of international interest as multinational companies vie for development rights. While development proceeds at a tremendous pace, Aboriginal inhabitants of the Northwest Territories have been negotiating a relationship with Canada for more than a century, attempting both to gain a degree of self-sufficiency, but also to exert control of and ultimately benefit from resource development on their traditional lands. Beginning with the negotiation of Treaties 8 (1899) and 11 (1921), Aboriginal inhabitants of the NWT—the Dene, Métis, and Inuvialuit—have struggled to find a relationship with Canada. Though comprehensive land claims—which many refer to as modern treaties—were signed with the Inuvialuit (1984), the Gwich'in (1992), the Inuit of Nunavut (1993), and the Sahtu Dene and Métis (1993), land claim negotiations continue in the southern reaches of the territory, as do self-government negotiations in most.[2] Part of a long and difficult process, self-sufficiency is the ultimate goal of these efforts.

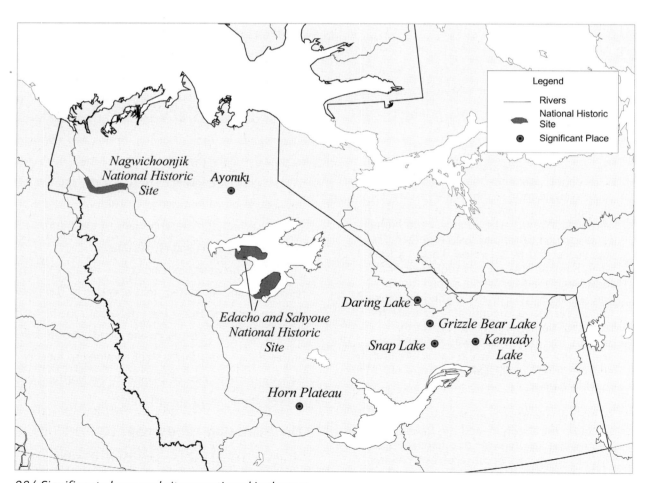

98/ Significant places and sites mentioned in the text.

99/ Drum Lake, Mackenzie Mountains, a Mountain Dene sacred site where oral tradition tells that the spirit of a giant mountain sheep lives underwater and must be avoided by travelers on the lake.

How have indigenous societies of the NWT moved to protect their cultural landscapes from the onslaught of market-driven forces? What impacts are occurring to cultural landscapes? Is the changing geopolitical landscape of the NWT straining perceptions of cultural landscapes? Have other social and cultural changes caused changes to the interpretation or appreciation of cultural landscapes? Though a detailed examination of these questions is beyond the scope of this paper, an attempt will be made to address them in a broad compass, providing a general perspective on cultural landscapes and change in the NWT today, by presenting a selected description of current or recent research approaches and projects directed at documenting and protecting cultural landscapes. However, in order to set the context for these, this paper will first review NWT social, political, and economic trends today.

The NWT Today

With twenty-eight communities and a total population of just over 42,000[3] in an area of 1,346,106 square kilometers (519,734 square miles), much of the NWT today is still remote and difficult to access. Although all of the communities are accessible by air, only half of them are linked by some 2,200 kilometers (1,367 miles) of all-season road. Winter roads link many of the remaining communities, as well as several large mines, though these roads are available for use only four months out of the year. A few communities are serviced by river barges or sealifts. Today all communities have access to telephone and electricity, though for the smallest and most remote, these services arrived only in the 1990s.

As a territory of Canada, the authority for responsible government in the NWT rests ultimately with the federal government. The territorial government has been gradually taking on a larger role as portions of these responsibilities are transferred through devolution agreements. However, whereas provinces in southern Canada hold title to land in right of the crown and consequently have broad legislative rights over provincial lands, in the NWT the federal government maintains title, and consequently also maintains legislative control over crown land. The largest private landowners in the NWT today are the Aboriginal land claim authorities where settled claims have been completed. For example, the Gwich'in of the Mackenzie Delta region received title to 22,422 square kilometers (8,657 square miles) of land in the NWT as a component of their land claim, representing forty percent of their settlement region. Continuing self-government negotiations will also change the political map of the NWT, as Aboriginal groups negotiate control of some government responsibilities over portions of their traditional lands. As these negotiations are still underway, it is premature to discuss their nature, but they have the potential for making significant adjustments to the way the NWT will be governed in the future.

Taxes generate only a small fraction of territorial government revenues, with the main cost of local government managed mostly through federal transfer payments, representing about sixty-one precent of nearly $800 million (CAD) required annually to finance public government. The government continues to be the largest employer in the NWT. Fur trapping, traditionally an important aspect of the subsistence economy, has suffered a dramatic decline over the last three decades, which many attribute to the campaign of the animal-rights movement and its effect on the fashion industry. In 1988, fur trapping generated almost $600 million in the NWT, compared with just $750,000, one decade later (GNWT 2000b). In contrast to this trend, resource development has been booming. In 1998, the value of mineral and oil and gas production in the NWT was worth $289 million while a year later (1999) it had risen to $861 million. This three-fold increase was due solely to the opening of a new diamond mine, owned by BHP

Diamonds, Inc., a subsidiary of the multinational BHP-Billiton. These figures will rise to much higher levels over the next decade as two new diamond mines begin production,[4] and there will be significant increases in gas production. Natural gas development is also booming, and the prospects of a new pipeline bringing gas from the Mackenzie Delta to southern markets is currently receiving much attention from government, industry, and Aboriginal groups. The latter have formed a consortium, the Aboriginal Pipeline Group, uniting Dene and Inuvialuit partners, to negotiate joint venture agreements with multi-national companies to develop and own a percentage interest in a new gas pipeline. Exploration activities are on the rise as companies rush to prove-up resources in the advance of a potential pipeline, already in the environmental review process.[5]

The economy of these projects often betters, and sometimes dwarfs, the cost of governing the NWT. Indeed, some of the larger multinational mining companies employ more people worldwide than the number of residents in the NWT. These are daunting facts, and they illustrate problems that both the territorial government and Aboriginal communities must overcome to negotiate meaningful partnerships and benefits.

The boom, bust cycle of development has created pressure on the delivery of government health and social services and programs. Social problems linked to drug and alcohol abuse are prevalent in many northern communities and seem to be exacerbated by the "bust" of the development cycle. However, many communities have chosen to battle these trends by ensuring that "wellness" and healing programs, supported by government and other agencies, are easily and widely available for those who request assistance.

A century ago, diseases introduced by Euro-Canadian newcomers decimated northern Aboriginal populations. Smallpox, scarlet fever, influenza, tuberculosis, and measles, among others, all had dramatic effects on northern populations. One estimate suggests (Krech, 1978:99) that between first contact with Europeans and 1860, eighty percent of the Gwich'in died from the introduction of new diseases, for which they had no immunity or treatment. Today, though most of these diseases have been eradicated or have been made manageable through medical advances, tuberculosis and influenza still result in some deaths each year.

Today, a few of the larger centers have hospitals; and the smaller communities have nursing stations, though it is often difficult to find and keep qualified nurses for those facilities. The Government of the Northwest Territories (GNWT) provides a medical air evacuation service, which brings patients to hospitals in Inuvik or Yellowknife; and when necessary, serious cases are medevaced to larger centers in southern Canada.

The Northwest Territories has eight official languages (Chipewyan, Dogrib, Slavey, Cree, Gwich'in, Inuktitut, English, and French). The Dene or Athapaskan group of languages (Chipewyan, Dogrib, Slavey,

100/ A Dogrib hunter and dead bull moose. Knowledge of areas where game might be encountered is critical to living in a subarctic landscape.

Gwich'in) represents the largest Aboriginal linguistic family, and many adults are fluent in both their first language and English. The worldwide trend of language homogenization has left many NWT Aboriginal languages in danger of disappearing, as fewer young people learn to speak their parent's language. Many Aboriginal communities are actively fighting this trend by implementing language revitalization programs and are hopeful that it will ensure language preservation.

Caribou hunting, long the touchstone of northern culture and the mainstay of the subsistence economy, continues to be important in both metaphorical and nutritive senses. In heavily forested areas of the NWT, where migratory caribou herds are absent, moose hunting (Fig. 100) is important. Fishing is also of critical importance, and perhaps because it is considered a more mundane activity—less romantic perhaps, than hunting—it is often under-represented in the literature on subsistence economy. For people who live off the land, however, it is easier and less expensive in terms of labor to catch fish every day than it is to hunt for caribou or moose, and consequently, people who live on the land eat fish more than they eat meat. Nonetheless, caribou are essential to northern subsistence and take a central place in the ideology of life in the North. As people moved in phase with the migration of caribou and the spawning runs of fish, living in and off the land (Helm 2000:35) meant a yearly round spent in the "bush." With the coming of the fur trade, periodic visits to the fur trade post were added to the yearly round, and the economy of trapping and trading fur was a new focus for families who made their life primarily on the land. Federal government transfer payments and the development of a Canadian social support network in the 1950s lead to people moving into town and a gradual erosion of "bush" life. Today northern communities flourish with modern homes and conveniences, with municipal and government services providing electricity, telephones, and satellite television.

Though country food is still an important part of northern diet, the practice of hunting has changed dramatically. In September 1999, I accompanied a group of Dogrib hunters to the barrenlands to partake in the traditional fall hunt, which I later described in a letter to anthropologist June Helm. In her recent book "The People of Denendeh," Helm (2000) excerpted part of the letter as a contrast to hunting techniques in the 1820s. Whereas hunting techniques of the 1820s included stalking with movements that mimicked caribou behaviour and the use of snares and a variety of drive techniques, today's hunters use modern conveniences to their benefit. Though the nature of the hunt has changed, it is still founded on a tradition and knowledge centuries old, as indicated in my letter to June Helm (2000:70-1):

> Hunts organized by the band councils of the four Dogrib communities [Rae-Edzo, Wha Ti, Gamiti, and Wekweti] were taking place at the same time and in the same general area. The camp locations had been chosen carefully the week before. Hunters first referred to satellite maps distributed weekly to the communities by the Department of Resources, Wildlife, and Economic Development (RWED), which show the locations of fourteen collared caribou cows. These are usually posted on a bulletin board near the band office and always attract lots of attention. The RWED study is designed to examine the impacts of recent diamond mine exploration and development on the Bathurst Caribou herd, which numbers nearly 350,000 animals. The satellite transmitters on the collars send signals once every five days for six hours. Biologists in Yellowknife download the location data and maps are prepared and sent to the communities. Once a general [hunt] location was chosen, the bands then chartered a small plane to scout for caribou, and ultimately, specific locations for the camps. The caribou are widely distributed in small groups ranging in size from a few animals to thousands, over an area of many thousands of square miles. The preparation in locating suitable sites is necessary because the bands use expensive aircraft charters to move hunters and camp supplies to the caribou. In contrast, just a generation ago hunters traveled to the barrenlands by canoe and were consequently much more mobile and able to cover large distances in pursuit of caribou. With the use of aircraft, the camps are set up at locations where caribou are fairly numerous and hunters range from camp on

foot. Consequently, it is important to choose areas where sufficient numbers of caribou are moving through to make a successful hunt.

> Though the satellite maps provide current data regarding the distribution of the herd, it only parallels Dogrib traditional knowledge of caribou movements and behaviour. Indeed the camp we visited had been used over many generations and the lakes and features in the area all have Dogrib place names. [For example,] Grizzly Bear Lake (known as Diga Ti, or "wolf lake" in Dogrib) is located on a traditional canoe route used to access the summer/fall hunting areas. Consequently, it was no surprise that we located two archaeological sites during our visit. One . . . consisted of an old stone ring measuring four metres in diameter, . . . a grave (surrounded by a picket fence, and [therefore] dating [it] to the twentieth century), and the remains of three birch bark canoes. Based on the state of preservation, the canoes are likely less than 100 years old. There were also a small number of stone flakes scattered throughout the site indicating a potentially much older use. A second site was located on a high bedrock hill . . . where we found a large surface scatter of stone flakes. The hunters we were traveling with had stopped there to rest and look for caribou. In discussing the [archaeological remains], they felt confident that the flakes were the result of an ancestor from long ago sitting on the top of the hill passing his time by working on a stone tool while waiting for caribou. It was interesting to reflect on these two episodes, separated by time and vast differences in technology, yet linked by the knowledge of the area passed down through the generations.

Today, the worldview of northern Aboriginal youth is different from that of their grandparents as television, the Internet, world travel, a southern-based education system, and a community-based life have created vastly different life experiences for young people. Partly due to a language barrier, where youth struggle to speak the first language of their elders, traditional knowledge and values are in danger of being marginalized—overwhelmed by dominant societal values of urban or southern Canada. Most young people today prefer the comforts of town life to the rigors of the bush and no longer pursue traditional lifestyles on a fulltime basis. As a result, an economy based on wages has gradually eclipsed one rooted solely in subsistence activities. Today, hunting, fishing, trapping, and bush life have become recreational activities for many Aboriginal northerners. Where just a generation ago young people were socialized and educated through travel and experience in a cultural landscape, where place was imbued with knowledge through stories, today children are largely educated in school settings and based in modern communities. These changes have come with a cost, and for many elders this situation represents a crisis. Elders are struggling to finds ways to ensure that the knowledge that guided them through life, passed down to them orally through many generations, is transmitted by other means to today's youth. If they no longer learn by traveling, by listening to the stories associated with place, are the North's cultural landscapes in peril too?

History of Cultural Landscape Research and Management in the NWT

> There are many stories about that hill, so when we get there I will tell stories about it. There will be many, many stories. We'll have to check all the areas mentioned in the story, and we will have to climb to the top of it. When we get to the hill there will be lots of work to be done (Harry Simpson, Rae Lakes, 1992—from Andrews and Zoe 1997:173).

Cultural landscape research in the NWT has a long history. Often partnered today with environmental assessment studies, documenting traditional ecological knowledge has become a part of doing business in the North. Natural gas producers in Alaska and Canada are currently debating routes for transporting Arctic gas reserves to market, one of which would see a pipeline constructed through the Mackenzie River valley. Recently a consortium of Inuvialuit and Dene organizations issued a statement in support of this proposal, indicating that they would be interested in negotiating a percentage ownership of the pipeline.

This statement was in stark contrast to the position taken by the same groups in the mid-1970s when a pipeline proposal caused outcry, launched a major study called the Mackenzie Valley Pipeline Inquiry (Berger 1977), and led to twenty-five years of land claim negotiations, which continue today in some areas.

Aboriginal organizations struggled during these decades to meet a government negotiating agenda by conducting ambitious land use and occupancy studies to document the context of cultural landscapes in the North. The Inuit Land Use and Occupancy Project (Freeman 1976), and the Dene Mapping Project (Asch et al. 1986) are two examples of these efforts from the area treated here. Funded through government loans advanced against the final compensation to be paid as part of the claim, these projects served to preserve a picture of landscape use which was under severe pressure from outside sources and which was undergoing tremendous change. Future generations of northern Aboriginal youth will find much of value in these studies as they grapple with new challenges.

In 1989, UNESCO Canada published an inventory of community-based resource management projects in Canada (Cohen and Hanson 1989). The chapter on the NWT (DeLancey and Andrews 1989) focused on resource use conflicts and inventoried a total of twenty-five projects designed to help communities prepare for negotiating their interests through comprehensive land claims. Most of the community-based research in the NWT in the 1980s was directed at documenting traditional lifeways, including knowledge about cultural landscapes as perceived by elders, for use in land claims negotiations or in environmental assessment hearings. The report (ibid.) classified community-based research efforts into a variety of categories, based on the subject of the research. The majority of these projects were designed to either document traditional lifeways in response to development pressures or to provide support for negotiations designed to empower local communities in managing resource use in their area. Though more than a decade has passed, today little has changed in this regard.

Large-scale development often serves to generate large sources of funding, which researchers from a variety of disciplines can draw on. The Northern Oil and Gas Action Plan of the 1980s and early '90s represented a consortium of industry and government that contributed equally to fund the collection of baseline data on the Mackenzie Delta region for a variety of disciplines. Managed by government, in its early days it made few allowances for Aboriginal research interests or needs. More recently, with the explosion of interest in diamond exploration and development in the mid-1990s, Aboriginal groups, industry, government, and environmental organizations partnered to create the West Kitikmeot/Slave Society (WKSS). Taking its name from the geological region in which diamonds are found (the West Kitikmeot and Slave geological provinces), the WKSS was begun in 1995 and was funded largely through contributions from industry, government, and environmental organizations. Aboriginal groups control more than half of the seats on the WKSS board. As reflected in the organization's vision statement, its objective "is to achieve sustainable development in the West Kitikmeot Slave Study area which respects Aboriginal cultural values, so that the land is protected, culture is preserved, and community self-sufficiency and reliance [are] enhanced" (WKSS 2000:iii).

Maintaining Cultural Landscapes Today: A Brief Survey

> So this place has a story, and it's a good story too (Harry Simpson, 1994—from Andrews et al. 1998:311).

Recognizing the continuing need to document and maintain cultural landscapes (Fig. 101), Aboriginal groups and their partners have been working diligently over the last decade. As in the recent past, a significant percentage of the ethnographic landscape research of the current decade is driven by resource use conflict—as the pace of development increases, so does the need to document cultural landscapes. Since a detailed inventory of current research is beyond the scope of this paper, instead I will discuss five different approaches to preserving cultural landscapes in the hope that these examples will demonstrate the direction that recent research is taking, as well as illustrating the diverse ways these projects are being managed.

Comprehensive Land Claims: Negotiating Preservation

Land claim negotiations in the Northwest Territories have been underway for nearly thirty years. Indeed, an entire generation of Dene and Inuvialuit youth has grown up thinking that negotiations are as much a part of life as is hunting. Summarized in brief compass, land claims completed to date empower Aboriginal groups by granting land ownership and management rights, by providing compensation for relinquishing certain rights, and by granting economic and social measures to provide for self-sufficiency. Many Aboriginal groups have begun to negotiate self-government provisions, either as a component of ongoing land claim negotiations, or through dedicated negotiations following the completion of a land claim.

Within these agreements, Aboriginal groups have used many strategies to maintain and protect cultural landscapes. Land selection allows Aboriginal groups to protect (through fee simple ownership) portions of their traditional lands that are deemed most important. However, the need to balance protection of cultural landscapes with economic self-sufficiency has meant that some land has been selected with an eye toward future development. The Gwich'in and Sahtu claims provide for the development of land use plans that are designed to sustain development through the establishment of land use policy. Conservation of cultural values is predominant in these plans. Some skeptics have wondered if the lobby to protect rights to mineral interests in these areas has caused government to pause before passing these plans; after years of negotiations, a new plan has finally been signed.[6]

101/ *Marking the confluence of the Bear and Mackenzie Rivers, Bear Rock (in the distance) is sacred to most NWT Dene groups; this is where Yamoria, a Dene culture-hero, stretched the hides of three giant beavers he had killed. Bear Rock is today depicted in the Dene Nation's corporate logo as a political symbol .*

The Sahtu Dene and Métis Comprehensive Land Claim (Government of Canada 1993) took a unique approach to protecting cultural landscapes. A clause in the chapter on heritage called for the creation of a joint working group charged with the responsibility of making recommendations to government on how specific places and sites should be protected. Representation on the joint working group included one representative from the federal government, one from the territorial government, and two from the Sahtu region. The four members elected a fifth person, a Sahtu resident, to act as chair. The Sahtu Heritage Places and Sites Joint Working Group released its report in January 2000 (T'Seleie et al. 2000), which presented recommendations on how to commemorate and protect forty sacred or cultural sites, or site groupings, in the Sahtu Settlement Area (see Fig. 97). It also presented an additional twenty-one general recommendations that ad-

dress the direction of future research and the need for cultural landscape protection and advocacy in the region. The Working Group met over a four-year period (1995–1999), often contracting elders and community experts to assist with the research.

Though many of the report's recommendations still await action by government and Sahtu land claim authorities, the Report has proved useful for developers wishing to avoid impacting Sahtu cultural sites, and to planners who are developing a land use plan for the region. As well, some teachers in the region have used the Report as resource material in the schools. These are positive advances and serve ultimately to protect Sahtu cultural landscapes.

Education: Taking the Classroom on the Land

Recognizing that the ethno-pedagogy of educating

youth through travel is disappearing, several Aboriginal groups have established annual educational trips using traditional trails where young people and elders interact in much the same way as they did in the past. For example, the Gwich'in have organized an annual snowmobile trip between Fort McPherson in the NWT and Old Crow in the Yukon. The trip, which follows a traditional dog team trail, allows families residing in both communities to connect and exchange greetings, and provides elders an opportunity to teach young people aspects of traditional life. Other groups have organized similar trips. In 1999 elders and youth walked from Colville Lake to Fort Good Hope, following a summer walking trail and recreating what was many years ago an annual event to trade at the Hudson's Bay Company post in Good Hope. The Yellowknives Dene First Nation have organized summer canoe trips, following traditional birchbark canoe trails, and designed specifically to provide learning experiences for youth.

In 1971, in his remarks on the occasion of the opening of the new high school in the Dogrib community of Edzo, Chief Jimmy Bruneau recognized the need to educate Dogrib students in both a southern Canadian-style school system and in Dogrib cultural ways. Reflecting the chief's perspective in her remarks to a meeting of Dogrib elders, educators, and education administrators working to develop a mission statement for the Dogrib school system in 1990, elder and education innovator Elizabeth Mackenzie, noted that "if children are taught in both cultures equally, they will be strong like two people." The Dogrib education board recognized the importance of this and adopted it as an educational philosophy for the Dogrib school system (Dogrib Divisional Board of Education 1991). The mission statement argues that if young people are provided a formal education in a southern Canadian-style school setting, in conjunction with instruction in Dogrib language, culture, and identity, they will grow to be "strong like two people," taking the best from both worldviews. Because much of Dogrib history and identity is tied to life on the land, this new educational

strategy uses every opportunity to take the classroom out on the land—or more relevant for this paper—to use the cultural landscape as a classroom. Through organizing cultural camps in all seasons, by canoe trips in summer, by bringing elders directly into the classroom, and by providing for formalized Dogrib language instruction, the Dogrib education system has forged a unique learning experience for Dogrib youth based on this collaborative philosophy.

Recognizing that their youth face a different world, Dogrib elders are working to bring the past into the education system, always guided by the pervasive philosophy of "strong like two people." Throughout the last decade, Dogrib elders have participated in a variety of research projects in partnership with linguists, anthropologists, and archaeologists.[7] In a general sense the research has been designed to apply Dogrib traditional knowledge within the theoretical and methodological constructs of these disciplines. However, for the elders a single objective has been tantamount: that these partnerships provide products that can be used to educate youth in the Dogrib school system (Fig. 102). As a result many of the research projects have been founded on complex partnerships with the Dogrib school system (see below).

Other efforts at using the cultural landscape as a classroom include the many science camps that have been organized in various regions of the NWT. Designed to combine Western scientific method and theory with traditional ethno-pedagogy in a land-based setting, these camps have met with much success. Since 1995, the Gwich'in Social and Cultural Institute (GSCI), with their head office located in Tsiigehtchic (formerly Arctic Red River), has organized a ten day "on-the-land" fall camp for high school students (Kritsch 1996). The curriculum focuses on the Gwich'in cultural landscape and involves instruction in a variety of topics including ethnobotany, renewable resource management, heritage resource management, and land claim history and implementation, presented by instructors from both Western and Aboriginal traditions.

The Tundra Science Camp, located at the Tundra Ecological Research Station (TERS)[8] at Daring Lake, about 150 kilometers (ninety-three miles) north of Yellowknife in the barrenlands, immerses high school students in a ten day program of hands-on scientific and cultural exploration (Strong and Hans 1996). Provided with an opportunity to participate in ongoing research programs being conducted at TERS, students gain an understanding of the cultural landscape of the barrenlands, through instruction in archaeology, botany, biology, geology, environmental research advocacy, and Dogrib culture. Science camps such as these follow the tradition of "strong like two people" using cultural landscapes as classroom.

Environmental Assessment: Mitigating Land Use Conflicts

Diamond mine exploration and development in the NWT has stimulated a wealth of research under the framework of environmental impact assessment. Recently enacted environmental protection legislation (Mackenzie Valley Resource Management Act 1998) gives high profile to the need to document traditional knowledge and for assessing potential impacts to cultural landscapes. As mentioned above, one outcome of this effort was the creation of the West Kitikmeot/ Slave Study Society (WKSS). Projects funded by WKSS include several community-based efforts directed at documenting aspects of the cultural landscape of the Chipewyan, Yellowknives, Dogrib, and Inuit. These projects have received significant funding and have been used to establish trained community-based research teams, which have been instrumental in directing changes to development plans to ensure that significant cultural sites are protected.

The "Habitat of Dogrib Traditional Territory Project" was undertaken by the Whaèhdǫǫ̀ Nàowoò Kǫ̀ (Legat 1998; Legat et al. 1999, 2001), a research institution under the aegis of the Dogrib Treaty 11 Council, and

102/ The importance of fish is often underestimated in anthropological literature, but here Dogrib elders make a point to teach youth how to properly clean a large lake trout.

funded through the WKSS. Staffed largely by Dogrib researchers, the Whaèhdǫǫ̀ Nàowoò Kǫ̀ group has carried out several projects designed to record and present Dogrib traditional knowledge, with specific reference to Dogrib classification of the environment. Focusing on place names, nomenclature for habitat, animal, and plant species occupying them, these projects have built a strong core of trained researchers, which the Dogrib Nation can employ in addressing other tasks.

The Chipewyan of Łutselk'e, located on the East Arm of Great Slave Lake, also undertook research funded by WKSS. Community researchers focused on documenting traditional ecological knowledge of elders and land users of the Łutselk'e Dene First Nation for a particular area within their traditional range. Known as Kache Kue, or Kennady Lake, the region was being intensively explored by Monopros, a subsidiary of

DeBeers Canada, the Canadian arm of the diamond-mining giant of South Africa. DeBeers Canada has applied for permission to open a mine at Snap Lake, a nearby site located about 100 kilometers (sixty-two miles) north of Łutselk'e, and at the time of writing (April 2002) had just submitted an environmental impact assessment report. The WKSS funds will assist the Łutselk'e Dene First Nation in presenting their own interests—particularly the documentation of the Chipewyan cultural landscape in the development area—and permit the people an opportunity to participate in the environmental review.

The use of innovative computer techniques, such as Geographic Information Systems (GIS), to record cultural landscapes ensures that traditional knowledge gathered through these projects will be archived and made available for future projects. These research projects also allow the Aboriginal groups to develop management strategies to monitor long-term and cumulative impacts from development on cultural landscapes. GIS computer technology is a tool designed to provide a way of managing place-based or geo-referenced information and is well fitted to recording traditional place names, trails, and other aspects of Aboriginal land use. As well as providing a tool for archiving and managing data, GIS technology allows Aboriginal youth to make significant contributions, by bringing new computer skills into the mix. By working with their elders to record land-based knowledge, and then together reviewing GIS-generated maps, young and old interact in new ways, providing a serendipitous opportunity to use the land as teacher.

Cultural Institutes: Taking Control of the Research Agenda

Created in 1992, the Gwich'in Social and Cultural Institute (GSCI),[9] has been working to inventory traditional place names and land use, sacred sites, and trails in the Gwich'in Settlement Region. The work has resulted in numerous research reports and publications that document the Gwich'in cultural landscape by recording an extensive body of traditional place names and associated narratives (Kritsch et al. 1994; Kritsch and Andre 1997; Heine et al. 2001). This work continues as a priority for the institute.

Working in a collaborative arrangement is a priority of GSCI, and they have entered several partnerships with southern and northern researchers. With GSCI help, the Gwich'in Tribal Council has drafted a traditional knowledge (TK) research policy[10] that outlines guidelines for all research activities conducted within the Gwich'in Settlement Region (GTC 2004). Designed to ensure Gwich'in collaboration, to protect Gwich'in intellectual rights to traditional knowledge, and to ensure that work is conducted in an ethical fashion, the policy strives to encourage all types of research in the region. The development of policies such as this helps ensure that research agendas are relevant to northern life and priorities. More important perhaps, it provides non-Gwich'in with a clear point of entry into establishing meaningful partnerships with Gwich'in researchers.

In 1997–1998 the Gwich'in partnered with Parks Canada to create a National Historic Site that commemorated a portion of the Gwich'in cultural landscape as being of national significance (Heine 1997; Neufeld 2001). Called Nagwichoonjik National Historic Site, it covers a 175 kilometer (110 mile) stretch of the Mackenzie River (see Fig. 98) and adjacent lands where the river flows through the center of the Gwich'in traditional land use area, making it one of the largest designated Aboriginal cultural landscapes in Canada, and among the first to be so commemorated (Buggey 1999, this volume). Presenting numerous named places, archaeological sites, cultural sites, and subsistence camps, the National Historic Site commemorates a synopsis of Gwich'in history and culture. These examples of collaborative research efforts serve as models for future efforts in preserving and managing northern cultural landscapes.

Museums: Partnership and Collaboration

103/ An elder examines archaeological remains of a birchbark canoe.

The Prince of Wales Northern Heritage Centre (PWNHC), a government-run territorial museum based in Yellowknife, has focused much of its research efforts on forging partnerships with elders, community organizations, and school boards that allow museum staff to develop close ties with many communities in the North. Through the 1980s and 1990s, these efforts were focused on projects in several regions, including:

—Ethnoarchaeological and traditional place name research with the Inuvialuit of the Mackenzie River Delta and Arctic coast region (Arnold 1988, 1994; Arnold and Hart 1991; Hart 1994).

—Inventory of trails, place names, and archeological sites in the Mackenzie Mountains, in partnership with the Mountain Dene (Hanks and Pokotylo 1989, 2000; Hanks and Winter 1983, 1986, 1989).

—Inventory of cultural sites and development of recommendations on how to preserve and protect cultural landscapes as part of the Sahtu Heritage Places and Sites Joint Working Group (T'Seleie

et al. 2000).

—Heritage resource inventories of Dogrib traditional birchbark canoe and dog team trails, and related projects (Andrews and Zoe 1997, 1998; Andrews et al. 1998; Andrews and Mackenzie 1998; Woolf and Andrews 1997, 2001).

Much of this work focused on building inventories of archaeological and cultural sites throughout the North, which permitted archaeologists at the Prince of Wales Northern Heritage Centre to serve as expert advisors in the land use review and environmental assessment process, providing recommendations on the potential for impacts to heritage sites from development.

Documenting place-names, trails, and cultural landscapes, and then using this information to locate archaeological sites, has made it possible to examine aspects of the temporal nature of cultural landscapes and in the process corroborate oral narratives that spoke of ancient times and events. The ethnoarchaeological research conducted with the Dogrib has demonstrated that place names themselves preserve knowledge of sources of raw material for making stone tools, demonstrating that the names encode centuries-old knowledge (Andrews and Zoe 1997:165–7; Hanks 1997).

Often these projects lead to related projects or follow-up research that usually starts because of an interest expressed by an elder or community member. For example, during the heritage resource inventories conducted in partnership with the Dogrib, archaeologists found the remains of thirty-five birchbark canoes at sites the elders had identified along the trails (Fig. 103). This provided the researchers with a new perspective on the role and importance of these craft for traversing the Dogrib cultural landscape. As a result a related project was undertaken to document by video the entire process of building a Dogrib birchbark canoe (Andrews and Zoe, 1998; Woolf and Andrews, 1997). Working within the Dogrib philosophy of "strong like two people," the project was conducted in partnership with the local school board, and several high school students served as apprentices to the six elders from Rae who made the canoe. While the canoe was being constructed, exhibit designers from the PWNHC worked with the industrial arts class at the school to build a display case for the finished canoe. Designed to roll through any door in the school, the canoe could be brought directly into classrooms and used by elders in instruction.

The Internet, which now links all NWT schools, provides an opportunity to introduce innovative new resources into northern classrooms. Following the ethno-pedagogical tradition of using the land as a teacher, the PWNHC, in partnership with the Dogrib Community Services Board, and the Inuvialuit Social Development Program, have developed a web-based virtual tour of northern cultural landscapes. Called "Lessons from the Land," the web resource provides students an opportunity to tour two cultural landscapes—the "Idaa Trail," a Dogrib birchbark canoe and dog team trail, and "Journey with Nuligak," which focuses on Inuvialuit culture and history (www.lessonsfromtheland.ca). Additional modules will be added in the future. Through photographs, illustrations, narrative, video and sound clips, and 3-D animation, students can opt to take a tour of these landscapes, with "on-line elders" as their guides. The web resource is structured to allow teachers to select specific features to make a lesson pertinent to the grade level being taught. Developed in conjunction with the GNWT Department of Education, Culture, and Employment, "Lessons from the Land" is featured as a component of the recently revamped Northern Studies curriculum. Using computers to create a virtual experience, "Lessons from the Land" takes the cultural landscape into the classroom, providing a learning alternative to taking the classroom out on the land.

Protecting Cultural Landscapes

The land is like a book. (Harry Simpson, Rae Lakes, 1998—Andrews and Zoe 1998:79)

Clearly these and other recent efforts have made great advances in documenting traditional knowledge and cultural landscapes across the NWT, creating sources of recorded knowledge that will be invaluable to future generations. How effective are these efforts in preserving and protecting cultural landscapes today?

Though the northern education system has made some advances in developing northern-based curricular material, broad-based advances are lacking. Currently, the NWT has only two elementary school curricula (Dene Kede GNWT 1993 and Inuuqatigiit GNWT 1997) based on Aboriginal worldviews. Though these curricula are used in several regions quite successfully, they are not used in all, and the resources to accompany them are scarce. The Dogrib have been very active in developing programs for their own schools. Special program curricula like "Trails of our Ancestors" (Dogrib Divisional Board of Education 1996), which provides for summer canoe travel through Dogrib cultural landscapes, are very popular with students. Though successful, these programs are expensive to operate, and the lack of published curricular material reflecting northern values and realities makes them difficult to deliver in a classroom setting. Land-based classes are always fun and instructive, but difficult and expensive to run. Funding for these programs is always difficult to obtain, and organizers are constantly searching for sources to draw from. As a result these programs are not widely available. Government needs to focus on developing northern curricula based on Aboriginal worldviews, and then funding school boards to move classrooms out onto the land whenever possible. The use of educational alternatives, which allow for innovation in the classroom through computers and the Internet, must also be maximized. These programs will provide future generations with an appreciation for the need to steward cultural landscapes as their ancestors have done (Fig. 104).

Though environmental assessment has supported traditional knowledge and cultural landscape research, thereby making a significant contribution to the northern knowledge base, the ability of these efforts to actually preserve and protect cultural landscapes has yet to be demonstrated. For community elders, who

104/ *Kwedoo* (blood rock), *a Dogrib sacred site. A spot is rubbed free of lichens from years of people kneeling here while leaving votive offerings in the rock crevice.*

hold vast amounts of knowledge pertinent to the cultural ecology of their lands, and who speak their Aboriginal language as a first language, the formality of an environmental hearing can be an intimidating experience and one not conducive to expressing an Aboriginal worldview. Furthermore, many communities find the process of participation in environmental proceedings to be little more than token efforts designed to appease political agendas. These programs are also tied to the boom and bust cycle of development and are therefore intermittent in their availability and patchy in their application. The WKSS, created in 1995, was designed with a lifespan of only five years. Though it was extended for two years, researchers must eventually look for alternate sources of funding. Consequently, although these projects add greatly to the documentation of traditional knowledge, they make minor practical impact on efforts in preserving cultural landscapes over the long-term. Community-based research capacity developed through these projects must be maintained through the bust part of

the development cycle that is almost certain to follow. Also, the use of GIS technology, and perhaps more importantly, the educational and training opportunities to learn how to use it, must be maximized in northern communities.

The commemoration of Aboriginal cultural landscapes is relatively new in Canada (Buggey 1999). In 1998 the community of Deline, in the Sahtu region, celebrated National Historic Site commemoration for a cultural landscape in their traditional territory— Sahyoue and Edacho National Historic Site.[11] As with the Nagwichoonjik National Historic Site, these designations serve to raise the profile of Aboriginal cultural landscapes through national commemoration, long part of the Canadian National Historic Site system plan (Parks Canada 2000; Buggey 1999, this volume). Though they cover large tracks of land, they offer little concrete protection because the commemorations are only honorific. The community of Deline has negotiated an interim land withdrawal for Sahyoue and Edacho National Historic Site, but the governments have dragged their heels in finding a permanent way of protecting these landscapes.

The interim withdrawal was granted through the auspices of the Protected Area Strategy (PAS), a joint federal-territorial program approved in 1999 (GNWT 1999). Designed to identify and establish protected areas in the NWT, the program seeks partnerships with northern Aboriginal groups in advancing areas for protection. The PAS secretariat (located in Yellowknife) has worked with communities to develop a plan to protect the Horn Plateau, a 10,000 square kilometer (3,861 square mile) area critical to both the Mackenzie Valley Slavey and Dogrib cultures.[12] While this interim solution protects it for five years, a permanent protection measure has not been developed.

With respect to the protection of cultural landscapes the report of the Sahtu Heritage Places and Sites Joint Working Group (T'Seleie et al. 2000:24-5) made the important observation that virtually all Canadian legislation designed to protect landscape or landscape features focuses on natural values instead of cultural ones. The laws designed to mark sites noted for their cultural value usually provide for honorific commemoration of these places only and do not protect them from incompatible land uses. Though cultural landscapes are mentioned in the PAS documentation, no special legislative tools were identified for protecting places of cultural value. The joint working group recommended that government move immediately to rectify this deficiency. Places exhibiting a natural value have a plethora of legislative tools available to protect them, which defines acceptable types of land use (such as tourism) and sets guidelines for their practice. Most importantly however, these instruments of law protect natural landscapes by protecting them from inappropriate forms of development. George Barnaby, a Sahtu Dene elder has remarked that "[w]e have no word in our language that means wilderness, as anywhere we go is our home" (Fumoleau 1984:59). This statement expresses a view that does not differentiate between the natural and the cultural—both are inseparable parts of a whole. The

Sahtu Dene worldview, which expresses an intellectual unity between the natural and cultural aspects of the environment, is in stark contrast to the philosophy of separating cultural from natural values represented in Canadian law and there is need to reflect this holistic view in new legislation designed to protect cultural landscapes.

The development of Aboriginal cultural institutes in the NWT is a major advance as it allows local communities to shape research agendas within their traditional lands. The Dene Cultural Institute, based in Hay River; the Whaèhdǫǫ Nàowoò Kǫ́, based in Rae; and the Gwich'in Social and Cultural Institute (GSCI), based in Tsiigehtchic, are all examples of community-based efforts striving to document cultural landscapes and preserve Aboriginal worldviews (Fig. 105). These are positive developments that encourage collaboration between research and Aboriginal communities. However, these organizations face several limitations. One of the most significant is the lack of stable funding needed to carry out long-term research and programs. For example, GSCI estimates that nearly fifty percent of its time and staff effort is spent on raising funds (Ingrid Kritsch, pers. comm.). Another problem faced by cultural institutes is one of scale. These institutes are often operated by a small number of dedicated people— and in the NWT it is most often women—who have been working consistently for many years. When interacting with government to access program funding or support, cultural institutes find they must respond to a bureaucracy many times larger. This often creates misunderstandings and makes it difficult for these small agencies to deal with government expectations. Significant and long-term funding must be found to support their activities, as it will be these groups who bring cultural landscapes forward for protection. Lack of funding is also an issue of constant concern for museum or government research projects. Competition among cultural organizations, museums, and government researchers for limited funding sources is ultimately counterproductive for preserving and protecting cultural landscapes in the NWT, as well as elsewhere in the Canadian North.

Though major advances have been made in the last decade toward documenting and protecting cultural landscapes in the NWT, much work remains to be done. Efforts in the coming decades must continue to focus on documentation as a priority. They must also strive to develop broad-based education programs that provide youth with an understanding about the cultural landscapes they live in. Northerners must urge governments to create legislative tools to protect cultural values. Finally, government must develop significant and stable funding sources for community-based cultural and heritage research.

Epilogue

"The land is like a book." I have worked with Harry Simpson, the Dogrib elder who spoke these words, for many years now, and after hearing him use this simile many times I have come to understand—I think—what he means. Clearly it captures the essence of the Dogrib ethno-pedagogy of using the land as a teacher—an aid in remembering the thousands of years of accumulated knowledge, transmitted to youth through an oral tradition and through travel. Moreover, this simile is really a carefully crafted translation of this Dogrib educational philosophy, because by making the comparison with a book, he has also made it relevant and easily understood by non-Aboriginal people who store their knowledge in books and not in oral narratives tied inextricably to a cultural landscape. Cultural landscapes are ultimately creations of a collective consciousness. They are places that are valued by society. If a society is to ensure that they are valued by future generations, then they must transmit that sense of value from generation to generation, something that the Dogrib and many other northern groups have done and continue to do with great eloquence.

In the struggle to protect their cultural landscapes, Aboriginal people in northern Canada have sought partnerships in the global community. Partnering with envi-

ronmental groups, lobbying national governments and international agencies, including UNESCO and others, and traveling to far-flung places to develop support networks have all become tools in the struggle for preserving and protecting the cultural landscapes at home. In September 2001, a group of Gwich'in from Canada and Alaska traveled to Washington, D.C., to lobby U.S. government representatives to vote against the proposed exploration for oil and gas reserves in the "1002 lands" on the Alaska North Slope. Though the Gwich'in representatives had been in Washington many times before on similar missions, the events of September 11, 2001 were to cause them much anguish. Family and friends in the North watched on television the terrorist attacks on the World Trade Center in New York and on the Pentagon in Washington worried for the safety of their loved ones so far from home. After several fretful hours of silence residents of the NWT learned that no harm had come to the Gwich'in representatives, and through a cell phone connection with CBC North radio in Canada heard familiar voices describing first-hand in the vernacular of the North, the atrocities that took place so far away. These terrible events—an attack on icons of the American cultural landscape, long thought to be impenetrable—serve to demonstrate that in today's world, cultural landscapes are indeed very fragile.

Acknowledgments

Over the years of my working and living in the Canadian North, I have been blessed with numerous rewarding friendships and experiences—many of which I have called on to write this paper. To the unnamed many who have helped form my understanding and appreciation of northern cultural landscapes I say *mahsi cho/* thank you. Several colleagues took time from their busy schedules to read and comment on a draft of this paper. I would like to thank Chuck Arnold, Susan Buggey, Melanie Fafard, June Helm, Mark Heyck, Ingrid Kritsch, Igor Krupnik, and Leslie Saxon for their helpful and insightful comments. If I have misrepresented a fact or omitted an important concept or issue, I bear this responsibility alone. I would also like to thank volume editor, Igor Krupnik, for inviting me to submit a paper, and for the support of both Susan Buggey and Ellen Lee, my Canadian compatriots, for suggesting me in the first place. Igor's lively and respectful encouragement at the beginning of this process was much appreciated. I wish also to thank Miles Davis of the Prince of Wales Northern Heritage Centre[13] GIS facility who, with his usual spirit of synergism, prepared the maps under tight time constraints, and to John Poirier, also of the PWNHC, who helped me format some of the images. Finally, to my wife, Ingrid, whose editorial skills I turn to most frequently, I express my sincere appreciation and thanks.

Notes

1. Readers wishing to read more about Dene, Metis, and Inuvialuit ethnography and history should consult Volumes 5 (Damas 1984) and 6 (Helm 1981) of the *Handbook of North American Indians*, published by the Smithsonian Institution. All Dene words are presented using the practical orthography of the Government of the Northwest Territories.

2. The Dogrib have been negotiating a land claim and self-government agreement with the federal government since 1992. In 2003 they signed a final agreement that will provide ownership to 39,000 square kilometers of land; co-management and hunting rights over a larger area; self-government rights, and $152 million CAD in financial compensation. As of June 2004, the Parliament of Canada had yet to pass the settlement legislation needed to give the agreement the force of law.

3. Approximately half of the NWT population is Aboriginal. Almost half of the population (18,000) lives in the territorial capital of Yellowknife. The next largest community is Hay River, population 4,000.

4. Diavik mine is located thirty-five kilometers from BHP-Billiton mine, and it began production in 2003. De Beers Canada, 150 kilometers northeast of Yellowknife, completed environmental negotiations in 2003 and should begin construction soon.

5. The Mackenzie Gas Project was proposed by a consortium of companies, including Imperial Oil, ConocoPhilips, Shell Canada, ExxonMobil, and the Aboriginal Pipeline Group. The project will see construction of a gas pipeline stretching from the Mackenzie River delta to northern Alberta, following the right bank of the Mackenzie River. If the project proceeds as expected, natural gas prodution could start in 2010.

6. See http://www.gwichinplanning.nt.ca/landUsePlan.html.

7. For example, see Andrews and Zoe 1997, 1998; Andrews et al. 1998; Legat 1998; Legat et al. 1999, 2001; Woolf and Andrews 1997, 2001.

8. The Department of Resources, Wildlife, and Economic Development established TERS to study tundra ecology and to create baseline data against which environmental impact assessment of diamond exploration and development might be measured. The science camp is organized by RWED, with assistance from the Prince of Wales Northern Heritage Centre.

9. Located in Tsiigehtchic, one of four Gwich'in communities, in the Mackenzie Delta region of the NWT

10. The policy is now available as a download from the Gwich'in Social and Cultural Institute's website at http://www.gwichin.ca.

11. Also known as Grizzly Bear Mountain and Scented Grass Hills. See Buggey (1999:21–3) for a discussion of the significance of this site in terms of the Canadian experience with cultural landscape designation.

12. Horn Plateau's Dene name is Edéhzhíe.

13. Prince of Wales Northern Heritage Centre, P.O. Box 1320, Yellowknife, NT X1A 2L9, Canada.

References

Andrews, Thomas D., and John B. Zoe
1997　The Įdaa Trail: Archaeology and the Dogrib Cultural Landscape, Northwest Territories, Canada. In *At a Crossroads: Archaeology and First Peoples in Canada*, George P. Nicholas and Thomas D. Andrews eds., pp. 160–77. Vancouver: Simon Fraser University Press.
1998　The Dogrib Birchbark Canoe Project. *Arctic* 51 (1):75–81.
Andrews, Thomas D., John B. Zoe, and Aaron Herter
1998　On Yamòzhah's Trail: Dogrib Sacred Sites and

the Anthropology of Travel. In *Sacred Lands: Aboriginal World Views, Claims, and Conflict*, J. Oakes, R. Riewe, K. Kinew, and E. Maloney, eds., pp. 305-20. Edmonton: Canadian Circumpolar Institute, University of Alberta.

Andrews, Thomas D., and Elizabeth Mackenzie

1998　*Tłı̨chǫ Ewò Kǫ̀nǫhmbàa: The Dogrib Caribou Skin Lodge: An Exhibit Guide*. Yellowknife: Prince of Wales Northern Heritage Centre, Yellowknife.

Arnold, Charles D.

1988　Vanishing villages of the past: Rescue Archaeology in the Mackenzie Delta. *The Northern Review*, Vol. 1:40-58.

1994　Archaeological investigations on Richards Island. *Canadian Archaeological Association Occasional Paper* 2:85-93.

Arnold, Charles D., and Elisa Hart

1991　Winter houses of the Mackenzie Inuit. *Society for the Study of Architecture in Canada* 16(2):35-9.

Asch, Michael, T.D. Andrews, and S. Smith

1986　The Dene Mapping Project on Land Use and Occupancy: An Introduction. In *Anthropology in Praxis*, P. Spaulding, ed., pp. 36-43. Occasional Papers in Anthropology and Primatology, Department of Anthropology. Calgary: University of Calgary.

Berger, Thomas R.

1977　*Northern Frontier, Northern Homeland: The Report of the Mackenzie Valley Pipeline Inquiry*. 2 vols. Ottawa: Supply and Services Canada.

Blondin, George

1990　*When the World was New: Stories of the Sahtu Dene*. Yellowknife: Outcrop.

Buggey, Susan

1999　*An Approach to Aboriginal Cultural Landscapes*. Ottawa: Historic Sites and Monuments Board of Canada, Parks Canada.

Cohen, Fay G., and Arthur J. Hanson, eds.

1989　*Community-based Resource Management in Canada: An Inventory of Research and Projects*. UNESCO Canada/MAB Working Group on the Human Ecology of Coastal Areas, Report 21. July 1989. Ottawa.

Damas, David

1984　*Arctic. Handbook of North American Indians*, Volume 5. Washington, D.C.: Smithsonian Institution.

DeLancey, Deborah J., and Thomas D. Andrews

1989　Denendeh (Western Arctic). In *Community-based Resource Management in Canada: An Inventory of Research and Projects*, F.G. Cohen and A.J. Hanson, eds., pp. 145-73. UNESCO Canada/MAB Working Group on the Human Ecology of Coastal Areas, Report 21. July 1989. Ottawa.

Dogrib Divisional Board of Education

1991　*Strong Like Two People: The Development of a Mission Statement for the Dogrib Schools*. Rae-Edzo: Dogrib Divisional Board of Education.

1996　*Gowhaèhdǫ́ǫ́ Gı̨ts'ǫ Etǫ Nı̨whereàa:Trails of our Ancestors: Course 15 Curriculum*. Rae-Edzo: Dogrib Divisional Board of Education.

Feld, Steven and Keith H. Basso, eds.

1996　*Senses of Place*. Santa Fe: School of American Research Press.

Freeman, Milton M.R.

1976　*Inuit Land Use and Occupancy Project*, 3 volumes. Ottawa: Indian and Northern Affairs.

Fumoleau, Rene

1984　*Denendeh: A Dene Celebration*. Yellowknife: Dene Nation.

Government of Canada

1993　*Sahtu Dene and Metis Comprehensive Land Claim*. Ottawa: Indian and Northern Affairs Canada.

Government of the Northwest Territories

1993　*Dene Kede: Education: A Dene Perspective. Curriculum K-6*. Yellowknife: Department of Education, Culture and Employment.

1997　*Inuuqatigiit: Curriculum K-6*. Yellowknife: Department of Education, Culture and Employment.

1999　*Northwest Territories Protected Areas Strategy: A Balanced Approach to Establishing Protected Areas in the Northwest Territories*. Northwest Territories Protected Areas Strategy Advisory Committee. Yellowknife: Department of Resources, Wildlife and Economic Development.

2000a　*Northwest Territories, Highway Traffic, 1999*. Yellowknife: Transportation Planning Division, Department of Transportation, GNWT, (www.gov.nt.ca/Transportation/documents/index,html).

2000b　*NWT Socio-Economic Scan, 2000*. Yellowknife: NWT Bureau of Statistics. (www.stats.gov.nt.ca/Statinfo/Generalstats/Scan/scan.html).

Gwich'in Tribal Council

2004　Gwich'in Traditional Knowledge Policy. Inuvik:GTC.

Hanks, Christopher C.

1997　Ancient Knowledge of Ancient Times: Tracing Dene Identity from the Late Pleistocene and Holocene. In *At a Crossroads: Archaeology and First Peoples in Canada*, George P. Nicholas and Thomas D. Andrews, eds., pp. 178-89. Vancouver: Simon Fraser University Press.

Hanks, Christopher C., and David L. Pokotylo

1989　The Mackenzie Basin: An Alternative Approach to Dene and Metis Archaeology. *Arctic* 42(2):139-47.

2000　Mountain Dene *In Situ* Adaptation and the Impact of European Contact on Mackenzie Drainage Athabaskan Land Use Patterns. *Anthropological Papers of the University of Alaska* 25(1):17-27.

Hanks, Christopher C., and Barbara Winter

1983　Dene Names as an Organizing Principle in Ethnoarchaeological Research. *The Musk-ox* 33:49-55.

1986　Local Knowledge and Ethnoarchaeology: an Approach to Dene Settlement Systems. *Current An-*

thropology 27(3): 272-5.

1989   The Traditional Fishery on Deh Cho: an Ethnohistorical and Archaeological Perspective. *Arctic*
44(1):47-56.

Hart, Elisa J.

1994   Heritage Sites Research, Traditional Knowledge
and Training. In *Bridges Across Time: The NOGAP
Archaeology Project*, J-L. Pilon, ed., pp. 15-27. Occasional Paper No.2. Ottawa: Canadian Archaeological
Association.

Heine, Michael

1997   *"That river, it's like a highway for us": The
Mackenzie River through Gwichya Gwich'in History and
Culture*. Ottawa: Historic Sites and Monuments Board
of Canada.

**Heine, Michael, Alestine Andre, Ingrid Kritsch, and
Alma Cardinal**

2001 *Gwichya Gwich'in Googwandak: The History and
Stories of the Gwichya Gwich'in.*. Tsiigehtchic: Gwich'in
Social and Cultural Institute.

Helm, June

2000   *The People of Denendeh: Ethnohistory of the
Indians of Canada's Northwest Territories*. Iowa City:
University of Iowa Press.

Helm, June, ed.

1981   *Subarctic. Handbook of North American Indians*, Volume 6. Washington, D.C.: Smithsonian Institution.

Hirsch, Eric and Michael O'Hanlon, eds.

1995   *The Anthropology of Landscape: Perspectives
on Place and Space*. Oxford: Oxford University Press.

Krech, Shepard

1978   On the Aboriginal Population of the Kutchin.
Arctic Anthropology 15(1):89-104.

Kritsch, Ingrid

1996   The Delta Science Camp. *Wild Times* (Fall):2-4.
Yellowknife: Department of Resources, Wildlife and
Economic Development, Government of the North-
west Territories.

Kritsch, Ingrid D., and Alestine Andre

1997   Gwich'in Traditional Knowledge and Heritage
Studies in the Gwich'in Settlement Area. In *At a Crossroads: Archaeology and First Peoples in Canada*,
George P. Nicholas and Thomas D. Andrews, eds., pp.
123-44. Vancouver: Simon Fraser University Press.

Kritsch, Ingrid, Alestine Andre, and Bart Kreps

1994   Gwichya Gwich'in Oral History Project. In
*Bridges Across Time: The NOGAP Archaeology
Project*, J-L. Pilon, ed., pp. 5-13. Occasional Pa-

per No.2. Ottawa: Canadian Archaeological Association.

Legat, Allice

1998   *Habitat of Dogrib Traditional Territory: Place
Names as Indicators of Biogeographical Knowledge*.
Annual Report of the Dogrib Renewable Resources
Committee to the West Kitikmeot Slave Study Soci-
ety, Yellowknife.

**Legat, Allice, Sally Anne Zoe, Madelaine Chocolate,
and Kathy Simpson**

1999   *Habitat of Dogrib Traditional Territory: Place
Names as Indicators of Biogeographical Knowledge*.
Annual Report of the Dogrib Renewable Resources
Committee to the West Kitikmeot Slave Study Soci-
ety, Yellowknife.

**Legat, Allice, Georgina Chocolate, Bobby Gon,
Sally Anne Zoe, and Madeline Chocolate**

2001   *Caribou Migration and the State of their Habitat: Final Report*. Submitted to the West Kitikmeot/
Slave Study Society, Yellowknife.

Neufeld, David

2001   Parks Canada and the Commemoration of the
North: History and Heritage. In *Northern Visions: New
Perspectives on the North in Canadian History*, K. Abel
and K.S. Coates, eds., pp. 45-75. Peterborough:
Broadview Press.

Parks Canada

2000   *National Historic Sites: System Plan*. Ottawa:
Department of Canadian Heritage.

Strong , Roseanna, and Brenda Hans

1996   Diamonds in the Rough: The Tundra Science
Camp. *Green Teacher* 48:24-6.

**T'Seleie, John, Isadore Yukon, Bella T'Seleie, Ellen
Lee and Thomas D. Andrews**

2000   *Rakekée Gok'é Godi: Places we take care of*.
Report of the Sahtu Heritage Places and Sites Joint
Working Group. Yellowknife: Sahtu Heritage and
Places Joint Working Group (available online at
www.pwnhc.ca).

West Kitikmeot/Slave Study (WKSS)

2000   *Annual Report: 99/00*. West Kitikmeot/Slave
Study, Yellowknife, NT.

Woolf, Terry, and Thomas D. Andrews

1997   *Tłįchǫ K'ıelà: The Dogrib Birchbark Canoe*. VHS video documentary; 30 minutes. Rae-Edzo:
Dogrib Divisional Board of Education.

2001   *Tłįchǫ Ekwò Nįhmbàa: Dogrib Caribou Skin
Lodge*. VHS video documentary; 30-minutes. Rae-
Edzo: Dogrib Community Services Board.

Documenting Ethnographic Landscapes in Alaska's National Parks

TONIA WOODS HORTON

In his travels through the Indian lands of the American West in the 1830s, the famed portraitist George Catlin was greatly affected by the threatened extinction of the buffalo herds throughout the Great Plains. Writing at a time in which traditional Indian hunting practices for subsistence were beginning to be overshadowed by the commercial and sport hunting practices laying waste to vast herds, his concern about the buffalo was not simply that of a species' extermination, but rather, was linked, inextricably, to the American Indian culture, which he saw "rapidly wasting away at the approach of civilized man... in a very few years, to live only in books or on canvass [sic]." As a consequence of this perceived lack of "preservation and protection," Catlin proposed, essentially, the first idea of a national park based on preserving the view of "Indian and the buffalo—joint and original tenants of the soil":

> And what a splendid contemplation too, when one (who has travelled these realms, and can duly appreciate them) imagines them as they might in the future be seen, (by some great protecting policy of government) preserved in their pristine beauty and wildness, in a magnificent park, where the world could see for ages to come, the native Indian in his classic attire, galloping his wild horse, with sinewy bow, and shield and lance, amid the fleeting herds of elks and buffaloes. What a beautiful and thrilling specimen for America to preserve and hold up to the view of her refined citizens and the world, in future ages! A nation's Park, containing man and beast, in all the wild and freshness of nature's beauty! (Catlin 1844/1973:261-62)

His romantic impulses and antiquarian view of culture as a curio show aside, Catlin's compelling argument for a "nation's Park" unwittingly—and naively—prefigured a view toward national parks that would not come to the fore until the late twentieth century: the concept of the ethnographic landscape and its preservation as cultural heritage.

Catlin's insistence on the "joint tenancy" of both man and beast within a protected landscape actually reflected more the reality of the American landscapes as parks than the credo of scenic nationalism exemplified in the panoramic expanses of Yellowstone, Grand Canyon, and Yosemite. The imperative to preserve grand scenery, which dominated the creation of national parks in the United States in its infancy, was argued in terms of both the frontier and of American exceptionalism (see Runte 1987:11–8). Catlin's "nation's Park" was an inhabited one in which the ecological relationships between man and environment—albeit fragmentary—were viewed as vestiges of culture worthy of preservation. Despite the emergence of distinctly historical and archaeological parks in the early twentieth century (such as Civil War battlefields and Southwestern Indian ruins) through both congressional legislation and the Antiquities Act allowing presidential proclamation, the overarching themes for park and monument designation were those related to nature—an idealized sanctuary in which man was the visitor and not the resident. Nature cast in the form of cultural heritage excluded the prime ecological agent: humankind.

In creating protected areas to be experienced "from the outside in," this model for a national park embodies institutional frameworks—in essence, historical perspectives—which not only prescribe what kinds of resources constitute a park, whether "natural" or "cultural," but the hierarchy of values that attend each category of resources. These perspectives profoundly influence not only the public perception of the parks as experienced through interpretive tourism, but the management of large-scale habitats and historical communities as discrete entities, as opposed to critically examining the integral relationship between them. The difficulty here occurs when the heritage resources of a national park, on an abstract level, are identified according to discrete categories of natural or cultural, in effect, mirroring an institutionalization process. This, in turn, sets the parameter for the interpretive paradigms by which parks are designated, managed, and "consumed" by the public, obscuring the fact that these models reflect distinctly historical concepts of nature and culture. A critical part to this is the designation of 'wilderness'; instead of its most commonly held perception as land in a pristine state of being, it is, rather, an idea about nature and culture that is time-bound, reflecting values of differing eras responding to the exigencies of cultural time and space (cf. Spence 1999).

This disjuncture between the national park model emerging from the late nineteenth and early twentieth century and contemporary ecosystem dynamics of protected areas is particularly evident when we view parks as landscapes, most notably ethnographic landscapes in which the human presence is key to their preservation as cultural heritage. The existence of opposing vantage points—whether seen from within or without, through the lenses of nature or culture—critically impacts our ability to view landscapes as the layered, multi-faceted, mutually dependent double helix of humans and environment.

How, then, do we begin to understand parks as landscapes in which cultural heritage is ethnographically conceived, i.e., cultural landscapes? How do these land-scapes reflect attitudes about culture and history that continue to evolve, rather than static portraits, artifactual in nature? What promise does the cultural landscape paradigm hold for the management of national parks? And critically, to what extent does the idea of the cultural landscape restructure history-writing, heritage production, and place-making themselves?

This paper will examine the concept of ethnographic landscapes within a discussion of this construct. The application of cultural landscape preservation, in essence, constitutes historical revisionism in terms of how environmental and Native American histories are written (or not)—and thus, heritage acknowledged—through the documentation and interpretation of heritage values in the landscape. Catlin's vision for a national park—though flawed and time bound—is not as irrelevant to a discussion of contemporary parks as it may seem upon first glance. This is particularly true when one considers the origin of Alaska national parks in the last quarter of the twentieth century, and the implications for defining park landscapes as "ethnographic."

Unlike the lower forty-eight states, Alaska's Native population was not subjected to a reservation system. Aboriginal land claims in Alaska, then, continued to exist until the discovery of oil on the North Slope. Though sparsely populated, much of Alaska continued to be traversed and used for a network of subsistence activities—inhabited—by Native peoples. The concept of parks as wilderness areas did not exist.

Before the 1970s, only three parks—two as national monuments, one as a national park and preserve—existed in Alaska: Katmai, Denali (established as Mt. McKinley), and Glacier Bay. With the massive changes wrought in the disposition of Native and public lands as a result of the desire for oil exploration and drilling, the resulting legislation, Alaska Native Claims Settlement Act (ANCSA, 1971) and the Alaska National Interest Lands Conservation Act (ANILCA, 1980; see Williss 1985), essentially reformulated the concept of a national park as an uninhabited place. In particular, ANILCA's passage determined the fate of 104 million acres; it created six new national parks, enlarged one existing park, established two new national monuments, added acreage to two existing monuments, and set aside two new national preserves. In the words of historian Roderick Nash (1982:272), ANILCA was the "single greatest act of wilderness preservation in world history," single-handedly doubling the number of acres in the entire National Park Service (NPS), and by adding an additional fifty-six million acres to the National Wilderness Preservation System, more than tripled its size.

Even more striking, ANILCA initiated an entirely new policy with respect to Native land rights: in this case, those of the Native Alaskans. As opposed to the national parks in the lower forty-eight states, the ANILCA parks recognized the land rights of pre-existing traditional cultures as legal, in particular, those related to hunting and gathering activities in a "traditional use of their subsistence resources" (Nash 1982:272).

Despite an enduring and highly political controversy over the subsistence issue since its passage, ANILCA reoriented planning and resource management in national parks toward the importance of ethnographic research, particularly in those parks it directly affected. The enabling legislation mandated a form of cultural conservation—in this case, Native subsistence culture—and created a legal obligation to preserve and protect the full array of resources people use to define and sustain their cultures.

The nexus of ethnography and history, of heritage and sustainability, cultural conservation is rooted in the concept of landscape—the physical matrix for cultural, natural, and symbolic threads of human existence. Interpreting park landscapes as ethnographic cultural resources, however limited by definitions and competing priorities, is an endeavor to portray how humans and land are inescapably woven together, a reciprocity that cannot be abstracted out of the historical portrayal of what a place is, how it has changed over time, and its importance to identity, belonging, and the traditional maintenance of the past through the present. Parks are

uninhabited, but their lands contain rich stories of occupation and use, memory and ritual, of seasonal rounds and ceremonial visits to sacred sites. Revealing the layered histories of these landscapes demonstrates the "provisional, conditional nature of the past" and is culturally empowering. This knowledge allows to reclaim place through stories—understanding landscapes as "storytelling with the shapes of time" (Hayden 1995:226).

The stories of two documented ethnographic landscapes in Alaska, Klondike Gold Rush National Historical Park (NHP) and Glacier Bay National Park and Preserve, illustrate how the process is being adapted to respond to the history of place—how re-visioning through the lenses of Native American and environmental history reinterprets park landscapes. As a baseline format for identifying, documenting, evaluating, and analyzing cultural landscapes within the national parks, the Cultural Landscape Inventory (CLI) is the first tier of research for constructing such landscape histories. Its methodology and application in the two Alaska parks under discussion is a "work in progress," but one which has begun to articulate new narratives of place.

These two parks represent a wide range of issues from memorialization to the recognition of traditional ecological knowledge as a key determinant of identity and cultural preservation. By viewing park lands as ethnographic landscapes—or at the very least, landscapes with ethnographic stories—the CLI process begins to acknowledge Native Americans as historical agents. This initial shift in perspective sets into place the importance of historical processes and their spatial dimensions:the functions of memory and identity within processes of cultural conservation, how contemporary perception and use shape the ideas of heritage and legacy, and the importance of recognition through interpretation—all tethered to physical places.

Dyea, the Chilkoot Trail, and Indian History in Klondike Gold Rush National Historical Park

In the late 1980s, a Deisheetaan clan potlatch ceremony

was held in a modest Legion Hall in the small South-eastern Alaska town of Skagway. Hosted by an elderly Native woman, Angela Sidney, from the Canadian village of Carcross in the Yukon Territory, the event celebrated the arrival and dedication of a grave marker for Tlingit/Tagish family members who had died between 1898 and 1901 at Dyea, otherwise known as the ephemeral gateway town at the foot of the famed Klondike Gold Rush's Chilkoot Trail. At the time of their deaths, Sidney's relatives had been buried at a "Native Cemetery" near the Healy and Wilson Trading Post at the western edge of the Taiya River, their graves marked by a "spirit house." Due to the dynamic river conditions—seasonal flooding and bank erosion—at Dyea, the spirit house marking the graves of her relatives, as well as much of the Native Cemetery, had washed away by the late 1970s. Before then, Sidney made periodic trips to visit the spirit house, which commemorated her three siblings and several other cousins who died in an outbreak of dysentery and German measles while her parents were at Dyea, trading with the Tlingits and the whites, Healy and Wilson.

Upon discovering that the spirit house had been washed away, Sidney was disturbed that there was no "mark" of her relatives' existence, no "spirit house on them." Returning to Carcross, Sidney spoke to another relative, Austin Hammond from Haines, about it:

> So I asked him. I told him all about those kids had a spirit house on them and I told him it's washed out. And I told him I want to put a gravestone on it. 'Do you think it will be all right if I do that? Just to put a mark on those kids? Just to know that they were there? That our people were there? (Angela Sidney in Cruikshank 1990:151–2).

Eventually, Sidney raised enough money for a stone marker upon which the names of about ten of her relatives were inscribed, and it was installed at the relocated Dyea Native Cemetery (Fig. 105).

From the small grave marker at Dyea to the larger Chilkoot Trail corridor, Native presence before, during, and after the Klondike Gold Rush has been a story in the shadows in the nearly thirty years of the Klondike

Gold Rush NHP's existence.[1] The park's enabling legislation and its National Historic Landmark status pegged its significance to the Gold Rush legacy, one in which the predominant image of the lone, burdened prospector setting out to strike it rich was juxtaposed against the teeming gateways of Skagway and Dyea, boomtowns springing up overnight in response to the discovery of gold in the Yukon River drainages. The romanticism of the trail and the swashbuckling exploits of frontier characters, along with the restoration of Gold Rush buildings within a historic district in the surviving Skagway, has been the primary narrative of both gold rush towns, with Dyea having quickly succumbed to abandonment when Skagway's White Pass and Yukon Railroad obviated the need for the arduous Chilkoot Trail route in 1900. Surviving physical resources from the Gold Rush era, such as a complement of historic buildings in Skagway, and the rich archaeological deposits at Dyea and on the trail buttressed the park's claim to exceptional historical significance.

Missing, however, from this narrative are two critical historical agents whose roles are intertwined: the Native people whose occupation preceded the 1898-1900 flurry of activity, and the influence of the landscape itself, particularly its natural systems and features. Interpretation of the park as an assemblage of historic sites related to the Gold Rush, while critical, has not addressed the complexity of the landscape as a continuum of cultural and ecological change. This is partly due to the fact that most visitors to the park, arriving predominantly by way of the summer cruise ships, experience the park through exhibits at the visitor center and the historic buildings in the Skagway Historic District—places in which the emphasis is focused almost exclusively on the years of the gold rush, a set of years frozen in time mirrored, for example, by the life-like tableaux exhibit of miners at a period bar in the Mascot Saloon. However, an increasing number of visitors are making their way into the large-scale landscapes—Dyea and the Chilkoot Trail—by tour groups, highlighting the interpretive potential of these sites as places

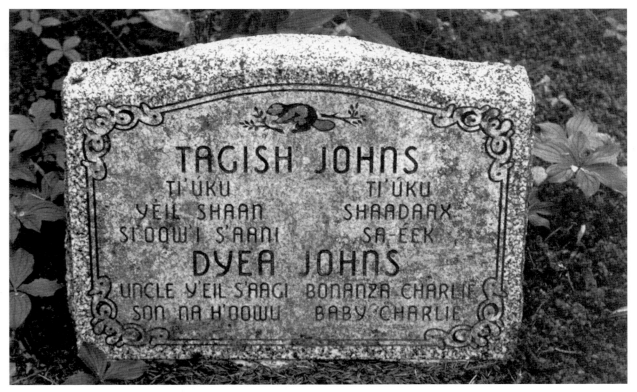

105/ Relocated Tlingit grave marker at Dyea Native Cemetery, 2001.

greatly altered from their gold rush days. The contrast is striking between the static urban grid of Skagway's historic district and the dynamic glacial hydrology of the Taiya River, which affects the trail and Dyea by seasonal flooding and bank erosion.

Linked to the National Register of Historic Places (NRHP – see Horton, this volume), and thus limited in terms of redefining Dyea and the Chilkoot Trail as ethnographic landscapes, both CLIs expanded the historical chronology of the sites by identifying them as Native territory, the sites of cultural interaction first between Tlingit and Tagish, and then Euro-Americans. In documenting the landscapes, strands of a story emerge that reflect a more palpable presence of occupation and use within both historical and environmental contexts. And while virtually none of this information is new, its inclusion as a part of the physical history of the site is critically important. Articulating Native patterns of territorial use and control keyed to the resources of a particular environment (read "place") re-

veals the larger dimensions of the history being constructed—that of a contact story in which centuries-old rhythms of seasonal occupation and trading are largely dislocated by an ephemeral event, the gold rush. In essence, this is a remapping of the landscape as a continuum of ecological relationships, rather than capsuling a select "period of significance" related to the gold rush. And while it may seem only a symbolic gesture—like the grave marker—the addition of an ethnohistorical aspect to the landscape history has the potential to mitigate the rigid typology of the NRHP by which salient aspects of sites as landscapes fall through the cracks.

The name, "Dyea," in fact, is derived from the Tlingit *dayei*, or "packing place," indicating the strategic value of the tidal floodplain for the entrepreneurial coastal Natives.[2] Consummate traders, the Tlingit predicated their wealth upon the movement of goods to and from the Athapaskan groups farther inland by controlling traffic along the passages to the interior, one of which was the Chilkoot Trail whose name by Euro-Americans recognized, if tacitly, its Native history. As one of only three non-glaciated passes connecting the Pacific coast with the interior of present-day Yukon Territory—especially the vast transportation network of the Yukon River drainage, the Chilkoot Trail was a vital trade corridor for at least two centuries before the Klondike gold rush. Trade between the coastal Tlingit and the interior Athapaskan people included a flow of marine products to the north, in particular dried fish, clams, seaweed, sea otter pelts, and fish oil, while the fur stocks of caribou, moose, and beaver were transported to the south. The importance of hooligan oil as a trade commodity gave rise to Euro-American explorers dubbing the route as the "grease trail." Traveling by family groups, the Chilkat/Chilkoot typically made two or three annual trips, the most important being the spring fur trade— allowing for a return to Dyea before the annual hooligan harvest at the mouth of the Taiya River in April. Similarly, the Tagish seasonal rounds also affected their trips to Dyea, as their trips coincided with the end of "beaver season" in the north, hunting mountain goats and groundhogs and other small game for drying during their camp at Dyea (Cruikshank 1990:151).

Dyea's location at the foot of the trail, as well as at the resource-rich tidal flats, established it not only as a staging area for the rugged trade corridor, but also as a seasonal camp for the Chilkat/Chilkoot Tlingit, whose permanent settlement was at Klukwan (Haines Mission), a few miles across the Lynn Canal. With the purchase of Alaska by the U.S. in 1867, and increased exploration and prospecting throughout the 1880s, the seasonal trade and subsistence rounds that had characterized Dyea shifted toward a more permanent settlement with the arrival of Healy and Wilson's trading post in 1884 (Fig. 106). By 1887, records noted that 138 Natives inhabited a settlement just north of the trading post, which eventually included the Dyea Native Cemetery. A decade before the gold rush, the importance of Dyea as a trading post resulted in a shift of goods and commodities; in addition to the local marine products from

the Tlingit, the Tagish brought their furs south to trade for guns, knives, and supplies at the trading post (Greer 1993:39). As Angela Sidney recounted,

> People used to go down to Dyea always all the time before Skagway—go back and forth from Tagish to the coast. It was just like going to the store—that's the only place they used to get their outfit, like flour and sugar and tea and stuff. They get enough stuff there for one whole winter's supply" (Cruikshank 1990:153).

At the outset of the gold rush fever, territorial conflicts between the Chilkoot and Sitka Tlingit over trail packing rights resulted in a violent confrontation in 1887 between the two groups; throughout the next decade, increasing traffic through Dyea to the trail irrevocably loosened the Chilkoot control over the packing trade to include not only the Sitkas and other Tlingit groups, but the Athabaskan (Tagish and Stikeen) packers as well. Ultimately, negotiations with the Chilkoot over use of the trail gave way in the face of thousands of stampeders, although their sense of ownership remained. Photographs taken during the 1897–1900 gold rush heyday on the trail generally depict Natives in the nearly invisible role of packers for the Euro-American prospectors. When Dyea collapsed as a boomtown gateway to the Yukon, the Native packing industry and trading post were abandoned as well. Left behind were the graves and markers, such as the spirit houses, of those in the Native Cemetery.

Although little is known of Tlingit occupation and use of Dyea and the Chilkoot Trail after 1900, at least one Native land claim with cabins was surveyed at Dyea before 1915; by the 1940s, subsistence activities in the area included at least one smokehouse, and known wood-gathering areas around Dyea.[3] Some families may have remained at Dyea for a short period after 1900, where at least one homesteading family, the Matthews, was the result of a Tlingit/Euro-American intermarriage. Interviews with Tlingit from nearby Haines (Klukwan) in 1946 indicated that Dyea was a traditional summer camp and that it continued to be an area of considerable resource gathering activities:

106/ *Tlingit village at Healy and Wilson trading post, Dyea, 1897.*

Dyea and Skagway are claimed by my people. There are three streams at Dyea, and there were three smokehouses there. The people did not live there the year around, but used the place a great deal. All three of these smokehouses were owned by Lukaax.adi people. They controlled a large area of land. This place was used for berries as well as for smoking fish. The Indian people [Tagish?] also hunted there and smoked meat. They generally went there in the fall of the year. Some of the people would go up to pick berries and then rush back to Chilkoot to put them up. During the hunting season, however, they stayed up there a long time (Paddy Goennette in Goldschmidt and Haas 1998:33).

With the establishment of the park in 1976, archaeological investigations at both the Dyea Townsite area and along the Chilkoot Trail focused primarily on artifacts from the Gold Rush era since these deposits were in abundance. This was partially due to the encroachment of the Taiya River during the past century; all

physical evidence of the Native village at the trading post, as well as the Native cemetery, was lost. Along the Chilkoot Trail, rock cairns and tree slashes marking the route were also subsumed, as early as the first wave of stampeders, with only the name recalling its cultural association before the gold rush (Brady 1997:76,110).

In order to fashion a more inclusive landscape history for Dyea and the Chilkoot Trail, both CLIs conducted began the landscape history with Tlingit occupation and use before the Gold Rush, despite the fact that little tangible "evidence" was available. Although not characterized as "ethnographic landscapes" in the inventories (rather, both are seen as vernacular landscapes), the ethnographic—in this case, Tlingit and Athapaskan—aspects of the landscape history were significant in that the case could be argued that indigenous subsistence and trade use of the area far outlived the transitory boomtown. Thus, the history of

Dyea as a cultural landscape originated in the earliest known uses by the Native people for its resource-rich environment as well as its strategic location at the beginning/end of the trail as a trade corridor. Determining the extent to which Tlingit and Tagish peoples participated in gold rush has proven elusive, as most documentation points to their support roles as packers.

Marginal as it may seem, the Native contribution to the park's historical narrative is an important one, for it is a largely unarticulated ethnohistory that speaks to the interrelationship of people and landscape. Perhaps even more importantly, it serves as an anchor for memory. Angela Sidney's lament that no one would know that her people had lived and been buried there led her to memorialize her relatives after the Native village and its cemetery had long since vanished. The Tlingit's land claim was subsumed under another homesteader, and documentation of subsistence use after 1946 is virtually nonexistent. Today, the legacy of the Chilkat/Chilkoot is one of traces—the names "Dyea" and "Chilkoot" and a small grave marker.

But, in attempting to capture the layers of the cultural landscape in these places, it becomes clear that the significance of Dyea and the Chilkoot Trail did not begin in 1898, nor did it end in 1900. A landscape of extremes, from the tidal flats to the towering summit at the pass, the Chilkat/Chilkoot territory was one that was clearly delineated in the minds of the Native Tlingit and visiting Tagish as valuable terrain before the arrival of the Euro-Americans; now, the "mark" of memory, though a grave marker, speaks to the efficacy of remembering a people's story, of heritage rooted to place.

Traditional Cultural Properties and the Wilderness Paradigm: Documenting Tlingit Homelands at Glacier Bay

With ANILCA's establishment of the Alaska national parks—and the recognition of Native peoples' rights to subsistence resources—ethnographic research came to the forefront of planning and management, primarily due to the legalities involved in resource management and land rights. Unlike the rest of Alaska, Natives of Southeast Alaska—primarily the Tlingit—were excluded from subsistence rights agreements incorporated into traditional and customary use of lands in the newly created parks. Nowhere is this more pronounced than, perhaps, the designation of the majority of lands within—and perception of—Glacier Bay National Park as a wilderness preserve. Although not part of the federal subsistence regime, expanded ethnographic research is gradually becoming a key aspect of park management. This is due, in part, to the park's increased cultural activities in support of closer relationships with the Huna Tlingit, who claim Glacier Bay as *Haa Aani* ("our land"), their ancestral homelands.[4]

Beginning in 1999, the National Park Service initiated Cultural Landscape Inventories (CLIs) in the park to support potential nominations of two places to the National Register of Historic Places as traditional cultural properties (TCPs): Dundas Bay and Bartlett Cove. Both places are of immense significance to the Huna Tlingit, who live on the north end of Chichagof Island at Hoonah, an hour's flight to the south of the park, but who maintain that all of Glacier Bay is Huna territory. Bartlett Cove, now the location of park headquarters, includes a small cluster of islands; the vicinity of the cove was an important resource procurement zone with at least one semi-permanent village, seasonal camps, and a turn-of-the century saltery. Mythologically, it may be one of the most significant cultural sites within Glacier Bay, as it is believed to be the landscape of the highly potent Kasteen and Shawatseek story validating Glacier Bay as a place of Tlingit origin and identity.

Farther to the west, the promontory, tidal flats, and waters of Dundas Bay contain archaeological remains that range from an eleventh century Tlingit fort and eighteenth century village site to late nineteenth-early twentieth century cannery, settlement site, cemetery, and seasonal camps; at least three Native allotments were filed on lands in Dundas Bay. The most dominant landscape vestiges of Tlingit historic occupation and use are found at the site of the adjacent Dundas Bay Cannery. The entire area continues to be important to the Huna as a prized berry habitat, although historically, Dundas Bay had several productive salmon streams, accounting for the documented remains of smokehouses indicative of seasonal use. Both landscapes constitute rich areas of traditional cultural use and association, borne out by historic patterns of site-specific resource harvesting, creation stories, oral histories, archaeological evidence, and place-names.

Mapping Dundas Bay and Bartlett Cove as cultural landscapes with a view toward identifying them as Traditional Cultural Properties (TCP), a designation for the National Register of Historic Places, poses distinct challenges, not the least of which is the construction of an alternative view of history in which environment and culture are inextricably woven in a designated "wilderness." As with Dyea and the Chilkoot Trail, this history is one in which human ecology (of the Tlingit) is the fundamental premise for cultural landscape recognition—and inherently, protection—within the legal framework of the National Historic Preservation Act.[5] The process of identifying and documenting Dundas Bay and Bartlett Cove as cultural landscapes essentially controverts a centuries-long continuum of identifying the landscape with Western ideas of origin and discovery. In its place, the cultural landscapes are revealed as integral repositories of history and identity for the Huna Tlingit, places of traditional ecological and cultural knowledge that retain their prominence despite the fact that decades have passed since the Huna actively fished and harvested there. Although truncated, the landscape histories in the Bartlett Cove and Dundas Bay CLIs reflect an intricately sophisticated physical, social, and symbolic matrix in which cultural values—homelands and wilderness—are at stake.

Part of this process is understanding how the wilderness paradigm—its "discovery," exploration, and in-terpretation—emerged from Euro-American perceptions of the Glacier Bay landscape, a far different perspective from that of Native Tlingit. The creation of Glacier Bay National Monument by President Calvin Coolidge on February 26, 1925, capped nearly fifty years of interest in its glacial landscape as an "ecological laboratory" worthy of preservation. In reality, the landscape of Glacier Bay had been largely constructed in the Euro-American imagination by narratives of exploration and discovery beginning with the first systematic survey of the Inside Passage, the expedition of Capt. George Vancouver, 1791, chronicled in the journal of Dr. Archibald Menzies (1793–1794), both surgeon and botanist for the expedition. Serious encroachment of glacial ice in the bay prevented ingress to the upbay areas; nevertheless, Menzies described portions of what would become park lands, including "a village with some natives" at Dundas Bay (Menzies 1993:161). Subsequent reports of Tlingit activity in Glacier Bay were limited primarily due to lack of glacial advance. However, a congressional report in 1882 included a population estimate of some 600–800 Tlingit at Hoonah, their largest concentrated, permanent settlement at Glacier Bay (U.S. Senate 1882:185).

The presence of the Tlingit in the shadows of the monumental glaciers was featured in the account written by Charles Wood, an American, whose reconnaissance of Southeast Alaska and the Yukon River headwaters nearly a century later than Menzies in April 1877 included Glacier Bay. Remarkably, Wood's account reflected more of his interaction with the Tlingits than his awe at the glaciers (Wood 1882:323–39).

Two years later in 1879, however, the arrival of John Muir at Glacier Bay heralded a more intense era of focus on the glacial landscape in which the Tlingit occupation was noted, but accorded little serious attention. An intrepid naturalist, Muir's fascination with Glacier Bay reflected the fusion of his beliefs in the "glacial gospel" espoused by Louis Agassiz with the legacy of Transcendentalism, in which human degradation of the natural world had resulted in the loss of an Edenic legacy. Muir's ideology of a paradise regained was implicit in his description of the glaciated Inside Passage of Southeast Alaska:

> To the lover of pure wildness Alaska is one of the most wonderful countries in the world. No excursion that I know of may be made into any other American wilderness where so marvelous an abundance of *noble, newborn scenery* is so charmingly brought into view" (Muir 1915/1998:13, emphasis added).

Muir's short statement, and his subsequent publications, outlined in essence what would become the philosophical imperative for the creation of Glacier Bay as a protected area. His acceptance of Agassiz's glacial origins theory, conjoined with the sense of an unspoiled landscape in which the sublime was evident at every view, constituted the basis for a latter-day scientific creation story. In fact, Muir's self-laudatory article recounting this visit was both ecstatic romanticism and portentous of the "natural" values by which Glacier Bay would come under the legal protection of the U.S. government as a national monument (Muir 1895:234–47).

Muir reckoned that here, as an inevitable retreat of glaciers, the "noble, newborn scenery"—encompassing the remains of ancient interstadial forests with the reestablishment of plant and animal life on the new land revealed by isostatic rebound—elevated this particular "wilderness" to distinction. "Fashioning the face of the coming landscape," the glaciers were the elemental force of a regeneration of earth" (Muir 1895: 247). In reality, Muir's assertion of the sublimity of the Glacier Bay landscape aligned very nicely with the sweeping tide of scenic nationalism parlayed into the creation of national parks, symbolic of an American heritage rivaling claims of European historical supremacy.

The Tlingit, whose presence Muir recorded and whose guidance was necessary in order for him to reach the limits of the up-bay regions, were, for the most part, anecdotal footnotes to the natural drama unfolding at Glacier Bay. Even in its muted details, Muir's tale—in essence, an ethnographic contact story—reveals the disparity between the landscape of "discovery" and the

landscape of habitation and use. The impetus for Muir's journey into Glacier Bay was his Chilkat Tlingit guide's childhood experience in the bay "full of ice" where the young man had been seal-hunting with his father. After entering and camping at one of the western inlets at the mouth of the bay, the group made contact with a small group of Huna seal hunters at a seasonal camp, more than likely in the vicinity of Bartlett Cove.[6] During the exchange, Muir's initial questions about the presence of the "ice mountains" were met with "counter questions as to our object in coming to such a place, especially so late in the year." As seal-hunters on a well-established seasonal round coming to a close (early November), Muir's sudden appearance was suspect for the Tlingit, leading them to ask if he was a missionary: "Was he going to preach to seals and gulls, they asked, or to the ice-mountains." After an exchange of tobacco, sugar, and other items, the Huna revealed that

> The main bay was called by them Sit-a-da-kay, or Ice Bay; that there were many large ice-mountains in it, but no *gold-mines*; and that the ice-mountain they knew best was at the head of the bay, where most of the seals were found" (Muir 1895:235–6).

Unfazed by the Tlingit questioning of his motives, Muir hired one of the seal-hunters to guide them up-bay. In the next few days, Muir "discovered" the landscape of "the five . . . huge glaciers. . . . [T]his was my first general view of Glacier Bay, a solitude of ice and snow and new-born rocks, dim, dreary, mysterious." While Muir's rapture was only slightly tempered by the daunting climatic conditions, the Natives knew the risks of traveling in the glacial waters, and feared the worst:

> The Hoona guide said bluntly that if I was so fond of danger, and meant to go close up to the noses of the ice-mountains, he would not consent to go any farther; for we should all be lost, as many of his tribe had been, by the sudden rising of bergs from the bottom" (Muir 1895:237).

Muir was able to convince the Huna guide to continue to the "head of the bay, and to the mouth of the northwest fiord, at the head of which lie the Hoona sealing-grounds. . . .[H]ere the Hoona guide had a store of dry wood, which we took aboard" (ibid.).

The contrast between Muir's pursuit of knowledge and the intimate knowledge of place revealed by the Tlingit is striking. The landscape that one party sought to explore and map as a *terra incognita* was, in fact, one in which the Huna imprint—however subtly perceived through seasonal camps, ecological knowledge, circulation networks, and place-names—had been in existence for centuries.

Despite the rise in steamship tourism that featured, at one point, the seal hunting camp at Bartlett Cove as somewhat of a local attraction in the 1880s and 1890s, the impetus toward imaginatively capturing Glacier Bay as a landscape of natural significance gained the upper hand in the first decades of the twentieth century, culminating in its designation as a national monument. In 1916, American ecologist William Cooper's foray into Glacier Bay initiated the first systematic study of the Glacier Bay landscape. Heavily influenced by Muir's accounts of the terrain, as well as the scientific publications emerging from expeditions before the earthquake-induced glacial activity after 1899, Cooper's interest in demonstrating the fledgling ecological model of plant community succession led him to the reemerging coastline of Glacier Bay. Echoing Muir's rapture with the landscape, Cooper's dedication to ecological study was to last nearly half a decade—and resulted in federal protection of Glacier Bay as a national monument.

Introducing his study to the scientific public, Cooper presented his case for the uniqueness of the Glacier Bay ecology, and its potential for revealing natural processes unavailable in other regions:

> An ecologist will seize with eager delight upon an opportunity to study the successional processes directly—a field where change is plainly evident from year to year; where the major part of a complete developmental cycle may be encompassed within the limits of a single lifetime. . . . In Glacier Bay we have a history of practically unbroken glacier retreat, known to extend back to 1794 and doubtless considerably farther. Since 1879 the changes in position of the various ice fronts have several times been accurately mapped, and the geology and especially the recent history have been well worked out. We thus have a continually expanding territory, quite fresh, exposed to plant invasion, and upon it we find the successive developmental stages displayed in a definite logical order, from pioneers to climax (Cooper 1923:93–4).

In setting forth a scientific investigation—studying plant quadrants to monitor reestablishment of plant communities, mapping remnants of interstadial forests, and recording climactic changes—Cooper was, in effect, continuing to map Glacier Bay as a scientific creation story, albeit with much more precision, and less bombast, than John Muir. As one of the first generation of ecologists, his view was shaped by a vision of nature in which balance, regeneration, and rational linear processes were at play. In this view, there was no human—cultural—interaction with the "ecological laboratory" of Glacier Bay; the teleological succession of plant and animal life as a result of glacial retreat constituted its own independent, autonomous history of place. The apparently seamless transition from Muir's philosophic romanticism to scientifically interpreting Glacier Bay as a "wilderness" devoid of human significance had been set into motion.

Strikingly parallel and yet wildly divergent, the Huna Tlingit view of Glacier Bay is not constructed on the absence of humankind within a creation myth, but on a presence intimately woven within it. Historically—and to the present day—the Huna Tlingit have claimed Glacier Bay as their place of origin and belonging. From the Tlingit perspective, even in their diminished role relayed by Muir's narrative, the landscape mapped by the Euro-Americans as Glacier Bay was a resource-laden homeland in which humans moved cyclically, with intimate knowledge of climate, natural processes, and wildlife, so since the beginning of their cultural time. Their geographic and practical knowledge of the ice-strewn bay areas was critical to "Muir's discovery."

In fact, the Glacier Bay area—both in times of glacial advance and in retreat—has been called *S'ix' Tlein*, or the "Big Dish," signifying its role not only as the physical "breadbasket" or "icebox" containing a rich panoply of life-sustaining resources, but perhaps more importantly, the shared conception of the landscape as *Tlingit A'ani*, Tlingit territory that persists to the present day. Chookaneidi elder Ken Austin described the meaning of "Big Dish":

> It is the Big Dish all year round....Amy Marvin (deceased Chookaneidi elder) told me 'We gathered for winter time all the food. We did it quickly. From the Big Dish area.' Summer, winter, summer, winter. That was our home, you know. So that's again, where, when we say 'Glacier Bay,' we are also saying 'The Big Dish' because that's where it all is. All the berries...it's there (Ken Austin, interview, September 2001, Anchorage).

For the Tlingit, the cognitive and symbolic mapping of Glacier Bay represents not only possessory rights to subsistence resources, but the very social organization underpinning the uniqueness of their cultural life and identity. Tlingit clans not only claimed their own distinctive locales through place-names, resource activities (berry-picking, sealing, seasonal fish camps) that may or may not have had visible impacts upon the landscape, but through symbolic ties as well, such as stories, crests, and ceremonies, they reciprocally acknowledged the territory of other clans. Clan property, the *at.oow*, then, was manifestly tied to places in an overall landscape of *ha aani*, or "our land."[7] Unlike other conceptions of contiguous or bounded property, however, the Tlingit recognition of specific clan territory was "conceptualized not in terms of large swaths of land, but rather as constellations of gathering, or historical and navigational landmarks." (De Laguna 1960:20).

With this culturally defined geography in mind, the identification of two cultural landscapes in the park—Dundas Bay and Bartlett Cove—set the stage for the initiation of the CLIs in 1999. The goal of the inventories was to synthetically document the two landscapes as places of cultural heritage for the Huna Tlingit in order to explore the potential for their nomination to the National Register as Traditional Cultural Properties (TCP). A TCP documents heritage as an active process in which the contemporary "property" demonstrates historically rooted beliefs, customary practices, and the maintenance of traditional knowledge—a task complicated by the fact that active Tlingit occupation and use of the sites effectively ceased due to park management policies in the late 1940s to early 1950s.[8] However, the vigor with which Tlingit elders still speak of Glacier Bay attests to the deeply held cultural sense of identity with its landscape and resources.

Fieldwork during the summers of 1999–2001, as well as supporting oral histories and historical research, focused on documenting the Tlingit historical association with these sites—an interdisciplinary methodology reflected in diverse and, perhaps, unconventional ways of interpreting cultural data. Four primary sets of cultural information were utilized: physical environs and remains, documented through existing conditions, photographic surveys, archaeological fieldwork, oral histories and interviews; available place-name data; and finally, historical and anthropological research (particularly that of anthropologist Thomas Thornton). Fieldwork included a study of traditional plant use interviews with four Tlingit elders: Winnie Smith, Esther Haze, Katherine Grant, and Jennie Lindoff, conducted in July, 2001, along with field identification of specific plants in the Bartlett Cove area.

This information was then interpreted through a site history, as well as an analysis of the significance of key landscape characteristics such as natural systems, spatial organization, land use, cultural traditions, and archaeological sites. The inventories concluded with an evaluation of the significance and integrity of these landscape characteristics as contributing to the potential designation of landscapes as TCPs.

Long the mainstay of historical construction for the National Register, the field survey documentation of archaeological evidence is the most problematic in the Glacier Bay sites due to the character of the glacial

107/ Tlingit village of Khart Heene [Gat-hi-ni], "Salmon Water." Photograph by George Emmons, 1889.

landscape. The advance and retreat of glacial ice sheets during the most recent "Little Ice Age," (approximately 1550-1850 AD), with its corresponding rise and fall of sea levels, isostatic rebound, and revegetation, destroyed Tlingit settlement and seasonal camp sites and other material evidence of occupation, complicating claims of ownership and use from the Western perspective.

One of the few exceptions to this paucity of known archaeological sites is found at Dundas Bay, *Tinaak'w* (Little Copper Shield), a glacial fjord on the north shore of Icy Strait, to which both the T'akdeintaan and Chookaneidi clans have traditional claims. Because this area had been in a state of glacial retreat since the Pleistocene (13,000 BP), it sustained an incredibly rich habitat for marine and plant resources harvested by the Tlingit. Corroborated by oral history, archaeological surveys have documented several historic settlements in the Dundas Bay area:

—The late eighteenth century village of *L'istee* (occupied late 1880s to 1910s);

—The recently rediscovered *Xakwnoowu* (Gravel or Dry Fort) dating to about 1100-1150 BP;

—Early twentieth century house pilings and a cemetery at the base of *Xakwnoowu* ;

—The remains of the Dundas Bay cannery (1900-1930), probably the most visible historic remnants of Tlingit occupation;

—A series of stone "nests" or monuments along the adjacent ridgelines, perhaps the oldest material evidence of occupation. Alluded to in stories as a place of refuge from bears during a period of flooding, this interpretations corresponds to the ice-free conditions present in Dundas Bay when the rest of Glacier Bay was under glacial advance in the Little Ice Age.

Bartlett Cove, by comparison, lacks the archaeological record of Dundas Bay due to its recent glacial history of advance and retreat. Historic occupation of this area can be dated to the remains of at least one salmon saltery (1888, possibly as early as 1883) and an associated Native cemetery at Lester Island. George Emmons' photograph from 1889 documents the presence of a sealer's camp and a village most likely at this site, which was also associated with a productive sockeye salmon stream (Fig. 107). Three Native allotments were recorded for Bartlett Cove; a claim survey in 1914 noted a log cabin "formerly used as a smoke-house for drying salmon," although no ruins exist today. At the time of the CLI fieldwork, there were several culturally modified trees dating approximately to 1900 within the immediate vicinity of the cove, and others located in adjacent areas. At least two uses for the peeled inner bark were described by contemporary elders—fibers stripped for basketry, and more common, the harvesting of the cambium layer as a foodstuff.[9]

However limited the physical record may be, critical oral histories conducted in the 1940s as part of a study of Tlingit and Haida land rights illustrate that all of Glacier Bay was described as *S'ix Tlein*, the Big Dish—the Huna "breadbasket," from which the material and spiritual sustenance originated (Goldschmidit and Haas 1998:25). Huna elders interviewed at that time recalled seasonal camps at both Bartlett Cove and Dundas Bay for marine and terrestrial resource harvesting as far back as the 1880s, with garden areas and thick patches of nagoonberries, strawberries, cranberries, soapberries, and raspberries, as well as rhubarb. The inter-tidal zone along the beaches was particularly rich with ribbon seaweed, crabs, and "gumboots" (especially at Bartlett Cove). Vital to the Tlingit diet, both salmon and seals were harvested in the waters at Bartlett Cove and Dundas Bay; both the story of *Xakwnoonu* and the 1889 photograph of *Gatheeni* seasonal village indicate sealing activities. Land otters, porcupines, martens, wolverines, wolves, and black bears were hunted and trapped in Bartlett Cove. The interviews also documented summer campsites, trap-lines, numerous smokehouses, gardens, and possessory rights to salmon streams, all multi-generational in ownership, indicating a long-term presence in both landscapes. Albert Jackson's statement revealed his family's activities and attachment to Bartlett Cove:

> Bartlett Cove was an important place for the Native people. I have a dwelling and two smokehouses there; also a garden...I had two trap lines around the lake above Bartlett Cove. The last time I trapped there was about eight years ago [1938], but since I have become too old my sons used these trap lines until it [Glacier Bay] was made a reserve. I have fish

lines and traps in my house. . . . I also have a trapping cabin on the lake—formerly had two or three cabins on the trap line. This place belongs to the T'akdeintaan clan and has belonged to my family for a long time. I am the fifth generation to use it (Goldschmidt and Haas 1998:55).

Similarly, oral histories recorded by Goldschmidt and Haas (1946) also confirm Tlingit occupation and subsistence activities at Dundas Bay, corroborating the archaeological surveys and recorded mythology concerning *L'istee* and *Xakwnoonu*. According to one interview,

> At Dundas Bay, where the creek flows into the Bay, there was a village called L'istee. On an island at the mouth of the stream was a fort called Xunakawoo Noowu. There was also a camp for drying fish and picking berries on this island. There were three big houses at L'istee, and these are now rotted away. There was also a graveyard for the "T'akdeintaan clan. . . . This was formerly a T'akdeintaan village and at one time, Mrs. Douglas's father homesteaded the place. A potlatch was given at this village about forty years ago [1906] (Goldschmidt and Haas 1946/1998:55-6).

The streams and tidal flats of the Dundas River drainage provided "humpies, sockeyes, cohos, nagoonberries, mountain blueberries, high-bush cranberries, porcupine, black bear, mountain goat, marten, otter, and mink" (Goldschmidt and Haas 1946/1998:55-6). In addition to the interviews, Native allotment claims dating from the 1920s at Dundas Bay also indicate the presence of active salmon streams, prime maintained berry patches, and at least three adjacent smokehouses and fish camps that had been in family ownership for several generations (Ibid:54-5).

The rediscovery of the fort remains of *Xakwnoowu* (c. 800 BP) in the mid-1990s is especially important not only in establishing the evidence of historic Tlingit occupation at Dundas Bay (800 BP), but in reaffirming ancestral ties for the both the Chookeneidi and Ka'gwaantan clans. In a story recorded in 1909 by John Swanton, the protagonist is a renowned hunter from *Xakwnoowu* who leaves the village after he returns from a trip to find all its inhabitants dead:

From Xakanuwu went a man of the Xakanukedi, who were named from their town. The people used to go out from there after seals, which, not having guns at that time, they hunted with long-shanked and short-shanked hunting spears always kept in the bow. . . . the people of that town were numerous and it was long (Swanton 1909:326–7).

The Menzies journal account for July 11, 1794, described a village—possibly *Xakwnoowu*—on the tidal flats at the mouth of Dundas Bay (Menzies 1993). Even Muir's return trip to Glacier Bay in 1880 included a side trip to Dundas Bay in a driving rainstorm; the party took refuge in a "hut" occupied by a Huna, Ka-hood-oo-shough, who offered to guide the American naturalist and his party to the upper reaches of Dundas Bay as a respite from berry-picking.

Contemporary interviews with Tlingit elders as part of the CLI fieldwork reflect the enduring physical and symbolic importance of Dundas Bay and Bartlett Cove as resource procurement areas that continue, even marginally, to provide traditional foodstuffs for personal and ceremonial use. Although seasonal rounds ostensibly ceased in the late 1930s to mid-1940s, traditional knowledge of plant and marine resources in the Big Dish still dominant their conversations about the Glacier Bay landscape, such as the much sought after Dundas Bay nagoonberries and the delicacies of Bartlett Cove gumboot clams. Dundas Bay, in particular, has been nicknamed *Tleikw Aani*, "Berry Land." According to anthropologist Thomas Thornton (1999:31) "These berry patches were not only owned and defended but celebrated and even cultivated by means of *heixwa*, or "magic," and other techniques believed to enhance productivity." In a letter supporting his claim to a Native allotment at Dundas Bay in November, 1924, Harry Shudake wrote that "and the berries that grow on the ground I all ways [sic] fertilize the ground like a garden."[10]

Several elders interviewed spoke in detail about berry-picking activities in Dundas Bay, including salient information on the changes in microclimate and berry production due to the Tlingits' decreased role in maintaining the landscape as a resource habitat. Not-

ing the vast changes in the appearance of the Dundas Bay berry patches since the late 1930s, the elders attributed this evolution to their absence. Without the historical practice of seasonally weeding out alder shoots from among the berry patches—a task relegated to the Huna children—much of the area has become overgrown with the alders, changing the environs from moist to dry—and, according to the elders, significantly reducing the availability of the nagoonberries. Ken Austin recalled his distress at being unable to recognize the landscape he visited as a youth upon returning with another elder, the late Amy Marvin, in the late 1990s to pick berries:

> My dad and I, we would be trolling around Point Adolphus, you know, close to Dundas Bay. About the middle or latter part of August, the aroma from the nagoon was so strong, he told me, 'It's almost time.'....Nagoon was all over the place...And all the berries we picked, we all went as families, you know, different clans. When I went back with Thornton [in 1999], oh I felt badly. I didn't recognize the place. There was few nagoon around. . . . Our traditional knowledge I got from Amy Knutsen (Marvin). . . . I ask her 'How come there are not too many berries here?' [She said] 'We are told by the white people not to pick berries around here anymore. The berries need to be picked; they need to be needed and wanted like we need to be needed. Since we didn't, they stopped growing because we're not there to do it anymore.'. . As soon as we stopped picking them, the nagoon didn't feel needed anymore, so they didn't come out like they usually did every end of August. Just hang on the branches, you know, now they're not there because we did not go back. That's traditional knowledge (Ken Austin, interview, September 2001).

The implication of such a changed landscape is vitally important for the Tlingit. It reveals an inability to sustain the reciprocal relationship between seasonal practices and the landscape resources that support Tlingit cultural life as a whole, such as the role of berries in diet, trade, and ceremonies, a loss of traditional ecological knowledge with the passing of time. As one elder prophetically voiced,

> It's changed a lot. The place where they had nagoonberries and strawberries, it's overgrown

by alderwood and all these different kind of little trees, and they wanted it to be a wilderness, so it is come, become a wilderness, and them not knowing it is where we get our food" (Winnie Smith, interview, July 2001).

Aligned with the archaeological record and information gathered from oral histories and interviews, compelling evidence of Huna Tlingit landscape identity and association is emerging through the ongoing interviews and collection of place-names with elders and clan members.[11] Though they are not "physical artifacts," place-names are tied to the very core of Tlingit identity; there is no separation between clan membership, place of origin, and means of territorial subsistence. To say that one is from the T'akdeintaan or Chookaneidi clans signifies a place of landscape origin and belonging—and, as a result, possessory rights to certain resource areas, such as salmon streams and berry patches, as the clan property, at'oow or "owned things."

Situating the cultural landscapes of Bartlett Cove and Dundas Bay within the Tlingit geography of Glacier Bay has particular resonance when attempting to frame these places as Traditional Cultural Properties. Analysis of place-names provides valuable ethnoecological clues to Tlingit landscape history, conveying a portrait of a glacial environment where the connections between major catastrophic events and Tlingit landscape history are evoked through toponyms. The pre-Little Ice Age village in Bartlett Cove, recalled as the site of the Kasteen and Shawatseek story, has been identified as L'awshaa Shakee Ann, or "Town on Top of the Glacial Sand Dunes," pointing to its location before another glacial advance prompting its abandonment except for the elderly Shawatseek. The settlement site recorded in 1889 as Gatheeni on Lester Island near the mouth of the Bartlett River—and more than likely the same location of seasonal camps during the next decade—translates as "Sockeye," designating a productive source of salmon. Place-names at Dundas Bay include the encompassing Tleikw Aani, or "Berry Land," the rarely used Tina'ak'w, or "Little Copper Shield," and Xakwnoowu, "Gravel" or "Dry Fort," perhaps referring to its location in an ice-free environment during the flood-

ing. The translation for the abandoned village site name, L'istee, is unknown. On a larger scale, the succession of place-names for Glacier Bay itself illustrates a Tlingit conception of landscape history that corresponds directly to the processes of glaciation: S'e Shuyee ("End of the Glacial Mud") at the inception of the bay at the base of a morainal valley; Xaatl Tu ("Ice Bay") as the size of the bay increased with glacial debris during its retreat, and the name used today, Sit' Eeti Geeyi, "The Bay in Place of the Glacier" (Thornton 1997b:223; Ken Austin, September 2001).

The conservation of place-names, like traditional ecological knowledge, speak to clan history and ownership, legitimately—in the Tlingit sense of place—validating their historical claim to their Glacier Bay homelands, ha'a aani. The legacy revealed by place-names, mythology, and oral history are indelibly inscribed upon the symbolic landscape of Glacier Bay, and are borne out by physical evidence found in the archaeological remains and contemporary resource habitats. Incorporating the cultural geography of place-names, traditional stories, oral histories, recent interviews, and field visits with Huna elders with more conventional historical documentation, the Dundas Bay and Bartlett Cove Cultural Landscape Inventories evince a profoundly ethnographic portrait of landscape far removed from the "pristine wilderness" paradigm.

By identifying and documenting places as cultural landscapes within a designated wilderness, the importance of an ethnographic context recognizing—and, perhaps, ultimately preserving—culture and nature in an intensely complicated environmental history is undeniable. The implicit connection between place and identity, between landscape and heritage, is borne out in the Tlingit concept of shagoon, loosely translated as "heritage" or "legacy" (Ken Austin, interview, September 2001). In fieldwork among the Angoon Tlingit, de Laguna described her perception of historical legacy reflected in shagoon:

It has been claimed with justice that every people live their own myths, that is, that their conduct in the present reflects what they believe their past to have been since that past, as well as the present and the future, are aspects of the 'destiny' in which they exhibit themselves as they think they really are. The Tlingit themselves sense this and use the term 'ha (our) cagun' for the origin and destiny of their sib [clan], including the totemic animal or bird encountered by the ancestors and the powers and prerogatives obtained from it, as well as their own place in the universe and the ultimate fate of their unborn descendants. This is something that goes beyond asking the historian to check the validity of native tradition, or attempting through native tradition to check the accuracy of historical documents. Rather it poses for us the problem of how a people view their history" (de Laguna 1960:202).

Elder Ken Austin specifically tied the concept—and evocative power—of *shagoon* to place:

> *Ha shagoon.* The Wooshketan ancestors lived there, in Bartlett Cove. [They say] 'Our ancestors lived here.' And the T'akdeintaan validated it. So, *ha shagoon* from their time to the present time. We still dance it, we still dance the songs. *Ha shagoon* comes to the present time to still validate it. And their oral history, their crests, *ha shagoon at.oow*, 'our ancestors owned it....Our grandchildren are going to own that crest, the names, the songs, and all that.' So, *ha shagoon* goes into the future. *Shagoon* covers past, present future in that way because of what they'll bring out, the crests again, at certain part of their potlatch. They want everyone to show it validates, presently validates, what they had long ago, and what they have now, and what their grandchildren will have. That's *shagoon.* Their *at'oow* is what they have, their songs, their *at'oow*, they will sing it. Again validating their own *shagoon*, Bartlett Cove, that's Wooshketan" (Ken Austin, September 2001).

In this respect, the recognition of Tlingit cultural landscapes within Glacier Bay National Park is essential in order to support the long term viability of cultural knowledge increasingly in danger of being lost as elders, who have specific knowledge of traditional practices, pass away. The cultural landscapes documented by the CLI process—even within the typological framework of the National Register—reveal an alternative historical vision of landscape through an authentic story of place, one that requires new avenues of interpretation and preservation. Large-scale patterns of spatial organization (recognized possessory clan rights to specific areas), historic land use patterns (the geographic network and seasonal rounds associated with resource harvesting), and most importantly, cultural traditions (stories, myths, place-names) connected with Dundas Bay and Bartlett Cove point to their efficacy as Traditional Cultural Properties as defined by the National Register, even with its problematic conceptions of history and place. As a result of the CLI process of documenting Tlingit history at Dundas Bay and Bartlett Cove, the Alaska State Historic Preservation Office concurred with the CLI findings of eligibility of these two landscapes as Traditional Cultural Properties in January 2004. The significance of this determination cannot be overstated. Though cultural ties to the landscape are now physically limited—precluding occupation and seasonal harvesting—the maintenance of traditional knowledge and association, and the recognition of the landscape's protected status as a result of the TCP designation are vital not only to the cultural survival of the Huna Tlingit, but increasingly to the preservation of Glacier Bay itself.[12]

Conclusion

In essence, this is a story of recovering landscape meaning—writing new histories, reconstructing cultural maps both literal and symbolic, and recognizing the potency of place—using a methodology of cultural landscape preservation that remains in its infancy. The production of historical narratives, in this case through the construction of ethnographic landscape histories, is, in itself, a cultural act that restructures the past as provisional and contingent, defying the pervasive belief in its representation as a scientific absolute. Perhaps nowhere is this more evident than in the contested terrain of national parks where the master narratives forged in executive proclamations and legislative mandates often obscure the richness of the storied landscapes they are designed to protect.

Like landscapes, memory and commemoration are

active processes that allow us to reclaim stories that range from the mythic to the personal, illustrating the "power of historic places to help citizens define their public pasts" (Hayden 1995:46). Tied to place knowledge, the interpretation of park landscapes is key to not only the protection of vital resources, but to the sustenance of American cultural diversity. Where ethnographic landscapes have not been acknowledged as historically significant, the revisioning of the past through the Cultural Landscape Inventories constitutes a powerful tool. It provides a unifying framework in which multiple histories can be told, and a forum where values attendant upon conflicting definitions of nature and culture can be negotiated.

From the subtleties of grave markers to the dramatic remapping of cultural territory, the recording of landscape history and evolution through the CLIs suggests not only a new vision of place history, but a reformulation of the landscape concept itself:

> The term *landscape* no longer refers to prospects of pastoral innocence but rather invokes the functioning matrix of connective tissue that organizes not only objects and spaces but also the dynamic processes and events that move through them. This is landscape as active surface, structuring the conditions for new relationships and interactions among the things it supports (Wall 1999:233).

In reading landscapes through the prism of historical and ethnographic time, the evolutionary dialogue of people and place is critical to the preservation of national park lands. Although naïve and antiquarian, Catlin's argument for a nation's park to preserve the traditional ecology of Indian and buffalo recognized the double helix of nature and culture as integral to American heritage. Documenting ethnographic landscapes is a daunting adventure that challenges long-standing categorical divisions between natural and cultural values, the linearity of historic progression, and, ultimately, the authorship of cultural stories embedded in place. It represents a decoding of historical sensibilities as much as a recapitulation of management philosophies, and allows those on the margins to participate in a po-

lyphony of voices retelling the stories of landscapes. Landscapes, indeed, are our legacy.

Notes

1. Three recently completed NPS projects, the Cultural Landscape Inventories (CLIs) for Dyea Historic Townsite and Chilkoot Trail, and the Ethnographic Overview and Assessment, are the first to specifically address the historical Native presence in the history of the park's lands.

2. The naming of the "Taiya" River reflects Tlingit origins: "taiya" is a derivative of *dayei*—Tlingit for "packing place." See "Dyea Historic Townsite CLI," ethnographic information section (NPS 2001).

3. The allotment known as the "Nan-Sook" Claim was just north of the Healy and Wilson claim. Early Skagway native J. Bernard Moore recalled that he hired Nan Sook to help build the Moore residence in Skagway, and that the Tlingit had come over from Dyea with Healy (Brady 1997:87).

4. The distinction between "Huna" and "Hoonah" is significant. "Huna" is the Tlingit people's name for themselves; Hoonah is the central settlement site of the Huna people. In 1995, NPS and the Hoonah Indian Association signed a Memorandum of Understanding aimed at promoting better relations between the two parties. In recognition of this important connection, the park has initiated and collaborated on culturally significant resource studies and activities that address Huna place-names in Glacier Bay, traditional harvesting of gull eggs, seals, berry habitats, and other traditional uses. In addition, a 1997 master-planning effort by NPS included Huna recommendations for construction of a cultural center along the beach trail in the Bartlett Cove area. Another collaborative project along Bartlett Cove trails resulted in two tree carvings of clan crests—octopus and eagle—on living trees within the NPS administrative area.

5. NHPA authorized the National Register; Sections 106 and 110 of the NHPA specifically apply to the protection of recognized National Register properties and to requiring compliance review of undertakings that may impact historic resources. The law also requires mitigation of damages and impacts to these properties in the event of adverse effects of undertakings.

6. This may have been the village, *Gatheeni*—

see the Tlingit sealing camp photo taken by George T. Emmons in 1889 (Fig.107).

7. Ken Austin described the Huna "*ha aaní*" boundaries as "from the mountains, all around Glacier Bay, except for the entrance, all encircled by mountains." Clan territories are associated with the three main clans: Chookeneidi, Ta'kdeintaan, and Wooshkeetan (Ken Austin's interview, 2001).

8. Glacier Bay's waters were closed to Tlingit seal hunters in 1974.

9. Winnie Smith recalled, "[A]nd we used to get—it's called 'sax' –we used to get it from up the bay, and it comes from hemlocks. . . . my grandmother used to start a place from the bottom, and they made of sticks, and we'd just go like this, and the whole bark would just fall off the tree. And then she'd sit there, and she'd have her knife, it's like this, and she used to take the insides off and dry it and put it in seal oil, and it's good, it's sweet, and we used to eat it." Interview, July 24, 2001.

10. Harry Ship Dick, (Shudake), to U.S. Land Office, Anchorage, Alaska, IA 04489, November 26, 1924. GLBA Park Archives, Native Allotments.

11. The collection and mapping of Tlingit place-names has been an ongoing collaborative project since 1993 (with Hoonah Indian Association and the Alaska Department of Fish and Game). Other project members have included the Southeast Native Subsistence Commission, and significantly, the National Park Service. NPS cultural resources staff at the park continue to focus on the creation of a "talking map," an ArcView based model of Glacier Bay replete with Tlingit place-names with hot links to Native pronunciation, as well as video and oral histories of the sites.

12. Since Dundas Bay and Bartlett Cove are now eligible for the National Register listing as TCPs as of 2004, their recognition as historically significant cultural resources will allow park management to address potential impacts and adverse effects of undertakings that may affect their integrity. In essence, this will institute a more formal process of cultural resource protection because of the mandates of Sections 106 and 110 of the NHPA.

References

Brady, Jeff, ed.
1997   *Skagway in Days Primeval: The Writings of J. Bernard Moore, 1886-1904*. Skagway, AK: Lynn Canal Publishing.

Catlin, George
1973   *Letters and Notes on the Manners, Customs, and Conditions of the North American Indians*. Letter No. 31, Mouth of Teton River, Upper Missouri. Marjorie Halper, ed. New York: Dover Publications. 1st edition 1844.

Cooper, William S.
1923   The Recent Ecological History of Glacier Bay, Alaska. 1. The Interglacial Forests of Glacier Bay" *Ecology*, IV(2):93–4.

Cruikshank, Julie, ed.
1990   *Life Lived Like a Story: Life Stores of Three Yukon Native Elders*. Omaha: University of Nebraska Press.

De Laguna, Frederica
1960   The Story of a Tlingit Community. *Bureau of American Ethnology Bulletin* 172. Washington, DC: Government Printing Office, Smithsonian Institution.

Goldschmidt, Walter R., and Theodore H. Haas
1998   *Ha'aa Aani: Our Land, Tlingit and Haida Land Rights and Use*. Thomas Thornton, ed. Seattle: University of Washington Press. Originally issued in 1946 as Indian Claims Document, "Possessory Rights of the Natives of Southeastern Alaska," typescript.

Greer, Sheila, ed.
1995   *Skookum Stories on the Chilkoot Trail*. Carcross, YT.

Griffiths, Tom
1996   *Hunters and Collectors: The Antiquarian Imagination in Australia*. NY: Cambridge University Press.

Hayden, Dolores
1995   *The Power of Place: Urban Landscapes as Public History*. Cambridge, MA: MIT Press.

Menzies, Archibald
1993   *The Alaska Travel Journal of Archibald Menzies, 1793-1794*. Fairbanks: University of Alaska Press.

Muir, John
1895   The Discovery of Glacier Bay by its Discoverer. *Century Magazine* 50(2):234–47.
1998   *Travels in Alaska*. New York: Houghton Mifflin (original edition 1915).

Nash, Roderick
1982   *Wilderness and the American Mind*. New Haven: Yale University Press.

Runte, Alfred Runte
1987   *National Parks: The American Experience*. Lincoln: University of Nebraska Press.

Spence, Mark David
1999   *Dispossessing the Wilderness: Indian Removal and the Making of the National Parks*. New York: Oxford University Press.

Swanton, John R.
1909   The Story of the Ka'gwantan. *Bureau of American Ethnology Bulletin* 39:326–7. Washington, DC: Smithsonian Institution.

Thornton, Thomas

1997a   Anthropological Studies of Native American Place Naming. *American Indian Quarterly* 21(2):209–28.

1997b   Know Your Place: The Organization of Tlingit Geographic Knowledge. *Ethnology* 36(4):295–307.

1999   *Tleikw Aani*, the "Berried" landscape: The Structure of Tlingit Edible Fruit Resources at Glacier Bay, Alaska. *Journal of Ethnobiology* 19(1):27–48.

U.S. Senate

1882   *Reports of Captain L.A. Beardslee, U.S. Navy, Relative to Affairs in Alaska.* U.S. Senate, Ex. Doc No. 71, 47th Congress, 1st Session. Washington, DC: Government Printing Office.

Wall, Alex

1999   Programming the Urban Surface. In *Recovering Landscape: Essays in Contemporary Landscape Architecture.* James Corner, ed. New York: Princeton Architectural Press.

Williss, Frank

1985   *Do Things Right the First Time: The National Park Service and the Alaska National Interest Lands Conservation Act of 1980.* Washington, DC: National Park Service.

Wood, Charles

1882   Among the Tlingits in Alaska. *Century Magazine*, 24(3/July):323–39.

Cultural Heritage in Yamal, Siberia:

Policies and Challenges in Landscape Preservation

NATALIA V. FEDOROVA[1]

The protection and use of individual objects cannot be effective outside the historical and natural space surrounding them (Shul'gin 1994:4).

The Yamal Peninsula, the northern extremity of the Western Siberian plain, is an exceptional region from many perspectives: geographical, cultural-historical, and economic. Located some 2,500 kilometers (1,550 miles) and two time zones east of Moscow and the center of European Russia, the peninsula is the northernmost section of one of the most dynamic regions of the Russian North, the Yamal-Nenets Autonomous Area (okrug), with its booming oil-and-gas industry.[2] The fact that this crossroads area is the home of the indigenous Nenets people, with their vibrant culture of traditional nomadic reindeer herding, makes the peninsula truly distinctive among all other areas of the Russian Arctic. Therefore, preservation of Native culture and economy as well as of its lasting heritage should occupy a central position in policymaking for "sustainable economic development" in the region.

The Yamal Peninsula, about 750 kilometers (466 miles) long, is a strip of flat tundra extending from south to north. Situated on the border of Europe and Asia, Yamal is essentially the last outpost of Europe in Siberia. To the west, the peninsula opens onto the Bolshe-zemelskaya Tundra, a broad swath along which the nomadic Reindeer Nenets migrate from east to west and west to east. This critical linkage connects the expanses of Northeastern Europe and Northwestern Siberia, just

as the zone of great steppes much farther south unites Europe and Inner Asia. To the east, Yamal is linked with the sparsely populated areas of the Central Russian Arctic—the Gydan and Taimyr peninsulas and the coasts of the Laptev and East Siberian Seas. Farther eastward and east of the mouth of the Kolyma River, begins a culturally different world, a coastal area of sea mammal-hunting cultures that share historical-cultural links with the Eskimo cultures of North America.

The lack of large rivers flowing longitudinally has made an indelible imprint on the processes of human settlement and on the domestic and economic adaptation of the indigenous population. The peninsula is a cultural nucleus, a core area for the nomadic culture of the Siberian Nenets indigenous people. It is a unitary, historical-ethnographic landscape, with a unique, profound history and a subsistence economy that is alive today, based on the year-round, nomadic travel of reindeer-herders with their herds of reindeer, from the arctic tree-line to the barren polar tundra (Fig. 108). Such a type of subsistence economy has been in existence in Yamal for hundreds of years. However, there is a marked difference between the economy of ancient times and that of today. During the first millennium and the beginning of the second, Native lifestyle was based on nomadic travel following herds of wild reindeer [or caribou], with a small number of domestic reindeer for transportation (Fedorova 2000, 2000a). Today, Native herders move year-round; and they have much larger herds of domestic reindeer, whereas little hunting is

343

practiced because of the almost total extermination of wild reindeer.

With its continued, unbroken practice of traditional, nomadic reindeer herding, the Yamal Peninsula—and the Yamal District as its administrative unit—are truly special among all other areas of the Russian Arctic. In a cultural sense, the Yamal Peninsula is the most "visible" component of the Yamal-Nenets Autonomous Area [sometimes refered to simply as okrug below] and also its best-known symbol among the public at large.

Problem Statement

Important, fundamental questions can and should be asked about the living, indigenous culture of Yamal: questions about its prospects of survival and sustainability in the modern world and questions about how well its heritage is being preserved under the modern administrative system and in connection with economic development of the Russian North.

The basic questions addressed in this paper can be summarized as follows:

—Does an effective system exist for protecting historical-cultural heritage in the Yamal-Nenets Autonomous Area as a whole and on the Yamal Peninsula in particular?

—If there is such a system, does it incorporate in any way the concept of "historical-cultural (ethnographic) landscape" in its operations"?

—If there is an effective system that incorporates such a concept, then how is this concept reflected in legislative documents and the daily practice of agencies that protect cultural heritage?

Contemporary Demographic Status of the Yamal-Nenets Autonomous Area

The Yamal-Nenets Autonomous Area covers 750,300 square kilometers (290,000 square miles), with a population of 500,500 people (here and hereinafter, figures are from Yamal 2000:13, 63–91, 92). The average population density in the okrug is 0.7 person per square kilometer (by comparison, there are 8.6 persons per square kilometer in the Russian Federation as a whole). The okrug includes seven cities, eight industrial towns,

and 103 rural communities. The administrative capital is the city of Salekhard.

Since the collapse of the centrally controlled Soviet economy in the early 1990s, the basic economic activities of the indigenous population—reindeer breeding, fishing, the processing of reindeer and fish products, and so on—have begun to develop as commercial market enterprises. Gas and petroleum exploration, which arrived in the region in the 1960s and 1970s, is the engine that drives regional economic development. However, at the same time, this industry creates many problems for preserving the living cultures of local indigenous people. There are serious questions about this rich culture's survival in an economic matrix that is increasingly dominated by industrial development.

The oil-and-gas industry has brought about pivotal changes in the okrug, not only in social and economic status, but also in demographic composition. Barely sixty years ago, according to data from the All-Union Census of 1939, the okrug population was 45,734, including 15,348 nomadic reindeer herders (33.56 percent of the total population). In 1959, on the eve of oil-and-gas development, the population increased to 65,000 persons, of whom 28,000 were indigenous residents. By the year 2000, the total population of the okrug had increased by nearly 800 percent, to 506,800 persons.

Of today's okrug residents, Russians constitute nearly 62.8 percent; Ukrainians, 5.8 percent; and Tatars, 5.8 percent, whereas the portion represented by indigenous people (Nenets, Khanty, Komi, and others) dropped to 8 percent. The urban population of the okrug is now 419,600 and predominately non-Native. Of the current rural population of 87,181, only a little more than one-third are indigenous residents. Among these indigenous rural residents, 13,285 are still leading a nomadic way of life. The majority of those people are living on the Yamal Peninsula that now makes the Yamal District (*Raion*), one of seven administrative districts of the okrug. The Yamal District Administration and all

108/ *Nenets herders visiting the Yarte site archaeology camp in Central Yamal.*

basic services for the district (including a small district museum) are located in the district capital, the town of Yar-Sale (population 3,800).

There can be no doubt that the okrug population has changed significantly in the last four decades—because of Russian and other newcomers. These new settlers came to the North primarily to earn higher wages and other benefits. Most of them did not see their own or their children's futures as connected in any way with this land. The settlers often used the term "mainland," or simply "the land," when referring to Russian territory outside Yamal and outside Siberia in general. After living in (what is now) the Yamal-Nenets Okrug for many years and having made its cities and villages their own, many of these people still feel like winter workers at isolated polar stations, who live with the knowledge that they will be replaced at any time and return to "the Big Land."

During the most recent decade (after 1991), another significant population of new arrivals appeared—immi-grants from former republics of the USSR and areas of military and interethnic conflict within the boundaries of Russia. Compared with the previous influx of immi-grants, these people initially had even less cultural and emotional connection with the land of Yamal and its earlier cultural history. Issues concerning preservation of local heritage, much less protection of the natural and cultural landscape, were the last things that con-cerned this pragmatic, economically oriented newcomer population.

However, as the various groups of settlers gradu-ally were cut off from their places of origin, many were compelled to stay and settle in the area. Professional careers and family homes were built over several de-cades. Children were born to the new settlers, and are already adults for whom this territory has become a "native" land. Hence, the recognition of certain local "roots" gradually became important not only to the in-digenous people, but also to all categories of new-comers. This remarkable shift in attitude toward local cultural heritage has begun to be exhibited distinctly in public discourse and in people's consciousness, particularly during the 1990s. The shift is also reflected today in local media coverage of various historical-cultural topics and heritage issues, and, to a certain extent, in the legislative activity of the Yamal-Nenets Okrug government and local authorities.

Cultural Heritage Preservation in Yamal: Legislative Base and Actual Situation

Whatever legislative base exists today for protection of local historical-cultural heritage in the Yamal-Nenets Okrug has essentially been developing during the last ten years—that is, since the okrug became a component of the new Russian Federation in 1992. Until that time, national heritage legislation had been in effect throughout the okrug, as across the entire territory of the former Soviet Union. The 1978 All-Union Law, "On Protection of Monuments of History and Culture," was the cornerstone of that legislation.

It was in 1993, however, that the first piece of relevant regional legislation was enacted—the "Regulation for Protection of Monuments of History and Culture." This law was adopted on May 22, 1993, by Decree No. 117 of the Head of the Okrug Administration. In that decree, responsibility for the "protection of monuments of history and culture in territories under its jurisdiction" was assigned to town and district administrations (municipal communities). Essentially, the decree only *recommended* that local administrations add heritage preservation specialists to the staffs of district and okrug departments of culture. As the regulation is worded, this task is not mandatory.

With a series of later bureaucratic reorganizations, the situation worsened: for example, district and okrug departments of culture were reorganized as "cultural administrations," and finally, as "committees on culture, youth policy, and sports," further diluting the administrations' legal obligation to employ preservation specialists. For these and other reasons, to this day [as of 2003], only two of seven Yamal-Nenets Okrug districts,

Priuralsk (Cis-Ural) and Krasnoselkup, have some type of heritage preservation specialists on their administrative staffs. It should be noted, however, that the main reason for this lack of necessary specialists is not so much the "non-mandatory" wording of the 1993 decree as the lack of appropriately qualified specialists in the area.

In 1996, another piece of regional legislation was introduced—the "Regulation for the Execution of Historical-Cultural Evaluation in the Yamal-Nenets Autonomous Area." A similar piece of legislation, enacted earlier in the neighboring Khanty-Mansi Autonomous Area, was used as a basis for the new regulation. The new regulation has not yet been put into effect (as of 2003) because it has not been approved by the Okrug Department of Minerals and Natural Resources. In the absence of such a regulation, historical-cultural evaluation (survey) of areas approved for industrial construction or other economic development is likely to be the exception rather than the rule. In today's practice, the execution of such surveys depends mainly on the attitudes of individual employees of local administrations or, rather, on the perseverance of archaeologists and other cultural specialists, who usually receive information on the proposed activity in passing.

On October 16, 1998, Okrug Law No. 40, "About the Protection of Monuments of History, Culture, and Architecture in Yamal-Nenets Autonomous Area," was enacted. As a result, the new Yamal-Nenets Okrug Inspectorate for the "Protection and Use of Monuments of History and Culture" was established in the capital city of Salekhard. The inspectorate currently possesses a generalized, but not finalized, list of the okrug's monuments of historical-cultural heritage. For the time being, this "list" is a card file, but it is being developed gradually as a computer database.

The database includes the following:

—Archaeological monuments, namely, sites, burial grounds, ancient ritual sites, and so on; 269 are registered in the database [as of 2002]

—Local historical monuments, such as "The Geographical Center of the Russian State," established by means of a mathematical survey by Dimitry I. Mendeleev in 1906 and designated as a memorial site (with a special plaque) in 1985. Another example is the preserved remains of many abandoned forced labor camps of the early Soviet era {the so-called GULAG], such as the famous "Construction Site No. 501," a huge labor camp of the 1940s and 1950s, which is located along the abandoned railroad that was built by the thousands of GULAG prisoners

—Municipal and architectural monuments, including monuments dedicated to victory in World War II; buildings constructed in the 1930s; commemorative signs and billboards; and Russian Orthodox churches and other temples

—Natural and cultural monuments, that is, sites and areas having universal value as "joint creations of nature and man from the perspective of history and ethnology," including local centers for Native crafts. Russian Federation legislation includes this category of heritage monuments under "historical monuments."

Legislation about protecting historical monuments of the Russian Federation and the corresponding version adopted in the Yamal-Nenets Autonomous Area also includes such concepts as "ensemble of monuments of history and culture" and "objects of urban development." However, neither of these pieces of legislation includes a concept of "monuments of ethnic culture" or "historical-ethnographic landscape." Meanwhile, in the Yamal-Nenets Okrug and other regions across the Russian North, these particular categories of local heritage are of special importance.

The status and preservation of monuments of ethnic culture and historical-ethnographic landscapes are critical issues that should be incorporated in any local policy (and politics) concerning indigenous residents of the area. While ancient archaeological monuments, as a rule, are already perceived as "no one's," the Native people regard sites of living ethnic culture, such as, abandoned village sites, modern camps, graveyards, active ritual, and memorial sites as "theirs." The connection of living sites with the present-day landscape is obvious to them.

The Yamal-Nenets Okrug now has a substantial package of legislative documents that theoretically allow fully viable work concerning the preservation and use of local historical and cultural heritage. Is it, therefore, possible to conclude that everything in this context is satisfactory, that the monuments of historical-cultural value included in the okrug administration's preservation database are well protected, and that active work is being conducted for identifying new sites and entering them in the database? Unfortunately, nothing of the kind has occurred.

The problem is not that there is no (or not enough) legal basis for adequate protection of historical-cultural monuments, but that the existing system is simply not working. Of course, there are many reasons for this failure, including the lack of funds and trained staff for agencies of heritage protection, at every level. More detrimental, however, is the low level of awareness among the general population and in local administrations about the value of the historical-cultural monuments that they are obligated to protect.

As an illustration, I will cite the unfortunately typical story of the ancient site of Ust-Poluy at the capital city of Salekhard. The Ust-Poluy site dates back to the first century BC and represents the remains of what we believe was once an ancient, intertribal ritual center. The site is internationally renowned because of its unique archaeological artifacts, among which there is a large quantity of precious art objects, including pieces made of bronze and gold. The site has been publicized in numerous articles, books, and catalogs, beginning with pioneer publications by two Russian archaeologists, Valerii N. Chernetsov and Wanda I. Moszinska. These authors—through their long-term excavations, numerous writings, and academic presentations—have made the site widely known to Russian and foreign professional audience alike (i.e., Chernetsov and Moszinska 1974).

In the early 1990s, when our archaeological team from the Ekaterinburg-based Institute of History and Archaeology of the Russian Academy of Sciences (Urals

Branch) began new series of excavations at Ust-Poluy, according to the then-federal heritage records, there were only two historical monuments of importance in the entire Yamal-Nenets Okrug. One was the abandoned town of Mangazeya, the remains of a seventeenth-century Russian fortress and a symbol of the early colonial era in Siberia. The other was the above-mentioned Ust-Poluy archaeological site. Because the site area is within modern city boundaries, it is formally under the jurisdiction of the City of Salekhard Cultural Administration. Accordingly, municipal agencies should bear the responsibility for the condition of the monument and for its protection. However, to my great surprise, the Cultural Administration personnel had neither any knowledge of this monument's precise location, nor any concept of the manner in which the site should be protected.

Because of many years of total ignorance and neglect, the monument once excavated by Chernetsov and Moszinska, and their team, is now seriously damaged by dirt roads and various small construction projects. In gullies surrounding the monument site, local residents have created garbage dumps. In addition, for a long while, the riches of the site have been attracting amateur "archaeologists" or, actually, site-diggers. These intruders have contributed considerably to the site's destruction and the plunder of archaeological valuables. In summary, the monument, already designated for the highest level of federal preservation and located literally in sight of cultural authorities for Yamal-Nenets Okrug, has not been protected by anyone in any way. Whereas the Ust-Poluy site is the most renown archaeological monument of the Yamal-Nenets Okrug, the one listed in every historical textbook and local guidebook, is it worthwhile to even mention the status of protecting and documenting heritage monuments in many remote rural communities—much less on the open tundra?

Again, it should be emphasized that this situation is not attributable to an absence of necessary legislation. The chief factors behind such failures are the weakness of local preservation agencies and the non-compliance at all levels—from official bodies to private enterprise—of federal and regional legislation for preservation of historical-cultural heritage and its individual monuments. Many managers and landowners simply are not aware of their responsibilities in this area. An effective measure to overcome such non-observance or ignorance would be participation by both okrug and municipal heritage-preservation agencies when permits for any kind of economic activity are issued. All areas that require construction permits, from a large oil-and-gas pipeline to a new cowshed, should go through mandatory historical-cultural evaluation. During the evaluations, professional archaeologists should survey the given areas, identifying any significant historical-cultural sites that should be protected.

Unfortunately, in all the above-mentioned legislative acts, issues of identification, registration, protection, and possible use of historical-cultural monuments are resolved exclusively through an approach that uses "specific" monuments, that is, "individual and highly localized objects" (Shul'gin 1994). Nowhere are these monuments being evaluated in conjunction with the surrounding landscape (Fig. 109). Accordingly, nowhere is such surrounding landscape being protected legislatively, and nowhere is it being evaluated for its special or cultural value.

For the last ten years, regular archaeological evaluations have been conducted at new construction sites in only one district of the Yamal-Nenets Okrug—the Pur District in the southernmost part of the region. Purneftegaz, a regional oil-and-gas company, is financing this work. As a result, in the Pur District alone, sixty-eight new archaeological monuments and ethnic cultural monuments have been discovered. An understanding is gradually developing among the local oil-and-gas industry, the local administration, and the general population about the importance of considering ancient and traditional Native sites as historical-cultural (ethnographic) landscapes.

Purneftegaz is not the only large, local company

109/ Nenets domestic reindeer graze at an ancient site, Vary-Khadyta-2.

that allocates funds for conducting archaeological evaluations. From the late 1980s through the early 1990s, a Tobolsk Teachers' College archaeological-ethnographic team (led by Dr. Andrei V. Golovnev) received funding from the Lengiprotrans enterprise. Lengiprotrans was a large government enterprise charged with producing a feasibility report for the construction of the Ob–Bovanenkovo Railway. Another example was the joint Russian-American heritage program called "The Living Yamal." Under this three-year program (1994–1996), significant work was carried out in documentation of historical and cultural heritage on the Yamal Peninsula. The program was financed by an American oil company, AMOCO-Eurasia, and carried out with assistance from the local Russian gas company, Nadymgazprom (Fitzhugh 2000; Krupnik and Narinskaya 1998).

In fact, my experience of many years confirms that it is often easier for archaeologists to work with large companies for several reasons:

—The mass media now covers their ventures constantly, and this coverage is frequently critical. The media attention includes coverage from the perspective of preservation of the environment and/or historical-cultural heritage.

—Legislative control and the pressure of public opinion are much more effective in ensuring proper heritage awareness for larger projects by "big business."

—In today's Russia, large oil-and-gas companies have the ability to finance historical-cultural evaluation of the areas allocated for industrial construction and/or mineral development.

In contrast to prosperous industrial companies, municipal agencies such as city and district administrations commonly have no funds to sponsor historical-cultural work. For example, for the past three years, the Priuralsk District Administration has been trying to launch a program for identifying and registering archaeological monuments in watersheds of the Longot-Yegan and Shchuchya (Pike) Rivers. In 1999, and again in 2000, this work was shut down because of lack of funding. For the same reason, a similar survey begun in 1994 in the Shuryshkar District of the Yamal-Nenets Okrug has not been completed. This list of hobbled projects, unfortunately, continues.

Monuments of Ethnic Culture

"Monuments of living culture" are a special category of historical-cultural heritage monuments. These monuments include ritual places (shrines, sacrificial sites, sites of ceremonial practice, and so on); funerary complexes (such as, cemeteries, separate tombs, and *khalmery*—aboveground burial places; Fig. 110); settlements, including nomadic reindeer-herder camps; sites related to various subsistence activities; and ethnographic landscapes that have special value for the local population. As they continue functioning, these imprints of human presence on the landscape have a specific, distinguishing attribute—they can be moved or partially destroyed, intentionally or unintentionally, in the course of daily activities or by ignorant intruders.

The study, documentation, and possible protection of these monuments of living culture are complicated precisely by their aliveness—their active use by contemporary local residents, who frequently do not wish to share information about them. Ritual sites can be taboo for several categories of people [see Khar-yuchi, this volume]. Surveys and even visits by outsider researchers frequently cause negative reactions among local indigenous residents. In addition, in the current practice of Russian archaeology, these traces of living culture(s) are "too young" to be studied by archaeologists; and Russian ethnographers almost never engage in the mapping and detailed documentation of such sites, like Native graveyards and other burial places that are absolutely necessary for any protective measures to be taken.

Resources of Local Agencies for Heritage Registration and Protection in Yamal

The main agency of the okrug administration in charge of registering and protecting monuments of history and culture is called the "Okrug Inspectorate for Protection and Use of Monuments of History and Culture." This agency is a branch of the okrug's Department of Culture, Youth Policy, and Sports and is located in Salekhard. The inspectorate's long name reflects the essence of this establishment fully enough: the agency is, for the present, still a non-independent link in a long, complicated chain of administrative command and bureaucratic paperwork. Therefore, the agency simply has neither the power nor the opportunity to enact any independent policy, particularly if a dispute arises that involves the powerful construction or oil-and-gas companies.

Nevertheless, in comparison with even the recent past, some positive shifts are evident. Just a few years ago, in 1999, there was only one employee working on all these issues for the documentation and protection of historical-cultural monuments in a territory of about 750,000 square kilometers [almost half the area of the state of Alaska]. The Okrug Inspectorate staff now has six permanent employees—the Chief of the Inspectorate; two specialists in registration and protection of monuments of architecture, history, and culture; two archaeological monument specialists; and one document technician/archivist (as of 2002). However, the staffing situation is much worse at the district level, with historical protection specialists on administration staffs in only two of seven districts.

It is clear that these severely limited personnel resources are totally inadequate for carrying out viable, comprehensive work in registering and protecting monuments. The problem is complicated further by conditions specific to the Yamal-Nenets Okrug, primarily, by the huge size of areas in which there simply are no roads, the difficulty of communicating with various distant arctic regions, and the small number of permanent settlements. These obstacles, together with the major industrial development of areas far removed from populated locations, mandate the development of specific, innovative approaches to the protection of heritage and historical-cultural landscapes.

110/ Khalmers, *traditional Nenets burial sites like this one, are always located on top of hills or on drier sand-covered uplands.*

In 2001, under orders of the Committee on Coordination of Scientific Research of the Yamal-Nenets Okrug Administration, a new initiative titled "Program for the Identification, Study, and Use of the Historical-Cultural Heritage of the Yamal-Nenets Autonomous Area" was outlined. The executor was the Institute of History and Archaeology of the Urals Branch of the Russian Academy of Science in Ekaterinburg, with two archaeologists, Drs. Konstantin G. Karacharov and Natalia V. Fedorova, acting as primary investigators for the program (Fedorova 2000a). In the program's outline, all current legislative documents in heritage preservation, at both federal and okrug levels, were reviewed; and the status of heritage protection in the area was analyzed. A set of measures to improve protection of Yamal-Nenets Okrug monuments and historical-cultural heritage sites was presented.

A program PI, Dr. Konstantin Karacharov, introduced the program in August 2001 at the 11th International Congress of Innovative Technologies for the Oil-and-Gas Industry, Energy, and Communications (CITOGIC) in Salekhard. For the first time, a special workshop on issues related to indigenous people was included on the Congress agenda. Dr. Karacharov spoke about the Yamal heritage program during the roundtable discussion, which was titled "The Culture and Lifestyle of Peoples of the North Under the Conditions of Oil-and-Gas Development." Incidentally, at the last plenary session of the Congress, when the discussions in all the Congress workshops were summarized, that particular workshop was simply overlooked. Its chair, anthropologist Dr. Andrei Golovnev, was not even given the opportunity to present his very thoughtful summary of the panel deliberations.

However, despite the various setbacks, the program leaders very much hope that, when new normative documents are enacted to implement our recommendations, the public attitude toward historical-cultural heritage will change and Yamal-Nenets Okrug heritage preservation agencies will be able to work more effectively. Therefore, we have proposed several new types of activity for the identification and inventory of historical-cultural sites.

Significant roles in these activities would be assigned to local indigenous people. Such activity could include, for example, correspondence work such as gathering information about monuments of archaeology and ethnic culture in the places where correspondents live and filling out questionnaires about the monuments, marking their locations on a map, and describing their external appearance and condition. In the program's prospectus, a similar questionnaire for describing ritual sites was proposed. To my knowledge, that questionnaire was already being used in summer 2001 by participants of a group engaged in documentation of Native sacred sites in the Taz District of the okrug.

Status of Heritage Preservation Efforts in Yamal Today

The status of many historical-cultural monuments on the Yamal Peninsula is quite familiar to the author, as I have worked as a field archaeologist in this area since 1994. During that time, I have had the opportunity to engage not only in field surveys for identifying new monuments of archaeology and ethnic culture, but also in many stationary site excavations. Over several years, our field archaeology teams interacted closely with the local Nenets people; often their summer tents were within accessible range of our site camp.

In this long-term study of the ancient cultures of Yamal, and in daily contact with the living culture of today's Nenets herders, the recognition blossomed that northern surroundings are a truly organic unit. In other words, the natural and human environment in the Arctic is unified: the river, tundra, lakes, birds and fishes, and dwarf tundra birches; the remains of the ancient monuments that we uncovered; and the modern Nenets, who often use the same sites as their distant ancestors,

are unified. I came to acknowledge that no archaeological monuments exist solely on their own merits (no simple task for a site archaeologist). They are all parts of a unified historical-ethnographic landscape, in which it is impossible to comprehend either ancient or modern cultural development without living on the land for a time.

In August 2001, our group surveyed the downstream area along the Venga-Yakha River near the town of Yar-Sale in the southernmost area of the Yamal Peninsula. The survey was that rare case when the actual idea of identification of local heritage sites for the purpose of protection had come from district authorities, from the Committee on Affairs of Youth, Culture, and Sports (analogous to the Yamal-Nenets Okrug department in charge of heritage preservation mentioned above). It was no surprise that this rare department head was the professional museum worker and trained archaeologist Konstantin Oshchepkov. He is an old friend and like-minded person who takes everything concerning local heritage closely to heart: monuments of archaeology, ethnic culture, or history, and other matters. He is virtually the only Yamal administration executive who tries to put industrial expansion on the Yamal Peninsula under some sort of control, at least by the historical-cultural evaluation of the areas approved for new construction and oil-and-gas development.

In the course of two weeks we found more than ten ancient settlements—more accurately, complexes of old settlements—in an area about three kilometers on the left bank of the Venga-Yakha River. All the monuments had a similar feature: they were located on a high portion of a bedrock bench and thus were situated on natural, sandy knolls formed as a result of freezing processes. We managed to identify at least three types of dwellings, clearly localized according to season. Some of them were summerhouses built on high, breezy sites oriented toward the river (their remains look like shallow, rounded pits). Others were winter houses constructed on the lee side of the heights, with well-defined traces of corridor-like outlets. The rest were

111/ The Tiutey-Sale 1 (Walrus Cape; Russian: Morzhovyi) site, long considered critical evidence for the existence of an "Eskimo type" sea-mammal hunting culture on the Yamal Peninsula (see Fitzhugh 2000).

traces of portable tent dwellings, constructed on elevated platforms that are quite similar to modern reindeer herders' tents.

The dating of the settlements was done through artifacts collected during the excavation, mainly fragments of ceramic and stone tools. The largest portion of the finds is associated with the Bronze Age, the particular time when the shore of the Venga-Yakha River was populated most densely. The Venga-Yakha River has a large fish population; in addition, herds of wild reindeer (caribou) used to pass through the valley on their seasonal migration. For these reasons, these sites provided an area superbly suited to the complex hunting-and-fishing economy so typical of the area's Bronze Age population.

The settlements we found are so well suited to the surrounding environment that together they represent a tightly knit complex, a unique natural-archaeological landscape, which should be evaluated as such.

Today, on the Yamal Peninsula, more than 100 ar-

chaeological monuments of various times are known. The most ancient site, Yuribey 1, dates back to the Mesolithic Age, or about 9,000 years ago. Many sites from the Neolithic and Bronze ages are known; but by far the greatest number is associated with the Iron Age, that is, from the third century BC to the fourteenth century AD. Like the sites along the Venga-Yakha River that we discovered during the 2001 season, all the sites are inscribed in the environmental landscape and merged with it, and cannot be studied and preserved without it (Fig. 111).

Sites of living ethnic culture are part of the special category of heritage monuments. Like historical-cultural monuments, there is no doubt about the connection of these monuments with the landscape. Stated more correctly, through their very existence, they are fully connected with a certain type of landscape. For example, sacred sites were frequently connected with certain natural features, cemeteries were created on high, outlying locations (see Fig. 110), and so on. However, it has been only in recent years that sites left by the present-day Nenets population or its ancestors began to be registered and designated for preservation.

In summer 2001, a group composed of Galina P. Kharyuchi, Michael N. Okotetto, and Leonid A. Lar conducted major work in identifying and describing modern sacred places in the Taz District [Kharyuchi, this volume]. Some Native graveyards of the eighteenth through the beginning of the twentieth century were identified and documented by our field parties. In 2001, a detailed study of one historical Native cemetery, first surveyed in 1909, was published after many years of delay (Murashko and Krenke 2001). I believe that the publication of the latter volume will promote the further study and better protection of many similar sites. At present, Native cemeteries are in an extremely miserable condition: in addition to destruction due to uncontrolled oil-and-gas exploration, they are now threatened by numerous collectors of antiquities and gravediggers (Fedorova 2000a:11). There are plentiful bronze ornaments at many historical cemeteries, and glass and metal cookware and utensils lie on the surface, quite accessible to such collectors.

When an ethnic-cultural landscape that contains a valuable historical monument is destroyed or is transformed by modern construction, the monument's very existence becomes senseless, and its value to the local indigenous people vanishes. We witnessed one such situation in 2001 (as in many previous years). Our group had found a Native cemetery of the early nineteenth century within the boundaries of the modern village of Salemal. No one in the community reportedly knew anything about the cemetery, and even the human bones that teenagers had dug up periodically had not aroused in the populace a desire to come to terms with the situation. This situation was, surprisingly, occurring in an area where the memory of ancestral cemeteries has been kept for several centuries. Apparently, the reason the cemetery appeared forgotten was the destruction—in this case, for modern construction—of the ethnographic landscape that contained it.

It is clear that there is little sense in framing Yamal heritage preservation policy in the context of protecting individual cultural monuments, because they have always been inscribed in their surrounding environments. Thus, an integrative approach governed by the concept of historical-cultural (ethnographic) landscape will ensure not only better protection of the monuments for the future, but also their study in a real context.

New Trends and Prospects

This short overview demonstrates that, in recent years, some changes have occurred regarding heritage protection in Yamal. Some newer trends that are furthering the protection of local monuments of historical-cultural heritage are also worth mentioning.

—*First*, the establishment of the Research Center for Humanitarian Studies on Indigenous Peoples of the North in Salekhard, with its all-Native staff, has made a significant difference. The center was created about 10 years ago, and the documentation and study of local sacred sites of the Yamal indigenous population is featured very highly on its agenda (Kharyuchi, this volume – ed.).

—*Second,* in recent years, the initiative for heritage evaluation of areas that are to undergo economic development, particularly oil-and-gas development, is coming more often from the departments of indigenous peoples at the okrug and district level, instead of from business ventures or other agencies. For example, the above-mentioned survey of the Longot-Yegan River area, where exploration work for gold extraction has been under way, was initiated by the Priuralsk District Administration, or by its Department of Indigenous Peoples, to be more precise. The staff members in many departments of indigenous peoples are Native. These employees understand perfectly well the value of the ethnographic components of cultural heritage and the importance of protecting relatively "young" cultural monuments, that is, living sites and actively used sacred places.

—*Third,* there has been a noticeable trend for business organizations and gas companies to approach scientific institutions (such as academic institutes and universities) with a request to conduct a historical-cultural evaluation of areas allocated for development. These trends are encouraging, but the scale of progress is still insufficient.

Summary

The concept of historical-cultural landscape is integral to the entirety of the environment and the many occupational imprints left by ancient and modern human groups on the Yamal Peninsula. Ideally, this integrative concept should become a cornerstone in policymaking for local agencies that regulate protection and use of cultural-historical heritage. To date, however, the work of these agencies has been oriented toward the concept of separate, individual historical monuments and sites that need documentation and protection. Unfortunately, no effective agency or system for protection of local historical-cultural heritage yet serves the Yamal-Nenets Autonomous Area as a whole or the Yamal Peninsula in particular. Neither designation for heritage preservation nor even the term "historical-cultural landscape" yet figures in the legislative acts and practices of local government agencies. However, some favorable new trends with regard to protection of cultural heritage have appeared in recent years—in both Russia as a whole and the Yamal-Nenets Okrug—which I have tried to summarize in this article. It is especially important to emphasize the increasingly active participation of the local Native people in this process. All of these new trends offer hope for possible shifts toward a better situation in the near future.

Acknowledgments

This article was written with assistance from Grant No. 01-01-00412a from the Russian National Scientific Fund. The author is grateful to Igor Krupnik for many valuable editorial comments and to Natalia Narinskaya and Konstantin Oshchepkov for information on policies and resources of local agencies that are active in heritage preservation in Yamal.

Notes

1. Translated by Georgene Sink; edited by Igor Krupnik.

2. See more on the current economic and administrative status of Yamal in Galina Kharyuchi's paper, this volume—ed.

References

Chernetsov, Valery N., and Wanda I. Moszhinska
1974   *The Prehistory of Western Siberia.* Translated by Henry N. Michael. London and Montreal: Arctic Institute of North America/McGill-Queens University Press.

Fedorova, Natalia V.
2000a   Sem' let Yamal'skoi arkheologicheskoi ekspeditsii (Seven years of the Yamal Archaeological Expedition: results from the past and a task for the future). *Nauchnyi vestnik. Bulletin* 3:4–12. Salekhard.
2000b   Olen', sobaka, kulaiskii fenomen i legenda o sikhirtia (A reindeer, a dog, the Kulai phenomenon, and the legend of Sikhirtia). In *Drevnosti Yamala* 1, Andrei Golovnev, ed., pp. 54–66. Ekaterinburg and Salekhard: Russian Academy of Sciences, Urals Branch.

Fitzhugh, William W.
2000   V poiskakh Graalia (Searching for the Grail: Virtual Archaeology in Yamal and the Circumpolar Theory). In *Drevnosti Yamala* 1, Andrei Golovnev, ed., pp. 25–53. Ekaterinburg and Salekhard: Russian Academy of Sciences, Urals Branch..

Krupnik, Igor, and Natalya Narinskaya
1998   *Zhivoi Yamal/Living Yamal.* Bilingual exhibit catalog. Moscow: Sovetskiy Sport.

Murashko, Olga, and Nikolai Krenke
2001   *Kul'tura aborigenov Obdorskogo Severa v XIX veke. Po arkheologo-etnograficheskim kollektsiiam Muzeia antropologii MGU* (The culture of indigenous people of Obdorsk North in the nineteenth century. From materials of the archaeological-ethnographic collections, Museum of Anthropology, Moscow State University). Moscow: Nauka.

Shul'gin, Pavel İ.
1994   Unikal'nye territorii v regional'noi politike (Unique areas in regional politics). In *Unikal'nye territorii v kul'turnom i prirodnom nasledii regionov*, Iu. L. Mazurov, comp., pp. 35–43. Moscow: Institut Naslediia..

Yamal
2000   *Yamal: Na rubezhe tysiachelietiia/ Yamal: On the Edge of the Millennium.* Salekhard and St. Petersburg: Artvid and Russian Collection (parallel Russian and English editions).

Sámi Cultural Heritage in Norway:

Between Local Knowledge and the Power of the State

TORVALD FALCH AND MARIANNE SKANDFER

Sámi (Saami) history in northern and middle Fenno-Scandinavia extends far back in time. As with all deep prehistory, many aspects of early Sámi history are unknown. In Norway, the strong and rather systematic Norwegianization of the Sámi from the end of the eighteenth century to approximately 1980, plus the lack of written documentation from the Sámi themselves, makes the recent Sámi past largely unknown, obscured or hidden. All Sámi cultural sites and monuments older than 100 years have been protected by law since 1978, and since 1994 the responsibility for Sámi cultural heritage management has been in the hands of the Sámi Parliament.

In this article, we will attempt to portray how the management of Sámi cultural heritage has stressed the importance of living, local knowledge both as a long-term objective and as a strategy to further the cause of preservation, and how this management relates to the power structures in the Norwegian government system. An institutionalized indigenous self-management of cultural heritage is quite exceptional. We will give an account of how Sámi cultural heritage management is organized and how it works, using some examples of the Sámi cultural landscape and the efforts to document them. Even though Sámi cultural heritage management in Norway is institutionally rather exceptional, there is still a reason to evaluate critically whether such an institutionalization has given the Sámi the authority to work with their cultural heritage to the extent that such an organization suggests.

Organization of Sámi Cultural Heritage Management in Norway

In 1990 the management of Norwegian cultural heritage was reorganized into a more decentralized and clearer political administrative organization. The regional administration charged with cultural heritage management was moved away from the four regional museums in Tromsø, Trondheim, Bergen and Oslo into a cultural department within each of the 19 county administrations. The Directorate for Cultural Heritage (Riksantikvaren) in Oslo became the central professional institution with responsibility for creating a coherent national policy and coordinating collaborative tasks. Simultaneously, Sámi cultural heritage management was partially separated from national cultural heritage management. However, it was another four years, until 1994, before a separate administration for Sámi cultural heritage became operational, with authority and responsibilities equivalent to the county heritage management administrations. The reorganization came as a natural consequence of the Norwegian Parliament passing amendment §110a to the Norwegian Constitution, as well as the law that established the Sámi Parliament and other Sámi rights (*Sameloven* – the Sámi Act) in 1987. The Norwegian Constitution now requires the state to provide the conditions and rights that allow the Sámi to preserve and develop their language, culture, and social life.

After the ratification of the constitutional amendment and the Sámi Act, the Sámi Parliament was established in 1989 as a body elected by the Sámi for the Sámi. In 1994 Sámi cultural heritage management was organized with a council nominated by the Sámi Parliament. The *Samisk kulturminneråd* (Sámi Cultural Heritage Council) was politically and administratively subject to the Sámi Parliament and professionally subject to the Norwegian Ministry of the Environment and the Directorate for Cultural Heritage. The administration of Sámi cultural heritage was further decentralized by the Sámi Cultural Heritage Council, which established regional offices in Snáasa (Snåsa), Ájluokta (Drag in Tysfjord), and Romssa (Tromsø), as well as a regional office and a coordinating main administration in Vuonnabáhta (Varangerbotn). In January 2001, the administrative authority for Sámi cultural sites was transferred from the Sámi Cultural Heritage Council to the Sámi Parliament itself. The administrative authority granted by the Cultural Heritage Act is so far the only law management function the Sámi Parliament has in Norway.

The importance of a Sámi-run cultural heritage management sector has grown in concert with increasing political and cultural consciousness in the Sámi people. During the 1970s and 1980s, the Norwegian State planned and accomplished several big development projects in the Sámi territories, including a hydroelectric plant in the watershed of the Alta-Kautokeino River in Finnmark. This area encroachment issue, which had consequences for the maintenance and development of Sámi culture, language, and life style, demonstrated to the Sámi the importance of the right of co-determination. In 1973, the first job position for Sámi cultural heritage was established at the Tromsø Museum, now part of the University of Tromsø, as a direct consequence of the planned water power expansion in northern Norway. The 1978 Norwegian Cultural Heritage Act gave preservation status to Sámi cultural sites more than 100 years old for the first time, and in 1992 the law was revised to include cultural landscapes, a central idea in Sámi cultural heritage. The Cultural Heritage Act states specifically that all Sámi cultural monu-

ments and sites older than 100 years are automatically protected by law, including those sites that are linked to historical events, either by belief or tradition. In contrast, although the cultural landscapes are not automatically protected by law, they are considered a part of the cultural heritage and identity. The Sámi Parliament provisionally designates a cultural site or monument as Sámi, but if other participants in the regional cultural heritage apparatus disagree, the Directorate for Cultural Heritage makes a final decision (Holme 2001:142).

Practical Management

The Sámi Parliament´s cultural heritage management department is the authority for all Sámi cultural monuments and sites that are included in the Cultural Heritage Act, and the Parliament gives statements concerning all proposed projects that imply land seizure in the Sámi settlement area. Today nine executive officers have the responsibility to give written feedback regarding protected Sámi cultural monuments and sites, valuable Sámi landscapes subject to plans for area encroachment, the maintenance of sites and landscapes, and the use of these sites and landscapes for research or public purposes. The department receives approximately 1800 inquiries per year. Earlier survey and site registration projects in Norway did not direct attention to Sámi cultural sites or the types of cultural sites and monuments that are most naturally interpreted within a Sámi context. There is no complete summary of Sámi cultural sites and monuments, and in large areas with both early and contemporary Sámi settlements the systematic documentation of Sámi cultural heritage and their associated environmental settings is still imperfect. Fieldwork involving inspection, registration and interviews of local informants in connection with concrete development projects, is therefore a big and important part of cultural heritage management. To provide an impression of the fieldwork, it can be mentioned that the 2000 field season registered 343 protected, but previously unknown, Sámi cultural sites and monuments spread out over 173 locations (Sametinget, Samisk kulturminneråd 2000).

Several circumstances make it difficult to document Sámi cultural sites, the evidence of earlier Sámi presence and manner of living. The Sámi possessed little or no written documentation of their daily life and culture prior to 1900. During World War II, when Norway was occupied by Nazi Germany (1940-45) and, particularly during the last year of German occupation in the North (1944), virtually all buildings in the majority of the Sámi settlement areas were burned down and the population was removed coercively. After 1945 the northern areas, like the rest of northern Europe, experienced fast and extensive technological and material growth. That growth resulted in basic changes in the people's everyday life and activity and also caused a great deal of traditional knowledge about landscape use, behavior toward nature, and manufacture of handicrafts to be gradually lost. To the Sámi Parliament, living tradition and human memory is therefore an equally critical source for understanding history and prehistory as the physical cultural monuments and sites. Older people who are connected with local places can share concrete and often extremely detailed narratives about, and interpretations of, physical structures and wider cultural landscapes. This approach can be accused of reproducing the much held view that Sámi culture was static, unable to develop (Olsen 1986), but the lack of a so-called "scientific basis" cannot negate the testimonies about their own past that one encounters in Sámi communities. Local Sámi understanding gives good and relevant additional information about cultural sites, monuments, and landscapes, because activities, events, beliefs, visions, and traditions are written into the physical remains (Skandfer 2001). This approach is therefore important as a contrast and corrective to what we as cultural heritage managers often assume, without local understanding: we read activities *out of* the cultural sites and monuments based on a more general knowledge. Local understanding has also often greater relevance

and value for modern people living in the local context than interpretations from outside.

During the last several years, the Sámi Parliament has experienced a possible shift in this attitude towards local vs. public/scientific knowledge of cultural heritage. Local communities ask to have their cultural sites registered, including sacred places, and thereby made public or available for public use or research. We are beginning to see the contours of increasing local interest in generalizing knowledge on cultural heritage and an acceptance of the Sámi Parliament's effort to manage Sámi cultural heritage. It is a great challenge to find working forms for managing knowledge of Sámi cultural heritage that are considered legitimate within both Sámi society and the larger, national administrative apparatus.

In addition to its mandated administrative authority, the Sámi Parliament's cultural heritage management department implements special projects, such as the protection of Sámi buildings and the documentation of eastern Sámi history in Norway, Russia, and Finland.

Sámi Cultural Landscapes and Local Understanding

Sámi cultural heritage is a broad concept because, naturally enough, the categories that fall under that concept span large distances in both time and place. Cultural sites can be regarded as parts of Sámi cultural heritage when they are known either from written historical or living Sámi tradition to have been explicitly used within a past Sámi cultural context. Sámi tradition or sites can also be regarded as Sámi cultural remains when orally transmitted local Sámi knowledge more implicitly relates them to the Sámi cultural sphere. Cultural heritage can be physical manifestation of Sámi activities, such as resource procurement or religious practice; where tradition and knowledge of past customs is lost, only the cultural sites themselves testify to an earlier Sámi presence. Certain types of cultural sites can also be regarded as related to Sámi prehis-

112/ Remains of a traditional goahti (Sámi turf house) and legally protected Sámi farm buildings are parts of the same cultural landscape. Lille Molvik, Berlevaag municipality, coastal Finnmark.

tory insofar as they are physical manifestations of the processes, which led to the establishment of the Sámi cultural character as known historically (Samisk kulturminneplan 1998-2001:1). The concept of cultural environment stresses the idea of sites that can be part of spatial, temporal, and cultural units. A cultural landscape is a large geographic or topographic unit that can include several cultural environments.

How the landscape is used depends particularly on how the landscape is understood, that is, on people's knowledge about the land and the associations they feel with it. Sámi culture springs from a lifestyle that is closely connected to their use of the land, and there is a tight relationship between subsistence and religious beliefs. The Sámi cultural landscape is a Sámi understanding of the land (Bjøru 1994:32; Gaukstad 1994: 38) articulated in the interplay between practical experience and historical consciousness. In accordance with Tim Ingold (1987) these cultural landscapes could be

termed "taskscapes". The Sámi cultural landscape includes many types of landscapes, from the oldest hunting, fishing, and catching (whales, seals, etc.) landscapes to the different reindeer exploitation landscapes ranging from the small-scale reindeer herding of the 1500s to the extensive reindeer herding of the 1900s, and further to the fishing-hunting-farming landscapes along the sea coast and major rivers. Sámi land use includes coastal and inland areas, mountain plateaus, forests, and river valleys. These have provided the basis for divergent forms of adaptation to the local environment. Just as there are different Sámi ways of living there are also different ways of understanding and relating to the landscape. Despite the differences, there are nevertheless similarities in storytelling, in landscape-form and place-name traditions, as well as in transmitted oral knowledge about the environment. This makes it possible to talk about a distinctive Sámi form of land-use (Gaski 2000:18).

The Sámi language has a rich and detailed terminology for describing landscape changes and terrestrial forms. The language thereby becomes a topographic tool, through which large territories can be visually described with just a few words. A place name can quickly and precisely convey, whether the place is steep, passable, forested, windswept, or sheltered along wide territorial areas. In this way, for example, reindeer migration routes between diverse landscape areas can be visualized (Mathisen 1997). The Sámi place-names can tell how certain landscape space or landscape elements were used or understood because of the distinctive weather conditions that the animals often met there; where people have lived before; where they fished or hunted; where water crossings are; where reindeer stopped at different times of the year; and where the dead are buried (J.Jernsletten 1994:234). In all parts of the Sámi area the local population emphasizes that the "Sámi way" of traveling in open terrain is not to leave any clear traces on the land. Another general attitude, especially among the elders, is that any buildings should preferably be constructed in such a way that they resemble nature and can go back to it after being used (Fig.112). Therefore, it is often not the cultural sites themselves that are evaluated as the most important element in a local context, but the stories about the happenings and activities connected to the landscape in which the cultural sites are located.

A certain landscape can be directly related to traditional Sámi subsistence, such as reindeer herding, hunting, fishing, trapping, cultivation, or tending domestic animals, such that cultural sites will be identified and related to these subsistence activities (Schanche 1995). These can encompass different types of turf hut (goahti) and house foundations, houses, tent rings, settlement areas, storage depressions in stone-scree, and constructions used to catch, mark, or milk reindeer (Fig.113). The landscape itself can also contain elements that have had value and meaning in the Sámi way of life without any identifiable human impact being visible in the terrain. These elements can be pastures or paths connected to reindeer migration, sedge grass bogs or alder woods that represent important domains of natural resources tied to daily life, or fishing site marks on the shore that permit the re-finding of the fishing grounds used previously.

Holy mountains, stones, forests, and lakes are examples of landscape elements understood to a great extent in a spiritual and mythical sense. The pre-Christian Sámi religion was a hunter-gatherer religion marked by ideas of nature wrapped in spiritualism (Hultkrantz 1965). The landscape offered natural resources one could harvest; but the landscape and its resources also allowed contact with a spiritual dimension. Sámi believed that one should bring sacrifices to sacred stones (sieidier) to receive good outcomes in hunting or fishing expeditions, and that one should honor holy mountains because they are nests (homes) for holy beings. They also believed that graves should be likewise respected and treated with caution. The dead were even more a part of the landscape than the living, inscribed in it through physical presence and cultural tradition. In former times it was customary to formulate wishes to the reindeer pastures and to ask places in the terrain for permission to set up a tent and stay overnight (Oskal 1995:145). Local narratives about helpful ghosts and what happens to someone who does not behave properly towards places in the landscape are very popular throughout the whole Sámi area. These stories constitute a form of collective memory and knowledge about the proper mindset concerning a local environment (Nergaard 1997:72). Many of the stories, legends, and attitudes toward the landscape that had their origin in Sámi pre-Christian religion are still valid in Sámi local societies today, including those concerning cultural heritage.

Sámi cultural heritage management is one way to relate to and preserve the human traces in the landscape. It allows the local Sámi population to have the opportunity to see their territories in light of a long time perspective, and it tries to appreciate the tradition and the meaning that is added to these traces locally.

113/ Remains of a traditional Sámi goahti ('turf hut') for goats. Devddesvuoppmi, Inner Troms.

In the management of Sámi cultural heritage, the value of the cultural environment also depends on cultural ascription and point of view (Samisk kulturminneplan 1998-2001:1). Sámi cultural heritage management stresses local knowledge because cultural heritage is a central resource and reference point in the struggle for a cultural survival and acknowledgment. Local stories and local knowledge are often the only narratives the Sámi can tell about themselves. This form of heritage management allows for different and sometimes opposing understandings of sites and landscapes. The inclusive attitude towards local knowledge and understanding can be seen as an expression of an ethical commitment towards living communities in the management of culture heritage (Skandfer 2002).

In local Sámi communities, knowledge of cultural sites and cultural environments is very important to one's identity and self-understanding. Being a bearer of tradition, history, and cultural retention, and also of the landscape's economic, social, and religious mean-

ing has a value of its own. It encompasses knowledge of how Sámi in past times related to and utilized their surroundings, and, no less important, the knowledge and understanding of how they can and should relate to the surroundings today. Tales of events in the landscape have traditionally been the means by which local Sámi communities have shared knowledge and cultural ideas between generations. This socializes the younger generation into the landscape so that they learn to travel in it and use it, conducting themselves well, in order to take part in the previous generation's adventures, as they become the beneficiaries and users of that knowledge (Gaski 2000; J. Jernsletten 2000; N. Jernsletten 1994; Nergaard 1997).

The landscape is a cultural construction, man-made and seen through a human perspective. The landscape therefore becomes not only a physical presence, but also the meaning that diverse cultural groups place on the landscape. Local knowledge and local attitude are essential for how the landscape is understood and valued. The small local stories that perhaps only give meaning to those who know the landscape intimately can be of decisive importance to the landscape's worth and meaning. This includes knowledge about the former locations of good snare places for trapping grouse, or places where the spring water is so clear that to wash one's eyes in it improves one's vision. The association of cultural environments with various locales is likewise applicable when various culture groups use the same landscape in different historic periods. In locales where the Sámi are a minority, stories can be tales of landscapes now lost to others.

In this regard, one can mention the Sámi Parliament's survey registration of Sámi cultural sites in 1997 related to the creation and expansion of national parks in the Trøndelag district, the more southern part of the Sámi settlement area. A district pattern occurred: cultural landscapes including Sámi dwelling sites, reindeer milk storage pits, and spring water sources were registered, but the pasture sites for reindeer—normally associated with such localities—were missing. Instead, in these landscapes summer mountain pastures were connected to nearby Norwegian farms. Not coincidentally, pastures for reindeer gathering and milking are preserved only at places where no Norwegian summer mountain pastures are listed on the registry. When border commissioner Major Schnitler traveled through Tydal in 1742, he observed what many of today's informants can tell, namely, that the fertile and nutrition-rich Sámi pasture sites have been confiscated by the Norwegian farmers for dairy production (Fjellheim 1998:44).

The Reindeer Landscape: A Sámi Cultural Landscape

We want to provide a general overview of the reindeer herding landscape and its attached cultural sites as an example of one particular type of Sámi cultural landscape. A reindeer herding landscape is marked both by human activities and by the grazing habits of the reindeer. The reindeer will seek the pastures they know (Paine 1994:44) and the animals thereby represent a stable element in the landscape. By watching the reindeer's habits, the Sámi herdsman learns about the dynamics between the reindeer herd and the landscape. This creates a continuum over the generations in the relationship between humans, animals, and landscape (Henriksen 1986:68 in J.Jernsletten 2000:81).

During the winter time, the reindeer herds in most parts of the Sámi herding area choose to stay inland where they graze relatively close to each other. The winter dwelling places of the reindeer-herding families lie in a sheltered place in the terrain, often in a small valley. In order to avoid the frost mist that accompanies the freezes in late fall and possible slush ice during the winter, the dwelling places were located slightly distant from big rivers or lakes. The whole society lived together in the winter dwelling places: children, women, men, young and old. The buildings were often sturdier constructions than those used during other seasons. The traditional winter building of the reindeer-herding Sámis is a *goahti* or *gamme*, which was either made of a bent birch wood frame clad with birch bark and thick turf, or of timber. Even very recent *goahti* foundations can be nearly invisible on the surface today; they are faint, round or oval banks of turf with a stone-set hearth in the middle. In the eastern Sámi area on the border between present-day Norway, Finland, and Russia, it is documented ethnographically that the Sámi communities had to change their winter dwelling places every 5-10 years in order to secure access to firewood.

All members of the society stayed at the winter dwelling places over a longer period every year, allowing the government and the church to have more extensive contact with the Sámi population. Churches and local sheriff stations were built, and the dwelling places gradually developed a more village character. A few of the old dwelling places that started to be used year round were Karasjok and Kautokeino in Norway, and the populous so-called "*samebyer*" (Sámi villages) in Sweden: among them Karesuando, Jokkmokk, Arvidsjaur and Arjeplog.

In early spring (March/April) the reindeer started to

move; in the northern Sámi areas, usually toward the coast, and the Sámi herders followed. The migrations took place along the natural trails of the reindeer over ridges and along watersheds. The community then split up into smaller units, but all family members undertook the trek. The migration took place with the reindeer pulling sleds while the ice still lay on rivers and lakes. On the way the reindeer herd was driven and tended, and the dwelling places were only along the long route toward the coast and in the calving grounds. In the snow-covered winter landscape, when it was difficult to find stones to frame a fireplace, they could either use wood sticks, which we know were also used in winter dwellings in inland Sweden, or sometimes they even brought stones to the area with them in the sleds. Those living places of a very short duration are almost impossible to find today.

The families established a spring camp for some weeks on the calving grounds before they moved on. The calving had to take place in warm and sheltered surroundings, areas where cold spring nights were not a threat to the newborn calves. Therefore, the spring dwelling areas are found in the forest, but near the treeline and preferably slightly toward the bare mountain top where the snow could still carry the reindeer hooves, as well as sleds and skis. The dwelling areas could be located without immediate access to running water, since snow could be used in early spring. For the spring dwelling, the Sámi built stone-set fireplaces and used wooden frames to make a *goahti*, or they erected a *lavvo*, the Sámi tent, and drew a felt canvas over it. In certain places the winter family belongings were stored until the next fall, while the summer equipment was taken into use. In such places food storage holes can be found in moraines or stone scree that became snow-free early and stayed frost-free in the spring. Here they could find meat, cheese, and soured milk that had been stored in the fall. The spring and fall places lay close to each other, since supplies and equipment had to be stored and retrieved on the way to and from summer sites. Some herds and Sámi herdsmen still had quite a

114/ *Frame of a recent Sámi summer herding tent,* lavvo *in Øverbygd, Inner Troms.*

distance to cover before arriving to the summer dwelling area, while others had already traversed most of the distance and only had to go a short way.

The summer dwelling sites were used into the late fall. The *lavvo* (summer tents - Fig.114) were set up again near running water or good fishing places and with easy access to reindeer pastures that lay in the high mountains or on islands off the sea coast, where the reindeer were less bothered by insects. Several stone-set fireplaces are often found in one of these dwelling places. Recent excavations of such fireplaces in Mid-Troms, central in the Sámi settlement area of Norway, showed that many dwelling places had been used over several hundred years (Sommerseth 2001, 2004). The datings show that the steady landscape use has preserved the local landscape understanding and knowledge through many generations. Another sign of an old summer dwelling site is fertile, perennial meadows, often with few old trees in the middle, near the former fireplace. These are reindeer milking pastures. The does were tied to the trees during the milking process, but otherwise they went free with their calves in the enclosure. At the summer sites, several activities also took place that did not leave direct physical traces: marking the calves with the owner's marks, fishing, and collecting sage grass, alder bark, and berries.

During the fall, Sámi moved to the winter dwelling places. In October, the breeding-month, the herd was left in peace during rutting. The animals could not be moved then. The late fall was also the slaughtering season, so guiding and slaughter fences were set up in the open terrain. The last trek to the winter dwelling places took place with all the sleds tied together in a row after the snow had covered the ground.

Many aspects of specific knowledge are preserved and kept alive in the local Sámi communities, such as when the reindeer herd could move through a certain landscape; how the ownership marking took place; where the watering holes and washing places were located; which pastures were of good quality in different times of the summer, depending on local weather patterns; how meat, milk, leather, or bark were processed, stored, and used; and how the dwellings were constructed.

Sámi cultural heritage management realizes the need to obtain and preserve this local knowledge, and utilizes much of its resources for that part of its work. But it is necessary to be aware that written descriptions and map drawings of activities and events also have influence on local knowledge and its transmission.

The Management of Sámi Cultural Heritage and Local Knowledge

In arguing for a Sámi cultural heritage management the meaning of identity management has been stressed. Cultural heritage gives the Sámi identity an historic perspective, which is important both for cultural legitimacy and cohesion (Sametingsplanen 1991:10). The relation between the people of today and the cultural

traces of the past is understood as an emotional dimension having to do with knowledge and cultural self-maintenance. The Sámi Parliament, therefore, considers the management of Sámi cultural heritage as a tool to strengthen the ties between the people and their cultural characteristics (Schanche 1994). Emphasizing the identity—forming a meaning of cultural heritage—implies that the Sámi Parliament, in its cultural heritage management role must be in constant communication with local communities that have the knowledge of cultural sites and of their identity-forming meaning (Fig.115). Local knowledge of use, stories, and concepts of landscape makes the individual aware that there are others who do not have this knowledge or who do not use the landscape in the same way. Knowledge and the shared cultural entitlement granted through use and understandings of the landscape provide both a common empirical worldview and a means to discover differences between people. Identity is shaped through one's own understanding of the landscape and by balancing other, often contradictory understandings of the landscape (Gaski 2000:18-9).

In arguing for self-management of Sámi cultural heritage, local knowledge has perhaps been vaulted to the top because Sámi local knowledge stands in a direct opposition to the Norwegian cultural heritage management system. The preservation of Sámi cultural heritage depends more on claiming local legitimacy than does the preservation of the Norwegian cultural heritage remains. The ambiguous geographic borders of the Sámi territory mean that the Sámi often have to expend energy to define what is "Sámi." Such a demand is seldom or never placed on Norwegian cultural heritage. The national historic narrative frame upon which prehistory is produced, seems to render a Sámi prehistory impossible (Hesjedal 2001: 291). Recognizing a Sámi prehistory is therefore extremely difficult, because this implies an initial deconstruction of the national Norwegian prehistory, constructed and reconstructed also within the frame of the Norwegian governmental system. As a counterweight against the Nor-

115/ Bjørnesteinen ("The Bear stone") in Ceavccegeadgi/Mortensnes, Unjargga/Nesseby municipality. Many local Sámi stories are connected to this stone.

wegian institutional monopoly on knowledge, local knowledge of the landscape argues strongly for an exclusive Sámi cultural competence (Kalstad 1991:8). Placing an importance on local knowledge can therefore also be seen as indirectly subverting the majority's pre-defined dichotomies, where the majority represents scientific knowledge and the minority represents traditional and local knowledge (Schanche 1993).

The context in which cultural sites are placed is therefore crucial to acquiring an understanding and acceptance that the cultural sites are *associated* with the Sámi prehistory and history. As an added benefit, there is a balance between cultural sites and local communities. Local Sámi communities and their knowledge are important to establish a site's cultural connection. At the same time, cultural sites offer a direct physical manifestation of the Sámi prehistoric and historic presence in the area, and with that they become the basis for forming Sámi culture and society.

Mauken-Blåtind: Sámi Reindeer Herding History in a Norwegian Farming Area

Mauken and Blåtind are two mountains on the border between Sweden and Norway in an area called Inner Troms. This area was first colonized by Scandinavian farmers from southern Norway at the end of the eighteenth century and the dominant local history is a pioneer story about clearing the fields and establishing farm settlements. Today's population is extremely aware of its particular south Norwegian culture; this expresses itself, among other things, through dialect, a different way of building, and strong musical traditions. However, written sources show that a Sámi presence in this area goes back at least several hundred years. Sámi reindeer-herders who live in Sweden during the winter still use mountain regions within the Norwegian national borders as summer pastures; but in the 1920s Norwegian national authorities closed these pastures in Mauken and Blåtind. Since the 1950s the area has been used for military training fields, but because of its qualities as a reindeer pasture area, in the 1960s two Norwegian Sámi reindeer herding families established themselves on an annual basis around Mauken and Blåtind. The long Sámi history has been ignored in the presentations and understandings of the area's past.

Between 1998 and 2001, the Ministry of Defense planned to expand and connect the artillery ranges around Mauken and Blåtind, so the Sámi Parliament undertook examinations of Sámi cultural sites within the planned field (Skandfer 1998; Sommerseth 1999-2001, 2001). One cultural site survey had already taken place in 1989 and 1990, with the conclusion that the planned military activities involved great wear and tear on, harm to, and in the worst case, destruction of the legally protected cultural sites, and that the enlargement and connection of the artillery ranges would likely bring further threat to a long list of hitherto unregistered Sámi cultural sites. It was concluded that from a cultural heritage preservation point of view, it was impossible to accept the plans. Nevertheless, the plans were approved by the Norwegian Parliament in 1996, and in the winter of 1998 the Ministry of Defense started the project. In spring 1998 the Sámi Parliament instituted an operation to fulfill its judicial administrative obligation toward cultural heritage management by gathering new information through registration work, place-name investigations, and reviews of written sources that address Sámi tradition in the area, creating a great deal of new data that needed to be processed. In spring 1999 a project worker was employed to administrate the great amount of new information. The work was completed in the fall of 2001, with a summary report finding that 214 registered structures were spread out over 133 sites (Sommerseth 2001). Most of the registered sites can be tied directly to the tradition of Sámi reindeer herding, but some findings date back to the Stone Age hunting and fishing economy. Other cultural sites are historic remains dating from after the establishment of Sámi farm settlements. The registered

sites and excavated archaeological materials now form part of the empirical database for Ingrid Sommerseth's ongoing Ph.D. project for the University of Tromsø on the transition from hunting wild reindeer to reindeer pastoralism and herding (Sommerseth 2004).

Most of the registered structures were stone-set fireplaces that once were located in the middle of the *lavvo* (Sámi tent), some of which have been excavated with interesting results (Fig.116). Several charcoal horizons show that the same fireplace was used several years in a row, and that fireplaces at the same site can vary in age by several hundred years; the oldest excavated in the area went back to the fifteenth century (Sveen 2000 in Sommerseth 2001). Information about the dating and seasonal use period implies that at least two separate herd migration routes were established in this area by the fifteenth century, making the Sámi reindeer herding tradition in Inner Troms stretch as far back in time, as others have documented, in what are today the more central parts of the Sámi settlement area. The results also support seventeenth and eighteenth century written records that described many Sámi activities around the Mauken-Blåtind area. The investigations also show that there is a certain correlation between the Sámi reindeer herding settlement sites and the older hunting and fishing seasonal camps, as in so many other places in the Sámi area. This suggests that there is a close connection between the local landscape knowledge of the reindeer-herding Sámi communities and the older hunting and fishing understanding and use of the landscape. With the help of local informants—among others, older Swedish Sámi reindeer herders and those who travel with the reindeer today—one can see spring, summer, and fall habitation areas that seem to spring out of the landscape. Seen in the light of how knowledge and understanding is passed on from generation to generation as a way to teach people how to behave toward both the landscape and the community, it can be claimed that an extended, probably, several-thousand-year-old record of habitation and utilization in Sámi reindeer herding areas can be relevant to the local Sámi self-understanding. It is equally reasonable to claim that the present-day local Sámi self-understanding and knowledge is relevant to the general understanding of such ancient cultural sites.

The mandated research of the Sámi Parliament brought to light a neglected and virtually forgotten Sámi past in Inner Troms. The Sámi population that had used the area around Mauken-Blåtind following migration routes established long before the 1923 closure of the national border between Norway and Sweden became excluded from its history simply because the border was shut to a population technically residing in Sweden. The current nearby immigrant Norwegian population knew neither about the Sámi place-names nor about the sites that bear witness to previous Sámi presence. However, the deep historic roots and the close cultural correlation between the modern reindeer economy and the long tradition it is part of provide the basis for appraisal and recognition of Sámi presence and Sámi rights. The Sámi Parliament's work caused the Ministry of Defense to adjust some of its plans so that selected Sámi cultural sites can be preserved for the future. As a result, the Sámi Parliament's work can perhaps contribute to both the local awareness of the long Sámi history in the area (which in the course of the last 200 years was surrounded by a Norwegian farming landscape) and to the increase of knowledge in Sámi societies about their own (pre)history in an area to which they now have little or no access.

The Management of the Cultural Self-Concept

The Sámi Parliament's weighting of local knowledge in its management of cultural sites is the good part of the story. In its management, local knowledge is respected. Through everyday efforts, one realizes that part of the management of knowledge is not just giving, but—probably more importantly—receiving. The management of cultural sites is an exercise in making conscious and justified choices. The cultural sites' local

meaning, presence, and the continued use of areas have vital importance to the choices that have to be made. The focus on local knowledge in the preservation of Sámi cultural heritage provides management practice with a sense of social proximity and immediate meaning. In the management of Sámi cultural heritage, the Sámi Parliament to a large degree is ensuring that the local Sámi communities have the opportunity

116/ Fireplace at a Sámi reindeer herding camp excavated in 2002 as a part of the ongoing Ph.D project by Ingrid Sommerseths, at Devddesjávri, Inner Troms. The camp was probably used during the fall time, and dates back to AD 1400-1445.

to tell and learn to recognize their own history, to form their own identity, and thereby master greater ability to select among various options in the formation of their own lives and culture (Føllesdal 1999). In this way, the preservation of Sámi cultural heritage will contribute to increased equality for cultural maintenance and development. This simultaneously minimizes signals of inferiority and cultural domination, and works to equalize distribution of culture and history as common benefits. The Sámi Parliament cannot on its own declare which is the "true" Sámi identity or what individuals' understanding of their own culture should be. The Sámi Parliament's role is to contribute so that the Sámi people can view themselves in light of both the past and present, and so that change and reinterpretation of one's identity and self-awareness is an ongoing process in which cultural sites and heritage are themselves important reference points (Fig.117).

Prioritizing local knowledge in the effort to preserve Sámi cultural heritage has been a very important goal because it is primarily in the local communities that cultural sites possess and give meaning. But placing a priority on local knowledge can simultaneously be seen as a strategy in the struggle for cultural survival and self-awareness, steered by the limitations that the power structures offer to the Sámi population.

The Norwegian Government System and the Sámi Voice

The system of government tells us about how power is organized, divided, and channeled in a state. Roughly said, the Norwegian system is built upon the state, county, and municipal levels. Formal power in Norway is organized and divided among these three hierarchically defined levels. When it comes to cultural heritage the Ministry of the Environment and the Directorate of Cultural Heritage represent the state as the central steering and controlling institutions; the counties represent the regional management and executive level; and the municipalities represent the local preparatory and fulfillment level. All public management is tied to a formal political organ and political power, and cultural heritage management is no exception.

Politics has been called the authoritative distribution of values (Easton 1953:127-32). Cultural heritage and cultural sites are thus values and benefits administered and distributed. Heritage management is as much about protecting and managing values as it is about the physical past represented by heritage artifacts, sites, and places (Smith 1994). Cultural heritage management therefore meets different cultural heritage values, represented by different interest groups and local communities, and it also exercises political power.

How the power is systematized, structured, and institutionalized influences strongly which values reach their goal and what decisions are made.

In this simplified outline of the formal division of power in the Norwegian system, we have not mentioned the Sámi Parliament. The Sámi Parliament is the popularly elected body by and for the Sámi people in Norway. It chooses for itself what issues to concern itself with, but it has a certain limited authority to distribute economic funds for culture, industry, language, and education. In addition, the Sámi Parliament has been delegated the authority for managing the Cultural Heritage Act insofar as it relates to Sámi cultural sites. The establishment of the Sámi Parliament has to be understood as an attempt to raise the Sámi voice in the Norwegian government system. The Sámi Parliament's place in the Norwegian government system is, however, not easy to describe, and there have been few attempts to do so.

From a corporate perspective, the Sámi Parliament can be understood as an expression of political design. One description of a corporative system—a system where representation of interests goes via uniformed organizations that are specialized in their defined areas, established and recognized by the state, and granted monopoly right to represent their own field by observing certain rules concerning election and the way demands are introduced—is strikingly similar to a description of the Sámi Parliament's role towards the central authority. Corporatism is in its nature equivocal, in the sense that it is hard to decide whether the organization conquers the government or if the government has conquered the organization. In the desire and necessity to secure the politics concerning the Sámi people, the state authorities guarantee a Sámi structural influence. The Sámi Parliament becomes an institution that shapes effective coordination of organizations to advance and consolidate Sámi politics, including Sámi cultural heritage politics. The establishment of the Sámi Parliament could in many ways be understood as a way to secure better governance capacity

117/ Pre-Christian Sámi grave at Gaparas/Klubben, Unjarga/Nesseby municipality represents a continual grave tradition between ca. 2000 BC and AD 1600. Due to different building material and place in the landscape, these stone-built graves can take a variety of forms.

over the Sámi people, and in this context the state authorities strive to reach a structuralized control of the potential, which is in the Sámi cultural heritage for the Sámi people to achieve power in the present.

Cultural heritage management cannot be discussed as if it is detached from the political system and from the value-struggle and value-distribution that take place in this governmental system. Management is therefore called politics with different means. Cultural heritage management is one part of the cultural and environmental politics, and one part of the fight and debate around history and identity, where heritage managers' interests are one of many interests and far from those of an innocent and neutral bystander (Smith 1994). To place the heritage management in a political organ opens the possibility for competing heritage values to be expressed. Granting the Sámi Parliament management authority over Sámi cultural heritage could be understood as an acknowledgment of the Sámi people's

right to be empowered for more equal participation in the value distribution of the cultural heritage. The establishment of the Sámi Parliament is probably an attempt to empower the Sámi people in their work for cultural maintenance and development. The Sámi Parliament has also achieved a degree of power when it comes to cultural heritage management, in the sense that power does not only involve realizing its interests, but also forming its own opinions and preferences (Føllesdal 1999).

As mentioned, the equivocal role of the Sámi Parliament in the Norwegian governmental system creates a tension in the state's relationship with the Sámi Parliament. This has consequences for the weight and status of Sámi cultural history when it comes to acknowledgment and resources. The Sámi Parliament is an independent, democratically elected body, but in cultural heritage management the Sámi Parliament is relegated to the status of a subordinate county administration. In practice, the Sámi Parliament's political and professional opinions and decisions can be reviewed by the Ministry of the Environment and the Directorate for Cultural Heritage. One example of the fact that the Ministry of the Environment treats the Sámi Parliament as a subordinate administrative organ is in the rules specified in the Cultural Heritage Act. The Directorate for Cultural Heritage has the delegated authority to exempt Sámi sites—as well as other cultural sites—from the protection automatically granted in the Cultural Heritage Act so planned encroachments in the landscapes can be done. Such a dispensation is given after a recommendation from the Sámi Parliament and the county governments regarding its areas of responsibility. The Sámi Parliament is not given in principle or in practice a role beyond that granted to county governments in such matters. The Sámi Parliament as a representative organ for an indigenous people—with the international obligations pressed thereby onto the state— carries little (or no) weight in the performance of practical administration.

The Sámi Parliament's cultural heritage management has an equivocal role in the governmental system. On the one hand, the regulations of the Cultural Heritage Act clearly state that the Sámi Parliament is delegated an authority which can be reviewed by the Ministry of the Environment and the Directorate of Cultural Heritage. On the other hand, the establishment of the Sámi Parliament with its own cultural heritage management is an expression of a desire to recognize the Sámi as a people and to give them the right to fully manage their own cultural heritage. This is a dilemma. Therefore, the Sámi Parliament has expressed an explicit desire to develop an equal partnership with the government, with consultations and necessary compromises, even in the cultural heritage management field. This right of consultations carried out in good faith with the objective of achieving agreement or consent is now under development. The government and the Sámi Parliament are now discussing procedures for this.

The emphasis on the Sámi voice in the Norwegian

governmental system is a difficult story for Sámi cultural heritage management. Even if the Sámi Parliament is empowered in the management of cultural heritage, it has to function within the limits of the Norwegian governmental system. The Sámi Parliament's economic resources are directed completely by the Storting (Norwegian State Parliament) and so far the Sámi Parliament has many fewer resources to disperse for the preservation of Sámi cultural heritage than the Norwegian cultural heritage system, even for the same geographical areas. (This is despite the fact that between these two northernmost populations, Sámi history in the North is certainly both longer and more comprehensive than Norwegian history). The Sámi Parliament must operate within a framework established by law and by regulations, over which the Sámi Parliament has little influence. Even in the field of cultural heritage protection, where the Sámi Parliament is given considerable power compared to most other fields, it has to conduct itself and undergo a one-sided adjustment toward the already established Norwegian governmental system, a governmental system with a clear Norwegian cultural character. The Sámi people have been given a voice through the Sámi Parliament; but it is still the Norwegian naturalized governmental system, which is decisive in categorizing what is valuable and nationally meaningful cultural heritage (Andreassen 2001).

It is a fact that the politics of Norwegian cultural heritage is divided into three levels, where the national level is most important, the regional level is somewhat important, and the local level is the least important. From these categories come the priorities and the distribution of resources. A convention with such a hierarchy of values is in itself a reason enough for discussion. In this connection we are satisfied, however, with calling attention to the telling coincidence between these value categories and the main levels in the Norwegian governmental system. The coincidence is hardly accidental. There are no fixed procedural rules for categorizing values. But there is a reason to assume that those who decide to which category a cultural site or environment belongs base their decision on the level of government from which the initiative or the request arrives. This, again, is related to the cultural character of the governmental system. One wonders, under which category does the Sámi cultural heritage find its home?

As mentioned above, the emphasis on local Sámi knowledge in the Sámi cultural heritage management is both an important goal and a chosen strategy. There is a reason to believe that this is the chosen strategy because it has been the only possibility for granting the Sámi cultural heritage a certain recognized value. Nevertheless, the Sámi cultural sites receive legitimacy primarily at the local level; at other levels, there remains an instituted demand for "proof" before the acceptance of a cultural site's connection to the Sámi culture. The strategy can accordingly be understood, in a certain way and to some extent, as having been chosen for the Sámi Parliament. The effect of the Sámi Parliament`s emphasis on local knowledge in its heritage management could to some degree have been detrimental, since Sámi cultural heritage has become unimportant, or at least less important.

Rock Art: Sámi and Non-Sámi Visions of the Landscape

One type of cultural heritage that has received great attention, and great devotion of personnel and economic resources from the government is rock art. Most of the rock art has been assumed to be so ancient that it is not considered to belong to any particular ethnic group. The result is that rock art is understood to be of no relevance for Sámi culture, even though in many cases the Sámi are the only ethnic group known to have lived in specific areas in pre-history. Over the last few years, new rock art has been registered in Sámi use and settlement areas.

Rock paintings were found in Cuppopgieddi in the Porsanger municipality during the summer of 2001. Cuppogieddi is a local Sámi community. The Sámi Parliament took the responsibility for announcing the find

and for its documentation and security, including, of course, actively involving the local Sámi population. The Sámi Parliament also interpreted the rock paintings in a Sámi cultural-historic framework. Despite this, the Directorate for Cultural Heritage signaled early on that the rock art could hardly be considered a Sámi cultural site or as having anything to do with the Sámi ethnicity. It remains to be seen if the directorate considers rock paintings to be so important that they must be administered by "neutral" county governments rather than by the Sámi Parliament.

In Bøla in the Steinkjer municipality during the summer 2001, a rock carving of a person apparently on skis was found. Prior to this, other carvings were registered in the same place, including one that showed a large reindeer, called the *Bøla* reindeer. Both skiing and reindeer herding and hunting can be associated with the Sámi people over an extensive period of time, but these rock carvings are probably so ancient that one hardly can consider them as reflecting a Sámi or, for that matter, Norwegian, ethnicity. The Sámi Parliament was never notified or informed about the new find of the skier, nor about the decisions and actions taken in regard to the Bøla reindeer. The effect of this management blackout has been that the Sámi people have been unable to see themselves in an emotionally meaningful relationship to these cultural sites, making it impossible to link the Bøla reindeer to the Sámi culture and people in the area. To a large extent, the identity and independence of the Sámi living in this area can be tied to a picture of a reindeer cut in a rock just by the simple fact that the motif is a reindeer. The only known people to depend upon the reindeer in both prehistory and today in that area are the Sámi.

It will be intriguing to find out to what extent the Directorate for Cultural Heritage will follow up the rock art find in Cuppopgieddi, beyond the declaration that it is of the "national importance." Likewise, one can speculate as to whether the Bøla reindeer would have received the central and national attention that it did if the Sámi Parliament had been the coordinating management authority with a weighty local value dimension. Perhaps one should not draw negative conclusions from conjectures. Sometimes, however, unknown motivations and ideas influence and give meaning to hidden factors, of which the actors themselves are unaware, but which nevertheless impregnate their attitudes and actions (Haaland 2001). The Norwegian governmental system's cultural character is a hidden factor the Sámi Parliament is confronted with in its cultural heritage management; this can be especially seen in the management of rock art in the Sámi area. It may appear that the Directorate of Cultural Heritage regards rock art to be of universal value, where discontinuity and cultural universality are emphasized at the expense of cultural continuity and historical identity. The foundation for a Sámi version of prehistory is not placed side by side with the almost cemented, objectified, and naturalized Norwegian narrative about prehistory, which frames understanding to such an extent that it is probably almost impossible to deconstruct (Hesjedal 2001:291). This narrow-minded "objective" emphasis in the interpretation of prehistory has the effect of further overshadowing Sámi history.

Conclusion: Sámi Past – Sámi Power

In this article we tried to discuss the organization, tasks, and inner-workings of Sámi cultural heritage management in Norway. By presenting an example of a type of the Sámi cultural landscape and the documentation work on that landscape, we wanted to show the practical challenges we face in the management of Sámi cultural heritage.

Our survey illustrates that the preservation of cultural sites depends on local knowledge and that the preservation of Sámi cultural heritage has been largely approached in this manner. At the same time, we tried to underscore that the Sámi Parliament's emphasis on local knowledge has also been an intentional strategy to support the legitimacy of Sámi cultural heritage, a

choice largely dictated by the possibilities provided within the power structure of the Norwegian government system.

Placing priority on local knowledge in Sámi cultural heritage management has clearly been advantageous, but it also has certain weaknesses. This is because it is difficult for Sámi cultural history to become more than "local values," with the limited attention and restricted resources for research, management, museums, and cultural centers that this implies.

The Sámi Parliament in Norway has been given a voice in the struggle over cultural values and in this distribution of values the cultural heritage management is a central part. That voice must, however, be heard within the established Norwegian government system and its structures. We suggest that this gives the Sámi themselves a definite say in the formation of their own past and identity; but this can only happen by sitting at the table that the state has set and not through an equal dialogue at a communal table. The Sámi past is only given the opportunity to be formed as a peripheral and local past, which would be safe for the Norwegian state. The issues in Sámi prehistory that the state, represented by the Directorate for Cultural Heritage, feels are important have been usurped as universal and decontextualized, such that the local Sámi association becomes barely relevant or even irrelevant. In those cases, the Sámi are being alienated from their own history (Fig.118), and that history becomes neutralized as a tool in a serious battle for culture and resources.

In the cultural heritage management oversight in Norway, the Sámi Parliament has a difficult role to play. It must simultaneously be engaged in a dialogue with the local Sámi communities, and pursue and struggle for the understanding of and respect for Sámi prehistory and identity against the state authority. The Sámi Parliament can be a go-between for local knowledge and state power, with local Sámi knowledge being a true asset for the Sámi Parliament, but not for the state. The local Sámi knowledge allows no impetus for the

118/ Pre-Christian Sámi grave (prior to AD 1600) in Veidnes, Unjarga/Nesseby municipality.

development of a modern, inclusive Sámi community, which is truly fundamental for the formation of a cohesive Sámi society in an established nation-state.

Although the power to preserve Sámi cultural heritage is to a large degree unilaterally bound and determined by the power of the state, one should not necessarily underestimate the ability to improve the system's infrastructure and operations from the inside. For instance, the cultural landscape concept that was included in the Cultural Heritage Act in 1992 is partly the result of Sámi professional and research branches' work on this theme.

The Sámi Parliament's steady, growing emphasis on Sámi prehistory will in time be able to challenge the research apparatus to take Sámi history as a starting point in its work. The fact that there is already an independent Sámi cultural heritage management system creates, therefore, an internal dynamics that chal-

lenges the non-Sámi cultural heritage management as well. A government 'white paper' will be published at the end of 2004, concerning the politics of cultural heritage management in Norway. There is a basis to say, with some anticipation, that the choice will be most likely to give the preservation of Sámi cultural heritage a stronger Sámi-nation voice, hopefully at the expense of today's strictly hierarchically organized government system.

Acknowledgments

Thanks to Elisabeth Ward and Iris Hahn. Elisabeth Ward made a preliminary translation of a first draft submitted in Norwegian, and revised the preliminary translation of a second draft, based on the work of Iris Hahn; both Elisabeth and Iris then worked at the Arctic Studies Center, National Museum of Natural History, Smithsonian Institution. Thanks to Bryan Hood, Institute of Archaeology, University of Tromsø, who offered valuable editorial comments to the final English version of this paper. Finaly, thanks to Audhild Schanche, Director of the Nordic Sámi Institute in Kautokeino, who recommended that the authors be invited as contributors to this international collection of papers.

References

Andreassen, Lars
2001 Makten til å kategorisere – samepolitikk og vern av natur. *Dieðut* 2:134–54.Ájluokta/Drag: Árran lulesamisk senter.

Bjøru, Heidi
1994 Hva er det med en kultur som etter hundre års intenst fornorskningspress enda er så sterk at den bokstavelig talt bryter i stykker norske typehus? *Utemiljø* 1:32–9. Oslo: Norsk anleggsgartnerforbund.

Easton, David
1953 *The Political System – An Inquiry into the State of Political Science.* New York: Alfred A. Knopf.

Fjellheim, Sverre
1998 *Samiske kulturminner innen planområdet for nasjonalpark.* Fylkesmannen i Nord-Trøndelag, Rapport nr. 1. Steinkjer.

Føllesdal, Andreas
1999 Hvorfor likhet – hva slags likhet? Normative føringer på forskning om makt og demokrati. *Tidsskrift for samfunnsforskning* 15(2):147–72. Oslo.

Gaski, Lina
2000 Landskap og identitet. *Fortidsvern* 26(2):18–20. Oslo.

Gaukstad, Even
1994 Kulturlandskapsbegrepet. Kulturminnevernets teori og metode. Status og veien videre. Seminarrapport, Utstein kloster 8.- 11. mai 1989. In *FOK - NAVFs program for forskning om kulturminnevern,* pp.135-144. Oslo:Norges allmenvitenskapelige forskningsråd.

Hesjedal, Anders
2001 *Samisk forhistorie i norsk arkeologi 1900-2000.* Ph.D. Thesis, Stensilserie B, no.63. Tromsø: Institute of archaeology, Universitety of Tromsø.

Holme, Jørn
2001 *Kulturminnevern. Lov. Forvaltning. Håndhevelse.* Oslo: Økokrim.

Haaland, Torstein
2001 *Tid, situasjonisme og institusjonell utakt i systemer.* Internet. LOS-senteret. Bergen: University of Bergen.

Hultkrantz, Åke
1965 Type of Religion in the Arctic Hunting Cultures:

A Religio-Ecological Approach. In *Hunting and Fishing : Nordic Symposium on Life in a Traditional Hunting and Fishing Milieu in Prehistoric Times and up to the Present Day.* Hvarfner, Harald, ed., pp.265-318. L uleå: Norrbottens museum.

Ingold, Tim
1987 *The Appropriation of Nature. Essays on Human Ecology and Social Relations.* Manchester: Manchester University Press.

Jernsletten, Jorunn
2000 *Dovletje jirreden: kontekstuell verdiformidling i et sørsamisk miljø.* Unpublished Masters thesis. Tromsø: Institute of religion science, University of Tromsø.

Jernsletten, Nils
1994 Tradisjonell samisk fagterminologi. In *Festskrift til Ørnulf Vorren.* D. Storm, N. Jernsletten, B. Aarseth and P.K. Reymert, eds. *Tromsø museums skrifter* XXV:234-53. Tromsø: University of Tromsø.

Kalstad, Johan Albert
1991 *Noen trekk ved fagfeltet samisk kulturminnevern.* Tromsø: Tromsø Museum.

Nergaard, Jens-Ivar
1997 De samiske grunnfortellingene - En kulturpsykologisk skisse. In: *Filosofi i et nordlig landskap.* A. Greve and S. Nesset, eds. *Ravnetrykk* 12:68-80. Tromsø: University of Tromsø.

Olsen, Bjørnar
1986 Norwegian Archaeology and the People Without (Pre-)History: Or How to Create a Myth of a Uniform Past. *Archaeological Review from Cambridge* 5(1):25-42.

Oskal, Nils
1995 *Det rette, det gode og reinlykken.* Unpublished Ph.D.Thesis. Tromsø: Institute of Social Science, University of Tromsø.

Paine, Robert
1994 *Herds of the Tundra. A Portrait of Sámi Reindeer Pastoralism.* Washington, DC, and London: Smithsonian Institution Press.

Sametinget, Samisk kulturminneråd
1998-2001 *Samisk kulturminneplan* (Sámi Cultural Heritage Plan). Varangerbotn: Sametinget.
2000 *Samisk kulturminneråds årsmelding* (Council of Sámi Cultural Heritage, Annual report). Varangerbotn: Sametinget.

Schanche, Audhild
1993 Kulturminner, identitet og etnisitet. *Dugnad* 4:55-64.
1994 Samisk kulturminnevern. *Vern og Virke: årsberetning fra Riksantikvaren og den antikvariske bygningsnemnd* 14:28-33. Oslo: Riksantikvaren.
1995 Det symbolske landskapet – landskap og identitet i samisk kultur. *Ottar* 207(4): 38-45.

Skandfer, Marianne

1998   *Registreringsrapport. Mauken-Blåtind øvings- og skytefelt.* Tromsø: Sametinget.

2001   Etikk i forvaltning - forvaltning av etikk. *Viking* 64:113-31. Oslo:Norsk arkeologisk selskap.

2002   Etikk i møte med Det Fortidige. In *NIKU Tema 5: Verneideologi.* Elisabeth Seip, ed., pp.51-60. Oslo: NIKU.

Smith, Laurajane

1994   Heritage Management as Postprocessual Archaeology? *Antiquity* 68(3):300-09.

Sommerseth, Ingrid

1999-2001   *Registreringsrapport. Mauken-Blåtind øvings- og skytefelt.* Tromsø: Sametinget.

2001   *Den samiske kulturhistoria i Mauken-Blåtind.* Varangerbotn: Sametinget.

2004   Fra fangstbasert reindrift til nomadisme i indre Troms. Etnografiske tekster og arkeologiske kontekster. In: *Samisk forhistorie. Rapport fra konferanse i Lakselv 5.-6. September 2002.* M. Krogh and Kjersti Schanche, eds. *Várjjat Sámi Musea Èallosat* 1:150-61. Várjjatvuonna (Varangerbotn).

119/ View from Iyat, known in English as Serpentine Hot Springs, a place of healing and spiritual renewal used by Iñupiat of Northwest Alaska, especially residents of Shishmaref. Two Alaska Native NPS maintenance employees, Al Mazonna of Bering Land Bridge National Preserve in Nome and Ed Viglione of the Western Arctic Parklands office in Kotzebue hike toward the south ridge and tors associated with the hot springs.

part 4

COMPARATIVE PERSPECTIVES

Joining the Dots:

Managing the Land- and Seascapes of Indigenous Australia

CLAIRE SMITH AND HEATHER BURKE

Much recent archaeological literature has highlighted a growing concern with the fracture between current cultural heritage management practice and the concerns of Indigenous[1] peoples. Chief amongst these criticisms is the undue emphasis placed on sites as the dominant units of cultural heritage management and the inflexibility of this approach in the face of the more abstract knowledge systems belonging to Indigenous peoples. These knowledge systems of the Indigenous Australians view contemporary Indigenous landscapes as physical manifestations of the actions of ancestors during a creation era known as the Dreaming. These landscapes are full of meaning, inherently powerful and potentially dangerous. Many of the places in these landscapes that are important to Indigenous peoples in Australia cannot be identified by traditional archaeological methods. Grounded in a Western, literary way of viewing the world, archaeology as a discipline has traditionally sought discontinuity and boundedness. As a result, archaeological classification systems have tended to rely on the identification of firm and fixed boundaries, both in time and space, overlooking the possibility of drawing on the more complex and nuanced systems of Indigenous peoples. This occurs not only at the level of site identification, but also in the ways in which archaeologists approach cultural heritage management issues.

One solution that has been advocated is to shift the emphasis away from the site and toward cultural landscapes as the units of study (Ross 1996). The idea is that this will allow the interconnections between sites to be given as much attention as the physical remnants themselves. This concept has gained currency over the last five years amongst many archaeological consultants and other cultural heritage professionals in Australia; but the rhetoric tends to break down in practice, most noticeably in urban and rural areas that are not under the direct control of Indigenous peoples. Our intention in this paper is to explore why this may be. We interpret contact between Indigenous and non-indigenous peoples in Australia as the meeting of Western and Indigenous systems of knowledge. We argue that conflict is inherent in this contact, as these ways of knowing are grounded in and driven by, fundamentally different and possibly irreconcilable, concepts of time and space. Conflicting approaches to the treatment of land, heritage, and documentation arise from this, as well as very different perspectives on preservation, with concomitant implications in terms of the documentation, preservation and management of ethnographic/cultural landscapes.

These differences are being played out within a changing legislative framework. During the 1970s, increased community concern with protecting cultural and environmental resources resulted in a plethora of state and federal cultural heritage and environmental legislation. The Australian cultural heritage legislation prompted the initial recording and assessment of cultural heritage sites (but not landscapes) throughout the country.

Indigenous attempts to gain control over their lands manifested in the case of Mabo v. Queensland, in which Eddie Mabo and others from the Murray Islands, in Queensland's waters, argued successfully that native title to their lands had never been sold, transferred or extinguished. The Mabo decision resulted in the "Native Title Act 1993—An Act about native title in relation to land or waters and for related purposes." This act recognizes a form of native title, which, in those cases where it has not been extinguished, reflects the entitlement of the Indigenous Australians to their traditional lands, in accordance with their laws or customs. This act overturned the notion of *terra nullius* (land with no people), as the legal basis for appropriation of Aboriginal Australia. At the time of making the Mabo decision, the High Court of Australia applied the principles in question to the country as a whole with the clear implication that native title may have survived in other parts of Australia. Since then, Indigenous Australians have made hundreds of applications for native title to their traditional lands. Approved determinations of native title by the High Court, Federal Court, and/or a recognized body are contained in the National Native Title Register (NNTR), a register maintained by the National Native Title Tribunal. This tribunal maintains a number of registers and databases that hold accurate and comprehensive records of native title applications, determinations and Indigenous land use agreements (ILUAs) made under the Native Title Act. For example, the Mabo decision is recorded as a native title determination on the National Native Title Register.

Western and Indigenous Ways of Knowing

This paper keys into an emerging debate among Australian archaeologists and cultural heritage managers about the most appropriate ways to identify and manage the living heritage of Indigenous Australians, the land and seascapes of Australia. This is a direct outgrowth of recent cooperative research with Aboriginal people and has resulted in concerted attempts to develop a more culturally sensitive approach to cultural heritage management (Fullagar and Head 1999; Greer 1996; Ross 1996).

The most common criticism of contemporary cultural heritage management practice in Australia, as elsewhere, is that it fails to take into account Indigenous peoples' needs (Isaacson 2003). In its strict scientific approach to classifying, assessing and documenting sites, cultural heritage management tends to overemphasize the material aspects of culture:

> Until recently, the concept of "heritage," as an archaeological or scientific construction, has been almost universally applied. In this construction, "heritage" may be defined as elements from the past, *most particularly archaeological sites or places where there is visible evidence of that past.* Within this, heritage preservation is aimed at preserving or conserving these elements which are the 'fabric' of the past. (Greer 1996:103, emphasis added)

This results, inevitably, in an undue emphasis on specific sites or locales which, by definition, must be spatially bounded in order to distinguish those areas that possess physical evidence from those that do not. In Australian practice, this is as much a bureaucratic decision as it is a Western scientific one. With a focus on discrete sites, management, too, can be easily bounded and decisions about recording and salvage, or destruction, can be tightly defined using archaeological arguments (Ross 1996:11).

In Australia, the concept of the "site" became enshrined in cultural heritage management practice as a direct result of the development of state and federal cultural heritage legislation in the 1970s, which was the first concerted attempt by government to record and protect cultural heritage. Cultural heritage management is at heart a relative process and in order to be effective requires some foundational pool of information from which to draw comparisons. The administration of the heritage legislation thus required the establishment of registers of the cultural resources existing within each of the eight states and territories of Australia.

The enormous amount of descriptive archaeological survey work that accompanied this push has often been characterized as the "dots on maps" approach: compiling lists of sites into a database with little or no exploration of the possible relationships between sites or areas (Clarke and Hamm 1996:82). Statewide cultural heritage registers created during the 1970s and 1980s were intended to provide a measurable index of cultural value—hence the common use of the term "resource" to describe the material components of culture. This very notion of conceiving of culture as a resource, however, is a reflection of the underlying chasm separating Western and Indigenous ways of knowing.

The Western worldview is often characterized as based on essentialized and dichotomized hierarchies, such as male/female; sacred/secular; culture/nature; self/other. This way of viewing the world seeks and finds discontinuity and boundedness (Wobst and Smith, in press). Expressed in the development of scientific instruments, from globes, telescopes and microscopes, to watches, compasses and clocks, this was part of a mindset that viewed the world as being precisely managed by mathematical principles. Under such processes, space is thought of as less an arena for social relations and more as a neutral, physical commodity. From a Western viewpoint, control over space ceases to be a matter of custom and becomes a matter of formalized, abstracted knowledge (Johnson 1993:347).

Our intent here is to emphasize the widely held notion that the cultural segmentation of space and time—which allowed them to be viewed in measurable, interchangeable segments—is part of a particular way of looking at the world, rather than a natural phenomenon (cf. Handsman and Leone 1989:33; Johnson 1996; Thomas 1993:21). In this way, new notions of space and time became closely linked to the capitalist experience of assessing value through monetary relationships and exchanges of equivalence.

Like all Western preserves, archaeology and cultural heritage management are firmly grounded in such modes of viewing the world. Assessing the significance of "cultural resources" is more a process of assessing exchanges of equivalence: for example, comparing the relative value of sites in a region by determining what constitutes, or does not constitute, a "representative sample." Such financial/economic terms, however, are inadequate ways to represent the complexity of Aboriginal notions of heritage.

Indigenous constructions of knowledge, on the other hand, arise from the fluidity and flexibility of oral traditions. They recognize a plethora of social and cultural distinctions and are based on the premise that knowledge is owned and that access to knowledge will be determined upon each person's specific position within society. The most significant difference in the ways in which Indigenous and non-Indigenous peoples construct knowledge is that Indigenous knowledge is not "open" in the sense that all people have an equal right to acquiring that knowledge. In Indigenous Australian systems, for example, knowledge is rarely definitive and often is restricted. Grounded in oral traditions, knowledge has many levels and is open to alternative interpretations according to the particular situation. It is a source of power and is curated by people with the appropriate qualifications and personalities. Often, only a few people will know the knowledge that is most crucial to the spiritual regeneration of the group. In terms of managing the land, this means it is essential that developers and cultural heritage managers obtain their information about sacred or important sites from the correct people, the people who hold the appropriate knowledge of those sites.

Conflict in these approaches to constructing knowledge is at the basis of many recent controversies over the management of land and seascapes in Indigenous Australia. These differences emerge in clashes between oral and literary traditions, as well as in how Indigenous and non-Indigenous peoples conceive of time and space.

Concepts of Space

Western concepts of space also arise from the capitalist disposition to separate, bound and control. Grounded in a habit of classification, archaeologists deal with space at a number of different scales: from individual finds to regional territories or continent wide transects. Invariably, like time, they conceive of space in terms of discrete and bounded entities. One of the fundamental ways in which archaeologists control space is through defining boundaries. One effect of this is to position Indigenous peoples within defined territories, facilitating administration by bureaucracies and a close counterpart to the process of colonialism (L. Smith 1999:53; Wobst and Smith 2003).

In contrast, Australian Indigenous peoples conceive of space in terms of the inter-relationships that exist between places and peoples, as laid down during the Dreaming era. Indigenous places always exist in relation to other Indigenous places. In terms of land management, this means that each individual site has to be managed as a small facet of a wider cultural landscape. What happens at one site will necessarily impact other sites within a web of inter-relationships that can span the entire country and extend into territorial waters. Morphy (1998:108) argues that:

> The whole of creation, all of human life, is mapped on the landscape, to which ancestral beings are inextricably connected. Almost anything that exists has its place in the Dreamtime, whether it is an animal . . . an object . . . a ritual practice . . . or even an illness. And everything that has a place in the Dreamtime is likely to have a place associated with it on earth.

This is not to say that Indigenous Australians do not have a traditional conception of bounded areas. They do, but the way in which they do this is paradoxically through creating linkages, like interlaced fingers or the checkered patterns on a chessboard. Sharp, linear boundaries do occur in some places, usually where quite clear geographical delineations, such as rivers,

allow them to be readily defined. An example of this is along the Mann River in central Arnhem Land, which acts as a boundary between the lands of Jawoyn and Ngalkpon peoples. Overall, though, Indigenous land boundaries are diffuse, and Indigenous conceptions of territory are focused on the core areas that are indisputably owned by particular groups, rather than on the lines that delineate the territories between them (Hiatt 1987).

In many parts of Australia, the management of Indigenous lands is structured by a web of complex and sophisticated social inter-relationships. In Arnhem Land, for example, "owners," called *gidjan* and "custodians," called *junggayi* have a primary custodial relationship to the other group. All people have birthrights that place them in an ownership relationship to particular tracts of land and in a custodial relationship to neighboring tracts of land. This system of reciprocal rights and responsibilities is all pervasive, since all people are owners for some tracts of land and for particular ceremonies and custodians for others. At a general level, the society is divided into two moieties, Dhuwa and Yirritja. Yirritja people will be the workers in ceremonies, such as *Gunapippi*, that are owned by Dhuwa people and Dhuwa people will be the workers in ceremonies, such as the *Jabuduruwa*, that are owned by Yirritja people. This reciprocal responsibility ensures that ceremonies and land are cared for properly even if people of the preferred "skin" group are not available. Ultimately, all Dhuwa people are custodians for all Yirritja land and all Yirritja people are custodians for all Dhuwa land (C. Smith 1999).

The Western conception of defining space in terms of boundaries is apparent in the failure until recently to grapple with Indigenous notions of sea rights within the existing system of cultural heritage management in Australia. Grounded in a Western tradition of classification, the physical boundary between land and sea has always been treated as a self-evident territorial boundary. From a Western perspective, the point at which the land joins the sea is clearly the place where

Indigenous country must end. This view has been challenged by Indigenous conceptions of territory and of land management and these views have been publicized through the Internet (http://www.nlc.org.au/nlcweb/land_and_sea_rights). The traditional country of coastal Indigenous groups in Australia often extended out to sea. Dreaming trails can include underwater sites, extending Indigenous territory well beyond the shore. Indigenous peoples in coastal areas claim comparable rights over areas of the sea that are contiguous to their lands and see this as a logical extension of land rights:

> Some eighty percent of the Northern Territory coastline is Aboriginal-owned land. Coastal or "Saltwater" Aboriginal people in the Top End of the Northern Territory have a strong attachment to "sea country." Connection to land does not stop at the water's edge. The land and sea are one, providing sustenance. There are sacred sites and dreaming tracks in and under the sea, just as there are on the land (Northern Lands Council 2001).

The principal test case involving native title rights to 3,300 square kilometers (1,275 square miles) of sea was pursued by the traditional owners of Croker Island, which is located off the coast of Arnhem Land, Northern Territory. The original determination by Justice Howard Olney of the Federal Court in 1998 decided that native title sea rights did exist, but that they were non-exclusive and non-commercial. He reasoned that the *Native Title Act 1993* itself allowed recognition of native title offshore by explicitly extending the operation of the Act to coastal seas and any waters over which Australia asserts sovereign rights. However, common law recognition of a public right to fish and to navigation prevented an acceptance of a native title right to exclusive possession, occupation, use and enjoyment of the same areas. On appeal, native titleholders have argued for exclusive possession, while the Commonwealth of Australia has argued that native title cannot exist beyond the low water mark. In 1999 two out of three judges of the full Australian

Federal Court rejected both claims and approved Justice Olney's original decision (http://www.atsic.gov.au). This result was disputed by the people of Croker Island; and in October 2001 the High Court of Australia affirmed that native title rights extended out to sea, but refused to give Indigenous Australians the right to veto offshore fishing, tourism and mining activities (Haslem and Toohey 2001:8).

The way in which this dispute was played out highlights some congruence between Indigenous and non-Indigenous notions of space. Both the Croker Island people and the Australian government had a notion of territory extending beyond the shoreline. In terms of land management, the difference is that the Australian government had not thought in terms of Indigenous peoples having a notion of territorial waters. From an archaeological perspective, this seems a perfectly logical contention, given the long-term land use patterns of the Australian continent and the submerging of large tracts of Indigenous lands by the early Holocene rising of the seas. The interesting point here is that these underwater sites remain incorporated into contemporary Indigenous land management strategies, around 8,000 years after they were originally submerged.

Oral vs. Literary Traditions

In contrast to Western systems of knowledge, which are grounded in the written word, Indigenous knowledge systems are based primarily on oral traditions and were communicated through dance, story, art, song and everyday practice. Such knowledge—of the past, of the land and its resources and of other groups of people—was the major device used by Indigenous peoples to occupy the continent and successfully manage the range of Australian environments. Oral traditions are more fluid and subtle than written systems of communication. Oral forms of communication place power directly in the hands of senior people, who are the respected holders and interpreters of Indigenous law. In many parts of Australia, Indigenous religious and cultural knowledge is separated into "women's business" and "men's business" (Hamilton 1981; Bell 1993). Under this system, the rights to knowledge must be earned; and information is revealed to people gradually, at particular stages in their lives and as they prove themselves worthy of being entrusted with this information and its attendant responsibilities. There is not a simple gendered division of knowledge, as the right to hold such cultural wisdom is dependent on each individual's personal qualities and particular position in Indigenous Australian society. Affiliation to land, specialist knowledge, age, initiated status and so forth are all dimensions that come into play when the transfer of knowledge is being decided.

Moreover, there is great variation across Indigenous Australia in the manner in which Indigenous knowledge is culturally organized (Fig.120). In the Western Desert, for example, gender-based distinctions are a conspicuous feature of cultural organization (Bell 1993), while in Arnhem Land such distinctions are much less obvious to an outsider's eye (Hamilton 1981; Smith 1994).

The most significant difference in the ways in which Indigenous and non-Indigenous Australians construct knowledge is that Indigenous knowledge is not "open" in the sense that all people potentially have an equal right to acquiring that knowledge. In Indigenous systems, knowledge rarely is definitive and often is restricted. Grounded in oral traditions, knowledge has many levels and is open to alternative interpretations according to the particular situation. It is a source of power and is curated by people with the appropriate qualifications and personalities. Responsibility for caring for this knowledge is not something like that everyone could theoretically aspire to, as in Western systems of knowledge. In terms of managing the land, this means it is essential that developers and cultural heritage managers obtain their information about sacred or important sites from the correct people, the people who hold the appropriate knowledge of those sites.

Hierarchical Knowledge: A Case Story of the Hindmarsh Island Bridge

A clash between oral and written traditions lay at the heart of recent controversy over the building of a bridge to Hindmarsh Island, near Adelaide in South Australia. Ngarrindjeri women from the area, because the bridge's construction would disturb an important site related to restricted women's business, objected to this development. Other Ngarrindjeri women, however, challenged the objection, asserting that they were unaware of this "women's business." The Federal Labor government in 1994 stopped the bridge after an inquiry found it would offend Aborigines because of secret women's business. Subsequently, a Royal Commission was called and anthropologists appeared, supporting both sides of the debate. In 1995, the South Australian Hindmarsh Bridge Royal Commission concluded that secret women's business associated with the island was impossible. According to the commission's statement, the Ngarrindjeri women and others who had made these assertions had fabricated their beliefs for the purpose of obtaining a declaration under the Heritage Protection Act to prevent the construction of the bridge (Stevens 1995). This finding was based on a determination that no secret women's business could have existed in Ngarrindjeri culture before the controversy regarding the building of the bridge. In August 2001, the Federal Court of Australia denied an application by Wendy and Thomas Chapman, the developers of the Hindmarsh Island Marina, for compensation from the Commonwealth, the relevant minister and academics, on the grounds that they had been financially disadvantaged by the delay in building the bridge.

It is our view that the determination of the Hindmarsh Bridge Royal Commission was faulty and that this emerged from a clash between Indigenous and non-Indigenous worldviews. This discord is evident in two principal respects: the manner in which the commission privileged evidence from oral and literary

120/ Indigenous Women's Dreaming Site, near Barunga, Northern Territory, Australia.

sources and the inability of the commission to properly grasp the manner in which Indigenous cultural knowledge is formed and disseminated.

Embedded in a Western tradition of dichotomized hierarchies, the commission consistently gave greater credence to historical and ethnographic sources by white people than to Indigenous oral histories. As Nicholls (1996:62) writes, these ways of ranking oral and literary traditions appear so natural that the ethnocentrism on which they are based has become masked. Grosz points out that:

> Dichotomous thinking necessarily
> hierarchises and ranks the two polarised
> terms so that one becomes the privileged
> term and the other its suppressed, negative
> counterpart. The subordinated term is merely
> the negation or denial, the absence or
> privation of the primary term, its fall from
> grace; the primary term defines itself by
> expelling its other and in this process
> establishes its own boundaries and borders
> to create an identity for itself (Grosz 1994:3,
> cited in Nicholls 1996:63).

It is not utterly surprising that the Hindmarsh Island Royal Commission gave greater credence to literary rather than oral sources. In Western modes of thought the former are characterized as detached, objective and reliable, while the latter are viewed as emotional, subjective, and changeable. This leaves oral evidence open to challenge when sites are identified that are likely to obstruct development, unless there is independently generated written substantiation of the information presented in oral evidence. As Bell (1998:34) states, "no texts, no sites" was the mantra of the Royal Commission. From this perspective, Indigenous knowledge only achieves legitimization in the transformation of oral evidence into written texts.

Seeing the world from the Western perspective of relatively open access to knowledge, the commission was unable to come to grips with Indigenous ways of segmenting knowledge and, more importantly, with variation in how such knowledge could be distributed. In trying to understand the idea of culturally segmented knowledge, the commission grasped upon the notion of a simple, exclusive gender division. From this perspective, evidence that not all Ngarrindjeri women were aware of the significance of the Hindmarsh Island area in terms of women's business was taken as evidence that this women's business did not exist. The commission did not entertain the view that gender-specific knowledge could be segmented at many levels, creating a fine and intangible cultural web. It failed to recognize that this knowledge was probably always restricted to a select group of women. Deane Fergie, the anthropologist who documented Ngarrindjeri women's secret-sacred knowledge in a report to the Aboriginal Legal Rights Movement, also attributed the Royal Commission's findings to a clash in worldviews:

> Importantly, the Commission seemed incapable of anything but the most literal interpretation of evidence. There is no recognition by the Commission of the existence of idioms for conveying meaning . . . what came to light and was tested was largely assumption and inference. This is the inferential tautology and the fatal flaw of the Commission's findings (Fergie 1996:17).

The commission's findings drew heavily upon the evidence of two white males, an historian, Phillip Jones, and an anthropologist, Phillip Clarke, who argued that there was no gender-based separation of knowledge within Ngarrindjeri culture. Jones and Clarke arrived at this conclusion on the basis of their analyses of a range of historic and ethnographic sources, rather than a more comprehensive anthropological method of field-based research aimed at assessing the claim of restricted women's business through fieldwork with Aboriginal people. Clarke contrasted the reliability of the sources he used in developing a historical account of Ngarrindjeri culture with the "new formulation" presented by the proponent Ngarrindjeri women, obtained, in his view, from a concentration of material from a range of oral sources (cited in Hemming 1996:32). It is notable that while both formulations of knowledge derive from an analysis of several sources, the reliability of historical and ethnographic sources was consistently privi-

leged over that of oral sources. Hemming criticizes this aspect of Clarke's testimony to the Royal Commission, arguing that:

> This passage highlights the clash occurring in this Commission between Indigenous, oral accounts of history and the Western empiricist tradition dominating the legal system and both Clarke and Jones' style of anthropology and history. Clarke's approach to the discovery of "truth" through the assembling of scientific facts, leads him to what can only be characterised as a "traditionalist" understanding of Aboriginal culture (Hemming 1996:33).

A flaw in Clarke's and Jones' methods that Hemming identified is their failure to conduct fieldwork aimed at testing the notion of restricted women's business or to discuss these issues with the Ngarrindjeri people concerned. Jones defended his position, asserting that ethnography often involves the practitioner in "just a desk-based, library-based, archive-based exercise" (Lucas 1996:43). This method of conducting ethnography, however, not only privileges the views of white colonists over those of Indigenous peoples, but also fails to recognize that these early colonists may not have had access to all forms of information in Indigenous societies and, indeed, that some important forms of knowledge—especially women's business—may have been actively hidden by Indigenous peoples. The majority of early ethnographers were European men who, understandably enough, tended to work mainly with Aboriginal men. Often, these ethnographers consciously avoided inquiring into the "preserves of the other sex" (Elkin 1939:xx). Their failure to discover information about women's business has been the basis for many misconceptions about women's roles in Indigenous Australian societies (Bird 1991; Smith 1993). From this viewpoint, the Hindmarsh Island debacle can be interpreted as a failure to seek Indigenous alternatives to Western assumptions about how Indigenous knowledge is constructed and disseminated.

Concepts of Time

As part of the Western penchant to separate, bound and classify, Western concepts of time are linear, with the past being quite separate from the present. In fact, people in the West go so far as to order their lives down to the unit of seconds, hours, and years. The special expertise of archaeologists is that they can track people's behavior through time; and the further back in time archaeologists are able to delve, the more satisfaction they derive. This way of looking at time relates to how archaeologists view the significance of sites. For most archaeologists, a Pleistocene site is self-evidently more important than a late Holocene or contact site. Moreover, this manifestation of Western control over the very distant past serves to distance the subject of analysis from the investigators of the present, keying into the complementary Western notion of the objectivity of science.

Indigenous peoples, on the other hand, view time in a more holistic manner, in which the past is thought of as impacting actively upon the present. Among Indigenous Australians, time is intricately tied to the notion of a Dreaming that exists in and somehow directs, the present. Morphy (1998:68) describes the Dreaming as existing independently of linear time and the temporal sequence of historical events:

> Indeed, the Dreaming is as much a dimension of reality as a period of time. It gains its sense of time because it was there in the beginning, underlies the present and is a determinant of the future; it is time in the sense that once there was only Dreamtime. But the Dreamtime has never ceased to exist and from the viewpoint of the present . . . is as much a feature of the future as it is of the past.

For Indigenous Australians, the past is never past. They have no concept of a distant past that does not impact upon people in the present. The spirits of relatives who have died inhabit contemporary landscapes and their assumed wishes have to be taken into account. Working together, ancestral beings and dead relations monitor and regulate not only the limits of territory but also the appropriate ways in which country can be used. Indigenous peoples relate to burial sites and occupation sites in a way that is dictated by their traditions associated with death, burials and

campsites associated with the "old people." Steve Hemming discusses this matter in terms of the Ngarrindjeri people of southern Australia:

> Burial sites provide contemporary Ngarrindjeri people with a physical and spiritual connection with their ancestors and their "country." For Ngarrindjeri people the spirits of the ancestors are still present at these sites and they believe that they can have an impact on contemporary people and events. If disturbed they can be very dangerous (Hemming 2000:62).

The intricate interconnections between the Dream-time and the present, between the ancestors and living people, have far reaching implications for what Indigenous peoples consider to be a "site." For Indigenous Australians, the land is the creation of the ancestral beings who, in their journeys across it, produced the various features of the landscape and left behind them songs and story cycles, sacred objects and practices that commemorate their creative acts (Morphy 1993:232). The physical places associated with these acts continue to represent important aspects of traditional life and continue to be vital reference points for delineating group territory and governing people's movements within it. This means that Indigenous peoples may give relatively similar significance to recent sites and to sites of great antiquity. Equally, a site does not need to contain physical traces (i.e., artifacts) for it to be considered significant by Indigenous peoples.

Responding to Indigenous ways of constructing landscape, when the Australian government established the National Aboriginal Sites Authorities Committee (NASAC), it was structured so that it distinguishes between two types of "Aboriginal sites" in Australia as follows:

(1) Archaeological sites, i.e., places that fall within the standard definition of archaeological sites, whose significance is defined "on the basis of scientific enquiry and general cultural and historical values;" and

(2) "sites that are the tangible embodiment of the

121/ Luma Luma, a female ancestral being who traveled throughout northern Australia and whose image exists in rock art throughout the region, material proof of her existence.

sacred and secular traditions of the Aboriginal peoples of Australia." The latter may include the former, of course; but the Aboriginal custodians only may determine the relative significance of these latter sites.

One implication of this is that what some may regard as "ancient" or "old" archaeological sites with no real connections to living Indigenous peoples, are actually places that have very particular cultural meanings for those people. Barbara Bender (1993:14) has expressed this conflict as the difference between landscapes *of* memory (where the landscape is given value by its place in history, typical of the Western notion of time as a linear sequence) and landscapes *as* memory (where creation myths are superimposed upon the land in the present, thereby turning a temporal sequence into a spatial grid). Western notions of objectivity often relegate this conflict to the arena of contemporary politics, a particular "primitivist" construction of Aboriginal culture as a people without politics (Sutton and Rigsby 1982). Therefore, contemporary urban or rural Aborigines are often represented by contrast as a people with politics but without culture (Hemming 2000:59).

An analysis of this situation leads to the recognition of a key limitation in the current cultural heritage management process in Australia. Traditional European notions of "sites" as pristine entities firmly bounded in time completely lack the fluidity of Aboriginal notions of heritage places as something to be used and changed, in the present. From an Indigenous viewpoint, sites are kept alive by being used, which keys into the ancestral power that is inherent in each locale.

Such differences in the way in which Indigenous and non-Indigenous peoples conceive of time can be inherent in conflicts over cultural heritage management strategies, most notably in the debate over the repainting of ancient rock art in Western Australia's Kimberley region. This project involved senior custodians and young Aboriginal people in the repainting of several major rock art galleries as part of an Indigenous cultural continuity and revitalization project. The

project elicited protests from non-indigenous station owners and others, who saw the repainting of these images as a desecration of national cultural heritage (Walsh 1992). The overwhelming response from Australian archaeologists who had conducted extensive fieldwork with Aboriginal groups, however, was to affirm the rights of Indigenous Australians to control their cultural heritage (Mowlarjarli et al. 1988; Vinnicombe 1992; Walsh, 1992; Ward 1992).

While the issues surrounding this debate are particularly complex, the point we will focus on here is the clash between Indigenous and Western conceptions of time and the implications for cultural heritage management. The Western view of time privileges the original authenticity of an artifact and a past that is ideally kept pristine. The conservation of images in Western culture focuses on restoring the original image, as in restorations of the Sistine Chapel. This can be contrasted with the Indigenous view that conservation is ensured through a use that keeps the power inherent in the object alive (Fig.121). This view incorporates change in a dynamic process of on-going cultural experience. David Mowaljarli, the Ngarinyin elder who supervised the Kimberley repainting project, highlights this: "We must draw. Repainting is allowed; we must keep it going; it must glow; must not be put out" (Mowaljarli, cited in Ward 1992:32).

Spaces and Places

Many of the places that are important to Indigenous Australians appear simply as "natural" to non-indigenous peoples. Lacking visible artifacts, the reasons behind their importance are not readily apparent. The successful management of these places has posed a challenge to conventional cultural heritage management strategies. Archaeological management recommendations are consistently based on a distinction between space and place, or nature from culture, a separation that is not a part of Indigenous constructions of the land. From an Indigenous viewpoint, the Australian continent is traversed by Dreaming tracks or songlines, which link the spaces between the successions of place-based events that occurred during the creation era. The individual locales that are encoded in stories are linked to other places within the region (Lewis and Rose 1988).

This is demonstrated in the Western Desert style painting (Fig. 122) depicting individual sites (shown as roundels in the painting) in terms of the activities of an ancestor that took place during the Dreaming. Sites are linked not only in terms of other sites, shown through the barred lines joining sites, but also through the ancestor's travels in non-designated areas, the latter of which is indicated through the rock wallaby's tracks. This painting shows a worldview that emphasizes interconnections and is not congruent with the notion of places as individual locales that are separated from the surrounding landscape.

This notion of being part of an interconnected world also exists in Arnhem Land art (Fig. 123). Here, the lines at the joints of the figures are described by the artist,

Paddy Babu, as "power lines," threads that have an invisible link to other parts of the culture. While the significance of these lines is restricted knowledge, not open to sharing with academic researchers, their existence demonstrates a worldview that emphasizes linkages, rather than boundaries, even when the manifestation appears to be segmentation.

From this perspective, Australia can be seen as a landscape covered by a cobweb of fine linkages—strong, resilient, powerful, and not always perceptible to an untutored eye. The integrity of each individual place is thus linked to all other places, both visible and invisible, by the topogenic narratives of the Dreaming. McWilliam discusses this matter in terms of the current criteria being used to assess compensation to Aboriginal communities for damage to places of cultural or mythological significance:

> The spatial and material connection between sites is merely inferred and created by the narrative or song. In such cases, successful

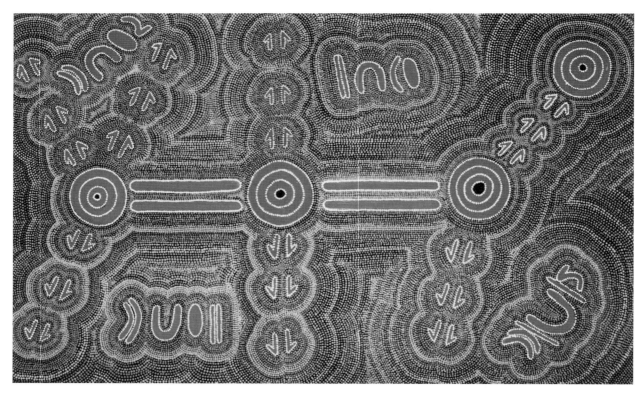

122/ Wakulyarri Tjukurrpa *(Rock Wallaby), acrylic on canvas painting by Lyn Nungarrayi Sims and Wendy Nungarrayi Brown.*

123/ Untitled acrylics on canvas painting by Barunga artist Paddy Babu, 1992.

compensation for damage or obstruction to such significant un-named spaces may be difficult to achieve. In other instances, the linkage between sites may well correspond to a distinctive feature in the landscape. For example, in the Victoria Rivers District, a 60 km limestone ridge represents the shed skin of the walujapi black-nosed python Dreaming, as it moves along its mythological path. As far as I am aware, this tract of land is not named as a specific site, yet clearly damage or destruction to the limestone ridge would certainly be challenged by Aboriginal custodians (McWilliam 1998:9).

Wilderness Areas

The fundamental difference in Western and Indigenous worldviews also underpins the conflict between archaeological and Indigenous approaches to the management of wilderness areas—in Australia, as elsewhere. Non-indigenous peoples tend to characterize "wilderness" as being exempt from

manipulation by humans. Such areas are perceived to be pristine, unaltered and, above all, natural (Head 1990; Ross 1996:12). From an Indigenous viewpoint, however, wilderness areas are as much cultural as any other part of the Australian landscape. Ancestors travelling during the creation era created these areas, they are owned by particular Indigenous groups and they are attributed with social identity in the same way as other tracts of land. From an Indigenous Australian perspective, both wilderness and non-wilderness areas are artifacts of Indigenous cultural and religious beliefs.

The Western separation of culture from nature was one of the mainstays of colonial arguments for the appropriation of Aboriginal lands in Australia. The view that the land was effectively unowned was accepted because the Aboriginal system of land ownership was not understood and because, to Europeans, the natural resources of the land did not seem to be effectively exploited or managed by Aboriginal people. The overturning of the notion of *terra nullius* by the Mabo decision, however, necessitates a re-thinking of the idea of wilderness, since the legal basis for the occupation of Australia now accepts that the whole of Australia, including wilderness areas, was occupied and managed by Indigenous peoples before white colonization (Ross 1996:12). Archaeological evidence in fact shows that Indigenous peoples occupied the full range of Australian environments by around 20,000BP (Mulvaney and Kamminga 1999). During that time Indigenous peoples developed a wide range of land management techniques, including the use of fire to maintain grasslands (Jones 1969; Hallam 1979), the building of weirs and fish traps on rivers and streams (Allen 1979; Godwin 1988) and the construction of fish traps in lakes, rivers and estuaries (Lane and Fullagar 1980; Godwin 1988).

Archaeological evidence that the entire Australian landscape is a cultural artifact is not compatible with the views of some environmentalists who retain the stereotype of Aborigines as "children of nature," living in equilibrium with the land (Toyne and Johnson 1991; Stevens 1994; Ross 1996:12). The potential for conflict becomes activated when archaeologists challenge this stereotype, pointing to substantial evidence for Indigenous manipulation of the land in both the recent and the distant past. As Ross (1996:12) points out, this occurred during the debate over the building of a dam on the Franklin River in Tasmania, when the environmentalists' argument for the area's being a pristine wilderness was seriously challenged by archaeological evidence that Aboriginal people had lived in the area before there were rainforests (Head 1990). The area was saved, partly based on archaeological research that demonstrated Pleistocene antiquity for Indigenous occupation of the region and the international significance of this for human colonization (Mulvaney and Kamminga 1999:184, 189); but the source of discord remains.

The conflict has implications for the management of wilderness areas. While archaeologists recognize that all of Australia was occupied by Indigenous peoples, they are still influenced by a Western mindset that equates wilderness with nature, rather than with culture. This means that wilderness areas do not receive the same kind of archaeological attention as areas that have substantive material evidence of Indigenous occupation. Around the world, archaeologists tend to avoid places where there is little evidence of human occupation and to seek other, more obviously fruitful, landscapes to analyze. Both the absence and the presence of artifacts, however, are the result of specific social strategies. Both speak about contexts, in which (via artifacts or via their absence) particular social strategies were pursued as part of society's reproducing itself. An Indigenous approach to archaeological analysis could well redress this archaeological bias. Such an approach may find space for the analysis of wilderness areas and buffer zones as well as that of massive material finds and may integrate folklore and oral histories into data collection (Wobst and Smith 2003). There is no doubt that this will produce more insightful and holistic interpretations of both past and present societies.

This is easier said than done, however, particularly in rural and urban areas, which are not under the direct control of Indigenous peoples. It is in these areas that development is often most intense. Being directly predicated on the notion of space-as-commodity, however, such development requires the focus of attention on small parcels of land and often the framing of mitigation strategies to deal with individual sites.

Changes are occurring at a legislative level. Queensland's Integrated Planning Act, 1997 requires a coordinated approach to land use, development, and infrastructure planning. Once fully implemented, this Act will bring together sixty separate state approval processes from thirty statutes through the Integrated Development Assessment System. The approval processes gathered under the Act will eventually include those mandated by the Cultural Record (Landscapes Queensland and Queensland Estate) Act, 1987 and the Queensland Heritage Act, 1992. The process is designed so those triggers to agencies with the relevant jurisdiction occur early in the planning process, allowing better management of community concerns and streamlining the development process. Each shire is required to conduct an inventory of known valuable features, which may include significant Aboriginal and non-Aboriginal sites and/or areas of cultural heritage sensitivity. This inventory will form the framework for planning triggers, although there is no provision in the Act as to how such features are to be dealt with.

Under Queensland's Integrated Planning Act of 1997, local governments *in that state* have to deal with ways of identifying and managing the cultural heritage of their shire/city. Simply establishing lists of heritage places within the shire is viewed as inadequate by the Environmental Protection Agency, the statutory authority that administers cultural heritage legislation in Queensland, which is encouraging a focus less on specific site data and more on the shires as cultural landscapes. This trend is occurring Australia-wide. Of primary concern in this process is the establishment of meaningful and effective planning codes to manage this heritage. It is one thing to identify an area as a cultural landscape, but quite another to define this in a spatial sense that is meaningful under a town, or shire-planning, scheme. Paradoxically, while the cultural landscape may have been the unit under study initially, all such schemes operate under Western administrative systems and therefore require sites to be spatially defined in some way. This runs the risk of either reducing the outcome, once again, to the seemingly inevitable list of sites, or generalizing the entire process so that it merely provides a forum for establishing protocols for Indigenous consultation. While limited, this latter approach can seek to identify "areas of concern" or "areas of cultural sensitivity," which can still function as planning triggers.

New Approaches to Interpreting Landscapes

One possible solution to this dilemma has been a landscape approach, such as that advocated by Clarke and Hamm (1996:80), who argue for a planning process that creates a space for the explicit recognition and demonstration of community or social values beyond those given the imprimatur of expert testimony by archaeologists, historians, architects, and the like. Done properly, this is a lengthy process, the outcome of which may be a reshaping of the project and a renegotiation of land management strategies. Clarke and Hamm imply that this more inclusive approach will broaden the types of sites that will be conserved, addressing the problems of disarticulated land management strategies, in which individual sites and clusters survive but their relationships to the landscape are lost.

New ways of managing ancestral lands and waters are also emerging from a collaboration of Indigenous and archaeological approaches. These new approaches have begun to incorporate Indigenous ways of constructing knowledge into the strategies and practices governing the management of land and seascapes. One of these strategies is the Australia-wide development of Indigenous Land Use Agreements (ILUAs), which set out a framework for voluntary cooperation between different interest groups regarding the access, use, and development of land. A direct response to the post-Mabo regulatory landscape, ILUAs are mechanisms for Indigenous empowerment through establishing regional alliances with pastoralists (ranchers in northern hemisphere parlance), mining and conservation interests. The Native Title Act of 1993 allows for local and state government and industry to negotiate land use agreements at a local or regional level with native titleholders. Although the successful use of these agreements requires negotiations based on good faith, once registered they allow for the consideration of Indigenous culture and experience when making decisions about future land management issues.

One of the first such agreements was negotiated in Cape York Peninsula, the northern tip of Queensland. Stemming from a comprehensive study into existing land use and management of the region and the compilation of a comprehensive inventory of its natural, cultural, development and infrastructure assets, various stakeholder groups (including the conservation, Indigenous, commercial herding, mining, local government and tourism sectors) signed an historic pact intended to establish a consensual approach to land management issues in Cape York. Despite the agreement lacking any enforceable provisions and neither the Queensland nor federal governments being party to it, the Cape York ILUA established a set of guidelines for the future use and management of Cape York, including continuing rights of access for traditional owners to pastoral properties for traditional purposes and a commitment to developing sustainable management regimes. Once registered, however, an ILUA is legally binding on the people who are party to the agreement and all native title holders for that area.

The success of such land use agreements for industry partners is apparent in the response by Jim Petrich, CEO of the Cape York Peninsula Development Association:

> What we started in Cape York can be used as a template around regional and rural Australia. Indeed, it can be used in urban Australia to give people some power back on the ground to make decisions—and it is win/win across the board (Petrich 2001).

One creative theoretical attempt at joining the dots is Bill Boyd's, Maria Cotter's, Wave O'Connor's and Dana Sattler's advocation of social construction theory as "an analytical tool with which to tackle the complexities of multiple meanings inherent in social landscapes" (Boyd et al.1996:123). This is their attempt to take into account the modern social landscape and the often conflicting claims of different groups (both Indigenous and non-indigenous) with interests in the same landscape:

> For each party a site is defined by some constructed meaning and represents a point within a particular landscape, that point being but one node within a network of linkages, pathways, edges, landmarks and areas within the landscape. . . .The site is rarely viewed by any party as an isolated individual point; its landscape relationship is constructed in terms of individuals' cognitive maps, these representing the cumulative effects of a wide range of social and cultural influences. . . .Such construction is not confined to the present and indeed forms the basis for much of the archaeological interest in cultural landscapes (Boyd et al. 1996:125).

Rather than getting bogged down in the minutiae of verifying the truth of one claim over another, Boyd and his co-authors advocate to shift the emphasis away from assessing the validity of any one perspective and toward the analysis of social issues. For them, in order to manage the cultural heritage, it is enough to accept that these competing claims exist, rather than to privilege one over another:

> For each party, the site represents a point within a particular physical, social and political landscape; neither the point nor the landscapes are static. ... The emphasis... is not on the validity of the meanings but with the reality of their existence and the outcome for cultural resource management in general includes a greater understanding of the processes of interaction between parties. (ibid.:135–7)

While this approach has tackled the interpretation of the modern cultural landscape, by drawing upon Indigenous notions of an interconnected world, Fullagar and Head (1990) explore the possibility of making interpretations of landscapes of the distant past more multi-dimensional. Integrating both ethnographic and archaeological evidence, the authors argue for the Pleistocene antiquity of mapped landscapes in the Keep River area of the Northern Territory. They use the material manifestations of links between specific places in the present in order to broaden the dimensionality of analyses of archaeological excavations:

> This cannot be attempted simply by transposing stories reflecting present-day perceptions backwards in time. What we have

argued is that, by demonstrating links between these perceptions and archaeologically visible materials, which, in this case, consist of stone, ochre and starch plants, we can begin the task of tracing changes in attachment to landscape over time (Fullagar and Head 1999:332-3).

The accommodation of Indigenous agendas into archaeological practice is reinforced by the structure of the Australian government's National Competitive Grants Programme (NCGP), the most recent manifestation of which was introduced in 2001. The Australian Research Council's (ARC) Linkage-Projects program, in particular, is structured so that research is shaped by more than the agendas of the academy. The aim of this program is to "encourage and develop long-term strategic research alliances between higher education institutions and industry in order to apply advanced knowledge to problems, or to provide opportunities to obtain national economic or social benefits" (ARC 2001). For archaeologists, a major reservoir of industry partners is Indigenous organizations. Moreover, ARC-Linkage applications require that the applicant identify specific benefits that the research will produce for the industry partner. This provision encourages archaeologists seeking funding from this source to shape their projects so that they further the agendas of their industry partners. If the partner is an Indigenous organization, the project is shaped in accordance with the agendas of Indigenous peoples.

A recent example of this is Bird and Frankel's (1998) analyses of archaeological site recordings that had been conducted under the auspices of the Victorian state government by the Victoria Archaeological Survey during the 1970s and early 1980s. There was a need for a regional integration of the material, as most of it was unpublished or published in a summary form only. The project has implications for Indigenous heritage management in the region, the quality of which should be enhanced by the more detailed regional analyses. Both the aims and outcomes of Bird and Frankel's research indicate an accommodation of academic and Indigenous agendas:

The study of this material will allow a new synthesis of regional prehistory, forming the basis for the preparation of educational material to meet the needs of local Aboriginal communities, as well as for site management of sites in the region. . . .A central aspect of the project is the explicit recognition of the importance of Aboriginal community interests in the material and its interpretation. . . .Our work will therefore provide the basis for a range of products developed specifically to address the requirements of local communities. Possible outcomes include pamphlets, posters and display materials on various aspects of Victorian Aboriginal archaeology. (Bird and Frankel 1998:36-8)

While this particular project still uses Western ways of classifying material, it is producing outcomes that are of benefit to the local Indigenous community. It is a small step to move beyond this consultative approach that shapes research outcomes to include Indigenous as well as archaeological products, to one of negotiation, in which integrated programs of collaborative research are shaped by Indigenous Australian as well as Western ways of knowing.

"Indigenous Archaeology:" The New Approach to Landscape Management/Preservation

Our intention in this chapter has been to explore the ways in which Indigenous and Western ways of the constructing the world have engendered current debates about the management of Indigenous land and seascapes in Australia. Recent areas of conflict can be interpreted in terms of a clash of worldviews, particularly in terms of capitalist and Indigenous approaches to the construction of space, time and knowledge. Recent cooperative research with Indigenous peoples, however, has resulted in concerted attempts to develop a more culturally sensitive approach to cultural heritage management (Greer 1996; Fullagar and Head 1999; Ross 1996).

As practiced in Australia, Indigenous archaeology—an archaeology informed by Indigenous values and agendas—is going through a period of rapid change. Archaeologists are moving beyond research *about*

Indigenous peoples to focus on research that is conducted with and for these peoples. In doing so, archaeologists are developing a greater knowledge of and appreciation for, Indigenous values, experiences and ways of knowing. Australian archaeologists recognize that Western methods are not the only valid ways of managing land and seascapes. Increasingly, they are willing to tackle the challenge of developing new approaches that are culturally appropriate to Indigenous knowledge systems. This trend is likely to continue as Indigenous peoples pursue greater input into the day-to-day practice of archaeology; as part of the ongoing recognition of land and sea rights; and as the Australian government continues to direct major support into collaborative funding programs. The trend will be augmented by the increasing numbers of Indigenous peoples who are training as professional archaeologists. This process is producing a new kind of synergism, with the potential for innovative and diverse outcomes.

A different kind of archaeology is gradually emerging in Australia, with new approaches to the documentation and management of Indigenous cultural landscapes. With informed Indigenous ways of thinking, the possibility arises of an opening up of new vistas of land management strategies, encompassing areas of research that previously have been neglected or discriminated against by archaeologists. This Indigenous archaeology is self-consciously aware of entrenched Western mindsets and is willing to address the intellectual challenges involved in engaging with the complexities of Indigenous knowledge systems. Moving beyond the fetters of Western modes of thought, this archaeology is likely to show greater interest in absence, as well as presence, in oral as well as literary forms of knowledge and in the interconnections of space and place (Wobst and Smith, in press). It promises to be an intellectually exciting, and more socially valuable, archaeology.

Conclusions

In summary, the flexibility of Indigenous notions of space and time views the landscape as an interconnected whole that is far more than just the sum of its parts. Indigenous Australians tend to view sites at this landscape level of abstraction, rather than in the spatially bounded sense commonly understood by Europeans, who habitually regard land as a commodity and partition it into discrete parcels. From an Indigenous Australian viewpoint, detrimental effects to one part of the cultural landscape affect all other parts of it; individual sites cannot be separated from the cultural context that gives them meaning.

Changes in the intensity of working relationships between archaeologists and Indigenous Australians have led to a recognition that lists of sites ('dots on maps') are an inadequate way to represent the complexity of Aboriginal notions of heritage. For Indigenous Australians, these dots are always joined and any focus on one dot in isolation will give only a partial and inadequate view. From a cultural heritage management point of view, the challenge becomes not only to join the dots, thus seeing the bigger picture, but also to develop more inclusive and thoughtful planning mechanisms that will make it possible for cultural landscapes to be regarded as a standard unit of cultural heritage management practice.

Acknowledgments

We thank the Indigenous peoples with whom we have worked and, in particular, Phyllis Wiynjorroc, the traditional owner for the Barunga-Wugularr region of the Northern Territory, Australia, and her senior custodians, Peter Manabaru and Jimmy Wesan. Also, we thank Igor Krupnik for inviting us to write this paper and for providing detailed editorial guidance.

Notes

1. Following the increasingly common practice among Indigenous authors, we use the term

"Indigenous peoples" in this paper. The capital "I" here emphasizes the nationhood of individual groups while use of the plural "peoples" internationalizes Indigenous experiences, issues, and struggles (L. Smith 1999:114-5).

References

Allen, Harry

1979 Aborigines of the Western Plains of New South Wales. In *The Aborigines of New South Wales*, C. Haigh and W. Goldstein, eds., pp. 22-43. Sydney: New South Wales National Parks and Wildlife Service.

ARC (Australian Research Council)

2001 *Australian Research Council Web Site*, online: http://www.arc.gov.au (accessed October 10, 2001).

ATSIC (Aboriginal and Torres Strait Islanders Commission)

2001 *Aboriginal and Torres Strait Islander Commission Web Site*, online: http://www.atsic.gov.au (accessed October 10, 2001).

Bell, Diane

1993 *Daughters of the Dreaming*. Melbourne: McPhee Gribble/George Allen and Unwin.

1998 *Ngarrindjerri Wurruwarrin: A World That Is, Was and Will Be*. Brisbane: Spinifex.

Bender, Barbara

1993 Introduction: Landscape—Meaning and Action. In *Landscape: Politics and Perspectives*. B. Bender, ed., pp. 1-18. Oxford: Berg.

Bird, Carolyn

1993 Woman the Toolmaker. In *Women and Archaeology: A Feminist Critique*. H. du Cros, and L. Smith, eds., pp. 22-30. Occasional publication, Department of Archaeology and Anthropology, Research School of Pacific Studies. Canberra: Australian National University.

Bird, Carolyn, and David Frankel

1998 University, Community and Government: Developing a Collaborative Archaeological Research Project in Western Victoria. *Australian Aboriginal Studies* 1:35-9.

Boyd, Bill, Maria Cotter, Wave O'Connor and Dana Sattler

1996 Cognitive Ownership of Heritage Places: Social Construction and Cultural Heritage Management. In *Australian Archaeology '95: Proceedings of the 1995 Australian Archaeological Association Annual Conference*, S. Ulm, I. Lilley and A. Ross, eds., pp. 123-40. *Tempus, Archaeology and Material Culture Series in Anthropology*. St Lucia: University of Queensland.

Clarke, Annie, and Giles Hamm

1996 Stumbling over Stones: Site Management at Lake Condah. In *Issues in Management Archaeology*, L. Smith. and A. Clarke, eds., pp. 79-82. *Tempus, Archaeology and Material Culture Series in Anthropology*. St Lucia: University of Queensland.

Elkin, Adolphus Peter

1939 Introduction. In P. Kaberry's *Aboriginal Woman: Sacred and Profane*, pp. xvii-xxxi. London: George Routledge and Sons Ltd.

Fergie, Deane

1996 Secret Envelopes and Inferential Tautologies. *Journal of Australian Studies* 48:13-24.

Fullagar, Richard, and Lesley Head

1999 Exploring the Prehistory of Hunter-gatherer Attachments to Place: An Example from the Keep River Area, Northern Territory, Australia. In *The Archaeology and Anthropology of Landscape. Shaping Your Landscape*. P. Ucko and R. Layton, eds., pp. 322-35. *One World Archaeology* 30. London and New York: Routledge.

Godwin, Luke

1988 Around the Traps: A Reappraisal of Stone Fishing Weirs in Northern New South Wales. *Archaeology in Oceania* 23:49-59.

Greer, Shelley

1996 Archaeology, Heritage and Identity in Northern Cape York Peninsula. In *Australian Archaeology '95: proceedings of the 1995 Australian Archaeological Association annual conference*, S. Ulm, I. Lilley and A. Ross, eds., pp. 103-6. *Tempus, Archaeology and Material Culture Series in Anthropology*. St Lucia: University of Queensland.

Grosz, Elizabeth

1994 *Volatile Bodies*. Sydney: Allen and Unwin.

Hallam, Sylvia

1979 *Fire and Hearth*. Canberra: Australian Institute of Aboriginal Studies.

Hamilton, Annette

1981 A Complex Stratigraphical Situation. Gender and Power in Aboriginal Australia. In *Australian Women: Feminist Perspectives*, N. Grieve and P. Grimshaw, eds., pp. 69-85. Melbourne: Oxford University Press.

Handsman, Russel G., and Mark P. Leone

1989 Living History and Critical Archaeology in the Reconstruction of the Past. In *Critical Traditions in Contemporary Archaeology. Essays in the Philosophy, History and Socio-politics of Archaeology*. V. Pinsky and A. Wylie, eds., pp. 117-35. Cambridge: Cambridge University Press.

Haslem, Benjamin, and Paul Toohey

2001. Native Title Leglislation Confirmed Seaworthy. *The Australian*. October 12, 2001, p. 8.

Hemming, Steven J.

1996 The Invention of Ethnography. *Journal of Australian Studies* 48:25-39.

2000   Ngarrindjeri Burials as Cultural Sites: Indigenous Heritage Issues in Australia. *World Archaeological Bulletin* 11:58-66.

Hiatt, Les
1987   Aboriginal Political Life. In *Traditional Aboriginal Society*, R. Edwards, ed., pp. 174-88. Melbourne: McMillan.

Isaacson, Ken
2003 Building for the Future. In *Indigenous People and Archaeology. Proceedings of the 29th Annual Chacmool Conference*, T. Peck and E. Siegfried, eds. Calgary:Archaeological Association of the University of Calgary.

Johnson, Matthew
1993   Notes toward an Archaeology of Capitalism. In *Interpretative Archaeology*, C.Tilley, ed., pp. 327-56. Oxford: Berg.
1996   *An Archaeology of Capitalism*. Oxford: Blackwells.

Jones, Rhys
1969   Fire-stick Farming. *Australian Natural History* 16:224-8.

Lane, L, and Richard Fullagar
1980   Previously Unrecorded Stone Alignments in Victoria. *Records of the Victoria Archaeological Survey* 10:134-51.

Leone, Mark P.
1988   The Georgian Order as the Order of Merchant Capitalism in Annapolis, Maryland. In *The Recovery of Meaning. Historical Archaeology in the Eastern United States*. M. P. Leone and P. Potter Jr., eds., pp. 235-61. Washington: Smithsonian Institution Press.

Lewis, Darrel, and Deborah Bird Rose.
1988   *The Shape of the Dreaming*. Canberra: Aboriginal Studies Press.

Lucas, Rod
1996   The Failure of Anthropology. *Journal of Australian Studies* 48:40-51.

Mulvaney, Derek John and Johan Kamminga
1999   *A Prehistory of Australia*. Sydney: Allen and Unwin.

McWilliam, Andrew
1998   Negotiating Desecration: Sacred Sites Damage and Due Compensation in the Northern Territory. *Australian Aboriginal Studies* 1:2-10.

Morphy, Howard
1991   *Ancestral Connections. Art and an Aboriginal System of Knowledge*. Chicago: University of Chicago Press.
1993   Colonialism, History and the Construction of Place: The Politics of Landscape in Northern Australia. In *Landscape: Politics and Perspectives*. B. Bender, ed., pp. 205-44. Oxford: Berg.
1998   *Aboriginal Art*. London: Phaidon Press Ltd.

Mowaljarli, David, Patricia Vinnicombe,

Grameme K. Ward and Christopher Chippindale
1988   Repainting of Image on Rock in Australia and the Maintenance of Aboriginal Culture. *Antiquity* 62(237):690-6.

Nicholls, Christine
1996   Literacy and Gender. *Journal of Australian Studies* 48:59-72.

Northern Lands Council
2001   *Northern Lands Council Web Site* online: http://www.nlc.org.au/nlcweb/land_and_sea_rights/documents/04_body_sea_rights_the_land_and_sea_are_one.html (accessed October 10, 2001).

Petrich, James
2001   *The Brisbane Institute Web Site* online: http://www.brisinst.org.au/papers/petrich_foundations.html. Cape York Partnership Plan: the Foundations. (accessed October 10, 2001).

Ross, Annie
1996   Landscape as Heritage. In *Issues in Management Archaeology*, L. Smith. and A. Clarke, eds., pp. 9-17. Archaeology and Material Culture Series in Anthropology. St Lucia: University of Queensland.

Smith, Claire
1993   The Negotiation of Gender through Western Desert Art. In *Women and Archaeology: A Feminist Critique*, H. du Cros and L. Smith, eds., pp. 161-70. Occasional publication, Department of Archaeology and Anthropology, Research School of Pacific Studies. Canberra: Australian National University.
1994   Situating Style: An Ethnoarchaeological Study of Social and Material Context in an Australian Aboriginal Artistic System. Unpublished PhD thesis, University of New England.
1999   Ancestors, Place and People: Social Landscapes in Aboriginal Australia. In *The Archaeology and Anthropology of Landscape. Shaping your Landscape*, P. Ucko and R. Layton, eds., pp. 189-205. *One World Archaeology* 30. London and New York: Routledge.

Smith, Laurajane T., and Annie Clarke, ed.
1996   *Issues in Management Archaeology*. Archaeology and Material Culture Series in Anthropology. St Lucia: University of Queensland.

Smith, Linda Tuhiwa
1999   *Decolonizing Methodologies. Research and Indigenous Peoples*. Second edition. London: Zed Books.

Stevens, Fran
1994   An Analysis and Rebuttal of Arguments Presented in Opposition to the Rights of Aboriginal and Torres Strait Islander Peoples to Hunt in National Parks in Queensland. Online: http://nativenet.uthscsa.edu/archive/nl/9402/0015.html (accessed 15, October 2001).

Stevens, Iris

1995 *Report of the Hindmarsh Island Royal Commission.* Adelaide: State Print.

Sutton, Peter, and Bruce Rigsby

1982 A People with 'Politicks:' Management of Land and Personnel on Australian's Cape York Peninsula. In *Resource Managers: North American and Australian Hunter-Gatherers,* N.M. Williams and E.S. Hunn, eds., pp. 155–72. Boulder: Westview Press.

Thomas, Julian

1993 The Politics of Vision and the Archaeologies of Landscape. In *Landscape: Politics and Perspectives,* B. Bender, ed., pp. 19–48. Oxford: Berg.

Toyne, Phillip, and R. Johnson

1991 Reconciliation, or the New Dispossession? *Habitat Australia* (June 1991):8–10.

Vinnicombe, Patricia

1992 Kimberley Ideology and the Maintenance of Sites. In *Retouch, Maintenance and Conservation of Aboriginal Rock Imagery,* G.K. Ward, ed., pp. 10–11. Melbourne: Australian Rock Art Research Association.

Ward, Graeme

1992 Ochre and Acrylic: Conflicting Ideologies and Divergent Discourses in the Issue of Repainting of Aboriginal Imagery. In *Retouch, Maintenance and Conservation of Aboriginal Rock Imagery,* G. K. Ward, ed., pp. 31–8. Melbourne: Australian Rock Art Research Association.

Walsh, Grahame

1992 Rock Art Retouch. Can a Claim of Aboriginal Descent Establish Curation Rights over Humanity's Cultural Heritage? In *Rock Art and Ethnography,* M. Morwood and D. Hobbs, eds., pp. 46–59. Melbourne: Australian Rock Art Research Association.

Wobst, H. Martin, and Claire Smith

2003 "Unothering" Theory and Practice in Archaeology. In *Indigenous People and Archaeology. Proceedings of the 29th Annual Chacmool Conference* T. Peck and E. Siegfried, eds., pp. 211–25. Calgary: Archaeological Association of the University of Calgary.

124/ *Early spring time in the reindeer herders' tundra camp on the Yamal Peninsula, West Siberia. Nomadic reindeer herders use the tundra landscape and fill it with stories, legends, and memories from the past days and the time immemorial.*

epilogue

Landscapes, Perspectives, and Nations: What Does It All Mean?

ELLEN LEE

When Igor Krupnik asked me to write this epilogue for the international collection on northern ethnographic landscapes, my first intention was to draw from the various chapters to provide some kind of summary or overview of the issues raised throughout the book. Once I had read all the chapters, I realized what a daunting task this would be. When I considered the contributions to this volume coming from nations as diverse as Canada, Russia, Australia, and Iceland, several questions jumped out at me that I would like to address in this concluding section. Three fundamental questions relate to the entire topic of northern ethnographic landscapes. First: *What are northern ethnographic landscapes?* Second: *What is it about northern ethnographic landscapes that merits our attention and our energies?* Third: *What can we learn from northern ethnographic landscapes?*

The Definition: What Are Northern Ethnographic Landscapes?

The volume's Introduction discusses various terms used in different countries for what are called here "northern ethnographic landscapes." In order to understand the concept in another way, I would break the title into its three constituent parts—"northern," "ethnographic," and "landscapes"—and examine each term separately.

Why, in the first place, was it considered interesting or useful to look at northern landscapes as a group, as opposed to including landscapes from other regions? While this is not directly expressed in the Introduction or in the individual chapters, I would venture to suggest that within the northern hemisphere, it is in the more northerly areas of North America, Europe, and Asia that indigenous people are present and where industrial exploitation is relatively small (or moderate—when compared to other regions). One may say that the northern part of the northern hemisphere, as a generalized region, is mostly made up of relatively undeveloped land, in comparison to areas further south. As a result, fewer northern indigenous people have been displaced from their traditional lands, and more of them have retained their traditional languages and ways of life. While this is particularly true in the northern areas of Canada and Alaska, even in those geographical regions both languages and traditional ways of life have changed dramatically as a result of European contact. Nevertheless, northern communities are more likely than others to have been able to maintain their links with their traditional territories, and their cultural landscapes are more clearly recognizable. All residents of the North, whether indigenous or non-indigenous (including two latter examples reviewed in this book, the Icelandic "saga-travelers" and Norwegian fishermen), have a special relationship with northern landscapes, and one that merits our attention.

The second word, "ethnographic," has traditionally been used to describe the study of communities or groups that are culturally different from the modern dominant culture. As a Canadian, I find the use of the term "ethnographic" in this book intriguing; I am not aware of it being commonly used in conjunction with the word "landscape" in Canada. In this volume, an ethnographic landscape is generally seen as one associated with a group whose culture or history stands apart from the modern dominant society. It includes landscapes associated with or valued by indigenous or Aboriginal communities, as well as earlier groups of people who may not be considered indigenous to a particular area, but whose cultures nevertheless differ substantially from what is commonly called "Western culture." The fact of cultural differences between those associated with the landscape and those studying it or attempting to manage those landscapes is one of the major sources of question and debate on this topic. Therefore, "ethnographic" here stands for differences, for cultural distinctiveness, and peculiarities that are so crucial in the field of heritage preservation and landscape management.

The term "landscape" is interesting to examine and dissect, as well. A search of on-line dictionaries for the definition of landscape revealed that while there is some variation among the definitions, they generally include some reference to scenery: an expanse of scenery, a broad view, a single view, a large area of countryside, a portion of land or territory, and so forth. More than one source attributed the origins of the word to the scenery depicted in Dutch landscape painting. The essence of the definition of landscape and how its use has developed is summed up in the Canadian Oxford Dictionary (1998:801) as "natural or imaginary scenery, as seen in a broad view." Landscape refers not only to the physical nature of the land itself, but also to how it is imagined or perceived.

So, putting these three words together, northern ethnographic landscapes are areas or regions of land in the northern part of the northern hemisphere. They are associated with cultural groups that are chronologically or culturally distinct from the modern dominant cultural groups. Further, they are imagined, perceived, remembered, or interpreted in a particular way because of their physical nature and their relationship with a particular cultural group or tradition. Those three

themes—the North, cultural distinctiveness, and specific visions or perceptions—all come together and are addressed in one way or another in every chapter of this book.

The Value: What About Northern Ethnographic Landscapes Merits Our Attention?

In other words, why do we care about these landscapes? While the aspect of being in the North gives all of these landscapes something in common in terms of environmental elements and the relative lack of development, the landscapes' presence in the North, in and of itself, does not give rise to major challenges. What is critical is that the study of northern ethnographic landscapes opens up the ways to learn how to preserve biodiversity and at the same time encourage the cultural survival of the people associated with these landscapes. The study of traditional ecological knowledge in these areas presents tremendous opportunities for understanding how cultural values and behaviors affect and enhance the sustainability of ecological zones, and vice versa. It is because of the North, its peoples, and the ways we communicate with them—politically, historically, and scientifically—that we have the possibility of coming to understand how cultural systems and natural systems are integrated, and are, in fact, part of each other.

Understanding and Communication: What Can We Learn from Northern Ethnographic Landscapes?

The most problematic aspect of northern ethnographic landscapes seems to be the cultural differences between the communities associated with the landscape and the dominant (usually governing) cultural group—in other words, the ethnographic aspect. These differences show up in all facets of identification, evaluation, protection, management, and interpretation of these landscapes. In fact, even listing these activities separately reveals clear cultural differences. Aboriginal groups who live in and are part of a landscape do not think about "identification," "evaluation," "protection," "management," and "interpretation" of the land they live in. Simply, they use other words and have other feelings toward their lands. To look at landscapes from the outside is the perspective of a dominant cultural group and of the system of dealing with the land it created.

The first, and in some ways the most basic, challenge is the factor of *unequal power* between the parties involved with these landscapes. Because of indigenous peoples' lower political status and recognition, in many situations these groups have little or no power to affect the disposition of their traditional land and how it is used. And where they do have some influence, they are invariably forced to work within the parameters set by the dominant culture or government. While the existence of a situation of unequal power is now recognized by both parties in these cases, often the implications of differing cultural approaches is inadequately understood by either side. The issue becomes one of failed cross-cultural communication. For such relationships to be productive, there needs to be recognition that there are ways of seeing the world that are different from one's own, but just as valid.

The ways that governments manage the kinds of landscapes referred to in this volume—by identification, evaluation, protection, management, and interpretation—are clearly developed by the dominant cultural perspective. They are now a reality for indigenous peoples as well, because of the political situation most indigenous northern groups find themselves in. Therefore, the most useful way to address these challenges might be to examine each step with the goal of trying to understand how it might be perceived by or might affect the respective indigenous or traditional group.

The first step here is to identify a landscape in terms of its interest to a particular group and/or government (in our case, to a governmental agency in charge of the land and/or heritage preservation). It is important to recognize that even though it appears to be a simple, straightforward step, identification itself can be an intervention in an existing ethnographic landscape. Identification carries cultural baggage; the categories favored by government will invariably not recognize the unique richness of meaning a particular landscape holds for its indigenous residents (Lee 2000:4–5). The "protected landscapes" concept used by IUCN (World Conservation Union) has great potential to work around this difficulty as it provides "opportunities to directly engage local communities in stewardship" (Mitchell and Buggey 2000: 40-1) and thus avoid reducing the landscapes to biophysical models. Who identifies a cultural landscape and what terminology they use to categorize it could have a major impact on later decisions.

With identification usually comes documentation. Documentation protocols need to be tailored to meet both the cultural needs of the resident population and the institutional needs of the relevant government program. It is crucial to ensure that the words used to document and describe the landscape are carefully defined, so that the words have commonly understood meanings, particularly when there are language as well as cultural differences. It is important to document both the physical and the intangible characteristics of the landscape. In some cases, the work needed to document such a landscape may actually contradict the intangible values inherent in the landscape. In such instances, intangible values may not fit within standardized government programs and established documentation patterns. In reading through the different stories presented in this volume, one gets the sense of not only the complexity of ethnographic landscapes, but also of the diverse possible dimensions that any given landscape might have. For example, the patterns of ethnographic landscapes may not necessarily match our common view of geography. What one thinks of as the normal horizontal and vertical dimensions of a landscape take on new meaning when one looks at a seascape (as in the case of fishermen's knowledge) or at a traditional tribal landscape lived with and built around hundreds of place-names, old stories, travel narratives, and ancestral paths. Time and seasonality are important, although often undocumented, dimensions of many landscapes. The boundaries of ethnographic landscapes may also be problematic in many cases. They may not be part of the traditional cultural conception of the landscape, and may therefore be artificially imposed for the purposes of some institutional need. Groups often see all of their traditional territory as important, even where it overlaps with the territory of others, and are unwilling or unable to choose smaller areas for the purposes of protection.

The challenges of documenting ethnographic landscapes also extend into the challenges of evaluation. An ethnographic landscape refers to a group or collective concept of land and place, so group values are paramount in determining the landscape's importance and meaning. However, not only do values placed on landscapes differ between local, indigenous people and the dominant culture, but they also vary between the male and female perspectives and among the different generations within a community. While there are group understandings of landscapes, each person also carries an individual and unique cultural landscape in his or her head and heart, based on personal experiences. Thus it is important to be aware of the layering of values and the potential for conflicting values, even between members of the same cultural group.

In considering the values associated with landscapes, it is important to remember that in the scientific approach, we tend to think of landscapes as concrete, physical things, with the values layered onto the place. However, the origins of the word "landscape" in Dutch landscape painting, suggest the original use of the concept as an abstract representation of land, that is, a way of *thinking* about the land. "The quintessential nature of the use of the term cultural landscape is that its definition and meaning are in the eye of the beholder" (Lee 2000:3). So if we think of landscapes as imaginary, or as creations of our experience, behavior, and memories, evaluating them becomes more dif-

ficult, or at least more complex. When landscapes are creations of memory, dreaming, or ritual, they require us to reach further than our usual scientific recording and evaluation techniques.

The challenge increases manifold when we are dealing with more than one language. Place-names in original languages are often the mnemonic devices that help to continue to connect the stories and the culture of the people to their land. Concepts are often not easily (if at all) translatable from one language to another, especially where cultures are radically different. Many indigenous peoples have identified the two most important mechanisms for sustaining their culture as language retention and a continuing relationship to the land. The transmission of these values from one generation to the next in the face of global, electronic communications is an enormous challenge facing indigenous people today.

Protection and Management

After government agencies and local people have succeeded in identifying, documenting, and evaluating an ethnographic landscape, the next step is to find a way to protect and sustain it. Assuming that the values have been adequately defined to accurately reflect the essence of the landscape, it should not be difficult to identify management practices that can help to ensure that the ethnographic landscape is sustainable. However, in some cases, culturally inappropriate activities may be necessary because of clashes with modern economy. Government protection might be necessary – for example, setting an area of land aside to prevent inappropriate commercial exploitation. Even though it may not be part of the traditional relationship between the landscape and the people, there may be a need to map and document places that previously were never written down, or were culturally protected because of their acknowledged power or sensitivity. Unusual protective mechanisms may sometimes be required. In some cases, restoration of spiritual value may be carried out through the conduct of

CATEGORY	PROTECTED AREAS (e.g. National Parks)	HISTORICAL SITES	ETHNOGRAPHIC LANDSCAPES
EVALUTAION CRITERIA	Natural values	Cultural or historic values	Cultural and natural values
SIZE OF GEOGRAPHICAL AREA	Large geographical areas to protect ecosystems, watersheds	Small geographical areas to protect buildings building complexes and archaeological sites	Large geographical areas to encompass all values
TANGIBLE OR INTANGIBLE VALUES	Primarily tangible values (biophysical)	Primarily tangible values (cultural resources)	Both tangible and intangible values
BALANCE OF NATURAL AND CULTURAL VALUES IN AREA MANAGEMENT	Cultural or historical values secondary	Natural values secondary	Cultural and natural values integrated

appropriate rituals. The accumulation, documentation, and appropriate transmission of traditional knowledge can also be a mechanism for sustaining a landscape. Participation of the associated local people in the management regime should, therefore, help ensure that these activities are appropriate and are properly monitored.

In most of the countries represented in this volume, finding a management regime for an ethnographic landscape is difficult. This is because existing protected area regimes tend to separate cultural and natural landscapes, with different foci and characteristics. Thus we find that cultural landscapes often fall between the cracks, not fitting very well into either type of protected area. Table 7 is modified from one published elsewhere (English and Lee 2003:51); it demonstrates the characteristics of the two types of regimes in comparison to the general nature of cultural (or in this case, ethnographic) landscapes. This table illustrates that most of the existing statutory mechanisms for natural protected areas and for historic sites do not adequately address the important characteristics of ethnographic

landscapes; instead, these landscapes fall somewhere in between. Currently, if a management regime is established for an ethnographic landscape, it ends up being created as a modified version of either a historic site or a natural protected area.

While I have spoken of the interpretation of ethnographic landscapes as a separate activity, in fact interpretation, if done appropriately, should be part of protecting or sustaining such landscapes. Since community elders see the transmission of knowledge and understanding of ethnographic landscapes as one of their biggest challenges, it is only natural to look at the potential to use these landscapes as classrooms and teaching tools. In the end, sustaining human relationships with landscapes is the way to sustain the landscapes themselves.

Conclusions

In analyzing northern ethnographic landscapes and trying to get at their essential nature, I have tried to elicit what we can learn from these fascinating examples of cultural interaction. Ethnographic landscapes fall somewhere between the cultural and the natural, between tangible and intangible, between preservation and use, and between local and national. It appears to me that the examples in this volume give us the opportunity to step outside of the box in terms of how we view ourselves in the world we live in. Finding environmental and cultural sustainability means finding effective ways of negotiating landscapes between dominant and local or indigenous cultural groups. The necessity to always keep the external (that is, dominant) and the internal (that is, ethnographic) perspectives in mind is a pervasive theme to this discussion. To follow through with the theme of sustainability, we also have to address the question: "What are the limits of acceptable change? We will need to determine measures of health or sustainability and establish programs to determine the effects of our management practices." (English and Lee 2003:53).

One of the clear messages I have taken from this volume—and I hope will be also taken by landscape managers, scholars, and protection agencies—is that northern ethnographic landscapes, or cultural landscapes in general, are not static. They will continue to evolve, both tangibly and intangibly, and we must do our best to monitor and understand their evolution.

Our role in that evolution may be paraphrased from the Hippocratic Oath: Do no harm.

Acknowledgements

This paper draws substantially on the insights offered in the various papers in this volume, in addition to conversations with and the writings of Susan Buggey, Christopher Hanks, Thomas D. Andrews, Lisa Prosper, and Anthony J. English.

References

Canadian Oxford Dictionary
1998   *The Canadian Oxford Dictionary*. Edited by Katherine Barber. Oxford University Press Canada.
English, Anthony J. and Ellen Lee
2003   Managing the Intangible. In *The Full Value of Parks: From Economics to the Intangible*, David L. Harmon and Allen D. Putney, eds., pp. 43–55. Lanham, MD: Rowman and Littlefield Publishers, Inc.
Lee, Ellen
2000   Cultural Connections to the Land – a Canadian Example. In *Non-Material Values of Protected Areas*. Allen D. Putney, ed., pp. 3–12. *Parks: The International Journal for Protected Area Managers*, Special issue,10(2). Gland, Switzerland: IUCN.
Mitchell, Nora and Susan Buggey
2000   Protected Landscapes and Cultural Landscapes: Taking Advantage of Diverse Approaches. *The George Wright Forum* 17(1):35-46.

index

National Historical Preservation Act (NHPA), 51–52, 67, 331

National Historic Landmark (USA), 78, 326

National Historic Sites system (Canada), 23, 34

National Native Title Register (Australia), 380

National Park Advisory Board (USA), 65

National Park Service (NPS; USA): Applied Ethnography Program, 50, 53, 58, 72, 73; classification of cultural landscapes, 50; Cultural Landscape Inventory (CLI), 58, 325; Cultural Landscapes Program, 1, 3, 50, 51, 61–62, 67, 68–69, 70, 73, 322; definition of cultural landscape, 50, 68; early cultural resource studies, 67; ethnographic landscapes use of, 50; historic designed landscapes, 50; historic sites, 50; historic vernacular landscapes, 50; landscape histories of, 69; lands owned by in Alaska, 185; on importance of cultural landscapes, 68–69; selection of boundaries for traditional cultural properties, 33; subsistence management and, 55; Traditional Cultural Properties (TCP), 52, 60, 61, 72–75, 331, 334, 339

National Register Bulletin 38, 61

National Register of Historic Places (NRHP; USA), 42, 60, 66, 67–68, 73, 75, 327, 330, 331

National Science Foundation, 225, 231, 235, 249

Native American Graves Protection and Repatriation Act (NAGRPA; USA), 1, 52

Native Title Act (Australia), 380, 383, 393

Nature Conservancy Act (Norway), 84–85

Navajo Nation (USA), 32

Nenets people (Russia), 105, 115. See also Yamal-Nenets Autonomous Area; Yamal-Nenets Autonomous Area, sacred sites mapping project

Newfoundland, 23, 265, 288

New Zealand, 2

Ngarrindjeri people (Australia), 384–386, 387, 389

Nicholls, Christine, 385

Ninaistákis (Chief Mountain), Canada, 37

Ningeulook, Davey, 242, 249

Ningeulook, Edgar/Nunageak, 231, 236, 241, 245

Ningeulook, Frieda, 242, 250

Ningeulook, Hattie, 230, 232

Njal, saga of, 260–263

Northern ethnographic landscapes: defining, 401–402; value of, 402; Western vs. Indigenous view; of identifying and managing, 402–404; of protection and management, 404–405;

Northern Khanty people , 132. See Khanty people (Russia)

Northern Native History initiative (Canada), 26

Northern Norway seascape: basic feature of, 278–280; compared with landscape, 277; current status of coastal fisheries in, 288–290; legal and general framework for, 290–292; management approach to, 292–295; preservation of, 295; value of fisherman knowledge, 295

Northwest Territories (NWT; Canada): cultural landscapes in, 301, 303; educating youth in, 311–313; history of cultural landscape research in, 309–310; maintaining cultural landscapes in, 310–319; mitigating land use conflicts,

313–314; negotiating preservation, 310–311; overview of, 305–309; pace and degree of change, 303–305; partnership with museums, 315–316; protecting cultural landscapes, 316–319; taking control of research agenda, 314

Norway: Ancient Monuments and Buildings Act, 82, 83; Church and Churchyard Act, 82; Cultural Heritage Act, 84, 85–87; cultural heritage management system overview of, 84–85; historical overview of legislation, 82–84; international treaties, 83–84; Listed Building Act, 82; Nature Conservancy Act, 84, 86–87; Planning and Building Act, 83, 84, 86; Planning and Zoning Act , 292, 294; role of Sámi Parliament in, 368–371, 372–373. See also Norway, Sámi cultural heritage in

Norway, Sámi cultural heritage in: conclusions about, 371–372; cultural management of Sámi landscapes, 87–88; definition of Sámi monument under, 90–97; organization of Sámi cultural heritage management system, 356–357; practical management of, 357–358; reindeer herding landscape, 362–364; role of local knowledge in managing cultural heritage, 358–362, 364–365, 368

Norwegian Conservation Act, 290–291

Norwegian Cultural Heritage Act and Sámi remains, 88–97; age of remains protected under, 88–89; definition of Sámi, 90–91, 98–101; main objectives, 89–90; protected Sámi cultural landscapes, 101–102; overview of, 88

Norwegian Cultural Inheritance Act, 291–292

Nova Scotia, Canada, 23, 24

Numto Lake Park (Russia), 119, 122

Nunavut, Canada, 17, 22; creation of, 301; Inuit perspective on history, 28; land claims at, 304; landscape protection at, 36

Nyamboy natural monument (Russia), 164

O

O'Connor, Wave, 394

Oil and gas: in Canada, 35–36, 306, 319; in Russia, 118, 120, 133, 134, 137–138, 139, 153, 155–156, 164, 166, 167, 343, 344, 348, 351, 352, 354

Okotetto, Michael, 170, 354

Okpowruk, Charley, 234, 236, 239

Old Fort Franklin, Canada, 28–29

Olsen, Bjørnar, 97

Oovi, Lloyd, 211

Oral history: in Australia, 383–384; knowledge of, 73; land ownership rights and, 17, 27; Sámi, 358, 359

Oseberg Viking ship, 82

Oshchepkov, Konstantin, 352

P

Paleontological natural monument, 164

Parks Canada: Aboriginal cultural landscape designation of, 75–77; Aboriginal cultural landscape protection and, 34, 37, 38, 39; commemorative integrity approach by, 24–25, 33–34; definition of cultural landscapes, 22; role in cultural landscape preservation, 18, 75

illustration credits

Title/ Photograph by John S. R. Hood, 2002.

1/ Photo courtesy National Park Service, Alaska Region.

2/ Photograph by Sergey Bogoslovkiy, 1981, courtesy Arctic Studies Center, Smithsonian Institution.

3/ Photograph by Thomas D. Andrews, 1991.

4/ Map produced by Dan Pag, courtesy Parks Canada, Archaeological Services Branch.

5/ Photograph by Ellen Lee. Courtesy of Parks Canada, Archaeological Services Branch.

6/ Photograph by Lyle Henderson, Parks Canada.

7/ Photograph by Lyle Henderson, Parks Canada, 1991.

8/ Photograph by David Neufeld, courtesy Parks Canada, Archaeological Services Branch.

9/ Photograph by Morris Neyelle, courtesy Parks Canada, 2000.

10/ Photograph by Thomas D. Andrews.

11/ Photograph by John McCormick, courtesy Parks Canada, 2000.

12/ Courtesy Parks Canada, Archaeological Services Branch.

13/ Courtesy National Park Service, Alaska Region.

14/ Courtesy National Park Service, Alaska Region.

15/ Courtesy Alaska and Polar Regions Department, Elmer E. Rasmuson Library, University of Alaska Fairbanks, Stephen Foster Collection, #69/92/330.

16/ Map source: Office of Subsistence Management, USFWS.

17/ Map source: Office of Subsistence Management, USFWS.

18/ Map source: Office of Subsistence Management, USFWS.

19/ Courtesy National Park Service, Alaska Region.

20/ Map adapted from Hætta 1996:6.

21/ Photograph by Ingegerd Holand, 2000.

23/ Photograph by Ingegerd Holand, 1997.

24/ Photograph by Ingegerd Holand, 1992.

25/ Photograph by Ingegerd Holand, 2000

26/ Map produced by Marcia Bakry, Smithsonian Instituttion; adapted from Espeland and Sveen 1989:162.

27/ Photograph by Ingegerd Holand, 2000.

28/ Photograph by Arve Kjershei, NIKU, 2000.

29/ Photograph by G. Lebedev, 1911.

30/ Photograph by Pavel Shul'gin, 1991.

31/ Photograph by G. Lebedev, 1911.

32/ Photograph by Pavel Shul'gin, 1999.

33/ Photograph by G. Vedmid', 1999.

34/ Photograph by Olga Shtelle.

35/ Photograph by Olga Shtelle.

36/ Photograph by Vladimir Evladov, 1928. Courtesy Arctic Studies Center, Smithsonian Institution.

37/ Map courtesy Andrew Wiget.

38/ Photograph by Andrew Wiget.

39/ Map courtesy Andrew Wiget and Olga Balalaeva.

40/ Photograph by Andrew Wiget.

41/ Map courtesy Andrew Wiget.

42/ Map courtesy Andrew Wiget.

43/ Photograph by Andrew Wiget.

44/ Photograph by Andrew Wiget.

45/ Photograph by Andrew Wiget.

46/ Map produced by Igor Krupnik and Marcia Bakry, Smithsonian Institution.

47/ Photo courtesy Galina Kharyuchi.

48/ Photograph by William Fitzhugh, courtesy Arctic Studies Center, Smithsonian Institution.

49/ Photo courtesy Galina Kharyuchi.

50/ Photograph by Vladimir Evladov, 1928. Courtesy Arctic Studies Center, Smithsonian Institution.

51/ Photograph by Galina Kharyuchi.

52/ Photograph by Galina Kharyuchi.

53/ Photograph by Vladimir Evladov, courtesy Arctic Studies Center, Smithsonian Institution.

54/ Photo courtesy National Park Service, Alaska Region.

55/ Photo courtesy National Park Service, Alaska Region.

56/ Photo courtesy National Park Service, Alaska Region.

57/ Relief map courtesy National Park Service, Alaska

Region.

58/ Map courtesy National Park Service, Alaska Region.

59/ Ahtna place-names map courtesy National Park Service, Alaska Region.

60/ Graph adapted from Halpin 1987:31.

61/ Photograph courtesy National Park Service

62/ Mentasta caribou herd density dependant model courtesy Don Callaway.

63/ Photograph by Igor Krupnik, 1999, from the panel photo at Sivuqam Inc., Gambell, Alaska.

64/ Map reproduced from Collins 1937: 32.

65/ Photograph by Peter Bonnett, 1889. Courtesy NAA-SI 85-814.

66/ Photograph by Leuman M. Waugh, 1930. Courtesy National Museum of the American Indian, Smithsonian Institution, N42787.

67/ Photograph by Riley D. Moore, 1912. Courtesy NAA-SI, neg. SI 76-705.

68/ Drawing by Willis Walunga, 2001.

69/ Photograph by Henry B. Collins, Courtesy NAA-SI, neg.2000-4459.

70/ Photograph by Peter Bonnett, 1889. Courtesy NAA-SI 85-815.

71/ Photograph by Igor Krupnik, 2001.

72/ Photograph by Igor Krupnik, 2001.

Pg. 228/Courtesy Sandra Haldane, 2004.

73/ Photograph by James Magdanz, Kotzebue, 1993, courtesy of the photographer.

74/ Map courtesy Susan Fair. Cartography by Nadia Hlibka, Ikarus Design, Tucson, AZ.

75/ Hand-drawn map, 1902. Courtesy Kathleen Lopp Smith and Verbeck Smith, Seattle.

76/ Watercolor courtesy Alaska State Library, Wickersham Collection, MS 107, Box 73, Folder 6, #35.

77/ Photograph by Fred Machetanz. Courtesy Alaska and Polar Regions Department, Elmer E. Rasmuson Library, University of Alaska Fairbanks, Fred Machetanz Collection, #73-75-452.

78/ Photograph by James Magdanz, Kotzebue, 1997, courtesy of the photographer.

79/ Photo by Glen Simpson, Fairbanks, 1987, courtesy of the photographer.

80/ Photograph by Edward L. Keithhahn, courtesy National Park Service, Alaska Region, Keithhahn collection, neg.047.

81/ Courtesy Edgar Ningeulook and Shishmaref IRA Village Council (SH/EN-83-F012-6).

82/ Photograph by Susan W. Fair, 1998.

83/ Photograph by Elisabeth Ward, 2001.

84/ Illustration courtesy Gisli Sigurdsson.

85/ Map adapted from Hreinsson et al., 2000b:388.

86/ Photograph by Elisabeth Ward, 2001.

87/ Photograph by Elisabeth Ward, 2001.

88/ Photograph by Elisabeth Ward, 2001.

89/ Photograph by Elisabeth Ward, 2001.

90/ Photograph by Elisabeth Ward, 2001.

91/ Photograph by Elisabeth Ward, 2001.

92/ Photograph by Anita Maurstad.

93/ Photograph by Anita Maurstad.

94/ Photograph by Anita Maurstad.

95/ Photograph by Anita Maurstad.

96/ Photograph by Thomas D. Andrews, 1992.

97/ Map produced by Miles Davis, Archaeology GIS Facility, Prince of Wales Northern Heritage Centre, Yellowknife, NWT, Canada.

98/ Map produced by Miles Davis, Archaeology GIS Facility, Prince of Wales Northern Heritage Centre, Yellowknife, NWT, Canada.

99/ Photograph by Thomas D. Andrews, 1996.

100/ Photograph by Thomas D. Andrews, 1991.

101/ Photograph by Thomas D. Andrews, 1996.

102/ Photograph by Thomas D. Andrews,1992.

103/ Photograph by Thomas D. Andrews, 1993.

104/ Photograph by Thomas D. Andrews, 1991.

105/ Photo courtesy National Park Service, Alaska Region, 2001.

106/ Photo courtesy Anchorage Museum of History and Art, Anchorage, B70.22.14, #271.

107/ Photograph by George T. Emmons, 1889. Courtesy Dept. of Library Services, American Museum of Natural History, New York, neg. 41619.

108/ Photograph by Mikhail Sherhsnev, 1995.

109/ Photograph by Mikhail Shershnev, 1997.

110/ Photograph by Natalia Fedorova, 1995.

111/ Photograph by Natalia Fedorova, 1996.

112/ Photograph by Marianne Skandfer.

114/ Photograph by Marianne Skandfer.

115/ Photograph by Marianne Skandfer.

116/ Photograph by Marianne Skandfer.

117/ Photograph by Marianne Skandfer.

118/Photograph by Marianne Skandfer.

119/ Photograph by Thetus Smith, 2001.

120/ Photograph by Claire Smith

121/ Photograph by Matt Schlitz.

122/ Photograph by Claire Smith.

123/ Photograph by Claire Smith.

124/ Photograph by David Dector, 1995. Courtesy Arctic Studies Center, Smithsonian Institution.

OTHER TITLES IN THE SERIES

CONTRIBUTIONS TO CIRCUMPOLAR ANTHROPOLOGY

Vol.1: *Gateways: Exploring the Legacy of the Jesup North Pacific Expedition, 1897–1902.* Edited by Igor Krupnik and William W. Fitzhugh. Arctic Studies Center, National Museum of Natural History, Smithsonian Institution. Washington, DC. 2001. xvi+335 pp.

Vol. 2: *Honoring Our Elders. A History of Eastern Arctic Anthropology.* Edited by William W. Fitzhugh, Stephen Loring, and Daniel Odess. Arctic Studies Center, National Museum of Natural History, Smithsonian Institution. Washington, DC. 2002. xvi+319 pp.

Vol. 3: *Akuzilleput Igaqullghet. Our Words Put to Paper. Sourcebook in St. Lawrence Island Yupik Heritage and History.* Edited by Igor Krupnik, Willis Walunga, and Vera Metcalf. Compiled by Igor Krupnik and Lars Krutak. Arctic Studies Center, National Museum of Natural History, Smithsonian Institution. Washington, DC. 2002. 464 pp.

Vol. 4: *Constructing Cultures Then and Now. Celebrating Franz Boas and the Jesup North Pacific Expedition.* Edited by Laurel Kendall and Igor Krupnik. Arctic Studies Center, National Museum of Natural History, Smithsonian Institution. Washington, DC. 2003. xviii+364 pp.

Vol. 5: Leonid P. Khlobystin. *Taimyr. The Archaeology of Northernmost Eurasia.* Edited by William W. Fitzhugh and Vladimir V. Pitul'ko. Arctic Studies Center, National Museum of Natural History, Smithsonian Institution. Washington, DC. 2004 (in press).